Alva W. Steffler

4 Find the REFERENCE NUMBER in the TABLE OF FIRST LINES and it will give you the correct first line of the hymn you are seeking.

425 Fade, fade, each earthly joy
426 Fair as a beauteous, tender flower
427 Fairest Lord Jesus, Ruler of all nature
428 Faith of our fathers! living still
429 Far and near the fields are teeming

NOW TO YOUR HYMNAL!

5 Using your own hymnal, look up the first line in the index. This will lead you to the hymn.

Eternal God, whose power upholds ... 535
Eternal Ruler of the ceaseless round 506
Eternal Spirit, evermore creating ... 161

Fairest Lord Jesus ... 261
Faith of our fathers, living still ... 348
Father Almighty, bless us with Thy blessing ... 344

Fairest Lord Jesus

261 CRUSADER'S HYMN. 5. 6. 8. 5. 5. 8.

German, 17th century

From Schlesische Volkslieder, 1842
Arr. by Richard S. Willis, 1819–1900

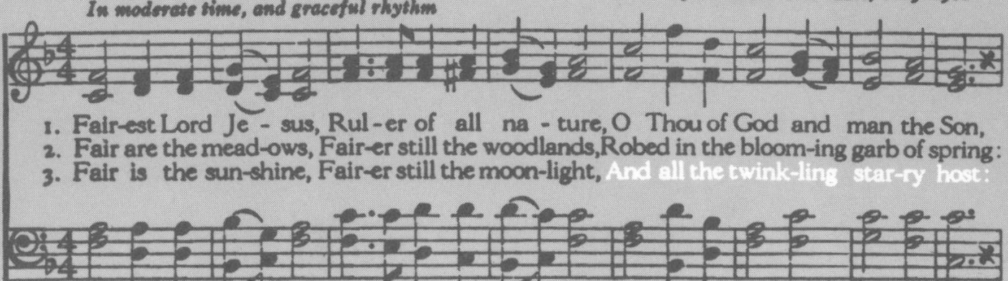

In moderate time, and graceful rhythm
1. Fair-est Lord Je - sus, Rul - er of all na - ture, O Thou of God and man the Son,
2. Fair are the mead-ows, Fair-er still the woodlands, Robed in the bloom-ing garb of spring:
3. Fair is the sun-shine, Fair-er still the moon-light, And all the twink-ling star-ry host:

D1266580

Because new hymnals are co... old ones going out of print, reference to specific hymn... is concordance.

JUDSON CONCORDANCE TO HYMNS

JUDSON CONCORDANCE TO HYMNS

Thomas B. McDormand
Frederic S. Crossman

THE JUDSON PRESS: VALLEY FORGE

JUDSON CONCORDANCE TO HYMNS

Valley Forge, Pa.

Library of Congress Catalog Card No. 65-15009

PRINTED IN THE U.S.A.

CONTENTS

FOREWORD

How OFTEN MINISTERS, CHOIR LEADERS, YOUTH LEADERS, AND leaders of church organizations have wanted the right hymn for the right theme or occasion, but could not find it! They may remember a striking line from the very hymn they want, but cannot recall how the hymn starts. And the first line is essential to locating the hymn since most hymnals are indexed in this fashion.

Examples of this awkward, and frequently-recurring, embarrassment are plentiful, but one will suffice. The line remembered may be "Our brethren shield in danger's hour," but the first line does not come to mind. In this Concordance the key word "brethren" provides the clue by which both versions of the first line may be located, "Almighty Father, strong to save" (number 81) and "Eternal Father, strong to save" (number 418). Thus the appropriate hymn for the desired occasion is found.

This Concordance treats nearly 2,400 hymns from 27 hymnbooks in common use, including those of many major denominations of the United States and Canada, as well as a number of youth hymnals and gospel songbooks.

The names of hymnbooks dealt with are not listed for the following reasons:

(1) Any well-known hymn will appear in almost every reputable hymnbook. It would not be practicable to attempt to list for all such hymns (hundreds of them) the many hymnals in which they would occur.

(2) The hymnbooks of denominations change from time to time, though probably at least 90 percent of the hymns in new

books have appeared previously. So it is deemed unwise to "date" this concordance by reference to specific present-day hymnals.

At some future date, the preparation of a supplement may well be considered, dealing with newer hymns which will be constantly appearing. Such a supplement would not outdate the present volume, however, for the great bulk of hymns presently listed will be loved and used for generations yet to come.

THOMAS B. MCDORMAND
FREDERIC S. CROSSMAN

HOW TO USE THIS CONCORDANCE

1. The book is used in much the same manner as a Bible concordance, but with some adaptations. The key word in a remembered line is looked up in the Line Index of this book. When the line is found, a reference number appears with it which, in the Table of First Lines, indicates the first line of the hymn sought.

For example, one remembers the word "birds" in the line: "The birds their carols raise." The line is found in the Line Index under the word "birds." Following the line is a number, 2012. This number in the Table of First Lines reveals that the line comes from the hymn whose first line is, "This is my Father's world." One then turns to a hymnal (most pastors, churches, and choir directors have a collection of these) to locate the actual hymn by its first line.

2. The first lines of hymns are not listed by key words in the Line Index, since they appear in the Table of First Lines.

3. The general rule is that *the first common noun or the first verb* of any remembered phrase or sentence is used for listing purposes. Thus, in the hymn mentioned under section 1 above, the line is listed under "birds," the first common noun. Only *one* word is listed for a given line, since it is sufficient to make the required identification, and this policy greatly reduces the size and cost of the Concordance without reducing its usefulness.

4. Proper names, and names of Deity (God, Jesus, Lord, and so forth) are not used for listing purposes *except* when no other identifying word appears.

5. The verbal forms (infinitive, participle, and gerund) are not used as key words unless no identifying noun or verb appears, but they must be used occasionally. In the line, "To know thee as thou art," for example, it is evident that the infinitive form of "know" should be used because no other word meets the requirements.

6. Names descriptive of Deity, such as "Shepherd," "Friend," "Guide," and "Guardian," are used when they appear as the first nouns in their respective lines.

7. The verb "come" appears so often as the opening word of a line that it is not regarded as the key word *except* in cases where no other identifying word is available.

8. Nouns used in adjectival forms are not listed as key words. Thus, in the phrase "mountain crest," the noun "mountain" is used adjectivally, so the noun "crest" would be used for listing.

9. In the case of verbal phrases, only the main verb is used for listing purposes. Thus, in such a phrase as "Let us make," the verb "make" would constitute the key word.

10. When a thought unit runs into two inseparable lines, only an identifying word of the first line is used. For example, the following two lines represent one thought, and one could scarcely be recalled without the other:

Jesus, the Savior, this gospel to tell,
Joyfully came, joyfully came. . . .

Thus the key word for the entire unit would be the first common noun, "gospel."

11. For listing purposes, a line may not be printed in full, but only enough to identify it with certainty. For example, a listing might be: "That in thy sunshine's blaze." It is not necessary to add the words "its day." Such abbreviation often avoids the use of two lines for an entry, thus reducing the size of the book considerably without sacrificing its clarity.

12. As in the case of a Bible concordance, try a second word if the desired line is not located by the first word you try. Few rules can be followed with absolute consistency, and a line you would expect to find under one key word might be listed under another.

TABLE
OF
FIRST LINES

TABLE OF FIRST LINES

A

1 A better day is coming
2 A blessing for you
3 A call for loyal soldiers
4 A charge to keep I have
5 A few more years shall roll
6 A gladsome hymn of praise we sing
7 A glory gilds the sacred page (see also 1933)
8 A holy air is breathing round
9 A little child the Savior came (see also 706)
10 A little more giving, a little less greed
11 A little seed lay fast asleep
12 A mighty fortress is our God
13 A name above all names
14 A noble life, a simple faith
15 A parting hymn we sing
16 A perfect day is coming
17 A river of crimson flows down from the tree
18 A ruler once came to Jesus by night
19 A safe stronghold our God is still
20 A Savior who died our salvation to win
21 A song of spring once more we sing
22 A story sweet and wondrous
23 A thousand tongues to tell the story
24 A wonderful Savior is Jesus my Lord
25 A wondrous song was given
26 Abide with all thy favor
27 Abide with me; fast falls the eventide
28 Above the clear, blue sky
29 Above the hills of time the cross
30 According to thy gracious word
31 After thy loving-kindness
32 Again, as evening's shadow falls
33 Again the morn of gladness
34 Ah, dearest Jesus, Holy Child (see also 513, 528)
35 Ah, holy (dearest) Jesus, how hast thou
36 Ah, think not the Lord delayeth
37 Ah! what a sound! The infinite
38 Alas! and did my Savior bleed
39 All as God wills, who wisely heeds
40 All beautiful the march of days
41 All creatures of our God and King
42 All for Jesus! all for Jesus
43 All glory be to God on high
44 All glory, laud, and honor
45 All hail, Adored Trinity
46 All hail, the pageant of the years
47 All hail the power of Jesus' name
48 All hail, thou Son of David
49 All hail to thee, Immanuel

50 All lands to God, in joyful sounds (see also 361)
51 All my days I should be saying
52 All my heart this night rejoices
53 All my hope on God is founded
54 All nations whom thou mad'st
55 All nature's works his praise declare
56 All people of the earth
57 All people that on earth do dwell
58 All praise to thee, for thou, O King
59 All praise to thee, my (O) God, this night
60 All that I am or hope to be
61 All the happy children
62 All the past we leave behind
63 All the sorrows of thy life
64 All the toil and sorrow done
65 All the way my Lord is leading
66 All the way my Savior leads me
67 All things are thine; no gift have we
68 All things bright and beautiful
69 All things come of thee
70 All to Jesus I surrender
71 All unseen the Master walketh
72 All ye that fear God's holy name
73 All ye that pass by
74 All ye who seek for Jesus
75 All ye who seek for sure relief
76 Alleluia! Alleluia! hearts to heaven (see also 663)
77 Alleluia! sing to Jesus
78 Alleluia, song of sweetness
79 Alleluia! the strife is o'er (see also 1937)
80 Almighty Father, hear our prayer
81 Almighty Father, strong to save (see also 418)
82 Almighty Father, who dost give (see also 1079)
83 Almighty God, thy word is cast
84 Almighty Lord, with one accord
85 "Almost persuaded," now to believe
86 Alone thou goest forth
87 Am I a soldier of the cross
88 Amazing grace – how sweet the sound
89 Amidst us our Beloved stands
90 An endless line of splendor
91 An exile for the faith
92 Ancient of Days, who sittest throned in glory
93 And are we yet alive
94 And can it be that I should gain
95 And did those feet in ancient time
96 And have the bright immensities
97 And let our bodies part
98 And now beloved Lord
99 And now, O Father, mindful of the love
100 And now the wants are told
101 Angel voices, ever singing
102 Angel voices, high and lowly (see also 104)
103 Angels, from the realms of glory
104 Angels holy, high and lowly
105 Angels we have heard on high
106 Another year is dawning
107 Another year of setting suns
108 Anywhere with Jesus I can safely go
109 Approach, my soul, the mercy seat
110 "Are ye able," said the Master
111 Are you burdened with sin and sadness
112 Are you weary, are you heavy-hearted
113 Arise, my soul, arise
114 Arise, O Lord, our God, arise
115 Arise, O youth of God
116 Arm of the Lord, awake
117 Around the throne of God a band
118 Around the throne of God in heaven
119 Art thou weary, art thou troubled (languid)
120 As comes the breath of spring
121 As darker, darker fall around

122 As far as the west is removed from the east
123 As light, O Christ, thou cam'st to earth
124 As now the sun's declining rays
125 As pants the hart for cooling streams
126 As the Father's boundless love
127 As the sun doth daily rise
128 As when the Hebrew prophet raised
129 As with gladness men of old
130 As your journey through life
131 Ask ye what great thing I know
132 Asleep in Jesus! blessed sleep
133 At all times praise the Lord
134 At Calvary's cross I met a Friend
135 At any cost to self, O Lord
136 At even, when (ere) the sun was set
137 At evening time may there be light
138 At length there dawns the glorious day
139 At one with God, how rich is my condition
140 At the Cross, her station keeping (see also 1263)
141 At the feet of Jesus
142 At the Lamb's high feast we sing
143 At the Name of Jesus
144 At thy feet, our God and Father
145 At work beside his Father's bench
146 Author of Faith, eternal Word
147 Awake, and sing the song
148 Awake! awake! and sing the blessed story
149 Awake! awake! O Christian
150 Awake, awake, O heart of mine
151 Awake, awake to love and work
152 Awake, my soul, and with the sun (see also 545)
153 Awake, my soul, in joyful lays
154 Awake, my soul, stretch every nerve
155 Awake, my tongue, thy tribute bring
156 Awake, O Christian, from thy sleep
157 Awake, our souls! away, our fears
158 Awaken from thy sinful sleep
159 Away in a manger
160 Away with gloom, away with doubt
161 Awhile in spirit, Lord, to thee

B

162 Backward we look, O God of all our days
163 Be a golden sunbeam, radiant and bright
164 Be glad in the Lord, and rejoice
165 Be known to us in breaking bread (see also 1716)
166 Be merciful to me, O God
167 Be not aweary, for labor will cease
168 Be not dismayed whate'er betide
169 Be not weary or cast down
170 Be of good cheer, the Master said
171 Be present at our table, Lord
172 Be silent, be silent, A whisper is heard
173 Be still, my soul, for God is near
174 Be strong! We are not here to play
175 Be thou faithful unto death
176 Be thou my Guardian and my Guide
177 Be thou my Vision, O Lord
178 Be with me, O my Savior
179 Beautiful city of God
180 Beautiful star of promise
181 Beautiful valley of Eden
182 Because I have been given much

183 Because I knew not when my life
184 Before Jehovah's awful throne
185 Before the cross of Jesus
186 Before the day draws near its ending
187 Before the ending of the day
188 Before thy throne, O Lord of heaven
189 Before thy throne, O God, we kneel
190 Begin, my tongue, some heavenly theme
191 Behold a sower from afar! (see also 1445)
192 Behold, a stranger at the door
193 Behold, all ye that serve the Lord
194 Behold th'amazing gift of love
195 Behold the Lamb of God
196 "Behold, the Master passeth by!"
197 Behold the messengers of Christ
198 Behold! the mountain of the Lord
199 Behold us, Lord, a little space
200 Behold we come, dear Lord, to thee
201 Believe not those who say
202 Beloved, let us love: love is of God
203 Beneath the cross of Jesus
204 Beneath the forms of outward rite
205 Beneath the shadow of the cross
206 Beyond the holy city wall
207 Beyond the sunset, O blissful morning
208 Birds are singing, woods are ringing
209 Bless, O my soul! the living God
210 Bless the four corners of this house
211 Bless thou the gifts
212 Blessed are they that undefiled
213 Blessed assurance, Jesus is mine
214 Blessed be the Fountain of blood
215 Blessed be the Lord God of Israel
216 Blessed, blessed be Jehovah
217 Blessed city, heavenly Salem (see also 281)
218 Blessed hope that in Jesus
219 Blessed hour, when we are meeting
220 Blessed Jesus, at thy word
221 Blessed Jesus, here are we
222 Blessed Jesus, thou didst go from Gethsemane
223 Blessed Lord, in thee is refuge
224 Blessed Master, I am yearning
225 Blessed Master, I have promised
226 Blessed Redeemer, full of compassion
227 Blessed Savior, we adore thee
228 Blessing and honor and glory and power
229 Blest are the pure in heart
230 Blest be the dear uniting love
231 Blest be the everlasting God
232 Blest be the tie that binds
233 Blest Creator of the light
234 Blest feast of love divine (see also 1805)
235 Blest Jesus, grant us strength
236 Blest land of Judea
237 Blest morning! whose first dawning rays (see also 1677)
238 Blest the man who fears Jehovah
239 Blow, golden trumpets, sweet and clear
240 Blow, winds of God (see also 1428, 2181)
241 Blow, ye the trumpet, blow
242 Book of books, our people's strength
243 Book of grace, and Book of glory
244 Bowed low in supplication
245 Bread of heaven, on thee we feed
246 Bread of the world, in mercy broken
247 Break, day of God, O break

248 Break forth, O beauteous heavenly light
249 Break thou the bread of life
250 Breathe on me, Breath of God
251 Brethren, we have met to worship
252 Brief life is here our portion
253 Bright the vision that delighted (see also 1178, 1673)
254 Brightest and best of the sons of the morning
255 Brightly beams our Father's mercy
256 Brightly gleams our banner
257 Bring a torch, Jeanette, Isabella
258 Bring, O morn, thy music
259 Bring ye all the tithes
260 Broken is the seal of death
261 Brother and Lord, among thy people sitting
262 Bugle calls are ringing out
263 Built on the Rock the church doth stand
264 Buried with Christ!
265 By all whom thou hast made
266 By Christ redeemed, in Christ restored
267 By cool Siloam's shady rill
268 By the Holy Spirit sent
269 By thy birth and by thy tears
270 By what means shall a young man learn

C

271 Call Jehovah thy salvation
272 Calm on the list'ning ear of night
273 Can a little child like me
274 Captain of Israel's host, and Guide
275 Captains of the saintly band
276 Cast thy burden on the Lord
277 Children of the heavenly King
278 Christ for the world we sing
279 Christ in his heavenly garden
280 Christ is coming! let creation
281 Christ is made the sure foundation (see also 217)
282 Christ is risen, Christ is risen
283 Christ is the world's Redeemer
284 Christ, of all my hopes the Ground
285 Christ of the upward way
286 Christ shall have dominion
287 Christ the Lord is risen again
288 Christ the Lord is arisen today, Christians
289 Christ, the Lord, is ris'n today, Alleluia!
290 Christ, the Lord, to us is born
291 Christ, who knows all his sheep
292 Christ, whose glory fills the skies
293 Christian, dost thou see them
294 Christian, rise, and act thy creed
295 Christian, seek not yet repose
296 Christian soul, the times are calling
297 Christian, work for Jesus
298 Christians, awake! salute the happy morn
299 Christians, lo, the star appeareth
300 Christ's life our code, his cross our creed
301 City of God, how broad and far
302 Come, all ye shepherds
303 Come and rejoice with me
304 Come, Christians (children), join to sing
305 Come, dearest Lord, descend and dwell
306 Come down, O Love divine
307 Come, everblessed Spirit, come
308 Come, every soul by sin oppressed
309 Come forth, ye men of every race
310 Come, gracious spirit, heav'nly dove (see also 319)
311 Come, Holy Ghost, in love
312 Come, Holy Ghost(!) in us arise
313 Come, Holy Ghost (Spirit), our souls inspire

314 Come, Holy Ghost, who ever one
315 Come, Holy Spirit, come
316 Come, Holy Spirit, Dove divine
317 Come, Holy Spirit, God and Lord
318 Come, Holy Spirit, heavenly Dove
319 Come, Holy Spirit, heavenly Dove, My (see also 310)
320 Come in, dear angels
321 Come, kingdom of our God
322 Come, labor on. Who dares stand idle
323 Come, let us join our cheerful songs (see also 671)
324 Come, let us join our friends above (see also 1067)
325 Come, let us join with thankful (faithful) souls
326 Come, let us sing of a wonderful love
327 Come, let us to the Lord our God
328 Come, let us tune our loftiest song
329 Come, let us use the grace divine
330 Come, my soul, thy suit prepare
331 Come, O Lord, like morning sunshine (sunlight)
332 Come, O thou God of grace
333 Come, O thou traveler unknown
334 Come! Peace of God, and dwell again on earth
335 Come, risen Lord, and deign to be our Guest
336 Come, sinners, to the gospel feast
337 Come, sound his praise abroad
338 Come, thou almighty king
339 Come, thou everlasting Spirit
340 Come, Thou Fount of every blessing
341 Come, thou holy Paraclete
342 Come, thou Holy Spirit, come
343 Come, thou long-expected Jesus (see also 658)
344 Come to Jesus, ye who labor
345 Come to me, Lord, when first I wake
346 Come to our poor nature's night
347 Come to the Savior, make no delay
348 Come to the Savior now
349 Come unto me, when shadows darkly gather
350 Come unto me, ye weary
351 Come, we that love the Lord
352 Come, with all your sorrow
353 Come with thy sins to the fountain
354 Come, ye children, sing to Jesus
355 Come, ye disconsolate
356 Come, ye faithful, raise the anthem
357 Come, ye people, rise and sing
358 Come, ye sinners, poor and needy (wretched)
359 Come, ye thankful people, come
360 Come, ye that fear Jehovah
361 Come, ye that fear the Lord, and hear (see also 50)
362 Come ye yourselves apart, and rest awhile
363 Comfort, comfort ye my people
364 Command thy blessing from above
365 Commit thou all thy griefs
366 Comrades known in marches many
367 Courage, brother! do not stumble
368 Cradled all lowly
369 Cradled in a manger meanly
370 Creation's Lord, we give thee thanks
371 Creation's Lord, who from thy heaven
372 Creator of the starry height
373 Creator of the stars of night
374 Creator of the world, to thee
375 Creator Spirit, by whose aid
376 Crown him with many crowns
377 Crown him upon the throne

D

378 Dare to be brave, dare to be true
379 Day by day, dear Lord
380 Day by day the manna fell
381 Day is done, gone the sun
382 Day is dying in the west
383 Dear Father, loud the ocean rolls
384 Dear Father, whom we cannot see
385 Dear God, our Father, at thy knee confessing
386 Dear Lord and Father of mankind
387 Dear Lord, I cannot see where thou art leading
388 Dear Lord, take up my tangled strands
389 Dear Lord, who sought at dawn of day
390 Dear Master, in whose life I see
391 Dear Master, in thy way
392 Dear Refuge of my weary soul
393 Dear Shepherd of thy people, hear (see also 651)
394 Deck thyself, my soul, with gladness
395 Depth of mercy! can there be
396 Dismiss me not thy service, Lord
397 Dismiss us with thy blessing
398 Do not be ashamed to own him
399 Do not wait until some deed of greatness
400 Do you ever stop, my friend, to think
401 Does Jesus care when my heart is pained
402 Down at the Cross where my Savior died
403 Down in the valley with my Savior
404 Down to the sacred wave
405 Draw nigh to thy Jerusalem
406 Draw thou my soul, O Christ
407 Dying with Jesus, by death reckoned mine

E

408 Each morning brings us fresh
409 Earth below is teeming
410 Earth thou dost visit, watering it
411 Earthly pleasures vainly call
412 Easter flowers are blooming bright
413 Encamped along the hills of light
414 Enduring Soul of all our life
415 Ere I sleep, for every favor
416 Ere we take our homeward way
417 Eternal beam of light divine
418 Eternal Father, strong to save (see also 81)
419 Eternal God, whose power upholds
420 Eternal Light! Eternal Light!
421 Eternal Ruler of the ceaseless round
422 Eternal Spirit, evermore creating
423 Eternal, unchanging, we sing to thy praise

F

424 Face to face with Christ, my Savior
425 Fade, fade, each earthly joy
426 Fair as a beauteous, tender flower
427 Fairest Lord Jesus, Ruler of all nature
428 Faith of our fathers! living still
429 Far and near the fields are teeming

430 Far away in the depths of my spirit
431 Far away the noise of strife upon my ear
432 Far down the ages now
433 Far, far away, in heathen darkness dwelling
434 Far off I see the goal
435 Father, again in Jesus' name we meet
436 Father Almighty, bless us with thy blessing
437 Father, before thy throne of light
438 Father eternal, Ruler of creation
439 Father, fill us with thy love
440 Father, give thy benediction
441 Father, hear the prayer we offer
442 Father, hear thy chidlren's call
443 Father, I know that all my life
444 Father, I stretch my hands to thee
445 Father in heaven, who lovest all
446 Father, in high heaven dwelling
447 Father, in thy mysterious presence kneeling
448 Father, lead me day by day
449 Father, let me dedicate
450 Father, long before creation
451 Father, loving Father
452 Father of heaven, whose love profound
453 Father of Jesus Christ, my Lord
454 Father of lights, in whom there is no shadow
455 Father of love and pow'r
456 Father of men, in whom are one
457 Father of mercies, in thy Word
458 Father of mercy, Lover of all children
459 Father of peace, and God of love
460 Father, our children keep
461 Father, take my heart, incline it
462 Father, the watches of the night
463 Father, to thee I come
464 Father, to thee we look
465 Father, to us thy children
466 Father, we greet thee, God of love
467 Father, we praise thee, now the night is over
468 Father, we thank thee for the night
469 Father, we thank thee who hast planted
470 Father, who on man dost shower
471 Father, whose will is life and good
472 Fear not, little flock, from the cross
473 Fear not, O little flock, the foe
474 Fierce and wild the storm is raging
475 Fierce raged the tempest o'er the deep
476 Fierce was the wild billow
477 Fight the good fight with all thy might
478 Fill thou my life, O Lord my God
479 Fling out the banner! let it float
480 "Follow me," the Master said
481 For all the blessings of the year
482 For all the Lord has done for me
483 For mercy, courage, kindness, mirth
484 For the beauty of the earth
485 For the brave of every race
486 For the bread, which thou hast broken
487 For the might of thine arm we bless thee
488 For the tempted, Lord, we pray
489 For thee, O dear, dear country (see also 961)
490 For them whose ways are in the height
491 For those we love within the veil
492 For thy mercy and thy grace
493 For ever here my rest shall be
494 "For ever with the Lord!"
495 Forget them not, O Christ, who stand

496 Forgive, O Lord, our severing ways
497 Forgive them, O my Father
498 Forth from God's throne, into this world of woe
499 Forth in thy name, O Lord, I go
500 Forty days and forty nights
501 Forward through the ages
502 Founded on thee, our only Lord
503 Fountain of good, to own thy love
504 Free from the law, O happy condition
505 Friend of the home: as when in Galilee
506 Friends all around me are trying to find
507 From age to age they gather
508 From all that dwell below the skies
509 From all the dark places
510 From all thy saints in warfare
511 From every stormy wind that blows
512 From Greenland's icy mountains
513 From heaven above to earth I come (see also 34, 528)
514 From homes of quiet peace
515 From ocean unto ocean
516 From over hill and plain
517 From the eastern mountains
518 From the Pilgrim's rock-bound coast
519 From the table now retiring
520 From thee all skill and science flow

G

521 Galilee, bright Galilee
522 Gather us in, thou love, that fillest all
523 Gentle Jesus, meek and mild
524 Gentle Mary laid her Child
525 Gird us, O God, with humble might
526 Give ear unto me when I call
527 Give ear unto my words, O Lord (see also 1176)
528 Give heed, my heart, lift up thine eyes (see also 34, 513)
529 Give me a passion for souls, dear Lord
530 Give me the wings of faith to rise
531 Give of your best to the Master
532 Give praise and thanks unto the Lord
533 Give thanks to God, call on his name
534 Give thy heart's love and labor
535 Give to our God immortal praise
536 Give to the winds thy fears
537 Give ye to Jehovah, O sons of the mighty
538 Giver of the perfect gift
539 Glad that I live am I
540 Glad was my heart to hear
541 Glorious things of thee are spoken
542 Glory be, glory be, Glory be to God on high
543 Glory be to God the Father
544 Glory be to Jesus
545 Glory to thee, who safe hast kept (see also 152)
546 Go forth to life, O child of earth
547 Go forth to serve, as Jesus went
548 Go forward, Christian soldier
549 Go home and tell to those you love
550 Go, labor on: spend and be spent
551 Go, tell it on the mountain
552 Go to dark Gethsemane
553 Go to the deeps of God's promise
554 God, be merciful to (unto) me
555 God be with them while they stand
556 God be with you till we meet again
557 God bless our native land

558 God calling yet! shall I not hear
559 God from on high hath heard
560 God, give us Christian homes
561 God has given you his promise
562 God has shown his loving face
563 God himself is with us (see also 600)
564 God holds the key of all unknown
565 God is calling the prodigal
566 God is Love; his mercy brightens
567 God is my strong Salvation
568 God is near thee, therefore, cheer thee
569 God is now willing, in Christ reconciled
570 God is of mine inheritance
571 God is our Refuge and our Strength
572 God is the Refuge of his saints
573 God is true! yea, he is ever true
574 God is working his purpose out
575 God loved the world of sinners lost
576 God make my life a little light
577 God moves in a mysterious way
578 God of compassion, in mercy befriend us
579 God of earth and sea and heaven
580 God of grace and God of glory
581 God of heaven, hear our singing
582 God of mercy, God of grace
583 God of our fathers, known of old
584 God of our fathers, the strength of our people
585 God of our fathers, whose almighty hand
586 God of our life, through all the circling years
587 God of our saving health
588 God of our youth, to whom we yield
589 God of pity, God of grace
590 God of the living, in whose eyes (see also 1446)
591 God of the nations of the earth
592 God of the nations, near and far
593 God of the nations, who from dawn of days
594 God of the prophets! Bless the prophets' sons
595 God of the shining hosts
596 God of the strong, God of the weak
597 God, our Father, we adore thee
598 God reigneth, he is clothed (see also 1882, 1886)
599 God rest you merry, gentlemen
600 God reveals his presence (see also 563)
601 God save America
602 God sees the little sparrow fall
603 God send us men whose aim 'twill be
604 God speaks to us in bird and song
605 God, that madest earth and heaven
606 God, that touchest earth with beauty (see also 615)
607 God the all-merciful! earth hath forsaken (see also 608, 612)
608 God the all-mighty One, King (see also 607, 612)
609 God, the Father, gave us all
610 God, the Lord, a King remaineth
611 God, the Lord, is King: before him
612 God the Omnipotent (all-terrible)! King (see also 607, 608)
613 God, who created me
614 God, who made the earth
615 God, who touchest earth with beauty (see also 606)
616 God will I bless all times (see also 1902)
617 God's glory is a wondrous thing (see also 2321)
618 God's law is perfect, and converts
619 God's mercies I will ever sing
620 God's trumpet wakes the slum'-ring world
621 Golden breaks the dawn
622 Golden harps are sounding

623 Gone are my fears
624 Gone from my heart the world and all its charm
625 Good Christian men, rejoice
626 Good Joseph had a garden
627 Good King Wenceslas
628 Good unto all men is the Lord
629 Grace and truth shall mark the way
630 Grace, love and peace abide
631 Grace! 'tis a charming sound
632 Gracious Father, hear our prayer
633 Gracious Savior, gentle Shepherd
634 Gracious Savior, who didst honor
635 Gracious Spirit, dwell with me
636 Gracious Spirit, Holy Ghost (see also 1192)
637 Gracious Spirit, Love divine
638 Grander than ocean's story
639 Grant us, Lord, the grace of giving
640 Great God of nations, now to thee
641 Great God of wonders
642 Great God, to thee our hearts we raise
643 Great God, we sing that mighty hand
644 Great God, what do I see and hear
645 Great God who hast delivered us
646 Great is the Lord, and greatly he
647 "Great is thy faithfulness," O God my Father
648 Great King of nations, hear our prayer
649 Great Master, touch us with thy skillful hands
650 Great Ruler of the land and sea
651 Great Shepherd of thy people, hear (see also 393)
652 Guide me, O thou great Jehovah

H

653 Hail, gladdening Light
654 Hail, sacred day of earthly rest
655 Hail the day that sees him rise
656 Hail the glorious golden city
657 Hail the hero workers of the mighty past
658 Hail, thou long-expected Jesus (see also 343)
659 Hail, thou once despised Jesus
660 Hail to the brightness of Zion's glad morning
661 Hail to the Lord's Anointed
662 Hallelujah, fairest morning
663 Hallelujah, hallelujah! Heart and voice (see also 76)
664 Hallelujah, "he is risen!"
665 Hallelujah(!) Raise, O raise
666 Happy are they, they that love God
667 Happy the home when God is there
668 Hark! a herald voice is sounding
669 Hark, creation's Alleluia
670 Hark! Hark, my soul! angelic songs
671 Hark how the adoring hosts above (see also 323)
672 Hark, my soul! it is the Lord
673 Hark! ten thousand harps and voices
674 Hark! the glad sound, the Savior comes
675 Hark, the herald angels sing
676 Hark! the song of jubilee
677 Hark! the sound of holy voices
678 Hark! the vesper hymn is stealing
679 Hark! the voice of Jesus crying
680 Hark! there comes a whisper
681 Hark! 'tis the Shepherd's voice I hear
682 Hark! 'tis the watchman's cry
683 Hark, what a sound, and too divine
684 Hark! what mean those holy voices

685 Hast thou not known, hast thou not heard
686 Hast thou, O Lord, a work to do?
687 Have faith in God, my heart
688 Have faith in God when your pathway
689 Have mercy, Lord, on me
690 Have mercy on us, God most high
691 Have thine own way, Lord
692 Have you any room for Jesus
693 Have you been to Jesus for the cleansing power
694 Have you failed in your plan
695 Have you heard the voice of Jesus
696 Have you read the story of the Cross
697 He dies! the Friend of sinners
698 He feedeth his flock
699 He is coming, the "Man of Sorrows"
700 He is risen, He is risen
701 He knoweth the way that I take
702 He leadeth me: O blessed thought
703 He liveth long, who liveth well
704 He that is down needs fear no fall
705 He was not willing that any should perish
706 He who, a little child, began (see also 9)
707 He who would valiant be (see also 2290)
708 Head of thy church triumphant
709 Hear, hear, O ye nations
710 Hear my words, O gracious Lord
711 Hear our prayer, O heavenly Father
712 Hear us, O Lord, from heaven thy dwelling place
713 Hear us, our Father
714 Heart and mind, possessions, Lord
715 Heaven and earth, and sea and air
716 Heaven is here, where hymns of gladness
717 Heav'nly Father, bless me now
718 Heavenly Father, send thy blessing
719 Help me to be holy, O Father of Light
720 Heralds of Christ, who bear the King's commands
721 Here at thy table, Lord, this sacred hour
721 Here at thy table, Lord, this
723 Here from the world we turn
724 Here my heart, O Lord, I give to thee
725 Here is my Rock! here is my Fortress
726 Here, Lord, we take the broken bread
727 Here, O my Lord, I see thee face to face
728 Here, Savior, we would come
729 "Hidden with Christ in God"
730 Hide me, Lord, in thy pavilion
731 High in the heavens, eternal God
732 High o'er the lonely hills
733 Hills of the north, rejoice
734 His are the thousand sparkling rills
735 His name for ever shall endure (see also 145, 4)
736 Ho, my comrades see the signal
737 Hold thou my hand(!) so weak I am
738 Holy Bible, Book divine
739 Holy Father, cheer our way
740 Holy Father, hear me
741 Holy Father, in thy mercy
742 Holy Father, thou hast given
743 Holy Ghost, dispel our sadness
744 Holy Ghost, my Comforter
745 Holy Ghost, with light divine
746 Holy God, we praise thy name
747 Holy, holy, holy is the Lord
748 Holy, holy, holy, Lord
749 Holy, holy, holy! Lord God Almighty

750 Holy, holy, holy, Lord God of Hosts
751 Holy, holy, holy, Lord, thy disciples
752 Holy Lamb, who thee confess
753 Holy off'rings, rich and rare
754 Holy Spirit, bending lowly
755 Holy Spirit, faithful Guide
756 Holy Spirit, from on high
757 Holy Spirit, hear us
758 Holy Spirit, heavenly Dove
759 Holy Spirit, lead us now
760 Holy Spirit, Lord of love
761 Holy Spirit, Truth divine
762 Hope of the world, thou Christ of great compassion
763 Hosanna, loud hosanna
764 Hosanna to the living Lord
765 Hosanna we sing, like the children dear
766 Hover o'er me, Holy Spirit
767 How are thy servants blest, O Lord
768 How beauteous are their feet
769 How beauteous were the marks divine
770 How beautiful! The morning star!
771 How beautiful the sight
772 How blest is he whose trespass
773 How blest the man that fears the Lord
774 How bright these glorious spirits shine
775 How excellent in all the earth (see also 1450)
776 How firm a foundation, ye saints of the Lord
777 How gentle God's commands
778 How glorious Zion's courts appear
779 How happy every child of grace
780 How I love thy law, O Lord
781 How lovely and how cheering
782 How lovely are thy dwellings fair
783 How lovely is thy dwelling-place
784 How near to us, O God, thou art
785 How oft, O Lord, thy face hath shone
786 How pleased and blest was I
787 How precious is the Book divine
788 How shall I sing that Majesty
789 How shall the young direct their way
790 How strong and sweet my Father's care
791 How sweet amid earth's wild alarms
792 How sweet, how heav'nly is the sight
793 How sweet the hour of closing day
794 How sweet the name of Jesus sounds
795 How tedious and tasteless the hours
796 Hush, all ye sounds of war
797 Hushed was the evening hymn

I

798 I adore thee, I adore thee
799 I am a stranger here, within a foreign land
800 I am coming to the cross
801 I am happy in the service of the King
802 I am happy today and the sun shines bright
803 I am not worthy, holy Lord
804 I am resolved no longer to linger
805 I am satisfied with Jesus
806 I am so glad that my (our) Father in heaven
807 I am so happy in Christ today
808 I am thine, O Lord, I have heard
809 I am thinking today of that beautiful land
810 I am trav'ling toward the sunset gate
811 I am trusting thee, Lord Jesus
812 I am walking ev'ry day with Jesus

813 I bind my heart this tide
814 I can hear my Savior calling
815 I cannot drift beyond thy love
816 I cannot put the Presence by
817 I cannot tell why he, whom angels worship
818 I cannot think or reason
819 I come to the garden alone
820 I could not do without thee
821 I do not ask, O Lord, that life may be
822 I do not ask to see the way
823 I do not know, I cannot tell
824 I do not know why oft 'round me
825 I dreamed I saw the Savior climb
826 I feel the winds of God today
827 I gave my life for thee
828 I greet thee, who my sure Redeemer art
829 I have a friend who abides
830 I have a Savior, he's pleading in glory
831 I have a Savior who's pleading above
832 I have a song I love to sing
833 I have a song that Jesus gave me
834 I have found a Friend in Jesus
835 I have walked alone with Jesus
836 I hear my risen Savior say
837 I hear the Savior say
838 I hear the words that Jesus spake
839 I hear thy welcome voice
840 I heard the bells on Christmas Day
841 I heard the Savior calling
842 I heard the voice of Jesus say
843 I joyed when to the house of God
844 I know I love thee better
845 I know my heav'nly Father knows
846 I know not how that Bethlehem's Babe
847 I know not what before me lies
848 I know not what the future hath (see also 2310)
849 I know not why God's wondrous grace
850 I know of a world that is sunk in shame
851 I know that my Redeemer lives
852 I know that my Redeemer liveth
853 I know whom I believed
854 I lay my sins on Jesus
855 I lift my heart to thee
856 I look to thee in every need
857 I love the Lord, because my voice
858 I love the Lord, his strength is mine
859 I love thy kingdom, Lord
860 I love to hear the story
861 I love to steal awhile away
862 I love to tell the story
863 I must have the Savior with me
864 I must needs go home by the way of the cross
865 I must tell Jesus all of my trials
866 I need Jesus, my need I now confess
867 I need not ask what time will bring
868 I need thee every hour
869 I need thee, precious Jesus
870 I never can forget the day
871 I own not the riches of silver or gold
872 I saw the cross of Jesus
873 I see the crowd in Pilate's hall
874 I serve a risen Savior
875 I sing a song of the saints
876 I sing the love of God, my Father
877 I sing the mighty power of God
878 I sought his love in sun and stars
879 I sought the Lord, and afterward I knew
880 I stand all amazed at the love Jesus offers
881 I stand amazed in the presence
882 I thank thee, Lord, for life
883 I thank thee, Lord, for strength of arm
884 I think when I read that sweet story
885 I to the hills will (wilt) lift mine eyes

886 I vow to thee, my country
887 I waited for the Lord my God
888 I walked one day along a country road
889 I want a principle within
890 I want my life to glorify
891 I was sinking deep in sin
892 I was wandering and weary
893 I will not question, Lord, today
894 I will sing of my Redeemer
895 I will sing the wondrous story
896 I will sing you a song of that beautiful land
897 I would be true, for there are those who trust me
898 If God himself be for me
899 If I can stop one heart from breaking
900 If I come to Jesus
901 If I have wounded any soul today
902 If, on a quiet sea
903 If the dark shadows gather
904 If thou but suffer God to guide thee
905 If you are tired of the load of your sin
906 If you from sin are longing to be free
907 If your own sorrows you want to forget
908 If you've found Jesus the friend that you need
909 I'll hear what God the Lord will speak
910 I'll of salvation take the cup
911 I'll praise my Maker while I've breath
912 I'll tell to all that God is love
913 I'm a pilgrim, and I'm a stranger
914 I'm not ashamed to own my Lord
915 I'm pressing on the upward way
916 Immortal, invisible, God only wise
917 Immortal Love, forever full (see also 2181)
918 In Bethlehem 'neath starlit skies
919 In Christ there is no East or West
920 In full and glad surrender
921 In heav'nly love abiding
922 In his love abiding
923 In homes where pride and splendor
924 In Jesus' name we pray
925 In life's earnest morning
926 In lovingkindness Jesus came
927 In memory of the Savior's love
928 In our dear Lord's garden
929 In our hearts celestial voices
930 In our work and in our play
931 In sorrow I wandered, my spirit oppressed
932 In sweet communion, Lord, with thee
933 In the bleak mid-winter
934 In the Cross of Christ I glory
935 In the early morning
936 In the gladness of the morning
937 In the hour of trial
938 In the land of fadeless day
939 In the land of strangers
940 In the lonely midnight
941 In the ranks so true there's a place for you
942 In the secret of his presence
943 In the shadow of his wings
944 In this, thy temple, Lord, we see thy face
945 Infant holy, infant lowly
946 Into the heart of the wildwood
947 Into the woods my Master went
948 It came upon the midnight clear
949 It fell upon a summer day
950 "It is finished!" Man of Sorrows
951 It is good to sing thy praises
952 It is the joyful Easter time
953 It may be at morn, when the day is awaking
954 It may be in the valley, where countless
955 It may not be on the mountain's height
956 It singeth low in every heart
957 It was alone the Savior prayed

J

958 Jehovah is thy God! O Israel, arise
959 Jehovah the Lord, our Savior and King
960 Jerusalem, my happy home
961 Jerusalem the golden (see also 489)
962 Jesu, from thy throne on high (see also 1009)
963 Jesu, grant me this, I pray
964 Jesu, meek and gentle (see also 999)
965 Jesu, our hope, our Heart's desire
966 Jesu, Sun of Righteousness (see also 1012)
967 Jesus! and shall it ever be
968 Jesus bids us shine
969 Jesus calls me, I must follow
970 Jesus calls us, o'er the tumult
971 Jesus Christ is risen today
972 Jesus, Fountain of my days
973 Jesus, Friend of little children
974 Jesus, Friend, so kind and gentle
975 Jesus himself drew near
976 Jesus, holy, undefiled
977 Jesus, I am coming home
978 Jesus, I am resting, resting
979 Jesus, I live to thee (see also 1250)
980 Jesus, I my cross have taken
981 Jesus is all the world to me
982 Jesus is coming to earth again
983 Jesus is our Shepherd
984 Jesus is standing in Pilate's hall
985 Jesus is tenderly calling thee home
986 Jesus, keep me near the cross
987 Jesus knows thy sorrow
988 Jesus, lead the way (see also 989, 1011)
989 Jesus, lead thou on (see also 988, 1011)
990 Jesus lives, and Jesus leads
991 Jesus lives and so shall I
992 Jesus lives! thy terrors now
993 Jesus, Lord of life and glory
944 Jesus, Lover of my soul
995 Jesus loves me, this I know
996 Jesus loves the little children
997 Jesus, Master, whom I serve (see also 998)
998 Jesus, Master, whose I am (see also 997)
999 Jesus, meek and gentle (see also 964)
1000 Jesus merciful, Jesus pitying
1001 Jesus, my all, to heaven is gone
1002 Jesus, my Lord, my Life, my All
1003 Jesus, my Strength, my Hope
1004 Jesus, priceless treasure
1005 Jesus, Refuge of the weary
1006 Jesus, Rose of Sharon, bloom within
1007 Jesus, Savior, pilot me
1008 Jesus shall reign where'er the sun
1009 Jesus, Son of God most high (see also 962)
1010 Jesus, stand among us
1011 Jesus, still lead on (see also 988, 989)
1012 Jesus, Sun of Righteousness (see also 966)
1013 Jesus, tender Shepherd, hear me
1014 Jesus, the children are calling
1015 Jesus, the Crucified, pleads for me
1016 Jesus the Great Physician came
1017 Jesus! the Name high over all
1018 Jesus, the sinner's Friend, to thee
1019 Jesus, the very thought of thee
1020 Jesus, these eyes have never seen
1021 Jesus, thine all-victorious love
1022 Jesus, thou divine Companion (see also 2006)
1023 Jesus, thou joy of loving hearts
1024 Jesus, thy blood and righteousness
1025 Jesus, thy boundless love to me
1026 Jesus, thy church with longing eyes

1027 Jesus, thy name I bear
1028 Jesus, to thy table led
1029 Jesus, united by thy grace
1030 Jesus wants me for a sunbeam
1031 Jesus, we look to thee
1032 Jesus, where'er thy people meet
1033 Jesus, with thy church abide
1034 Jesus, wondrous Savior
1035 Join all the glorious names
1036 Joy because the circling year
1037 Joy dawned again on Easter Day
1038 Joy is a fruit that will not grow
1039 Joy to the world!
1040 Joyful, joyful, we adore thee
1041 Joys are flowing like a river
1042 Judge eternal, throned in splendor
1043 Judge me, O Lord, for I have walked
1044 Just a few more days to be filled with praise
1045 Just as I am, thine own to be
1046 Just as I am, without one plea
1047 Just when I need him

K

1048 Keep on praying when the skies are gray
1049 King of love, O Christ
1050 King of my life, I crown thee

L

1051 Lamb of God, to thee we raise
1052 Lamp of our feet, whereby we trace
1053 Lead, kindly Light
1054 Lead me, Lord, lead me in thy righteousness
1055 Lead me now and lead me ever
1056 Lead me to some soul today
1057 Lead on, O King Eternal
1058 Lead us, Heavenly Father, lead us
1059 Lead us, O Father, in the paths of peace
1060 Let all mortal flesh keep silence
1061 Let all on earth their voices raise
1062 Let all the world in every corner sing
1063 Let all who enter here
1064 Let Christian faith and hope dispel
1065 Let everlasting glories crown
1066 Let our hearts be ever happy
1067 Let saints on earth in concert sing (see also 324)
1068 Let the beauty of Jesus be seen in me
1069 Let the church march on
1070 Let the song go round the earth
1071 Let the whole creation cry
1072 Let there be light, Lord God of Hosts
1073 Let us sing the King Messiah
1074 Let us with a gladsome mind
1075 Life is good, for God contrives it
1076 Life is like a mountain railroad
1077 Life of ages, richly poured
1078 Lift up, lift up your voices now
1079 Lift up our hearts, O King of Kings (see also 82)
1080 Lift up your heads ye gates eternal
1081 Lift up your heads, ye gates of brass
1082 Lift up your heads, ye mighty gates
1083 Lift up your hearts, ye people
1084 Light of life, so softly shining
1085 Light of light, enlighten me
1086 Light of the lonely pilgrim's heart
1087 Light of the world! for ever, ever shining
1088 Light of the world, how long the quest
1089 Light of the world, we hail thee

1090 Light up this house with glory
1091 Like a river glorious is God's perfect peace
1092 Like a rushing wind, O Holy Spirit
1093 "Like as a mother comforteth"
1094 Like children round a radiant light
1095 Like silver lamps in a distant shrine
1096 Like sweet music softly breaking
1097 Like wand'ring sheep o'er mountains cold
1098 Listen! the Master beseecheth
1099 Little children praise the Savior
1100 Little children wake, and listen
1101 Little drops of water
1102 Little stars are shining
1103 Little things that run and quail
1104 Living for Jesus a life that is true
1105 Lo, God is here! let us adore
1106 Lo! He comes, with clouds descending
1107 Lo, how a rose e'er blooming
1108 Lo! round the throne a glorious band
1109 Lo, the day of God is breaking
1110 Lo! the pilgrim magi
1111 Lo! what a glorious sight appears
1112 Long did I toil, and knew no earthly rest
1113 Long years ago o'er Bethlehem's hills
1114 Look away to Jesus
1115 Look away to the cross
1116 Look from thy sphere of endless day
1117 Look, ye saints, the sight is glorious
1118 Lord, a little band and lowly
1119 Lord, as to thy dear cross we flee
1120 Lord, as we thy name profess
1121 Lord, at this closing hour
1122 Lord, at thy table we behold
1123 Lord, bless and pity us
1124 Lord Christ, when first thou cam'st to men
1125 Lord, dismiss us with thy blessing
1126 Lord, enthroned in heavenly splendor
1127 Lord, for the mercies of the night
1128 Lord, for tomorrow and its needs I do not pray
1129 Lord, from the depths to thee I cried
1130 Lord God of Hosts, whose purpose
1131 Lord God of morning and of night
1132 Lord God, the Holy Ghost
1133 Lord, have mercy upon us
1134 Lord, hear my voice, my prayer attend (see also 1376)
1135 Lord, hear the right, attend my cry
1136 Lord, her watch thy church is keeping
1137 Lord, I am thine, entirely thine
1138 Lord, I hear of showers of blessing
1139 Lord, I want to be a Christian
1140 Lord, I was blind: I could not see
1141 Lord, I would own thy tender care
1142 Lord, in the fullness of my might
1143 Lord, in the morning thou shalt hear
1144 Lord, in the strength of grace
1145 Lord, in this thy mercy's day
1146 Lord, in thy name thy servants plead
1147 Lord, increase our faith today
1148 Lord, it belongs not to my care
1149 Lord Jesus Christ, be present now
1150 Lord Jesus, think on me
1151 Lord, keep us safe this night
1152 Lord lay some soul upon my heart
1153 Lord, let mercy now attend us

1154 Lord, now lettest thou thy servant
1155 Lord of all being, throned afar
1156 Lord of all power and might
1157 Lord of Good Life, the hosts of the undying
1158 Lord of health, thou life within us
1159 Lord of heaven, and earth and ocean
1160 Lord of light, whose name outshineth
1161 Lord of mercy and of might
1162 Lord of our life, and God of our salvation
1163 Lord of our life, God whom we fear
1164 Lord of the harvest, it is right that we
1165 Lord of the lands, beneath thy bending skies
1166 Lord of the living harvest (see also 1344)
1167 Lord of the worlds above
1168 Lord, save thy world: in bitter need
1169 Lord, send us forth to preach the word
1170 Lord, speak to me, that I may speak
1171 Lord, teach us how to pray aright (see also 1506)
1172 Lord, thee my God, I'll early seek
1173 Lord, this day thy children meet
1174 Lord, thou hast been our dwelling place
1175 Lord, thou hast known our joy
1176 Lord, thou shalt early hear my voice (see also 527)
1177 Lord, through this holy week
1178 Lord, thy glory fills the heaven (see also 253, 1673)
1179 Lord, thy mercy now entreating
1180 Lord, thy word abideth
1181 Lord, we come before thee now
1182 Lord, we thank thee for our brothers
1183 Lord, what a change within us
1184 Lord, when we bend before thy throne
1185 Lord, while for all mankind we pray
1186 Lord, who ordainest for mankind
1187 Lord, who throughout these forty days
1188 Lord, wilt thou in this temple reign
1189 Love came down at Christmas
1190 Love divine, all love(s) excelling
1191 Love him, love him, all ye little children (see also 1615)
1192 Love is kind and suffers long (see also 636)
1193 Love not the world, O Christian
1194 Love opened wide the door for me
1195 Loved with everlasting love
1196 Loving Savior, thou didst come
1197 Loving Shepherd of thy sheep
1198 Lovingly the Shepherd, seeking the lost sheep
1199 Low in a manger
1200 Low in the grave he lay

M

1201 Majestic sweetness sits enthroned
1202 Make me a captive, Lord
1203 "Man of sorrows," what a name
1204 March on, O soul, with strength
1205 Marching with the heroes
1206 Marvelous grace of our loving Lord
1207 Master, speak! Thy servant heareth
1208 Master, the tempest is raging
1209 May the grace of Christ our Savior
1210 Meet him in the morning
1211 Men and children everywhere

1212 'Mid pleasures and palaces though we
1213 Mighty God, we worship thee
1214 Mighty God (while) whose angels bless thee
1215 Mine eyes have seen the glory
1216 More about Jesus would I know
1217 More light shall break from out
1218 More like Jesus would I be
1219 More like the Master
1220 More love to thee, O Christ
1221 Morning has broken
1222 Must I go, and empty-handed
1223 Must Jesus bear the cross alone
1224 My country is the world
1225 My country, 'tis of thee
1226 My dear Redeemer and my Lord
1227 My faith looks up to thee
1228 My Father, for another night
1229 My Father is rich in houses and lands
1230 My God, accept my heart this day
1231 My God [and, my] Father, while I stray
1232 My God, and is thy table spread
1233 My God, how endless is thy love
1234 My God, how wonderful thou art
1235 My God, I love thee; not because
1236 My God, I thank thee who hast made
1237 My God, is any hour so sweet
1238 My God, my father, make me strong
1239 My God, my God, why dost thou me forsake
1240 My God, the spring of all my joys
1241 My gracious Lord, I own thy right
1242 My heart is resting, O my God
1243 My heavenly home is bright and fair
1244 My hope is built on nothing less
1245 My Jesus, as thou wilt
1246 My Jesus, I love thee
1247 My latest sun is sinking fast
1248 My life, my love, I give to thee
1249 My Lord has garments so wondrous fine
1250 My Lord, I live to thee (see also 979)
1251 My Lord, my Master, at thy feet
1252 My Master was a worker
1253 My Master was so very poor
1254 My own dear land, where'er my footsteps
1255 My song is love unknown
1256 My soul, be on thy guard
1257 My soul in sad exile
1258 My soul with expectation doth
1259 My spirit longs for thee
1260 My times are in thy hand
1261 My trust is in the Lord

N

1262 Naught have I gotten but what I received
1263 Near the Cross her vigil keeping (see also 140)
1264 Nearer, blessed Jesus, to thy wounded side
1265 Nearer, my God, to thee
1266 Nearer, still nearer
1267 "Nearer the Cross!" my heart can say
1268 'Neath the stars of the night
1269 Never be sad or desponding
1270 Never fear though shadows dark around
1271 Never further than thy Cross
1272 Never shone a light so fair
1273 New every morning is the love
1274 No burdens yonder
1275 No longer, Lord, thy sons shall sow
1276 No, not despairingly
1277 None other Lamb, none other name
1278 Nor silver nor gold hath obtained

1279 Not all the blood of beasts
1280 Not alone for mighty empire
1281 Not in dumb resignation
1282 Not now, but in the coming years
1283 Not so in haste, my heart
1284 Not what I am, O Lord
1285 Nothing but leaves
1286 Now cheer our hearts this eventide
1287 Now do we come, O God, to worship
1288 Now from the altar of my heart
1289 Now God be with us, for the night
1290 Now I have found the firm foundation
1291 Now in the days of youth
1292 Now just a word for Jesus
1293 Now let us all with one accord
1294 Now, Lord, upon thy sea of air
1295 Now, on land and sea descending
1296 Now praise we great and famous men
1297 Now rest beneath night's shadow
1298 Now sing we a song for the harvest
1299 Now thank we all our God
1300 Now that the daylight fills the sky
1301 Now that the daystar glimmers
1302 Now the day is over
1303 Now the laborer's task is o'er
1304 Now the light has gone away
1305 Now the spring has come again
1306 Now to him who loved us
1307 Now to the King of heaven
1308 Now to the Lord a noble song
1309 Now woods and wolds are sleeping

O

1310 O be joyful in the Lord
1311 O beautiful for spacious skies
1312 O beautiful, my country
1313 O blessed day of motherhood
1314 O blessed is the man whose sins
1315 O bless the Lord, my soul
1316 O Bread of Life, for all men broken
1317 O Bread of Life, from heaven
1318 O Breath of God, breathe on us now
1319 O brother man, fold to thy heart thy brother
1320 O brothers, lift your voices
1321 O children, hither do ye come
1322 O Christ, in thee my soul hath found
1323 O Christ, the way, the truth, the life
1324 O Christ, thou gift of Love Divine
1325 O Christ, thou hast ascended
1326 O Christ, thou Lamb of God
1327 O Christ, who holds the open gate
1328 O church of God, divided
1329 O church of God, our solitude
1330 O come, all ye faithful
1331 O, come, all ye that labor
1332 O come, and dwell in me
1333 O come and mourn with me awhile
1334 O come and sing unto the Lord (see also 1335)
1335 O come, let us sing to the Lord (see also 1334)
1336 O come, O come, Emmanual
1337 O come, sinner, come
1338 O come to the merciful Savior
1339 O could I speak the matchless worth
1340 O day of God, draw nigh
1341 O day of rest and gladness
1342 O dearest Lord, accept today the gifts
1343 O do not let the Word depart

1344 O Father, all creating (see also 1166)
1345 O Father, hear my morning prayer
1346 O Father, thou who givest all
1347 O for a closer walk with God
1348 O for a faith that will not shrink
1349 O for a heart of calm repose
1350 O for a heart to praise my God
1351 O for a thousand tongues to sing
1352 O for the peace which floweth as
1353 O God, above the drifting years
1354 O God, beneath thy guiding hand
1355 O God Creator, in whose hand
1356 O God, Eternal God! Thy name
1357 O God, give ear unto my cry
1358 O God, I cried, no dark disguise
1359 O God, in restless living
1360 O God, in whom we live and move
1361 O God, in whose great purpose
1362 O God, my heart is fixed
1363 O God, not only in distress
1364 O God of Bethel, by whose hand
1365 O God of earth and altar
1366 O God of God
1367 O God, of good the unfathomed Sea
1368 O God of light, thy Word
1369 O God of love, O King of peace
1370 O God of love, to thee we bow
1371 O God of mercy, God of might
1372 O God of our fathers, we praise
1373 O God of truth, whose living Word
1374 O God of youth, whose Spirit in our hearts
1375 O God, our help in ages past (see also 1596)
1376 O God, regard my humble plea (see also 1134)
1377 O God, the Rock of Ages
1378 O God, thou art the Father
1379 O God, thy summons still is heard
1380 O God, thy world is sweet with pray'r
1381 O God, we pray for all mankind
1382 O God, who workest hitherto
1383 O God, whose daylight leadeth
1384 O God, whose love is over all
1385 O God, whose smile is in the sky
1386 O gracious Father of mankind
1387 O gracious God, forsake me not
1388 O gracious God, whose constant care
1389 O grant us light, that we may know
1390 O greatly blessed the people are
1391 O happy band of pilgrims
1392 O happy day, that fixed my choice
1393 O happy home, where thou art loved
1394 O happy is that man and blest
1395 O hear my cry, be gracious now to me
1396 O help us, Lord; each hour of need
1397 O holy city, seen of John
1398 O Holy Ghost, thy people bless
1399 O holy night; the stars are brightly shining
1400 O Holy Savior, friend unseen
1401 O Holy Spirit, Comforter
1402 O Holy Spirit, enter in
1403 O Holy Spirit, Lord of grace
1404 O house of many mansions
1405 O Jesu, King most wonderful (see also 1409)
1406 O Jesus Christ, our Lord most dear
1407 O Jesus Christ, grow thou in me
1408 O Jesus, I have promised
1409 O Jesus, King most wonderful (see also 1405)
1410 O Jesus, Master, when today
1411 O Jesus, my Lord and Savior
1412 O Jesus, Prince of life and truth
1413 O Jesus, Savior and my Lord
1414 O Jesus, thou art standing
1415 O Jesus, we adore thee

1416 O Jesus, when I think of thee
1417 O Jesus, youth of Nazareth
1418 O joyous Easter morning
1419 O Lamb of God, still keep me
1420 O Lamb of God, that takest away
1421 O land of rest, for thee I sigh
1422 O let my heart an altar be
1423 O Light that knew no dawn
1424 O Light, whose beams illumine all
1425 O listen to our wondrous story
1426 O little own of Bethlehem
1427 O living Christ, chief Cornerstone
1428 O Lord and Master of us all (see also 240)
1429 O Lord, be with us when we sail
1430 O Lord, how are my foes increased
1431 O Lord, how happy should we be
1432 O Lord, how joyful 'tis to see
1433 O Lord, I unto thee do cry
1434 O Lord, make haste to hear my cry
1435 O Lord Most High, with all my heart
1436 O Lord my God most earnestly
1437 O Lord my God! When I in awesome wonder
1438 O Lord, my inmost heart and thought
1439 O Lord of heaven and earth and sea
1440 O Lord of hosts, the fight is long
1441 O Lord of hosts, whose glory fills
1442 O Lord of life, and love, and power
1443 O Lord of life, thy kingdom is at hand
1444 O Lord of life, thy quickening voice
1445 O Lord of life, to thee we lift (see also 191)
1446 O Lord of life, where'er they be (see also 590)
1447 O Lord of love, thou light divine
1448 O Lord, our fathers oft have told
1449 O Lord our God, arise
1450 O Lord, our Lord, in all the earth (see also 775)
1451 O Lord, thou art my God and King
1452 O Lord, thou hast me searched
1453 O Lord, thy benediction give
1454 O Lord, thy judgments give the king (see also 735)
1455 O Lord, to thee I cry
1456 O Lord, turn not thy face from me
1457 O Love divine and golden
1458 O Love divine, how sweet thou art
1459 O Love divine! that stoop'st to share
1460 O Love divine, what hast thou done
1461 O love of God, how strong and true
1462 O love of God most full
1463 O love that casts out fear
1464 O love, that passeth knowledge
1465 O love that wilt not let me go
1466 O Master, let me walk with thee
1467 O Master of the waking world
1468 O Master Workman of the race
1469 O men of God, go forth to win
1470 O Morning Star, how fair and bright
1471 O my Savior, lifted
1472 O my soul, bless thou Jehovah
1473 O Perfect Love
1474 O Risen Lord, within thy temple here
1475 O Sacred Head, now wounded
1476 O Sacred Head, surrounded
1477 O safe to the Rock that is higher
1478 O Savior, bless us ere we go (see also 1812)
1479 O Savior, I have naught to plead
1480 O Savior, may we never rest
1481 O Savior, precious Savior
1482 O Savior, where shall guilty man

1483 O send thy light forth and thy truth
1484 O set ye open unto me
1485 O serve the Lord with gladness
1486 O sing a new song to the Lord
1487 O sing a song (hymn) of Bethlehem
1488 O Sion, open wide thy gates
1489 O sometimes the shadows are deep
1490 O Son of God, incarnate
1491 O Son of Man, our Hero strong and tender
1492 O Son of Man, thou madest known
1493 O sons and daughters, let us sing
1494 O soul in the far-away country
1495 O Source divine, and Life of all
1496 O still in accents sweet and strong
1497 O that the Lord's salvation
1498 O the bitter shame and sorrow
1499 O, the friends that now are waiting
1500 O, the love so full and free
1501 O, the wondrous love, coming from above
1502 O they tell me of a home
1503 O think of the home over there
1504 O thou beautiful, O thou wonderful
1505 O thou, before whose presence
1506 O thou by whom we come to God (see also 1171, 1641)
1507 O thou eternal Christ of God
1508 O thou Eternal Source of life
1509 O thou, from whom all goodness flows
1510 O thou God of my salvation
1511 O thou great friend to all the sons
1512 O thou, in whose presence my soul
1513 O thou my soul, bless God the Lord
1514 O thou, my soul, forget no more
1515 O thou not made with hands
1516 O thou sweetest source of gladness
1517 O thou, the contrite sinner's Friend
1518 O thou, to whom our voices rise
1519 O thou, to whose all-searching sight
1520 O thou who by a star didst guide
1521 O thou who camest from above
1522 O thou who didst, with love untold
1523 O thou who gavest power to love
1524 O thou who hearest prayer
1525 O thou who through this holy week
1526 O thou whose feet have climbed
1527 O thou, whose glory shone like fire
1528 O thou whose gracious presence blest
1529 O thou whose hand hath brought us
1530 O thou, whose own vast temple (see also 2052)
1531 O troubled heart, there is a home
1532 O valiant hearts, who to your glory came
1533 O Voice that calls to me from
1534 O what am I that I should be
1535 O what can be more beautiful
1536 O what can little hands do
1537 O what, if we are Christ's
1538 O what their joy and their glory
1539 O where are kings and empires now
1540 O, where are the reapers
1541 O with thy tender mercies, Lord
1542 O why not say yes to the Savior
1543 O wondrous type, O vision fair
1544 O Word of God Incarnate
1545 O word of pity, for our pardon
1546 O worship the King, all glorious
1547 O ye angels, that excel
1548 O ye who taste that love is sweet
1549 O young and fearless Prophet
1550 O young mariner
1551 O Zion (Sion), haste, thy mission high

1552 O'er field and forest stealing
1553 O'er the trackless ocean guided
1554 O'er those gloomy hills of darkness
1555 Of him who did salvation bring
1556 Of Jesus' love that sought me
1557 Of mercy and of judgment
1558 Of the Father's love begotten
1559 Of the themes that men have known
1560 Oft in danger, oft in woe
1561 On a hill far away stood an old
1562 On Calvary's brow my Savior
1563 On Jordan's stormy banks
1564 On the cross for me
1565 On the good and faithful
1566 On this day, the first of days
1567 On this stone now laid with prayer
1568 On yonder hill of Calvary
1569 On Zion's hill I long to be
1570 Once again, dear Lord, we pray
1571 Once far from God and dead in sin
1572 Once in royal David's city
1573 Once my way was dark and dreary
1574 Once to every man and nation
1575 One day when heaven was filled with
1576 One holy church of God appears
1577 One is kind above all others
1578 One more day's work for Jesus
1579 One sole baptismal sign
1580 One sweetly solemn thought
1581 One there is, above all others
1582 One thing I of the Lord desire
1583 One thing needful, Lord, this treasure
1584 Only a step to Jesus
1585 Only a touch of thy hand, dear Lord
1586 Onward! Christian soldiers
1587 Open my eyes that I may see
1588 Open now the (thy) gates of beauty
1589 Our blest Redeemer, ere he breathed
1590 Our children, Lord, in faith and
1591 Our church proclaims God's love
1592 Our day of praise is done
1593 Our faith is in the Christ who walks
1594 Our Father in heaven, we hallow thy
1595 Our fathers' God, to thee we raise
1596 Our God, our help in ages past (see also 1375)
1597 Our lamps are trimmed and burning
1598 Our life is like a summer day
1599 Our Lord Christ hath risen
1600 Out in the darkness of sorrow and sin
1601 Out in the highways and byways of life
1602 Out of my bondage, sorrow and night
1603 Out on life's dark heaving ocean
1604 Outside the holy city
1605 Over the river faces I see

P

1606 Part in peace! Is day before us
1607 Pass me not, O gentle Savior
1608 Pass on the torch, pass on the flame
1609 Peace in our time, O Lord
1610 Peace, perfect peace
1611 Peacefully round us the shadows
1612 Pleasant are thy courts above
1613 Praise God from whom all blessings flow
1614 Praise God, ye peoples of the earth
1615 Praise him, praise him, all ye little (see 915, 1191)
1616 Praise him! praise him! Jesus, our blessed

1617 Praise him, ye heavens, rejoice all ye
1618 Praise, my soul, the King of heaven
1619 Praise, O praise our God and King
1620 Praise our God above
1621 Praise the Almighty, my soul, adore him
1622 Praise the Lord, for he is good
1623 Praise the Lord! His glories show
1624 Praise the Lord of heaven
1625 Praise the Lord who reigns above
1626 Praise the Lord! ye heavens, adore him
1627 Praise thou the Lord, O my soul
1628 Praise to God, immortal praise
1629 Praise to God for things we see
1630 Praise to the Holiest in the height
1631 Praise waits for thee in Zion, Lord
1632 Praise we the Lord this day
1633 Praise we the Lord who made all beauty
1634 Praise ye Jehovah, praise the Lord
1635 Praise ye the Father, for his loving
1636 Praise ye the Lord, for it is good
1637 Praise ye the Lord, the Almighty, the King
1638 Praise ye the Lord: with my whole heart
1639 Pray on, O soul of mine, pray on
1640 Pray, pray when things go wrong
1641 Prayer is the soul's sincere desire (see also 1506)
1642 Precious promise God hath given
1643 Precious thought, my Father knoweth
1644 Prince of Peace, control my will
1645 Purer in heart, O God
1646 Put forth, O God, thy Spirit's might

Q

1647 Quiet, Lord, my forward heart

R

1648 Redeemed and made perfect
1649 Redeemed, how I love to proclaim it
1650 Rejoice and be merry in songs
1651 Rejoice, O land, in God thy might
1652 Rejoice, O people, in the mounting years
1653 Rejoice, the Lord is King
1654 Rejoice, ye pure in heart
1655 Rescue the perishing
1656 Rest of the weary
1657 Return, O wanderer, return
1658 Revealing Word, thy light portrays
1659 Revive thy work, O Lord
1660 Ride on! ride on in majesty
1661 Ring, happy bells of Easter time
1662 Ring out the old, ring in the new
1663 Ring out, wild bells
1664 Ring the bells of heaven
1665 Ring, ye bells of joy and praise
1666 Rise, crowned with light, imperial
1667 Rise, my soul, and stretch thy wings
1668 Rise, my soul, to watch and pray
1669 Rise up, O men of God
1670 Risen with Christ! O boundless joy
1671 Rock of Ages, cleft for me
1672 Round me falls the night
1673 Round the Lord in glory seated (see also 253, 1178)

S

1674 Safe am I
1675 Safe in the arms of Jesus
1676 Safely through another week
1677 Salvation and immortal praise (see also 237)
1678 Saved to the uttermost
1679 Savior, again to thy dear name we raise
1680 Savior, blessed Savior
1681 Savior, breathe an evening blessing
1682 Savior, lead me, lest I stray
1683 Savior, like a shepherd lead us
1684 Savior, more than life to me
1685 Savior, now the day is ending
1686 Savior, sprinkle many nations
1687 Savior, teach me, day by day
1688 Savior, 'tis a full surrender
1689 Savior, thy dying love
1690 Savior, while my heart is tender
1691 Savior who thy flock art feeding
1692 Savior, whose love is like the sun
1693 Scattering precious seed by the
1694 Seal us, O Holy Spirit
1695 See how great a flame aspires
1696 See Israel's gentle Shepherd stand
1697 See the Conqueror mounts in triumph
1698 Seek not afar for beauty: lo, it glows
1699 Send down thy truth, O Lord
1700 Send forth, O God, thy light and truth
1701 Send out thy light and thy truth
1702 Send thou, O Lord, to every place
1703 Send thy Spirit, I beseech thee
1704 Servants of God, awake
1705 Servant of God, well done
1706 Serve the Lord in the days of youth
1707 "Serve the Lord with gladness"
1708 Set thou thy trust upon the Lord
1709 Shall I crucify my Savior
1710 Shall I empty-handed be
1711 Shall we gather at the river
1712 Shall we meet beyond the river
1713 She only touched the hem of his
1714 Shepherd Divine, our wants relieve
1715 Shepherd of eager (tender) youth
1716 Shepherd of souls, refresh and bless
1717 Shepherds are we, kneeling to thee
1718 Shepherds in the field abiding
1719 Shew me thy ways, O Lord (see 915, 2116)
1720 Silent night! holy night
1721 Simply trusting every day
1722 Since Christ my soul from sin
1723 Since Jesus is my Friend
1724 Sing, all ye Christian people
1725 Sing alleluia forth in loyal praise
1726 Sing hosannah, David's Son comes
1727 Sing, men and angels, sing
1728 Sing, my tongue, the glorious battle
1729 Sing praise to God who reigns above
1730 Sing the clouds away
1731 Sing the wondrous love of Jesus
1732 Sing them over again to me
1733 Sing to the great Jehovah's praise
1734 Sing to the Lord of harvest
1735 Sinners Jesus will receive
1736 Sinners, turn: why will ye die
1737 Sleep thy last sleep
1738 Smiling skies will bend above us
1739 So let our lips and lives express
1740 So near to the kingdom of heaven
1741 So precious is Jesus, my Savior
1742 Soft as the voice of an angel
1743 Softly and tenderly Jesus is calling
1744 Softly fades the twilight ray
1745 Softly now the light of day
1746 Soldiers of Christ! arise, and put

1747 Soldiers of the Cross, arise!
1748 Soldiers, who are Christ's below
1749 Some day the silver cord will break
1750 Some of these days all the skies will
1751 Some sweet day I shall enter
1752 Somebody came and lifted me
1753 Somebody did a golden deed (see also 1755)
1754 Somebody knows when your heart aches
1755 Somebody made a loving gift (see also 1753)
1756 Somehow I know that Christ is mine
1757 Someone is slighting the Savior of men
1758 Someone will enter the pearly gate
1759 Sometimes a light surprises
1760 Son of God, eternal Savior
1761 Son of Man, to thee I cry
1762 Songs of praise the angels sang
1763 Soon will our Savior from heaven appear
1764 Soul of mine, in earthly temple
1765 Soul, thy Redeemer hath broken death's prison
1766 Soul, why art thou anxiously striving
1767 Souls of men, why will ye scatter (see also 1999)
1768 Sound over all waters, reach out
1769 Sound the battle cry
1770 Sow flowers, and flowers will blossom
1771 Sowing in the morning
1772 Speak, I pray thee, gentle Jesus
1773 Speak just a word for Jesus
1774 Speak to my heart, Lord Jesus
1775 Speed thy servants, Savior, speed them
1776 Spirit Divine, attend our prayers
1777 Spirit of faith, come down
1778 Spirit of God, descend upon my heart
1779 Spirit of God, for every good
1780 Spirit of Life, in this new dawn
1781 Spirit of mercy, truth, and love
1782 Spirit of the living God
1783 Spread, O spread, thou mighty word
1784 Stand fast for Christ thy Savior
1785 Stand up, and bless the Lord
1786 Stand up! stand up for Jesus
1787 Standing at the portal
1788 Standing by a purpose true
1789 Standing in the market place
1790 Standing on the promises
1791 Star of peace to wanderers weary
1792 Stars all bright are beaming
1793 Still, still with thee, when purple morning breaketh
1794 Still will we trust, though earth seem
1795 Still with thee, O my God
1796 Strong of body, high of spirit
1797 Strong Son of God, immortal Love
1798 Such pity as a father hath
1799 Summer ended, harvest o'er
1800 Summer suns are glowing
1801 Sun of my soul, thou Savior dear
1802 Sunset and evening star
1803 Sunset to sunrise changes now
1804 Sweet are the promises
1805 Sweet feast of love divine (see also 234)
1806 Sweet hour of prayer
1807 Sweet is the breath of morning air
1808 Sweet is the promise
1809 Sweet is the solemn voice that calls
1810 Sweet is the sunlight after rain
1811 Sweet is the work, my God, my King
1812 Sweet Savior, bless us ere we go (see also 1478)
1813 Sweet the moments, rich in blessing
1814 Sweeter sounds than music knows
1815 Sweetly, Lord, have we heard thee calling

T

1816 Take my life, and let it be
1817 Take the name of Jesus with you
1818 Take thou my hands, dear Savior
1819 Take thou our minds, dear Lord
1820 Take time to be holy
1821 Take up the broken threads of life
1822 "Take up thy cross and follow me"
1823 "Take up thy cross," the Savior said
1824 Talk with us, Lord, thyself reveal
1825 Teach me, my God and King
1826 Teach me, O Lord, the perfect way
1827 Teach me, O Lord, the way of thy statutes
1828 Teach me thy will, O Lord
1829 Teach me to pray, Lord
1830 Tell me the old, old story
1831 Tell me the stories of Jesus
1832 Tell me the story of Jesus
1833 Tell the blessed tidings, children of the King
1834 Temper my spirit, O Lord
1835 Temple of God's Holy Spirit
1836 Ten thousand times ten thousand
1837 Thank and praise Jehovah's name
1838 Thank the Lord, for he is kind
1839 Thank you for the world so sweet
1840 That cause can neither be lost nor stayed
1841 That man hath perfect blessedness
1842 The Advent of our King
1843 The beauteous day now closeth
1844 The body, Lord, is ours to keep
1845 The church's one foundation
1846 The cross it standeth fast
1847 The cross that he gave is heavy
1848 The cross that he gave may be heavy
1849 The dawn of God's dear Sabbath
1850 The day hath now an ending
1851 The day is past and over
1852 The day is past; the shadows round are falling
1853 The day is slowly wending
1854 The Day of Resurrection
1855 The Day-star hath risen
1856 The day thou gavest, Lord, is ended
1857 The earth, with all that dwell therein
1858 The ends of all the earth shall hear
1859 The eternal gifts of Christ the King
1860 The fight is on, the trumpet sound
1861 The first Nowell the angel did say
1862 The glory of the Lord
1863 The glory of the spring how sweet
1864 The God of Abraham praise
1865 The God whom earth, and sea, and sky
1866 The gospel bells are ringing
1867 The great Physician now is near (see also 1968)
1868 The hand that was nailed to the cross
1869 The Head that once was crowned with thorns
1870 The heaven-born pilgrim now homeward is bound
1871 The heavens declare thy glory, Lord
1872 The Holy Ghost is here
1873 The king, O God, his heart to thee upraiseth
1874 The King of Glory standeth
1875 The King of heaven his table spreads
1876 The King of Love my Shepherd is
1877 The King shall come when morning dawns
1878 The kings of the east are riding

1879 The light along the ages
1880 The light of God is falling
1881 The lone wild fowl in lofty flight
1882 The Lord Almighty reigns (see also 598, 1886)
1883 The Lord ascendeth up on high
1884 The Lord be with us as each day
1885 The Lord bless thee
1886 The Lord doth reign, and clothed is he (see also 598, 1882)
1887 The Lord for ever doth endure (see also 1888)
1888 The Lord for ever sits as King (see also 1887)
1889 The Lord hath reigned, and reigns
1890 The Lord I will at all times bless
1891 The Lord is in his holy place
1892 The Lord is in his holy temple
1893 The Lord is King! lift up thy voice
1894 The Lord is my Shepherd, no want shall
1895 The Lord is ris'n indeed
1896 The Lord is true! His loving Fatherheart
1897 The Lord Jehovah reigns
1898 The Lord of heaven confess
1899 The Lord our God alone is strong
1900 The Lord our God is clothed with might
1901 The Lord will come and not be slow
1902 The Lord will I at all times bless (see also 616)
1903 The Lord's my light and saving health
1904 The Lord's my Shepherd, I'll not want
1905 The Lord's our Rock, in him we hide
1906 The love of Christ constraineth
1907 The love of Jesus is my song
1908 The man who once has found abode
1909 The Master hath come, and he calls us to follow
1910 The morning bright, with rosy light
1911 The morning light is breaking
1912 The name of Jesus is so sweet
1913 The nearer I reach the end of life
1914 The night is ended and the morning
1915 The one true Friend abides in heaven
1916 The Prince of Peace his banner spreads
1917 The race that long in darkness pined
1918 The radiant morn hath passed away
1919 The river of thy grace is flowing free
1920 The roseate hues of early dawn
1921 The royal banners forward go
1922 The sands have been washed in the foot-prints
1923 The sands of time are sinking
1924 The Savior calls; let every ear
1925 The Savior has died to redeem you
1926 The Savior who loves me and suffered
1927 The shadows of the evening hours
1928 The shepherds had an angel
1929 The ships glide in at the harbor's
1930 The Son of God goes forth for peace
1931 The Son of God goes forth to war
1932 The spacious firmament on high
1933 The spirit breathes upon the word (see also 7)
1934 The star of morn has risen
1935 The steps of those whom he approves
1936 The strain upraise of joy and praise
1937 The strife is o'er, the battle done (see also 79)
1938 The summer days are come again
1939 The sun declines; o'er land and sea

1940 The sun is sinking fast
1941 The time of the harvest was ended
1942 The touch of human hands
1943 The voice of God is calling
1944 The voice that breathed o'er Eden
1945 The whole wide world for Jesus
1946 The whole world was lost
1947 The wise may bring their learning
1948 The work is thine, O Christ our Lord
1949 The world looks very beautiful
1950 The world needs a friend like Jesus
1951 The world's a-stir! The clouds of storm
1952 The year is swiftly waning
1953 Thee will I love, my strength, my tower
1954 There are days so dark that I seek
1955 There are lonely hearts to cherish
1956 There are shadows of sorrow that darken
1957 There are stormy days of trouble
1958 There comes to my heart one sweet strain
1959 There is a blessed home
1960 There is a book, that all (who run) may read
1961 There is a fountain filled with blood
1962 There is a gate that stands ajar
1963 There is a green hill far away
1964 There is a holy sacrifice
1965 There is a land mine eye hath seen
1966 There is a land of pure delight
1967 There is a name I love to hear
1968 There is a name most sweet on earth (see also 1867)
1969 There is a place of quiet rest
1970 There is a Rock in a weary land
1971 There is a Shepherd who cares for his own
1972 There is a story more precious than gold
1973 There is joy in serving Jesus
1974 There is life for a look
1975 There is music in the air
1976 There is never a day so dreary
1977 There is no night in heaven
1978 There is no sorrow, Lord, too light
1979 There is rest, sweet rest, at the Master's feet
1980 There is sunshine in my soul today (see also 2001)
1981 "There shall be showers of blessing"
1982 There was one who was willing to die
1983 There were ninety and nine that safely lay
1984 There's a beautiful star
1985 There's a call comes ringing
1986 There's a church in the valley
1987 There's a fight to be fought
1988 There's a Friend for little children
1989 There's a garden where Jesus is waiting
1990 There's a great day coming
1991 There's a land beyond the river
1992 There's a land that is fairer than day
1993 There's a light upon the mountains
1994 There's a royal banner given for display
1995 There's a song in the air
1996 There's a Stranger at the door
1997 There's a voice comes ringing
1998 There's a voice in the wilderness crying
1999 There's a wideness in God's mercy (see also 1767)
2000 There's not a Friend like the lowly Jesus
2001 There's sunshine in my soul (see also 1980)
2002 There's within my heart a melody

2003 These things shall be: a loftier race
2004 They are gathering homeward
2005 "They say that man is mighty
2006 They who tread the path of labor (see also 1022, 2017)
2007 Thine are all the gifts, O God
2008 Thine arm, O Lord, in days of old
2009 Thine for ever! God of love
2010 Thine is the glory
2011 This child we dedicate to thee
2012 This is my Father's world
2013 This is the day of light
2014 This is the day the Lord hath made
2015 This joyful Easter-tide
2016 This rite our blest redeemer gave
2017 Those who love and those who labor (see also 2006)
2018 Thou art coming, O my Savior
2019 Thou art fairer than the morning
2020 Thou are my Shepherd
2021 Thou art the Bread of heaven
2022 Thou art the Everlasting Word
2023 Thou art the Way: to thee alone
2024 Thou comest, Lord, in kingly state
2025 Thou dear Redeemer, dying Lamb
2026 Thou didst leave thy throne and thy kingly crown
2027 Thou glorious God, before whose face
2028 Thou God of all, whose spirit moves
2029 Thou Grace divine, encircling all
2030 Thou gracious God, whose mercy lends
2031 Thou hast, O Lord, most glorious
2032 Thou hast said, exalted Jesus
2033 Thou hidden Love of God, whose height
2034 Thou hidden Source of calm repose
2035 Thou hitherto hast helped me, Lord
2036 Thou, in whose name the two or three
2037 Thou Judge of quick and dead
2038 Thou Life within my life
2039 Thou, Lord, by strictest search
2040 Thou Lord of light, across the years
2041 Thou Love, O how great
2042 Thou, my everlasting portion
2043 Thou, O Christ of Calvary
2044 Thou sayest, "Take up thy cross'
2045 Thou shalt arise, and mercy yet
2046 Thou spotless Lamb of God
2047 Thou to whom the sick and dying
2048 Thou who has known
2049 Thou who taught the thronging people
2050 Thou who thyself didst sanctify
2051 Thou whose almighty word
2052 Thou, whose unmeasured temple stands (see also 1530)
2053 Thou wilt keep him in perfect peace
2054 Thou, with thy counsel, while I live
2055 Though far you may wander away from the fold
2056 Though the angry surges roll
2057 Though the storm of life be raging
2058 "Though your sins be as scarlet
2059 Throned upon the awful tree
2060 Through all the changing scenes of life
2061 Through days of toil and sorrow
2062 Through the day thy love has spared us
2063 Through the gate of the city they led
2064 Through the land a call is sounding
2065 Through the love of God, our Savior
2066 Through the mist of years I can seem
2067 Through the night of doubt and sorrow

2068 Throw out the life-line across the dark wave
2069 Thy blessing, Lord, on all vacation days
2070 Thy bounties, gracious Lord
2071 Thy ceaseless, unexhausted love
2072 Thy hand, O God, has guided
2073 Thy kingdom come, O God, thy rule, O Christ
2074 Thy kingdom come, O Lord, wide circling
2075 "Thy kingdom come,"—on bended knee
2076 Thy kingdom, Lord, thy kingdom
2077 Thy life was given for me
2078 Thy loving-kindness, Lord, is good
2079 Thy mercy and thy truth, O Lord
2080 Thy mercy, Lord, is in the heavens
2081 Thy might sets fast the mountains
2082 Thy palm trees fed with dew and sun
2083 Thy way, not mine, O Lord
2084 Thy Word is a lamp to my feet
2085 Thy Word is like a garden
2086 Thy Word, O Lord, is morning dew
2087 Thy Word, O Lord, is my delight
2088 Thy work, O Lord, needs many hands
2089 "Till He come!" O Let the words
2090 'Tis from the mercy of our God
2091 'Tis midnight, and on Olive's brow
2092 'Tis so sweet to trust in Jesus
2093 'Tis the blessed hour of prayer
2094 'Tis the grandest theme through the ages ring
2095 'Tis the old-time religion
2096 'Tis well with me—when at his secret
2097 'Tis winter now; the fallen snow
2098 To all the nations, Lord
2099 To bless thy chosen race
2100 To build a world of brutal force
2101 To every man there openeth
2102 To God be the glory, great things he hath done
2103 To God my earnest voice I raise
2104 To God our hearts we lift
2105 To God the only wise
2106 To him that loved the souls of men
2107 To him who hallows all our days
2108 To Jesus ev'ry day I find my heart
2109 To Jesus I am clinging
2110 To the knights in the days of old
2111 To my humble supplication
2112 To render thanks unto the Lord
2113 To the work! to the work
2114 To thee before the close of day
2115 To thee, Eternal Soul, be praise
2116 To thee I lift my soul (see also 1719)
2117 To thee, my heart, eternal King
2118 To thee, O Comforter divine
2119 To thee, O dear, dear Savior
2120 To thee, O (Lord) God, our hearts we raise
2121 To thy temple I repair
2122 Together, Lord, we come to thee
2123 Touch me, Lord Jesus
2124 Toiling for the Master in the fields
2125 Traveling onward to a city
2126 Trembling soul, beset by fears
2127 Trials dark on every hand
2128 True-hearted, whole-hearted, faithful and loyal
2129 Trying to walk in the steps of the Savior
2130 Turn back, O man, forswear thy foolish ways
2131 Turn us again, O God of hosts
2132 'Twas on that dark and doleful night
2133 'Twas on that night when doomed to know
2134 Two empires by the sea

U

2135 Unbar the door! and let the Lord Christ in
2136 Under his wings I am safely abiding
2137 Unfold, ye portals everlasting
2138 Unto my Lord Jehovah said
2139 Unto the hills around do I lift up
2140 Unto the King, whose life was offered
2141 Unto us a Boy is born
2142 Unto thy temple, Lord, we come
2143 Up Calv'ry's hill Jesus patiently trod
2144 Up Calvary's mountain one dreadful morn
2145 Up to the bountiful Giver of life
2146 Upon a wide and stormy sea
2147 Upon the holy mount they stood

W

2148 Waiting on Jesus when I am weak
2149 "Wake, awake, for night is flying"
2150 Wake the song
2151 Walk in the light! so shalt thou know
2152 Walking in sunlight, all of my journey
2153 Watch, my soul, and pray
2154 Watchman! tell us of the night
2155 We all like sheep have gone astray
2156 We are climbing Jacob's ladder
2157 We are living, we are dwelling
2158 We are waiting, blessed Savior
2159 We are workers for the blessed Lord
2160 We bear the strain of earthly care
2161 We bless the name of Christ, the Lord
2162 We bless thee, Lord, for all this common life
2163 We cannot think of them as dead
2164 We come unto our fathers' God
2165 We dedicate this temple
2166 We gather together to ask the Lord's
2167 We give thee but thine own
2168 We hail thee now, O Jesu
2169 We have heard a (the) joyful sound
2170 We have not known thee as we ought
2171 We hope in thee, O God
2172 We journey to a city
2173 We know the paths wherein our feet
2174 We leave this (thy) house, but leave not thee
2175 We lift our hearts, O Father
2176 We lift our hearts to thee, O Day-Star
2177 We limit not the truth of God
2178 We love the place, O God
2179 We love the wonderful stories
2180 We march, we march to victory
2181 We may not climb the heav'nly steeps (see also 240, 917)
2182 We met them on the common way
2183 We mix from many lands
2184 We plough the fields, and scatter
2185 We praise thee, God, for harvests earned
2186 We praise thee, Lord, with earliest morning
2187 We praise thee, O God! for the Son of thy love
2188 We praise thee, O God our Redeemer
2189 We praise thy name, O Lord most high

2190 We sail along toward the harbor light
2191 We shall reach the river side
2192 We sing the praise of him who died
2193 We thank thee, Lord, thy paths of service
2194 We thank thee, O God, for the gifts
2195 We thank thee, O our Father
2196 We three kings of Orient are
2197 We worship thee, almighty Lord
2198 We would be building
2199 We would see Jesus, for the shadows lengthen
2200 We would see Jesus, lo, his star is shining
2201 Weary of earth and laden with my sin
2202 Weary of wandering from my God
2203 Welcome, delightful morn
2204 "Welcome, happy morning!" age to age shall say
2205 We'll to God's tabernacles go
2206 Were you there when they crucified my Lord
2207 We're going home, no more to roam
2208 We've a story to tell to the nations
2209 What a fellowship, what a joy divine
2210 What a Friend we have in Jesus
2211 What a wonderful change in my life
2212 What a wonderful Savior is Jesus
2213 What can I give to Jesus
2214 What can wash away my sin
2215 What child is this who, laid to rest
2216 What God ordaineth, he doth well
2217 What grace, O Lord, and beauty shone
2218 What means this eager, anxious throng
2219 What shall I render to the Lord
2220 What star is this, with beams so bright
2221 What various hindrances we meet
2222 When all my labors and trials are o'er
2223 When all thy mercies, O my God
2224 When by fear my heart is daunted
2225 When comes to the weary a blessed
2226 When courage fails and faith burns low
2227 When from care I seek repose
2228 When God of old came down from heaven
2229 When he cometh, when he cometh
2230 When, his salvation bringing
2231 When I can read my title clear
2232 When I fear my faith will fail
2233 When I need a friend and guide
2234 When I put out to sea
2235 When I shall come to the end of my way
2236 When I survey the wondrous Cross
2237 When I was but a little child
2238 When in the night I meditate
2239 When Israel, of the Lord beloved
2240 When Israel was in Egypt's land
2241 When Jesus comes to reward his servants
2242 When Jesus hung on Calvary
2243 When morning gilds the skies
2244 When morning lights the eastern skies
2245 When mothers of Salem their children brought
2246 When my life-work is ended
2247 When my love to God grows weak
2248 When on my day of life, the night is falling
2249 When peace, like a river, attendeth
2250 When spring unlocks the flowers

2251 When storms around are sweeping
2252 When the clouds are hanging low
2253 When the day of toil is done
2254 When the golden evening gathered
2255 When the Lord of love was here
2256 When the mists have rolled in splendor
2257 When the storms of life are raging
2258 When the sun shines bright and your heart
2259 When the trumpet of the Lord shall sound
2260 When the weary, seeking rest
2261 When this passing world is done
2262 When through the whirl of wheels
2263 When thy heart with joy o'erflowing
2264 When thy soldiers take their swords
2265 When upon life's billows you are
2266 When we walk with the Lord
2267 When wilt thou save the people
2268 When you long for Christ to bless
2269 When you my Jesus understand
2270 Where cross the crowded ways of life
2271 Where findeth the soul its dear homeland
2272 Where is my wandering boy tonight
2273 Where is your God? they say
2274 Where the great ships, passing, cleave
2275 Where the light forever shineth
2276 Where the olive grove stood darkly
2277 Where winds the road o'er hill and dale
2278 Wherefore, O Father, we thy humble servants
2279 While in sweet communion feeding
2280 While Jesus whispers to you, come
2281 While passing through this world of sin
2282 While shepherds watched their flocks by night
2283 While we pray and while we plead
2284 Whither, pilgrims, are you going
2285 Who goes there, in the night
2286 Who is he, in yonder stall
2287 Who is on the Lord's side
2288 Who is this so weak and helpless
2289 Who trusts in God, a strong abode
2290 Who would true valor see (see also 707)
2291 Whom oceans part, O Lord, unite
2292 "Whosoever heareth," shout, shout the sound
2293 Why do you wait, dear brother
2294 Why should I charge my soul with care
2295 Why should I fear the darkest hour
2296 Why should I feel discouraged
2297 Will our lamps be filled and ready
2298 Will your anchor hold
2299 Winter reigneth o'er the land
2300 Wise men seeking Jesus
2301 With friends on earth we meet in gladness
2302 With God I now am reconciled
2303 With happy voices ringing
2304 With joy we hail the sacred day
2305 With joy we meditate the grace
2306 With shepherds watching lambs
2307 With songs and honors sounding loud
2308 With the morn in radiance breaking
2309 Within my heart a song is ringing
2310 Within the maddening maze of things (see also 848)
2311 Within thy tabernacle, Lord

2312 Within thy temple, Lord, we on thy
2313 Within thy temple's sacred courts
2314 Wonderful fountain that cleanseth
2315 Wonderful grace of Jesus
2316 Wonderful love that rescued me
2317 Wonderful story of love
2318 Word of God, across the ages
2319 Word of Life, thou living water
2320 Work, for the night is coming
2321 Workman of God, O lose not heart (see also 617)
2322 Worship the Lord in the beauty of holiness
2323 Would you be free from the burden of sin
2324 Would you live for Jesus, and be always

Y

2325 Ye Christian heralds! go, proclaim
2326 Ye fair green hills of Galilee
2327 Ye gates, lift up your heads on high
2328 Ye heavens on high, praise ye the Lord
2329 Ye righteous, in the Lord rejoice
2330 Ye servants of God, your Master proclaim
2331 Ye servants of the Lord
2332 Ye that have spent the silent night
2333 Ye watchers and ye holy ones
2334 Ye who the name of Jesus bear
2335 Years I spent in vanity and pride
2336 Yield not to temptation
2337 You can know Jesus and love him today
2338 You cannot hide from God
2339 You may have the joy-bells
2340 Youth of the world, arise

Z

2341 Zion stands with hills surrounded
2342 Zion's King shall reign victorious

LINE INDEX

A

ABASE

Thou didst thyself *abase* 1715

ABASEMENT

In deep *abasement* bending 644

ABBA

He is my *Abba* true 2302

ABHORS

Lo, he *abhors* not the Virgin's womb 1330

ABIDE

Abide, dear Lord, e'er with us stay 1094
Abide in him always 1820
Abide with me from morn 1801
Abide with me when night is nigh 1801
Abide with us, that so, this life 1187
And *abide* with thee in bliss 744
And *abide* within my heart 369
Before the Lord shall he *abide* 1134
But let me still *abide* 1003
But thou wilt *abide* unchanging 1411
Come and *abide* 326
Dying let me still *abide* 963
If thou *abide* with me 27
Jesus! with us *abide* 1187
Let me evermore *abide* 963
Let me thus with thee *abide* 1647
Let me with thee *abide* 1645
Lord, with me *abide* 27
Safely *abide* forever 2136
Savior, *abide,* with us, and spread 165, 1716
Then come to him, with him *abide* 2
They with God himself *abide* 2017
This God for ever shall *abide* 2312
Thus may we *abide* in union 1209
With us *abide* this passiontide 2024
Within its portals fadeless joys *abide* 16

ABIDES

He *abides* with us forever 1041
Only Jesus Christ *abides* 1766

ABIDETH

God's truth *abideth* still 12

ABIDING

Am I in his grace *abiding* 51
Fruitful, if in Christ *abiding* 2065
In the house of God *abiding* 78

ABLE

"Are ye *able*" to remember 110
"Are ye *able*" when the shadows 110
"Lord, we are *able,*" our spirits are thine 110

ABOARD

I will *aboard* and quickly put 1533

ABODE

And at our Father's loved *abode* 1364
And watering our divine *abode* 572
God had his *abode* 2255
In heaven's bright *abode* 28
O blessed *abode,* O thou home 1870
Thine *abode* most lowly 740
To everlasting our *abode* 1174
To thine *abode* my heart aspires 1167

ABOUND

Abound with love and solace 2193
And righteous fruits *abound* 83

ABSENCE

Absence exchanged for a place 1763

ABSENT

Absent from him I roam 494
Though *absent* long, your Lord is nigh 733

ABSOLVED

Fully *absolved* through these 1024

ABSOLVER

O great *Absolver,* grant my soul 2201

ABSORBED

Absorbed in prayer and praise 376

ABSORBS

Absorbs not all the heart 100

ABUNDANCE

Which will all its full *abundance* 76, 663
Who with *abundance* of good things 1513
With the *abundance* of thy house 2079

ABUSE

With sore *abuse* and scorn 1475

ACCEPTED

Let our work *accepted* be 45

ACCLAIM

And thus our Christ *acclaim* 1930
Acclaim with joy thy wondrous 1368
Thus, in one great *acclaim* shall 1725

ACCOMPLISH

Thou shalt *accomplish* it 534

ACCORD

And all with one *accord* 28
And all, with one *accord* 329
Confessing, in a world's *accord* 496
In sweet *accord* will raise 28
Then let us all with one *accord* 1861
With one *accord* to offer ourselves 1529
With one *accord* we seek thy holy 454

ACCOUNT

A strict *account* to give 4

ACCOUNTS

He *accounts* us brethren still 1581

ACCUSER

I may my fierce *accuser* face 109

ACHIEVEMENT

For each *achievement* human toil 2162

ACKNOWLEDGE

Let me *acknowledge* too, O God 2039

ACT

And every *act* of brotherhood 204
As the dread *act* of sacrifice began 1545
In this dread *act* your strength 1333
May every *act*, word, thought 1025
To *act* as in thy sight 1291

ACTIONS

And with *actions* bold 635
And with *actions* brotherly 635

ACTS

Acts unworthy, deeds unthinking 1179
And in patient *acts* of kindness 2254
Lowly *acts* of adoration 753
My *acts* of faith and love 1521

ADD

But *add* a depth and sweetness 279

ADMIRE

But, most of all, *admire* that we 1122

ADMIRED

Which are to be *admired* 54

ADMIT

Admit him, for the human breast 192
Now *admit* the heavenly Guest 1996

ADOPT

We *adopt* the angels' cry 1178

ADOPTED

But I've been *adopted* 1229

ADORATION

Alone with thee, in breathless *adoration* 1793
And equal *adoration* be 375
And in your *adoration* 1083
Deep in *adoration*, bending low 1680
In endless *adoration* 1481
Receive this humble *adoration* 23
Richer by far is my heart's *adoration* 1481
Thee, with humble *adoration* 1159
With true *adoration* shall lisp 1546

ADORE

And *adore* the Lord our God 251
And ever thee *adore* 1409
And every voice *adore* 45
And gratefully *adore* him 1552
And nature's God *adore* 2176
And shall we not *adore* thee 2303
And thee as God and Lord *adore* 785
And thy great God *adore* 200
And to *adore* the Lamb 323
Come, *adore* on bended knee 105
He whom we *adore* shall keep thee 2139
Holy Spirit, we *adore* thee 597
I do *adore* thee, and will ever pray 35
I'll ever *adore* thee in heaven 1246
In that Babe *adore* 1110
Just to be near the dear Lord I *adore* 2222
Let us now *adore* him 563, 600
New-born worlds rise and *adore* 53
O, shall I not *adore* his name 1534
Only God our hearts *adore* 45
Son eternal, we *adore* thee 597
The God whom we *adore* 237, 671, 1677
The Lord your God *adore* 1785
Thee rightly to *adore* 1166
Thee we *adore*, for we are thine 1447
Then let us *adore*, and give him 2330
These all *adore* and praise him 33
Thus we *adore* thee 467
To God, the Father, whom I *adore* 207
We joyfully *adore* thee 708
We thee unseen *adore* 1317
Yea, amen! let all *adore* thee 1106

ADORED

And God the Father be by all *adored* 58
Be here and everywhere *adored* 171
Nor to be equally *adored* 2334

ADORING

O Triune God, with heart and voice *adoring* 92

ADORNED

Adorned with prayer, and love 1082
Adorned with wondrous grace 786

ADVANCE

Advance upon the strongholds 1328

ADVANCES

Onward the line *advances* 90

ADVENT

And silently thy promised *advent* 405
New *advent* of the love of Christ 1124
To greet his *advent* with the bridal 1352
With the last *advent* we unite 266

ADVENTURE

"*Adventure*" is your cry 2340

ADVENTURERS

Bold *adventurers* on the sea 485

ADVOCATE

Christ is our *Advocate* on high 1318
I have an *Advocate* above 2202
My *Advocate* see 73
Our *Advocate* with God 1325
Thou art our *Advocate* within 1318

AEONS

The *aeons* come, the *aeons* go 46

AFFECTION

Let all the soul's *affection* 1183
Since, with pure and firm *affection* 271
With *affection* kind and true 555

AFFLICTION

Even in *affliction*, peace 1431
In the midst of *affliction* my table 1894
On whom in *affliction* I call 1512
Where such a light *affliction* 1391
Willing to suffer *affliction* and loss 1104

AFFORD

Here *afford* us, Lord, a taste 1676

AFFRIGHT

Naught shall *affright* us 464

AFRAID

Anywhere with Jesus I am not *afraid* 108
Art thou *afraid* his power shall fail 685
Be thou not *afraid* 1787
How can I be *afraid* 2020
We will not be *afraid* 571

AGE

Age after *age* their tragic empires 2130
Age to *age*, and shore to shore 1623
And *age* comes on uncheered 1059
And shall from *age* to *age* endure 57
And still from *age* to *age* convey 1781
But no *age* is degenerate 14
Each *age* its solemn task my claim 594
From *age* to *age* his righteous reign 1692
From *age* to *age* more glorious 661, 1879
From *age* to *age* the same 12
From *age* to *age* the sons of men 1451
In an *age* on ages telling 2157
In ev'ry *age* adored 1121
In type from *age* to age 1366
So that, even as the eagle's *age* 1513
To serve the present *age* 648

AGED

When the *aged*, weak and grey 2260

AGELESS

But thou are *ageless* 1658

AGENTS

By feeblest *agents* may our God fulfil 322

AGES

A thousand *ages* in thy sight 1375
And *ages* move 566
And, all the *ages* through, past crumbling 593
And down the *ages* long 2104
For ever through the *ages* 1485
In all the *ages* with the fire and cloud 92
It doth through *ages* all remain 628
Long as eternal *ages* roll 1705
The God of ancient *ages*, and *ages* yet 2165
This my song through endless *ages* 66
This, through countless *ages* 1586
Through all the *ages* of our race 1174
Through endless *ages*, ever to be 1266
Through eternal *ages*, let his praises 1790
Through latest *ages* let it pour 2133
Through the *ages* as they change 64
Through the *ages* it has shown 1559
Today as in the *ages* lost to sight 29
That through the *ages* all along 313
Which, through the *ages* that have gone before us 37
While eternal *ages* run 543
While unending *ages* run 281

AGONY

And when such *agony* he bore 825
By thy bitter *agony* 1761
In *agony*, sorrow and woe 17
Jesus is dying, in *agony* sore 1015
O *agony* and dying 1476
The double *agony* in man 1630
There behold his *agony* 2247

AID

Aid us in our strife 2010
All must *aid* alike to carry 656
And *aid* my tongue to bless 1315
Ever near thine *aid* to lend 755
He is willing to *aid* you 2336
His *aid* for thee, and change 125
Jesus, thy timely *aid* impart 1519
Let each his friendly *aid* 1029
The *aid* that thou didst me 2035
Thine *aid* impart to me 1345
To save ourselves without thine *aid* 1168
What without thy *aid* is wrought 744
Without our *aid* he did us make 57

AIM

Be this thy constant *aim* 201
I *aim* at thee, yet from thee 2033
My constant *aim* is higher ground 915

AIR

And larger, ampler is the *air* 491
No more will fill the *air* 1
Rise mingling on the holy *air* 32
Wild through the frightened *air* 592

AIRS

And the same *airs* are blowing 236

ALARMS

From war's *alarms* 585
Safe and secure from all *alarms* 2209

ALIVE

Alive and quick to hear 797
Alive in him, my living head 94

ALL

All of self, and none of thee 1498

ALLAYING

Ne'er this searching quest *allaying* 51

ALLELUIAS

To thee our *alleluias* we raise 1329
To thee our *alleluias* we sing 1329

ALL-SUFFICIENT

God is *all-sufficient* 1787

ALLURED

Allured by Love 264
These have *allured* my sight 804

ALLUREMENTS

Its vain *allurements* flee 1193
Where sin's sore *allurements* ne'er 2271

ALMIGHTY

Come, *Almighty* to deliver 1190
Oh, 'tis a wonder how low the *Almighty* 1617

ALMS

Let thine *alms* be hope and joy 294

ALOES

For *aloes* had a part 1249

ALONE

Anywhere with Jesus I am not *alone* 108

ALPHA

Alpha and Omega be 1190
He is *Alpha* and Omega 1558

ALTAR

All for Jesus—at thine *altar* 42
Himself to his own *altar* comes 1488
On his *altar* laid we leave them 753
On the mean *altar* of my heart 1521
On thy holy *altar* pour them 753
Over this *altar*, Lord, we pray 1188
So to thine holy *altar* go 1043
Then to thy *altar* will I spring 1700
Then will I to God's *altar* go 1483
This *altar* that echoes
the message of grace 172
Upon thine *altar*, Lord, we lay 2120
Upon thy holy *altar* 1312
When onward to thine *altar* 1944
Will Kali's *altar* go 90

ALTARS

Even thine own *altars*, where she 783
The rival *altars* that we raise 496
Till all thy living *altars* 1155

AMBASSADOR

Ambassador to be of realms 799

AMBUSHED

Ambushed lies the evil one 295

ANCHOR

Come, *anchor* your soul in the "Haven 1257
For my *anchor* grips the rock 2056
I've an *anchor* safe and sure 2056
I've an *anchor* that shall hold 2056
My *anchor* holds within the veil 1244
'Tis the *anchor* of hope, and the lamp 130
We have an *anchor* that keeps 2298
We shall *anchor* fast by the 2298
Will your *anchor* drift or firm 2298

ANCHORED

Anchored safe within the veil 2018
I've *anchored* my soul in the "Haven 1257

ANCIENT

One with the *Ancient* of all days 195

ANGEL

An *angel* rolled away the stone 498
And bright with many an *angel* 961
Death's dark *angel* sheathes his sword 142
For lo, the *angel* of the Lord came down 260
No *angel* could his place have taken 1425
No *angel* of death enter in 1870
No *angel* in the sky can fully 376

The *angel* of the Lord came down 2282
The *angel* of the Lord encamps 616, 1902

ANGEL-BANDS

And *angel-bands* are waiting 1893

ANGEL-GUARDS

His *angel-guards* attend you 1850

ANGEL-HANDS

And by *angel-hands* be gathered 76

ANGEL-HOSTS

And, with *angel-hosts* encircled 217
Angel-hosts rejoicing 544
Yet *angel-hosts* adore thee 1476

ANGELS

And *angels* are attending 793
And *angels* of God are crowding 1095
And *angels* with their sparkling 76
And singing *angels* are 1928
And the *angels* echoed around 1983
And thronging *angels* never cease 1918
And with the *angels* bear thy part 152
Angels adore him in slumber 254
Angels and archangels may have 933
Angels and men before it fall 1017
Angels and shepherds together 302
Angels are ling'ring near 85
Angels are still the choristers 1113
Angels bend in anxious silence 479
Angels bright, their service bringing 1213
Angels brought the message down 1100
Angels came down o'er his tomb 1575
Angels caroled this sweet lay 412
Angels descend with songs 1008
Angels descending, bring from above 213
Angels descending, over him bending 1199
Angels descending, shepherds 1504
Angels do sing of him still 1617
Angels fall before thee 1034
Angels have in song 542
Angels, help us to adore him 1618
Angels hymn the King of glory 1718
Angels in bright rainment 2010
Angels in robes of light 1050
Angels now are hov'ring round us 1510
Angels o'er us join the chorus 208
Angels of Jesus, *angels* of light 670
Angels round his throne above 1623
Angels sang about his birth 524
Angels, shout; and men, reply 664
Angels, sing on, your faithful watches 670
Angels, swell the glad triumphant 1664
Angels to beckon me 1265
Angels with rapture announce it 2317
But God's *angels* watch o'er all 1102
Come in, dear *angels,* ye so pure 320
Come, with all thine *angels* 359
From *angels* bending near the earth 948
Glorious *angels,* downward thronging 282
Glory! Glory! How the *angels* sing 1664
God's *angels* still are near to save 319
Good *angels* know it well 1959
Here as there thine *angels* 1126
Him let all *angels* bless 1898
Holy *angels* round us stand 2284
Let *angels* prostrate fall 47
May *angels* guard us while we sleep 1151
May thine *angels,* pure and holy 711
May thine *angels* spread 1302
No *angels* on his errands sped 2326
None but the *angels* were watching 1199
Nor weary till *angels* shall greet you 1098
Now let the *angels* 353
Of *angels* in the height 133
Of glorious *angels* ever stand 117
Round us too shall *angels* shine 500
Safe with the *angels,* whiter than 1605
So *angels,* clad in white 1928
So *angels* from God's presence 2147
Than all the *angels* heaven can 427
The *angels* prostrate bow 559
The *angels* rejoicing and singing 1926
The *angels* tried to comfort them 626
The *angels* worshiped as he lay 9
Thine *angels* adore thee 916
Thine *angels* send us 1289
To sing among his *angels* 860
To thee, where *angels* know 1366
Well might *angels* tell the story 1100
Where *angels* soon shall gather 1166
Where the *angels* ever sing 971
While *angels* delight to hymn thee 1546
While *angels* in their songs 1641
While *angels* sing with pious mirth 513, 528
While *angels* sing with tender 34
While *angels* winging, his praises 302
Whom *angels* greet with anthems 2215
Whom the *angels* praise above 105
With *angels* in the heights 148
With *angels* round thy throne 117
With the *angels* I shall sing 833
Ye *angels,* dwell upon the sound 1308

ANGELS'

The *angels'* song resounds 1113

ANGEL-VISITANT

No *angel-visitant,* no opening 1778

ANGER

From *anger,* pride, and selfish care 1518
He who, no *anger* on his tongue 620

ANGUISH

How art thou pale with *anguish* 1475
Nevermore with *anguish* laden 1991
Suffering *anguish,* despised 1575
Sweet Savior, in my hour of mortal *anguish* 98
The *anguish* view of him who groans 697
Was it vain, thy Son's deep *anguish* 1136
What *anguish* he suffered 623
Will all my heart's wild *anguish* 1585
With what *anguish* and loss 1982
Yet he that hath in *anguish* knelt 2091

ANOINT

Anoint and cheer our soiled face 313
Anoint me with thy heavenly 1230
Anoint them heralds of thy peace 490
Anoint them kings 594
Anoint them prophets 594
Anoint them with the spirit 594

ANOINTED

All hail the Lord's *anointed* 48
Look, Father, look on his *anointed* face 99

ANOINTING

A blest *anointing* thou dost give 1376

ANSWER

An *answer* will expect 527, 1176
And *answer* all thy prayers 1639
Answer in love thy children's 436
Answer quickly when he calleth 679
Answer them, Lord most holy 2273
Gladly *answer* duty's calls 416
God will *answer* by his Spirit 561
He will *answer* every prayer 561
I'll *answer,* dear Lord, with my hand 955
Keep on praying, God will *answer* 1048
Our hearts, O Lord, make *answer* to 29
The Master made *answer* in words true 18
To *answer* to his call 185
Who is there will *answer* quickly 2064
Who will *answer,* gladly saying 679
Will he *answer* us, "Well done" 2241
Will you *answer* quickly 3
Yea, thou wilt *answer* for me 2201

ANSWERED

Answered his request in grace 72
Answered them in all their fear 611
But *answered* his request in grace 72
That hath *answered* for me 73
'Twas there he *answered* mother's prayer 870

ANSWERS

For God *answers* prayer 1048
His Spirit *answers* to the blood 113
Jesus kindly *answers* 680
Love *answers* love's appeal 86
Where Jesus *answers* pray'r 109
Wonderful *answers,* my pray'rs far 2314

ANTHEM

Alleluia is the *anthem* 78
And this shall be their *anthem* 2072
Bid we thus our *anthem* flow 253
Hark! how the heavenly *anthem* drowns 376
Hark, that everlasting *anthem* 669
Let every *anthem* rise 332
One *anthem* raise 2134
Pealing forth the *anthem* of the free 1664
The *anthem* rolled among the clouds 1113
While all their *anthem* sing to Christ 851
While the *anthem* rolls along 1272

ANTHEMS

Let cheerful *anthems* fill his house 1392
Let echoing *anthems* ring 1449
Loud with their *anthems* ring 272
Loud your *anthems* raise 1586
Our praise and prayer and *anthems* 44
Safely the *anthems* of Zion 1538
Supernal *anthems* echoing 2333
To thee, great Jehovah, glad *anthems* 2188
Too faint our *anthems* here 1592

ANTICIPATE

And thus *anticipate* by faith 927

ANXIOUS

Are you *anxious* what shall be 112

APOSTLES

Let what *apostles* learned of thee 1646
The *apostles* saw their risen Lord 1037
The *apostles* sing thy praise 1213

APPARELED

Appareled in omnipotence 1882

APPEAL

By this prevailing presence we *appeal* 99
Love answers love's *appeal* 86

APPEALING

Still *appealing,* still inspiring, 'mid the 2318

APPEAR

All who there *appear* 3
And ready all *appear* 1510
And when Jesus doth *appear* 1510
And with awe *appear* before him 563
Appear, Desire of nations 1836
God shall *appear,* and we shall rise 327
How precious did that grace *appear* 88
In word and life *appear* 15
In Zion do *appear* 782
See the day of God *appear* 1106
That with thee we may *appear* 500
Till thou *appear,* thy members 708
When we *appear* in yonder cloud 2025

APPEARED

And forthwith *appeared* a shining throng 2282
The Son of God *appear'd* 128
Till he *appeared,* and the soul 1399
Who once *appeared* in humblest 1511

APPEARS

But, O what sight *appears* 559
God *appears* on earth to reign 1106
While his dear cross *appears* 38

APPLE

Dear as the *apple* of thine eye 859
Quick as the *apple* of an eye 889

APPOINT

Appoint my soul a place 914

APPOINTED

In thine own *appointed* way 1181
The third, the *appointed* day 237
To its *appointed* end 124
To wait for the *appointed* hour 1026

APPOINTS

But he who *appoints* me my 1922
Where he *appoints* we go 230

APPROACH

Approach with joy his courts unto 57
Bold I *approach* th'eternal throne 94
Who shall *approach* his holy 1080

APPROVAL

She her Lord's *approval* won 141

APPROVE

If but thy God *approve* 201

APPROVED

And then, by him *approved* 1935

ARCH

Our rainbow *arch,* thy mercy's 1155
Rainbow *arch,* his covenant 1211
'Tis an *arch* of promise bright 169

ARCHER

The *archer* and the lion 1878

ARCHES

And heaven's eternal *arches* ring 674
Broader than heav'n's high *arches* 638
Heaven's *arches* rang 2026
When heaven's *arches* shall 2026

ARCHITECT

That without God as *architect* 1609

ARDOR

That my heart, fresh *ardor* gaining 140

ARISE

Arise, and come back to thy father 1494
Arise, and crown our days 46
Arise, and in his might shake 958
Arise, and never set 2073
Arise, and take thy stand 1328
Arise, and with thy morning beams 1086
Arise, in all your weakness 1292
Arise, O Lord, into thy rest 2205
Arise, O Lord; save me, my God 1430
Arise, O Morning Star 2073
Arise, to dare and do 516
Arise triumphant from the grave 237
Arise, ye Christian mothers 2005
Arise, ye guilty, he'll forgive 1555
Arise, ye needy, he'll relieve 1555
From whence *arise* 2139
Glorious now behold him *arise* 2196
In thee I shall *arise* 123
Let us all *arise* tomorrow 1685
Let us *arise,* all meaner service 2200
Quickly *arise* and away 985
The holy melodies of love *arise* 37
Then *arise,* O children of the light 547
Then may I *arise,* pure and fresh 1302

ARISEN

"But now hath Christ *arisen*" 952, 2015
Glorious and radiant
the Lord hath *arisen* 1765
Thou hast *arisen,* but thou 1087

ARK

They can to their *ark* repair 1612

ARM

And can an all-creating *arm* 685
And his holy *arm* spread o'er us 2180
And though his *arm* be strong to smite 327
Arm me with jealous care 4
Arm their faltering wills to fight 294
Arm us, Savior, for the war 492
Be thy strong *arm* our ever sure defense 585
By his strong *arm* defended 6
By thy strong *arm* their lives 490
Does not thine *arm* encircle us 435
God's own *arm* hath need 2157
Great Captain, now thine *arm* 473
His *arm* will safely keep 348
In thine *arm* I rest me 1004
Let thine almighty *arm* be their defense 514
No *arm* so weak but may do service 322
Nor short thine *arm* 1032
O Lord, be there thine *arm* made bare 1281
Since on thine *arm* thou bidd'st me 1400
Strong is his *arm,* and shall fulfil 1897
Strong is thine *arm* 712
Sufficient is thine *arm* alone 1375
The *arm* of flesh will fail you 1786
The *arm* of the Lord is strong 1998
Thine *arm* the victory gaineth 1419
Thy mighty *arm* make bare 1659
Thy strong *arm* will guide us 2188
'Tis thine *arm* alone that saves 1775
Trusting the *arm* that is strong 2129
When I fear, his *arms* enfoldeth 65
Whose *arm* doth bind 418
Whose *arm* hath bound the restless wave 81

ARMED

Armed by faith and winged 980
Armed with thy courage 1130

ARMIES

And *armies* of the sky 1325
And mighty *armies* still in war 2098
And we put to flight the *armies* 2180
For the *armies* of the faithful 1280
Him all his *armies* praise 1898
The *armies* of the ransomed saints 1836
Ye *armies* of the living God 1081

ARMISTICE

The *armistice* of might 2098

ARMOR

Keep thine *armor* bright 1114
Must in their Savior's *armor* 1505
The *armor* of his soldiers 283
To keep your *armor* bright 1746
To our souls' *armor* grant celestial 1873
With *armor* gleaming and colors 1860

ARMS

And his *arm* around me thrown 863
And in the *arms* of Jesus sink 1569
And in those *arms* to die 124
Arms, so strong to clasp 1672
Back to his dear loving *arms* 806
He with open *arms* received them 1099
His *arms* are near 477
His sheltering *arms* defend you 1850
In his *arms* he carries them 1616
In his *arms* he'll take and shield 2210
In my *arms* I'll fold thee 1808
In thine *arms* may we respose 2062
In thy kind *arms* enfold me 2016
Into thy Father's *arms* with conscious will 98
Leaning on the everlasting *arms* 2209
Let thine *arms* around them be 974
Lord, on the Cross
thine *arms* were stretched 124
Lord, thine *arms* are stretching 1471
Of him who, loving *arms* extending 1290
Put his loving *arms* around you 556
Safe in the *arms* of his infinite love 2145
That his *arms* had been thrown around 884
The *arms* of love that compass me 1017
The *arms* that are open 2
The eternal *arms,* their dear abode 2164
Their *arms* in surrender cast down 509
Then, with thy pitying *arms* enfold 1517
Those outstretched *arms* receive my latest 98
When his loving *arms* receive us 1848
Who from our mother's *arms* 1299

ARMY

A noble *army,* men and boys 1931
But the King's own *army* 2287
Like a mighty *army* 1586
One *army* of the living God 1067
'Tis the ransomed *army,* like a 1664

AROSE

For Christ *arose,* our precious souls 498
He *arose,* a Victor from the dark 1200
Jesus, thy Savior, victorious *arose* 1765
My Lord *arose* to save his own 498
The Lord *arose,* and saved them 1890
Then he *arose,* over death 1575

AROUSE

Arouse, ye soldiers brave and true 1860

ARRAY

He, bridegroom-like in his *array* 1862
In their great *array* 143
Whence all their white *array* 774

ARRAYED

Arrayed in garments washed in blood 1108
Arrayed in robes of stainless white 958
The saints *arrayed* in white 33

ARRIVES

Till each *arrives* at length 1167

ARROW

Though the *arrow* past us fly 1681

ARROWS

Bring me my *arrows* of desire 95
Thine are the *arrows* of the storm clouds 595

ART

And, rich in *art,* made richer still 1296
Consecrating *art* and song 1077
Craftsman's *art* and music's measure 101
Not by *art* of human word 275

ARTS

New *arts* shall bloom 2003
Satan all his *arts* employ 2257

ASCEND

Ah! when shall we *ascend* 1705
Ascend I heaven, lo, thou 1452
Come, *ascend* his Zion still 611
Evermore let us *ascend* 64
O let our heart
and mind continually *ascend* 97

ASCENDED

Jesus hath *ascended* 622
Lo! the incarnate God, *ascended* 358
Now is *ascended,* my Lord 1575

ASCENDETH

Ever *ascendeth* the song and the joy 228

ASCENSION

Mighty Lord, in thine *ascension* 1697

ASCRIBE

And I the glory will *ascribe* 54
Ascribe their conquest to the Lamb 530
Do ye *ascribe* unto the Lord 1486
To him all majesty *ascribe* 47

ASCRIPTIONS

Let our high *ascriptions* be 663

ASHAMED

Ashamed of Jesus, that dear Friend 967
Ashamed of thee, whom angels 967
My God, let me not be *ashamed* 2116
That Christ is not *ashamed* 967

ASHES

And in its *ashes* plant the tree 1319
Securely shall my *ashes* lie 132
The *ashes* of my heart 1142
With *ashes* who would grudge to part 1392

ASK

All I *ask*, a gift of grace 2227
All we *ask* thee is to keep us 929
And *ask* that thou wilt set us free 384
And *ask* the gift unspeakable 146
And I will *ask* for no reward 396
Ask, and he turns your hell 1555
Ask, and it shall be given 111
Ask, and they will not be denied 1333
Ask but his grace, and lo, 'tis given 1555
Ask for help the wand'ring one 1048
Ask for naught beside thee 1004
Ask freely of him, and receive 553
Ask not how this should be 1632
Ask not what may here befall us 1606
Ask of thy God and receive 1269
Ask the saved of all the race 524
Ask the Savior to help you 2336
Ask your Father's blessing 357
But I *ask* thee for a present mind 443
But still we *ask*, as the rocks 2190
Ever *ask*, "What shall we do?" 752
I *ask*, but for a life made up 478
I *ask* but to be thine 979, 1250
I *ask* no dream, no prophet 1778
I *ask* no higher state 1332
I *ask* no other sunshine 203
I *ask* not, need not ought 1400
I *ask* thee for a thoughtful love 443
I *ask* thee to stay 159
I *ask* them whence their victory 530
I do not *ask* my cross 821
I do not *ask* that thou shouldst take 821
I do not *ask* to know the path 387
I do not *ask* to see 1053
I will *ask* Jesus to help me 1030
If I *ask* him to receive me 119
If I but *ask* him, he will deliver 865
Lord, I *ask* it, hardly knowing 754
None can ever *ask* too much 330
Nor *ask* thee for a sign 1386
Nothing you *ask* will be denied 168
O what shall I *ask* of thy 1894
So I *ask* thee for the daily strength 443
Some *ask* a human image 522
Then *ask*, "O death, where is thy sting" 697
Thou art here, we *ask* not how 1126
We *ask* for Jesus' sake 2088
We *ask* for naught 100
We *ask* not that our service 1906
We *ask* thee, Lord, that thine shall be 1287
What have I to *ask* beside 66
You *ask* me how I know he lives 874

ASKS

Asks the work of his own hands 1736

ASLEEP

The little Lord Jesus, *asleep* on the hay 159

ASPIRE

Would earnestly *aspire* 1442

ASPIRINGS

There our last *aspirings* end 1271

ASS

Where *ass* and ox but lately fed 528

ASSEMBLED

Assembled in thy name 1031
Assembled in thy sacred name 764
Assembled round the great white throne 49
O God, on all *assembled* here 364
Since we *assembled* last 93

ASSEMBLIES

Where the *assemblies* of the just 1638

ASSEMBLY

Nor in the *assembly* of the just 1841
The *assembly* of ill men I hate 1043

ASSERT

Assert, O Christ, thy glory's name 1702

ASSIST

Assist his feeble praise 55
Assist me, Lord, to offer up 1288
Assist me to proclaim 1351

ASSURANCE

Let this blest *assurance* control 2249
What *assurance* in my soul 1041

ASSURED

Assured alone that life and death 848, 2310
Assured of his tender compassion 1494
Is my *assured* foundation 853

ATHIRST

And my soul *athirst* may be 66

ATONE

He dies to *atone* for sins not his own 73

ATONEMENT

For me a full *atonement* made 1024
For thou, in thy *atonement*, didst give 1104
Hath full *atonement* made 247
Th' *atonement* of thy blood apply 493
When Jesus made *atonement* on Calvary 139

ATTAINEST

Soon thy Canaan thou *attainest* 2153

ATTEND

Attend the Almighty Father's name 375
Attend with constant care 1746
Splendor, light and life *attend* him 53
Today *attend* his voice 337
Thou will *attend* when we earnestly 713
Ye children of men, *attend* to the word 18

ATTENDED

Our footsteps have *attended* 6

ATTENDING

Attending to my prayer 50

ATTENDS

Attends the softest prayer 365
God *attends* him 568

ATTENTIVE

Attentive to the trumpet's sound 2037

ATTRACTED

Attracted by those loving words 75

ATTUNE

Attune our lives to thee 1386
If thou *attune* the heart 1592

AUGHT

Nor should I *aught* withhold 1689
Sweeter by far than *aught* beside 1807

AUTHOR

Author of faith! to thee I lift 444
Author of liberty 1225
Author of the new creation 743

AUTUMN

For the golden *autumn* 409

AVAIL

"Almost" cannot *avail* 85
What can *avail* to wash it away 1206
What can for them *avail* 1261

AVENGER

That so the *avenger* may be quelled 775

AVERT

Avert our woes, and calm our dread 43

AVOWED

His first *avowed* intent 707

AWAIT

Await a new creative hour 1467

AWAITS

There my Savior *awaits* 1989

AWAKE

Awake! awake! and let your song of praise 148
Awake! awake! the earth is full of glory 148
Awake, my glory; harp 1362
Awake, my heart and tongue 1288
Awake, my love; awake, my joy 1288
Awake, my soul, and sing 376
Awake, my soul, awake my tongue 1308
Awake my soul when sin is nigh 889
Awake, O sons of privilege 309
Awake the purpose high which strives 1526
Christians, *awake!* your forces all 433
In his own likeness we shall then *awake* 16
Rising, shall *awake* and sing 2299
To serve my God when I *awake* 59
Where'er he be, *awake*, asleep 1406

AWAKENED

Awakened from silence deep 1585

AWAKES

Awakes our hearts as with the light of morn 29

AWARE

More *aware* of power 1359

AWAY

"Almost persuaded," turn not *away* 85

AWE

And with *awe* appear before him 600
As with trembling *awe* and wonder 394
Kneel in *awe* and wonder 52
Stand ye in *awe* before his face 72
To *awe* the bold, to stay 1116

B

BABE
A *babe* within a manger lies 918
Christ the *babe* was born for you 945
Christ the *babe* is Lord of all 945
Such a *Babe* in such a place 524
The *Babe* of the manger, though born 1926
The *Babe,* the Son of Mary 2215
The dear little *Babe* in his bed 1199
"The heavenly *Babe* you there shall find 2282
The holy *Babe* to greet 559

BABES
Such helpless *babes* thou didst 1590

BABY
The *Baby* awakes 159

BACK
Look not *back,* the past regretting 36

BACKSLIDINGS
And freely my *backslidings* heal 2202

BADE
And *bade* its waves be still 1487
And *bade* them depart 2245
He *bade* me cease to roam 1421
He *bade* them still attend him 2230
It *bade* me quickly come 2237
That *bade* death's gloomy fears 265
They *bade* men rise, and hasten 2072
When he *bade* me come 1500

BADEST
Who *badest* its angry tumult 418

BAD'ST
And *bad'st* the eye of sense 1522

BALL
On this terrestrial *ball* 47

BALM
A *balm* of care and sadness 1341
He has precious *balm* and comfort 344
Here is *balm* for all our woes 1588
Jesus, thy *balm* will make it 1555
The *balm* of life, the cure of woe 2192
To find a *balm* for woe 2167
What a *balm* for the weary 2093
With healing *balm* my soul 1729
With the *balm* of his counsel 2113

BAND
A *band* of hard-pressed folk 2122
A glorious *band,* in every age 1930
A glorious *band,* the chosen few 1931
All hail to Daniel's *band* 1788
In all the land, one stedfast *band* 84
O happy *band* of pilgrims, look 1391
One brave *band* of heroes 657
While young and old, in many a *band* 540
You a little, feeble *band* 2284

BANDS
My *bands* thou didst untie 910

BANE
Bane and blessing, pain and 934

BANISH
And *banish* all your fears 778
And *banish* ev'ry care 1385
And *banish* sin away 29
Banish all my dark misgivings 1772
Banish from my mind the night 758
Banish mist and shadow as you march 163
Banish our weakness, health 467
Banish our worldliness 705
Banish the fear, the falsehood 1087
He will *banish* every fear 2258
Lord, *banish* strife and variance 244
That *banish* us so long from thee 374

BANISHED
Banished unbelief and sadness 1041
He *banished* my sins, both the greatest 122
When are *banish'd* grief and 424

BANNED
Alas, I must be *banned* 1422

BANNER
And his *banner* gleameth 1800
And let his glorious *banner* be unfurled 148

Be the *banner* still unfurled 1747
Beneath thy *banner* bright 1412
God's *banner* exalted shall be 509
His *banner* is unfurled 510
His *banner* over us 413, 1860
His blood-red *banner* streams afar 1931
Keep love's *banner* floating o'er you 556
Of the crimson *banner* now the story 1994
Our *banner* is unfurled 1945
Our *banner* the Cross of Calvary 2180
See Jehovah's *banner* furled 676, 2150
That *banner*, brighter than the star 1081
The red-cross *banner* is unfurl'd 620
Thus deriving from their *banner* 541
Under his *banner* thus we sing 927
We stand beneath thy *banner* 48
Where'er our *banner* flies 1165
With the *banner* of Christ before 2180
With the *banner* of Christ unfurled 574
Your glorious *banner* wave on high 1654

BANNERS

Banners unfurled o'er all 2110
Their silken *banners* flare 923

BANQUET

Christ shall the *banquet* spread 2331
Hath this wondrous *banquet* 394

BANQUET-HALL

As to thy *banquet-hall* we enter 721

BAPTISM

The *baptism* of the heaven-descended 1778

BAPTIZE

Baptize their spirits in its light 479
Baptize them with thy spirit 9, 706
Baptize us with the courage thou 487
Baptize us with thy might 1169
Thine we *baptize* them in 505

BAPTIZED

Baptized in God—the Father, Son 2161

BAR

And may there be no moaning of the *bar* 1802
Before whose *bar* severe 2037

BARDS

By prophet *bards* foretold 948

BARK

And Christ my *bark* will use 826
And my *bark* its haven nears 1096
Guiding the lonely *bark* 180

BARQUE

When our *barque* shall sail 1991

BARQUES

Our little *barques* are frail 712

BARRENNESS

May *barrenness* rejoice to own 1776

BARRIER

Ev'ry *barrier* swept away 223

BARRIERS

Between us, then, all *barriers* were broken 139

BARS

The *bars* from heaven's high 1937
Ye *bars* of iron, yield 1081

BASE

The *base* to shun 456

BATHE

Bathe my trembling heart 766
Bathe, O *bathe* my heart 766
There shall I *bathe* my weary soul 2231

BATHED

Bathed in the light of heaven's 1254
E'en he who, *bathed* in Calvary's 1080

BATTLE

A little while of *battle* 2172
All the *battle* fought and won 64
And he must win the *battle* 12
And strong in *battle* is 2327
Battle bravely all the mighty hosts 2159
Courage, my soul, in the
battle beside thee 1765
Do thine own *battle* in our hearts 1373
Fierce and long the *battle* rages 736
Forward into *battle* 1586
"Forward" is the *battle* shout 262
Give ye to him who our *battle* hath won 228
Hard the *battle* ye must fight 1747
How hard the *battle* goes 174
In the mighty *battle* with the hosts 1997
Into the *battle* for truth 531
Onward then to *battle* move 1560
Shall conquer in the *battle* 19
That *battle* calls our marshaled ranks 370
The *battle* ne'er give o'er 1256
The *battle* to the strong 2226
Through the *battle* and the strife 863
Through the *battle*, through defeat 62
To us that still do *battle* here 2182
We *battle* now for Jesus 1945
When the *battle* thickens 1114
Who *battle* with the body's ills 471
You may *battle* with sin and with Satan 130

BATTLE-FIELD

And, in the darkest *battle-field* 617, 2321

BATTLE-LINE

Lord of our far-flung *battle-line* 583

BATTLES

And where the fiercest *battles* press 1412
Life's *battles* fought and won 1027

Lord of *battles,* God of armies 1697
The *battles* lost, or scarcely won 2170
What *battles* we have fought 2134

BATTLE-SHIPS

Not for *battle-ships* and fortress 1280

BEACON

A *beacon* to God 110
Beacon of hope and rest 180

BEAM

A *beam* from heaven is sent 793
A *beam* in darkness; let it grow 1797
And a brighter Easter *beam* 700
Beneath thy *beam* grow bright 191
Brightest *beam* of love divine 966, 1012
The *beam* that shines from Zion hill 198
Thine is the Parsee's sin-destroying *beam* 522
Thou burning sun with golden *beam* 41
'Tis the Spirit's rising *beam* 358

BEAMING

Abide with all thy *beaming* 26

BEAMS

And by its clear, revealing *beams* 185
Bright the *beams* that smile on me 1791
His *beams* are majesty and light 1061
In thy bright *beams,* which on me fall 1407
It *beams* above a manger 1878
Its *beams* in the valley reflected 1855
Let thy bright *beams* arise 315
O, let thine orient *beams* the night 2176
Pure religion's holier *beams* 1628
Radiant *beams* from thy holy face 1720
There *beams* above a manger 1878
Till thy mercy's *beams* I see 292
With *beams* of heavenly day 7
With the *beams* of truth unclouded 220

BEAR

And *bear* a song away 777
And *bear* our harvest home 1496
And *bear* the crown of life away 1962
And both of this *bear* witness 2072
And with him *bear* a part 792
Bear fruit eternal unto thee 458
Bear it onward, lift it high 1747
Bear me o'er life's fitful sea 2042
Bear the blessed tidings over land 1833
Bear the news to every land 2169
Bear us aloft, more glad, more strong 312
Bravely *bear,* and nobly strive 761
But *bear* it not alone 2160
Can you *bear* to let them go 251
Could we *bear* from one another 1581
Fain would we be and *bear* 1382
For me didst *bear* the nails 1235
"I *bear* this grief to set thee free" 825
I cannot *bear* these burdens alone 865
"I'll *bear* it all" 680
I'll *bear* the toil, endure the pain 87
Jesus will *bear* your burden 2280
Let him *bear* the burden 1210
Lord, send us forth as those who *bear* 1169
Make me *bear* more of thy gracious 1226
May we and all who *bear* 1286
O *bear* me away on thy snowy 1247
O *bear* me safe above 1227
O *bear* my longing heart to him 1247
O let me *bear* thy cross 888
Ours to *bear* the faithful witness 36
Shall *bear* his image bright 194
So *bear* thee in thy battles 1784
Some *bear* the wounds of combat 2182
Then he'll *bear* me safely over 895
Though some may *bear* their load alone 866
To *bear* the Cross and shame 109
Unless ye *bear* the child-like heart 949
We *bear* the burden of the day 2120
We *bear* with thee the scourge 1507
We too would *bear* the fruit devine 264
Who *bear* to every place 197
Who will *bear* the sheaves away 679
Would you have him *bear* your burden 2324
Ye who long pain and sorrow *bear* 41
Yea, whate'er we here must *bear* 1004

BEARER

O why was he there as the *Bearer* 1974

BEAREST

Our sins, not thine, thou *bearest* 86
Thou *bearest* every name 1325

BEARING

Bearing on Calvary my sin 1104

BEARS

All the pain thy bosom *bears* 63
Bears steadfast witness 'gainst the wrong 620
For only he who *bears* the cross 1823
He *bears* our sins upon the Tree 2192
He *bears* them all, and frees us 854
It *bears* thy name alone 826
Who patient *bears* his cross below 1931
Who so *bears* his brother's burden 299

BEASTS

Beasts wild and tame, your homage 2328
But the very *beasts* could see 2141
Prowling *beasts* about thy way 500
Then let the *beasts* of earth 1936

BEAT

A few more storms shall *beat* 5
As long as this poor heart shall *beat* 23
Not *beat* with cries on heaven's doors 1386

BEATEN

And oft hast *beaten* down my foes 1430
Beaten back by storm and sleet 488

BEATITUDES

For friendship's pure *beatitudes* 1779

BEAUTEOUS

And they are all so *beauteous* 2195

BEAUTIES

And still new *beauties* may I see 457
Beauties of thy truth and holiness 1006
His *beauties,* how divinely bright 1061
His *beauties* there may I 1308
How fair thy *beauties* shine 100
Its *beauties* like dewy blossoms 1411
The *beauties* and glories that greet us 2194
With holy *beauties* shine 198

BEAUTIFY

O, *beautify* our spirits 1359

BEAUTY

And let the *beauty* of the Lord 1541
And there doth *beauty* shine 1486
As thy *beauty* fills my soul 978
Beauty and wisdom all our ways 1873
Beauty is seen again 732
Beauty springeth out of nought 53
Beauty that around us glows 1158
But now the *beauty* of thy face 1140
For the *beauty* of each hour 484
Full of *beauty* is the pilgrim's 1066
His *beauty* paints the crimson 2097
His *beauty* shall enter them in 509
In *beauty* of his holiness 1486
In *beauty* of holiness kneel and 537
In the *beauty* of the lilies,
Christ was born 1215
In thy *beauty* all-resplendent 2018
Let me more of their *beauty* see 1732
No *beauty* can I plead 872
Not for more *beauty* would our eyes 385
Of thy bright *beauty* caught the view 2189
Some *beauty* may remain 388
Soon his *beauty* we'll behold 1731
That I, the *beauty* of the Lord 1903
The *beauty* of the Lord our God 1174
The *beauty* of the oak and pine 1441
The glorious *beauty* of thy name 1002
Their *beauty* this, their 1024
Thine *beauty* let me wear 1835
Thy *beauty,* Lord, and glory 1419
Till the *beauty* of Jesus be seen 1087
When *beauty* gilds the eastern hills 1877
When in his *beauty* I see the great 806
When in his *beauty* I see the great King 2235

BECAME

Became a prince in Egypt's land 2179
When I *became* a prodigal, and left 2237

BECKONS

And *beckons* thee his road 2321

BECOME

I through him *become* thy child 2121
Till he *become* the place 306

BED

And warmed its earthy *bed* 11
For his *bed* a cattle stall 945
Make thee a *bed,* soft, undefiled 34
The grave as little as my *bed* 59
Watching round my *bed* 1302

BEDS

Is by our *beds* of pain 240
On fever *beds* where sick men toss 734
On flowery *beds* of ease 87

BEES

Bees are humming round the hive 1305
Bees o'er the blossoms were 946

BEFALL

For I know, whate'er *befall* me 66
Strong through thee, whate'er *befall* us 605
Trusting him, whate'er *befall* 1721

BEFITS

What more *befits* the tongues 682

BEFORE

Before all them that fear thee 72

BEFRIEND

We are thine: do thou *befriend* us 1683

BEFRIENDED

Who hath our race *befriended* 43

BEGAN

With thee *began,* with thee shall end 1679

BEGIN

Begin this day to live anew 1821
We *begin* it at thy word 1301

BEGINNING

So from the *beginning* the fight 2166

BEGOTTEN

Begotten of the Father 43
First-*begotten* from the dead 1126

BEGUN

My journey's just *begun* 1949
Now it's *begun* within my soul 1722
What he hath once *begun* 166

BEHELD

Beheld thee fairer yet, while 2193
I *beheld* him bleeding on 1498
Nor *beheld* his children begging 1935
She *beheld* her Son despised 140
We *beheld,* it is no fable 1718

BEHEST

Nor how at thy *behest* they 491

BEHOLD

And *behold* them face to face 1712
And *behold* thy kingdom 974
And many who *behold* how good 887
And we *behold,* as pilgrims 1443
As we *behold* him face to face 847
Behold him, all ye that pass by 1460
Behold his hands and side 376
Behold his life, and thou shalt see 1935
Behold my hands, my feet" 1493
Behold our need, and hear our cry 43
Behold that blessed throng 1977
Behold, the bending orchards 1952
"*Behold* the man!" they say 1880
Behold the world's great tragedy 1568
Behold to thee, this festal 45
Behold us with a Father's love 364
Come and *behold* him 1330
For now, *behold,* to enter in 1857
Glorious now *behold* him arise 2196
He lives! *Behold* the empty bed 260
I *behold* thee as thou art 978
I shall *behold* his face 1864
O when shall I *behold* thy face 125
She shall yet *behold* thy glory 280
There *behold* his agony 2247
Till we *behold* the clearer light 787
Where we together thee *behold* 2174
Ye *behold* him face to face 1618
Ye who *behold* him, robed in his splendor 747
You *behold* the union depot 1076
Zion, *behold* thy Savior King 766

BEING

And our inmost *being* fill 342
Being of beings, may our praise 1105
God, who did your *being* give 1736
How great a *being,* Lord, is thine 788
If your *being* he is possessing 111
Let all my *being* speak 478
My inmost *being* thrills with joy 2238
That my whole *being* may proclaim 478
What is my *being* but for thee 1241

BEINGS

By whom, through whom, in whom all *beings* 2186
From God your *beings* are 1898
Which doth all *beings* keep 788

BELFRIES

The *belfries* of all Christendom 840

BELIEF

True *belief* and true repentance 358

BELIEVE

And we *believe* thy word 2167
Believe, believe the record true 1460
Believe his word, and trust 1806
Believe in him without delay 308
Believe on him, the work 1343
But we *believe* it was for us 1963
Come to Christ, on him *believe* 2283
I *believe* the promises he gave 2057
I now *believe* in Jesus 1867
I now *believe* thou dost receive 1248
If, seeking, ye truly *believe* 553
Only *believe,* and thou shalt see 477
Only *believe,* only believe 472
They who *believe* on his name 985
They who *believe* will find 858
Trusting him we *believe* that the 2093
You must *believe,* there is no other way 2337
Will you *believe,* or your Savior 2

BELIEVER

To ev'ry *believer* the promise 2102

BELIEVES

To him that in thy name *believes* 146

BELIEVETH

And who trustingly *believeth* will great 2319
That whosoever *believeth* in him 22
Whosoe'er *believeth* in him 1866

BELIEVING

"Am I now in Christ, *believing* 51
More of *believing* his marvelous Word 10
Then, in *believing,* thy peace receiving 60

BELL

And like a *bell,* with solemn, sweet 37

BELLS

All the *bells* are gladly ringing 354
And joining with the cadenced *bells* 816
Bells still are chiming and calling 263
Evening *bells* I seem to hear 810
Far, far away, like *bells* at evening 670
Flower *bells* are ringing 61
Gospel *bells,* how they ring 1866
Heavenly *bells* the while a-ringing 1718
Let the *bells* of heaven ring 1559
Soft *bells* of peace shall ring 496
Tell out, sweet *bells,* his praises 33
The *bells,* like angel voices 33
The *bells* of joy are ringing 2109
The *bells* of the city of God peal out 1095
The *bells* of the city of God ring out 1095
The gospel *bells* are joyful as they 1866
The gospel *bells* invite us to a feast 1866
The gospel *bells* give warning 1866
The merry *bells* ring out 952
The merry *bells,* the song 1629

BELONG

And I to him *belong* 1723
May we to Christ *belong* 84
To the precious Savior I *belong* 1907
To thee they all *belong;* to thee 1441

BELONGS

Belongs to God, who founded it 1857

BELOVED

Beloved, let us love: for they who love 202
Beloved, let us love: for love is rest (light) 202
Beloved, let us love: for only thus 202

BEND

And adoring *bend* the knee 746
Before him *bend* the knee 348
Bend at the mercy seat 540
Bend from heaven, thy dwelling-place 589
Bend from heaven thy gracious 993
Bend o'er us a pitying eye 756
Bend our pride to thy control 580
Bend the stubborn heart and will 342
Bend the stubborn will to thine 744
Here we *bend* before thy throne 1159
No, not distrustingly *bend* I 1276
Till before thee *bend* the knees 2138
We would not *bend* thy will 1386

BENDS

And *bends* them to his peaceful will 1614
And *bends* with eyes of pity 1464
But downward *bends* his burning 376
He *bends* in faithful watchfulness 1093

BENEATH

Beneath the earth's brown sod 11

BENEDICTION

And as a final *benediction* send 1287
And thy fullest *benediction* 281
God's *benediction* falls on souls 334
Thy *benediction* now bestow 1939

BENEDICTIONS

May *benedictions* here attend 1427

BENEFITS

For all the gracious *benefits* 2219
Of all his gracious *benefits* 1513
Who daily with his *benefits* 2031

BENIGHTED

Benighted, in this land of light 1116

BENT

Bent low beneath the burden 888

BEREFT

Thou who once wast thus *bereft* 2059

BESEECH

We *beseech* thee, hear us 442, 1033

BESET

Behind, before, thou hast *beset* 1452
Sin *beset* am I and tempted 224
Whoso *beset* him round 707, 2290

BEST

All the *best* we have we owe thee 242
Of the *best* that thou hast given 101
Our *best* is but thyself in us 1386
To be the *best* that I can be 1045

BESTOW

Bestow on every joyous thrill 1495
Bestow on us more than we think 1474
But my Savior will *bestow* 25
Thy quickening grace *bestow* 83
Till thou thyself *bestow* 1714
Who cry to thee *bestow* 75

BESTOWED

So let there be on us *bestowed* 1174
The Father hath *bestowed* 194

BESTOWER

Bestower of our rest 261
Chiming to the great *Bestower* 1665

BESTOWEST

That thou *bestowest* all our good 1495
Which thou *bestowest* day by day 2035

BETHLEHEM

How that in *Bethlehem* was born 599

BETIDE

And that, whate'er *betide* me 898

BETIDES

Whate'er *betides,* thy love abides 956

BETRAY

And let me ne'er my trust *betray* 4
Sword and crown *betray* his trust 53
While we *betray* so quickly 1549

BEWILDERED

Bewildered oft with doubt and care 1097

BIBLE

The *Bible* tells me so 995

BID

And *bid* farewell, farewell to 1821
And *bid* my heart rejoice 1824
And *bid* the choral song ascend 1900
And *bid* their conflicts cease 1328
And *bid* them every evening 117
And *bid* thy church increase 1646
And *bid* us all depart in peace 397
Bid darkness turn to day 1227
Bid her bear aloft its light 1033
Bid him come their hearts to win 1726
Bid him enter while you may 692
Bid its cruel discords cease 1760
Bid Jordan's narrow stream divide 1067
Bid my anxious fears subside 652
Bid my fears and doubtings 1644
Bid my many woes depart 745
Bid not thy wrath in its terrors 608, 612
Bid purest thoughts within me 345
Bid raging winds their fury 2325
Bid sadness and sorrow depart 164

Bid the fears and sorrows 1010
Bid the pow'r of sin depart 756
Bid the sad earth to join 239
Bid the whole earth, responsive 1086
Bid them gather everywhere 429
Bid them their lives to amend 1098
Bid thine angels shield us 256
Bid this struggling heart 1644
Bid thou our clamor cease 1359
Bid thou the blasts of discord 2013
Bid us hail the cheering ray 2253
Bid we thus our anthem flow 1178, 1673
Bid your heart be still 1565
By them *bid* fellowship increase 490
Come, blessed Lord, *bid* every shore 1086
Hast thou not *bid* me love thee 1778
He will *bid* us welcome 1771
I'll *bid* farewell to ev'ry fear 2231
Jesus will *bid* them depart 1269
Now *bid* thy banished ones 1024
Then I *bid* farewell to the way 864
Thou dost not *bid* us bend 1281
Thou hast *bid* us rise 742
Would *bid* us check the pride of sense 1300

BIDDEN

For God hath *bidden* all mankind 336
Whom God himself hath *bidden* 19

BIDDEST

And that thou *biddest* me come 1046
And what thou *biddest* we will do 1382
As thou *biddest* in thy saying 221
Thou *bidd'st* us not refuse 559
Who *biddest* the mighty ocean deep 81, 418

BIDE

Be thou with those who *bide* 2069
We'll *'bide* in him, then ev'ry hour 791

BIDS

And *bids* me at my Father's throne 1806
And *bids* the spring return 2307
And freely *bids* us come 1122
And he *bids* you to come meet him 1989
And since he *bids* me seek 1806
Bids me nestle closer to him 1643
Bids them come and stand 928
But he *bids* me go 819
He *bids* the moon direct the night 535
He *bids* the saints be glad 786
He *bids* the sun cut short his race 2307
He *bids* us draw near 172
It *bids* the strong be just 1281
Now he *bids* us tell abroad 287
That *bids* me scatter smiles 876
That *bids* our sorrows cease 1351
Thy Savior *bids* thy spirit 1659
Who *bids* all anxious fears 1912
Yea, *bids* us seize the whole 1397

BILLOWS

And *billows* toss and leap 2234
Billows his will obey 891
How often amid the wild *billows* 181
How the *billows* cease to roll 1041
In fathomless *billows* of love 430
Loud the angry *billows* roar 255
The *billows* are tossing high 1208
The sullen *billows* ceased to leap 475
When life's stormy *billows* roll 1682
Yea, though the mighty *billows* shake 571

BIND

And *bind* and heal the broken 1116
And *bind* thy church to thee 1497
And *bind* thy gospel to my heart 1065
And *bind* us all together 249
And the broken-hearted *bind* 1033
As thou didst *bind* two natures 1944
Bind all our lives together 1365
Bind my wandering heart to thee 340
Bind our souls to earth again 233
Bind strong the bond of brotherhood 471
Bind the old in slumber's bond 416
I *bind* my soul this day 813
I *bind* myself to peace 813
O *bind* us in that heavenly chain 1369
We *bind* it in sheaves from 1298
Which *bind* all hearts in one 1113
Which *bind* in sacred brotherhood 14

BINDS

And *binds* the ransomed nations 1652
He *binds* their wounds and gently 1636

BIRD

And the *bird* its nest 2026
Chanting *bird* and flowing fountain 1040
Each little *bird* that sings 68
"Now like a *bird* from peril 1261
When the *bird* waketh 1793

BIRDS

All the *birds* with joy are singing 354
And *birds* and streams repeat 1661
And *birds* upon the wing 55
Beneath thy mighty caring, the *birds* 1853
Birds above me fly 621
Birds, and beasts, and flowers 1302
Birds and flow'rs their carols 1975
Birds are brightly singing 61
Birds fill the air with joyous sound 1293
Birds in the branches were 946
Birds with gladder songs 1195
Birds, with morn and dew 1071
But *birds* and flowerets round us 1431
But now like the *birds* and the sunbeams 931
First let the *birds,* with painted 1936
For the *birds* and flowers 61
For the *birds* that sing of thee 273
Happy *birds* that sing and fly 1612
In *birds,* in sunshine, childish 1698
Now the little *birds* arise 976
The *birds* are on the wing 1938
The *birds* that wake the morning 2250
The *birds* their carols raise 2012
Thou by whom the *birds* are fed 976

Where *birds* and clouds go 1629
While *birds,* and flowers, and sky 2200

BIRD-SONG

Bird-song the valley fills 732

BIRTH

Be worthy of thy heavenly *birth* 546
But of lowly *birth* cam'st thou 2026
By thy lowly human *birth* 1022
By thy pure and holy *birth* 1761
Him whose *birth* the angels sing 105
Jesus, Lord, at thy *birth* 1720
Of Jesus' *birth* and peace 1487
Share but one common *birth* 56
Son of Man, whose *birth* incarnate 1760
Still mindful of thy heavenly *birth* 546
Thou art my joy, thou my new *birth* 123

BIRTHDAY

For this is the *birthday* of Jesus 1650

BIRTHRIGHT

The poor man's *birthright* 1810
Thou hast no common *birthright* 1312

BIRTHS

These new *births* more divine 1863

BITTERNESS

Our *bitterness* of tears 121

BLACK-BIRD

Black-bird has spoken 1221

BLACKNESS

It may be, perchance, that the *blackness* 953

BLADE

First the *blade,* and then the ear 359
The tender *blade* is hope's young dawn 191

BLAST

Defying ev'ry *blast* 1846
Not a *blast* of hurry 1091
The *blast* of war's great organ 37

BLAZE

Let us *blaze* his name abroad 1074
No more the *blaze* of glistering 2147
That in thy sunshine's *blaze* 1465

BLED

For the world's salvation *bled* 76
He *bled* and died to take away 1437
He who *bled* and died 622
Jesus hath *bled,* and there is remission 504
Who for us all hast *bled* 1175

BLEED

Bleed and suffer in my room 1814
On Calvary to *bleed* 549

BLEND

Blend it with thine; and take away 1231
Blend with ours your voices 1586
But *blend* our wills with thine 1386
We can *blend* our songs of praise 357

BLESS

All within me *bless* his name 1472
And *bless* each crystal window 210
And *bless* each place of 210
And *bless* his works, and bless 1811
And *bless* in death a bond 1392
And *bless* the door that opens 210
And *bless* the earth with peace 1449
And *bless* the Founder's name 1875
And *bless* the hearth, and bless 210
And *bless* the roof-tree 210
And *bless* the sacred hours 2203
And *bless* thee for the love 590
And *bless* thee while I live 1172
And *bless* this hallowed hour 1872
And *bless* us, more than in 1478, 1812
And *bless* where'er thy servants 471
And ever *bless* thy name 1448
And I the Lord will *bless* 1484
And I will ever *bless* thy name 1451
And sweetly *bless* this consecrated 1776
As thou didst *bless* the bread 249
Bless all our sisters and brothers 1014
Bless all the dear children 159
Bless and make them like to thee 718
Bless her works in thee begun 1033
Bless his care who guards 1606
Bless Jehovah, all his creatures 1472
Bless Jehovah, and forget not 1472
Bless, O God, to wise and simple 2318
Bless, O my soul! the God of grace 209
Bless, O my soul, the Lord thy God 1513
Bless our motherhood, we pray 634
Bless our union: through its 634
Bless the dark world with heavenly 1871
Bless the friends I love 1013
Bless the gifts we children 609
Bless the men, who, when night 416
Bless the prophets' sons 594
Bless the sailor's lonely pillow 1791
Bless the same boundless Giver 2164
Bless the sheep 1453
Bless the soul that sighs for thee 1791
Bless them, guide them 741
Bless these thy gifts, and grant 171
Bless those who kneel in worship 1188
Bless thou our fellowship 456
Bless thou the truth, dear Lord 249
Bless thou the work our hearts 211
Bless thou thy people as they strive 592
Bless thy church's new endeavor 1182
Bless thy little lamb tonight 1013
Bless thy people, *bless* our king 1159
Bless us, and keep us wherever 1611
Bless us in our daily labor 1022
Bless us tonight 455
Come all the faithful, *bless* 311

Come, and *bless* me now, O Lord 717
Come, *bless* the day that God 1704
Come near and *bless* us when 1801
Gladly we *bless* Thee 458
God *bless* His Word 1156
God *bless* these hands united 1457
God *bless* these hearts made one 1457
He doth forever *bless* 573
I *bless* the Lord because he doth 570
I will *bless* my Savior 311
I'll *bless* the hand that guided 1923
I'll *bless* the heart that planned 1923
Jesus alone can *bless* 425
Jesus, *bless* us ere we part 1685
Lord, *bless* me and protect me 2302
Lord, *bless* our souls' endeavor 2303
My God will *bless* in all distress 2216
O *bless* and keep the faithful 244
O *bless* and magnify the Lord 1547
O *bless* me now, my Savior 868
O *bless* the Lord, all ye his works 1547
O *bless* the shepherd 1453
O *bless* this sacred rite 728
O Father, *bless* our parish 244
O we would *bless* thee for thy ceaseless 435
So I will *bless* thee while I live 1436
To *bless* the love of God above 6
To *bless* the sacred name 323
We *bless* him for his holy Word 2161
We *bless* the Lamb with cheerful 1279
We *bless* thee for the friends 2128
We *bless* thy providential grace 2070
Where God shall *bless* his own 321
Ye who now will *bless* the poor 627

BLESSED (see also "blest")

And *blessed* be his glorious name 735, 1454
Blessed are they who to observe 212
Blessed be for evermore 665
Blessed be the dear Son of God 214
Blessed be thou, who, through 462
Blessed be thy gentle reign 1214
Blessed shall be her name 1632
Blessed them when their mothers 928
Blessed, yea, blessed is he 1621
He *blessed* little children 765
Now *blessed* be the Lord our God 735, 1454
So *blessed* for ever be Jesus 1650
That *blessed* are the pure in heart 1520
That they too may be *blessed* 549
To Jesus, who had *blessed* them 763
Who hath *blessed* us all our days 144
What can more *blessed* be 1535
Where the *blessed* evermore 1748

BLESSEDNESS

O the *blessedness* of peace awaiting 2252
Shall this *blessedness* attend 238
What a *blessedness*, what a peace 2209
Where is the *blessedness* I knew 1347

BLESSER

The *Blesser* and the blest 1457

BLESSEST

And gladly, as thou *blessest* us 2167

BLESSING

A *blessing* he'll surely bestow 1770
Abide with all thy *blessing* 26
Above all *blessing* high 1785
And, grateful for the *blessing* given 1186
And thy *blessing*, Lord, be granted 662
Asking for a *blessing* 1102
But at the last their *blessing* share 1522
For with *blessing* in his hand 1060
Glad shalt thou be, with *blessing* 1651
His *blessing* shine along the way 2269
I have not any *blessing* here 1141
Let thy *blessing* fall on me 70
Let us now a *blessing* seek 1676
O for that choicest *blessing* 2119
O let thy *blessing* evermore 1430
O Lord, thy *blessing* pour 244
O thou, above all *blessing* blest 100
The *blessing* of God will not fail thee 553
The *blessing* is never denied 553
The *blessing* shall be ours 1659
The primal marriage *blessing* 1944
Thee we would be always *blessing* 1190
There is always a *blessing* 1979
There's a *blessing* in prayer 1979
Thy *blessing* came; and still its power 1354
Thy *blessing* on the hearts they blend 1523
Thy *blessing* on their lives command 9, 706
To strive beneath thy *blessing* 1505
Whatever would be a true *blessing* 553
Willing with *blessing* your spirit 569
With thy *blessing* filling each who 2287
With thy tender *blessing* 1302
Yet possessing every *blessing* 1058

BLESSINGS

A thousand *blessings* on him rest 786
And *blessings* crown the board 1875
And *blessings* in our cup that brim 2185
And *blessings* more than we can give 323
And endless *blessings* paid 671
And the *blessings* that hallow 1992
Best of *blessings* he'll provide thee 1577
Blessings abound where'er he reigns 1008
Blessings all mine, with ten thousand 647
Blessings on his head hast showered 2308
By *blessings* like the sunshine 1952
Enough that *blessings* undeserved 39
For all the *blessings* earth displays 1439
For all the *blessings* life has 2030
For all the *blessings* of the light 59
For all the *blessings* that we prize 1518
For *blessings* passing number 1309
For *blessings* which he gives 2001
From every cloud his *blessings* break 6
Perpetual *blessings* from thy hand 1233
Rich *blessings* to bestow 308
Rich the *blessings* he will shed 63
Shall to thee his *blessings* send 238
Such *blessings* from thy gracious 1364

The *blessings* of our pilgrimage are 2199
The *blessings* thou dost crave 158
The *blessings* thy love hath bestowed 2194
Thousand thousand *blessings* 1792
Whose rich and tender *blessings* 1384
With *blessings* on our head 111
With *blessings* unmeasured my cup 1894
With numberless *blessings,* each moment 24

BLEST (see also "blessed")

And *blest* all nations shall him call 735
And *blest* in Jesus live 241
Blest be his compassion 544
Blest be the gracious power 1807
Blest be the Lord, who comes 2104
Blest be the Lord, who is to us 2131
Blest be the tempest 902
Blest by thee, with thee be passed 538
Blest is that tranquil hour 1237
Blest is the man to whom the Lord 1314
Blest is the man whom thou 1631
Blest the sign which thus reminds 2032
Blest through endless ages 544
Blest when our faith can hold thee 1023
But more *blest* the love that binds 2032
God shall be all, and in all ever *blest* 1538
How *blest* are they who have not 1493
Living, or dying, they are *blest* 1446
O, if you were never *blest* 562
Thrice *blest* is he to whom is given 2321
Thou hast *blest* us with thy favor 579
We shall be *blest,* and all the world 1123
While *blest* with a sense of his love 795
Whose waking is supremely *blest* 132
With Jesus the Savior his own
shall be *blest* 2271
Yea, *blest* be thou, O house of God 1569

BLIGHT

Free from the *blight* of sorrow 1675

BLIND

As of old when *blind* and lame 1559
Lord, thou hast made the *blind* 1140
Once I was *blind,* but now the light 624
The *blind* rejoiced to hear the cry 2218
Was *blind,* but now I see 88
Ye *blind,* behold your Savior 1351

BLINDED

Yet, weak and *blinded* though 1428

BLINDNESS

And I through *blindness* fail 434
Awhile his mortal *blindness* 1843
Lord, upon our *blindness* 1800

BLINDS

That *blinds* our eyes to thee 419

BLISS

And brighter *bliss* of heaven 859
And immortal *bliss* inherit 718
Bliss he wakes, and woe he 566
Earnest of the *bliss* on high 346
From the best *bliss* that earth 1023
Here little, and hereafter *bliss* 704
In *bliss* returns to reign 512
O for the *bliss* that by it 2119
O, the *bliss* of consecration 1688
O, the *bliss* of over there 2191
Private *bliss* and public wealth 1628
So that earth's *bliss* may be our guide 1236
The *bliss* till now unknown 1322
Till in *bliss* we see thy face 1153
To live in thee in *bliss* 979, 1250
What *bliss* beyond compare 961
What *bliss* till now was thine 1475
Why should we then our *bliss* delay 196

BLOOD

Abel's *blood* for vengeance 544
All the sprinkled *blood* receive 339
And cleansing through his *blood* 575
And hear the *blood* speak
that hath answered 73
And his the *blood* that can for all 2201
And in the *blood* of Christ have 774
And richer *blood* than they 1279
And some, as with heart's *blood* 1298
And with his *blood* mankind 1861
Because with his *blood,* he has washed 122
Blood of Christ, so rich and free 1138
Blood of the guiltless, like water 607
Blood of the Lamb of God 1276
But the *blood* of Jesus 544
But the *blood* that atones for the soul 1974
By thy *blood,* O spotless Lamb 998
For atoning *blood* has been sprinkled 1979
For us the Savior's *blood* was shed 43
Hath redeemed us by his *blood* 77
His *blood* atoned for all our race 113
His *blood* availed for me 1351
His *blood* can cleanse your heart 2324
His *blood* can make the foulest 1351
His *blood* flowed out in a crimson 1970
His *blood* hath made me whole 729, 802
His precious *blood* salvation bought 2140
His precious *blood,* to plead 113
His sacred *blood* hath washed 426
How, sown in martyr's *blood,* the Faith 91
Jesus' *blood* can cleanse from sin 759
Just to trust his cleansing *blood* 2092
Let thy precious *blood* applied 1684
Lord, let the cleansing *blood* 1276
My all to the *blood* I am bringing 1848
My *blood* I thus pour forth 2153
My precious *blood* I shed 827
My sins are all under the *blood* 17
Nothing but the *blood* of Jesus 2214
O by that *blood* so freely shed 435
O, wash me in thy precious *blood* 5
Pleading naught but Jesus' *blood* 755
Praise we Christ, whose *blood* was shed 142
Precious is the *blood* that healed us 2065
Pulsing in the hero's *blood* 1077
That *blood* which flowed for sin 234
That Jesus and his *blood* alone 898

The *blood* of Christ most precious 869
The *blood* of Jesus whispers peace 1610
The *blood* of pilgrim nations 1312
The *blood* of the Cross is my only 1278
The *blood* that flowed for sin 1805
Then the Savior's *blood* reveal 756
There is healing in his *blood* 1999
There where the *blood* of the Lamb 1206
They are singing of the *blood* of 1919
Through the *blood* of Christ, my Master 461
Through the rich *blood* that Jesus shed 1875
Thy *blood,* O Lord, was shed 2077
Thy *blood* through all eternity 836
Thy precious *blood* must be 820
Thy precious *blood* shall never lose 1961
Thy precious *blood* the wine 722
'Tis thine the *blood* to apply 1777
To feel for those thy *blood* 1371
To save us by thy precious *blood* 1482
To thee, whose *blood* can cleanse 1046
When by his sacred *blood* 459
Where the paschal *blood* is poured 142
Whose *blood* now cleanses from 1247
Whose precious *blood* redeemed 820
With his *blood* he purchased me 894
With his own *blood* he bought her 1845
With thy *blood* outpoured 1049
Yet not the less that *blood* avails 873

BLOOD-DROPS

Lord, whence are those *blood-drops* 1983

BLOOD-SHED

No *blood-shed* in the wrestling 90

BLOOM

Bloom in every meadow 2204
Bloom in radiance and 1006
Bloom the fair flowers the earth 349
This *bloom* of love so fair 1863

BLOSSOM

May it *blossom* forth and flower 219
We *blossom* and flourish as 916

BLOSSOMING

There, like an Eden *blossoming* 349

BLOSSOMS

Blossoms breaking, nature waking 208
For *blossoms* sweet and tender 2303
Let the *blossoms* of the earth 1071
Life *blossoms* to its goal 120
There are *blossoms* of gladness 903

BLOT

Blot out my transgressions now 554
Blot out our sins, O Father 244
Blot them out in boundless grace 554
For thy compassions great, *blot* out 31

BLOTTED

He *blotted* them out 122

BLOW

Blow, bugles of battle 1768
Blow soft upon the perfumed air 239
Blow your wildest, then, O gale 2056
Many a *blow* and biting sculpture 217

BLOWS

Blows the wind and it is gone 1618
With *blows* and outrage adding 1251

BLUE

Through the soft *blue* of echoing sky 239

BLUSH

No, when I *blush,* be this my 967
Or *blush* to speak his name 87

BOARD

Thyself at thine own *board* make 335

BOAST

All we can *boast,* till Christ 1038
For frantic *boast* and foolish 583
The *boast* of haughty error 1
Then let us make our *boast* 93
Till then I *boast* a Savior 967

BOASTING

In him shall all my *boasting* be 1890

BOAT

Tossing the *boat* in a tempest 1831

BOATS

When the fishing *boats* lay quiet 2254

BODIES

Bodies clear and spirits bright 470
Our *bodies* may far off remove 230
Pure and chastened *bodies* 1110

BODY

All one *body* we 1586
Here in the *body* pent 494
His *body,* broken in our stead 266
In the *body* and the blood 1060
In whose *body* joined together 677
Jesus for thee a *body* takes 1514
My *body,* Lord, is thine to keep 1844
"My broken *body* thus I give 2133
One *body* we, one *body* who 335
The *body* that was broken 2021
The *body* they may kill 12
"This is my *body,* broke for sin 2132
"This is my *body*": so thou givest yet 335
Thy *body* and thy blood 165
Thy *body,* broken for my sake 30
To rest my *body* hasteth 1297

BOLTS

His *bolts* have pierced the mighty 1889

BOND

As thou in *bond* of love 1403
O *bond* of perfect peace 205
O *bond* of union, strong and deep 205
O happy *bond,* that seals my vows 1392

BONDAGE

And from all *bondage* win a full 721
From ancient *bondage* freed the poor 1873
From *bondage* set me free 2119
From killing *bondage* free 191
No more in *bondage* shall they toil 2240
The *bondage* of sin 2
Then shall all *bondage* cease 249
Willing from *bondage* of sin 569

BONDS

Burst Satan's *bonds* 1366
But now the *bonds* of death are 965
From the *bonds* of sin release 1028
He hath burst his *bonds* in twain 282
In *bonds* my perfect liberty 2034
That from our *bonds* we might be freed 1168
These are the firm-knit *bonds* of grace 14
Walking in *bonds* of perfect love 1670
With *bonds* of peace serene 2134

BOOK

Book of love, in accents tender 243
"Holy Bible, *Book* divine 2087
Holy *Book* and pilgrim track 1077
O *Book* of life, of love 2087
O thou holy *Book* divine 738
The *Book* is his Word 850
Your life's a *book* before their eyes 2281

BOOKS

When the *books* are opened wide 1710

BOON

And may all who *boon* of heaven 1553
Shall come the *boon* of peace 46
That is the *boon* we ask 1942

BOONS

Above all *boons,* I pray 1423

BORDER

There on the *border* of boundless 1550

BORDERS

From Yukon's ice-bound *borders* 149

BORE

Faithfully he *bore* it 143
He *bore* it all alone 957
He *bore* the burden to Calv'ry 881
He *bore* the Cross, but I received a blessing 139
He *bore* the mighty load 426
He who *bore* all my blame 1268
He who *bore* all pain and loss 287
He who *bore* your load of sin 692
Hers, who *bore* God's Holy One 1263
O who like thee so humbly *bore* 769
She *bore* to men a Savior 1107
Suff'ring, he *bore* my shame 2143
They *bore* the cross, despised the shame 1108
They *bore* thee to Calvary 2026

BORN

Alleluia! *born* of Mary 77
Be *born* in us today 1426
Born a child and yet a King 343, 658
Born a King on Bethlehem's plain 2196
Born as a child, he was so lovely 1617
Born but for one brief day 425
Born in heaven and radiant 294
Born is the King of Israel 1861
Born of him, through grace 1218
Born of his Spirit, washed 213
Born of Mary, mother mild 609
Born of the one light 1221
Born of woman, would not weep 140, 1263
Born of woman, yet divine 798
Born that he might lead us 1792
Born that man no more may die 675
Born, the King of angels 1330
Born this day to save us 290
Born this happy morning 1330
Born thy people to deliver 343, 658
Born to give them second birth 675
Born to raise the sons of earth 675
Born to redeem, and strong to save!" 697
Born to reign in us forever 343, 658
Born to set thy people free 343, 658
Christ is *born* and Mary's calling 257
"Christ is *born* in Bethlehem!" 675
Christ, the Savior, is *born!* 1720
For Christ is *born* of Mary 1426
For the Son of Mary is *born* tonight 1095
He, then *born* to grief and pain 412
He that was *born* upon this joyful day 298
I am evil, *born* in sin 554
Is *born* on earth to dwell 559
Jesus Christ is *born* today 625
Jesus Christ was *born* for this 625
Jesus Christ was *born* to save 625
May we, *born* anew like morning 605
O be thou *born* within our hearts 559
The humble Christ was *born* 551
They only, are his sons, *born* from 202
Unto you is *born* a Savior 1866
"Ye must be *born* again." 18

BORNE

Borne aloft on angels' wings 1161
Borne on faith's strong wing 297
Borne thy witness in all ages 579
Borne upon their latest breath 1762
I've *borne,* I've *borne* it all for thee 827
Thou hast *borne* all for me 1050
Thou, Lord, hast *borne* for me 2077
What hast thou *borne* for me 827
Who hath *borne* all our sins 2187

BORROWS

It gives, but *borrows* none 7
While all that *borrows* life from thee 877

BOSOM

All the pain thy *bosom* bears 63
And in his *bosom* rest 1563
Let me to thy *bosom* fly 994
On Jesus' *bosom* nought but calm 1609
When on thy *bosom* it has leant 1202
Where, on the *bosom* of their God 1537

BOSOMS

Come, within our *bosoms* shine 342
Our inmost *bosoms* fill 311
With thyself our *bosoms* fill 1683

BOUGH

For lo, each *bough* proclaims 1921

BOUGHS

Through leafless *boughs* the sharp winds 2097

BOUGHT

Bought by him at such a cost 2232
Bought with a price, the blood 1278
Bought with blood, and *bought* 1197
For thou hast *bought* it 291
For thou has *bought* me; I am thine 60
I am *bought,* but not with gold 1278
Jesus, thou hast *bought* us 2287
That *bought* my guilty soul 1137
That *bought* us, once for all 99
Thou hast *bought* me with thy blood 1644
Thou hast *bought* us, thine we are 1683
Thy love has *bought* me 60

BOUND

And then for ever *bound* me 2119
Bound and bleeding 'neath the rod 1263
Bound by God's far purpose 501
Bound, every heart with rapturous joy 328
Bound to him eternally by love's 1790
Ever to thee I'm *bound* by love 1254
Fast *bound* in sin and nature's night 94
From earth's remotest *bound* 1134
I am *bound* for the promised land 1563
I to thee am closely *bound* 855
Nearer the *bound* of life 1580
None can *bound* the tender mercies 711
Once I was *bound,* but now 624
Satan *bound,* and banished sin 1136
Still praying as I onward *bound* 915
That *bound* the tomb where Jesus lay 260
That *bound* their hearts as one 487
They were *bound,* but thou hast freed 1775
While they are *bound* can we be free 309
Whose arm hath *bound* the restless wave 81

BOUNDLESS

'Tis *boundless* as eternity 150

BOUNDS

Till in the utmost *bounds* of earth 549

BOUNTIES

Each annual round with *bounties* crowned 21
For *bounties* of earth 959
May we thy *bounties* thus 2167
Why are its *bounties* all in vain 1232

BOUNTY

And all thy *bounty,* Lord 26
And may we for thy *bounty* give 383
Because of thy great *bounty,* Lord 182
By his incessant *bounty* fed 643
For thy *bounty* everywhere 273
God's free *bounty* glorify 358
His *bounty* hath expressed 857
It is from thy *bounty* that all 1594
'Mid thy *bounty* we uplift 1665
Since from his *bounty* I receive 1201
The *bounty* of thy perfect love 1346
Thy *bounty* freely gave 200
Whose *bounty* like the gentle rain 422

BOURNE

For, though from out our *bourne* 1802

BOW

All men shall humbly *bow* 13
And before him *bow* with 563
And *bow* before thy throne 200
And *bow* in penitence beneath 435
And *bow* to his command 1653
And silent *bow* before his face 1105
Bow down and hear our cry 1365
Bow down before him, his glory 2322
Bow down in adoration 770
Bow thine ear to us here 563
Bow thy meek head in mortal pain 1660
Bring me my *bow* of burning gold 95
I *bow,* and bless the sacred name 1864
Let us *bow* down withal 1335
Lord of all, we *bow* before thee 746
O God, our light, to thee we *bow* 32
O let us only lowlier *bow* 1522
Shall be constrained to *bow* 50
The *bow* of promise spans 1860
Then I shall *bow* in humble adoration 1437
We *bow* before thee humbly now 1356
We *bow* our hearts before thee 1415

BOWED

Bowed in sorrow, sighing 1263
Bowed with anguish, deeply grieved 140
In Jordan *bowed* his head 404
Jesus is *bowed* with the weight 1015
Meekly she *bowed* her head 1632
Nor *bowed* beneath thine awful 2170
They *bowed* their necks the death 1931
To thee, in reverent love,
our hearts are *bowed* 92
Yet when *bowed* down beneath the load 1531

BOWS

My Savior *bows* his head 1562

BOY

And of the sinless *Boy* 1487
For the Virgin's sweet *boy* 1995
O Jesus, once a Nazareth *boy* 1412
O, where is my *boy* tonight 2272
The *boy* of my tenderest care 2272
The *boy* that was once my joy 2272

BOYS

All the little *boys* he killed 2141

BRACE

And *brace* thy heart, and nerve 1823

BRAIN

On weary *brain* and troubled 2013

BRAKE

He *brake* the age-bound chains 1937

BRANCH

And that same *branch,* which for 2131
As a fruitful *branch* receiving 51
No *branch* of palm I merit 2248
Waving a *branch* of the palm-tree 1831

BRANCHES

For once thy favored *branches* 1921
The *branches* that we offer are 1604
The *branches* weighing down 107
Ye are the *branches* bearing fruit 170

BRAVE

And *brave* another cruise 826
Let me be *brave* and strong 1027
With him I'll *brave* death's chilling tide 1421

BREAD

All the *bread* he ever broke 990
And hungering for the *bread* of life 1659
Be known to us in breaking of the *bread* 335
Bread from stones around him laid 268
Bread of heaven, *bread* of heaven 652
Bread of our souls, whereon we feed 1052
Come, there's *bread* in the house 565
Feeds me with the living *bread* 66
For *bread* which satisfieth not 2155
From thy living *Bread,* O Lord 127
Giving in Christ the *bread* eternal 269
He can with *bread* of heaven 548
I am the *Bread* of life 1866
I, the *Bread* of heav'n, am broken 2006
Is here in this memorial *bread* 266
Lo, the *Bread* of heaven is broken 2017
My *bread* from heaven shall be 30
One *bread* of life we break 335
That living *bread,* that heavenly wine 165
The *bread* how sweet 89
The *bread* is always consecrate 204
The *bread* of life is here for you 362
The holy *bread,* the food 1327
Thine the broken *bread* 2007
Thou, the *Bread* of heaven, art broken 1022
To feed upon the *bread* and wine 234
With *Bread* of life earth's hungers 1576
With this true and living *bread* 245

BREAK

And *break* upon thee in a flood 1666
And *break* with self and sin 1442
And lo, I *break* the chains of my 1140
And shall *break* in blessings 577
As thou didst *break* the loaves 249
Break down every idol 964, 999
Break, ev'ry tender tie 425
Break every weapon forged in fires 334
Break forth in rapturous strains 1086
Break forth in swelling song 733
Break me, melt me, mold me 1782
Break, my tongue, such guilty silence 1214
Break off your tears, ye saints 697
Break the chains of sin 433
Break thou the bread 721
Break with thine iron rod 2073
By thee we shall *break* through 708
O *break,* O *break,* hard heart 1333
Or *break* his cruel bands 156
Or *break* the sacred chain 1064
The *break* of day will come ere long 1639
Thou Father, God eternal, didst *break* 2021
When shall *break* the promised day 1136

BREAKERS

And the fearful *breakers* roar 1007
Breakers crashing on the shore 1211
The *breakers* roar and the waves 2190
Then far beyond the *breakers* 1784

BREAKETH

Soundless and bright for us *breaketh* 732

BREAKS

Breaks the mingled tide of song 678
For yonder *breaks* a new and cloudless 1399
He *breaks* the power of cancelled 1351
Jerusalem *breaks* forth in songs 768
Soft it *breaks* upon the ear 678
Suddenly *breaks* on earth 732
Till thy Spirit *breaks* our night 220

BREAST

And heaven's within my *breast* 1208
And if, within thy *breast* 201
But, chiefest, in our cleansed *breast* 764
I on his *breast* recline 854
Leaning upon thy *breast* 1828
Meekly on each *breast* 1102
Nay, on thy *breast* engraven 1325
Safe on his gentle *breast* 1675
Soothing the weary *breast* 180
Speak peace to every *breast* 1675
The throbbing brow and laboring *breast* 98
Then, while leaning on thy *breast* 1007

BREATH

And *breath* of clover fields 1398
And the *breath* of God is moving 1993

And with unfaltering *breath* 2050
Breath of God-head, highest King 1516
Breath of our breath, in thee 1163
Breath of the holy 1656
Eternal Spirit, by whose *breath* 452
Happy, if with my latest *breath* 1017
How sweet the *breath,* beneath the hill 267
O may my last expiring *breath* 153
Purer than *breath* of morning 638
So, when my latest *breath* 494
Soft as the *breath* of even 1589
The *breath* of Christ is in the air 1380
Then shall my latest *breath* 1220
Were half the *breath* thus vainly spent 2221
When the *breath* of life is flown 2253
Wheresoe'er his *breath* has giv'n 1783
Yea, while a *breath,* a pulse remains 30

BREATHE

All that *breathe,* your Lord adore 1623
And *breathe* around thy perfect calm 2048
And *breathe* that heavenly air 1349
And *breathe* the Living Word 1777
Be silent, be silent,
breathe humbly our prayer 172
Breathe each day nearness 1793
Breathe into every wish thy will 406
Breathe into the music 757
Breathe, O *breathe* thy loving Spirit 1190
Breathe on us, Lord! our sins 1810
Breathe that holy name in pray'r 1817
Breathe the Holy Spirit into 1010
Breathe through the heats of our desire 386
Breathe thyself into my breast 637
Breathe thy life, and spread 643
Come Holy Spirit! *breathe* that peace 1349
Let all that *breathe* partake 1225
O *breathe* thy mighty power abroad 1440
O *breathe* thy peace, as flesh and spirit 98
Or *breathe* the prayer divinely 1231
Penitent we *breathe* thy name 442
Savior, *breathe* forgiveness o'er us 1058
We *breathe* the air of that blest clime 1661
We *breathe* thy breath 784

BREATHED

And *breathed* out my woe 1477
Breathed in the hour of loneliness 1545

BREATHER

O *Breather* into man of breath 590

BREATHES

He *breathes,* and there is health 120
It *breathes* in the air 1546

BREEDS

And from the *breeds* of earth 593
Or lesser *breeds* without the law 583

BREEZE

And in the *breeze* beside thee I am 1533
Each *breeze* that sweeps the ocean 1911
In every *breeze* a song 55

BREEZES

Come, O Lord, like mountain *breezes* 331
Let the stormy *breezes* blow 431
On the summer *breezes* winging 678
The *breezes* of thy love are 1919
While on summer *breezes* winging 678

BRETHREN

Brethren, let our tongues unite 1178
But thou hast needy *brethren* here 503
Fear not, *brethren,* joyful 277
For all are *brethren,* far and wide 1371
Our *brethren* shield in danger's hour 81, 418
To call thy *brethren* forth from want 1511
Where *brethren* meet, where Christ 1809
Wherever, Lord, thy *brethren* go 81

BRIDE

As a *bride* dost earthward move 217
To give away this *bride* 1944

BRIDEGROOM

As thou, for Christ, the *Bridegroom* 1944
O, be ready when the *Bridegroom* comes 2297
The *Bridegroom* comes 2149
Thou glorious *Bridegroom* of our hearts 89
When the *Bridegroom* cometh 693

BRIGHT

How *bright* their glories be 530

BRIGHTEN

Brighten the corner where you are 399
Brighten thou my Sabbath morning 1085
Holy Spirit, *brighten* little deeds 757
Will *brighten* the moments of earth's 10

BRIGHTENED

They *brightened* all the joy 956

BRIGHTENS

Now *brightens* dawn toward golden 1951
That *brightens* up the sky 68

BRIGHTNESS

And *brightness* of thy face 1172
And in the *brightness* of thy light 2079
Brightness from first to last 1087
Brightness of God's glory 1034
Brightness of my Father's glory 978
Brightness of my morning rays 972
Brightness of the Father's glory 1214
Brightness of the morning 2204
Brightness of uncreated light 2022
But its *brightness* shall only come 1990
Cause the *brightness* of thy face 2099
For the *brightness* of thy face 1612
From the *brightness* of thy face 76
In *brightness* of thy face 1390
Jesus in *brightness* revealed 1678
Lord, by the *brightness* of thy light 317
The *brightness* of the coming night 1927
The *brightness* of the day 1920
Thou heavenly *Brightness!* Light divine 1470

Thy *brightness* unto them appears 788
What great *brightness* did you see 105
When clothed in his *brightness* 24
With growing *brightness* shine 685

BRING

And *bring* all heaven before 1032
And *bring* an offering with you 1486
And *bring* but withered leaves 1285
And *bring* me safe to land 898
And *bring* me to thine holy hill 1483
And *bring* the glorious liberty 1332
"And *bring* the glorious years!" 312
And *bring* the grand sabbatic 1733
And *bring* them all to the good 1116
And *bring* to fullest triumph 1372
And *bring* us safe to heaven 1067
And *bring* your gifts 320
And changeful hours *bring* 1
And some *bring* strength 1947
And some may *bring* their greatness 1947
And thou wilt *bring* the young green 1327
And we would *bring* our burden 1849
And when we *bring* them to thy throne 1441
Be thou, O Father, near to *bring* 383
Bring a torch, to the cradle 257
Bring, and adore him 2322
Bring before us all the story 2279
Bring every day thy choicest 200
Bring greetings to yon heavenly 302
Bring healing in thy wings 944
Bring her bud to glorious flower 580
Bring him thy burden 985
Bring hope to the nations 1768
Bring justice to our land 1340
Bring love and justice home 1698
Bring in the day of brotherhood 1669
Bring me flesh, and *bring* me wine 627
Bring me, noble Guest divine 1516
Bring me pine logs hither 627
Bring near thy great salvation 1836
Bring, O *bring* the glorious day 673
Bring our ransomed souls 129
Bring peace to all mankind 1313
Bring relief for all complaints 1676
Bring that victorious hour 1916
Bring the child-like heart 925
Bring the nations help and healing 2342
Bring the wand'ring ones 681
Bring them home, dear Lord 1196
Bring them in from the fields 681
Bring them to thy heavenly rest 718
Bring thy mercy to us all 1685
Bring to every thankful mind 339
Bring to my remembrance 937
Bring to our troubled minds 1340
Bring to our world of strife 1340
Bring to tired children 935
Bring us, O Father, nearer thee 189
Bring us safe through Jordan 2010
Bring us to heaven, where thy saints 467
Bring us where all tears are dried 2253
Bring us your Savior 705
Bring your load of doubts 2252
Bring your praise for mercies 357
Bring your sweetest, noblest lays 659
Bring your troubles, not a few 2252
But *bring* him to me with all 2272
But, O, that he'd let me *bring* 830
Come then, my soul, *bring* all 200
For he it is that shall *bring* forth 2116
Give deeper calm than night can *bring* 32
He will *bring* relief 987
He'll *bring* me to the promised 1907
Her young ones forth may *bring* 783
I *bring*, I *bring* rich gift 827
I *bring* my guilt to Jesus 854
I could *bring* nothing but leaves 1941
It *bring* to pass shall he 1708
"It can *bring* with it nothing 1759
It will *bring* me no grief 1751
Lord, *bring* me nearer day by day 1928
Lord, we *bring* to thee the glory 542
Lord, we would *bring* for offering 1849
Naught can I *bring*, dear Lord 2201
O *bring* each one for whom 1640
O *bring* me, and all I love 1304
O *bring* the tribes of Israel 116
O *bring* thy great salvation in 82
O let them *bring* me to thy holy 1701
Shall I *bring* him golden sheaves 1710
Should *bring* our harvest offerings 1164
So *bring* him incense, gold 2215
Such ever *bring* thee where 1032

BRINGER

O *bringer* of salvation 1481

BRINGEST

O Zion, that *bringest* good tidings 1998

BRINGING

Bringing of our substance 1110
Bringing the weary to find rest 1104

BRINGS

And *brings* the truth to sight 1933
Brings every blessing from above 2221
Brings his frankincense to Jesus 299
He *brings* me near his throne 150
He *brings* the wicked low 1636
He *brings* us mercy from above 2192
O for trust, that *brings* the triumph 223
When to follow thee *brings* sorrow 2276

BRINK

Beyond the river's *brink* we'll lay 1962

BROKE

It *broke* his heart on Calvary 2242
She almost *broke* her loving heart 2237

BROKEN

Broken for mankind 3
Broken, humbled to the dust 554
Christ hath *broken* every chain 287
He has *broken* ev'ry fetter 411

Thy body, *broken* for my sake 30
Was in this *broken* bread made 469

BROKEN-HEARTED

When grieving, *broken-hearted* 22

BROOK

And every *brook* that flows 1384
Brook by the traveler's way 1052
By singing *brook* or cottage door 2277

BROTHER

And the *brother* near at hand 813
Brother and sister gone to that 1605
Brother clasps the hand of *brother* 2067
O Christ, the elder *Brother* of proud 1880
Once for all, O *brother,* believe it 504
Our Savior and our *Brother* still 1526
Somebody's *brother,* O who then 2068
Then with my Savior, *Brother,* Friend 1339
There is a *brother* whom someone 2068
Thy *brother* calls to thee 156
To thy God, and to thy *brother* 2263
Will you not, my *brother,* come 2283
With every *brother* that I see 182

BROTHERHOOD

And all the sin-stained *brotherhood* 2155
And holier dreams of *brotherhood* 82
Brotherhood and sisterhood of earth's 485
Brotherhood banish wail of the worker 601
In glad, exultant *brotherhood* 46
One *brotherhood* in heart are we 325
Our *brotherhood* still rests in him 2160

BROTHER-LOVE

Brother-love binds man to man 1040

BROTHERS

All are *brothers* coming to thee 1075
As *brothers* of the Son of Man 1669
Brothers ever let us be 366
Brothers in work to do 170
Brothers, lift your voices 1586
Brothers of the heart are we 366
Brothers, we are treading 1586
O Christian *brothers,* glorious shall be 1320
The *brothers* of thy well-beloved Son 421
Then, *brothers* brave and manly 1252
Thy *brothers* help, thy God revere 546

BROUGHT

And God *brought* near 1130
And I have *brought* to thee 827
And thou hast *brought* to me 2077
Brought it back victorious 143
Brought me lower, while I whispered 1498
Brought out their sick and deaf 2218
But he hath *brought* us gladness 350
Hath *brought* us by his love 93
He *brought* us to his fold again 184
He hath *brought* salvation near 1510
I *brought* my soul to Jesus 872
I was *brought* low 857
It *brought* my Savior from above 575
Our Christ hath *brought* us over 1854
They *brought* them in love to 1941
Thou hast *brought* a message 297
Thou hast *brought* thy people nigh 597
Thou hast *brought* us life and light 142
What *brought* them to that world above 118
While others *brought* fruit to 1941
Who *brought* this upon thee 35
What hast thou *brought* to me 827
What have I *brought* to thee 2077
Who *brought* God's revelation 2165

BROW

Ev'ry *brow* is beaming 409
His *brow* was pierced with 926
No *brow* to seek the dust 1281
No more to wear the *brow* of care 2207
On the Redeemer's thorn-crowned *brow* 1803
That his *brow* adorns 119
The throbbing *brow* and laboring 98

BROWS

Erect, clear-eyed, upon their *brows* 491
Their *brows* are enclosed in a golden 2004
Wreathing *brows* with roses plucked 163

BRUISED

And *bruised* by the fall 504
I was *bruised,* but Jesus healed 895

BRUSH

For I *brush* the dews on Jordan's 1247

BUCKLE

Go, *buckle* on the armor 1860

BUFFET

Though Satan should *buffet* 2249

BUILD

And *build* its glory there 1397
And finely *build* for days to come 1340
Build us a tow'r of Christ-like 1468
Build ye the road, and falter not 720
I *build* on this foundation 898
That they may *build* from age to age 445
That we may *build*
with all thy wondrous 1609
We *build* an altar here, and pray 1528
We *build* with thee, O grant 2198
Ye shall *build* more nobly 657

BUILDED

Builded for his habitation 263
They have *builded* him an altar 1215

BUILDER

Builder of life divine 1468

BUILDERS

We are *builders* of that city 656

BUILDETH

What with care and toil he *buildeth* 53

BUILDS

Builds on the rock that naught 904
The Lord our God *builds* up his church 1636

BUILT

And *built* in righteousness 1609
And *built* the lofty skies 877
As that which *built* the skies 190
Built by workmanship divine 1712
Built in our bodies his temple 263
Built on his faithfulness 572
Built on hope unswerving 1110
Built on the precious Corner-stone 1441
Built while they dream 2130
Formed the seas, or *built* the sky 356
Grafted, rooted, *built* in thee 245
He *built* the earth, he spread 535
He *built* the sky 1061

BULWARK

A *bulwark* never failing 12

BULWARKS

These are the *bulwarks* of the state 603

BURDEN

And his *burden* light 344
And the *burden*, and the lesson 62
And the *burden* of the day 203
Come with thy *burden* of grief 353
Content to bear the *burden* 1166
Ev'ry *burden* will be lighter 144
From our *burden* set us free 589
He taketh my *burden* away 24
Lay down the *burden* and the care 32
Let thy *burden* fall 689
May we now their *burden* share 2047
My *burden* and my cross 812
Never a *burden* that he doth not bear 407
Not a *burden* we bear 2266
On him your *burden* roll 1331
Perfectly willing your *burden* 569
Shall we from the *burden* flee 2032
Sorrow's *burden* share 2263
Taking away my *burden* 2315
The *burden* from my soul remove 889
The *burden* will fall 504
The *burden* will grow lighter 1252
Thou shalt lay the *burden* down 71
'Tis hard to take the *burden* up 956
Who didst for me the *burden* bear 2326
Why should I the *burden* bear 1647
With its *burden*, sad and tearful 51
Yet thy *burden* thou didst shoulder 2267

BURDENED

Are you ever *burdened* with a load 2265
So *burdened* with sin and distress 1257
When the *burdened* brings his guilt 2260

BURDENS

All the *burdens* are gone which he 2063
All the *burdens* of the years 2252
All thy *burdens*, all thy cares 63
And, 'neath the *burdens* there 2193
As the *burdens* press 401
Bearing my *burdens* all the day 1047
Bringing all my *burdens* 1471
Dost all our *burdens* share 1609
Giving for *burdens* pleasures 1047
He has all my *burdens* borne 835
His mother's daily *burdens* bore 145
How light the heavy *burdens* 16
In mighty *burdens* one are we 596
Others' *burdens* share 903
Our mutual *burdens* bear 232
Wearisome *burdens* will all be laid 167
What heavy *burdens* from our bosoms 1183
What if thy *burdens* oppress 1269
Whate'er your *burdens* be 348
Yes, the *burdens* of life can be borne 1751

BURIED

Buried, be my grave, O God 1516
Buried deep in the heart of my soul 430
Buried with my Lord to be 2032

BURN

Burn brighter through the cold 40
Burn, every breast, with Jesus' love 328
Burn up every base desire 759
O let it freely *burn* 306
Where *burn* the funeral pyres 720

BURNS

Burns the face of Love 279
The Southern Cross *burns* brightly 149

BURST

And *burst* the bars of iron 180
And *burst* their feeble chain 237
And Satan's pow'r is *burst* in twain 49
Burst into living flame 923
Burst the bars of death asunder 664
Christ hath *burst* the gates of hell 289
He *burst* the bonds of death 1704
He has *burst* his three days' prison 700
Now they *burst* upon the shore 610
O *burst* these bonds, and set it free 1519

BUSINESS

And that's my *business* for my King 799
I'm here on *business* for my King 799
'Tis all my *business* here below 1017

BUY

Buy up the moments as they go 703
Come to Jesus Christ and *buy* 358

C

CABLE

And the *cable,* though unseen 2056

CADENCES

Its *cadences* are sweet, and softly 2309

CALAMITIES

Until these sad *calamities* 166

CALL

A *call* from the ways untrod 1998
And *call* him Father from 317
And *call* it my supreme delight 1241
And Jesus *call* us to heaven's 1610
And one clear *call* for me 1802
And soon he will *call* me 830
And the *call* is gone out o'er 1987
And, when I *call,* in mercy 1434
And when thy last *call* comes 285
Answering when upon him I *call* 1047
But Christ shall *call* us home 231
But if you still this *call* refuse 2218
By thy *call* of mercy 2287
By thy *call* to heaven above 486
Call him to rescue 378
Call home thy thoughts 209
Call my heart away 225
Call to each wakening band 682
Call us, O Lord, to thine eternal 1679
Clear is the clarion *call* 2340
For God's *call* to labor 1098
How shall I *call* thee who art 2038
However we may *call* 956
I'd *call* them vanity and lies 1065
If thou shouldst *call* me to 1231
In duty's *call,* thy *call* 1492
In weakness and in want we *call* 67
Like him to answer at thy *call* 797
Lord, thy *call* we answer 928
Now as on Jesus we *call* 1981
O thou whose *call* our hearts 1496
On thee I'll *call* 85
Praise, Lord, to thee, for Matthew's *call* 196
Sent by my Lord, as you I *call* 336
Soon will he *call* you hence 147
Still he doth *call* today 2317
The *call* is thine: be thou 1526
The *call* to battle resounds 1987
The *call* to share his strife 1157
The gospel *call* obey 1911
The gracious *call* obey 1924
Then he'll *call* me some day 1561
Then he'll *call* us home 251
Then the *call* divine obeyed 1051
They *call* us to deliver 512
Thine is the *call,* and thine 1238
This is to me thy *call* 724
Thou shalt *call* on him in trouble 271
Thy Savior now doth *call* 158
Thy *call* has come to us 1329
Till Christ himself shall *call* thee 548
To *call* us sons of God 194
To thee I *call,* on thee rely 1434
We thy *call* have disobeyed 442
When they *call* he sends them 1565
When thou shalt *call* them home 1166
Whilst thou'rt calling, O *call* me 1138

CALLED

All are *called* to tasks divine 656
And *called* ambition duty 183
And *called* him to the sky 231
And *called* on him to save 1931
As they *called,* they found him near 611
Called home by the dip of the sun 1941
Called us to his glorious light 275
He *called* me long before I heard 926
He might have *called* us yonder 2061
How he *called* little children 884
I have *called* on thee, O God 135
None ever *called* on thee in vain 1369
They *called* on thee, they found 1239
Thou art *called* and chosen 1787
Thou hast *called* us to the journey 487
Thyself hast *called* me by my name 333
Who *called* us from the shades of death 197

CALLEST

If thou *callest* to the cross 449
Thou *callest* burden'd souls to thee 109
Thou *callest* me to seek thy face 1824

CALLETH

Calleth forth our gladdest strain 412
He gently *calleth* thee 348

CALLING

Calling each one by his name 1098
Calling for you and for me 1743
Earnestly, tenderly, Jesus is *calling* 1743
Forever *calling, calling* 841
My *calling* to fulfil 4
'Tis the Savior *calling* 680

CALLS

And *calls* aloud for thee 1086
And *calls* thee to his praise 133
And *calls* us sons, and takes us 1634
And, guarding, *calls* not thee 583
As that which *calls* me to thy feet 1237
Calls us to fellowship with God again 1545
Calls you one, and *calls* you all 625
God sweetly *calls* us every 196
Hark! how he *calls* 1696
He *calls* by name, and counts 1636
He *calls* me still; can I delay 558
He *calls* the hours his own 2014
He *calls* the warmer gales 2307
He *calls* to heaven and endless 196
He *calls* us to his service 510
He *calls* you, for he loves you 3
Jesus *calls* for soldiers 3
Jesus *calls* the children 928
She *calls* her sons to pray 33
Still he *calls* mankind his own 655
Still he *calls* them brethren 1581
That *calls* me from a world of care 1806
That *calls* thee from on high 154
'Tis Jesus *calls* me on 839
Which *calls* us, very sinners 350

CALM

All *calm* and courage, faith and hope 520
And *calm* our dread 43
Calm and subdue our woes 1927
Calm every doubt and fear 1774
Calm may my answer be 285
Calm my anguish into rest 717
Calm our despair 383
Calm our unwise confusion 1359
Calm the fears in me 2123
Calm thy foes' raging 1162
Calm thy sadness 568
Calm us to perfect rest 455
Calm with trust each anxious 440
Could *calm* the sea with gentle power 389
Give deeper *calm* than night can bring 32
Holy Savior, *calm* our fears 739
In the *calm* of the noon-day (tide) 1477
The *calm*, the breeze, the gale 1429
The holy *calm* and quiet 2119
This shall *calm* our trembling breath 992
Where all is *calm*, and joy, and peace 1519

CALMED

Calmed the tumult by his will 521
Till thou hast *calmed* our troubled 1480

CALMNESS

Thy *calmness* bends serene above 856

CALMS

And *calms* our lurking fear 817
And *calms* the troubled breast 794
Calms all my weary, troubled soul 1585

CAME

Amidst them *came* their Lord 1493
And *came* from the world of light 881
And he who *came* our souls 404
But, when he *came* the second time 2228
Came a vision of Holy Grail 2110
Came he to a world forlorn 2141
Came he to seek the lost 705
Came Mary to that garden 626
Came thy Son to set us free 1158
Came thy voice in summons 923
Came to show us what to be 1158
Came with the helpless and hopeless 326
For whom he once *came* down to die 173
He *came* back, his loved ones 1075
He *came* down to earth from 1572
He *came* from his blest throne 1255
He *came* from hours of rapture 2147
He *came* in power and love 2228
He *came* in tongues of living flame 1589
He *came* sweet influence to impart 1589
He *came* to raise our fallen state 128
He, the new Elias, *came* 1051
He who *came* to save us 622
Healing all who *came* in faith 521
Here *came* the wise men from Orient 1399
How *came* the everlasting Son 1482
How *came* they to the blissful seats 774
I *came* to Jesus, and I drank 842
I *came* to Jesus as I was 842
Jesus *came* forth to be born of 1575
Mine to tell me whence I *came* 738
None who to Jesus *came* 348
See how Jesus *came* to save thee 175
She *came* in fear and trembling 1713
Since Jesus *came* into my heart 2211
Son of God, who *came* to die 597
That 'twas for them he *came* to earth 549
The Lord *came* down to save me 860
Then *came* the sun, and decked 11
There *came* the holy women 626
There *came* to men the Master's word 1379
Till he *came* to the summit 2063
Until he *came* and spake the word 1493
Until it *came* and stood beside 1520
When he *came* through that which 1075
When Jesus *came* to die 22
Who *came* that he might claim 2309

CAMEST, CAM'ST

And thou, who *cam'st* on earth to die 1371
Cam'st down to earth, and took 371
Thou *cam'st* not in splendor bright 373
Thou *cam'st*, O Lord, with the living 2026
Thou *cam'st*, the Bridegroom of the bride 372

Thou *cam'st* to us in lowliness 58
Thou who *camest* from above 760
When he *camest*, the angels sang 1814
Yet thou *camest* to us 1034

CAMPAIGN

Dreary is the long *campaign* 1560

CAN

And *can* I be dismayed 921
And *can* you yet delay 1924
But in Christ I *can* be bold 2056
"*Can* a woman's tender care 672
I *can* if I but try 1030

CANDLE

An altar *candle* sheds its light 96
Like a little *candle* 968

CANOPY

Whose *canopy* space 1546

CAPTAIN

But if thy *Captain* sails 2146
Captain divine, his name enroll 2050
Christ is *Captain* of the mighty 1769
Christ is your *Captain*, fear only 378
For our *Captain* has broken the brazen 2180
Its *Captain* of salvation 284
Loyal to our *Captain* 1205
May we be true to him, our *Captain* 1205
The *Captain* is calling 941
Thee, the *Captain* of salvation 677
Thou who art our *Captain* ever 470

CAPTAINS

The *captains* and the kings depart 583

CAPTIVE

The *captive* to release 2167

CAPTIVES

All to ransom guilty *captives* 1214
Our *captives*, ransomed souls 1320
Where Satan's *captives* languish 923

CARE

And basely his kind *care* repay 558
And *care* is light, for thou hast 1478
And from the *care* and fret of life 1385
And in his *care* I saved shall be 564
And there, from *care* released 961
Away from the tender Shepherd's *care* 1983
Be thine a nobler *care* 1312
Beneath thy *care* parental 1457
Bravely over *care* I ride 2224
Care, anguish, sorrow melt 1025
Does he *care* enough to be near 401
Does Jesus *care* when my way 401
Earthly *care* and want distress 589
For all thy *care* this day 455
For his gentle *care* 928
For me that tender *care* 497
Free from *care*, from labor free 1745
From *care* he sets me free 2296
God's *care* like a cloak 1620
He shall, with all-protecting *care* 1908
He will ever *care* for you 1270
Hence all *care*, all vanity 1085
His *care* was on my frailty shown 1288
His constant, latest *care* 1579
I will *care* for thee 1808
I would be pure,
for there are those who *care* 897
In his *care* confiding, I will 1565
In the mother's tender *care* 936
Let thy *care* now be near 415
O, it is wonderful that he should *care* 880
O, let thy watchful *care* 1807
O Savior, with protecting *care* 764
Or *care*, or joy, or sorrow 6
Ready and waiting to take all your *care* 569
Safe alone beneath thy *care* 2009
Safe from corroding *care* 1675
Such *care* as was in him 1942
There is never a *care* or burden 1976
There is no anxious *care* too slight 1978
Thy bountiful *care*, what tongue 1546
Thy ceaseless *care*, thy signal grace 1595
'Tis enough that thou wilt *care* 1647
We shall soon from *care* be free 2252
We to thy guardian *care* commit 643
What with *care* and toil he 53
With watchful and unslumbering *care* 885

CARED

Nor *cared* I, but now how it grieves 1941
Nor *cared* that we are loved 2170

CARES

And all my *cares* and sorrows cast 861
And life's *cares* grow lighter 1338
By rude *cares* troubled 462
Cares for me day and night 1928
Cares of life have overtaken me 65
Earthly *cares* can never vex me 942
Free from the *cares* that would annoy 1670
From our worldly *cares* set free 1676
Graciously *cares* he for his chosen 1635
He all my *cares* and sorrows 865
He *cares* for me 790
He with earthly *cares* entwineth 566
Let *cares*, like a wild deluge 2231
Let no worldly *cares* nor pleasures 225
Let not the world's deceitful *cares* 83
No mortal *cares* shall seize 1811
Of simple *cares*, and love that grows 107
Tenderly *cares* he for his erring children 1635
To her my *cares* and toils 859
What if tomorrow's *cares* were here 564
When the *cares* of life all around 2258
When the *cares* of life oppress 562
When the vain *cares* that vex 464

CAREST

"*Carest* thou not that we perish?" 1208

CARETH

Careth for his child 1643
Careth for me 614
He *careth* fatherly 573
To know he *careth* day by day 791

CAROL

A *carol* to my King 1980, 2001
Carol we with you and them 1718
Sweetest *carol* ever sung 1867

CAROLS

Our sweetest *carols* gayly ring 918

CARPENTER

O *Carpenter* of Nazareth 1468
Thou, the *Carpenter* of Nazareth 1022

CARRIED

And he *carried* my sins with him 1982
Buried, he *carried* my sins 1575
He *carried* as your due 1391
Must I be *carried* to the skies 87

CARRIES

Jesus *carries* all thy sorrow 1577
Till it *carries* me into the city of gold 17

CARRY

All because we do not *carry* 2210
Carry the message to those in despair 1972
Carry the Sunshine where darkness 1601
He will *carry* you through 2336
It may be I must *carry* 954
Some *carry* burdens whose weight 506
We *carry* the tidings that make us 1926

CASKET

It is the golden *casket* 1544

CAST

And *cast* a wishful eye 1563
And *cast* our load 1431
And *cast* their altars to 116
And *cast* their crowns before thee 1320
And *cast* their idols all away 2245
And *cast* their lot with you 1548
And round it hath *cast* 1546
"*Cast* all your care on me" 348
"*Cast* away the dreams of darkness 668
Cast care aside, lean on 477
Cast down every idol-throne 745
Cast down our rancor, fear 1916
Cast foreboding fear away 380
Cast me not away from thee 554
Cast on him thy burden 987
Cast our crowns before thy feet 1271
Cast out our sin,and enter in 1426
Cast thy burden at his feet 276
Cast thy burden on the Lord 276
Cast thy dreams of ease away 295
Cast thy poor soul at the Savior's 402
Come, *cast* on me thy many cares 836
Come, *cast* your burdens on the Lord 777
He *cast* all my sins in the depths 623
He will not *cast* his work aside 1821
If *cast* on shores of selfish ease 826
I'll *cast* on him my ev'ry care 1806
Jesu, *cast* me not from thee 963
Nor *cast* away our crown 1920
Now *cast* out each idol 719
Now once more *cast* grief away 412
On thee I *cast* my care 1003
On thee we *cast* each earth-born care 1459
On thee we *cast* our burdening woe 1459
Or *cast* his words behind 329
Savior, I *cast* my hopes on thee 1964
Till we *cast* our crowns before thee 1190
We *cast* our crowns before thee 49
We may *cast* on him every grief 1979
When we *cast* our bright crowns 747
Why art thou then *cast* down 1483

CASTE

Ancient *caste* and creed 138

CASTETH

Keeping me safely, he *casteth* out 1678

CASTLE

Safe am I, within the *castle* 431

CASTS

And *casts* her soft and hallowed 640
Casts on the dear place where we dwell 383

CATCH

O that all might *catch* the flame 1695
To *catch* the simple unaware 189
We'll *catch* the broken threads 1282

CATTLE

The *cattle* are lowing 159

CAUGHT

Caught up through the clouds 953
Caught up to meet him in the skies 644, 982

CAUSE

And shall I fear to own his *cause* 87
And whatsoever *cause* is thine 514
Be of good cheer; your *cause* belongs 473
But those that without *cause* 2116
Cause thou all wrongs and strife 1595
Cause us to see thy goodness 587
Each worthy *cause* with a future 1840
Ere her *cause* bring fame and profit 1574
He my *cause* will e'er defend 845
He, the fatal *cause* demands 1736
Nor *cause* their hearts to fear 772
Now thy glorious *cause* maintain 2342
Of each good *cause* the shield 377
Or to defend his *cause* 914
Some great *cause*, God's new Messiah 1574
The *cause* despised loves most 620
The *cause* for which we stand 1948
The *cause* of truth maintain 1449

Though the *cause* of evil prosper 1574
Thy *cause* doth claim our souls 84
To do us harm, or *cause* us fear 117
While our *cause* we know 1769

CAUSED

And *caused* the blind to see 1556
Died he for me, who *caused* his pain 94
If I have *caused* one foot to go 901
That *caused* thy needless fear 536

CAUSES

Sometimes it *causes* me to tremble 2206

CEASE

And we shall be where tempests *cease* 5
And youthful vigor *cease* 685
But can never *cease* to love thee 2341
Cease from man, and look 367
Cease, my soul, then, cease to mourn 1667
Cease not to watch and pray 548
Cease now your heart to harden 2280
For strife will *cease* 1
I never will *cease* to love him 482
I will not *cease* from mental fight 95
May all contention *cease* 56
The echoing sounds grow fainter, and then *cease* 37
Thy sorrows make my own to *cease* 60
We *cease* to water gardens 1359
When you *cease* your toiling at the set 1997

CEASED

I have *ceased* from my wandering 2211

CEDARS

Jehovah the *cedars* of Lebanon 537
Thy *cedars* crowning Lebanon 2082

CEDE

To thee my all I *cede* 724

CELEBRATE

Celebrate his deeds and sing 1622
Celebrate th'eternal God with harp 1625

CELL

But in the spirit's secret *cell* 32

CENTER

Center and soul of every sphere 1155
Thou, the great and only *center* 1055
To find my *center,* and my rest (soul) 1055

CENTURIES

And o'er the *centuries* still we hear 2160
Behind us fade the *centuries* 46

CERTAINTY

Certainty shall make us strong 2018

CHAFES

So *chafes* weak nature's restless 1431

CHAFF

But like they are unto the *chaff* 1841

CHAIN

By one blest *chain* of loving rite 266
To break the captive's *chain* 1511
Unbroken be the golden *chain* 2164

CHAINS

And *chains* you to the shore 1900
Chains have been torn asunder 2315
In iron *chains* of fear and pride 1168
My *chains* fell off 94
See, the *chains* of death 282
There are *chains* to be severed 1987

CHALLENGE

Once more to hear thy *challenge* above 1549
The *challenge* of our tasks 1492
We *challenge* life without a fear 1951
Who *challenge* nations in thy name 2040

CHAMBER

A quiet *chamber* kept for thee 34, 513, 528

CHAMBERS

Them in thy *chambers* hide 460

CHANCE

Chance and change are busy 566
The *chance* of life that each day 1492

CHANGE

And *change* these sighs 125
And *change* to peaceful harmonies 388
And *change* with changing years 1988
Change and decay in all around I see 27
Change flash of hope to flame 1951
Change to flesh this heart of stone 461
Me through *change* and chance he guideth 53
No *change* my heart shall fear 921
O, what a *change* 1763
The wondrous *change* which grace 549
There is no *change* in thee 1087
Through the ages as they *change* 64
Weeping will *change* to a jubilant 1763

CHANGED

All will be *changed* by a glimpse 1763
Changed from glory into glory 1190

CHANGES

And the *changes* that are sure to come 443
And wise, and *changes* never 43
But no *changes* can attend 2341
Changes may come—I take, or I resign 1112
From all *changes* thou art free 1084
O, for faith that *changes* fighting 223
Who *changes* all my grief 876

CHANGEST

O thou, who *changest* not, abide 27
Thou *changest* not, thy compassion 647

CHANGETH

He *changeth* not, and thou art 477

CHANNELS

And be the *channels* of his grace 1469

CHANT

Chant his honor, ocean fair 1071
Chant thy praises merrily 208
Who *chant* their heavenly psalms 2003

CHANTED

Chanted by the angel-throng 1272

CHARGE

For who ought to my *charge* 1024
He shall *charge* his angel legions 271
O give thine angels *charge* 9

CHARIOT

Bring me my *chariot* of fire 95

CHARIOTS

His *chariots* of wrath the deep 1546

CHARITY

Let holy *charity,* mine outward 306
Nor that cold *charity* which shuns 1942
Of tender *charity,* and steadfast 1473
With thy *charity,* our zeal 1160

CHARM

A *charm* from the skies seems 1212

CHARMED

Charmed to confess the voice divine 1392

CHARMS

Ah! who against thy *charms* is proof 1555
Ten thousand thousand *charms* unfold 155

CHART

Chart and compass come 1007
It is the *chart* and compass 1544

CHARTER

Her *charter* of salvation 1845

CHARTS

In *charts* of science's skill 878

CHASE

And *chase* its gloom away 2013
And *chase* our gloom away 1132
Chase the dark night of sin 1023
Chase the darkness of our night 1681
Chase the shades of night away 745
Chase these doubtings from my heart 1644
To *chase* hence winter's breath 120

CHASED

Constantly *chased* away the night 1753

CHASTENED

Chastened by pain we learn 464

CHASTENING

His *chastening* turned me back 39

CHASTENS

He *chastens* and hastens his will 2166

CHEAT

Cheat our poor souls of good 1794

CHECK

Check every thought that turns 1807

CHECKS

That *checks* each fault, that calms 1489

CHEEKS

How he is white, his *checks* are rosy 257

CHEER

And *cheer,* and heal, and purify 1964
And *cheer* the thirsty ground 327
And *cheer* us on our way 787
Cheer it with a song 163
Cheer, my comrades, cheer 736
Cheer our desponding hearts 315
Cheer the pilot's vision 1791
Cheer this saddened heart of mine 745
Cheer thou our waiting sight 723
Cheer us this hour 311
Come, *cheer* our hearts and tell us 1292
None other can *cheer* and bless 111
Then dost thou *cheer* my solitude 1237
With a ready *cheer* 3
You may *cheer* many a pain-weary 907

CHEERS

Cheers each winding path I tread 66
It *cheers* with hope the gloomy day 2192
It sweetly *cheers* our drooping hearts 787
Who *cheers* the contrite 1634
Yet *cheers* both earth and sky 2176

CHERISH

And *cherish,* with adoring voice 1889
So I'll *cherish* the old rugged cross 1561
Thee will I *cherish* 427

CHERUBIM

Cherubim and seraphim 746, 749
Cherubim and seraphim thronged 933
Cherubim in heaven singing 1213
Cherubim, with sleepless eye 1060
O higher than the *cherubim* 2333
Where the *cherubim* adore him 611

CHIDE

Slow to *chide* and swift to bless 1618

CHIDED

Chided the billows 1831

CHIDETH

Even when he *chideth* 983

CHIEF

Me, the *chief* of sinners, spare 395

CHILD

A *Child,* and mother poor 559
Above his trusting *child,* the Lord 1093
And thou, *child,* shalt be called 215
As a little *child* relies on a care 1647
Can a *child* presume to choose 449
Child of heaven, shouldst thou repine 980
Child of sorrow and of woe 1817
For that *Child* so dear and gentle 1572
He who, a little *child,* began 9
His *child,* and forever I am 1649
Hush! hush! See how the *child* is sleeping 257
If some poor, wandering *child* of thine 1801
I'm a *child* of the king 1229
It is wrong when the *child* is sleeping 257
Jesus Christ her little *child* 1572
Let his little *child* come in 995
Let me as a *child* receive 1647
Lo! such a *child* whose early feet 267
May each *child* of thine be 2047
My *child,* just trust me 259
Not as of old a little *child* 1877
O holy *Child* of Bethlehem 1426
O'er each *child* as Guardian stand 416
The *child* of my love and prayer 2272
This *child,* now weak in infancy 248
This little *child,* of lowly birth 513
Thou has been a *child* 973
Thou wast once a little *child* 523
Though the *child* of Mary 940
Thy *child* accept and bless 1228
To us a *Child* of hope is born 1917
Waiting the penitent *child* to receive 1655
Welcoming his weary wandering *child* 1664
When the *child,* with grave fresh 2260
Wherein no blinded *child* can stray 39
Who is this *child,* so young and fair 528
Yet these a *child* may bring 1917
Yet thou, her *child,* whose head is crowned 2130

CHILD-HEARTS

The *child-hearts* growing wise 90

CHILDHOOD

And through all his wondrous *childhood* 1572
As *childhood* ripened into youth 2326
In *childhood,* manhood, age, and death 267

CHILDREN

All thy *children* sing with thee 78
And are his *children* weary 1535
And children's *children* shall proclaim 1858
And may thy *children* thee adore 1313
And to their children's *children* 1798
And to your *children* say 2312
Bidding thy waking *children,* come 1852
But *children* of the heavenly King 351
Children are we, kneeling 1717
Children forgiven, happy 385
"*Children* of God," O glorious calling 504
Children of men, falling and rising 584
Children of the day 1787
Children such as we 928
Children whose sins are all 118
Come, ye *children,* praise and pray 354
Christian *children* all must be 1572
Full in his sight his *children* 6
Frail *children* of dust, and feeble 1546
God will all his *children* keep 1096
God's *children* are gathering home 2145
God's *children* cannot live 2
God's own *children* 450
He will thy *children* bless 1636
His *children* to hear 2093
Hither our *children* bring 1715
Hosanna! sing the *children* 48
Jesus, the *children* are calling 1014
Joyful *children,* sons and daughters 238
Let all his *children* say 33
Let his little *children* say 354
Let thy *children* by thy grace 2007
"Let little *children* come to me" 9, 706
"Let the *children* come unto me 996
Little *children,* little *children* 2229
Little *children,* praise the Savior 1099
Little *children* sang his praises 1099
Little *children* thou dost love 1173
Little *children,* wake and listen 1100
Now these *children* come to thee 221
O, Holy Father, who hast led thy *children* 92
O let thy *children* share thy blessing 1524
O may our children's *children* 1595
Once more the *children* throng to bring 1604
Praying for his *children* 622
Safely the *children* are folded 1611
Sing, *children,* sing his name 33
So *children* are the seeds 11
So may his *children* gladly adore 747
So shall thy *children* with thankful 608
So we, dear Lord, would now the *children* 505
That he might his *children* show 268
The *children* all stood singing 2230
The *children* of the merciful 1935
The *children* of thy grace 33
The *children* of Zion must follow 1909
The *children* sang their praises 763
The needy's *children* save 1454
There are many little *children* 996
There with happy *children* 900
There, with thy blood-bought *children* 869
These thy *children,* Lord, defend 2264
Thither be all thy *children* led 1232
Thy *children* lift their cry 1168
Thy *children* to thy knee 100
Thy erring *children,* lost and lone 1170
Till all his waiting *children* know 626
To enfold thy *children* 1471
To show God's *children* of every land 1591
To teach thy questioning *children* 383

To thy *children* come 925
To whom the lips of *children* 44
We are *children* of thy freemen 487
We are of thee, the *children* of thy love 421
We are only little *children* 929
We are thy *children*, we turn 713
We, thy *children*, bless thy name 597
What shall we *children* bring 1947
Where *children* early lisp his name 667
While *children* shouted in their glee 2024
Ye are *children* of the light 682
Ye blessed *children*, come 147
Ye *children* of his chosen race 72

CHOICE

And the *choice* goes by forever 1574
Not mine, not mine the *choice* 2083
O happy *choice*, for earthly toil 2189

CHOIR

All heaven's triumphant *choir* shall sing 748
And straightway the celestial *choir* 298
And the *choir* of angels with song 2180
Choir of heaven! thou criest 1792
The shining *choir* of angels 33
Thus the *choir* of angels sings 543
While the *choir* with peals of glee 2141

CHOIRS

And heavenly *choirs* are ever free 374
And her *choirs* shall sing 2026
And the *choirs* that dwell on high 1936
Celestial *choirs*, from courts above 272
"Christ is born," their *choirs* are singing 52
Ever dear to *choirs* on high 78
Hark! the *choirs* of angel voices 1697
While the angel *choirs* are crying 1510

CHOOSE

By which alone we *choose* thee 1124
Choose for us, God 1794
Choose his guidance without delay 1706
Choose out the path for me 2083
Choose thou for me, my God 2083
Choose thou my good 2083
Choose ye to-day 2
O *choose* me in my golden time 1142
Or, if he *choose* to send us 984
Since what we *choose* is what we are 370
That thou must *choose* thy infant bed 528
Therefore, I *choose* my highest part 1444
To *choose* and to command 536
We fain would *choose* the better 2122

CHOOSETH

Chooseth the pure in heart 229

CHOOSING

And our blind *choosing* brings 1794
Not *choosing* what is great 1291
The Man of God's own *choosing* 12

CHORALE

The *chorale* from a city fair 1604

CHORDS

Chords that were broken will vibrate 1655
The vibrant *chords* of heaven ring 49

CHORISTERS

Choristers on high were singing 1718

CHORUS

At length the *chorus* clearer grows 138
In sacred *chorus*, with the throngs 133
In the loud-swelling *chorus* 2113
Let the mighty advent *chorus* 280
Rising to the Father, in a *chorus* strong 61
Singing in *chorus*, from ocean to ocean 607
The *chorus* of voices, the clasping 1768
With them loud *chorus* raise 55

CHOSE

Chose the meek disciple's place 141
Chose to abide on earth 263

CHOSEN

All thy *chosen* gathered in 1136
And thou shalt be our *chosen* God 1364
Chosen, called, and faithful 2287
Chosen of the Lord and precious 281
Chosen in the Christ before thee 597
Chosen not for good in me 2261
Chosen the darkness instead 1015
Coming to claim his *chosen* bride 982
Thy Zion thou hast *chosen*, Lord 114
Where thou hast *chosen*, Lord, to set 405
Within thy *chosen* place 33

CHRISTIAN

Christian, answer boldly 293
Christian, dost thou feel them 293
Christian, dost thou hear them 293
Christian, never tremble 293
Christian, up and smite them 293
Saying, "*Christian*, follow me" 970
Saying, "*Christian*, love me more" 970
Where *Christian* ne'er hath tread 149

CHRISTIANS

Christians, on this happy day 288
Christians, onward with your treasure 299

CHURCH

A faithful *church* shall love 360
And from his waiting *church* new 1652
And let thy *church* on earth 1776
And the great *church* victorious 1845
And while thy *church* is pleading 1880
Be as the *church* above 1401
Binding all the *church* in one 281
But, Lord, thy *church* is praying yet 1539
But the *church* of Jesus, constant 1586
Church of Christ, awake 2126
Come to the *church* in the wildwood 1986
His *church* as a bride's preparation 2041
Let his *church* with gladness 2010
Let thy *church* rise, strong 1567
Lord, may thy *church*, as with a mother's 505

May the *church* that waiteth for thee 486
May thy *church* the world deliver 470
Now on his *church* his grace 1883
O *church* of Christ's evangel 1328
O *church* of God, for thee our hearts 1329
O *church* of God, like bells 1329
O *church* of God, our love for thee 1329
O *church* of God, where sin and pain 1329
O *church* of God's anointing 1328
O living *church,* thine errand 1576
Once thou on thy *church* didst 1036
One *church* above, beneath 324, 1067
One *church* for all humanity 496
One *church,* united in Communion 335
So shall the *church* on earth 1401
Still o'er thy holy *church* preside 1781
That all thy *church* may holier 1453
The *church* by the side of the road 2066
The *church* from her dear Master 1544
The *church* her voice upraises 1341
The *church* is bright with flowers 952
The *church* on earth rejoices 33
The *church* our blest Redeemer 859
The *church* with psalms must 1062
The pilgrim *church* pursues 432
There, close by the *church* in the valley 1986
Thy *church,* and the work of our Christ 1372
Thy *church* doth in thy strength 2197
Thy *church* shall stand as stands 502
Till all the ransomed *church* 1961
With his holy *church* below 253, 1178, 1673

CHURCHES

Churches in thy church rejoice 1182

CIRCLE

Are you in the inner *circle* 695
Let earth's wide *circle* round 2243

CIRCLES

Their everlasting *circles* run 157

CIRCUIT

His *circuit* reaches to its ends 1862

CIRCUMSTANCE

Ev'ry *circumstance* is mingled 1957

CITIES

Thine alabaster *cities* gleam 1311

CITY

And in the dusty *city* 2195
And whether in the *city* 2195
City of God, eternal and supreme 1725
City of God, the bond are free 733
How long the holy *city* 1497
I seek a *city,* bright and fair 135
In the "*city* four-square," 938
In the glorious, golden *city* 2288
In the glorious, wonderful *city* 2212
Into the *city* I'd follow 1831
Once more beside a *city* the Son of 1604
Sion's *city* is in sight 277
The *city* of God remaineth 19
The *city* of our God 2074
The *city* of peace is eternally new 2271
The *city* of the mighty King 646
Th' eternal *city* stands 301
Though in David's *city* 940
Till it carries me into the *city* of gold 17
To the "*city* four-square," 938
To Zion's *city,* sing 7
Up to the *city,* where falleth no night 2145
Within the *city* of our God 646
Zion, *city* of our God 541

CLAD

Are *clad* in robes of white 961

CLAIM

And *claim* the crown, through Christ my own 94
And *claim* the kingdom of the earth 199
And *claim* whatsoever ye will 553
And Satan can never *claim* such 1922
By thy love's eternal *claim* 505
Can you his *claim* disown 957
Claim by thy love these souls 595
Claim the high calling angels cannot share 322
Claim the kingdom for thine own 1106
Here to thy *claim* our earthly service 1157
How he will *claim* his earthly 817
Mocking thus the Savior's *claim* 1117
Now I *claim* complete redemption 224
One *claim* unites all men in God 138
That we who *claim* a heavenly birth 1373
Thy cause doth *claim* our souls by name 84
Well thou may'st *claim* that heart of me 722
While the Lord shall *claim* his own 1994

CLAIMS

He justly *claims* a song from me 153

CLAMOR

And earthly monarchs *clamor* forth 49
Lest the *clamor* of our greed 309

CLAM'RING

And ev'ry *clam'ring* stills 2309

CLAN

Of battling tribe and *clan* 46

CLANGOR

And the city's crowded *clangor* 1042
The stormy *clangor* of wild war-music 1319

CLANK

The *clank* of chains, the curse 1467

CLAP

We *clap* our hands exulting 708

CLASH

The *clash* of arms still shakes 592

CLASHING

For not with swords' loud *clashing* 1057

CLASP

Lord, I would *clasp* thy hand 702
O *clasp* our children firmer 460

CLAY

From out the miry *clay* 887
I am the *clay* 691

CLEAN

Be *clean* and pure without 2281

CLEANSE

And *cleanse*, and keep me clean 493
And *cleanse* them of their hate 1699
Cleanse all our hearts from our 1916
Cleanse and comfort, bless and save 766
Cleanse it from guilt and 406
Cleanse it, grant it sweet 461
Cleanse me by thy washing 214
Cleanse me from its guilt 1671
Cleanse me from my sin 554
Cleanse me now from every stain 222
Cleanse my heart, dear Master 2123
Cleanse the body of this nation 1042
Cleanse this guilty heart of mine 745
Cleanse thou me and make me 754
Cleanse us, Lord, from sinful stain 744
I will *cleanse* my heart and ways 800
Lord, *cleanse* my sins, my soul 1871
Me *cleanse* from sin, and thoroughly 31
O *cleanse* and for thy use make meet 686
Thou canst *cleanse* from every sin 538
To *cleanse* the heart and banish 29
We are sinful, *cleanse* us, Lord 346

CLEANSED

And be *cleansed* in the blood 1115
And *cleansed* for life divine 1379
And hath *cleans'd* ev'ry stain 2187
Cleansed and conformed unto 469
Cleansed from unrighteousness; glory 1678
He *cleansed* it in his blood 872
Now I'm *cleansed* from sin 1501
That, *cleansed* from stain of sin 1423

CLEANSES

While he *cleanses* my heart 1982

CLEANSING

Come for a *cleansing* to Calvary's tide 2323

CLEARS

He gently *clears* thy way 536

CLEAVE

Cleave our darkness with thy 1042
Cleave the skies with shouts 356
Cleave the wood and I am there 2006
It shall not *cleave* to me 1557
To thee I *cleave*, dear land 1254

CLEFT

He hideth my soul in the *cleft* of the rock 24

CLIFFS

Cliffs where trembling seas have roared 102

CLIMB

Climb the steeps and cross 2169
Could we but *climb* where Moses 1966
If I ever *climb* to the heights 864
We may not *climb* the heavenly steeps 917

CLIMBED

They *climbed* the steep ascent 1931

CLIME

A far serener *clime* 5
Every *clime* and every tongue 1070
In every *clime*, by every tongue 1781
In every *clime* of every name 116
In yonder sun-bright *clime* 135
Should spread from *clime* to *clime* 91

CLIMES

And distant *climes* thy name 2117
In *climes* forever vernal 137
To different *climes* repair 97
To distant *climes* the tidings bear 2325

CLINGING

I am *clinging, clinging* close 1684

CLOSE

And *close* thine eyes against 1343
At the radiant *close* of labor 331
Close to thee, *close* to thee 2042
I cannot *close* my heart to thee 1465
Soon shall *close* thy earthly mission 980
Would *close* our ears from vanities 1300

CLOTHE

And *clothe* me round, the while 306
Clothe me in thy purity 1835

CLOTHED

And *clothed* in righteousness divine 94
And *clothed* in white raiment they rest 2004
And *clothed* my soul with righteousness 1194
Clothed in his righteousness 1244
Clothed in light as with a garment 2019
Clothed in our flesh with its sorrow 705
Clothed in robes of spotless beauty 669
In them thou mayest be *clothed* 503
That *clothed* in white, through 460
Thou hast *clothed* me, warmed 1013
Till, *clothed* in light forever 1377
When my spirit, *clothed*, immortal 66

CLOTHES

And *clothes* the boughs with 2097
Himself Jehovah *clothes* with strength 598

CLOUD

A *cloud* of witnesses around 154
And not a *cloud* to dim its sky 16
Cloud and rain and wild winds' 102
Ev'ry *cloud* wears a rainbow 903
For the *cloud* that bore thee 2158
From every *cloud* his blessings break 6
He who, to *cloud* and tempest 534
In *cloud* and storm be thou 490
No *cloud* in the heavens a shadow 1741
No *cloud* of sorrow passes 2172
No *cloud* will come between 1274
Now let thy *cloud* upon this house 1287
O may no earthborn *cloud* arise 1801
Out of the *cloud* and strife 732
The *cloud* of thy protecting love 274
The flying *cloud*, the frosty 1663
Through *cloud* and sunshine, O abide 27
Though the *cloud* from sight received him 77
While the long *cloud* of witnesses 530
Without a *cloud* between 197

CLOUDS

All, save the *clouds* of sin 1155
All the *clouds* have touched the sun 972
And *clouds* arise, and tempests blow 877
And, when *clouds* are drifting 1800
And wintry *clouds* o'ercast 1026
Angry *clouds* o'ershade the sky 2056
Back of the *clouds* it's waiting 1270
Back of the *clouds* the sun 1270
Beyond the sunset no *clouds* 207
But *clouds* are descending 1926
By him the *clouds* drop fatness 1734
Clouds and conflicts round us 2089
Clouds no more foretell the rain 1305
Fearing neither *clouds* nor winter's 1771
Like *clouds* they had gathered, obscuring 122
Nothing but *clouds* can see 463
The *clouds* be roll'd back as a scroll 2249

COAST

And from eastern *coast* to western 1554

COASTS

Snowbound *coasts* give back the hymn 1070

COFFERS

His *coffers* are full, he has 1229

COIN

His *coin* puts not to usury 2311
Precious is the lost *coin* 1198

COLD

Burn brighter through the *cold* 40
Cold and wet are quite forgot 1305

COLDNESS

All *coldness* from my heart 1025
Our icy *coldness* end 311

COLOR

Color awakes on earth 732

COLORS

He made their glowing *colors* 68

COLUMN

Thine to glimpse the fiery *column* 296

COMBINE

For thy praise *combine* 101

COME

Almighty God, we *come* to thee 650
And *come* before his presence with a song 1310
And *come* before his throne 1485
And *come* in thy great might 2073
And he at last will *come* for me 852
And he will *come* in and save 474
And I *come*, O Jesus 1471
And I *come* today 1471
And then, whate'er may *come* 1348
And when they were *come*, they their 1650
And, when thou at last shall *come* 976
As I *come* in deep contrition 1688
As the Savior who would have us *come* 1767
But *come* and dwell within 1463
But the Savior's "*Come*, ye blessed" 2256
Christ has *come*, the Prince of Glory 1272
Christ has *come* to save 474
Christmas-time again hast *come* 1504
Come, and reign over us 338
Come quickly from above 1350
Come then, O come, glad fruition 1742
Come thou also down to me 1588
Come thou, O Lord divine 1175
Come, with the healing 334
Dear Lord, if thou wilt *come* to stay 1528
Emmanuel shall *come* to thee, O Israel 1336
Even so, Lord, quickly *come* 359
Father, now we *come* to thee 581
For Christ has *come* again to greet 1724
For from thee *come* all things good 127
For the Lord our God shall *come* 359
"Freely *come* drink," words the soul 807
From God the Lord doth *come* 2139
Gladly we *come* our praise to sing 1591
Gladly we *come* to thy presence 584
Great Spirit *come*, and rest in me 1881
He shall *come* down like showers 661
Here we *come* thy name to praise 1676
"I *come*, I come," true youth 2340
I *come*, no more to roam 1097
I *come*, O Lord!—for thou dost call 173
I *come* to thee for rest 109
I *come* where life eternal I may drink 1569
I shall *come* and dwell with thee 1055
If He shall *come* at the dawn 2241
If we *come* to him in faith 2093
It is only till he *come* 2089
I've *come* to save you, do not fear 474
Jesus, *come* and fill me now 766
Jesus, Deliverer, *come* thou to me 476
Jesus, I *come* to thee 1602
Jesus is waiting, O *come* to him 985

Joshua now is *come* to Canaan 1697
Let Jesus *come* into your heart 905
Let them *come* out with Egypt's spoil 2240
Lo! glad I *come;* and thou blest 1001
Lord, I *come,* for thou art willing 798
Naked, *come* to thee for dress 1671
Nearer *come* and teach us 757
Nor once *come* near to him 1314
Now we are *come,* to the sun's hour 653
O *come,* and bowing down to him 1334
O *come,* and let us worship him 1335
O *come,* and reign, Lord Jesus 920
O *come,* and reign o'er every 1026
O *come,* for your exile will shortly 1338
O *come,* great Spirit, come 1776
O *come* in this sweet morning 803
O *come,* let Jesus have control 1331
O *come,* let us adore him 1330
O *come,* Lord Jesus, come and stay 2306
O *come,* O come, thou Lord of might 1336
O *come,* on Christ alone depend 1331
O *come* quickly, Hallelujah! come 1106
O *come* then to Jesus, whose arms 1338
O *come,* thou Day-spring come 1336
O *come* thou Rod of Jesse, free 1336
O *come* to my heart, Lord Jesus 2026
O *come* to the church in the vale 1986
O *come* to the Father 2102
O *come* to the Lord who forgives 1338
O *come* to the Savior 1257
O *come* to us, abide with us 1426
O *come,* together let us mourn 1333
O *come* with glad and true 1941
O *come* ye, O come ye to Bethlehem 1330
O *come* ye to the Savior's side 1333
O *come,* ye weary and opprest 1331
O Christ of God *come* near 1604
O God, we *come* in reverent praise 1356
O Jesus Christ, I *come* 1045
O Lord Jehovah, *come* thou nigh 1188
O Thou, by whom we *come* to God 1641
O whence shall *come* my aid 885
O who will *come* and go with me 1563
O who will *come* and share 1540
Savior, *come* and dwell in me 1583
So *come* I to thy mercy-gate 1456
So *come,* O King, and our whole being 828
So *come* with your sickles 1540
Tenderly saying, "*Come*" 347
That Jesus will *come* in the fullness 953
Then *come* rest and peace 256
Then *come* to him, with him abide 2
Then *come* to his feet, and lay 1338
Then will he *come* with meekness 2262
They have *come* from tribulation 677
Thou didst *come* to die a ransom 227
Thou hast *come* to join the workers 1022
Thou shalt *come* with joy untold 429
Thou who didst *come* to bring 2051
Till Christ shall *come* again 5
To us no harm shall now *come* nigh 43
Unless it *come* from thee 1259
We are *come* to sing to thee 1118
We *come* as those with toil far spent 1385
We *come* before thee now 1324
We *come* for this our parish 244
We *come* from our wanderings gladly 742
We *come* in the might of the Lord 2180
We *come* thy name to sing 1715
We *come* to feel thee more 2277
We *come* to live and reign 733
We *come* to offer on our knee 200
We *come* to thine altar 959
We *come* to worship at his feet 2306
We shall *come* rejoicing 1771
We shall *come* with joy and gladness 2256
We, too, shall *come* to the riverside 2004
When Christ shall *come* with shout 1437
When he shall *come* with trumpet 1244
When shall I *come* to thee 960
Who *come* to thee aweary 1404
Why not *come* to him now 2293
Why not *come* to Jesus now 2283
Ye all may *come* to Christ and live 336
Ye who are weary, *come* home 1743
Yea *come!* then, tried as in the fire 1373
Yes, *come* to the Savior, whose mercy 1338
Yes, my God, I *come* before thee 1588
You, too, shall *come* to know his favor 1425
You will never *come* at all 358

COMES

And it *comes* to age and youth 2064
And it *comes* with fuller swell 1993
And not empty-handed be when *comes* 1710
And when he *comes* in bright array 2294
Behold, he *comes* as first he came 309
Comes faint and far thy voice 2044
Comes night, all eyelids sealing 1552
Comes the chime of vesper bells 678
Comes the eastern sun 621
Comes the promise down from heaven 1096
Comes this message sweet to me 1096
Comes to claim his bride 282
Comes with its calm the thought 464
For her Lord *comes* down 2149
For when Satan *comes* to tempt me 942
He *comes* again: O Zion, ere thou 1551
He *comes,* from darkening scales of vice 674
He *comes* like dawning day 120
He *comes* like songs at morn 120
He *comes,* the broken heart to bind 674
He *comes,* the fainting soul to cheer 876
He *comes,* the prisoners to release 674
He *comes* "to bind the broken-hearted" 876
He *comes* to break oppression 661
He *comes* to break the barriers 816
He *comes* to give the world's starved heart 816
He *comes* to make his blessings 1039
He *comes* to reign with boundless sway 733
He *comes* to rouse the heart 120
He *comes* with thrill of life 120
He never *comes* too late 1283
It *comes* as cooling showers 1849
Now *comes* the hour of resting 1853
Onward *comes* our great Commander 736

That when next he *comes* with glory 668
Till *comes* the night, and labor 1444
Till he *comes* to earth again 282
Whatever *comes* must be his will 1640
When *comes* that final night 463
When *comes* the promised time 2073
When he *comes,* our glorious King 1203
Who *comes,* in God his Father's name 2014
Who is this that *comes* in glory 1697
Yet ever *comes* the thought of sadness 2301

COMEST

Thou *comest,* and all troubles 1363
When thou *comest* back to reign 280

COMETH

"And whosoever *cometh* I will not cast 350
He never *cometh* late 1283
My God, now through thee there *cometh* 2041
No man *cometh* unto the Father but by me 1097
Surely he *cometh* 683
Until he *cometh,* rest 1283
Whosoever *cometh* need not delay 2292

COMFORT

And *comfort* of my nights 1240
Are you sighing for *comfort* and rest 111
But God's Holy Spirit shall *comfort* 1909
Christ will *comfort* your heart 694
Comfort every sufferer 1302
Comfort it brings, and power 2034
Comfort, strengthen, and keep 2336
Comfort those in pain or sorrow 1685
Comfort those who sit in darkness 363
Comfort thy sorrows, and answer 2322
Comfort to me bring 1000
Comfort troubles; banish grief 1747
Every *comfort* to impart 2047
Finding in him sweet *comfort* 2148
For thou alone canst *comfort* 178
Heavenly peace, divinest *comfort* 66
He'll *comfort* me in trouble 1949
His *comfort* in sorrow 423
If you have *comfort* in being 908
My *comfort* by day and my song 1512
My *comfort* in the duty 2119
My *comfort* still is this 2243
Of *comfort* in the strife 2178
One tender *comfort* broods upon 138
Seeking for *comfort* from your heavenly 349
"So will I *comfort* you," declares 1093
Thine the solemn *comfort* of his staff 296
Thou feel the *comfort* of his love 201
To *comfort* and to bless 2167
With his *comfort* he'll surround thee 175
Wonderful *comfort,* abiding within 2314

COMFORTER

And let the *Comforter* and Friend 2052
Come holy *Comforter* 337
Comforter benignest who abiding 740
One with the *Comforter* in praise 195
There is a *Comforter* come from above 1971
Thou *Comforter* unfailing 43

COMFORTERS

Thou of *comforters* the best 342, 744

COMFORTS

And *comforts* flee 27
Comforts undeserved possessing 1159
It *comforts* grief and lightens care 2087
Let *comforts* that we cherish 2076
Still he *comforts* mourning hearts 521
When *comforts* are declining 1759

COMING

Coming for you and for me 1743
Coming now to thee 839
For Jesus is *coming* again 1926
Glad in his *coming* 683
He is *coming,* our loving Savior 699
I am *coming,* Lord 839
I am *coming* nearer 1267
Jesus is *coming,* is *coming* again 1926
Thou art *coming;* we are waiting 2018
Though *coming* weak and vile 839
Though he's on high, he's *coming* back 498
We are *coming* now to meet him 1726
When Jesus, my Savior, is *coming* 1926

COMMAND

And when I follow his divine *command* 2
And while at thy *command* we pray 161
At thy *command* he gave up all 2189
At whose supreme *command* 1864
Clear is our Lord's *command* 682
Command, and we obey 1943
Command thy blessing, in this hour 364
Command thy blessing, Jesus, Lord 364
Command to guide us in our way 117
For thy *command* is victory 1951
Going at our King's *command* 2284
Heeding God's *command* 1788
Onward! 'tis our Lord's *command* 2169
Ready at thy *command* 1027
Rise, and join the Lord's *command* 36
The Lord's *command* is pure 618
They heed their King's *command* 90
This is the King's *command* 799
Thy blessing on their lives *command* 9
To his *command* we bow 324, 1067
True and faithful to *command* 485
Waiting his *command,* firmly take 2159

COMMANDED

Thou hast *commanded* us to keep 212

COMMANDMENT

His new *commandment* Jesus gives 205
The holy *commandment* forbade me 1278

COMMANDMENTS

Abide with thy *commandments* 26

And mindful are always of his *commandments* 1798
Thy *commandments* in my heart 780

COMMANDS

And some, when he *commands* them, go 117
Ever thy *commands* obeying 461
For there the Lord *commands* 771
God *commands* her duty 1305
His *commands* may we revere 519
How wise and holy thy *commands* 1065

COMMEND

Commend, Lord, to thy care 514
To *commend* your soul to God 110
To him *commend* thy cause 365

COMMENDED

And *commended* his spirit to God 1115

COMMENDING

In perfect peace *commending* 98

COMMIT

I *commit* my spirit unto thee 714
Sinful, I *commit* myself to thee 714

COMMITTED

What I've *committed* to his trust 914

COMMONWEALTH

The *commonwealth* of man 2074

COMMOTION

In the tempest's wild *commotion* 1603

COMMUNE

I *commune* as friend with friend 808
Lord, we would *commune* with thee 1745

COMMUNION

And mystic, sweet *communion* 1845
And thou in each *communion* 2168
Be our *communion* shown 15
Her sweet *communion*, solemn 859
Holding *communion* with my Lord 1216
The sweet *communion* with thee here 2140

COMPANION

Companion of this sacred hour 1388

COMPANY

Company blessed of all faithful 2278
Making strong our *company* 1182
My *company* before is gone 333

COMPARE

None can with him *compare* 1896

COMPASS

And *compass* lost 488
Though many thousands *compass* me 1430

COMPASSETH

Compasseth me round with 978

COMPASSION

For me was that *compassion* 497
God's *compassion* is my story 450
He is of great *compassion* 2058
His *compassion* and his covenant 450
In *compassion* now descend 1181
In thy *compassion*, helper of 458
Jesus, thou art all *compassion* 1190
Nailing in thy vast *compassion* 1049
O depth of sweet *compassion* 497
O infinite *compassion*, still revealing 1545
Plenteous in *compassion* thou 554
The great *compassion* of his heart 912
The same *compassion* show 1590
With tender *compassion* he loves you 1925
With thy most sweet *compassion* 1476

COMPASSIONATE

The Lord is most *compassionate* 1638

COMPASSIONS

For thy *compassions* great, blot out 31
Thy *compassions*, they fail not 647

COMPEL

Compel the wanderer to come in 550

COMPLAIN

Do not *complain* that you've 907

COMPLAINT

Lord, it is my chief *complaint* 672
To my *complaint* wilt thou no answer 1239

COMPLAINTS

Against the world's *complaints* 547

COMPLETE

Complete thy purpose that we may 649

COMPLETED

And *completed* the work he begun 1974

COMRADE

As a *comrade* brave come 941
Comrade of the faithful, in the 2274
Must be a *comrade* too 1252

COMRADES

Comrades bound by memories many 366
Comrades of the strong 1205
Comrades tried in dangers many 366
For *comrades* loyal-hearted 941
For our *comrades* and our plays 273
With *comrades* missed or gone 456

COMRADESHIP

In the *comradeship* of school 930
Thy *comradeship* so graciously 2069

CONCEAL
May we never more *conceal* it 219

CONCEALED
Concealed as yet this honor lies 194

CONCEDE
Thou wilt *concede,* God is 922

CONCEIVED
Was by the Holy Ghost *conceived* 1865

CONCERN
A jealous, just *concern* 1003

CONCERT
In the *concert* bear your parts 1623

CONDEMN
Not to *condemn* the sons of men 128
Who now can *condemn* us 1599

CONDEMNATION
But "there's no *condemnation*" 1982
No *condemnation* now I dread 94
There's no *condemnation* 504

CONDEMNED
Condemned was he,
but I received a pardon 139

CONDESCEND
To us he'll *condescend* 304

CONDESCENDEST
And yet thou *condescendest* 1464

CONDESCENDS
With whom he *condescends* to dwell 192

CONDESCENSION
So great the *condescension* 2168
Wondrous the *condescension* 638

CONDITION
Yet how rich is my *condition* 980

CONDUCT
Conduct me as thine own 1245
Conduct me safe, *conduct* me far 319
Thou dost *conduct* thy people 708
Thou wilt *conduct* me safely 180

CONE
As in the *cone* the tree 1571

CONFERRED
Conferred on me thy favor 2035

CONFESS
Alike *confess* thy sweet control 2029
And *confess* thee, Lord of might 101
And there *confess* my sin 1279
Confess his judgments fair 954
Confess with joy that thou art 1474
Fairest they *confess* thee 1034
For my transgressions I *confess* 31
Him our God *confess* 1110
I *confess* thy judgment just 554
"I will *confess* unto the Lord 1314
Jesu, may all *confess* thy name 1405
Let all, who Christ *confess* 311
Let every tongue *confess* with one accord 58
Lord, I *confess* to thee sadly 1276
O Jesus, we *confess* thee 1415
That we *confess* the Father, Son 1402
To all who now *confess* the need 1094

CONFESSED
One true eternal God *confessed* 364
When I *confessed* transgression 772
Your Lord you have *confessed* 549

CONFESSING
Now as to God we're *confesssing* 1981

CONFESSION
And pouring forth *confession* meet 648
And still through his *confession* flows 785
Be this *confession* given 391
Come to Christ, *confession* make 2283
No withholding, full *confession* 1688
Our common, glad *confession* be 300

CONFESSIONS
And our *confessions* pour 1184

CONFIDE
Did we in our own strength *confide* 12

CONFIDED
They, O Lord, in thee *confided* 1553

CONFIDENCE
A strong, desiring *confidence* 1506
Our *confidence* and joy shall be 248
Their *confidence* in thee will place 1435
Their *confidence* will place 1887
While in the *confidence* of prayer 767
With *confidence* I now draw nigh 113
With *confidence* we seek thy face 1029
With holy *confidence* to sing 132
With humble *confidence* look up 1003

CONFIDENT
But *confident* in self-despair 333

CONFIDING
Happy, still in God *confiding* 2065

CONFIRM
Confirm the tidings as they roll 1932
Confirm the will of eager lives 1526
Confirm thy soul in self-control 1311
Jesus, *confirm* my heart's desire 1521

CONFIRMED

Confirmed and sealed for evermore 459

CONFIRMS

'Tis Jesus who *confirms* 839

CONFLICT

By thy *conflict* in the hour 269
By thy fearful *conflict* there 269
Fierce may be the *conflict* 2287
Forth to the mighty *conflict* 1786
How oft in the *conflict,* when pressed 1477
If in ev'ry *conflict* you would 1997
In all the *conflict* of thy sore 1177
Not long the *conflict:* soon the holy war 1204
One the *conflict,* one the peril 2066
Only in thee abiding, the *conflict* 1419
So, amid the *conflict,* whether great 2265
Soldiers for the *conflict* 3
Still on in *conflict* pressing 1320
Through life's *conflict* guard us all 2264
Thy *conflict* and thy vict'ry too 1226
To a *conflict* long 'gainst a foe 941
What though in the *conflict* for right 164
Willing the *conflict* within you 569
Your Redeemer's *conflict* see 552

CONFLICTS

And all your *conflicts* passed 1746
What *conflicts* have we passed 93

CONFOUNDED

I'll never be *confounded* 853

CONFOUNDS

Confounds their dark designs 1897

CONFUSED

Confused at the grace that so fully 880

CONFUSION

Beyond our fierce *confusion* 2076
Satan in *confusion* 544

CONFUSIONS

Confusions vast, and endless 2135

CONGREGATION

Let thy *congregation* escape 2166
The *congregation* of thy saints 619
The great *congregation* his triumph 2330

CONQUER

And *conquer* if I can 613
And more than *conquer* all 1064
He will *conquer* all 1114
I can *conquer* ev'ry foe 1848
Not alone we *conquer* 501
Shall *conquer* in the battle 19
That we may *conquer* base desire 465
We *conquer* only in that sign 479
We, through him, can *conquer* sin 268
Why *conquer* so slowly this nature 719

CONQUERED

Be *conquered* by my instant prayer 333
Our Christ has *conquered* death today 239
They have *conquered* death and Satan 677
Thou hast *conquered* in the fight 142
When he who *conquered* sin and death 2326

CONQUERING

Conquering, holding, daring, venturing 62

CONQUEROR

And *Conqueror* of time 96
Be thou our *Conqueror* over death 1424
Sudden the *Conqueror* arose 237
The *conqueror* of hate 510
Thou *conqueror* renowned 1405, 1409

CONQUERORS

More than *conquerors* ye shall 1560

CONQUESTS

But for *conquests* of the spirit 1280
Not for *conquests* of the sword 1280
To further *conquests* go 97

CONSCIENCE

Here *conscience* ends its strife 1805
How shall a stained *conscience* 719
In vain the trembling *conscience* 1065
Let not *conscience* make you linger 358
The tender *conscience* give 889
Thy presence keeps my *conscience* clean 60
With *conscience* by the world unstained 1300
With *conscience* free, we rest in God 2161

CONSCIOUS

Conscious of hidden deity 1488
Conscious of weakness, ignorance 465

CONSCIOUSNESS

So does this blessed *consciousness* 1793

CONSECRATE

And *consecrate* as his abode 1964
And *consecrate* it for our future 1287
And *consecrate* to thee my all 1137
And *consecrate* today 2005
Consecrate every part 531
Consecrate me now to thy service 808
Consecrate thee to the task that nearest 296
Consecrate them all upon the altar 259
Doth *consecrate* his gen'rous youth 620
Great God, to thee we *consecrate* 55
I'll *consecrate* my life to thee 1248
To *consecrate* myself to thee 1045
To thee I *consecrate* my days 1233
We *consecrate* ourselves to thee 1948

CONSECRATION

May this solemn *consecration* 1690
More *consecration* for work 1219

CONSENT
In sweet *consent* unite your 1936
With full *consent* thine I would be 1137
With one *consent* we meekly bow 648

CONSIDER
Consider all the worlds thy hands 1437
Consider ye her palaces 646

CONSOLATIONS
Having thy sweet *consolations* 743
While thy gracious *consolations* 1553

CONSOLES
Who *consoles* my saddest woes 131

CONSTANCY
Let him in *constancy* 707

CONSTANT
They have his *constant* care 11

CONSTELLATIONS
'Neath gleaming *constellations* 149
The shining *constellations* join 1936

CONSTRAINED
Shall be *constrained* to bow 50

CONSULT
Consult the chart and day 2146

CONSUME
Consume the ill; purge out the shame 189

CONSUMMATION
Yet, ere its *consummation* 2076

CONTEMPLATE
And *contemplate* with awe 2104
We *contemplate* thy grace, O God 2313

CONTEMPLATION
Beneath thy *contemplation* 961
In holy *contemplation* 1759

CONTEND
As thou with Satan didst *contend* 1187

CONTENT
But I am *content* with the treasures 871
Content if thou, my Guide, art ever 387
Content to ask no wages 1344
Content to bear the burden 1344
Content to bloom in native bower 576
Content to fill a little space 443
Content to let the world go by 203
Content to pray in life and love 1386
Content to suffer while we know 1459
Content, whatever lot I see 702
Content with beholding his face 795
Content with death and shame 947
I am *content* with what I have 704

CONTENTION
May all *contention* cease 56

CONTENTMENT
And Lord, *contentment* still I crave 704
Deep your *contentment* in that blest 1532
This gift of sweet *contentment* bringing 23

CONTINENT
As o'er each *continent* and island 1856

CONTINUE
That life-giving stream will *continue* 17
We would *continue* with thee day 1177

CONTINUED
And so it *continued* both day 1861

CONTRITION
Kneeling there in deep *contrition* 1607

CONTROL
Control its raging motion 2251

CONVERSATION
In *conversation* be sincere 152

CONVERSE
For *converse* which the world has never 362
Then, fresh from *converse* with your Lord 362

CONVERTS
And *converts* the soul in sin 618

CONVICT
Convict the world of sin 1401

CONVINCE
Convince us of our sin 315

CONVOCATIONS
To holy *convocations* the silver 1341

CONVULSIONS
Convulsions shake the solid world 572

COOL
Or *cool* one pain 899

COOLNESS
Grateful *coolness* in the heat 342

COPY
A *copy,* Lord, of thine 1350

CORD
When the silver *cord* is broken 2019

CORDS
By thine own *cords* of love 855
Round us golden *cords* of love 144
When my *cords* are strained 730

CORN

A golden ear of *corn* 11
And *corn* in valleys grow 2307
Than they, even then, when *corn* 526
The *corn* that makes the holy bread 1327
The young green *corn* divinely 1327
The young green *corn* forever 1327
With *corn* the vales are covered 2081

CORNER

From the utmost *corner* of the land 1357
You in your small *corner* 968

CORN-FIELDS

In our fertile *corn-fields* 2300

CORRECT

Correct me where I go astray 2039
Correct us with thy judgments 648

CORRIDORS

Through *corridors* sublime 96

CORRUPTION

And from *corruption,* thou, O Lord 2238
Corruption give to see 570

COST

Looking to Jesus, minding not the *cost* 433

COT

Who is he, in yonder *cot* 2286

COTTAGES

And *cottages* possessing thy blessedness 1457

COUCH

But thy *couch* was the sod 2026
Lighting the *couch* of sorrow 180

COULD

Who *could* it be but Jesus 1752

COUNSEL

Be thou our *counsel,* strength 2036
By his unerring *counsel* led 643
By thy same sure *counsel* led 485
Counsel and aid he doth afford 1621
God doth the *counsel* bring 2329
His *counsel* shall appear 536
O but the *counsel* of the Lord 2329
Thy *counsel* through my earthly 932
With his *counsel* guards and guides 812

COUNSELOR

By thou my *counselor,* my pattern 1035

COUNSELS

And *counsels* wiser than a friend 2087
By his *counsels* guide, uphold 556
His steady *counsels* change the face 2307
How deep thy *counsels,* how 1811
Naught are their *counsels* at life's last 1621

COUNT

All else we *count* but loss 1415
And *count* all else as loss 84
And *count* each lost and misspent 1285
And *count* each sacred wound 1959
And, if thou *count* us worthy 708
And they *count* not time by years 938
But *count* as dross its treasures 1193
Can he always *count* on me 805
Count on him 2268
Count your blessings 2265
Count your many blessings 2265
For Christ *count* everything 1994
For this we *count* the world but loss 2192
God will *count* but vain 744
I can always *count* on Jesus 805
I *count* all but loss that I 1583
I *count* it a privilege here 954
If I should *count* them, than the sand 1452
So *count* on his presence 472
To spend thyself, nor *count* the cost 151
We may not *count* her armies 886

COUNTENANCE

And did the *countenance* divine 95
But of thy *countenance* the light 526
He of my *countenance* is the health 1483

COUNTRY

A *country* far from mortal sight 779
And there's another *country* I've heard of 886
And thou, O my *country,* from many 709
Do thou our *country* save 557
For our native *country* is our 2300
Here in this *country,* so dark 913
My native *country,* thee 1225
O, sweet and blessed *country* 489
O sweet and blessed *country* 961
Who more than self their *country* 1311
Wonderful *country,* O wonderful song 2314

COUNTS

And *counts* the stars of night 1636

COURAGE

A little more *courage* to do 10
And *courage* in the evil hour 685
And put a cheerful *courage* on 157
By the *courage* where the radiance 1160
Courage almost gone 736
Courage and service bring 2340
Courage, brother! do not stumble 367
Courage, my soul, in the battle 1765
Courage our fainting souls to keep 1171
Courage then, my soul, for thou 991
High *courage* grant, the outlook 2040
Increase my *courage,* Lord 87
Let strengthened *courage* lead o'er land 1873
Longing for *courage* and strength 1600
The *courage* that we lack 185
'Twas not their *courage* nor their sword 1448
To stand with humble *courage* for truth 1549
What though your *courage* sometimes 473

When all *courage* leaves us 352
When *courage* fails us, and when faith 1545
With noble *courage* lead 2100
Your *courage* rise with danger 1786

COURSE

A clearer *course,* a nobler goal 1523
And oh, when my *course* is finished 1411
And their earthly *course* is run 1499
But spite of hell, shall have its *course* 19
If, in our daily *course,* our mind 1273
In all the *course* the seasons run 2277
Onward shall be our *course* 1156
When our *course* is o'er 988
When the Christian's *course* is run 1744
When this earthly *course* is run 480

COURSES

Their mighty *courses* run 414

COURT

Through pillared *court* and temple 763

COURTS

And into his *courts* with praise 1310
Approach with joy his *courts* 57
Come ye into his *courts,* and bring 1486
In heavenly *courts* a warrior band 1859
In thy *courts* with willing feet 1173
Pleasant are thy *courts* below 1612
Still may these *courts* proclaim 1175
That he within thy *courts,* O Lord 1631
That in the Father's *courts* my 2201
Thy *courts* with grateful fragrance 1105
Up to the *courts* of heav'n with 1895
Waiting in his *courts* today 1676
When the *courts* of heaven ring 833
Within the *courts* of God's own 910

COVENANT

And his faithful *covenant* show 629
And to remember his holy *covenant* 215
God there with us his *covenant* 263
His eternal *covenant* he will 1787
In a perpetual *covenant* 329
In this the *covenant* is sealed 2133
The *covenant* we this moment make 329
Thy gracious *covenant,* Lord, fulfil 114
To those that do his *covenant* keep 2116

COVER

Cover my defenseless head 994
Till it *cover* all the earth 684

COVERED

And *covered* by sheltering pinions 2271
Though thou art *covered* with 1015

COVERS

And *covers* me there with his hand 24
This *covers* all my wants 564

COVERT

And in thy *covert* keep me 730
And under *covert* of thy wings 1357
To *covert* of thy wings 1134

COVET

We *covet* most, of thy gifts 636

COWARD

While the *coward* stands aside 1574

CRADLE

And a lowly *cradle* found 1100
And his *cradle* was a stall 1572
Cold on his *cradle* the dewdrops 254

CRADLED

Cradled in a stall 1792
Cradled in a stall was he 2141

CRADLE-SONG

That sweetest ancient *cradle-song* 34

CRAFT

God's word, for all their *craft* and force 19
His *craft* and power are great 12
Strong mail of *craft* and power 19

CRAG

Crag where eagle's pride hath soared 102

CRAVE

Some *crave* a spirit vast as life 522
We *crave* a brother's smile 389
We *crave* the power to do thy will 185
Who *crave* thy rest and peace 1385

CRAVED

But *craved* to touch those hands 785
The all, that so for self I *craved* 2140

CREATE

And new *create* the whole 315
Create a clean heart, Lord, renew 31
Create in them the will for peace 371
Create in us the splendor that 1549
Create soul-thirst for thee 1659
He can *create,* and he destroy 184

CREATED

Ah, Lord, who hast *created* all 528
For being *created* and quickened 2194
You all *created* were when he 1898

CREATEST

For thou *createst* all things new 1380

CREATION

All *creation* find a voice 282
And *creation* swells the chorus 1712
Creation lives and moves in thee 591
Creation stirs to hail the light 770
Fairer than earth's most
wonderful *creation* 1254
For our world's *creation* 357
Him *creation* all adore 1070

Let all *creation* join in one 323
Let *creation* from her groans 280
Let *creation* praise its Lord 1558
Lord, Lord, thy fair *creation* groans 1086
On thee, at the *creation* 1341
She is his new *creation* 1845
The humbler *creation,* though feeble 1546
Thy mighty *creation* in beauty 423
'Tis the Lord of all *creation* 2288
To God, who all *creation* made 1936
Yea, without thee all *creation* 2319

CREATIONS

Before thy first *creations* 1377

CREATOR

Creator of the rolling spheres 376
Creator of the world, we pray 2114
God the Almighty, the great *Creator* 1621
He is the great *Creator* 1485
Him, their true *Creator,* all his works 2204
Let all things their *Creator* bless 41
Thee, O *Creator* of the world, we praise 1725
To our *Creator* true praises belong 1707

CREATURE

Let every *creature* rise and bring 1008
Let every *creature* sing 1625
Let every *creature* speak his praise 1893
Lord of every grateful *creature* 2308

CREATURES

All *creatures* great and small 68
And when his *creatures* sinn'd 328
Are you blacker than all other *creatures* 1338
But we are fallen *creatures* here 374
Life and death, thy *creatures* praise thee 258
Little *creatures* everywhere 1103
Till all thy *creatures* own thy 1856
Why, ye thankless *creatures,* why 1736
Ye *creatures* of the earth and sea 2328

CREED

Breathing in the thinker's *creed* 1077
Not to defend some ancient *creed* 603

CREEDS

The cries of clashing *creeds* 14
With *creeds* they go from Scotland 90

CRESCENT

The fiery *crescent* gleams 149

CRIB

At his *crib* they worship 1110
No *crib* for a bed 159

CRIED

At last he *cried* on Calvary 2242
Cried to a dying comrade 818
How he *cried,* "They know not what 696
I *cried,* "Lord Jesus," and he spoke 888
I *cried,* "O Christ, and must it be 825
I, with my mouth unto him *cried* 50
Where he *cried* in his anguish 1115

CRIES

And *cries* exulting unto thee 1281
And *cries,* "It shall be done!" 453
From little children's *cries* 1397
He *cries* to thee across the deep 156
That *cries,* "All souls are mine" 1916
The *cries* of agony, the endless groan 37
The *cries* of clashing creeds 14
The futile *cries* of superstition's 1467
Their furious *cries* I hear 873

CRIME

Shall *crime* bring *crime* forever 2267

CRIMES

To die for *crimes* which thou hast done 209
Where are *crimes* of blackest dye 1747

CRIMSON

And *crimson* the stains 122
The *crimson* of the sunset sky 1920

CROSS

A *cross* it cannot be 1292
Alone upon the *Cross* he hung 957
And every *cross* grows light 1978
And from the *Cross* on Calvary's height 1803
And I *cross* the mystic sea 805
And in the *Cross* of Jesus I found 872
And lo, a *cross* for me appeared 888
And not the less that *Cross* prevails 873
And of the *Cross* where my Savior 1831
And on the *Cross* on high 1630
And the *Cross* his body o'ercame 214
And the *Cross* the world shall sway 1994
And there's a *cross* for me 1223
And through the *Cross* attain 235
Around the *Cross* the throng 873
As Christ upon the *Cross* in death 1940
At the *Cross* of Christ I bow 717
At the *Cross* of Jesus 680
Bearing his *Cross* 2063
Bearing his *Cross* in service glad 1374
Before the *Cross* of him who died 1230
Beneath thy *Cross* abiding 1476
Beside the *Cross* once Mary stood 1313
But on the *Cross* God's love reveals 1652
By the *Cross* are sanctified 934
By the *Cross* of Jesus bringing 1160
By thy *Cross* and dying cries 269
By thy guardian *Cross* uphold me 1263
Christ, beneath thy *Cross,* we blame 442
Christ the red *Cross* ascended 283
Cross of the high 1656
Does the *cross* seem heavy you are 2265
Down before the *Cross* we cast them 711
Each other's *cross* to bear 1029
Even though it be a *cross* 1265
Faithful *Cross,* thou sign of triumph 1728
For me thou to the *Cross* didst go 123
For the *Cross* is now my glory 1573

For 'twas on that old *Cross* Jesus 1561
From the *Cross* of Jesus flowing 1084
From the *Cross* where thou hast died 1055
From the *Cross* the radiance 934
From thy *Cross* our frailty borrows 950
He who is ready for the *cross* 620
He who on the *Cross* did suffer 1697
He who on the *Cross* a ransom 663
Here, at that *Cross* where flows 1137
His conquering *Cross* no kingdom 438
His *Cross* our creed 300
Hold thou thy *Cross* before 27
Humbly at thy *Cross* I bow 800
If you cannot *cross* the ocean 679
In the *Cross* and its banner our glory 2113
In the *Cross*, in the *Cross* 986
In the old rugged *Cross*, stained 1561
It is the old *Cross* still 1846
It was a *Cross*, a *Cross* I knew 888
Lifting up the *Cross* of Jesus 2159
Long as the *cross* we bear 1714
Low before his *Cross* to lie 1813
Marching with thy *Cross* their banner 677
May thy *cross* be bravely borne 1120
My *cross* I'll carry till the crown 888
Near the *Cross*, a trembling soul 986
Near the *Cross* I'll watch and wait 986
Near the *Cross*, O Lamb of God 986
Near thy *Cross*, O Christ, abiding 1263
Nearer the *Cross* from day to day 1267
Nearer the *Cross* where Jesus died 1267
Never shall the *Cross* forsake 934
No, there's a *cross* for ev'ry one 1223
Not even the lifted *Cross* can harm 205
Now above the *Cross*, the trophy 1728
Now, the blazoned *cross* 2157
O *Cross* that liftest up my head 1465
O cruel *Cross* of Calvary 1324
O, that old rugged *Cross* so despised 1561
Of thy *Cross* the wondrous story 1686
On that dread *Cross* of Calvary 2242
On the *Cross* for sinners shown 144
On the *Cross* he sealed my pardon 894
On the *Cross* he suffered for my sake 2057
On the *Cross* his life he gave 1500
On the cruel *Cross* he suffered 894
Our *cross* to bear, and thee 2189
Our daily *cross*, whate'er it be 235
Preaching but the *Cross* of shame 275
Simply to thy *Cross* I cling 1671
So around the *Cross* we sing 1846
So, while here the *cross* I'm bearing 2257
Still passing by the *Cross* 1415
That *Cross* he bears, he is bearing 2143
That on the *Cross*, my burden 1437
The consecrated *cross* I'll bear 1223
The *Cross* despise for that high prize 708
The *Cross* has been victorious 1320
The *Cross* hath won the field 1081
The *Cross* he bore is life 1869
The *Cross* is all thy splendor 489
The *Cross* is in the field 1081
The *Cross* is not greater than his grace 1848
The *Cross!* it takes our guilt 2192
The *Cross* it would attain 724
The *Cross*, O Christ, thy wondrous 29
The *cross* of pain, the cup 1482
The *cross* of your Lord 2
The *Cross* on which the Savior 479
The *Cross* shall surely conquer 1945
The *Cross* shines forth in mystic 1921
The *Cross* that Jesus carried 1391
The luster of thy *Cross* 84
The Savior's *Cross* is winning 1853
Then shall our *cross* be exchanged 167
There at the *Cross* where he took me in 402
There is a *Cross* where the Savior died 1970
There is never a *cross* so heavy 1976
Thine was the *Cross*, with all 1086
Through Christ on the *Cross* peace 1958
Through thy *Cross* made pure 1271
Thy blessed *Cross* has sealed 60
Thy *Cross* before to guide me 1876
Thy *Cross* is lifted o'er me 1057
Thy *Cross* is my only plea 2026
Thy *Cross* may bring us 86
Thy *Cross* we lift on high 1175
Thy holy *Cross* now let him bear 1406
Till I *cross* the rolling tide 863
To bear the *Cross* and agony 1562
To make a wooden *Cross* thy throne 2024
To the *Cross* of deepest woe 1214
To the *Cross* of sin and shame 227
To the *Cross* where he suffered and bled 1115
To the old rugged *Cross* I will ever 1561
To them the *Cross*, with all its shame 1869
To this dear *Cross*, the eyes of men 29
To thy *Cross* we look and live 245
To thy dear *Cross* turn thou mine eyes 98
To thy dear *Cross* we flee 404
'Twas on the *Cross* he bled for me 1562
'Twas there on the *Cross* Jesus suffered 17
Upon a *Cross* they bound thee 1124
Upon the *Cross* embrace 1235
Upon the *Cross* he mirrored 1356
Upon the *Cross* of Jesus mine eyes 203
We shall *cross* the stormy tide 2191
When heavy the *cross* I must bear 701
When on the *Cross* he died 150
When on the *Cross* he shed his blood 1080
When the crimson *Cross* is so near by 1970
When to the *Cross* I turn mine eyes 30
While upon thy *Cross* we gaze 1028
Who, by his *Cross* have found their life 666
Who by thy *Cross* didst save us 762
Who didst once upon a *Cross* 971
Who upon a *Cross* didst die 1009
Whose *cross* has bought them, and 1532
With the *Cross* of Jesus going on 1586
With the *Cross* our only standard 1182
With the *Cross* that turns not back 1574
With the *cross* which we must bear 480
With us the *Cross* to bear 278
Yet in the *Cross* I glory 872
Yet upon the *Cross* extended 1005
You will *cross* the bridge of strife 1076

CROSSES

The *crosses* that now I bear 1411

CROST

When I have *crost* the bar 1802

CROWD

We'll *crowd* his gates with thankful songs 184
With thee amid the *crowd* 1795

CROWDS

Shall *crowds* of slain deplore 198

CROWN

A *crown* of brightest glory 1988
A *crown* of life shall be 1786
A shining *crown* of gold 11
Alone the *crown* of thorns 957
And an immortal *crown* 154
And casting down each golden *crown* 437
And claim the *crown* 94
And *crown* him Lord of all 47, 1109
And *crown* the Savior Lord of all 116
And *crown* the years with blessing 2175
And *crown* thee their eternal King 300
And *crown* thy gifts with strength 99
And *crown* thy good with 1311
And *crown* thy gospel with success 1026
And *crown* with tongues of flame 1401
And the immortal *crown* 2050
And their *crown* of life is won 1499
And with *crown* of thorn 2026
Arise, and *crown* our days 46
Be thine the *crown* of glory 1086
Bright shall the *crown* of glory be 1537
But manhood's noble *crown* to win 546
Crown all high endeavors 1372
Crown for the valiant 1538
Crown him as your Captain 143
Crown him, *crown* him, all ye little 1615
Crown him, *crown* him, Lord of all 2286
Crown him! *crown* him! prophet and 1616
Crown him the
Lord of love (peace, years) 376
Crown, O God, thine own endeavor 1042
Crown of the humble 1656
Crown the Savior, angels 117
Crown the Savior, King of kings 117
Crown thine ancient church's story 580
Crown with life beyond the grave 271
For his *crown* made meet 297
For there's a *crown* for me 1223
He will *crown* his gracious deeds 990
He will *crown* with glory 3
His bright *crown* adorning 2229
Lord, *crown* our faith's endeavor 1377
Nearer gaining the *crown* 1580
Nearer the *crown* I soon shall wear 1267
Our *crown* beyond the cross 1794
Praise we the goodness that doth *crown* 92
Soon thy *crown* and palm 2153
That *crown* he wears still in visions 2143
That he thy *crown* with saints 1406
The *crown* awaits the conquest 1057
The *crown* of heavenly life 2189
The *crown* that Jesus weareth 1391
Their sov'reign King to *crown* thee 49
Theirs, not a jeweled *crown* 594
Then *crown* him king 850
There's a *crown* for little children 1988
There's a *crown* for thee, believe it 175
Thine an everlasting *crown* 673
Thorny was the *crown* 21
Thy thorny *crown,* thy cross 1482
To weave a *crown* for May 21
When we shall *crown* him King 982
Yea, a *crown,* in very surety 119

CROWNED

And at last by thee be *crowned* 1051
And, *crowned* with victory, at thy feet 154
And thou art *crowned* at last 1705
But *crowned* with glory like the sun 1877
Crowned in mockery a king 659
Crowned with majesty divine 2019
Crowned with thine own purity 442
Each annual round, with bounties *crowned* 21
Is Christ the Lord
with endless glories *crowned* 16
Now is *crowned* with glory 622
The *crowned* and palm-decked martyrs 33

CROWNS

Casting down their golden *crowns* 749
Crowns and thrones may perish 1586
Crowns become the Victor's brow 1117
He *crowns* the year with goodness 1734
He *crowns* thy life with love 1315
Immortal *crowns* of majesty 2105
We cast our *crowns* before thee 49
Where *crowns* of gold are given 1297
With numberless blessings each
moment he *crowns* 24

CRUCIFIED

All for Jesus *crucified* 42
Caring not my Lord was *crucified* 2335
I *crucified* the Christ of God 873
I *crucified* thee 35
Is *crucified* for me and you 1460
Jesus, our Lord, is *crucified* 1333
Jesus, the *Crucified,* breathes my 1015
Jesus, the *Crucified* pleads for me 1015
Once! Oh once! I *crucified* him 1709
The *Crucified* thy praise 489
'Twas there my Lord was *crucified* 1562
Where the dear Lord was *crucified* 1963

CRUCIFY

Shall I *crucify* again 1709
Shall they *crucify* him yet 1709
Then "*crucify,*" is all their breath 1255

CRUMBLED

Crumbled have spires in every land 263

CRUSADE

We join the glorious new *crusade* 138

CRUSHED

And *crushed* the power of sin 1480
Carelessly *crushed* life's fairest 1755
Crushed by the tempter 1655
Crushed them with sorrow 506

CRY

A *cry* comes o'er the mountains 149
And at the thrilling *cry* rejoices 2149
And *cry*, "All Hail, O King!" 48
And *cry* aloud and give to God 708
And *cry* aloud, "Hosanna 2230
And *cry*, with joy unspeakable 1777
And Father, abba Father, *cry* 48
And humbly, with united *cry* 648
And whate'er our *cry* may be 589
Be this the *cry* of every heart 1714
But, O, dear Lord, we *cry* 2044
By thy supplicating *cry* 1145
Cry thy groping nations 258
Cry out, dominions, princedoms 2333
Cry out, O stately cedars 510
Hark, that *cry* that peals aloud 2059
Henceforth a *cry* can bring 1727
His *cry* of agony doth yet 816
I'll *cry* to God, who is most high 166
In us, "Abba Father," *cry* 346
It is a *cry* no wind can hurl 1533
Let all *cry* aloud, and honor 2330
My *cry* for help is turned to praise 361
My pleading *cry* to hear 887
Needy and sorrowful, to thee I *cry* 2078
Oh, blessed *cry* for you, for me 2242
O, that warning *cry* obey 363
Or *cry* in the desert for bread 1512
The *cry* from the past, and the call 709
The *cry* is "Come and help us 149
The *cry*, "to arms," is heard afar 1860
The yearning *cry* comes forth 149
They *cry* with us 1366

CRYING

No *crying* he makes 159

CRYSTAL

In *crystal* and in rose 40
The *crystal* of the snow 40

CUMBERED

Cumbered with a load of care 2210

CUP

And *cup* the portion sure 570
And doth thy *cup* with love 1232
And my *cup* overflows 1904
Bitter the *cup* of woe 1537
Even thy *cup* of grief to share 1050
Let this *cup* pass from me 1268
Salvation's *cup* my soul will take 2219
Such a *cup* of sorrow drinking 140
The blessed *cup* is only passed 204
The *cup* in token of his blood 927
The *cup* of water given for thee 2270
The *cup* that I drink not more 1848
This blest *cup* of sacrifice 245
Thy testamental *cup* I take 30
To drink thy *cup* of agony 2189

CURE

Cure thy children's warring 580
The *cure* for its desolation 1950

CURED

And he *cured* the leper's sore 2254

CURSE

From the *curse* to set me free 894
O Father, from the *curse* of war 592
The *curse* of greed 1467

CURSED

Cursed by the law, and bruised 504

CURSES

Their *curses* fill mine ear 873

CURTAINS

And my *curtains* riven 730

D

DALE

As through a fruitful watery *dale* 782

DANGER

And calmly every *danger* brave 1823
As far from *danger* as from fear 274
Danger cannot fright me 403
From all *danger* keep them 974
If in *danger*, for him call 1721
In *danger* still our guardian be 640
Never a *danger*, but there on the throne 407
That when in *danger* knows no fear 1348
There's *danger* and death in delay 2293
When in *danger*, make me brave 448
Where the *danger* least thou fearest 2153

DANGERS

A Pilot who knoweth the *dangers* at hand 20
And *dangers* and sorrows are 1909
Dangers from which to flee 2190
In midst of *dangers*, fears and death 767
Though there are *dangers* untold 529
Through him all *dangers* we'd defy 1064
Through many *dangers*, toils and snares 88
When *dangers*, like a stormy sea 648
When from its *dangers* shrinking 2251

DARE

America for God, we *dare* 1608
And *dare* the truth to tell 325
And never *dare* offend thee 2202
And shall I *dare* his Spirit grieve 558
Dare I turn away 1471
Dare to answer promptly 1997
Dare to be a Daniel 1788
Dare to have a purpose, firm 1788
Dare to make it known 1788
Dare to stand alone 1788
Dare to stand among the few 2064
Dare to stand where others 1997
Father, we *dare* by our great Brother 466
I *dare* not ask to fly from thee 1465
I *dare* not choose my lot 2083
I *dare* not climb without my Guide 915
I *dare* not take one step 737
I would be brave
for there is much to *dare* 897
None may *dare* to pierce 394
That love may *dare* thy work to share 84
Ye *dare* not trust your own 1786

DARED

For thee they *dared* the sea 1361

DARES

And *dares* to take the side 617
Who *dares* to bind to his dull sense 2177

DARK

And after that the *dark* 1802
Dark and cheerless is the morn 292
Dark was the night 476
For *dark* and light are both alike 1679, 1852
So trust in God, however *dark* the way 16

DARKNESS

A solemn *darkness* veils the skies 697
And *darkness* fast is creeping 1309
And *darkness* is as morning 2306
And the *darkness* falls on me 224
And the *darkness* rolled away 2158
And through life's *darkness*, danger 1374
And when in *darkness* lost 2104
As makes a world of *darkness* shine 7
As the *darkness* deepens o'er us 1295
Better in *darkness* just to feel 821
But though *darkness* hide, he is there 1954
By conquering *darkness* banished 1552
By *darkness*, foe of day 1552
Christ to our earthly *darkness* 2048
Clear before us through the *darkness* 2067
Darkness be over me 1265
Darkness cannot hide from thee 1681
Darkness is not dark with thee 739
Darkness must fly 476
Darkness now is drawing nigh 233
Darkness veils thine anguished 2059
Do thou on our *darkness* shine 966
Eternal *darkness*, black as death 912
For the *darkness* shall turn to dawning 2208
Groping on in *darkness* 755
In *darkness* and temptation 567
In *darkness* deep and drear 149
In *darkness* feels no doubt 1348
In the *darkness* may be lost 255

Let it in my *darkness* shine 222
Lie in deepest *darkness* shrouded 220
Many in *darkness* are waiting 1972
Many kinds of *darkness* 968
My *darkness* turns to light 1436
My *darkness* vanish in thy light 1407
Never shall *darkness* veil thee 1089
New *darkness* waits its deathless 2040
No *darkness* have we who in Jesus 1946
Now the *darkness* gathers 1302
O'er *darkness* and the grave 2008
"Once all was *darkness,* but now 1678
Onward through the *darkness* 517
That in the *darkness* and the night 1323
The *darkness* and the light of day 1438
The *darkness* deepens;
Lord, with me abide 27
The *darkness* disappears 1911
The *darkness* falls at thy behest 1856
The *darkness* shines as light 586
The *darkness* will not always 2146
Those, whom *darkness* doth enfold 2227
Though *darkness* shroud the deep 2234
Though *darkness* surround you by day 164
Though the *darkness* hide thee 749
Through *darkness* and perplexity 1150
Through terrestrial *darkness* 964
Through the *darkness* be thou 1013
Through the thick *darkness* covering 438
Through the thick *darkness* thy kingdom 607
To thee the *darkness* and the light 1452
Trusting when in *darkness* 1264
When *darkness* hides his lovely face 1244
When the *darkness* melts away 2253
When the *darkness* of the tempest 1957
Will not the deepening *darkness* 1742
With thee there is no *darkness* 1939
With thee when *darkness* 1795
Yea, *darkness* hideth not from 1452

DARLING

Sweet little *darling,* light of 1605

DARTS

And fiery *darts* be hurled 2231

DAUGHTER

Daughter of Sion, rise to meet 1842

DAUGHTERS

And Zion's *daughters* poured their lays 2239
From China's unloved *daughters* 149
Let Judah's *daughters* praise 2312
Lo, Salem's *daughters* weep around 697

DAUNT

Let nothing *daunt* your ardor 1469

DAWN

As *dawn* fades flickering candle 1359
As in the *dawn* the shadows fly 1131
Dawn on our darkness and lend us 254
Dawn upon this soul of mine 761
E'en from the *dawn* of creation 2317
If, at the *dawn* of the early morning 2241
Let mercy's *dawn* dispel 1174
On the *dawn* your hearts be setting 36
Sweet is the *dawn,* when skies 1807
The *dawn* is near at last 149
The *dawn* of heaven breaks 1923
The *dawn* of peace is nigh 1860
The *dawn* shall bring us light 327
There will *dawn* a brighter day 169
Till like the *dawn* it spread 2135
Until the *dawn* of perfect day 867
When *dawn* her judgment–days that 2226
With the *dawn* of redeeming grace 1720
With thee when *dawn* comes in 1795

DAWNING

And the *dawning* to noonday 2208
O, for that holy *dawning* 1
Since Eden's *dawning* day 92
The holy *dawning* of thy perfect day 1443
'Twas but the *dawning,* yet to grow 2177

DAWNS

Brightly at last, *dawns* a day 1737
Clearer still and clearer *dawns* 1680
Dawns the sweet consciousness 1793
Lo, *dawns* the new era 709

DAY

A *day* of holy love 1341
A *day* of resurrection 1341
A *day* of sweet refection 1341
Ah, blessed he who all *day* long 1598
All *day* I cry, by night no rest 1239
All *day* long, in every way 976
All *day* serve thee, in all that we 1289
All this *day* thy hand has 1013
All through the *day,* I humbly 1910
And all our *day* with joy 1174
And all thy *day* be bright 842
And *day* and night she prayed 2237
And *day* by *day,* we humbly ask 235
And, *day* far spent, the very 2174
And every *day* uncloses a host 1724
And grief's dark *day* come on 1119
And here all *day* they rise 1242
And I upon thee all the *day* 1719, 2116
And may each *day* be Christmas 2306
And now, on this our festal *day* 2120
And O let heaven's eternal *day* 1127
And on the *day* of judgment 1422
And some glad *day* his sun 817
And the *day* is at the spring 1993
And to life's *day* the glorious 1473
And we this *day,* both old and 1442
And, when life's brief *day* 2062
And when the *day* is done 1027
And, where the gospel *day* sheds 2051
Are you ready for that *day* 1990
Are you ready for the judgment *day* 1990
As heavenly *day,* now night 2332
As the swift *day* rolls on 1934
Asking not the *day* or hour 2018

Be not by the evil *day* 1668
Be our unchanging *day* 1087
Be thou with us every *day* 962, 1009
Before the dawning *day* 1842
Blackest *day* of nameless anguish 1709
Blest *day* of God! we hail 1810
But a blessed *day* is coming 424
But his triumph *day* is breaking 1993
But some *day*, I'll understand 824
But, when life's *day* is over 1843
By *day*, along the astonished lands 2239
By *day*, by night, at home 1795
By *day*, by night the sacred courts 774
Come the great *day*, the glorious 1061
Day and night thy beams 1084
Day breaketh at last 1599
Day by *day* his sweet voice 970
Day by *day* his tender mercy 1498
Day by *day* like us he grew 1572
Day by *day* new vict'ries 1048
"*Day* by *day*," the promise reads 380
Day by *day* with strength supplied 245
Day fills up all its blue 1087
"*Day* is passing 929
Day of all the week the best 1676
Day unto *day* declareth speech 1862
Day when first the light 1036
Each *day* he grows still sweeter 2108
Each *day* I live 182
Each *day* let thy supporting 1407
Each *day* returning to begin 1795
Each present *day* thy last esteem 152
Earth's *day* of storm is dying 137
Every *day* and hour supplying 811
Every *day* will be the brighter 144
For *day* by *day* the joy of life 882
For even our life's longest *day* 1598
For groping, *day* by *day* along 1942
For some *day* I shall understand 824
For that *day* my heart is yearning 1044
For the *day* and for the night 273
For the *day* to God is holy 1085
For the great *day* thyself prepare 152
For them by *day* the golden corn 712
For 'tis a holy *day* 540
From *day* to *day*, let good the ill 1027
From our bright baptismal *day* 760
Guarding guiding all the *day* 930
Hailing the *day* when all discords 601
Hallowing our happy *day* 1173
Happy is my *day* of rest 1085
Him *day* and night they ceaseless praise 1108
Him *day* and night united choirs 1105
His *day* is marching on 1215
"I am with you, this *day* 1316
In the *day* of health and peace 993
In the *day* of Satan's power 993
Infinite *day* excludes the night 1966
"Jesus," ev'ry *day* the same 1912
Just beyond is shining one eternal *day* 1808
Let the *day* with thee be ended 662
Let this *day* praise thee 1127
Lo, a triumph *day* is coming 2064
Lord, may we *day* by *day* 2170
Lord of the *day*, let thy Spirit 1611
Making *day* with radiance bright 233
May we, in this our trial *day* 644
More like Jesus *day* by *day* 1218
My soul for that great *day* 5
Not alone the *day* of rest 1173
Not one *day* of service give 1222
Now anew the *day* is dawning 1085
Now at the ending of the *day* 1692
Now the battle *day* is past 1303
Now the new-born *day* 2308
Now with the new-born *day* 1228
O *day* for which creation and all 1836
O *day* of joy and light 1341
O gracious *day* of motherhood 1313
O let me from this *day* 1227
O precious *day* of motherhood 1313
O wondrous *day* of motherhood 1313
On this *day* the eternal Son 1566
On this *day* the Spirit came 1566
On this most holy *day* of days 1493
One *day* a message came to me 2237
One *day* he rested, from suffering 1575
One *day* he's coming, O glorious day 1575
One *day* kind, the next day grieve 1577
One *day* the grave could conceal him 1575
One *day* the skies with his glory 1575
One *day* the stone rolled away from 1575
One *day* the trumpet will sound 1575
One *day* they led him up Calvary's 1575
One *day* they left him alone 1575
One *day* they nailed him 1575
One *day* when sin was as black 1575
Our triumphant holy *day* 971
Outlived on earth its *day* 2100
Praising my Savior all the *day* 213
Resounding all the *day* 1255
Rise glorious at the awful *day* 59
Seemed every *day* afresh to hear 196
Shining to the perfect *day* 292
So life's brief *day* is sinking 124
So we, when this new *day* is gone 1300
Some *day* from tears I shall be free 824
Some *day* he'll make it plain 824
Some *day* his glorious face 829
Some *day* I'll know, come weal or woe 2216
Some *day* it will all be over 1847
"Some *day*" may be too late 1740
Some *day* my earthly house 1749
Some *day*: till then I'll watch 1749
Some *day*, when fades the golden 1749
Some *day* you plan to enter 1740
Some *day* your heart will be asking 984
Some *day* when I his face 824
Some more convenient *day* 85
Some sweet *day*, some sweet day 2191
Soon the delightful *day* will come 1339
Sweet is the *day* of sacred rest 1811
Swift to its close ebbs out life's little *day* 27
That each departing *day* 1689
That so throughout the coming *day* 1345
That with the new unsullied *day* 1383
The *day* declared his glory 1552

The *day* in whose clear-shining 2075
The *day* is done, its hours 1478
The *day* is gone, its hours have run 1812
The *day* of dawning brotherhood 138
The *day* must dawn, and darksome 670
The *day* of grace is past and gone 644
The *day* of his appearing will come 874
The *day* of march has come 1057
The *day* of perfect righteousness 2075
The *day* of rest will dawn for thee 1531
The *day* wears on to night 2171
The full *day* yet shall be 507
The lengthening *day*, the shortening 2027
The promised *day* of God 2075
The smiling *day* has come again 1418
Then welcome, *day!* and farewell 2199
There's a bright *day* coming 1990
There's a new *day* dawning 547
There's a sad *day* coming 1990
This *day* God was my sun 1288
This *day* hath God fulfilled 298
This *day* is born a Savior 298, 599
This *day* is born in Bethlehem 796
This *day* so long foretold 1632
This *day* the noise of battle 1786
This is now the *day* of grace 759
This is the *day* God made 1484
This is the *day* of peace 2013
This is the *day* of prayer 2013
This is the *day* of rest 2013
Thou art brighter, brighter than the *day* 2019
Though long our *day* of testing 1853
Though this new *day* with joy 1131
Through all life's changeful, shadowed *day* 815
Through life's long *day* and death's 1478, 1812
Through many a *day* of darkness 2072
Through the *day* thy care has led 446
Through the *day* thy love has fed 446
Through the long *day* we labor 1927
Thus when life's toilsome *day* 861
Till the perfect *day* before us 1681
'Tis the *day* of the Lord, foretold 850
Who on that first glad Easter *day* 1293
Who the *day* for toil hast given 605
With eternal *day* before us 1738
With thee when *day* is done 1795
Wonderful *day* my beloved ones 1575
Yet hoping ever for the perfect *day* 1511

DAY-DAWN

Fairer than the *day-dawn* 1034

DAYLIGHT

As the *daylight* fades into deep 401
Lovelier than *daylight* 1793
The *daylight* dies 1940
The *daylight* is serene 961
Where the *daylight* has its birth 1070

DAYS

According as the *days* have been 1541
Ancient of eternal *days* 1214
Ancient of everlasting *days* 1864
And all our earthly *days* 1175
And *days* of darkness fall 1064
And so let all our *days* 1127
And so through all the length of *days* 1876
And through these *days* of penitence 1187
And till our pilgrim *days* shall end 2313
And when life's working *days* 2036
And you will be singing as the *days* 2265
And wintry *days* appear 2307
As in the *days* of long ago 2
But when trav'ling *days* are over 1731
Days of darkness still come o'er me 895
Days of lengthening light 2204
Days of toil and hours of ease 970
Days that never can return 2253
For, lo! the *days* are hastening on 948
For our *days* of gladness 935
From *days* of old, through swiftly 1368
He in the *days* of feeble flesh 2305
I would to everlasting *days* 1339
In early *days* their hearts secure 1590
In latter *days* shall rise 198
In youthful *days,* when joys 1363
Its *days* shall all be holy time 496
My *days* of praise shall ne'er 911
New *days,* brave, free 120
Oh! may these our lenten *days* 538
Savior, may our Sabbaths be *days* of 1744
Say not the *days* are evil 174
Singing thus through all our *days* 1628
Some of these *days* all the burdens 1750
Some of these *days,* in the deserts 1750
Some of these *days,* let us bear 1750
Sunny *days* are past and gone 2299
That all *days* of my life I may 1903
The summer *days* are come again 1938
The summer *days* are past 1952
The three sad *days* have quickly 29, 1937
The unseen *days* will changes bring 882
Three *days* he lay within that dark 498
Through *days* of joy and pain 2061
Through *days* of preparation 1057
Till, throughout our earthly *days* 357
Trusting as the *days* go by 1721
When *days* are filled with pure 1370
When for vanished *days* we yearn 2253
When our *days* of toil shall cease 755
When our *days* shall know 1991
When the *days* are weary 401
When the forty *days* were o'er 77
When the harvest *days* are past 1710
While the *days* are going by 1955
Who, from of old to our own *days* 2115
Ye *days* of cloudless beauty 1936
Yet till forty *days* were past 268

DAYSPRING

But *dayspring* is at hand 1923
Dayspring from on high, be near 292
O *Dayspring,* rise upon our night 2013
Whereby the *Dayspring* from on high 215

DAYSTAR

Daystar, in my heart appear 292
The *daystar* ever bright 284
The *Daystar* hath risen 1855

DEAD

Christ was *dead,* but lives 2191
Dead to herself, and *dead* 1940
Dead to the world am I 729
"God is not *dead,* nor doth he sleep 840
Him from the *dead* thou broughtest 459
Holy Jesus, may I be *dead* and buried 1566
Jesus, the *dead,* revives again 697
Lo! the *dead* is living 2204
O let the *dead* now hear 1024
Once I was *dead,* but now in Christ 624
Our *dead* are living unto thee 590, 1446
The *dead* and living swell 764
The *dead* in Christ are first 644
Then shall the *dead* in Christ 982
Though once *dead* he liveth 1198
We who are *dead* and not our 1670
When from the *dead* he raised 231

DEAF

The *deaf* to hear, the dumb 1140

DEALINGS

Who God's *dealings* wisely heed 1622

DEALS

Who with thee so kindly *deals* 1472

DEALT

Freely *dealt* at thy good pleasure 1516

DEAR

And thou art *dear* 477

DEATH

A *death* to be feared 2
All is chill and drear as *death* 2299
And after *death,* at thy right 1260
And after *death,* in distant worlds 2223
And by *death* to life immortal 677
And by that *death* did life procure 1921
And by thy *death* was God's salvation 58
And *death* has lost its sting 1083
And *death* is known no more 872
And *death* is now but my entry 991
And *death* itself cannot unbind 666
And *death* the gate of heaven 1230
And *death,* when *death* shall be our lot 767
And *death* with cruel rigor 1476
And for his *death* they thirst 1255
And gentle *death* at last, for heaven 434
And his *death* revived our souls 426
And in *death* by all forsaken 140
And in *death* find happiness 744
And in *death* thy comfort lend 2264
And in *death* we sweetly slumber 1991
And in his perfect *death* was 466
And in whose *death* our sins 246
And with God the Lord from *death* 2031
And what that *death* involved 975
Away with *death* and welcome 160
By *death,* I shall escape from *death* 494
By his *death* and endless life 2169
Christ's *death* proclaiming 2278
Daring *death* thy soul to rescue 474
Death, and darkness, and the tomb 2089
Death cannot affright us 1599
Death cannot harm my soul 729
Death cannot keep his prey 1200
Death ere the morrow 2
Death for aye has lost his sting 664
Death hath lost its sting 2010
Death hath many captives 2308
Death hath no more sting 1735
Death he overcame 498
Death in vain forbids him rise 289
Death is conquered, man is free 700
Death is good, for man survives it 1075
Death, like a narrow sea, divides 1966
Death, like winter, standeth nigh 2299
Death of *death,* and hell's destruction 652
Death, sin and hell no longer 49
Death, sin, and Satan are beaten 1765
Death the mighty love resigned 990
Death thy sting is gone forever 991
Death will come one day to me 963
Death with life abundant 1034
Death with thee is bright 1800
Faithful unto *death* be found 1051
For *death* is drawing near 2168
For *death* may soon be calling you 1337
For even *death* cannot divide 1370
Free and faithful, strong as *death* 672
From *death* and dark despair 762
From *death* thou hast delivered me 2219
From *death* to life eternal 1854
From *death* unto life he went 472
Gone from *death* forever 260
Grant, Lord, when I from *death* 152
He by *death* has spoiled 1697
He from *death* to life hath brought me 894
He who *death* overcame 2137
He will even unto *death* us guide 646
His *death* is my plea 73
His *death* of pain 1366
His *death* will be a triumph song 1598
Humbling thyself to *death* 58
In *death* my everlasting life 2034
In life, in *death,* O Lord, abide 27
Not at *death* I shrink 1222
Not even *death* can harm me 1949
Now no more can *death* appall 142
O Christ, o'er *death* victorious 762
O *death* that set us free 1324
O *death,* we defy thee 1599
O saving *death,* O wounds 1251
O'er *death* today rose triumphing 1493
Of *death* the cords and sorrows 857
Our *death,* our doubt and sin 1401
Passing from *death* to life at his call 504
Savior, by whose *death* we live 1748
Seeking through *death* our Savior's 391

Showing not thy *death* alone 2018
Steadfast unto *death* endure 718
Still for us his *death* he pleads 655
So whene'er in *death* I slumber 415
That *death* hath lost his venomed 132
That *death* seems but a covered 39
That unto *death* we may be thine 1482
The *death* of my Savior could only 1278
The *death* of my Savior now maketh 1278
The *death* of my Savior redemption 1278
The *death* of my Savior removeth 1278
The God-like *death* he died 816
The Lord arose! from *death* 260
There is no *death* in heaven 1977
There, where *death* will reach us 1738
There'll be no pain, no *death* 260
There's no *death*, no pain 938
Thou o'er *death* hast won 2010
Though cruel *death* my flesh assaileth 852
"Through *death* immortal life 239
Thy *death* has broken Satan's might 1948
Thy *death*, O Christ, means life 60
Thy *death* of anguish 35
Till *death* thy endless mercies seal 1521
'Tis a *death*, whose bonds ne'er riven 2319
To live apart from God is *death* 932
"To the *death* we follow thee." 110
Victorious *death* accord 311
When *death* and shame would woo 947
When *death* these mortal eyes 1020
When from *death* he passed 143
Who the *death* of *death* 131
Whom *death* a little while alone 1393
With Christ close at hand, it is not *death* 2225
Yet strong in *death* 98
Yet thy sinless *death* has brought 1005

DEATHBEDS

Deathbeds are coming 1743

DEBATE

The wise *debate* of statesmen 592

DEBT

Discharging all thy dreadful *debt* 1514
My *debt* by his death was all 1958
The *debt* of love I owe 38
'Twas here the *debt* was paid 1846
Where your *debt* was paid by the precious 696
Your *debt* he hath paid 73

DECAY

Change and *decay* in all around I see 27
Earthborn they are and soon *decay* 1621

DECAYED

The upper room has not *decayed* 2174

DECEIVE

For he will ne'er *deceive* me 2216
Jesus will not *deceive* you 2280

DECKED

Then came the sun, and *decked* it all 11

DECLARE

Declare his mighty deeds abroad 1435

DECLARED

He *declared* thy kingdom nigh 1051

DECLINE

No more from thee *decline* 1230

DECREE

By his *decree* you cannot pass 1898

DEDICATE

And unto thee we *dedicate* 1127
We *dedicate* our strength and youth 1412
We now *dedicate* this symbol 2041

DEDICATION

Now in grateful *dedication* 579

DEED

By some *deed* of faith and love 2043
Each kindly *deed* a prayer 1319
Every *deed* of love and kindness 1022
Every *deed* of love and mercy 2006
Hating every *deed* of sin 233
Just a little *deed* of kindness now 400
May be in very *deed* thine own 1441
Nothing good in *deed* and thought 342
Skilful *deed* or wisest thought 744
Some *deed* of kindness done 1689
The mighty *deed* was done 1713

DEEDS

And all its ancient *deeds* of wrong 82, 1079
And all thy *deeds* with mercy 2313
And by *deeds* of kindly love 1628
And the *deeds* of all are tried 1710
And we their *deeds* record 2072
By many *deeds* of shame 2073
Christian soul, great *deeds* await thee 296
Deeds full of grace 1831
Deeds of mercy do each day 2339
Deeds of noblest right 657
From *deeds* and words and thoughts 650
His *deeds* among the nations tell 1435
His mighty *deeds* proclaim 33
In *deeds* of love, and when our hopes 1329
In kindly *deeds* be fruitful 1402
In living *deeds* that prove 1490
Let there be *deeds*, instead of boasts 1072
Life's common *deeds* build all 1698
Little *deeds* of kindness 1101
Little *deeds* of love may shine 962
O, that my *deeds* might witness 890
O thou, whose *deeds* and dreams 390
Thy *deeds* shall fill the world 1451
To *deeds* of pure self-sacrifice 205
To men his *deeds* make known 533
What *deeds* our fathers wrought 2134
With *deeds* of love and mercy 1057

DEEM

And *deem* that our redemption's 1026

DEEP

A *deep* where all our thoughts are 155
Deep on *deep* its wonder lies 1075
Glorious is the breaking *deep* 610
The angry *deep* sank like a little 475
The sea's dark *deep*, and no man's land 1881
Within the primal *deep* our 2104

DEEPEN

Deepen our spirits for a love like 385
Deepen our spirits to receive 385

DEEPENS

Love *deepens* round the hearth 40

DEEPS

What *deeps* the sons of God 1658
When in its dread *deeps* sinking 2251

DEFEAT

Through the battle, through *defeat* 62
When *defeat* seems strangely near 223

DEFEATS

Who *defeats* my fiercest foes 131

DEFENCE

And for *defence* against my foes 1357
And our *defence* is sure 1375
For God is our *defence;* and He 1390
God shall be thy sure *defence* 271
He only is my sure *defence* 1258
How sure is their *defence* 767
Jehovah thy *defence* on thy right hand 2139
My sure *defence* in every strait 858
Thou strong *defence*, thou holy light 317
Whose providence is our *defence* 6

DEFEND

He'll *defend* thee when around thee 568
O *defend* us to the end 2009
Our Savior, King *defend* us 515
Since, Lord, thou dost *defend* us 707

DEFENDED

By his strong arm *defended* 6

DEFENDER

Be thou our *defender* in all time 959
Thou alone, our strong *Defender* 1126
Thou art my *defender* 740

DEFENDS

God *defends* him 568

DEFERENCE

Such *def'rence* to thy Father's will 1226

DEFILED

Reaching the most *defiled* 2315

DEFILETH

Where nought that *defileth* may enter 179

DEGENERATE

But no age is *degenerate* 14

DEGREE

And love beyond *degree* 38
Proclaiming thy royal *degree* 2026

DEIGN

And *deign* with them to hasten 1166, 1344
Deign to fill this temple lowly 1085
Deign to make us thy co-workers 1160
How canst thou *deign* to enter 803
O Father, *deign* these walls to bless 67
Yet *deign* our Hope to be 1415
Yet he would *deign* with us to dwell 263

DEIGNED

He who *deigned* for me to die 991

DEIGNS

Christ *deigns* to manifest today 1543
When Jesus *deigns* the guests to meet 89

DEIGN'ST

And yet thou *deign'st* to come 1367

DEIGNETH

Yet to dwell with thee he *deigneth* 394

DELAY

Come, and no longer *delay* 985
Delay thou not thy Lord to praise 770
Do not *delay*, but come 347
Do ye not *delay* 126
Don't *delay* our preparation 2297
For how can you longer *delay* 1925
Hang on a moment's *delay* 2
O, why wilt thou longer *delay* 1494

DELECTATIONS

Not for *delectations* sweet 62

DELICATES

And with their *delicates* 1433

DELIGHT

And here will I *delight* to dwell 114
Be thou alone my soul's *delight* 1407
Delight of men in the fray 613
Delight thyself in God 1708
O the pure *delight* of a single hour 808
'Tis my *delight*, thy face to see 1241

DELIGHTEST

Thou *delightest* not in sin 710

DELIGHTS

Delights our evil to remove 2071
That *delights* and stirs me so 131
This *delights* and stirs me so 131

DELIVER

Come, Almighty to *deliver* 1190
Deliver thou my soul, O Lord 857
Deliver us from every touch of ill 99
O *deliver* us, good Lord 993
Our God is able to *deliver* thee 2094

DELIVERANCE

Deliverance he affords to all 2060
To us *deliverance* bring 1448

DELIVERED

Delivered to the saints 547
"I *delivered* thee when bound 672
That we, being *delivered* out of the hand 215

DELIVERER

Be thou our great *Deliverer* 2008
Strong *Deliverer,* strong 652

DELIVERETH

And them *delivereth* 1902

DEMAND

Each *demand* of thy high 1049

DEMANDS

Demands our choicest songs 1733

DEMONS

Or *demons,* or men, or whatever 1208
Slaying the hidden *demons* 90

DENIAL

Lest by base *denial* 937

DENIED

It cannot be *denied,* for such 1094
It was *denied* thee 35
No longer Thomas then *denied* 1493

DENY

And come for the pardon God cannot *deny* 73
To those who *deny* him what patience 2055
Who shall then *deny* his name 1109
Will you, like Peter, your Lord *deny* 984

DEPART

And ne'er from us *depart* 338
But do not then *depart* 165, 1716
Depart from evil, and do good 1935
Depart from ill, do good 1321
From him I'll never, no, never *depart* 1971
O Lord, that we may thus *depart* 793
O let me not from thee *depart* 789
Prone from my Savior, to *depart* 153
That I from God may ne'er *depart* 319
That we from God may ne'er *depart* 310
Though vile I am, do not *depart* 838

DEPEND

Then on Jesus I *depend* 2227

DEPENDENT

Dependent on thy bounteous breath 267

DEPTH

And in the *depth* be praise 1630
Ere from the *depth* the mountain fastness 725
From the *depth* of nature's blindness 993
In *depth* of care I lie 1239
In the *depth* of midnight blasting 271
Mysterious *depth* and height 1457
Thy *depth* would every heart 1495
Whose *depth* unfathomed, no man 2033

DEPTHS

And from the *depths* of sin and shame 926
And out of sorrow's lowest *depths* 1387
Below all *depths* thy saving mercy 2038
Deeper than the *depths* beneath 672
Depths no man hath ever sounded 394
For him no *depths* can drown 917, 2181
From *depths* of hell thy people 1336
From the *depths* unto the skies 676
He hideth my life in the *depths* 24
That in thine ocean *depths* its flow 1465
The *depths* of earth are in his hand 1334, 1335
The *depths* of my sad heart 1208
The hidden *depths* of many a heart 1170
When in the *depths* the patient miner 2262

DERIDED

By foes *derided,* by thine own rejected 35

DERIVE

To thee, from whom we all *derive* 1439

DESCEND

Descend and bring salvation 2014
Descend, celestial Dove, with all 2203
Descend in all thy power 1132
Descend, O Holy Spirit, like a dove 421
Descend to us, we pray 1426
Descend with all thy gracious 1776
Now let the dew of heaven *descend* 83

DESCENDETH

Ever *descendeth* the love from on high 228

DESCENDING

From Lebanon *descending* like dew 781
Suddenly the Lord, *descending* 103

DESCENDS

It *descends* to the plains 1546
Lo! from the opening heaven *descends* 559

DESERT

And when in the *desert* they roam 698
Fasting alone in the *desert* 1832
I will not *desert* to his foes 776
Into the *desert* would we flee 161
Jesus, to the *desert* went 268

Journeying o'er the *desert* 256
Lo, in the *desert* rich flowers 660
Out in the *desert* dark and drear 681
Out in the *desert* he heard its cry 1983
Out in the *desert* hear their cry 681
The *desert* thy temptations 1226
Through life's *desert,* dry and dreary 718
Through the *desert* thou didst go 1058
We shall not in the *desert* stray 274

DESERTS

And *deserts* learn the joy 768
The *deserts* bloom and spring 1734

DESIGN

All I *design,* or do, or say 152, 545
Thyself the fair *design* 1468

DESIRE

A pure *desire* that all may learn 1003
And all *desire* the other's good 1930
But if we *desire* him 2300
Dear *Desire* of every nation 343
From whom the great *Desire* of earth 1865
If you *desire* a new life to begin 905
May this *desire* my spirit 1345
May we *desire* all thou dost 1474
Nothing *desire,* nothing esteem 230
Only my heart's *desire* cries out 1277
Seek the great *Desire* of nations 103
Thou dost *desire* my worthless heart 1367
What but thyself canst thou *desire* 1367

DESIRED

Long *desired* of every nation 658

DESIRES

O not for thee my weak *desires* 1142
There he *desires* to dwell 2205
Those warm *desires* that in thee 1657
To teach our faint *desires* to rise 1032
With warm *desires* to see 1167

DESIREST

Thou *desirest* truth within 552

DESOLATION

And *desolation* cease 1340

DESPAIR

And *despair* no more be mine 1772
And in *despair* I bowed my head 840
In dark *despair,* by foes 1239
No one to lighten their *despair* 918
Not wandering in unknown *despair* 590
Out of *despair* into raptures 1602
Then in *despair* I breathed a prayer 878
Waiting on Jesus lest I *despair* 2148
When dark *despair* distresses 2251
With long *despair* the spirit 1065

DESPISE

Lord, thou wilt not *despise* 31

DESPISED

He was *despised* and afflicted 1832

DESTINED

Destined, dedicate, and willing 1728
Destined for their fathers' places 1553
Destined to behold thy face 673

DESTINY

One common birth, one *destiny* 56

DESTITUTE

Destitute, despised, forsaken 980

DESTROY

Can *destroy* her peace 1069
The rising plant *destroy* 83

DESTROYED

In thee *destroyed* thrones of tyrants 1873

DESTRUCTION

Though *destruction* walk around us 1681

DETAIN

Do not *detain* me, for I am going 913

DEVIL

When the *devil* at his side 268

DEVILS

And *devils* fear and fly 1017
And though this world with *devils* filled 12
And were this world all *devils* o'er 19

DEVOTE

May I *devote* my life wholly 1645
Would he *devote* that sacred head 38

DEVOTION

And our *devotion* dies 318
And pure *devotion* rise 1530, 2052
In grateful *devotion* our tribute 2188
Jesu, may her deep *devotion* 140
May true *devotion* sweep 454
With fervent *devotion* to thee 1648
With pure *devotion* glow 2304

DEVOUR

And watching to *devour* us 19

DEW

And like the *dew* is fresh from day 422
As *dew* upon the tender herb 327
Come as the *dew;* and sweetly 1776
From Lebanon descending like *dew* 781
In the calm *dew* and freshness 1793
Like the *dew* thy peace distil 346
Now let the *dew* of heaven descend 83
O gentle *Dew,* from heaven now fall 1402
Once he was pure as morning *dew* 2272
The *dew* of heaven is like thy grace 1960
The early *dew* of morning 1830

Then, Lord, as morning *dew* come down 1373
While the *dew* is still on the roses 819

DEWDROPS

As *dewdrops* in the morning light 2138
Chilly *dewdrops* nightly shed 500

DEWS

And aye the *dews* of sorrow 1923
Thirsting, as for *dews* of even 1686
'Tis like the *dews* that fill 771
When the soft *dews* of kindly sleep 1801
While the night *dews* are distilling 446

DIADEM

A royal *diadem* adorns 1869
Bring forth the royal *diadem* 47
Hath he *diadem,* as monarch 119

DID

And all he *did,* and all he bare 1078
And *did* above all fears me raise 1902

DIED

All for Jesus—thou hast *died* 42
And *died* on earth that man 1551
And there he *died* in agony 1568
As he *died* to make men holy 1215
As thou hast *died* for me 1227
But our Jesus *died* to have us 1581
Died he for me, who caused 94
Died himself, that ye might 1736
Died upon the tree 297
For he *died* for me on the cruel 1501
For he who *died* on Calvary 1487
For Jesus who *died,* and is now 2187
For me the Savior *died* 493
For thou hast *died* for me 376
For thou has *died* that I 1248
Gladly, Lord, with thee they *died* 677
He *died* of a broken heart for you 696
He *died* on Calvary 2335
He *died* on the cross for me 864
He *died* that I might live 729
He *died* that we might be forgiven 1963
He *died* to bear the guilt of men 426
He *died* to make us good 1963
He gladly *died* for my salvation 1915
He has *died* to set me free 805
He hath *died* in my place 73
He hath *died* upon the Cross 282
He, to redeem you, *died* 906
He who *died* for their release 1303
"I *died* for you, my children 1414
In him we *died* and live again 160
Jesus Christ, who *died* for me 424
Jesus *died* for all mankind 631
Jesus *died* my soul to save 837
Jesus has *died* for me 1675
Jesus hath *died* to save from death 433
Knowing not it was for me he *died* 2335
Let it not be in vain that thou hast *died* 195
Lord, I am lost, but thou hast *died* 1018
O Christ, who *died* to give men life 1916
O thou who *died* on Calvary 1248
Of him who *died* to save 13
Of him who *died* upon the Cross 2192
Of Jesus who *died* on the Cross 130
On Calvary the Savior *died* 1469
Once I *died* for thee 680
Th' incarnate God hath *died* for me 1460
The son of God for me hath *died* 1460
The Savior *died,* but rose 1064
Thou who hast *died,* thy victory 1702
To the Christ, who *died* for me 813
'Twas there my Savior *died* for me 1562
What a Savior *died* to win 980
When Christ, the mighty Maker *died* 38
Where Jesus *died* a bitter death 626
Who *died* that we might live 5

DIES

Dies safely through thy love 1475
Dies that we may die no more 356
For he who *dies* believing 1475
He *dies* to atone for sins not 73
Nor *dies* the strain of praise 1856
Soon as *dies* the sunset glory 1295
Who *dies* is crowned victor by Jesus 1987

DIFFUSED

Thine eye *diffused* a quickening ray 94

DIM

And not a cloud to *dim* its sky 16
So *dim* our anxious will 1359

DIMNESS

The very *dimness* of my sight 564

DIN

Above the *din* of toil 604
And in that *din* of voices rude 873
For above the *din* and striving 1095
From anger's *din* would hide 1300
Through *din* of market, whirl 2160

DIRECT

All our days *direct* us in the way we go 256
Direct, control, suggest this day 152, 545
He shall *direct* thy wandering feet 365
I early will *direct* 527, 1176
Thus *direct* them, and protect 633
To thee will I *direct* my prayer 1143

DIRECTION

By thy *direction* led 391
We shall not full *direction* need 274

DISAPPOINTMENT

Where no *disappointment* hinders 2275

DISCERNING

O that we, *discerning* its most 1180

DISCIPLE

E'en the *disciple* that he loved 2091
Thine own *disciple* to the Jews 1251

DISCIPLES

And thy *disciples* quailed 1429
As the first *disciples* did in 2300
As the first *disciples* followed 695
May we thy true *disciples* be 364
The stern *disciples* drove them back 2245
Thus the first *disciples* found him 2017
Thy *disciples* ever through the ages 751
Thy *disciples* gather in devotion 751

DISCLOSE

Disclose a Savior's love 2203
Disclose to us the greatness 1474
When we *disclose* our wants 1184

DISCLOSES

The Son of God *discloses* 819

DISCORD

Discord filled my heart 2002

DISCOURAGE

What should *discourage* thee 1483

DISCOURAGED

Discouraged in the work of life 856
Do not be *discouraged,* God is over all 2265
We should never be *discouraged* 2210
When you are *discouraged,* thinking 2265

DISCOURAGEMENT

There's no *discouragement* 707, 2290

DISDAIN

Disdain not, Lord, our meaner 1105

DISEASES

Thy *diseases* all who heals 1472
Who thy *diseases* all and pains 1513

DISGRACE

That from sin's deep *disgrace* 1715

DISHEARTENED

Disheartened by its load 856

DISLOYALTY

To doubt would be *disloyalty* 617, 2321

DISMAY

Let no ill *dismay* 126

DISMAYED

Be thou not *dismayed* 1787
O be not *dismayed* 776

DISMISS

Dismiss me not, I pray 396
Dismiss thy fears 836

DISPEL

And *dispel* with purest light 966, 1012
Dispel all idle fear 1385
Dispel the darkness from our minds 315
Dispel the gloom of error's night 419

DISPELS

God *dispels* our fear 1004

DISPERSE

Disperse my sins as morning dew 152
Disperse the gloomy clouds 1336
Disperse thy warring factions 1328

DISPERSED

But Christ their legions hath *dispersed* 79
Then shall Israel, long *dispersed* 2342

DISPLAY

For such a bright *display* 7
More and more thyself *display* 292

DISPLEASE

Yet they at these themselves *displease* 1255

DISPOSE

Let him *dispose* and govern 534

DISPOSSESSED

For the *dispossessed* of earth to God 309

DISQUIETED

Be not cast down, *disquieted* 464

DISSEMBLERS

Nor with *dissemblers* gone 1043

DISSOLVE

Dissolve my heart in thankfulness 38

DISTANT

The *distant* and the dear 121

DISTILS

And sweetly *distils* in the dew 1546

DISTRESS

And in our sore *distress* 149
From all *distress* redeemed 616, 1902
In deep *distress* 922
In my *distress* he kindly will help me 865
Mine to comfort in *distress* 738
Out of *distress* to jubilant psalm 1602
Those in *distress* the Lord will not 2078
To rescue those in dire *distress* 1412
To strengthen in *distress* 2165
When in *distress* to him I called 2060
Who is he, in deep *distress* 2286

DISTRESSED

Art thou sore *distressed* 119
Distressed, they cried; the Lord 1890
Within me why *distressed* 1700

DISTRIBUTOR

Great *Distributor* of grace 743

DISTRUST

From *distrust* and envy free 1647

DISTURB

Disturb not her rest in the vale 1986
Disturb the sparrow's nest 1900
Disturb this sleep of death 1659
Disturb those peaceful years 198
Let no ill dreams *disturb* my rest 59

DITCH

They will almost *ditch* your train 1076

DIVIDE

I shall *divide* my gifts from thee 182
Who then can e'er *divide* us 1064

DIVIDED

Never must you be *divided* 62
No more *divided* be, ye families 796
Though now *divided* by the stream 324, 1067
We are not *divided* 1586

DIVINE

Blest too is he who can *divine* 617

DO

All we can *do* is nothing worth 574
And *do* what thou wouldst *do* 250
And *do* what thou wouldst have us *do* 1291
And ever *do* they will 2011
And justly *do* always 532
And may I bravely *do* my part 1152
And more than thou canst *do* 2226
And those about that *do* him fear 1902
And what I *do* in anything 1825
But *do* thine own part 904
Come early and *do* now awake 1598
Do all in Jesus' name 1228
Do but themselves confound 2290
Do his will and walk 1706
Do more than pardon; give us joy 1478
"*Do* this," he cried, "till time shall 2132
Do what he willeth 804
Do your duty, never fail 1076
Early let us *do* thy will 1683
I could not *do* without thee 820
I'll *do* thy will with a heart 955
In all I *do* be thou the way 1825
In all we *do* in work or play 468
It will *do* when I am dying 2095
Let me *do* thy will, or bear it 1690
Let us *do* with our might what 2113
Like thee to *do* our Father's will 1119
Making glad whate'er they *do* 555
May I *do* the good I know 448
O *do* the Lord adore 1486
That he, in all we *do* or say 1300
"This will I *do* with Jesus 984
What will you *do* without him 2280
Whate'er for thine we *do* 2167
Whate'er I *do*, things great 1228
When I *do* thee upon my bed 1172
"When you *do* this, *do* in remembrance 1316
While we *do* his good will 2266
Would you *do* service for Jesus 2323

DOCTOR

And one was a *doctor* 875

DOCTRINE

May she one in *doctrine* be 1033

DOEST

O God, thou *doest* all things 1378

DOETH

He *doeth* all things well 1896
Jesus *doeth* all things well 66

DOING

This is the *doing* of the Lord 1484

DOINGS

The *doings* of Jehovah are 1638
Wondrous are thy *doings* unto me 714

DOMINION

All throughout his vast *dominion* 1472
For he shall have *dominion* 661
From sin's *dominion* free 1089
His large and great *dominion* 1452
In glorious *dominion* 283
May our *dominion* ever be 1165
Satan's *dominion* will then be o'er 982
World *dominion* is his right 1069

DOMINIONS

All *dominions*, bow before him 1558
In his *dominions* everywhere 1547
May thy lasting wide *dominions* 1554

DONATIONS

Come, thou best of all *donations* 743

DONE

Have *done* with lesser things 1669
He has *done* so much for me 805
Of all thou hast *done* for the children 2194
The ill that I this day have *done* 59
The powers of death have *done* their worst 79
Till you have *done* what he tells 2337
'Tis *done!* the great transaction's *done* 1392
What God hath *done* for you 549
What thou, the Lord, hast *done* for me 23
When the battle's *done* 1769
Why, what hath my Lord *done* 1255

DOOM

"Almost persuaded," *doom* comes at last 85
And the rebel sinner's *doom* 738
For, lo, his *doom* is sure 12
For why? his *doom* is writ 19
My soul from lasting *doom* 13
On to *doom* 'tis swiftly driving 474
Who, when sin's primeval *doom* 1161

DOOMED

And *doomed* to death, must bring 1124

DOOR

And bless the *door* that opens wide 210
And let their *door* a gateway be 67
For the open *door* to manhood 1280
He is standing at the *door* 1996
Kneeling lowly at thy *door* 1145
No *door* can keep them out 1062
Now the *door* is open, enter 2292
Some humble *door* among thy many 2248
The *door* swung wide, and wider 2135
The *door* that leads to God 1194
The *door* that leads to pow'r 1194
The *door* that leads to rest 1194
The *door* to pard'ning grace 1194
Within that lowly *door* 559
Yet halting at the *door* 1740

DOORS

The *doors* of heaven are open 1418
The *doors* wide open fling 778
Thy *doors* are open wide 1404
Ye *doors* that last for aye 2327
Ye everlasting *doors* give way 1857

DOST

For thou art God that *dost* to me 1719

DOTH

And all he *doth* shall prosper 1841
For he alone *doth* all my sorrows 2096
For he alone *doth* wondrous works 735, 1454

DOUBT

All *doubt* remove 1828
Can I *doubt* his tender mercy 66
Dispelling every *doubt* 832
Do not *doubt,* do not fear 1956
Doubt, and care, and self 1195
Doubt and fear and things of earth 431
Doubt and terror are withdrawn 2154
Doubt to chase, and faith to lift 754
Ev'ry *doubt* and fear remove 2279
He is willing, *doubt* no more 358
How can I *doubt* him when he 2148
No more we *doubt* thee 2010
Nor *doubt* our inmost wants 904
Or *doubt* his royal promises 1893
Though *doubt* and temptation may 1909
Then *doubt* not thy welcome 1974
To check the rising *doubt* 1778
We will never *doubt* thee 1800
What if thou *doubt?* his steadfast word 133
Why should I *doubt* or fear 1260
Why should you *doubt* or fear 1773
Why will you longer *doubt* him 2280

DOUBTINGS

Just now, your *doubtings* give o'er 905

DOUBTS

All my *doubts* and questions stilling 1096
And all their *doubts* were solved 975
And *doubts* appall 1059
Away with gloomy *doubts* and faithless 322
Free from my *doubts* and fears 1675
Our *doubts* and fears remove 315
Soon shall our *doubts* and fears 902
The *doubts* that trouble pass away 2
Those gloomy *doubts* that rise 1966

DOVE

Come as the *dove;* and spread 1776
Come Holy Spirit, heavenly *Dove* 318
Let thy holy *Dove* descending 1685
Life-giving, holy *Dove* 2051
Like the wandering *dove* that found 1612
The *dove* of peace sings in my heart 1980, 2001

DOWER

And thine the golden *dower* 489
Of love, his richest *dower* 120

DOWNRIDDEN

Full soon were we *downridden* 19

DRAIN

And *drain* the bitter dregs of woe 2189

DRAINED

Alone he *drained* the bitter cup 957

DRANK

He *drank* all the bitter in 472

DRAW

And closer, closer *draw* me 737
And *draw* the wondering eyes 198
But Jesus, *draw* thou nearer 1408
Dear Savior, *draw* reluctant hearts 1924
Draw firmer round us thy protecting 460
Draw from my timid eyes 1238
Draw me and keep me closer to thee 226
Draw me, in thy mercy 1471
Draw me, my Savior, so precious 1266
Draw me nearer, nearer 808
Draw me with the magnet 1471
Draw near, O Lord, *draw* near 975
Draw our hearts to thee above 1173
Draw them to thee day by day 634
Draw through the child the parents 505
Draw us, Holy Jesus 999, 964
Draw us, to thy wounded side 1028
I *draw* the closer to him 2296
I would *draw* closer, Lord, each hour 893
Jesus, *draw* near with kindly aid 650
Nearer, ever nearer, Christ, we *draw* 1680
O *draw* us to thy feet 99
O to *draw* back the grim curtains 506
So that he *draw* but nigh 2076
Thou who shalt *draw* all men to thee 634
To Jesus *draw* nigh 73

To visit me *draw* near 532
Unto us *draw* nearer 563
We *draw* our blessings thence 1167
We may, we must *draw* near 1171
While I *draw* this fleeting breath 1671

DRAWEST

So that thou *drawest* me 1828

DRAWETH

He *draweth* near, he standeth by 312

DRAWN

And be closer *drawn* to thee 808
Drawn out in living characters 1226
Is upward *drawn* to God 267

DRAWS

But he *draws* me back to the upward 1954
Draws thee with love's own cord 158
Homeward *draws* our spirit 258
It *draws* me unto thee 1462
Nearer and nearer *draws* the time 574
When the Savior *draws* near 2093

DREAD

And calm our *dread* 43
Dread not his rage 473
In thee there is no *dread* of death 960
No *dread* of ill shall make my soul 737
Nor *dread* the shock 502
Teach me to live, that I may *dread* 59
That I may *dread* thy gracious power 2202
Thou shalt *dread* no hidden snare 271
We *dread* thee no more 1599
What have I to *dread* 2209
Why should I *dread* the morrow 2109

DREAM

Dream not of greatness afar 1098
Dream not of noble service 1698
Hailing the *dream* for which they 1275
I *dream* of thy rest—sweet rest 181
Life's *dream* is past, all its sins 1737
Like a passing *dream* 16
Nor *dream* of peaceful rest 548
O beautiful for patriot *dream* 1311
The cherished *dream* of watchers 1443
Then soon from my *dream* I was 1941
Though what I *dream*, and what I do 390
We *dream* of days beyond these 1951

DREAMED

I *dreamed* I saw him hanging 825

DREAMERS

"Yea," the sturdy *dreamers* answered 110

DREAMS

And holier *dreams* of brotherhood 82, 1079
Bright be the *dreams* of the troubled 1611
Fair are my *dreams* of thee 1913
Farewell, ye *dreams* of night 425
For daring *dreams*, for friends 1388
For youth's invigorating *dreams* 1779
From broken *dreams* and shattered 944
Holy *dreams* and hopes attend as 605
In *dreams* no more in selfish 1496
Let no ill *dreams* disturb my rest 59
May our *dreams* be of thy kingdom 929
O thou whose *dreams* enthrall the heart 1507
Our *dreams*, our aims, our work 1386
What holy *dreams* of brotherhood 1217
Yet in my *dreams* I'd be 1265

DRESS

The healing of his seamless *dress* 917
The healing of the seamless *dress* 2181
The healing of thy seamless *dress* 240

DREW

As *drew* the world to eventide 372
Drew me back into his way 895
He *drew* me, and I followed on 1392
He *drew* me closer to his side 1822
Yea, patiently *drew* near 887
When that which *drew* from out 1802

DRIFT

I cannot *drift* so far away 815
Of those who *drift* in storm 389
Soon will they *drift* to eternity's shore 2068
Thou wilt not let me *drift* 826

DRIFTING

Be near me when all else
is from me *drifting* 2248
From *drifting* to despair 120

DRINK

And *drink* and never die 1924
And *drink* the wine believing 726
Drink the rivers of thy grace 1691
Drink the wine, and break 2089
Here *drink* with thee the royal wine 727
I *drink* and yet am ever dry 1555
If I must *drink* this bitter cup 1324
More deep I'll *drink* above 1923
Now they *drink*, as from a river 677
We *drink* of thee, the Fountainhead 1023
We shall *drink* of life's clear river 2284
Who best can *drink* his cup 1931

DRIVE

And *drive* me to that grace again 889
And he'll *drive* the gloom from 1754
But he can *drive* the clouds away 845
Drive the dark of doubt away 1040
It cannot *drive* the world 1202
O *drive* them not away 2245
O *drive* these dark clouds from my sky 795
Shall *drive* the gloom away 1
'Twill but *drive* me to thy breast 980

DRIVES

And *drives* away all doubt 1907
And *drives* away his fear 794

O Christ, who *drives* the furrow 1327
Which *drives* us nearer home 902

DROOP

Come unto me all ye who *droop* 349

DROP

Drop thy still dews of quietness 386
I'll *drop* my burden at his feet 777
They *drop* on desert's pastures 410
To spill no *drop* of blood, but dare 2003

DROPS

Bright with the *drops* of showers 771
But *drops* of grief can ne'er repay 38
Drops of blood were on thy forehead 2276
Let some *drops* descend on me 1138
Who is this? behold him shedding *drops* 2288

DROSS

I am counting all but *dross* 800
Let no *dross* in me remain 222
The *dross* consume, the gold refine 686

DROVE

And *drove* thee from my breast 1347

DROWNS

The shout that every prayer
for mercy *drowns* 37

DRYNESS

On our *dryness* pour thy dew 342

DRY-SHOD

Through seas *dry-shod* 92

DULLNESS

The *dullness* of our blinded sight 313

DUMB

And when these failing lips grow *dumb* 30

DUNE

On *dune* and headland sinks 583

DUNGEON

I woke, the *dungeon* flamed with light 94

DUSK

If in the *dusk* of the twilight 1742

DUST

All valiant *dust* that builds 583
Crumbling *dust* of passing pleasure 1766
Dust and ashes—such are they 488
From the *dust*, when I arise 1516
Her very *dust* to them 2045
Here in the *dust* and joy 1157
Let *dust* in *dust* and silence lie 788
The *dust* that lives by lure 1727
Though *dust* and ashes in thy sight 1171
Through *dust* of conflict, and through 1532
To the *dust* their hearts were bowed 611
When from the *dust* of death 1024
When in *dust* and ashes 937

DUTIES

Alas! the *duties* left undone 2170

DUTY

And *duty* marked each step 2326
Do your whole *duty*, and preach 907
Doing each *duty* in his holy name 1104
Duty marked each step 2326
In *duty* grown divine 2273
No *duty* can seem lowly 1880
The simple *duty* that awaits 1698
Where *duty* calls, or danger 1786

DWELL

And *dwell* in peace at home 1421
And *dwell* in perfect peace 778
And *dwell* with thee forever 1325
And let me *dwell* in light 1423
And to *dwell* eternally where 2227
And we shall *dwell*, when life is past 117
And *dwell* thou with us in this place 2142
Because thou only me to *dwell* 526
Do always *dwell* together 781
Dwell in the depths of his mercy 1269
Dwell in this holy place 332
Dwell in each breast 311
Dwell in us, and may we be 439
Dwell, therefore, in our hearts 315
Dwell thou within my heart 1828
Dwell with us, sweetest Savior 2168
Dwell within my heart alone 1566
Dwell within this heart 745
God is now willing within you to *dwell* 569
Here by faith in him to *dwell* 66
I shall *dwell* in the land of delight 1751
I'll *dwell* with him for evermore 1756
Let all that *dwell* above the sky 671
Let my Savior *dwell* in me 1218
May hymn and pray'r forever *dwell* 32
Now and forever *dwell* thou in me 226
O may we *dwell* in peace and unity 56
Soon thou shalt *dwell* in its brightness 1269
That we may *dwell* in perfect unity 828
Though some may *dwell* where these 915
To *dwell* forever at his side 2
To God the powers that *dwell* on high 55
To him who doth in Zion *dwell* 1435
We shall *dwell* with God forever 2284
We'll *dwell* with the Savior forever 2212
What will it be with thee to *dwell* 1413
Where I shall *dwell* eternally 832

DWELLERS

Dwellers all in time and space 1618
No *dwellers* in darkness with 1946

DWELLING

And for his *dwelling* and his throne 229
In yonder blissful *dwelling* 1464
Of thine high eternal *dwelling* 610
Thou in me *dwelling*, and I with thee one 177

Up to the *dwelling* where cometh 2145
Where and what his *dwelling* 627

DWELLING PLACE

Another *dwelling-place* will own 1964
My *dwelling-place* shall be 1904
Safe in the same dear *dwelling-place* 2164
Thy *dwelling-place* the highest one 1908

DWELLINGS

Even where thy *dwellings* be 1483
The *dwellings* of thy love 1167

DWELLS

And *dwells* within my heart 1907
Dwells in the heart of the Father above 326
He *dwells* in God's own country 1880
He *dwells* with men, his people they 1111
He *dwells* within our soul 1872
The Lord in Zion *dwells* 1261
There *dwells* the Lord our King 1864
Though I'm not worthy he *dwells* 1971
Who *dwells* in cloudless light 2151

DWELT

And they that *dwelt* apart shall 1914
Dwelt among men, my example 1575

DYING

Be near when I am *dying* 1476

E

EAGLE

Swift as the *eagle* cuts the air 157

EAR

And as on Israel's awe-struck *ear* 2228
Besieging thine attentive *ear* 1432
In reason's *ear* they all rejoice 1932
No *ear* may hear his coming 1426
Nor deaf thine *ear* 1032
That, "Follow me," his faithful *ear* 196
The green *ear,* and the golden grain 1146
The hearing *ear,* the seeing eye 651
To entrance the prophet's *ear* 253

EARNEST

Earnest of our coming bliss 2018
The *earnest* of his rest 201
There is one thing in *earnest*
I wish you to do 130

EARS

And to my listening *ears* 2012
But the fruitful *ears* to store 359
His *ears* are open to their cry 1321
How happy are our *ears* 768
Nor my *ears* hear the dashing 236
Then the golden *ears* of harvest 76, 663
Thou didst *ears,* and hands, and voices 101
When to our *ears* there come divine 2198

EARTH

Against me *earth* and hell combine 2295
All *earth* his broad dominion 1906
All *earth* to him her homage 1858
All on *earth* shall worship thee 50
All on *earth* thy scepter claim 746
All the *earth* shall own his sway 2342
All the *earth* shall sing of his glory 747
All the round *earth* I claim 1224
And all the *earth* find peace 419
And all the *earth* lies dead 2097
And all the *earth* shall hear 631
And *earth* exchanged for heaven 1667
And *earth* has ne'er so dear a spot 1020
And *earth* in humbler strains 1704
And *earth* is filled with praise 1320
And *earth* itself looks fairer 33
And *earth* repeat the loud amen 1008
And *earth* with her ten thousand tongues 184
And having thee, on *earth* is naught 932
And in the *earth* whom I desire 2054
And lisping this, from *earth* I'll rise 1514
And nightly, to the listening *earth* 1932
And on the *earth* again shall stand 852
And, saved from *earth,* appear 241
And the *earth* rejoices 683
And, therefore, though the *earth* remove 571
And thus on *earth* possessing 2119
And to the *earth* be peace 2282
And to the *earth* it gave great light 1861
And whom but thee have I in *earth* 2038
As of old on *earth* he stood 1060
As when on *earth* they walked 2163
But the sleeping *earth* shall wake 2299
By *earth* and heaven confessed 1864
"Christ o'er all the *earth* doth reign" 1109
Christ our God to *earth* descended 1060
Dear mother *earth,* who day by day 41
Earth, air and mighty seas combine 155
Earth and heav'n reflect thy rays 1040
Earth and heaven render thee 101
Earth and sky, all living nature 104
Earth and sky the Lord adoring 770
Earth and the starry height 559
Earth around is sweeter green 1195
Earth can now but tell the story 280
Earth does but reflect his light 1305
Earth has no abiding city 1411
Earth has no resting place 425
Earth has no sorrows that heaven
cannot heal (cure) 355
Earth hath forsaken thy ways 607, 608, 612
Earth in all her glory waking 2308
Earth in darkness was 542
Earth is poised, to swerve no more 610
Earth is with its fullness
stored 253, 1178, 1673
Earth might be fair and all men 2130
Earth, receive our treasure 1737
Earth shall be fair, and all her people 2130
Earth shall keep her jubilee 2169
Earth shall then her fruits afford 582
Earth shall to freedom and truth 607

Earth, soft rushing through the air 1071
Earth stood hard as iron 933
Earth takes up the angel cry 1673
Earth takes up the angels' cry 253, 1178
Earth, tell it out abroad 1854
Earth that long in sin and pain 275
Earth thy bed 500
Earth thy footstool, heaven thy 77
Earth to heaven, and heaven 1623
Earth wearies and wastes 709
Earth with all thy nations wait 611
Earth with joy confesses 2204
Even on *earth,* as through a glass 2261
Even on *earth,* Lord, make me know 2261
Evil this *earth* 666
Far above the *earth* below 1472
For *earth* and trees and seas 2162
From *earth* I rise, and seek the joys 1864
From *earth* unto the sky 1854
Great God of all the *earth* 56
Headlong to the *earth* would fall 1788
Here on *earth,* may faithful be 76
Here on *earth* thy will be done 1760
High above *earth* his temple stands 263
Hosanna, *earth* replies 48
I all on *earth* forsake 1864
In *earth* and heaven, are one 324
In God the *earth* rejoiceth still 2250
Is there on *earth* a closer bond 855
Let *earth,* and all that live therein 2329
Let *earth,* and sea and all 2078
Let all the *earth* keep silence 1892
Let all the listening *earth* be 1781
Let *earth* and heaven adore 1625
Let *earth* and sea and sky 2243
Let *earth* arise in glad commotion 1889
Let *earth* her song begin 1854
Let *earth,* let heaven, hosannas sing 764
Let *earth* receive her King 1039
Let *earth* tell forth the story 1325
Let *earth* to heaven draw near 2013
Let me on *earth* thy likeness wear 2326
Let the *earth* hear his voice 2102
Let the whole *earth* adore his grace 209
Let the whole *earth* his power confess 209
Let the whole wide *earth* rejoice 700
Likewise let all the *earth* 1486
Long as thou on *earth* shall dwell 238
Naught on *earth* my hold on him 259
Nevermore can *earth* allure me 835
None on *earth* to aid us 1289
Nor *earth,* nor hell with all their crew 473
Nor *earth* sustain 933
"Not till *earth,* and not till heaven 119
Now let the *earth* by joyful 1083
Now o'er *earth* is shed abroad 363
O *earth,* adore thy glorious king 1883
O Lord, our Lord in all the *earth* 775, 1450
Of *earth* the calm 1810
Often when *earth* has no balm 2136
Old now is *earth,* and none may 2130
On *earth* begin, in heaven complete 1725
On *earth* his kingdom cometh 507
On *earth* is not his equal 12
On *earth* is not his fellow 19
On *earth* receiveth praise 28
On *earth* they loved his name 118
On *earth* they sought the Savior's grace 118
On the *earth* he shall reign 699
Once more the glad *earth* yields 1938
Or *earth* received her frame 1375
Over all the *earth* we see 1213
Over *earth* his footstool 1624
Ringeth the *earth* with his glory 220
Shall flood the *earth* and sky 1
Should *earth* against my soul engage 2231
Since thou on *earth* hast wept 1245
So shall the wide *earth* seem 1319
So we on *earth,* to their great song 1157
Some from *earth,* from glory some 2089
Soon to come to *earth* again 1161
That all the *earth* thy ways 1123
The *earth* from waters dark 725
The *earth* he viewed from heaven 2045
The *earth* her fruit shall yield 1123
The *earth* his power displays 1485
The *earth* is circling onward 507
The *earth* is full of song 1951
The *earth* is not too low 1062
The *earth* shall be full of his 509
The *earth* shall tremble 'neath our tread 413
The *earth* thy mercy fills 2081
The *earth* with its store of wonders 1546
The *earth* with strife is worn 247
The former *earth* and skies 1111
The Lord of *earth* is he 775
The whole *earth* let his glory fill 735, 1454
The wide *earth* saw and started 1889
Then from this *earth,* he'll carry us 498
Then was *earth* made anew 2135
Then, when on *earth* I breathe 1231
"This *earth,*" he cries, "is not my place 779
This wicked *earth* redress 1901
Thou did's't o'er the foaming *earth* 233
Thou on *earth* both Priest and victim 77
Thou on *earth* our food and stay 77
Though *earth* despise me 1808
Though the *earth* be shaking 1004
Through the *earth* and sky 621
Through the *earth* proclaim 286
Till all the *earth* shall lose its weight 148
Till *earth,* as heaven, fulfil 406
Till *earth* thy sway shall own 1169
Till on *earth* by every creature 1686
To bless the *earth* thou sendest 2081
To spread through all the *earth* 1351
Trusting him till *earth* be past 1721
Until in all the *earth* thy kingdom 1130
Weary of *earth,* myself and sin 1018
When *earth* and hell my way oppose 153
When *earth* grows dim, and round me 98
When *earth* shall feel his saving 1061
When lo, above the *earth* 551
When shall *earth* thy rule obey 1136
When the *earth* shall be filled 574
When we no more on *earth* adore thee 186
Where yearning *earth* draws nearest 2069
Which on *earth* we sing to thee 208

While on *earth* her faith is tried 1033
While on *earth* we tarry 563
While thou didst on *earth* appear 752
Who *earth* and heaven commands 365
Who on *earth* for thee labored 297
Whom *earth* and heaven adore 1299
Whom have I on *earth* beside thee 1607
Yea, to *earth* he condescends 665
Yet she on *earth* hath union 1845
Yet this *earth* he still remembers 356
Yet this fair *earth* is in the shadow 422

EASE

Ease their pain 458
From *ease* and plenty save us 1943
If I can *ease* one life the aching 899
Let not *ease* and self enthrall us 605
Not for *ease* or wordly pleasure 2042
Not for *ease* that prayer shall be 410
On flowery beds of *ease* 87
Thou art not here for *ease* or sin 546

EAST

And *east* and west the nations 1906
And from farthest *east* and west 357
Coming, in the opening *east* 2018
Far as *east* from west is distant 1472
From utmost *east* to utmost west 574
To *east* and west his kingdom 1652

EASTER

At the last to keep thine *Easter* 78
Easter came because the master 1075

EASTER-NEWS

Yet when thine *Easter-news* 785

EAT

And we shall *eat* the marriage 2132
Eat of me, thou hungry soul 1866
Eat we manna from above 142
Thou shalt *eat* of thy hands' labor 238

EBBS

Swift to its close *ebbs* out life's little day 27

ECHO

And *echo* back the mighty strain 49
And *echo* in thy prayers 1325
And *echo* to thy voice 1824
And *echo* with our shout 413
Does this *echo* ever roll 1096
Echo back ye ocean caves 2169
Echo his praises, and tell of his power 228
Echo the words from Galilee 838
Let it *echo* o'er the sea 2150
O may we *echo* on the song 2186
Sweetly *echo* the gospel call 1732

ECHOES

And through the dark, its *echoes* 670
Clearer than mountain *echoes* 638
Echoes of mercy, whispers of love 213
Heaven's *echoes* ringing 302
In living *echoes* of thy tone 1170
It *echoes* through the skies 48
Its *echoes* stirred his spirit still 196
Like *echoes* to sweet temple bells replying 29

ECHOING

Echoing their brave delight 105

ECLIPSE

Lo! our sun's *eclipse* is o'er 289

ECSTASIES

In *ecstasies* of praise 1705

ECSTASY

This new-born *ecstasy* of song 1863

EDIFIED

Who would be *edified* 1094

EFFACE

Our sins from us *efface* 26

EFFLUENCE

What are they save the *effluence* 1391

EFFORT

By *effort* true, to meet each test 1492
Less wearied with our *effort* 1359
More earnest *effort* to bring 1219
Weak is the *effort* of my heart 794

EFFORTS

And our weak *efforts* fail to win 1440

ELATE

Yet *elate* with gratitude 380

ELECT

Elect from every nation 1845

ELECTED

Elected of God, created new 1670

ELEMENTS

In three *elements* free 613
The *elements* sweetly rest 1208

EMANCIPATION

To their *emancipation* we devote 309

EMBLEM

Blest *emblems* of the crucified 89
Emblem of eternal rest 1676
Emblem of my Savior's grave 2032
The *emblem* of suffering and shame 1561

EMBRACE

And joyfully *embrace* thy cause 316
To rest in his *embrace* 1667
Which now I *embrace* 73

EMMANUEL

Emmanuel, in glory, ascends 1325

EMPIRE

And be his *empire* all mankind 192
And Satan's *empire* fell 2014
By the *empire* all thine own 269
Founding an *empire* on brotherly kindness 601
How grandly hath thine *empire* 301
Our wide extending *empire* 1165
Thine is the *empire* of vast China's 522

EMPLOY

Building for thine *employ* 1174
For thee delightfully *employ* 499

EMPLOYMENT

Such our whole *employment* be 752

EMPOWER

Empower the hands and hearts 471

EMPTINESS

Fill with thy love their *emptiness* 67

ENABLE

Enable with perpetual light 313

ENCAMPMENTS

Receive in thine *encampments* 26

ENCIRCLED

Encircled with the rainbow 869

ENCOMPASSED

Wherewith *encompassed,* great and small 1960

ENCOMPASSETH

And round *encompasseth* 616, 1902

ENCOURAGED

But now, *encouraged* by thy voice 435

END

And at the journey's *end* 975
And cannot *end* the union here 1393
And *end* the night of wrong 1669
And in thy blessing *end* 1301
And its *end* far out of sight 367
And let them to the *end* endure 1590
And the *end* of sorrow 293
And to observe it to the *end* 1826
Christ is the *end* 683
End of faith, as its Beginning 1190
For the *end* of my journey I see 1503
He to the *end* my Friend shall be 1915
Nearer the *end* of toil and care 1267
Our *end,* the glory of the Lord 274
Soon *end* in joyous day 536
That once in the *end* of the world 1974
The *end* is nearing fast 1952
The *end* of every heart's desire 377
Then the *end;* thy church completed 1136
Unto earth's remotest *end* 2018
When shall *end* the night of weeping 1136
When the *end* is reached 810
Wilt be with me to the *end* 2092

ENDEARED

And each to each *endeared* 1029

ENDEAVOR

All my *endeavor,* world 1656
Through *endeavor,* failure, danger 441
Till we by strong *endeavor* 1325
Valiant *endeavor,* and loving 2128
With him no true *endeavor* dies 2340

ENDEAVORS

Vain are all our weak *endeavors* 1603

ENDED

As this which has *ended* our sighs 1095
Ended is night for us 732
When the battle's *ended* 1997

ENDING

What is the final *ending* 90

ENDOW

Their souls with saving grace *endow* 9

ENDS

Is soon to evil *ends* betrayed 1168
It *ends* not as the day goes past 408
The *ends* of earth are in thy hand 1881
The *ends* of the universe praise 1617
When *ends* life's transient dream 1227

ENDUE

Endue the creatures with 1441
Endue their home with growing 505
Pray *endue* thy word with power 219

ENDURANCE

Long *endurance* wins the crown 71

ENDURE

And doth *endure* forever 618
And shall from age to age *endure* 57
Endure no self-denial 923
His rage we can *endure* 12
His steadfast word, unchanging shall *endure* 133
What did thine only son *endure* 444

ENDURED

He *endured* it for us, and no word 2063
Who *endured* the cross and grave 971
Who for us *endured* the strife 287

ENDURES

And firm *endures,* while endless years 157
As long as life *endures* 88
God *endures* unchanging on 1618

ENDURETH

God's great goodness aye *endureth* 53

ENEMIES

All thy *enemies* shall perish 951
Enemies may strive to injure 2257
Mighty are your *enemies* 1747
Put thine *enemies* to flight 470
Your *enemies* almost prevail 164

ENEMY

And all for one who was thine *enemy* 1235
Does the *enemy* attack 2268
E'en though I was his *enemy* 2140
The *enemy* restrained 775

ENERGIES

A Holy Spirit's *energies* 420

ENERGY

By the *energy* of prayer 380
That with *energy* undying 470

ENFOLD

In thy dying, Christ, *enfold* me 1263
Now *enfold* them in thy 974

ENFOLDED

Enfolded deep in thy dear love 856

ENFOLDS

Enfolds and understands 818

ENGAGE

O may it all my powers *engage* 4

ENJOY

And *enjoy* it ever there 1612

ENJOYED

Nor Sabbaths be *enjoyed* in vain 2203

ENJOYMENT

For all the *enjoyment* and pleasures 2194
In his *enjoyment* to be blest 319
Not for us the tame *enjoyment* 62

ENJOYS

Zion *enjoys* her Monarch's love 572

ENKINDLED

Enkindled by thy word 515

ENLARGE

Enlarge, expand all Christian souls 2177

ENLARGED

Thou hast *enlarged* me in distress 526

ENLIGHTEN

Enlighten me, with love endow 2302

ENLIST

Then *enlist* beneath his standard 941
Then *enlist* today 941

ENLISTED

Others have *enlisted* 3
Will you be *enlisted* 3

ENMITY

Old *enmity* forget 796

ENOUGH

Are they not *enough* for thee 1983
Enough for all 2071
Enough for each (evermore) 2071

ENRICH

Enrich its golden store 1313
Enrich that temple's holy shrine 307
Enrich the poor 1801
Enrich our life with heavenly 2122
Enrich our souls in secret 1359

ENSAMPLE

Ensample true for all, for me 1534

ENSIGN

As an *ensign* fair we lift it 1994
Like an *ensign* lifted high 1051

ENSLAVE

Enslave it with thy matchless love 1202

ENTER

And *enter* now unto thy rest 114
And free to all who will *enter* in 1970
And I shall *enter* into rest 1749
And I shall *enter* my heav'nly home 1249
And those who *enter* in 1404
But let me *enter* in 1456
Dear Savior, *enter, enter* 1414
Enter, and chase them forth 405
Enter and claim thine own 1090
Enter every trembling heart 1190
"*Enter,* faithful servant, welcome home 1808
Enter his courts with song 1707
Enter into my Master's joy 1824
Enter our lives, all veils 1316
Enter, then, O Christ most holy 369
Enter, ye nations who obey 778
How we, too, may *enter* heaven 287
If you would *enter* the mansions 905
No, I'll *enter,* no 2032
O *enter* before 'tis forever too late 1740
O *enter* then his gates with praise 57
O, ye who would *enter* that glorious 18
Still will I *enter* in 804
Then will I *enter* into them 1484
Who *enter* through thy portals 1404
Wilt thou pitifully *enter* 369
With him I may *enter* in 1735
Zion, let me *enter* 1588

ENTERED

And I *entered* the "Haven of rest" 1257
Jesus *entered* Jordan's wave 2032
Then *entered* in those wise men 1861
Thou within the veil hast *entered* 77

ENTERS

He *enters* all rooms, "the doors 472
He *enters,* condescends to stay 2218
Now our heavenly Aaron *enters* 1697

ENTERTAINED

Ne'er *entertained* so kind a guest 192

ENTHRALL

Nothing worldly shall *enthrall* me 411

ENTHRONED

Jesus, *enthroned* in the glory above 705

ENTRANCE

But thou art seeking *entrance* 784

ENTREAT

Entreat the Lord with them to stay 1569
O Lord, I thee *entreat* 2116
Soft and sweet, doth *entreat* 52
Then will the Spirit *entreat* 2

ENTRENCHED

It matters not how deep *entrenched* 174

ENVY

Envy banish, strife will vanish 1402
When, free from *envy,* scorn and pride 792

ERECT

Erect thy temple-throne 1090

ERR

May they who *err* be guided 2052

ERRED

Have I *erred* along the way 2227
When I have *erred,* and gone astray 1517

ERRING

Erring hearts to right incline 744

ERROR

Oft in *error,* oft in anguish 656
The boast of haughty *error* 1

ERRORS

So our little *errors* 1101

ESCAPE

"*Escape* thee for thy life 1866

ESCAPED

And oft *escaped* the tempter's snare 1806

ESPOUSAL

Still in the pure *espousal* 1944

ESSENCE

And *essence* all-divine 1630

ESTABLISH

Establish them each one 1541
Establish thou, and make it stand 1174
Establish thou forevermore 1507
Establish thou Messiah's throne 114

ESTABLISHED

Established evermore by thee 1174

ESTATE

How my lost *estate* to save 894

ETERNAL

Eternal and yet ever new 1461

ETERNITY

A blest *eternity* I'll spend 1339
A life for all *eternity* 60
And through *eternity* shall live 1514
And to *eternity* love and adore 338
Be thine through all *eternity* 1137
Changeless through *eternity* 1213
Dawning day of thine *eternity* 1094
Eternity then will be mine 701
From *eternity* the same 1837
I am safe for all *eternity* 2057
Leading, guiding to *eternity* 1919
Look away to Jesus, through *eternity* 1114
Safe in thine own *eternity* 1446
That through *eternity* thy glory 2077
Then through all *eternity* 1173
Vast as *eternity* thy love (his love) 184
We are sailing to *eternity* 1919
Yet to *eternity*
standeth thy word 607, 608, 612

EVADE

You can *evade* him as Pilate 984

EVANGEL

In thee is God's *evangel* heard 1569

EVENING

And *evening* calms the mind 1795
And *evening* steals o'er earth and sky 186
And from *evening* prayer time 451
Each *evening* closer than before 2146
Heavenward, then, at *evening* 429
One *evening* in that garden 626
Sowing in the *evening* 1693
Till *evening* ends the varied 1410

EVENTIDE

At *eventide* descend 124
At *eventide,* renewed upon the 389
At that dread *eventide* let there be light 98
Once more 'tis *eventide,* and we 136
That *eventide* may still be light 1692

EVERLASTING

And to *everlasting* God 2288
He is God from *everlasting* 2288
Thou wert from *everlasting* 1914

EVERYTHING

Everything rejoices in the mellow 1800
Till *everything* that's human 1089

EVERYWHERE

And *everywhere* his heat extends 1862
I am with thee *everywhere* 2006

EVIL

All, all the present *evil* teach 1431
And from all *evil* keep them 458
And from *evil* still defend us 1153
Evil let me shun 621
Evil shall not dwell with thee 710
Evil to lash with love's pure 594
From every *evil* shall he keep 2139
From *evil* he will keep thee safe 885
Long has *evil* reigned within 800
Neither shall *evil* dwell with thee 527, 1176
No *evil* shall upon thee come 1908
Something of *evil* die 1345
Though *evil* would assail me 1297
Would you o'er *evil* a victory 2323

EVILS

Or when *evils* come alluring 988

EXALT

Come, *exalt* him, all the living 611
Come, *exalt* me to the skies 1516
Exalt goodwill again 1916
Exalt him in the highest 1485
Exalt his matchless worth 510
Exalt our low desires 311
Exalt the Giver of them all 1309
Exalt the glory of him whose 1627
Exalt the name of Jesus 1627
Exalt them evermore 1455
Exalt them over every fear 495
Exalt thy precious name 1659
Exalt thy tow'ring head 1666
With me *exalt* his name 2060

EXALTED

And though *exalted*, feels afresh 2305
Be thou, O God, *exalted* high 1362
O Lord, *exalted* be thy name 166
To thee, now high *exalted* 44
Thou, O Lord, on high *exalted* 951

EXALTS

And *exalts* to highest honor 991

EXAMINE

Examine me, and do me prove 1043

EXAMPLE

He the great *example* is 1804
His *example* while beholding 519
Thou shalt my *example* be 523

EXCELLENCE

On *excellence* divine 100

EXCHANGE

And *exchange* it some day 1561
I'll *exchange* my cross for a starry 1044

EXCLUDED

Boasting *excluded*, pride 1262

EXCLUDES

But it ne'er *excludes* his face 1848

EXCUSES

No vain *excuses* frame 348
Nor weak *excuses* frame 1875

EXEMPT

O to live *exempt* from care 380

EXILE

And how can we, in *exile* drear 374

EXILED

Tho' *exiled* from home, yet still 1229

EXILES

Long thine *exiles* have been pining 280
Mourning *exiles* now are we 78
Thine *exiles* long for home 1836

EXPAND

Expand thy quickening wing 1449

EXPANSES

O'er white *expanses*, sparkling 40

EXPECTANT

And *expectant* I will bring 710

EXPECTATION

With longing *expectation* 405

EXPEL

Expel with thy brightness my darkness 719

EXPERIENCE

Experience will divide 2060
Would you *experience* what I know 2

EXPLORE

May I *explore* the mine 2085

EXPRESSED

In thee most perfectly *expressed* 2022

EXTEND

Extend thy blessed reign 1449
That he should *extend* his great love 880

EXTENDED

While *extended* there, we view 950

EXTENDS

And God *extends* grace to each 991

EXTINGUISH

Extinguish passion's fires 311

EXTOL

And *extol* our God and King 1558
And how *extol* thy matchless fame 1002
Extol the Lamb of God 241
Extol the Lamb with loftiest song 328
Extol the Lord with me 616
I will *extol* thee every day 1451
My tongue did him *extol* 50
We all do *extol* thee 2166

EXULTS

In them *exults* the Holy Ghost 1859

EYE

And God the Lord from every *eye* 774
And his *eye* the way must guide 863
And thine *eye* beheld them good 748
And your *eye* upon the rail 1076
Beneath his watchful *eye* 777
Ev'ry *eye* rejoices 409
Every *eye* shall now behold 1106
Eye and heart long for thy gladness 1470
Eye cannot see nor heart 491
From every weeping *eye* 1111
Guarding with watchful *eye* 557
He hath with a piteous *eye* 1074
His *eye* is fixed on you 2338
His *eye* is on the sparrow 2296
His *eye* our secret thoughts 2338
His watchful *eye* ne'er sleepeth 1729
If his ever watchful *eye* 1218
Mine *eye* at times can see 203
Mortal *eye* can scan 101
No *eye* can to thy throne ascend 1423
No *eye* hath seen its glories 2172
No *eye* upon thy sins but one 133
No mortal *eye* can bear 1897
Nor *eye* hath seen, nor ear 2149
One with thyself, may every *eye* 2217
So now beneath his *eye* 1940
The *eye* of faith e'en now 1080
The *eye* of faith is dim 1148
Thine *eye* detects the sparrow's fall 1163
Thou whose all-pervading *eye* 1745
Though the *eye* of sinful man 749
To thine aspiring *eye* 154
What though no *eye* beholds 2303
With a pitying *eye* behold 589
With his *eye* of love looking 2180
With his loving *eye* looking 2180
With pitying *eye* behold our 648

EYE-BALLS

And on the *eye-balls* of the blind 674

EYELIDS

And with sweet sleep mine *eyelids* 59
When mine *eyelids* close in death 1671

EYES

And *eyes* are on you as you run 1608
And let our wondering *eyes* 116
And our *eyes* at last shall see 1572
And our *eyes* behold the splendor 2158
And to wipe the weeping *eyes* 443
And with long weeping our *eyes* 705
And wondrous in our *eyes* 1484
As, to our *eyes*, the tender grace 2027
But in the *eyes* of men, redeemed 2193
But when our *eyes* behold thy word 1871
Eager *eyes* are watching 255
Eyes art thou unto us, the blind 784
Eyes of love are on thee 939
For *eyes* to see, and ears 1346
For mine *eyes* have seen thy 1154
For weary *eyes* and aching hearts 121
Full of sad and weeping *eyes* 1955
God's *eyes* are on the just 1321
His *eyes* behold the sons 1261
His pitying *eyes* thy grief 1657
How blessed are our *eyes* 768
If now, with *eyes* defiled and 89
In whose *eyes* vile men are 2311
Kind *eyes* that marked the lilies 1491
Lift your *eyes*, ye sons 277
Little *eyes* are sleeping 1102
Lord of angels, on our *eyes* 382
May our *eyes* be ever turning 1005
May our sinful *eyes* thy light 1092
Mine *eyes* look up thy loving 1395
Mine *eyes* their vigils keep 489
Mine *eyes* uplifted be 1433
Mine *eyes* upon the Lord 2116
My *eyes* in the gath'ring mist 1913
My *eyes* shall seek the faithful 1557
My *eyes* with tear-drops start 1249
Nay, which is precious in his *eyes* 1964
Nor my *eyes* see the cross which 236
O how oft thine *eyes*, offended 1005
O those dim *eyes* never turning 1263
O what can little *eyes* do 1536
On which, with sorrowing *eyes* 1116
Our *eyes* are blind and sightless 149
Our *eyes* see dimly 'till by faith 1794
Pure *eyes* and Christian hearts 1960
Softly let the *eyes* be closing 446
Soon shall my *eyes* behold thee 1419
Than human *eyes* can know 548
The *eyes* of men are turning 29
The little *eyes* can upward look 1536
Then *eyes* with joy shall sparkle 1836
These *eyes*, new faith receiving 1475

Thine *eyes* have searched the ancient 1533
Thine *eyes* of holy love can see 2122
To my *eyes* thy precepts show 780
To our admiring *eyes* 1111
Unto thee their *eyes* are turning 296
When our *eyes* behold the splendor 2158
When our *eyes* behold, through 2298
When our *eyes* shall see the beauty 1993
While before our *eyes* unfold 2191
While their eager *eyes* behold him 1697
Who with the *eyes* of early youth 1468
Whose *eyes* mine inmost substance see 499
With *eyes* that dimmed and softened 818
With our *eyes* his glory see 2252

F

FACE

Although his *face* I cannot see 812
Always looking on his smiling *face* 2002
And as for me, I thine own *face* 1135
And *face* a frowning world 2231
And *face* to face in stern array 1860
And let the *face* of God shine 1358
And we his *face* shall see 1877
And when thy *face* I see 1689
Are there no foes for me to *face* 87
Before his *face* I fall 1578
Before his *face* my grief 2103
Before thy *face;* and they, O Lord 54
Before thy *face* shall I abide 1376
Before whose *face* his angels bow 173
But sweeter far thy *face* to see 1877
Face to face in all his glory 424
Face to face I shall behold him 424
Face to face with my Redeemer 424
Face to face with those that love us 2256
For thou shalt go before the *face* 215
From him he has not hid his *face* 72
God's blessed *face* to see above 2332
Here have we seen thy *face* 15
His blessed and his gracious *face* 533
His *face* in its beauty at last 1868
In the shining of thy *face* 106
Just to be there and to look on his *face* 2222
Keeping *face* forward up the hill 285
Let your *face* be like the morning 1955
Lord, let thy blessed *face* 1828
Nature's *face* all gleaming 1792
No *face* was so bright, no heart 2272
O God, we *face* its test 185
Our mother's *face,* the bright blue 1629
Seeking thy *face* 584
Should thy *face* be clouded 925
Singing, till thy *face* I see 1687
That fading *face* 734
There thy *face* unclouded see 655
Thus might I hide my blushing *face* 38
Thy blessed *face* one moment's space 2044
Thy *face* hide from my sin 31
Thy *face* with reverence and 503
Thy steadfast *face* set forward 1549
Till at last thy *face* we see 442
'Tis good his *face* to seek 932
To see thee *face* to face 1805
Until thy blessed *face* I see 1170
Until thy holy *face* one day 1645
We *face* the sterner fights of life 588
We *face* the storm with a heavy heart 2190
Where the *face* of sorrow brightened 716
Who will *face* the foe 2287
With open *face* they see 2172
With shining *face* and bright array 1543
You that are longing to see his *face* 1206

FACES

And kindly *faces* to my own 2248

FADE

Behind us *fade* the centuries 46
Fade every evil thought 1407
So *fade* within our heart 1927
Thou canst not *fade* nor flee 1087

FADES

Fades the chime of vesper bells 678
Or *fades* my earthly bliss 2243
Soft it *fades* upon the ear 678

FADETH

When *fadeth* the day, and dark 2225

FADING

The nearer the *fading* of the leaf 1913

FAIL

"Almost," is but to *fail* 85
And that cannot *fail* 1586
But God doth *fail* me never 2054
For should all *fail* proclaiming 2230
He never will *fail* me, I know 701
He will never *fail* us 1787
Jesus will not *fail* us 1004
Nor ever *fail* us 291
Then can I never *fail* 494
Thine can never *fail* 811

FAILINGS

Each can his brother's *failings* hide 792

FAILS

Fails my heart, I know not how 627

It never *fails* my heart 1912
Never *fails* from age to age 541

FAILURE

Failure cuts the way to triumph 1075
Failure will change to perfection 1763
In my *failure*, sin, and sorrow 835
Out of my shameful *failure* 1602
There to work, where free from *failure* 2275

FAILURE'S

Here are earth's splendid *failures* 2182
Not in our *failures* only 1491
The *failures* half divine 2182
With my *failures* patient be 2227

FAIN

I *fain* would take my stand 203
Such as thou art, I *fain* would be 1964
To God I *fain* would go 1097
Who would not *fain* be resting 1531

FAINT

And *faint* before the truth 201
And ye will *faint* beside 362
Faint for the flaming of thine 683
Faint not! much doth yet 1560
Faint not! nor fear, his 477
For the *faint* and feeble 1787
O *faint* not by the way 1945
Shall neither *faint* nor falter 1906
The *faint* and overborne 278
When I *faint*, his grace upholdeth 65
Who can *faint* while such a river 541

FAINTING

And should I *fainting* be 1475

FAINTS

Yea, *faints* thy courts to see 783

FAITH

A *faith* that keeps the narrow way 1348
A *faith* that shines more bright 1348
A sweet unmurmuring *faith* 797
And all our *faith* he will complete 791
And by *faith* we can see it afar 1992
And *faith* be lost in sight 2168
And *faith* delights to prove 1805
And *faith* demands the world 1945
And *faith* has still its Olivet 917, 2181
And *faith* perceives alone 99
And *faith*, rekindling all its powers 1931
And *faith* stands leaning on 1739
And *faith*, taking hold of the Word 1257
And if your *faith* be dim 1292
And in simple *faith* to plunge me 2092
And our *faith* so dim 99
And their *faith*, like David 718
And thus our *faith* with water 2161
And trembling *faith* is changed 1459
And when *faith* is dim 1545
And yet whose *faith* hath constant 1493
But by *faith* their refuge 1402
But, should my *faith* prove frail 434
But when by *faith* I catch 737
By *faith*, and faith alone 1797
By *faith* I'll rise and go 893
By *faith*, on heaven's table-land 915
By faith they, like a whirlwind's 413
By *faith* we know thee strong 146
By *faith* we see the glory 708
By *faith* we take the bread of life 927
Cold and wavering *faith* increase 1028
Constant still in *faith* 1813
E'en though my *faith* be failing 573
E'er since by *faith*, I saw 1961
Even now by *faith* I claim him 575
Even now by *faith* we join 324
Even when my *faith* is small 1721
Faith and hope and love we see 636, 1192
Faith believes, nor questions 77
Faith can sing through days 2065
Faith, hope, and love all warmed 1453
Faith in him who died 131
Faith in the future, its light 1750
Faith in the only sacrifice 1171
Faith is certain to be blest 1147
Faith is our battle token 1320
Faith is sure that all is best 1147
Faith is the victory, we know 413
Faith like its Finisher 146
Faith, mighty faith, the promise 453
Faith sees no longer the stable 1095
Faith shouts in triumph 1238
Faith still receives the cup 335
Faith that mountains could 636
Faith that triumphs over wrong 2043
Faith to make our prayers 1147
Faith to sight, and prayer 980
Faith will lead to perfect rest 1147
Faith will vanish into sight 636, 1192
For *faith*, and will to win 593
For *faith* renewed, for hope 1807
For *faith* to conquer doubt 1346
For the *faith* in truth and freedom 487
Freest *faith* assailed in vain 294
Have *faith* in God and wait 1283
Have *faith*, leaving all in his 1640
Here by *faith* in him to dwell 66
Here *faith* is ours, and heavenly 1920
In childlike *faith*, believing 2096
In *faith* address our prayers 651
In *faith* and patience may we live 1121
In *faith* present our prayers 393
In *faith* sow the word of the Master 1770
It may the *faith* of one restore 400
Learning here, by *faith* and love 1762
Let *faith* each weak petition 1184
Let *faith* in thee, and in thy might 1407
Let human *faith* abide 1526
Let not *faith* and hope forsake 989
Like them in *faith* to bear 1537
Lord, send us forth, the *faith* supply 1169
May *faith* grow firm and love 1530, 2052
May we in *faith* receive thy word 651
Mine to show by living *faith* 730
My *faith* burns low 1277

My *faith* is strong and clear 822
My *faith* to test 824
My *faith* would lay her hand 1279
My feeble *faith* looks up 1689
No much-tried *faith* like gold 1274
Nor would we, their *faith* despising 1553
Now the living *faith* impart 339
O for the *faith* to grasp heaven's 1352
O Lord of hosts, our *faith* renew 325
Of *faith,* that never waxes dim 576
Of *faith* that overcomes the world 912
One common *faith* unites us all 138
One in the *faith* of all thy prophets 1443
Our *faith,* by God increased 1313
Our *faith* is built upon thy promise 828
Our *faith* shall never yield to fear 572
Our *faith* springs like the eagle 1281
Ours is the *faith,* the will 211
Patient *faith* the crown to win 760
Put your *faith* in our Father 130
Rich in *faith* I still would be 1218
Spirit of *faith,* descend and show 1777
Still by *faith* I'll tread the narrow 2057
Strong in *faith* resist the foe 1748
Stronger in *faith,* more clear I see 1267
Such *faith,* O God, our spirits 1360
The *faith* by which alone God's 1474
The *faith* by which they conquer'd 413
The *faith* by which ye see him 1391
The *faith* sure and steadfast 423
The *faith* that burns, the 2040
The *faith* that makes men brave 2028
The *faith* that triumphs o'er the dust 2048
The *faith* we keep in goodness 185
Their steadfast *faith* our unity 1646
Theirs is the steadfast *faith* 1859
Then let our humble *faith* address 2305
There by wrestling *faith* obtain 752
There in trembling *faith* to leave them 753
This is our *faith* tremendous 90
Thou in the *faith* dost 317
Though dim our *faith* 2167
Though *faith* and hope may long 1400
Through *faith* we shall conquer 2336
Thus *faith* approves itself 2090
Thy *faith* hath made thee whole 1713
Till *faith* shall dawn and doubt 1116
True *faith* waits not to prove 133
Walking by *faith,* and not by sight 1370
Walking by *faith,* change 1763
When all alone, if my weak *faith* 2096
When *faith* has heard the Master's 1487
When for deeper *faith* I seek 2247
When for stronger *faith* I seek 2247
When my *faith* would surely 224
When my wavering *faith* in trials 259
When their first warm *faith* 2264
Where *faith* and hope shall vanish 2175
Where *faith* bids fear depart 1515
Where *faith* in sight is swallowed 1714
Where *faith* is lost in sight 1959
Who from the saving *faith* 1621
With *faith,* my soul, pray on 1639
With *faith* that glows, and love 1469
With thee, in thee, by *faith* 1795
Yea, *faith* can pierce the cloud 559
Zion, one *faith* is thine 1579

FAITHFUL

O may I ever *faithful* be 1248
On the *faithful,* who adore 342
That all the *faithful* might enjoy 128

FAITHFULNESS

And for thy *faithfulness,* O God 1387
And in thy *faithfulness* and love 2244
And to declare thy *faithfulness* 2112
His *faithfulness* shall ever be 1908
Of *faithfulness* and grace 106
Thy *faithfulness,* even in the heavens 619
Thy *faithfulness* make to be known 619
Thy *faithfulness* unto all men 2084

FALL

And *fall* beneath his feet 1653
And *fall* on sea and earth 1103
And humbly *fall* before his feet 109
And though they *fall,* held by his 1935
Before him we adoring *fall* 1109
Faint *fall* the footsteps in city 1611
Faint was I from many a *fall* 895
Fall down on their faces 2330
Fall on your knees 1399
In thee I *fall* asleep 1444
Let *fall* on every college hall 84
Let *fall* thy rod of terror 1497
Let thy blessing *fall* on me 70
Low, we *fall* before thee 357
Never let me *fall* 811
Not alone we *fall* 501
Sweet the rain's new *fall* 1221
Tenderly watching lest I should *fall* 1047
To raise up them that *fall* 1525
To those who *fall,* how kind 1019
Tower and temple *fall* to dust 53
We at his feet may *fall* 47
Without him I would *fall* 981
Ye ransomed from the *fall* 47

FALLEN

Fallen the engines of war 660

FALLS

And round me *falls* the night 98
Falls steady, clear, and sure 185
For nothing *falls* unknown 6

FALSE

You can be *false* to him 984

FALSEHOOD

Falsehood and wrong shall not tarry 607, 608
Hating *falsehood,* loving right 780

FALTER

Just when I *falter,* just when 1047
May I not *falter,* Lord, nor 893
Need we ever *falter* 925

Never *falter,* never quail 1076
Though my weary steps may *falter* 66
We must never yield or *falter* 62

FAME

And all inspiring *fame* 1224
And the *fame* of their exploits 1987
For much his *fame* should be 1898
Nor for *fame* my pray'r shall be 2042
Where'er thy glorious *fame* extends 2313

FAMILY

One *family* God made of men 2098
One *family,* we dwell in him 324, 1067

FANCIED

The half cannot be *fancied* 2108

FANCIES

Then *fancies* flee away 707
Then *fancies* fly away 2290

FANCY

And I shall *fancy* his blessing 1831
Till I *fancy* but thinly the veil 896

FANG

And *fang* and claw 2100

FARE

Fare forth beyond the thunder of 2069
Wherever they may *fare* 956

FASHION

And every changeful *fashion* 1325
Father who didst *fashion* me 1566

FASHIONS

He *fashions* and rules by his word 164

FAST

"Always *fast* and vigil 293
Our *fast* with thee in spirit keep 161

FASTENED

Fastened to the Rock which cannot 2298

FATALIST

Not like the nerveless *fatalist* 1281

FATE

But whatever *fate* betide us 366
Of the *fate* which doth await 1866

FATHER

A *father,* torn with anguish 2147
Abba, *Father,* give me grace 2121
Almighty *Father,* who dost give 1079
And he who would the *Father* 2023
And to the *Father* cry 1988
But thou, eternal *Father* 1952
Come thou *Father* of the poor 342
Father, as in highest hear 1160
Father, give us this day 712
Father, grant thy wearied one 2253
Father in heaven, to thee are known 121
Father in heaven, we thank thee 273
Father, in thy gracious keeping 1303
Father, let thine eyes now be 2227
Father, now we thank thee 935
Father of all, life's source and spring 1920
Father of Jesus, love's reward 1234
Father of love and light 1156
Father of the poor, draw near 341
Father, thy mercies past 1733
Father, thy name be praised 1289
"*Father,* thy will be done." 1119
Father, we obey the summons 929
Father, we thank thee 273
Father, what can to thee be given 1439
Father, who the crown dost give 1478
For the *Father* waits over the way 1992
From God, our heavenly *Father* 599
For whate'er my *Father* doeth 1643
Great *Father* of glory 916
I have a *Father,* to me he has given 830
I have but thee, my *Father* 2248
My *Father,* for his sake I pray 1228
My *Father,* still I strive to say 1231
No earthly *father* loves like thee 1234
O *Father,* grant this child-like heart 949
O *Father,* in thy mercy great 1939
O *Father,* soothe all troubled thought 1385
O *Father,* while we sleep 1853
O God, our *Father,* bless this day 1313
O Spirit, whom the *Father* sent 81
One with the *Father,* thought and deed 1130
Praise him, *Father,* friend 104
See! the *Father* meets him out 1664
Sure that the *Father,* who is nigh 1431
Tenderly the *Father* welcomes 1198
That God is my dear *Father* 898
The *Father* on his sapphire throne 1660
Thou my great *Father,* I thy true son 177
Thou our *Father,* Christ our brother 1040
Thou wast, O God, creatively the *Father* 725
Though *father* or mother forsake us 2055
'Tis a loving *Father* calls the 2292
To God the *Father,* equal praise 1037
To our bountiful *Father* above 1992
Where the one almighty *Father* 2067
While our *Father* calls you home 2283
Who is the immortal *Father* 653
Yes, our heavenly *Father* leads us 1066

FATHERHOOD

Thy joy thy tender *Fatherhood* 67

FATHER-LOVE

Father-love is reigning o'er us 1040

FATHERS

As thee their God our *fathers* 1448
Fathers and mothers safe in 1605
Fathers themselves are God's 1014
For thee our *fathers* suffered 1312
God of our *fathers,* be the God 1364
God of our *fathers,* help us share 1217
In the way the *fathers* trod 277
In thee our *fathers* trusted 1873, 1361

It has saved our *fathers* 2095
On thee, O God, our *fathers* put 1239
Our *fathers* owned thy goodness 2072
Their *fathers* would not know 2239

FATHOM

I cannot *fathom* though often 1971

FATNESS

They with the *fatness* of thy house 2080

FAULT

That without *fault* or fear 285

FAULTS

Humbly confessing our *faults* 584
Our *faults* and failings he forgives 1093

FAVOR

And in thy *favor* shall our horn 1390
For the *favor* he shows 2266
For thy *favor* and thy mercies 770
Free and changeless is his *favor* 2065
I am longing for thy *favor* 1138
Nor the proud thy *favor* win 710
That, with thy wonted *favor* 2114
There is *favor* now at the mercy-seat 1979
Thy *favor* I entreat 1455
With *favor* thou wilt compass him 527
With the Holy Spirit's *favor* 1209
Wonderful *favor* from heaven above 2314

FAVORED

Favored beyond measure 1034

FAVORS

His *favors* claim thy highest praise 209

FEALTY

He who, in *fealty* to the truth 620

FEAR

A Godly *fear* of sin impart 2202
All *fear* before thy presence 1025
All that *fear* God, come, hear 50
And all *fear* of want remove 541
And *fear*, and love, and serve 2170
And *fear* not, 'tis Jesus 1338
And *fear* to launch away 1966
And from *fear* of cloud and 730
And if, perchance, dread *fear* 2234
And shall I *fear* to own 87
And the *fear* that sends me 1242
And those about that do him *fear* 1902
And with *fear* and trembling 1060
Anywhere with Jesus I need *fear* 108
Before all them that *fear* thee 72
But those that God do *fear* 2311
But to those that *fear* him 1565
But unto them that do him *fear* 1798
Do not *fear* to join our standard 2064
Do not *fear* to trust him 987
Do you *fear* the gath'ring clouds 112
Ever great to them that *fear* him 1472
Fear God, his saints, none that 616
Fear him, ye saints, and you will 2060
Fear I cannot know 108
Fear not, brethren, joyful stand 277
Fear not, for he doth hold 1282
"*Fear* not, I am with thee . 776, 2002
"*Fear* not, I will pilot thee" 1007
Fear not, little flock, he goeth 472
Fear not, little flock, whatever 472
Fear not, O land, in God 1651
"*Fear* not," said he, for mighty dread 2282
Fear not the secret foe 548
"*Fear* not, then," said the angel 599
Fear not though death all its 1765
Fear not to enter his courts 2322
Fear not when shadows 906
Fear ye not the way so lonely 2284
He'll *fear* not what men say 2290
Herod then with *fear* was 2141
Hushing every *fear* 1787
I can no longer *fear* 113, 2046
I *fear* no foe, with thee at hand 27
I *fear* to call thee mine 392
I shall not *fear* the battle 1408
I will not *fear*, though darkness 822
I'll *fear* not what men say 707
In every *fear* and conflict 872
In them that *fear* him he delights 1636
In thy *fear* will worship there 710
Let no *fear* of death appall us 1125
Lord, should *fear* and anguish 2059
Make us *fear* whate'er is wrong 1118
May *fear* continually 54
Naught I *fear* when I abide 963
Never *fear*, only trust and obey 2266
No *fear*, no woe shall dim 132
No *fear* nor angry sorrow 2109
No more by *fear* and doubt 1446
None that him *fear* shall be with want 616
Nor *fear* the storms 502
Nor *fear* to tread below 1959
Nor *fear* what waiteth there 162
O *fear* not, and doubt not 1338
O *fear* not, faint not, halt not 1081
O how I *fear* thee, living God 1234
O'er *fear* and doubt, o'er black 1368
Onward then, and *fear* not 1787
Surely to such as do him *fear* 587
Surely to them that *fear* the Lord 909
That none might *fear* that world to see 590
The *fear* that turns the heart 2122
Then shall I *fear* no gathering 137
They shall thee *fear*, while sun 1454
They that *fear* and love the Lord 629
Thus all our raging *fear* controls 572
We need not *fear*, though all 1429
We will *fear* no evil 983
What shall we *fear* with thy power 578
When I *fear*, his arms enfoldeth 65
While thou art near we will not *fear* 2289
Who would not *fear* his holy 1785
With those that *fear* him is 2116
Yet will I *fear* none ill 1904

FEARED

That *feared* thou mayest be 1129
We have not *feared* thee as we 2170

FEARFUL-HEARTED

Come, ye sad and *fearful-hearted* 700

FEARS

Above all *fears* me raise 616
All my guilty *fears* remove 637
All the *fears* of men allay 2227
All the *fears* that press the soul 1096
And from my *fears* he set me 1890
Fears to stir or step alone 1647
From midnight *fears* and perils 1927
From our *fears* and sins release 343
From the *fears* that long have bound 580
He all my *fears* within doth quell 2216
Let not faithless *fears* o'ertake 989
Let not *fears* your course impede 1560
Lo, on him that *fears* Jehovah 238
No *fears* to quell 967
No gloomy *fears* their souls dismay 644
Our *fears*, our hopes, our aims 232
Secure from all our *fears* 1151
The *fears* that brace 1146
The *fears* that hold us back 185
To thee our *fears* and joys 1491

FEAST

And be thy *feast* to us 246
And the *feast* is spread 1114
And the *feast* is waiting there 565
Come to the *feast* of love 355
Hail, sacred *feast*, which Jesus 1232
Here let me *feast*, and feasting 727
In the Eucharistic *feast* 77
Jesus, thy *feast* we celebrate 2132
Lord of our *feast*, to thee as is 261
O Lord, this *feast* receiving 1317
Of the endless *feast* 1114

FEATURES

And upon thine upturned *features* 2276

FED

Fed by thy living bread 721
May we, with thee, O Christ, be *fed* 161
They shall be *fed* and satisfied 72

FEEBLE

All the *feeble*, gently leading 1691
We are so *feeble*, and thou 713

FEED

And *feed* on his word 1820
And *feed* on thee, and make thee 173
Feed in pastures ever vernal 1691
Feed me till I want no more 652
Feed me with food divine 803
Feed me with thy food 1000
Feed the faint and hungry 1042
Feed them with nourishment 774
Feed thy saints with joys 1516
Feed us, we pray 721
Feed us with thy body 1049
He shall *feed* his flock like a 1998
Here would I *feed* upon the bread 727
I *feed* in green pastures 1894
O *feed* me, Lord, that I may 1170
Safe they *feed* upon the manna 541
We are his flock, he doth us *feed* 57

FEEDS

And *feeds* the widow and the 1319
And he who *feeds* the ravens 1759
Feeds me with the living bread 66
He *feeds* the poor 911
That *feeds* the strength of every saint 157

FEEL

And *feel* at heart that One above 1431
And *feel* his brother's care 1029
And *feel* his hands on me 949
And *feel* that I am frail 176
And *feel* the blessed pledge within 234, 1805
And *feel* the promise is not vain 1465
And in my heart I *feel* the thrill 2
Can we *feel* that thou art near us 101
Come, *feel* with me his blood applied 1460
Do you not *feel*, dear brother 2293
Feel thy presence with them in 2274
I can *feel* the anchor fast 2056
I *feel* as if she still were here 870
I *feel* his hand 564
I *feel* his presence sweetly near 812
I *feel* my strength is small 434
I *feel* the winds of God today 826
I *feel* thy love enfolding 893
I *feel* thy strong and tender love 856
I *feel* thy tender touch 2
I may only *feel* the touch 822
I must *feel* his presence near me 863
I would not *feel* my strength 1142
If what ye *feel* ye can fully 1538
Just now I *feel* his cleansing 482
Let all within us *feel* his power 1105
Let me *feel* the Holy Spirit 70
Let me *feel* the Spirit's power 1688
Let me *feel* thy cleansing pow'r 1684
Let us *feel* thy power 339
Let us *feel* thy presence near 1676
Lord, let me *feel* thy fresh'ning 826
May we *feel* thee near us 451
O let me *feel* thee near me 1408
O let us *feel* thee near in loving power 721
O may we *feel*, as low we kneel 437
Often I *feel* my sinful heart 153
Somehow I *feel* that he is near 1756
Then, only then, we *feel* our interest 1777
Thou didst *feel* its keenest woe 1058
'Tis only in thee hiding, I *feel* 1419
We *feel* our hearts within us 2174
We *feel* the love in thy blood-stained 1316
We *feel* the resurrection near 779
We *feel* thy calm at evening hour 591
When each can *feel* his brother's sigh 792
When they *feel* the conqueror's pride 2264

When we *feel* our mortal weakness 993
Ye that *feel* the tempter's power 552
Yet I *feel* a blessed assurance 1847
You *feel* your sins forgiven 1292

FEELETH

And he *feeleth* for our sadness 1572

FEELINGS

Feelings lie buried that grace 1655
For *feelings* do not stay 348

FEELS

But *feels* the death that all must die 1508

FEET

Ah! who shall at the Savior's *feet* 1285
And *feet* on mercy's errand swift 1576
And *feet* that from thee rove 121
And *feet* that go astray 1604
And if my *feet* would go astray 822
And missing thee, my trembling *feet* 737
And round his pierced *feet* 376
And swift our *feet* shall move 205
And to guide our *feet* into the way 215
And what if my *feet* may not tread 236
And where their pilgrim *feet* have 1354
As their weary *feet* touch 2004
At his *feet* I'll lay ev'ry burden 1044
At his *feet* the six-winged 1060
At his *feet* we humbly fall 2286
At the *feet* of Jesus, is the place 141
At the *feet* of Jesus, risen now 141
At the Master's *feet* 1114
At thy *feet* adoring fall 1612
At thy *feet* I bow 811
At thy *feet* I lay them 1471
At thy *feet* their tribute pay 582
At thy *feet* we are reclining 219
At thy *feet* we humbly bow 1181
At thv sacred *feet* I bow 766
At whose *feet* the shepherd fall 2286
Be near me when my *feet* 1580
Before his *feet* the clouds were riven 2228
Before thy *feet,* abashed 186
Christ, thy bleeding *feet* we track 1574
Falling prostrate at his *feet* 1817
For *feet* to run on errands 1346
For weary *feet* awaits a street 2008
Guiding my *feet* lest I should 1752
Humbly at thy *feet* we fall 442
In his *feet* and hands are 119
Let marching *feet* and joyous song 720
Let the naked *feet* be shod 2007
Little *feet* are still 1102
Lord, my *feet* have grown so weary 224
Low at his *feet* lay thy burden 2322
My *feet* no straying know 1463
Never higher than thy *feet* 1271
O beautiful for pilgrim *feet* 1311
O *feet* so strong to climb 1491
O let my *feet* ne'er run astray 1035
O thou, whose infant *feet* were found 267
Of thine advent *feet* 683
Our willing *feet* shall stand 540
Savior, at thy *feet* I fall 1644
Thankful at thy *feet* to be 798
That, wheresoe'er my *feet* have swerved 39
The *feet* are slack 2044
The *feet* that wait for God 1283
The *feet* that walked the stormy 206
The wandering and the wavering *feet* 1170
Then shall my *feet* no longer rove 1021
There, adoring at his *feet* 552
They with unwearied *feet* shall tread 685
Thine own before thy *feet* we lay 67
Thy blessed *feet* shall glitter 1327
Thy *feet* the path of suffering trod 1525
Till at thy *feet* in triumph 2138
Till at thy *feet* we lay it down 235
Till we meet at Jesus' *feet* 556
To follow till my falt'ring *feet* 1818
To guide the *feet* that own 1186
To his *feet* thy tribute bring 1618
We at his *feet* may fall 47
We, at thy *feet* pour forth our song 642
When my *feet* stumble 1656
When tyrant *feet* are trampling 1281
While at thy *feet* we bend 723
Yea, at his *feet* we're playing 1535

FELL

Never *fell* so sweet a song 1272

FELLOW

On earth is not his *fellow* 19

FELLOWSHIP

But one great *fellowship* of love 919
Fellowship with him possessing 2032
I have a *fellowship* with hearts 443
May *fellowship* increase 56
Of that enduring *fellowship* 1379
One Christian *fellowship* of love 1652
The *fellowship* of kindred minds 232
The *fellowship* with noble souls 2162
Then in *fellowship* sweet we will sit 2266
Whose joyous *fellowship* we share 1388

FELT

And *felt* thy presence here 15
Felt in the movement of 784
Felt the sharp and piercing sword 140
I *felt* its weight and guilt 1001
I have *felt* his presence 835
Nothing *felt* but doubts 1775
She *felt* that from him virtue 1713
We've *felt* thy touch in sorrow's 2193

FENCE

Securely *fence* our gates 1301

FETTERS

All *fetters* fall 249
Fetters never more will bind us 1738
The iron *fetters* yield 674
My *fetters* fell off, and I anchored 1257
Thy *fetters* break 1514
World *fetters* all be riven 2077

FEUDS

The ancient *feuds* forgetting 284

FEW

The faithful *few* fought bravely 2072

FIELD

And when the *field* is fresh 1327
Field and forest, prairie sod 518
Field and forest, vale and mountain 1040
Field and fountain, moor and 2196
From *field,* and streets and prison 2183
From his *field* shall in that day 359
Lo, all my hearts' *field* 1327
Of many a gloried *field* 46
The *field* is white, the laborers few 686
Though all the *field* should wither 1759
Upon the well-contested *field* 588
When from the *field* of mimic strife 588
Where *field* and forest mark 2277

FIELDS

Across wide *fields* of melting snow 1661
And our *fields* are far apart 2256
But more for *fields* whereon the sun 2185
Fields are white and harvests waiting 679
For even I, in *fields* so broad 396
Henceforth in *fields* of conquest 1057
In *fields* where they lay keeping 1861
Its death-strewn bloody *fields* 1916
Or in the *fields* they dwell 2195
Our *fields* with plenteousness 1185
Over the *fields* of glory 1675
Sweet *fields* beyond the swelling 1966
The *fields* all are ripening 1540
The *fields* are wet with diamond dew 151
The *fields* no longer mourn 2307
The *fields* strive in vain 795
They through the *fields* of Paradise 1936
Up, the ripening *fields* ye see 1783
What parched *fields* refresh 1183
When in from the *fields* came 1941
Where *fields* of strife lie desolate 334
Where golden *fields* spread fair 2120
While *fields* and floods, rocks 1039

FIGHT

A second Adam to the *fight* 1630
And hard the *fight* 492
And now we *fight* the battle 252
Fight, and I must prevail 494
Fight for us, once again 473
Fight manfully onward 2336
Fight, nor think the battle 1560
Fight on, my soul, till death 1256
Fight the fight of faith and love 262
Fight the fight though worn with 1560
Fight then, good soldiers, fight and 378
Fight we the fight with sorrow 574
Fight with sin bravely 378
From the *fight* returned 1117
Firm to the *fight* I stand 567
He who would *fight* for thee on earth 1373
In the *fight* to set men free 580
Little things that *fight* and fail 1103
Sure I must *fight* if I would reign 87
The *fight* is fierce and long 350
Their *fight* with death and sin 1836
We *fight* for truth, we fight for God 1373
Though hot the *fight,* why quit 2295

FIGHTINGS

Fightings and fears within 1046
Fightings without and fears within 93

FIGHTS

But for us *fights* the proper man 19

FIGURES

Figures too great for victory 2182

FILL

And *fill* our fellow-creature's ear 2221
And *fill* them with thy fullness 1334, 1166
And *fill* this place with humbling 364
And *fill* us now with watchful care 2037
And *fill* with all thy love 803
And *fill* with music all the hills 734
Come, *fill* my soul 1462
Come, *fill* our hearts with inward 305
Fill all our hearts with love 1121
Fill all our lives with love 585
Fill and nerve this will of mine 761
Fill brightest hours with labor 2320
Fill each heart with thy love 2187
Fill every part of me with praise 478
Fill me full of heaven 637
Fill me in abundant measure 1516
Fill me just now with power 1829
Fill me now 766
Fill me, Radiancy divine 292
Fill me with joy and strength 1470
Fill me with life anew 250
Fill me with thy grace 978
Fill me with thy hallowed presence 766
Fill me with thy love 70, 222, 1566
Fill me with thyself today 754
Fill my life completely 1006
Fill my soul with joy divine 637
Fill my soul with peace and love 1218
Fill our hearts with heavenly joy 1058
Fill our hearts with joy 1125
Fill our hearts with love 964, 999
Fill our hearts with love divine 1028
Fill our hearts with prayer 579
Fill our hearts with thoughts of Jesus 1118
Fill our hearts with thy rich grace 1181
Fill the heavens with sweet accord 746
Fill thou our hearts with faith 1353
Fill thou our hearts with zeal 1374
Fill thou the cup that brings 721
Fill thy church with light divine 582
Fill up each hour 703
Fill up the roll of thine elect 1836
Fill us with heart—searching 1145
Fill us with love that never 195
Fill us with the light of day 1040

Fill us with thy love and pity 1760
Fill us with thy pow'r again 1092
Fill with power, and fill me now 766
Fill with thy Spirit till all 691
No more will *fill* the air 1
O *fill* me with thy fullness 1170
O *fill* us now, thou living 414
On a *fill*, a curve, a trestle 1076
Shall *fill* his courts with 184
She shall *fill* thy house with 238
So *fill* us all with mutual love 1403
That *fill* the earth with joy 120
That *fill* the heavenly train 1201
Thou canst *fill* me, gracious Spirit 766

FILLED

And *filled* my longing soul 1907
And *filled* the gloom and darkness 1083
And, *filled* with true devotion 515
Daily more *filled* with thee 1407
Filled his temple, and repeated 253, 1673
Filled with grace and sanctity 1051
Filled with his goodness, lost in his love 213
Filled with solace, light, and grace 1588
Filled with thy majesty 332
He hath *filled* the garner floor 1619
Thou hast *filled* my heart with 951
When thy heart is *filled* with fear 63

FILLETH

He *filleth* with his fullness 1734

FILLS

Fills my ev'ry longing 2002
Fills my soul with heavenly music 1973
He *fills* and satisfies my longing 2108
He *fills* our eyes, our ears 312
He *fills* the sun with morning light 535
It *fills* and thrills, gives joy 2309
It *fills* the church of God 2228
It *fills* the realms above 150
It *fills* the sinful world 2228
Sweet music *fills* the world abroad 55

FILL'ST

Thou *fill'st* our being's hidden 784

FIND

And *find* a harvest-home 703
And *find* a heaven within 1349
And *find* at last, beneath thy trees 2248
And *find* deliverance 1134
And *find* it ever new 1759
And *find* my heaven in thee 1824
And *find* my joy in duty 770
And *find* thy perfect blessing 2273
And I shall *find* my peace 249
And may we *find* that as our day 728
And none shall *find* his promise 911
And thou shalt *find* thy heart 2151
And we shall *find* our strength for 721
And when we *find* thy blessed mind 84
And you'll *find* that care and trouble 1270
But what to those who *find* 1019
Can never *find*, although they seek 1236
Come and *find* rest unto your soul 1331
Come back and *find* the Savior 1919
E're in thee may *find* its ending 770
Faithful and true would he *find* us 982
Faithful to him will he *find* us 2241
Find in me thine all in all 837
Find our heaven of heavens in thee 655
Find that Jesus is the Life, the Truth 1919
Find the true and upward way 2043
Find their fulfilment, Lord in thee 300
Here *find* the rest of God's own peace 32
How may I *find* the way 1097
I can always *find* a rest 562
I *find*, I walk, I love, but O 879
I *find* myself by hands 2248
If I *find* him, if I follow 119
In Jesus you will *find* 345
Jesus, what didst thou *find* in me 1002
Let us *find* our rest in thee 343, 658
Let us *find* the promised rest 1190
More than all in thee I *find* 994
Nor *find* thee to fail 1546
O my Savior, thou canst *find* 1735
Should *find* a welcome place 1122
That we may *find* in thee pardon 721
There I *find* comfort, and there 2136
Thou shalt *find* the winter's rage 627
Thou shalt *find* thy hopes 991
Thou wilt *find* a solace there 2210
Till it *find* its full fruition 1280
To them that *find* thee All in all 1023
We can *find* our surest rest 716
We *find* him not by seeking long 1891
We our life in him will *find* 64
We sadly *find* at last 1285
We'll *find* for thee a footpath 534
When shall I *find* my willing heart 1458
Where thou wilt *find* sweet relief 353
Where we *find* thee and adore thee 1588
Where we shall *find* peace at thine 959
While he can *find* one humble heart 1589
Wilt thou *find* this one thing 1583
Wouldst thou *find* a refuge 680
You can *find* the heathen nearer 679
You will *find* him your dearest 1331
You will often *find* obstructions 1076

FINDS

Blessed are those whom the Lord *finds* 2241
Finds thought in thy compassion 1325
"He *finds* his life who loseth it," 507

FINGER

Tis written by his *finger* 19

FINISH

And *finish* what we here began 1282
Finish, then, thy new creation 1190

FINISHED

"It is *finished!*" hear him cry 552
That thou has not yet *finished* man 370

'Tis *finished,* all is *finished* 1836
" 'Tis *finished* for eternity!" 2242

FINISHETH

Who *finisheth* in my behalf 166

FIRE

And *fire* thy church with 1440
And *fire* us for the fight 283
By the *fire* of thy chastening 607, 608
Come as the *fire;* and purge our 1776
Fire ascending seeks the sun 1667
Fire, that love might burn 1036
From sacred *fire,* on mountain 1088
His purifying *fire* 1090
In the *fire* the tares to cast 359
Let the *fire* and cloudy pillar 652
My glowing *fire,* my loaf 182
Refining *fire* go through my heart 1021
The *fire* divine their steps 2164
The *fire* that molds and 2183
Thou *fire* so masterful and bright 41
Thou searching, cleansing *fire* 1401
To bring *fire* on earth he came 1695
With thy living *fire* of judgment 1042

FIRED

And *fired* his hope, and nerved 196
Till, *fired* with true devotion 515

FIRES

Let the fierce *fires,* which burn 189
Mid *fires* of evil falling 2251
O not for thee my fading *fires* 1142
The *fires* that rushed on Sinai's 2228
Though passion's *fires* are in 546

FIRMAMENT

The *firmament* displays 1862
The *firmament* to him is for 1862
To spread abroad the *firmament* 81

FIRST-BORN

Now the *first-born* from the dead 288

FIRST-FRUITS

Christ is risen, Christ the *first-fruits* 76
To thee our *first-fruits* give 2167

FISHER

Thou didst the humble *fisher* call 2189

FISHERMEN

Fishermen talk with him 2300
To *fishermen* beside the lake 838

FISHERS

Fishers of men always to be 838
Where the lonely *fishers* 2274

FIT

And *fit* it for the sky 4
And *fit* us by thy grace 1026
And *fit* us for heaven 159
And *fit* us to fulfil 1291
Fit us for perfect rest above 1273
Fit us for the heav'nly clime 219
Fit us for the promised crown 492

FITNESS

All the *fitness* he requireth 358
Nor of *fitness* fondly dream 358

FITTED

Thou soon shalt be *fitted* 1820

FIX

Come, *fix* thy glorious presence 502
Fix in us thy humble dwelling 1190
Fix on his work thy stedfast eye 365
Fix them, Lord, above 1471
He whom I *fix* my hopes upon 1001
That we might *fix* our hearts on thee 1523

FIXED

And *fixed* the starry lights 535
But *fixed* his word, his saving 1666
Fixed on this blissful center 1392
Here *fixed* his loved abode 778

FLAG

Its *flag* can only be unfurled 1202
My *flag* with stars impearled 1224
What though our *flag* in glory 923

FLAME

A *flame* that through the earth 2086
A little *flame* that burneth bright 576
But, keen as lightning *flame* 2147
It doth not *flame* and wane 2183
O for the living *flame* 1785
O God, be with us in the *flame* 189
Love's pure *flame,* and wisdom's 1686

FLAMES

Flames out the sunshine of the great 2262

FLARES

No more shall *flares* and rockets 1275

FLATS

And in between, on the misty *flats* 2101

FLATTER

Some will *flatter* 367

FLED

I have *fled* to my refuge 1477
To Jesus Christ I *fled* for rest 1421

FLEE

And comforts *flee* 27
And shadows *flee* away 16
"*Flee* from woe and danger 52
Flee to thee from day to day 77
To thee alone we *flee* 244
Will ye *flee* in danger's hour 1560

FLEETS

Where the stately *fleets* so swiftly 2274

FLESH

All *flesh* shall come to thee 1631
And all *flesh* shall see the token 363
And my *flesh* in confidence shall rest 570
And our *flesh* in hope shall rest 2299
Flesh and blood control 2153
Flesh or spirit should assail 500
For thy *flesh* is meat indeed 245
If the *flesh*, more dangerous still 963
Let *flesh* retire 386
My *flesh* and heart doth faint 2054
My *flesh* in hope shall rest 2015
My *flesh* longs in a dry parched land 1172
Our *flesh* and sense must be denied 1739
Our very *flesh* and bone 1325
That *flesh* and blood which did in 1630
Though *flesh* and heart should faint 932
To bear what *flesh* would have us shun 559
To shun what *flesh* would choose 559

FLIES

As winter *flies* away 21
Northward *flies* the swallow 1305

FLIGHT

Save all who dare the eagle's *flight* 81
Wing your *flight* o'er all the earth 103
Wings its *flight* to realms of day 66

FLING

Fling open wide the golden gates 1836
Fling wide the portals 1082

FLOAT

Let it *float* skyward and seaward 479
Let it *float* there wide unfurled 1747

FLOATETH

It *floateth* like a banner 1544

FLOATS

And *floats* upon the breeze 149
Floats down from days of yore 21
Lord, while the music round us *floats* 55
See where *floats* the conqu'ring sign 262

FLOCK

A wandering *flock*, and bring 1116
No more the simple *flock* shall bleed 1488
O here with his *flock* the sad Wanderer 236
One *flock* and but one Shepherd 781
Our gathered *flock* thine arms 2030
Still by him the *flock* are fed 356
Thy chosen *flock* to greet 2178
Thy *flock* we are, thy house 2174
We are his *flock*, he doth us feed 57
We'll *flock* around his banner 2230

FLOCKS

Flocks that whiten all the plain 1628
Flocks were sleeping 945
Nor *flocks* nor herds be there 1759
Of *flocks* and herds, of beasts 775
The *flocks* in pastures graze 2081
They to their *flocks*, still praising 298
Watching o'er your *flocks* by night 103
With *flocks* the pastures clothed 410

FLOOD

And he'll *flood* it, O he'll *flood* it 2233
Death's *flood* hath lost his chill 2015
Flood thou our souls, thou presence 422
In *flood*, in flame, in dark 495
In the crimson *flood* 811
Must I not stem the *flood* 87
My sins rolled away in the *flood* 17
Our helper, he, amid the *flood* 12
Thunder like a mighty *flood* 77
Wading deep the dismal *flood* 755
With God's full *flood*, thou givest 410
With thy full *flood* of holiness 314
Yes, he'll *flood* it all on me 2233

FLOODED

Flooded with beauty 385

FLOODS

Across the *floods* of fear 1217
Floods of joy o'er my soul 2211
Floods of light the earth 1272
Hurling *floods* of tyrant wrong 1077
No whelming *floods* shall reach 772
Surely, when *floods* of waters 1314
The *floods* have lifted up 598, 1882
The *floods*, O Lord, have lifted up 1886
The *floods* of deepest anguish 1874
To some are the *floods* of the river 2004
When rising *floods* my soul 1519
Ye *floods* and ocean billows 1936

FLOOD-TIDES

Come, O Lord, like ocean *flood-tides* 331

FLOOR

O for the golden *floor* 1920

FLOURISH

Will *flourish* by and by 1

FLOW

And endless *flow* of pleasures 1377
And started the life-giving *flow* 17
Flow my praise, forever *flow* 1214
Flow still in the prophet's word 1077
Flow thou to every nation 1911
Flow through the world until all 584
In time's resistless *flow* 46
Let them *flow* in ceaseless praise 1816
O precious is the *flow* 2214
When our tears for sin must *flow* 78
Which from thy heart doth *flow* 75

FLOWED

From thee have *flowed*, as from a pleasant 92
O why from his side *flowed* 1974

FLOWER

And from the sod the *flower* 6
As *flower* in field he grows 1798
Each *flower* and tree reposeth 1843
Each little *flower* that opens 68
Flowers with deeper beauties 1195
Frail as summer's *flower* we 1618
It is a *flower* blooming at thy door 1698
Like unto the with'ring *flower* 2319
That childhood's *flower* and manhood's 437
The growing *flower,* the waving tree 1629

FLOWERET

It came a *floweret* bright 1107

FLOWERETS

Many tiny *flowerets* 928

FLOWERS

All the *flowers* are gaily springing 354
And blooming *flowers* greet my 867
And never-withering *flowers* 1966
Fair *flowers* of Paradise extend 376
Flowers bloom below 621
Flowers gay and golden bloom 1293
Flowers of thy heart, O God 2267
For now the *flowers* of Nazareth 1487
In *flowers* along the countryside 1363
In the *flowers,* in the bird song 936
Its *flowers* shortly wither 1193
Like the *flowers* of the field 1998
May I the fragrant *flowers* glean 2085
New-born *flowers* shall burst 2299
Sweet *flowers* and fruits, thy love 1439
That *flowers* with grace divine 321
The *flowers* and fruits that in thee 41
The *flow'rs* of grace appear 1980
The *flow'rs* that withered long ago 1821
Where the *flow'rs* are blooming 403
White *flowers* of love its walls 496
With no *flow'rs* my way 1044

FLOWETH

Perfect, yet it *floweth* 1092

FLOWING

Flowing inland from the sea 331

FLOWS

And *flows* forever through 2248
And often for each other *flows* 232
Around me *flows* thy quickening 856
Ever *flows* thy thirst to assuage 541
The year in beauty *flows* 40
Where *flows* the crystal river 2120

FLUNG

All else is being *flung* away 703

FLY

And *fly* to this most sure relief 1514
Fly abroad, eternal gospel 1554
Let me *fly* to the land of the blest 1503
They *fly* forgotten, as a dream 1375
Why must I either *fly,* or yield 2295

FOAM

Foam glimmered white 476

FOE

Against the *foe* in vales below 413
Against the *foe* prevailing 43
And a *foe* to be met ere the set 1987
And will shield thee from each *foe* 63
Braving each *foe,* escaping 1284
Do not let the *foe* prevail 1147
Every *foe* of man defying 470
For still our ancient *foe* 12
For the *foe,* well we know 1608
I fear no *foe,* with thee at hand 27
If the *foe* be near 989, 1011
Let no *foe* our peace molest 2062
Let not the *foe* of Christ and man 83
Never a *foe* that his eyes cannot 829
Never *foe* can follow 1091
No *foe* alarm me 1674
O'er every *foe* victorious 661
Our great *foe* is baffled 1599
Strong may be the *foe* 2287
Strong to meet the *foe* 1769
The *foe* is stern and eager 350
Though the *foe* may rage 1994
Till every *foe* is vanquished 1786
What *foe* have I to fear 567
What *foe* or what disaster 898
When the *foe* within is killed 2253

FOEMAN

Fierce is our subtle *foeman* 1505

FOEMEN

Like *foemen* in the night 1328

FOES

All her *foes* shall be confounded 2341
All inward *foes* help us destroy 1412
And thou hast been from *foes* 1134, 1376
Are more than the *foes* which assail 164
Are there no *foes* for me to face 87
Backward shall thy *foes* be driven 1577
Fierce our *foes,* and hard 492
Foes may beset me 804
Foes who would molest me 1004
From *foes* without, from ills 650
He is greater than our *foes* 480
Her *foes* in fear are therefore fled 646
Lo! what embattled *foes* 1156
My *foes* are ever near me 1408
No *foes,* no violence I fear 1519
No *foes* shall stay his might 707
Nor *foes* triumph o'er me 2116
Not the *foes* without 1069
Our *foes* are all conquered 1599
Our *foes* repel, our wrongs 1026
Shall all thy *foes* subdue 548
Ten thousand *foes* arise 1256
The *foes* of all things wrong 1291

Thou art in the midst of *foes* 295
Though thy *foes* with power 2126
Through thy great power thy *foes* 50
Thy *foes* are vanquished 49
Thy *foes* might hate, despise 2217
Thy *foes* their ruler own thee 2138
Thy *foes* will rejoice when my sorrow 1512
Till all his *foes* submit 1653
What *foes* and snares surround 1419
Whose are my *foes* to fight 613

FOIL

What but thy grace can *foil* the tempter's 27

FOLD

A great *fold* stands with its portals 1970
And *fold* the hands and acquiesce 174
And *fold* the lambs to 1998
And *fold* them to my bosom 2245
And *fold* your wings 320
Far from the Shepherd's *fold* away 681
Fold me, O *fold* me, close 1266
Fold the young lambs in thy bosom 1014
Fold them in thy gracious arm 1691
O *fold* them closer to thy mercy's breast 99
Returning to the *fold* 348
Then within thy *fold* eternal 1691
To the *fold* of thy embrace 382
When the Shepherd's *fold* is so near by 1970

FOLDED

Folded in his bosom 983

FOLDS

And beneath its *folds,* as soldiers 1994
And *folds* them in his arms 1696
For our use thy *folds* prepare 1683
He *folds* me to his bosom when 2108

FOLIAGE

None in *foliage,* none in blossom 1728

FOLK

Enough to share with loveless *folk* 883
It is Jesus, good *folk* of the village 257
Still the weary *folk* are pining 1042
To his *folk* he'll speak peace 909
We are his *folk,* he doth us feed 57

FOLLIES

For thee all the *follies* of sin 1246
Its *follies,* and its fashions 1193
The hourly *follies* of our lives 209

FOLLOW

And *follow* thee to heaven 1119
And *follow* where thy feet 2270
And we still will *follow* thee 277
And we'll *follow* till we die 2127
And when I *follow* his command 2
As they *follow* their Shepherd 765
But I will *follow* Jesus 1949
Can we not *follow* thee 2044
Dauntless, untired, I *follow* thee 1519
Follow ev'ry hour 969
Follow ev'ry passing day 969
Follow him alway 969
Follow him today 969
Follow his leading, and give 1104
Follow, I will *follow* 969
Follow me, I'll guide thee home 755
Follow, obey him, he asks 2337
Follow the gleam 2110
Follow the path the master trod 2011
Follow thee more nearly 379
Follow to the judgment hall 552
Follow with reverent steps 1319
For I will *follow* Jesus 1949
Gladly *follow* his command 398
Go, Lord, we *follow* thee 2044
How can I *follow* thee 2044
How should we *follow* thee 2044
If you *follow* its guidance 130
I'll *follow* on with all my heart 838
I'll *follow* then my glorious Lord 2016
Jesus, I'll *follow* thee 984
Let us *follow* still thy 988
Let us *follow* the path that our 2113
Only let us *follow* 983
So today, we, too, may *follow* 695
Still *follow* my steps till I meet 1894
Still *follow* thy Lord 1820
That unto those that *follow* me 1387
Then might we *follow* thee 2044
Thou, that we might *follow* 1680
To Bethlehem of fair renown we *follow* 2306
To *follow* truth, and thus to *follow* thee 421
Upward, still upward we'll *follow* 2129
We *follow* him with pure delight 2161
We *follow,* not with fears 1057
We *follow* the Savior and cannot 1909
We *follow* thee and only thee 1951
We *follow* thee from afar 1984
We *follow* till the halls 2149
We *follow* where he leads the way 432
We *follow* where the Master leads 2160
We still will *follow* thee 277
We will *follow* calm and fearless 989
We will *follow,* ever ready 988
We will *follow* Jesus 480
We will *follow* the steps 1815
Who *follow,* gain the goal 1526
Who'll *follow* the banner 1987
Would you *follow* the will of the risen 694
Yet we would *follow* thee 2044

FOLLOWED

And they *followed* the right, for Jesus' 875
Followed the world in my selfish 1015
From Olivet they *followed* 763
I rose, went forth, and *followed* thee 94
Though thou hast *followed* thy 1015

FOLLOWER

A *follower* of the Lamb 87
His faithful *follower* I would be 702

FOLLOWERS

And thus to all his *followers* spoke 2133
Followers of thy holiness 752
To all thy tempted *followers* 1714

FOLLOWING

And, *following* their incarnate 530

FOLLOWS

He *follows* in his train 1931
He *follows* our footsteps 2055
He patiently *follows* their footsteps 698
If only he *follows* the flag 1987
Who *follows* in his train 1930, 1931
Who *follows* in their train 1931

FOOD

And by this *food*, so awful and so sweet 99
And verily have *food* 1707
Be our immortal *food* 1716-165
Food from labor, rest from toil 1665
God's gift to man, our daily *food* 11
Her *food* I'll greatly bless 2205
The *food* I eat, the clothes 1141
The *food* unpriced 1327
Thou on earth our *Food*, our *Stay* 77
What *food* luxurious loads the board 89
With *food* celestial feedeth 1876
With heavenly *Food* supported 244

FOOLISH

Where the *foolish* see no God 296

FOOLS

And we are *fools* and blind 1794
Nor *fools* stand in thy sight 527, 1176
We are *fools* and slight 1797

FOOT

Down at the *foot* of Calvary 25
Foot it bravely 367
He will not let thy *foot* 885
Till, where'er man's *foot* 1049

FOOTPRINTS

And all thy *footprints* shine 534
Footprints of Jesus that make 1815

FOOTSTEP

And with faithful *footstep* 988

FOOTSTEPS

And all their *footsteps* guide 744
And his *footsteps* follow still 863
And let the Lord his *footsteps* guide 400
And our *footsteps* guideth 1180
And then the Bridegroom's coming *footsteps* 1352
Causing my *footsteps* from God 1262
Footsteps of faithfulness 2129
His *footsteps* cannot err 1901
In his *footsteps* tread 1114
In their *footsteps* will we tread 485
Let not my slippery *footsteps* slide 176
Our *footsteps* hath attended 6
Slow are our *footsteps* 1014
So that my *footsteps* may not slide 1135
Then our straying *footsteps* 1066
There thine unknown *footsteps* 2274
To guide my doubting *footsteps* 869
Thus with quickened *footsteps* 1010
Thy *footsteps* tracing eagerly 300
Walking in *footsteps* of gentle 2129
Walking in his *footsteps* till 403
We still in Jesus' *footsteps* tread 230
Where hallowed *footsteps* never trod 1081

FOOTSTOOL

And at his *footstool* bow 2205
And at thy *footstool* lay 121
At thy *footstool* kneeling 632
Earth thy *footstool*, heaven thy throne 77
Yet still to his *footstool* in prayer 884

FORBID

Are they *forbid* the children's bread 1232
Forbid false love of country, that 1549
Forbid it, Lord, that I should boast 2236
Forbid, O Lord, that hymns of hate 371
"*Forbid* them not, unless ye bear 949

FORCE

Force me to render up my sword 1202
Fresh *force* to do our daily part 1131
Let *force* and greed be overcome 1930
Whose *force* may stay temptation's 1440
With *force* of arms we nothing 19

FORCES

The *forces* at his hand 1505
To show, where earthly *forces* fail 1238

FORDS

The *fords* of sorrow rough 847

FOREFATHERS

Darkling our great *forefathers* went 2177

FOREHEAD

And on thy shining *forehead* 1312

FOREORDAINED

Foreordained the Prince of princes 356

FORERUNNER

Blest *forerunner* of the Lord 1051

FORESIGHT

With *foresight* and with care 534

FOREST

From *forest* and field, from valley 959
Right against the *forest* fence 627

FORESTS

Inland *forests*, dark and dim 1070

FORETASTE

A *foretaste* of Eden this moment we share 172
A glorious *foretaste* here below 575
Have a *foretaste* inly given 1085
O what a *foretaste* of glory divine 213
Sweet *foretaste* of the endless day 654

FORETOLD

Isaiah 'twas *foretold* it 1107

FOREVER

In that far-off sweet *forever* 1991
Where, in all the bright "*forever*" 1712

FORGAVE

But their Father God *forgave* them 611

FORGET

And I will not *forget* thy law 789
But cans't thou, Lord, *forget* 1325
But they *forget* the mighty God 157
Forget the steps already trod 154
He never will *forget* me 860
He'll not *forget* his little ones 602
I never can *forget* the hour 870
I never can *forget* the voice 870
"I will not *forget* thee," 1808
I would be giving, and *forget* 897
If ever I *forget* thy love 826
Lest I *forget* Gethsemane 1050
Lest I *forget* thine agony 1050
Lest I *forget* thy love for me 1050
Lest I *forget* thy thorn-crowned 1050
Nor him *forget* who left his throne 1514
O ne'er shall I *forget* my home 1569
Shall our hearts *forget* his promise 77
Though I *forget* him 806
We, alas! *forget* too often 1581
With thee conversing, we *forget* 1824
You'll *forget* all your troubles 903

FOREGETFUL

Yes, she may *forgetful* be 672

FORGETS

Forgets his selfish being 1843
He *forgets* not his own 2166

FORGETTING

O may I never be *forgetting* 2140
With thee is no *forgetting* 1089

FORGIVE

All that has been amiss, *forgive* 397
As we *forgive* those done to us 1103
Forgive, and love, and guide me 387
Forgive, forgive, O Lord, we cry 189
"*Forgive* him, O forgive," they cry 113
Forgive me if too close, I lean 848
Forgive me, Lord, for thy dear Son 59
Forgive me, too, Lord Jesus 497
Forgive our transgressions, and teach us 1594
Forgive the guilty past 244
Forgive the secret sins I do not see 901
Forgive the sins I have confessed 901
Forgive the wrong this day we've done 1939
He shall *forgive* thy sins untold 1651
He will *forgive* if they only 1655
He'll *forgive* your transgressions 2058
Lord, *forgive* and save 589
Lord, *forgive* each sinful thought 1685
Master, *forgive* and inspire 705
"My Father, *forgive*." 73
O *forgive* and rescue me 1138

FORGIVEN

And both *forgiven* through thy abounding 2248
Lest we, *forgiven* much, forget 1930

FORGIVENESS

But yet with thee *forgiveness* is 1129
Forgiveness free of evil done 445
Make *forgiveness* feel so sweet 2261
To read *forgiveness* in thine 1780
Unwearied in *forgiveness* 2217

FORGIVES

Who *forgives* all thy transgressions 1472

FORGIVING

Faithful and just art thou, *forgiving* 1276
Forgiving others, take your part 41

FOREGO

Make us for a while *forego* 78

FORGOT

And *forgot* its misery 2254
But though I have him oft *forgot* 153

FORGOTTEN

The one *forgotten* I had cast 888
Will be *forgotten* in that blessed 16

FORM

And *form* one family 557
And *form* our souls for heaven 1119
Come in the viewless *form* 2273
Himself a servant's *form* put on 1842
In human *form* thou speakest 1490
Or ever thou didst *form* the world 1356
Our poor human *form* he took 290
The very dying *form* of one 203
Though in the *form* of God he was 2334
Though the lowliest *form* may veil 1126
What if thy *form* we cannot see 136
Who in their *form* didst send 458

FORMED

And *formed* us men 184
Formed the seas, or built the sky 356
Formed thee for his own abode 541
He *formed* the creatures with his word 877
He *formed* the deeps unknown 337

He *formed* us by his word 337
Or ever thou hadst *formed* the earth 1174
Thou who *formed* the earth's 579
Till Christ is *formed* in all mankind 419
Who *formed* the earth and sky 685

FORMS

And all the *forms* of love 1339
And ancient *forms* of party strife 1662
Confusing *forms* and creeds 1069
In diverse *forms* a common soul 522
Should all the *forms* that men devise 1065
When alluring *forms* are nigh 488
Which *forms* and saves a church 1090
Whose *forms* are bending low 948

FORSAKE

He will not *forsake* 1787
He will not *forsake* you 3
I all for thee *forsake* 247
I'll never, no never, no never *forsake* 776
My Lord doth ne'er *forsake* 867
Should we *forsake* him and our love 2055
That they never may *forsake* thee 1402
Them that *forsake* thee wantonly 2054
We will no more our God *forsake* 329

FORSAKEN

For thou hast ne'er *forsaken* them 1435
For thou hast not *forsaken* them 1887, 1888
Forsaken then by God and man 957
Forsaken thus by all 857
Friendless, *forsaken,* betrayed by all 984
Yet he never has *forsaken* me 65

FORSAKES

He never *forsakes,* he never 472
The rising God *forsakes* the tomb 697

FORSAKINGS

Though *forsakings* and betrayals 2276

FORSOOK

God never yet *forsook* at need 904

FORSPENT

Forspent with love and shame 947

FORTRESS

Her *fortress* is a faithful heart 886
My *fortress* high, my shield 858

FORTUNE

Though dark be the *fortune* on earth 1338

FOUGHT

All the battle *fought* and won 64
Fought for their lives, but gave 2135
Fought the fight, the battle won 289
The battle's *fought,* the race 1705
While others *fought* to win 87

FOUND

And *found* in thee alone 1322
And *found* in thee its life 1202
And *found,* with Joseph and the blessed 298
And I have *found* a mighty arm 303
And I have *found* a treasury 303
And I've *found* a resting-place 562
And when *found* he ever keeps 2126
For I have *found* a Friend 303
For I have *found* there's joy 977
Found it tired and hungry 1198
Found the sheep that went 895
I *found* a home, a rest 1112
I *found* in him a resting place 842
I *found* the Lord of Love 878
I once was lost, but now am *found* 88
If you have *found* him a Savior 908
It was not I that *found* 879
Jesus hath *found* me, happy my 1262
No, I was *found,* of thee 879
O may I then in him be *found* 1244
O may we thus be *found* 2037
On the Rock of Ages *found* 175
There the Lord I *found,* it is 2066
They *found* the Messiah 1650
They *found* thee good and just 1239
'Tis *found* beneath the mercy-seat 511
When Christ has *found* you, tell 830
When they have *found* each other 1880
With him I *found* a home 1112
Yet he *found* me; I beheld 1498

FOUNDATION

Foundation which unmoved shall 1290
No other *foundation* is laid 1958
Nor can her firm *foundation* move 572

FOUNDATIONS

And her *foundations* strong 1539
Deeper than earth's *foundations* 638
Hell's *foundations* quiver 1586
That we, who these *foundations* 1441
When all *foundations* are destroyed 1261

FOUNT

Fount of life, and source of love 663
Fount of love and sanctity 76
Fount of love, Redeemer kind 140
God's the *fount* whence all things 1305
No other *fount* I know 2214
O *Fount* of grace redeeming 1317
The *fount* of beings wondrous sea 1495
The *fount* of heavenly wisdom 283
Thou *Fount* of life 1023, 1409
Thou *Fount* of living fire 1405
Who hast the mystic *fount* of life 422

FOUNTAIN

A *fountain* brimming o'er 1377
A precious *fountain,* there uncovered 2140
At the *fountain;* full and free 759
By St. Agnes' *fountain* 627
Come as thou art to the *fountain* 353

Dear *fountain* of refreshment 489
Foul, I to the *fountain* fly 1671
Fountain for guilt and sin 493
Fountain in life's desert 1005
Fountain of good, all blessing 1367
Fountain of good, and God of love 642
I'm drinking at the *fountain* 431
It springs from the *fountain* 17
Jesus, to that *fountain* of thine 214
May I to that *Fountain* be led 214
O Christ, he is the *fountain* 1923
O precious *fountain;* so rich 402
O precious *fountain;* that saves 402
Silver *fountain;* clearly gushing 104
The *fountain* of eternal life 2079
There a precious *fountain* 986
There's a *fountain* flowing 693
Thou art a cooling *fountain* 1341
Thou art the *fountain* whence 464

FOUNTAINS

For glorious *fountains* of water 959
Fountains for cleansing are flowing 905
Or along by Siloam's *fountains* 1815
Where Afric's sunny *fountains* 512

FOUNTS

The *founts* where he drank 236

FOXES

The *foxes* found rest 2026

FRAGRANCE

Diffusing *fragrance* round 327
Its *fragrance* reached to this heart 1249
Like *fragrance* on the breezes 854
Upon the *fragrance* of the flowers 1927

FRAGRANCY

And *fragrancy* of prayer 1863

FRAMED

He *framed* the globe 1061
Nor *framed* with stones of price 1515

FRANKINCENSE

Frankincense to offer have I 2196

FRAUD

No *fraud,* while thou, my God, are near 1519
Nor *fraud* is found therein 1314

FREE

And *free* them that are doomed 2045
And *free* us from all ills 1299
Free from every earthly stain 1264
Free from sorrow, free from sin 359
Free from the fret of mortal 491
Free our hearts to faith and praise 580
Nothing *free* from taint of ill 342
Now to serve its God is *free* 275
Thine own to be, from sin set *free* 21
Till thou, Redeemer, shouldest *free* 373
We are *free* from death's dark prison 700

FREED

But he *freed* me from them all 895
Freed from sin, that worst of tyrants 1073
Has *freed* our brethren too 1320
Of nations *freed* from war 46

FREEDOM

A day of peace and *freedom* 16
Bringing *freedom,* spreading truth 242
Freedom her bondage breaks 284
Here *freedom* spreads her banner 640
Into thy *freedom,* gladness 1602
Ours, for where *freedom* lives not 2183
Wonderful *freedom* when Christ 2314

FREES

And *frees* us from the accursed 854

FREIGHTED

Freighted with thy sevenfold dower 1516

FRESHNESS

The *freshness* of the fragrant breeze 1461

FRIEND

A *Friend* before the throne of love 2202
A *Friend* to guide when paths 866
A *Friend* who never changes 1988
A loving *Friend* and kind 348
And be to the friendless, a *friend* 1098
And *friend* hold fellowship 888
And he's a *Friend* of mine 2294
And no other *friend* will do 1950
And yet no *Friend* is so meek 2000
Be a *Friend* to me 973
Be my never-failing *Friend* 758
Be thou my *Friend* and Guide 1645
Be with me when no other *friend* 1318
But O my *Friend,* my *Friend* indeed 1255
But this *Friend* will ne'er deceive 1577
Come, tenderest *Friend* 311
Ever be my *Friend* 973
Ever present, truest *Friend,* ever near 755
For he is a *Friend* indeed 2252
For Jesus is a *Friend* of mine 2294
For our *Friend* above is a Friend 1979
Friend and guide, and brother 751
Friend of helpless sinners, hear 973
Friend of sinners, shield 1603
Friend of sinners was his name 1581
Friend of the young who lovest me 1045
Friend to friend unfaithful prove 2341
He is a *Friend* that's well-known 112
He is a kind, compassionate *Friend* 865
He is my truest *Friend* 1896
He is the sinner's *Friend* 866
He's my *Friend* 981
I would be *friend* of all 897
Is this vile world a *friend* to grace 87
Jesus is a *Friend* in need 1581
Jesus is the *Friend* you need 2258
More than *friend* or life to me 2042
My constant *Friend* is he 2296
My *Friend* in trials sore 981

My *Friend,* my *Helper* he became 1016
My *friend* to me his heart 1915
No better *friend* we've had 1535
No *friend* like him in times of deep distress 866
No *friend* like him is so high 2000
No other *friend* can read 820
No other *friend* will do 866
Nor to his *friend* doth hurt 2311
O *friend,* without Jesus 831
O how could I this *Friend* deny 981
Our *Friend,* our Brother, and our Lord 1428
Still the *Friend* of all is he 521
Such a *Friend* is he indeed 2258
The constant *Friend* who thinks 1593
The *friend* who loves me most 898
The Lord almighty is our *Friend* 1064
This *Friend* is always worthy 1988
This is my *Friend,* in whose sweet 1255
Thou loving *Friend,* and Savior 1393
Thou my best and kindest *Friend* 1304
To be a *Friend* to everyone 145
To him, my never-failing *Friend* 1700
To our own eternal *Friend* 64
To the God, the poor man's *Friend* 813
To thee, their *Friend,* who from 1393
Where *friend* holds fellowship 511
With so blest a *Friend* provided 144
Yes, he's a *Friend* of mine 2294
Yet this glorious *Friend* and Brother 1581

FRIENDLESS

"Thou art *friendless,* homeless 939

FRIENDS

All thy false *friends* and thy true 63
And earthly *friends* and hopes 1400
And *friends* betrayed him to his foes 2132
And so, good *friends,* we wish you 918
As *friends* who share the Maker's plan 370
Best of *friends* of all is he 805
Do thy *friends* despise, forsake thee 2210
Earthly *friends* may fail 1577
Earth's *friends* are few 573
For all the *friends* we hold so dear 481
For *friends* and brethren dear 540
For *friends* and teachers—all who 1346
For *friends* who stirred the fragile 1388
For there my *friends* and kindred 786
For troubled, sick and weary *friends* 145
Friends, and home, and all 1775
Friends at his table, priests 466
Friends may oppose me 804
Friends of mine are lost in sin 1056
Friends on earth, and friends above 484
Friends will be there I have loved long 2222
Here loyal *friends* are very rare 1915
My *friends* and kindred nearest 1309
No; for *friends* unseen are near us 2284
O *friends,* in gladness let us sing 2333
Old *friends,* old scenes will lovelier 1273
Other *friends* may fail me, he is still 108
Our earthly *friends* may fail us 1988
Our *friends,* beloved and dearest 1850
The *friends* of Jesus are 97

FRIENDSHIP

And *friendship* spanned 2134
Dearer than any *friendship* 638
Needing his *friendship* so holy 1754
No *friendship* can ever be severed 1870
Old *friendship* knit again 796

FRIENDSHIPS

What knitting severed *friendships* up 1836

FRONT

It may not be at the battle's *front* 955

FROST

Hath sent the hoary *frost* of heav'n 40
His hoary *frost,* his fleecy snow 2307

FROWN

Not a *frown* or a cross 2266
Or bursting *frown* of thunder 2273

FRUIT

All the *fruit* is budding 1305
By ripening *fruit* may we be 2082
For *fruit* of the tree 959
For the *fruit* upon the tree 273
Fruit unto his praise to yield 359
None in *fruit* thy peer may be 1728
Ripened *fruit* not faded leaves 1710
Where no *fruit* appears 1775

FRUITS

And righteous *fruits* abound 83
Bearing the *fruits* of righteousness 1670
Celestial *fruits* on earthly ground 351
Christ the first *fruits* of the holy 663
Fair *fruits* of self-denial 1849
For *fruits* of the garden and field 1298
For the *fruits* of tree and field 1799
For the *fruits* of wood and field 518
May the *fruits* of grace abound 1676
May the *fruits* of thy salvation 1125
That *fruits* of earth shall wake 21
The flowers and *fruits* that in thee 41
The *fruits* of grace belong 958
The *fruits* of labor garnered in 2185
The *fruits* of peace and joy 83
The ripe *fruits* in the garden 68
There *fruits* of heavenly joy 1038
To bring forth *fruits* of love 83

FRUIT-TREES

The *fruit-trees* bow beneath 1164

FULFIL

Fulfil of old thy word 2074
Fulfil thy blessed word 2245
Fulfil thy task sublime 1576
Fulfil to us thine own 2036
I may *fulfil* thy purpose 285

Its patient working doth *fulfil* 1360
My calling to *fulfil* 4

FULFILLED

Fulfilled is all his words 1921
So shall they be *fulfilled* 904
'Tis now *fulfilled* what God 2220

FULLNESS

All *fullness* dwells in him 854
And filled with his *fullness* divine 24
And with thine own *fullness* fill 754
For thy *fullness,* God of grace 1612
Fullness to such a burden is 704
In the *fullness* of this trust 2093
In the *fullness* of thy grace 710
In thee all *fullness* dwelleth 1481
May the Spirit's *fullness* 1036
More of his saving *fullness* see 1216
O, the *fullness* of his love 66
Or the *fullness* of the sea 676
O thou in whom a holy *fullness* dwelleth 422
Since the *fullness* of his love came in 1573
The *fullness* comes to the tasselled corn 1929
The *fullness* of my heart 1142
The *fullness* of thy love 1805
There to an ocean *fullness* 1923
With God's perfect *fullness* 1583

FURLED

That never shall be *furled* 48

FURNACE

In the *furnace* God may prove thee 2341
While in affliction's *furnace* 708

FURNISHED

And *furnished* well with joyful 1232

FURROW

On *furrow* long, in village street 2277

FURROWS

From the *furrows* of the grave 76
Its *furrows* thou dost water 410
On the foaming *furrows* of the restless 2274
When these darkened *furrows* 464

FURY

When the *fury* of disaster 1957

FUTILITIES

The fierce and foul *futilities* 46

FUTURE

All my *future* he doth undertake 2057
And, whate'er the *future* brings 449
Dark the *future,* let thy light 492
Down the dark *future* 37
Future and past subsisting now 146
The *future,* all to us unknown 643
The *future* bright, the past 1274
My *future* is concealed 387

G

GAIN

And every *gain* divine 1311
And *gain* from thy exhaustless store 2221
And turn to *gain* each earthly loss 235
And where the higher *gain* appears 1353
Apart from thee all *gain* is loss 240, 1428
Counting his earthly *gain* as loss 196
For our *gain* he suffered loss 282
For they who *gain* that shore 1977
Into the glorious *gain* of thy cross 1602
My richest *gain* I count but loss 2236
Of selfish greed and fruitless *gain* 82
The *gain* of this one thing all loss 1583
To know no *gain* nor loss 203
Turning all my *gain* to loss 449
We *gain* but things by strain 1359
What they *gain* from thee forever 281

GAINED

He has *gained* the victory 1697
I've almost *gained* my heavenly home 1247
They *gained* the promised rest 530
Who has *gained* the victory 76

GALE

In every high and stormy *gale* 1244
Softer than *gale* at morning prime 2228

GALES

And calming passion's
fierce and stormy *gales* 92

GARB

In dainty *garb* of green 11

GARDEN

And in the *garden* secretly 1630
For me it was in the *garden* 881
In the *garden* of dew-ladened breeze 1268
In the quiet of the *garden* 936
O *garden* of Gethsemane 1324
O the beautiful *garden* of prayer 1989
'Tis the beautiful *garden* of prayer 1989
To the beautiful *garden* of prayer 1989
Within his *garden* fair 11

GARDENER

Christ, the loving *Gardener* 928

GARDENS

Where beautiful *gardens* of roses 1870

GARDEN-SPICES

The *garden-spices* shall spring 1398

GARMENTS

Are your *garments* spotless 693
Aside its *garments* casteth 1297
His *garments* too were in cassia 1249
In *garments* glorious he will come 1249
The *garments* he assumes 1897
Their travel-stained *garments* are all 2004

GARNER

We *garner* it in from the cloudland 1298

GARNERED

Garnered truth of sage and prophet 2318

GATE

A *gate* which opens wide to those 1456
And watchful at his *gate* 2331
At the beautiful *gate* may be watching 18
Christ by the *gate* stands 279
No *gate* of pearl, no branch 2248
No wider is the *gate* 432
"Still by the *gate* I stand 279
That *gate* ajar stands free 1962
That *gate* was left ajar for me 1962
The *gate* of every sense 1301
Then the *gate* of life eternal 2042
This is the *gate* of God 1484
Through the city's open *gate* 144
While mercy's *gate* is open 1962

GATES

All the *gates* of pearl are made 938
And the *gates* of that city appear 1922
And the *gates* of the city 2211
And the *gates* shall never close 938
Bright thy *gates* of pearl 217
Far off from the *gates* of gold 1983
Gates of hell can never 1586

Heaven's *gates* unfold above thee 1325
Its *gates* are open wide 2172
Jerusalem, within thy *gates* 843
O enter, then, his *gates* with praise 57
O for the pearly *gates* of heaven 1920
Pearly *gates* are opened 622
Soon the pearly *gates* will open 1731
The *gates* of brass before him burst 674
The *gates* swing wide to every 1467
Through open *gates* thy power flows 1386
Through the *gates* of the city 2246
To the *gates* of heaven striding 51
Where the *gates* swing outward 1044
Ye *gates,* lift up your heads 2327

GATEWAY

And let their door a *gateway* be 67

GATHER

And *gather* all, by earthly homes 505
And *gather* together the golden grain 1540
And oft as here we *gather* 1529
And thankfully we *gather* 6
And we *gather* to Jesus, our 2093
And we shall *gather,* Savior, with thee 347
But *gather* them all for the home 1540
Gather all the nations in 1033
Gather in the heathen 517
Gather in the outcasts 517
Gather now the sheaves of gold 429
Gather one by one 3
Gather our rival faiths within 522
Gather thou thy people in 359
Gather us like little sunbeams 929
Gather us who seek thy face 382
Gather with the saints at the river 1711
He shall *gather* his chosen people 699
He will *gather,* we will gather 2229
Here we *gather* faith to die 1271
Here we *gather* love to live 1271
Let us *gather* jewels for a crown 1985
Now we may *gather* with our king 263
Silence all, as you *gather* around 257
Up to where they *gather* on the hills 403
We *gather* every day 68
We *gather* here, O Lord 1094
We *gather* here, with hymn and prayer 121
We *gather* in these hallowed walls 32
We shall *gather* round the throne 2256
When we *gather* in the morning 2256

GATHERED

All is safely *gathered* in 359
And by angel-hands be *gathered* 76
And, *gathered* all above 1426
And these have been *gathered* 1298
And we'll be *gathered* home 1421
Gathered by the crystal sea 895
Gathered out of every land 1837
Gathered with thine arms and 633
Proudly you *gathered,* rank on rank 1532
Till, at last, her sons are *gathered* 42
Till we are *gathered* to thy home above 29

GATHERS

Gathers 'round its head 934
He *gathers* the lambs to his bosom 698

GAVE

But when I *gave* to one in need 878
Christ *gave* himself for such as we 1568
For God *gave* up his Son to death 128
For thee I *gave* my life away 836
Gave his life that we might live 1306
Gave speech and strength 2008
Gave up his glory above 531
Gave us every pledge that love 1306
God his beloved Son *gave* 531
He freely *gave,* my life to save 1194
He *gave* Himself for your ransom 531
He *gave* Himself so lovingly 2140
He *gave* Himself to save His own 957
He *gave* His all and knew 1253
He *gave* the blind their sight 1255
He *gave* the seas their bound 337
He *gave* us eyes to see them 68
"I *gave* my life to ransom thee 1822
Jesus, who *gave* Himself for me 1267
Jesus, who *gave* Himself for you 75
Lo, he *gave* his only Son 542
That *gave* the sick man strength 206
That he *gave* his only begotten Son 22
The God who *gave* all worlds that are 151
The hand that *gave* it still supplies 7
To him who *gave* thee powers to sing 155
When Jesus *gave* his all 888
Who *gave* the light its birth 614

GAVEST

And *gavest* light, and life, and peace 418
And those thou *gavest* us to love 514

GAV'ST

As Eve thou *gav'st* to Adam 1944
But *gav'st* him for a world undone 1439
For me thou *gav'st* thy blood to flow 123
Thou *gav'st* thyself for me 2077

GAZE

And *gaze* from Olivet 1325
Here I *gaze* and gaze upon thee 978
My *gaze* fixed on before 2234
O may we *gaze* upon thy Cross 1480
Or *gaze* upon the sky 877
There as we *gaze,* may we become 1480

GAZING

Gazing thus our sins we see 1271

GEM

A precious *gem* of thy right hand 2107

GEMS

Bright *gems* for his crown 2229
Gems of the mountain and pearls 254
Living *gems* at his feet to lay 809
Priceless *gems* to offer 297

GENERATIONS

And *generations* yet unborn 2045
Then coming *generations* will 2005
Through *generations* he shall live 1134
Through long *generations* 37
To endless *generations* 1377

GENTILES

Gentiles and Jews the blest vision 660

GENTLE

They shall be *gentle,* brave 2003
Thou art *gentle,* meek and mild 523

GENTLENESS

That *gentleness* and grace that 2217
Thou hast the true and perfect *gentleness* 828
Thy *gentleness* has made me great 858

GET

Get thee up to the heights 1998
When we all *get* to heaven 1731

GETHSEMANE

For me, in dark *Gethsemane* 123

GHOST

So the Holy *Ghost* is given 1041

GHOSTS

We are the *ghosts* of a valiant war 2285

GIANT

He'll with a *giant* fight 2290

GIANTS

Many *giants,* great and tall 1788

GIFT

All hail, the *gift* of Christ 839
And he who is himself the *gift* 1352
And that a higher *gift* than grace 1630
As Jesus' parting *Gift* is near 1872
But every *gift* surpassing 1879
By thy *gift* of peace restored 486
Even as we, the *gift* from thee 454
For his *gift* a baby small 609
For the glorious *gift* of his love 1992
For the great *gift* of thy Son 273
For the priceless *gift* of freedom 1280
Gift of God to age and youth 243
God's *gift* from highest heaven 762
God's *gift* to man, our daily food 11
Great *gift* of our ascended King 1398
His *gift* of peace on all 1884
How silently, how silently,
the wondrous *gift* 1426
Like Mary's *gift,* let my devotion 2201
My humble *gift* to own 150
Our fervent *gift* receive 1291
That some little *gift* of love 1710
The *gift* of Jesus' love 241
The *gift* of life to all who live 82
The *gift* of salvation through Jesus' 1868
The *gift* of sweet contentment 23
The song is mine, a *gift* of grace 25
This *gift* so divine 139
This wondrous *gift* we own 1879
Thus the *gift* of love sufficed 2017
Thy *gift* of peace on earth 1286
Thy infilling is the *gift* 754
Was e'er a *gift* like the Savior given 2000
When by the *gift* of his infinite 2222
Where, in that *gift* so precious 334
Wonderful *gift* from above 1958

GIFTS

All good *gifts* return with her 2204
All their *gifts* and praise to bring 1570
And daily his *gifts* are to me 623
And *gifts* for prayer 1984
And *gifts* of friendly service bring 1591
And these are *gifts* that even 1947
As they offered *gifts* most rare 129
Bearing *gifts* we traverse afar 2196
Before his *gifts* earth's richest boons 1634
Freely have thy *gifts* been granted 1760
Gifts in differing measure 501
Gifts of heaven to men below 1036
Gifts unto thee we would bring 1717
God's *gifts* you may have squandered 2280
Great *gifts* thou broughtest me 2077
In thy sevenfold *gifts* descend 342
Lord of all *gifts,* to offer thee 67
Of all his *gifts,* the sum and 2118
Of all thy *gifts* from heaven above 642
Such *gifts* will make the lowliest 1453
Ten thousand, thousand precious *gifts* 2223
Than richest *gifts* without them 1947
The *gifts* I owe to Jesus 898
The Spirit, and the *gifts* are ours 12
There are *gifts* of love for the seeking 1979
Thou, who dost all *gifts* impart 1566
Thy dying *gifts* receiving 726
Thy *gifts* are every evening new 1233
Thy *gifts* so free 1689
Thy sacred *gifts* impart 311
'Tis our God, who *gifts* and graces 2288
Vainly with *gifts* would his favor 254
Who dost thy sevenfold *gifts* impart 313
With countless *gifts* of love 1299
With *gifts* his hands are filled 1167
With sevenfold *gifts* of grace 307

GILD

Gild its holy pages 757

GIRD

Christ will *gird* himself 251
Gird each one with the Spirit's sword 1702
Gird me with thy sword 613
Gird on thy mighty sword 338
Gird our lives that they may be 580
Gird thee for the battle 293
Gird those brave souls upon 422
Gird thy heavenly armor on 295
Gird up your loins, as in his sight 2331

Gird up your loins, ye prophet 2075
Gird us for the task that calls us 605
Gird you then for action 1997
Gird you with your armor 1747
Gird your armor on 1769
He will *gird* thee by his pow'r 276
They *gird* the earth with valor 90

GIRDED

And *girded* round with might 1882
And *girded* with praise 1546
But *girded* for our Father's work 1496
He hath *girded* him with might 610
When *girded* right, with holy 1

GIRDS

And *girds* about with might 598
Girds with strength the weak 1634

GIRT

And *girt* about with might 1886
And *girt* about with tenderness 1363
Girt with the love of God 1284

GIVE

Ah, *give* me, Lord, the tender heart 2202
All else, though it first *give* pleasure 1583
All for Jesus thou wilt *give* 42
All to him I freely *give* 70
And *give* a song for tears 388
And *give* an ear unto my voice 1433
And *give* for wild confusion, peace 418
And *give* him the glory 2102
And *give* new strength to fainting 572
And *give* refreshing showers 1659
And *give* thee peace 1885
And *give* them victory o'er 1336
And *give* thy word success 338
And *give* thy workers might 1442
And *give* to God the praise of 708
And *give* to the weary rest 1998
And *give* to them the shelter 595
And *give* up your will 569
And *give* us eyes to see 1777
And *give* us grace through ampler 1353
And *give* us hearts and tongues 1132
And *give* us men to guide 1526
And *give* us strength in every 828
And he will surely *give* you 308
And I will *give* you rest 75
And the least you *give* for Jesus 679
And therefore *give* him praise 1455
And thy Holy Spirit *give* 976
And unto me *give* ear 1321
And will *give* me a throne 1229
But *give* it root in every heart 83
But *give* us grace to stand 1291
Can aught but Jesus *give* him light 156
Come and he'll *give* you rest 1331
Come, *give* your all in gratitude 957
Could *give* the guilty conscience peace 1279
Did'st *give* man food for all 469
Give and to you shall be given 531
Give as 'twas given to you 1601
Give but a ray of peace 821
Give deep humility 1506
Give dreams, O Lord, to me 1383
"*Give* ear to me, ye continents 574
Give ear unto our cry 1524
Give every fettered soul release 397
Give heart and soul and mind 1669
Give him first place 531
Give him his armor, all of light 2050
Give him thanks in humble zeal 294
Give him the best that you have 531
Give him your heart's adoration 531
Give him your loyal devotion 531
Give his angels charge at last 359
Give it and speak of his love 1398
Give life and order, light and love 1398
Give me a faithful heart 1698
Give me a heart to find out 1960
Give me at thy side a place 1612
Give me but Jesus, my Lord 1266
Give me daily bread 621
Give me, Lord, my daily bread 380
Give me on thee to wait 1003
Give me one soul today 1056
Give me the good stout arm 285
Give me the heart to hear 285
Give me the single eye 265
Give me their message 1831
Give me thy easy yoke to bear 417
Give me thy obedient heart 523
Give me thy work to do 406
Give me to bear thy easy yoke 499
Give me to live that higher life 1349
Give my goods the poor to feed 636
Give my heart 933
Give of thy wealth to speed 1551
Give oil of joy for mourning 1497
Give our hearts to thine 970
Give peace, O God, give peace 1369
Give pure happiness in leisure 470
Give rest with all thy saints 2036
Give skill to those who now 1355
Give steadfast wills thy cross 2036
Give such a force of holy thought 465
Give sweeter songs than lips 32
Give thankful hearts thy gifts 2036
Give thanks for all his mercy 791
Give thanks to God, for he 1484
Give thanks to him, the Giver 1843
Give the golden light its birth 233
Give the winds a mighty voice 2169
Give the word, and of the preacher 1686
Give the word in every nation 1136
Give them joys that never end 342
Give them life to live for thee 760
Give them light thy truth to see 760
Give them peace and joy 718
Give them the peace, the courage 2069
Give them thy salvation, Lord 342
Give them virtue's sure reward 342
Give these and then
thy will be done 1171, 1506
Give thine heart, thine all to him 1577
Give those that learn the willing ear 1453

Give those that teach pure hearts 1453
Give thou that peace, O Savior 1692
Give thy gift of charity 744
Give thy peace before we part 440
Give thy strength to serve thy brother 2263
Give to all anxious hearts 383
Give to all who teach and guide 974
Give to each flying minute 2320
Give to gods of wood and stone 1570
Give to him what he gave 1706
Give to me my daily bread 976
Give to our land wise laws 1440
Give to the Lord of lords renown 535
Give to thy sons to bear 1551
Give to thy word impressive 1402
Give to us, o'erladen, rest 744
Give to us peace in our time 607, 608
Give understanding unto me 1826
Give up ourselves through Jesus 329
Give us a conscience bold and good 1468
Give us a conscience quick 189
Give us a purpose true 1468
Give us a respite from our toil 1927
Give us compassion 86
Give us each day our daily bread 1364
Give us grace to lead our children 634
Give us his clear-eyed faith 1374
Give us holy freedom 964, 999
Give us, O God, the strength to build 1397
Give us, O Lord, fresh hopes 1927
"*Give* us our bread from day 161
Give us purity 2049
Give us stout hearts ablaze 525
Give us strength for days to come 711
Give us strength to serve 144
Give us sure faith in darkest 525
Give us that light for which 408
Give us the Bread eternal 2120
Give us the faith that follows on 1780
Give us the mind of Christ 1819
Give us the peace of vision clear 1072
Give us the valiant spirit 1374
Give us thy good, and save 436
Give us thy patience 525
Give us thy Spirit from above 525
Give us thy strength to face 2122
Give us thy vision 1780
Give us to build above the deep 2173
Give us to lie with humble hope 315
Give us, we pray, a loyal heart 785
Give us wisdom, courage 470
Give we the glory and praise 228
Give what is best 1220
Give, what thine eye delights 1171, 1506
Give ye heed to what we say 625
Give ye the glory to the Lord 1486
Give ye to Jehovah the glory 537
Give you vict'ry o'er the foe 2268
Gladly to thee, my Savior, I *give* 584
God calling yet! and shall I *give* 558
God can *give* as we implore 743
God *give* thy wayward children 1072
God *give* us Christian homes 560
He will *give* me grace and glory 814
He will *give* me pleasure 900
He will *give* me victory 714
He will *give* to all the faithful 1060
He will *give* you what is best 561
Heavy-laden, he will *give* you 344
He'll *give* thee strength, whate'er 904
He'll *give* thine heart's desire 1708
Here *give* the troubled conscience 393, 651
Here I *give* my all to thee 800
Here, Lord, I *give* myself away 38
Holy Spirit, *give* us each 757
How Christ will *give* me yonder 1297
I can but *give* the gifts he gave 2310
I *give* myself, or suffer loss 2140
I *give* myself to thee 920, 1104, 2077
I *give* thee back the life I owe 1465
I *give* up every plea beside 1018
I'll *give* my all to Jesus 2213
I'll *give* my life to Jesus 2213
I'll *give* my strength to Jesus 2213
I'll *give* my voice (wealth) 2213
I will be glad and *give* thee thanks 1435
I will ever *give* to thee 652
I will *give* thanks and sing 1242
I will still *give* thee aid 776
I would *give* them to my Savior 1222
I would not *give* the world 1142
If you cannot *give* your thousands 679
"Jesus, I *give* thee my heart 984
Lord, *give* a pure and loving 2170
Lord, *give* ear and acceptation 2111
Lord, *give* me such a faith as this 1348
Lord, *give* the zeal, and give 2170
Lord, *give* thy angels every day 117
Lord, *give* us faith and strength 720
Lord, *give* us faith to know 2170
Lord, *give* us grace that we 1845
Lord, *give* us light thy truth 2170
Lord, *give* us peace and make 828
Lord, I *give* myself to thee 70
Lord Jesus, *give* us grace 2178
Lord, we are thine, we *give* 2200
Loving Savior, thou didst *give* 1197
May I *give* myself to thee 1566
May we *give* thee of our best 1628
Myself to thee entirely *give* 1025
Never *give* up the battle 903
Never *give* up to thy sorrows 1269
Now as we *give* it thee 1175
Now we *give* thee thanks 486
O *give* me grace to follow 1408
O *give* me Samuel's ear (heart, mind) 797
O *give* thine angels charge 9, 706
O *give* thine own sweet rest 1170
O *give* to the name of Jehovah 537
O *give* to us daily our portion 1594
O *give* to us the will to live 2098
O *give* us brother-love 438
O *give* us faith to face 1604
O *give* us hearts to love like thee 2217
O *give* us noble purpose 1505
O *give* us now repose 1927
O *give* us strength in thee 1187
O *give,* we pray, yet more 1948

O God, *give* us the strength to build 1604
O Savior, *give* us then thy grace 1520
Or *give* me a trial too much 1922
Savior, *give* me of thy Spirit 1835
Should *give* his life, my soul 1534
So *give* this child of thine 1406
So *give* us hearts to pray 393
Still *give* us grace to adore 584
That thou shouldst *give* thy life 1562
The Lord doth *give* the blind 1394
The Lord will *give* thee peace 567
Thee, who didst *give* thy flesh 803
Then *give* our hands a touch 1410
Therefore *give* us love 636, 1192
They ever *give* thee praise 783
They *give* strength and cheer 2066
Thou dost *give* thyself to me 1566
Thou shalt thy Spirit *give* 453
Thou wilt *give* peace in thy time 607
Thou wilt *give* us sweet content 42
Thou who dost *give* us daily bread 2120
"To Christ I *give* my all." 2340
To *give,* and give, and give again 151
To *give* or to withhold 39
To thee I *give* myself 173
To thee will I *give* the glory 1411
We *give* our heart's devotion 1464
We *give* our lives with glad 1412
We would *give* our lives to thee 579
What can I *give* him 933
What may I *give* thee, save 2038
Who would not *give* his heart 1367
Yet *give* us strength to trust 1177
Yet what I can I *give* him 933
You can *give* the widow's mite 679

GIVEN

All so freely *given* 1732
As thou hast *given* a place 651
As thou hast *given,* so would we 726
For God hath *given* to love to keep 2163
For thou hast *given* me the peace 844
Hast *given* us joys, tender and true 1236
Have you *giv'n* your life to Jesus 695
Now I've *giv'n* to Jesus everything 2335
Shall we, to whom is *given* 923
Then let all praise be *given* 86
Thou hast *given* me the heritage 1357
Thou hast *given* thy Son to save us 579
Thou who hast *given* me eyes 1960
Thrice blest is he to whom is *given* 617
To Zion shall be *given* 859
What hast thou *giv'n* to me 827
What have I *given* for thee 2077

GIVER

Giver of all gifts, be here 341
Giver of every good and perfect gift 454
Giver of grace for our needs 578
Giver of immortal gladness 1040
O *Giver* of the life within 590
The *Giver* who gladdens our days 1298

GIVES

And *gives* me victory 1247
And *gives* to love the power 1523
And he *gives* them o'er and o'er 981
But *gives* us strength while life 408
But to us he *gives* the keeping 255
Gives exercise to faith and love 2221
Gives himself, the living Bread 356
Gives his body for the feast 142
Gives his sacred blood 142
Gives me his Spirit, a witness 1678
God *gives* us reward 1620
Grace sufficient *gives* his own 71
He *gives* himself unto his own 173
He *gives* his precious life for you 697
He *gives* me joy in place of sorrow 876
He *gives* me love that casts out 876
He *gives* me "oil of joy" 876
He *gives* me strength for ev'ry day 482
He *gives* me sunshine for my shadow 876
He *gives* release, offers you 1617
He *gives* the conquest to the weak 685
He *gives* thee bread from heaven 173
He *gives* them rest, sweet rest 1535
He *gives* to all those heav'nly 155
He *gives* us as our own to share 1078
He *gives* us solace for our grief 791
It *gives* a light to every age 1933
It *gives,* but borrows none 1933
It *gives,* returns a thousand-fold 2087
Something he *gives* you to do 908
That *gives* thee glory, love 100
When the Lord *gives* you his love 908
Who *gives* the lilies clothing 1759
Yea, he *gives* them food 356

GIVEST

And *givest* each his task 1468
And when thou *givest* dreams 1383
More thou *givest* every day 449
Thou *givest* our wishes heavenward 784
Who *givest* all 1175, 1439

GIVETH

And *giveth* me songs in the night 1649
He *giveth* me strength as my day 24

GIV'ST

O God, who *giv'st* the winter's cold 2097
Thou *giv'st* the Spirit's blessed dower 1439

GLAD

And still be *glad* in thee 1541
Be *glad* in the Lord and rejoice 164
Glad for the cause that binds 454
Glad for the crowning gift 454
Glad my eyes and warm my heart 292
Glad thy summons to obey 1125
Glad to learn each holy way 1009
Glad when thy gracious smile 1023
I am so *glad* I have entered in 402
Then are they *glad* because at rest 773
To meet the *glad* with joyful smiles 443

GLADNESS

And *gladness* bring to me of Christ 2309
And *gladness* fills my breast 2238
And *gladness* fills thy days 133
And *gladness* girds each hill 410
And in *gladness* hear thy voice 554
For *gladness* breaks like morning 1057
For the Lord of *gladness* 1004
Gladness in my heart 621
Holier *gladness* ours shall be 500
In *gladness* and in woe 1654
In the *gladness* of God's worship 662
More *gladness* I have found 526
On with singing, *gladness* bringing 2159
The Passover of *gladness* 1854
Then let us all with *gladness* 1418
There is *gladness* in my soul today 1980, 2001
Watching in *gladness* and not 982
With *gladness* we confess 391

GLANCE

And naked to thy *glance* 1428
Then let a kindling *glance* 1184
Thy kind but searching *glance* 136

GLANCES

Forward be our *glances* cast 64

GLARE

From the *glare* of noon-day 730

GLEAM

Broader and brighter the *gleam* 1550
Each *gleam* of truth a glowing spark 1088
Gleam, ye starry train 282
How *gleam* the watch-fires 301
Some softening *gleam* of love 1273
Thou silver moon with softer *gleam* 41

GLEAMED

They *gleamed* on this wonderful night 1095

GLEAMINGS

And *gleamings* of eternal joy 2048

GLEAMS

But before us *gleams* the vision 1760
For Pisgah *gleams* of newer 2162
Now *gleams* at last upon our 1443
Rain, and dew, and *gleams* of glory 76

GLEAN

We *glean* it from meadow 1298

GLIMMER

From the dawn's first *glimmer* 451

GLIMPSE

Just one *glimpse* of him in glory 1731
O if this *glimpse* of love 234, 1805
One *glimpse* of Jesus and all 506
To take a *glimpse* within the veil 1038
When I caught a *glimpse* of heav'n 25

GLINTS

Soft *glints* of light 1088

GLOBE

About the *globe* from zone to zone 816

GLOOM

Chasing far the *gloom* and terror 2067
From the *gloom* and the darkness 903
From the *gloom* of night, into 1501
Gloom around thee and within 2059
Let me, like Mary, through the *gloom* 1050
'Mid deepest *gloom* and darkest night 156
Shall drive the *gloom* away 1
Shine through the *gloom* and point me 27
The *gloom* is past, and the morn at last 1095
The *gloom* of land and sea is lit 592
Through thickest *gloom* I see 2038
When *gloom* and sorrow compass 2103
Where else might be but *gloom* 1410

GLOOMS

To chase all *glooms* away 120

GLORIES

And shut his *glories* in 1089
But the bright *glories* of thy grace 641
Glories stream from heaven afar 1720
His *glories* shine with beams 1897
How transcendent are thy *glories* 1073
Is Christ the Lord with endless *glories* 16
Its *glories* pass away 27
The brightest *glories* earth can yield 859
The *glories* of my God and King 1351
Then, amid the *glories* 1114
Thy *glories* gild earth's darkest 1965
When shall these *glories* meet our eyes 982
Whose *glories* now with radiance 770
Whose *glories* shine through endless 967

GLORIFIED

He was *glorified* with light 542
In us let God be *glorified* 1174

GLORIFIES

And *glorifies* with duty 1089

GLORIFY

A God to *glorify* 4
Glorify thy name 449
Him *glorify* sun, moon, and stars 1898
Now *glorify* the Son 1401
Thy name shall *glorify* 54

GLORY

A *glory* gilds the sacred page 1933
All *glory* and power, all wisdom 2330
All *glory* and praise to the Lamb 2187
"All *glory* be to God on high 2282
All *glory,* Holy Ghost to thee 100, 1403
All *glory* to God, I'm the child 1229

All *glory* to our risen Head 79, 1937
All *glory* to the dying Lamb 1867
All *glory* to the Father 100, 124
All *glory* to the Son 1403, 1842
All his *glory* hiding 1792
All singing, "*Glory*, glory" 1928
An unremaining *glory* 1377
And, as thy *glory* fills the sky 1362
And *glory* beam from Zion's gates 1026
And *glory* crowns the task 1951
And *glory*, glory dwelleth 1923
And *glory*, laud and praise 585
And *glory* of the star 1891
And *glory* rests on all the ground 771
And *glory* shall ere long appear 587
And *glory* shone around 2282
And his *glory* is flooding my soul 430
And I the *glory* will ascribe 54
And in the coming *glory* 1378
And in the *glory* of thy face 391
And 'mid the *glory* of these days 588
And O may this my *glory* be 967
And the *glory* of his presence 835
And the *glory* of his resurrection 2259
And the *glory* of that vision 835
And thine be the *glory* forever 1594
And to be the *glory* of thy people 1154
And to *glory* take us 990
And to thy *glory* afterward 2054
Around us all his *glory* shall display 298
At the *glory* of thy presence 2019
Be thy *glory* seen on earth 1006
Because the *glory* of their strength 1390
Bright is their *glory* now 1537
But who of *glory* is the King 2327
Calling them to *glory* 622
Did'st hear thy perfect *glory* 9
Did'st yield the *glory* to thy name 49
Eternal *glory* is the goal 912
Eternal *Glory* to thy name 49
Everywhere his *glory* shineth 566
For a *glory* and a covering 541
For *glory*, Lord, to thee belongs 770
For the *glory* of the Lord was passing 2254
For the *glory* of the skies 484
For the *glory* that illumines 1280
For thee the *glory* of my prime 1142
For us his *glory* veiled 2334
Glory all around him 524
Glory and praise! Amen 1366
Glory and praise to Jesus 93
Glory and power, Amen 1366
Glory be to God on high 118, 684
Glory be to him who bought us 543
Glory be to thee, O Lord 543
"*Glory*, blessing, praise eternal!" 543
Glory do ye unto the Lord 1486
Glory find beyond the grave 1553
Glory, glory, thine the glory 1182
Glory, glory, thine the kingdom 1182
Glory, glory, thine the power 1182
Glory in the highest 412
Glory in the highest for this 1792
"*Glory* in the highest glory 684
Glory in the highest I will shout 1790
Glory in thy perfect love 1190
"*Glory*, laud and honor 1586
Glory let creation sing 1619
Glory to God, and praise 1351
"*Glory* to God in the highest" 1330
Glory to God who bids us 1157
Glory to God who thus to man 1157
Glory to his name 402
Glory to our bounteous King 1619
Glory to our Savior giving 992
Glory to the church's King 54
Glory to the heroes 1205
Glory to the King of angels 543
Glory to the King of kings (nations) 543
Glory to the Lamb that's slain 2191
"*Glory* to thee for all the grace 1242
"*Glory* to thee for strength withheld 1242
Glory to their Maker give 1625
God in his *glory* shall appear 2045
God's *glory* be by man extolled 2328
Hallelujah, thine the *glory* 2187
He is thy *glory* and thy strength 1636
He's fairer than the *glory* of the gold 2108
His *glory* broken upon me when 2108
His *glory* has filled my soul 802
His *glory* let the people know 1061
His *glory* tell, his praise proclaim 72
I *glory* in the grace and strength 1224
I only for his *glory* burn 1021
In *glory* and in darkness 1818
In God's eternal *glory* blest 1108
In God my *glory* placed is 1258
In his *glory* they shall share 2241
In the *glory* of God the Father 699
In thee be all our *glory* now 965
In them the Father's *glory* shone 1859
In thy *glory* all transcendent 2018
In whom God's *glory* dwelleth 1490
It will be *glory* then to say 2294
Jesus, be thou our *glory* now 1019
Jesus, to thee be *glory* given 1330
Lamb of God, thy *glory* 1034
Let *glory* from the church arise 1121
Let thy *glory* e'er shine 978
Let thy *glory* shine in this heart 1672
Looking to Jesus till *glory* doth shine 407
Lord, from thine inmost *glory* 1530
Lord, thy *glory* fills the heaven 1178, 1673
May thy *glory* meet our eyes 1676
More of thy *glory*, O my God 1284
My *glory* and my plea 820
Nor let thy *glory* cease 1449
Not unto us: in *glory* 1320
Now above all *glory* raised 1581
Now to *glory* born again 412
O Christ, for thine own *glory* 515
O that will be *glory* for me 2222
Of *glory* that the church shall share 1543
Of Jesus and his *glory* 1830
On high his *glory* raise 1898
Our *glory*, only in the Cross 479
Pride of man and earthly *glory* 3
Round the Lord in *glory* seated 253

Safe to *glory* he will guide thee 1577
That gives thee, *glory*, love 100
That *glory* is ever the highest 1098
That *glory* in our land again 909
That the *glory* of the Lord is passing 2254
That this world's empty *glory* 1830
That where thou art in *glory* 1408
That will be *glory* for me 2222
The apostles' *glory*, let us sing 1859
The future *glory* and the present 1352
The *glory* of his endless fame 958
The *glory* of my brightest days 1240
The *glory* of that love 1090
The *glory* of the kingdom that shall be 1443
The *glory* of thy kingdom show 628
The *glory* shall be all thine own 1659
The *glory* that excelleth 1481
The God of *glory* down to men 1111
The Lord of *glory* dies for men 697
Then sweeping up to *glory* 834
There let it for thy *glory* burn 1521
There saw in *glory* him 91
There with him in *glory* stand 1697
They shall with me in *glory* 2245
Thine is the *glory*, gleaming 467
Thine shall the *glory* be 1050
Thou, my soul's *glory*, joy and crown 427
Though no heavenly *glory* 940
Thy *glory* by the morning star 422
Thy *glory* ever showing 1402
Thy *glory* flames from sun 1155
Thy *glory* is thy childhood's good 67
Thy *glory*, Lord, proclaim 775, 1450
Thy *glory* may I seek 1228
Thy *glory* on our banners shed 1412
Thy *glory* thou hast spread afar 1450
Till *glory* breaks upon my view 7, 1933
Till in *glory*, parted never 1005
Till in his *glory* there is light 2048
Till safe in *glory* my anchor 1266
Till thy *glory* breaks 144
'Tis the *glory* hallelujah Jubilee 1991
To bear the *glory* to its goal 1608
To God be the *glory* 1262
To *glory* in his holy name 533
To him be *glory* given 1307
To his great name be *glory* 6
To our God all *glory* be 1211
To show the *glory* 1578
To thee the *glory* of thy power 453
To thee the *glory* we ascribe 1448
To thy great *glory*, Lord, we place 642
Unto thee be *glory* given 1178, 1673
What a *glory* he sheds on our way 2266
When his *glory* shall be seen 424
When the *glory* dawns, 'tis drawing 1994
Where Christ in *glory* dwelleth 1193
While heaven's *glory* flasheth 937
Who dost now in *glory* 517
Who hast thy *glory* spread afar 775
Whose *glory* shines mirrored 466
With a *glory* in his bosom 1215
With *glory* and with dignity 775
With his Father's *glory* 1830
Yes, and when that world's *glory* 1830
Yours is the *glory* bright 682

GLOW

And *glow* of summer air 1938
By morning *glow*, or evening 1729
For the *glow* of eventide I wait 810
Glow within this heart of mine 761
The *glow* of life decays 1476
This new-born *glow* of faith 1863

GLOWS

And warmer *glows* her light 2097
Bright *glows* amid our joys 2040
For it *glows* with the light of 1989
Glows with thy fire divine 250
Lo! it *glows* in dew-wet grasses 1698
Lo! it *glows* with peace 934
Than *glows* in any earthly sky 1980

GO

Lord, obediently we *go* 277

GOES

If Jesus *goes* with me 954
Onward *goes* the pilgrim band 2067
When my Savior *goes* before me 969
Where *goes* a loyal comrade 1252
Who *goes* there, at the dawn 2285
Yet cheerful he to suffering *goes* 1255

GOING

Going forth with weeping 1771

GOLD

A shining crown of *gold* 11
And *gold* and incense bring 661
Bringing *gold* to Bethlehem 299
Far and near their *gold* is gleaming 429
For *gold* which the mine and the 1298
Gold and serene again dawneth 732
Gold I bring to crown him again 2196
Gold of obedience, and incense 2322
May God thy *gold* refine 1311
More bright than *gold* or gem 1515
Of pure *gold* are fashioned 217
The *gold* and silver, make them thine 1441
They more than *gold*; yea, much 618
Thine the *gold* and thine the silver 1760
We have *gold* for tribute 1984
With *gold* and myrrh and incense 2306

GONE

All who've *gone* astray 517
And now that she has *gone* to heaven 2237
Gone are my sins and all 624
Gone forever parting, weeping 1136
Gone is thy shame 1921
Gone the sun, from the lake 381
I had *gone* astray from the narrow 1501
Is *gone* up in triumph 622
Jesus is *gone* up on high 664
Let him in ere he is *gone* 1996

Our great High Priest hath *gone* 1883
Since all have *gone* astray 1097
There with the loved ones who've *gone* on before 167
They have but *gone* before 2163
We might have *gone* astray 2061
With those who've *gone* on before us 2317

GOOD

All *good* may be had for the asking 553
And all their *good* seems turned 1370
And be thou doing *good* 1708
And future *good* implore 861
But surely it is *good* for me 2054
But the *good* shall live before thee 951
Divinely *good* thou art 311
For why the Lord our God is *good* 57
God *good* and upright is 2116
Good that we have left undone 1179
Him from whom all *good* proceeds 1625
In others' *good* he finds his own 456
Naught of *good* that I have done 2214
Naught but *good* shall e'er betide 1577
O God, of *good* the unfathomable Sea 1367
O, the *good* we all may do 1955
O thou on whom our human *good* 422
Only *good* and only true, God unknown 53
Something of *good,* be born in me 1345
That I thy chosen's *good* may see 532
The *good* I have is from his stores 1112
The *good* that you do brings 907
Though for *good* we render ill 1581
Thy glory is thy children's *good* 67
To visions of a larger *good* 82
Who in all *good* delighteth 44
Yes, yes! be *good* and true 273

GOOD-BYES

No parting yonder, and no sad *good-byes* 1274

GOODNESS

And all his *goodness* show 1636
And each thy *goodness* sings 437
And for thy *goodness* great 1719
And resting on his *goodness* 2296
And with the *goodness* of thy house 1631
Ever reflecting his *goodness* 1030
For his *goodness* bides eternally 1838
God's great *goodness* aye endureth 53
Goodness and mercy all my life 1904
Goodness and mercy ever shall follow 2020
His *goodness* stands approved 777
His *goodness* we'll adore 304
In all *goodness,* now and always 936
In his *goodness* to the righteous 951
Let all thy *goodness* by our minds 465
Let *goodness* and mercy, my bountiful 1894
Let us all thy *goodness* share 2009
No more thy *goodness* grieve 889
O how marvellous thy *goodness* 978
O Lord, thy *goodness* makes me raise 72
O thank him for his *goodness* 43
Of all thy *goodness* I am singing 23
On us thy *goodness* rest 1377
Such *goodness,* Lord, and constant care 1141
The *goodness* must endure 2071
There's a little of his *goodness* in 1957
Thy bounteous *goodness* nourish 585
Thy *goodness* all our hopes shall raise 643
Thy *goodness* and mercy our tongues 2194
Thy *goodness* and thy truth to me 2071
Thy *goodness* in full glory shines 731
Thy matchless *goodness* and thy grace 1451
With *goodness* thou dost crown 410
With thy *goodness* fill my chalice 754
Wherever *goodness* reigneth 1879
Whose *goodness* faileth never 1876
With his *goodness* I am satisfied 2057

GOODS

Goods, honor, children, wife 19
Let *goods* and kindred go 12

GOOD-WILL

Good-will henceforth from heaven 2282

GOSPEL

His *gospel* calls for living men 1593
His *gospel* we'll proclaim 516
Jesus the Savior, this *gospel* to tell 326
Let his *gospel* and his word 1726
Nor shall thy spreading *gospel* 1871
The *gospel* of his grace 197
The *gospel* makes the simple wise 1871
The *gospel* of salvation that Jesus did 853
Their *gospel* of redemption 2072
'Tis for the *gospel* they hunger 1972
To young and old the *gospel* gladness bear 322
We would be faithful to thy *gospel* 762

GOSPEL-TRUMPET

Let the *gospel-trumpet* sound 1136

GOVERNED

Governed by thy only will 752

GOVERNS

He *governs* land and sea 2005

GRACE

All *grace* and glory be to thee 1423
All *grace* and power divine 1481
Almighty God, thy *grace* proclaim 116
Am I in his *grace* abiding 51
And all thy *grace* declare 2071
And all thy *grace* discern 1805
And by his *grace* are striving 1292
And by his *grace* I know 624
And by his *grace* vict'ry o'er 991
And by thy *grace,* I never will 270
And for his *grace* so rich and free 482
And for thy *grace* our love shall be 2161
And *grace* beyond degree 638
And *grace* divine is his 377
And *grace* revive a dying world 1026
And *grace* subdues the pow'r of sin 1739

And *grace* to lead us higher 1920
And *grace* will lead me home 88
And heaven's eternal *grace* 2133
And plenteous *grace* from Christ 2096
And this thy *grace* must give 1148
And through the *grace* he gives 260
And thy refreshing *grace* 125
Are you fully trusting in his *grace* 693
Blessing his *grace* eternally 1670
But we thy *grace* receive 455
By adding *grace* to welcomed 839
By *grace* the Comforter comes nigh 2161
By *grace* we, "Abba, Father," cry 2161
By his *grace* I shall not fail 2056
By thy *grace* divine 2287
By thy *grace* forever blest 597
"By thy *grace* we will." 736
Come, Lord, when *grace* hath made 1148
Every *grace* that brings you nigh 358
For all thy *grace* and power 2118
For God, by *grace,* shall dwell in thee 2151
For his *grace* and power are such 330
For his *grace* it is, that daily 1066
For his redeeming *grace* 93
For the wonderful *grace* of Jesus 2315
For thy *grace* and tender mercy 811
Grace of God, so strong 1138
Grace our spirits will deliver 1711
Grace, pardon, life to us extend 452
Grace sufficient gives his own 71
Grace sufficient he will give 2339
Grace taught my soul to pray 631
Grace taught my wandering feet 631
Grace that exceeds our sin 1206
Grace that is greater than all 1206
Grace that will pardon and cleanse 1206
Grace! 'tis a sweet, a charming 1308
Grace to cleanse, and power 1683
Grace to cover all my sin 994
Grace to keep the trusting soul 1573
Grace, which, like the Lord the Giver 541
Jesus, all *grace* supplying 1476
Jesus his *grace* to us accords 263
Knowing thy *grace* o'er us 162
Let *grace* our selfishness 1119
Let that *grace,* now (Lord) like a fetter 340
Let thy spirits' *grace* and power 966, 1012
Long-suffering is thy *grace* 1874
Looking to him for the *grace* freely 2129
Lord, may that *grace* be ours 1537
Lord, give us *grace,* like him 91
Lord, God, whose *grace* has called us 1130
Marvellous, infinite, matchless *grace* 1206
May thy rich *grace* impart 1227
More full of *grace* than I of sin 2202
More of his *grace* to others show 1216
More of thyself, in all thy *grace* 1284
My God, how excellent thy *grace* 731
Needed *grace* he will bestow 2268
Nor yet his *grace* from me 50
O by thy soul-inspiring *grace* 1918
O for *grace* our hearts to soften 1581
O for *grace* to trust him more 2092
O, let thy *grace* inspire my soul 631
O let thy *grace* prevail 434
O, the *grace* that brought it down 2335
O to *grace* how great a debtor 340
Of his *grace* and love appraised 1766
Of wondrous *grace* that brought me 1556
On thy *grace* I rest my plea 554
Only what thy *grace* has taught us 1005
Or who has *grace* so rich and free 641
Perfect is the *grace* that sealed us 2065
Plenteous *grace,* eternal cheer 1766
Plenteous *grace,* with thee is found 994
Quickened by the Spirit's *grace* 127
Rich in *grace,* by sin 542
Rich with the same eternal *grace* 2164
Sending them his *grace* 622
Shed upon us heavenly *grace* 76
Some *grace,* that seeks my heart 1345
Still leading me onward from *grace* 1648
Still our *grace* whate'er befall 2318
Strong to follow in thy *grace* 1687
Such *grace* to mine be given 1536
Surely his *grace* will keep us from falling 504
That by thy *grace* our souls are fed 246
That *grace* and pow'r are in his hand 852
That we may through *grace* eternally 542
The children of thy *grace* 33
The *grace* of God here shone 1846
The *grace* that sought and found 1419
The *grace* those sinners that subdued 2164
The *grace* which all may find 1777
The spirit's interceding *grace* 1714
The three-fold *grace* is said 1944
Then, for thy *grace* to grow 593
There is *grace* and pow'r in 1954
There is *grace* for all the lowly 1573
There is *grace* to help in our time 1979
These are the firm knit bonds of *grace* 14
Thine is the *grace* of freedom 1312
Thou by whose *grace* alone we live 2036
Through *grace* he lifted me 926
Through *grace* he will lead me 701
Through *grace* set me apart 134
Through the *grace* of Jesus 925
Thy all-abounding *grace* has banished 391
Thy *grace* alone can save us 244
Thy *grace* and love in me 1082
Thy *grace* has taught me 60
Thy *grace* impart; in time to be 496
Thy *grace,* O father, give 1423
Thy quickening *grace* bestow 83
Thy reigning *grace* I sing 1035
Thy saving *grace* impart 1497
Till by thy *grace* I see thy holy 2020
Till *grace* the sightless eyes 1322
'Tis *grace* that brought me safe 88
'Tis *grace* that makes us free 234, 1805
To thy little ones, Lord, may such *grace* 765
To us and ours, O God of *grace* 1590
To us thy saving *grace* extend 452
Transformed by his wonderful *grace* 17
Triumphant in his *grace* 1339
Triumphant through *grace* I shall some 1868

'Twas *grace* that gave me to the Lamb 631
'Twas *grace* that taught my heart 88
'Twas *grace* that wrote my name 631
'Twas *grace* which kept me 631
We too will his *grace* implore 611
We with thee, by *grace* co-workers 1049
What but thy *grace* can foil 27
What strange, surprising *grace* is this 1122
When by his *grace* I shall look 2222
When, by thy *grace,* the victory's won 702
When through wonderful *grace* 809
While for thy *grace,* Lord, their voices 1538
Will ye not his *grace* receive 1736
With all its *grace,* is given 1869
With all lowly *grace* 1173
With all thy glorious *grace* 2037
With all thy pard'ning *grace* 26
With every *grace* endued 1845
With *grace* on his brow 953
With quickening and confirming *grace* 364
With thy *grace* our triumphs 1160
Wonderful *grace,* all-sufficient 2315
Wonderful *grace* of my wonderful King 2314
Wonderful the matchless *grace* of Jesus 2315

GRACES

And dost his sevenfold *graces* 1439
And more *graces* for the good 1999
Be all thy *graces* now outpoured 317
New *graces* ever gaining 1341
To make our *graces* grow 393

GRAIN

As *grain* once scattered on 469
Then the harvest *grain* 1620

GRAINS

Little *grains* of sand 1101
Yet *grains* of wheat; before they grow 1948

GRANDEUR

For the *grandeur* of thy nature 1214
Of thy *grandeur* and thy beauty 2019
Thy *grandeur* in the march of night 591

GRANT

All Gracious! *grant* to those who bear 1186
Amen, Lord Jesus, *grant* our prayer 473
And *grant,* as morning grows 505
And *grant* that I may be 1053
And *grant* the glad new song 1863
And *grant* the grace of holy fear 2170
And *grant* us grace to look 312
And *grant* us, in thy love 325
And *grant* us, Lord, thy blessing 1342
And *grant* us nevermore to part 99
But, weeping, *grant* us faith 374
Father, *grant* thy wearied one 2253
God *grant* us grace that height 2332
God *grant* you courage to carry 378
Grant forgiveness unto me 2227
Grant, God, a triumph not too dear 2182
Grant, Lord, that hope of seeing thee 2189
Grant, Lord, when I from death 545
Grant me an assurance 1772
Grant me now my supplication 1498
Grant me the cleansing 1266
Grant me the filial awe 889
Grant me to see the brightness 1239
Grant me thy power, boundless 1829
Grant me thy voice to hear 1423
Grant, O Christ, that we may overcome 2049
Grant, O grant, our hope's fruition 1760
Grant one poor sinner more 1137
Grant our burdened heart 1036
Grant our womanhood may be 634
Grant patience, rest, and kind relief 1509
Grant peace on earth, and after 1162
Grant that all may seek and find 1181
Grant that all we, who here 1441
Grant that I never part, Savior 1828
Grant that knowledge, still increasing 1160
Grant that our daily toil 1934
Grant that they may see thy wonders 2274
Grant that we fall not from 1920
Grant that we will never vainly 1092
Grant that we with them thy 2275
Grant that with true and faithful 2011
Grant the mercy we implore 538
Grant them the joy 1473
Grant them the peace which 1473
Grant them thy truth, that they 1162
Grant them who watch the gleam of 1294
Grant thine own abiding peace 1036
Grant those who turn for healing 2069
Grant thy grace, and we shall be 742
Grant thy sustaining arm 463
Grant to little children 1302
Grant to them thy dearest 974
Grant to us a deep compassion 974
Grant to us each that greater wealth 588
Grant to us now a refreshing 1981
Grant, too, that they my need 1410
Grant us, as we come to die 739
Grant us, blessed Trinity 78
Grant us courage 580
Grant us, dear Lord, from evil ways 1812, 1478
Grant us, every closing day 739
Grant us, Holy Ghost, we pray 357
Grant us in all our thoughts 1819
Grant us in our latter years 739
Grant us, like him, with heart-felt awe 1522
Grant us, Lord, who cry to thee 744
Grant us that way to 2023
Grant us the joy that works no ill 1508
Grant us, the life eternal 642
Grant us the purpose, ribbed 2173
Grant us the seeing heart 1508
Grant us the skill to aid 389
Grant us the Spirit's quickening light 1090
Grant us the strength to labor 2173
Grant us the will to fashion 2173
Grant us thine impress, we pray 1694
Grant us thy help till backward 1162
Grant us thy illumination 743
Grant us thy peace 1326
Grant us thy peace through this 1679

Grant us thy peace throughout 1679
Grant us thy peace upon 1679
Grant us thy sustaining graces 988
Grant us thy truth to make 1155
Grant us to find, with reverent mind 1417
Grant us to join thy harvest home 712
Grant us to know and serve 1398
Grant us to march among 1130
Grant us to mourn for deeds 374
Grant us we pray, who thus explore 1294
Grant us who breathe and are akin 1508
Grant us wisdom, grant us courage 580
Grant us with all thy blessed 195
Grant we may not faint 500
Grant we may thy footsteps follow 634
Grant when our race is ended 1317
Holy Jesus, *grant* us tears 1145
Like unto Lydia *grant*, we plead 1094
Lord *grant* that we aright 1052
Lord, *grant* thy servants who implore 1523
Lord, *grant* to us remission 1415
O *grant* enduring worth until 2198
O *grant* that nothing in my soul 1025
O *grant* the consummation 1481
O *grant* the grace that hath 463
O *grant* us light that we may learn 1389
O *grant* us light that we may see 1389
O *grant* us peace, almighty Lord 1524
O *grant* us power to pray 1171, 1506
O *grant* us so to use thy grace 307
O *grant* us still in thee 1495
O *grant* us then that Cross 124
So *grant* the precious things 1146
Yea, *grant* us the fruition 1415
Yet *grant* us, Lord, the seeing eye 1508

GRANTS

And *grants* his name to know 1869
And *grants* the prisoner sweet 911
He *grants* the soul again 1759

GRAPES

The *grapes* to store 396

GRASP

Grasp it, thyself, O my God 1834
Here *grasp* with firmer hand 727

GRASPED

Who *grasped* a nation's fate 368

GRASS

As the new-mown *grass* for rain 1686
In the rustling *grass* I hear 2012
In waving *grass*, and ocean spray 1384
Of springing *grass*, of tender buds 107

GRASSES

For *grasses* of upland and lowland 1298
Or *grasses* in the meadows 1377

GRATITUDE

And *gratitude* my voice 1700
Deep *gratitude* and praise 1422
If my *gratitude* I'd show 1710
The *gratitude* declare 2223
Yet, beating through our *gratitude* 2040

GRAVE

From the furrows of the *grave* 76
From the *grave* "His own" will bring 664
Grave thine image there 461
He from out the *grave* arose 1109
He who from the *grave* arose 1697
Mary did her Savior, for the *grave* 141
No more to fear the *grave* 13
Now no more the *grave* 142
The *grave* and death are conquered 1418
The *grave* and hell are captive 1883
The *grave* as little as my bed 59
The *grave* had not the pow'r 260
The *grave* has lost its triumph 1083
The *grave* hath lost its prey 1895
The *grave* no more has power 1418
Up from the *grave* he arose 1200
When the *grave* must claim its own 2253
Who is he, that from the *grave* 2286

GRAVEN

And *graven* on thy hand 859
Graven in our hearts forever 1005
'Tis *graven* on my heart that thou 2035

GRAY

Gray wakes to green again 732

GREAT

Because thou art exceeding *great* 54
How *great* is God almighty 68
How *great* thou art 1437

GREATNESS

And of thy *greatness* I will tell 1451
His *greatness* he for us abased 2334
His *greatness* is beyond our thought 1451
I am finding out the *greatness* 978
O, the *greatness* of thy mercy 2019
Thy *greatness* shelt'ring me 893
Thy very *greatness* is a rest 100

GREED

Of selfish *greed*, and fruitless gain 82, 1079
Till *greed* and hate shall cease 419

GREET

And *greet* from all their holy heights 272
And *greet* the blood-besprinkled bands 324
And we *greet* in his cradle 1995
Greet the morrow 945
Greet the sunlight every day 1066
I *greet* thy going forth 1863
Or *greet* the morning on his knees 1088
Our song shall rise to *greet* thee 33
Thee we *greet* triumphant now 289
Till thou shalt *greet* in heaven 1371
Yea, Lord, we *greet* thee 1330

GREETING

And a hallelujah *greeting* 2297

GREETINGS

O then what raptured *greetings* 1836

GREETS

Lovingly he *greets* thee 2010

GREW

And as he *grew* to be a man 145
And *grew* in grace with man and 2326
From his loving, *grew* his praise 2255
It *grew* so straight, and tall, and fair 11

GRIEF

And by each *grief* and pain 1952
And *grief*, and fear and care 417
Bearing *grief*, reproach and shame 521
But through all *grief* distressing 1729
Come, and for every *grief* 348
From woman's *grief*, man's burdened 2270
Grief and guilt my soul oppress 554
Grief cannot come too near 1949
Grief nor pain, nor any sorrow 71
Grief was his close companion 426
Here for *grief* reward thee double 271
I *grief* and trouble found 857
In *grief* he renders consolation 1915
Like some fresh *grief* from yesterday 816
My *grief* a burden long has been 1001
My *grief* is in the dullness 2119
Never was *grief* like thine 1255
Not a *grief* or a loss 2266
One with the *grief* that trembles unto 421
Should *grief* or sickness waste away 1231
So shall *grief* be gone forever 1772
There *grief* is turned to pleasure 252
There is never a *grief* or loss 1976
There is no *grief* in heaven 1977
To me in *grief* he comfort gives 851
What though in lonely *grief* 1231
When for my deep *grief* I find no 401
With *grief* and shame weighed 1475

GRIEFS

All thy *griefs* he carried 1114
And *griefs* and torments 1235
And *griefs* around me spread 1227
And sharing not our *griefs*, no joy 438
By thy human *griefs* and fears 269
For the *griefs* that wrought 1813
From all our *griefs* and fears, O Lord 767
Griefs like billows o'er me 2056
He all my *griefs* has taken 834
My childhood *griefs* and trials 2237
O by thy *griefs* that dreadful day 206
Our brethren's *griefs* to share 1119
Out of my stony *griefs*, Bethel 1265
Yet all the *griefs* he felt were ours 426

GRIEVE

And *grieve* thou hast no more 200
Do not *grieve* for their coming 903
He would *grieve* to look upon 1118
How I would *grieve* my mother 2237
It shall *grieve* and be weary no more 1098
Like thee, O Lord, to *grieve* 2217
O *grieve* not then the Spirit 1337

GRIEVED

Grieved him by a thousand falls 395

GRIEVES

And that which *grieves* thee most 534
Brethren come; from all that *grieves* you 52

GRIM

Look *grim* as e'er he will 19

GROAN

By thy spirit's parting *groan* 1761
Let us *groan* thine inward groaning 339
The cries of agony, the endless *groan* 37
To hear the prisoner's mourning *groan* 2045

GROANED

Groaned in Satan's deadly chain 275
He *groaned* upon the tree 38

GROPE

And *grope* in faithless strife 1843
To those who *grope* for light 1169
Which here I *grope* for 291
Who *grope* as in the night 149

GROUND

All other *ground* is sinking sand 1244
And from the *ground* there blossoms red 1465
Like seed into the *ground* 83

GROUNDED

Eternally he *grounded* 853
Grounded firm and deep 2298

GROVES

Ye *groves* that wave in spring 1936

GROW

And fain would *grow* in holiness 1398
And *grow* it shall, our glorious 2177
And we *grow* quiet, folded 464
Grow in all things like our 519
Grow to bless the nations 1101
Lest they *grow* self-satisfied 2264
Let us not *grow* weary 1985
May we daily *grow* in grace 756
May we *grow* from day to day 1009
May we *grow* like thee 930
Shall *grow*, with living waters 1116
That all may *grow* in grace 244
To *grow* more loving every day 468
We *grow* not wise by struggling 1359

GROWETH

Perfect yet it *groweth* 1091

GROWS

All secretly it *grows* 2076
It *grows* in splendor more and more 2087
No slacker *grows* the fight 432
Sweeter it *grows*, glory 1559
Swift *grows* the light for us 732
Wider *grows* the kingdom 501

GROWTH

Trusting the Lord for *growth* 1693

GUARDIAN

Be the *Guardian* of our way 1683
Be thou our *Guardian*, thou our 310
Jesus, thou our *Guardian* be 2062
Lord Jesus is my *Guardian* 1928
Since thou art my *guardian* 1894
Thy *guardian* never sleeps 885

GUARDIANS

We are *guardians* of an altar 487

GUERDON

Our *guerdon* and our guide 1951
Our *guerdon* lies beyond the hour 1794
What his *guerdon* here 119

GUESS

For none can *guess* its grace 306

GUEST

A gracious willing *Guest* 1589
An ever-welcome *guest* 1872
Gentle, awful, holy *Guest* 346
Here every welcome *guest* 1805
High heavens, Lord, our hearts' dear *Guest* 1386
Jesus, be thou our *Guest* 261
O rich man's *Guest*, be with us 1491
O Savior, *Guest* most bounteous 1344
Of so divine a *Guest* 1259
Thou the heart's most precious *Guest* 744
Thou the soul's most welcome *Guest* 342

GUESTS

And where among the *guests* there never 1393
For the *guests* are bidden 1114
Nay, let us be thy *guests* 335
When Jesus deigns the *guests* to meet 89

GUIDANCE

For their *guidance* hath he made 1626
Thy *guidance* and goodness through 1372

GUIDE

A *Guide*, a Comforter bequeathed 1589
A wonderful *Guide* is he 2190
An awful *Guide*, in smoke 2239
And *guide* and guard us through 1807
And *guide* me in thy perfect 2039
And *guide* me o'er death's river 178
And *guide* my steps, that I 1367
And *guide*, of all our ways 162
And *guide* our steps forever 2289
And *guide* the steps of all 1527
And *guide* them in the homeward 1466
And *guide* us through the night 2168
And *guide* us when perplexed 1299
And *guide* where we should go 515
Be her Savior, Lord, and *Guide* 1033
Be thou my *Guide* 319
Be thou my *Guide*, my Strength 2083
Be thou our *Guide* 586
Beside us to *guide* us 2166
But he'll *guide* us with his eye 2127
Ever be thou our *Guide* 1715
For he has been the *Guide* of this 2104
Forever he will *guide* 885
Guide and guard my erring 1612
Guide and guard us with 711
Guide me, help me in thy way 1703
Guide me through a world of sin 1612
Guide me with counsel sweet 1645
Guide of heroes, saints and sages 950
Guide of the nations 421
Guide our way, and feed us 1792
Guide, subdue our wayward will 161
Guide the steps that go astray 342
Guide their steps 718
Guide them by the brightness 517
Guide them, Jew and Gentile 517
Guide them, lead them, go 718
Guide them on their way 517
Guide thou our ordered lives 1819
Guide thou our way 1934
Guide unfailing, strength eternal 2318
Guide us by thy hand 988, 989, 1011
Guide us, O God, with swift 525
Guide us safely to the shore 1603
Guide us to seek the things 456
Guide us to the better land 2284
Guide us to the realms of day 2009
Guide us to thy perfect light 2196
Guide where our infant Redeemer 254
He is my *Guide* 847
He is our *Guide* and Friend 304
He will *guide* thee here below 63
He will *guide* 'till the day 2000
He will *guide* you if you look 1048
He'll *guide* me to my "Father's house," 1097
I am trusting thee to *guide* me 811
I will *guide* me with mine eye 1642
If he be my *Guide* 119
Jesu, be thou our constant *Guide* 1067
Let him be thy *Guide* 1820
Lord Jesu, be our *Guide* 1977
May *guide* us on our way 1301
May she *guide* the poor and blind 1033
Mine thou art to *guide* 738
None but he shall *guide* us 983
Now *guide* us and send us 2004
O *guide* me, love me 901

O let them *guide* me to the brink 893
O Savior, *guide* me 434
O Savior, if thou wilt be my *Guide* 955
Only do thou *guide* my way 1690
Our *Guide* and Chart, wherein 1052
Shall *guide* me and control 932
Tenderest *Guide,* in ways of 436
The only *guide* of age and youth 2087
They *guide* me through the night 1896
Thou hast been their constant *Guide* 760
Thou hitherto hast been my *Guide* 2035
Thou our *Guide* and Helper be 1603
Thou promised *Guide* divine 1401
Through him, our only *Guide* 1380
Thus will I let him *guide* me 2216
'Twill *guide* thee to a better home 1823
Where thou art *Guide* 313
Wherever he may *guide* me 921
Who, like thyself, my *Guide* 27
Who through life has been my *Guide* 66

GUIDED

And *guided* by thy hand 1438
And *guided* where I go 443
As thou hast *guided* us 1287
Guided along the road 1276
Guided by a star 517
Guided on their journey 2300
Safely has he *guided* 2061

GUIDES

And *guides* from afar 1081
And he whose wisdom *guides* 6
Guides a sparrow 1214
He *guides* us with unerring 1282
Into his faithful keeping who *guides* 534
My Savior *guides* with a loving 867
The Lord who *guides* my steps 858

GUIDING

Holy, through the Spirit's *guiding* 2065

GUILE

Guile nor violence can harm 271

GUILT

But now my *guilt* is washed away 624
May we ne'er by *guilt* depressed 233
My *guilt* and my need his great love 122
My *guilt* was all upon him 1422
Or *guilt* the soul oppress 75
The *guilt* is ours, but grace is thine 648
The *guilt* on my conscience too heavy 1278
Thy *guilt* assumes, thy fetters 1514
When from my *guilt* and grief 926
When I've no *guilt* to wash away 967

GUILT-BURDENED

Guilt-burdened and lowly I bow 719

GUILTY

Guilty and vile as I could be 2316
Though we are *guilty,* thou art 397
Who was the *guilty* 35

GULF

O, the mighty *gulf* that God did span 2335
So be the *gulf* between 2134

GUSHING

Gushing from the Rock before me 66

H

HABITATION

In his secret *habitation* 271
'Round each *habitation* hovering 541
The *habitation* of thy house 1043
What a peaceful *habitation* 1041

HABITATIONS

In our fairer *habitations* 1553

HAIL

All *hail* the Lord's Anointed 48
And *hail* him as thy matchless King 376
And we *hail* it with a song 1993
Great God, we *hail* the sacred day 2304
Hail Eternal Hope on high 288
Hail him, all his happy subjects 1073
Hail him, *hail* him, highest archangels 1616
Hail him, *hail* him, Jesus the crucified 1616
Hail him, Prince of Peace 1833
Hail his triumph now 2204
Hail in the time appointed 661
Hail quiet spirit, bringing peace 654
Hail the Bright and Morning Star 1109
Hail th' incarnate Deity 675
Hail, the King of Glory 524
Hail the Lord of all the skies 282
Hail thee as conqueror 1157
Hail, thou agonizing Savior 659
Hail to the millions from bondage 660
Happier all who *hail* his coming 369
I *hail* the glory dawning 1923
I *hail* thy kind return 2203
In thee, O Christ, we *hail* the dawn 1088
We *hail* thee by the shore 751
We *hail* thee, God, before whose 559
We *hail* thee now, O Jesu 2168
We *hail* thine august majesty 1507

HAILS

As he *hails* their wreck 474

HALL

Let fall on every college *hall* 84

HALLELUJAH

Hallelujah for the Cross 1846
Hallelujah, what a Savior 1203
I'll sing the *hallelujah* song 23

HALLOW

Hallow all our lives, O Lord 486
Hallow each thought, let all 1519

HALLOWED

Hallowed forever, Lord, to thee 307
We gather in these *hallowed* walls 32

HALLS

And let these *halls* thy temple 1899
In lordly *halls* of state 923

HALT

Ne'er shall *halt* till swells 1109

HAND

And by his *hand* the rising 1334
And every willing *hand* 1529
And lo, his *hand* is scarred 1414
As thy prosp'ring *hand* hath blest 1628
As with a mother's tender *hand* 1729
At my right *hand* I throne thee 2138
At thy right *hand* are pleasures 570
Be thou at my right *hand* 494
Beneath whose awful *hand* we hold 583
But the *hand* that bled to make 1242
But thy right *hand,* thy powerful 1448
By his *hand* I'm safely led 895
By his own *hand* he leadeth me 702
Even from your humble *hand* the bread 399
God's own *hand* shall guide 980
His full *hand* supplies their need 1074
His gracious *hand* shall wipe 1111
His *hand* shall heal thine inward 1657
His *hand* the wonders wrought 2012
His *hand* will hold the helm 2234
His right *hand* me embraces 854
How wise, how strong his *hand* 536
Into thy *hand* of love I would 1245
My Father's *hand* will never cause 1260
My *hand* in his own 701
My *hand* in the hand that 1868
My *hand* in thine hold fast 434
My *hand* shall wipe away 836
My *hand* thou holdest in thy 932

My Savior is at *hand* 898
No *hand* thy *hand* may feel 2303
O let thy *hand* be still upon 2131
O let thy *hand* support me 1519
On ev'ry *hand* the foe 413
One soft *hand* blinds our eyes 2029
Should the *hand* of sorrow press 589
Still 'tis God's *hand* that leadeth 702
Still 'tis his *hand* that leadeth 702
Strong in his own right *hand* 1156
Strong the *hand* stretched out 2065
That *hand* which bears all nature 777
The clean of *hand*, the pure 1857
The *hand* my cruel sins 1260
The *hand* of Jesus turned 1194
The *hand* of my Savior I see 1868
The *hand* that gave it still 1933
The *hand* that gives the flowers 1933
"The *hand* that made us is divine" 1932
The *hand* that rocks the cradle 2005
The *hand* that shaped the rose 40
The *hand* that was wounded 1868
The *hand* that wrought wonders 1868
Though his *hand* may lead me 108
Thou that, by the right *hand* 1135
Thy *hand* hast led across 593
Thy *hand* I can trace 1648
Thy *hand* in all things 856
Thy *hand* moves, but in blessing 534
Thy *hand* the victory won 1525
Thy *hand* unseen amidst us 67
Thy *hand* upholds me, lest 858
Thy *hand* was heavy on me 772
Thy *hand* we see 586
Thy loving *hand* will guide 815
Thy right *hand* doth sustain 1172
To his guiding *hand* forever 801
When his guiding *hand* I cannot 259
Where his own *hand* prepareth 1193
Whose *hand* contains the earth 1865
Willing both in *hand* and heart 2047
With his *hand* to lead me 403
With tender *hand* he lifted 926
With thy right *hand* to help 2072
Without thy guiding *hand* we go 1059

HANDIWORK

Thy *handiwork* on high 1450

HANDIWORKS

Our *handiworks* established thou 1541

HANDS

And from the *hands* of all that hate us 215
And O, his certain *hands* 818
And stronger far the clasped *hands* 592
And that which the *hands* cannot 1298
And the uplifting of my *hands* 1433
And to his Father's *hands* 1940
And to thy Father's *hands* thy soul 1176
And weak our *hands* that labor 1906
For *hands* to serve and arms 1346
Her *hands* reach out in service 1591
His are the *hands* stretched out 2201
If other *hands* should hold the key 564
In his *hands* he gently bears us 1618
In my *hands* I'll hold thee 1808
In thy gracious *hands* I am 523
Join *hands*, then, brothers of the faith 919
Let eager *hands* restore 309
Little *hands* are folded 1102
Little *hands*, whose wondrous skill 1570
"Lord, whence are thy *hands* so rent 1983
May our *hands* ne'er falter when 2198
O, the kindly *hands* of Jesus 1709
O wounded *hands* of Jesus 1124
The *hands* that touched the blind 206
The *hands* that work preserve 1441
The little *hands* some work 1536
Then in his *hands* the cup 2133
Thy *hands* have brought salvation 1065
To *hands* that work and eyes 2008
When the *hands* are on them laid 760
While his *hands* uphold and guide 71
With *hands* and feet of healing 818

HANG

Did *hang* in pain and bleed 206
They *hang* the trumpet in the hall 198

HANGETH

Who is this that *hangeth* dying 2288

HANGS

Hangs my helpless soul on thee 994
Hangs o'er all the thirsty land 1695

HAPPINESS

No true, lasting *happiness* ever 1583
Soon their *happiness* shall see 277

HAPPY

And be *happy* all thy days 238
Happy in her loving service 238
I in my Savior am *happy* and blest 213

HARBINGER

Harbinger of human race 655

HARBOR

In heaven's *harbor* my anchor 2235
In this safe *harbor* from the tossing 1533
O happy *harbor* of the saints 960
Someone far from *harbor* you may 399
'Tis better than in *harbor* 1533
Trying now to make the *harbor* 255

HARDNESS

The *hardness* from my heart 889

HARDSHIPS

Through *hardships* and through danger 145

HARK

Hark, hark, thy Savior 680
Hark, the glad celestial hymn 746
Hark, those bursts of acclamation 1117

Hark, those loud triumphant 1117
Hark to the advent voice 733

HARM

From *harm* and danger keep 1679
No *harm* can befall with 1894
No *harm* from him can come to me 848, 2310
To do us *harm,* or cause us fear 117
To us no *harm* shall now come nigh 43

HARMONY

For the mystic *harmony* 484
So rich in heaven's *harmony* 25

HARMS

He *harms* us not a whit 19

HARP

And on the *harp* with solemn sound 2112
And with his *harp* at eventide 2179
Let no *harp* remain unstrung 280
My *harp* I will employ 1483
With *harp,* and with organ 164

HARPERS

The white-robed *harpers* of the sky 1592

HARPS

And with *harps* in our hands 896
Angel *harps* forever ringing 101
Glory, glory, how the loud *harps* ring 1664
Harping on their *harps* hosannas 669
Loud our golden *harps* shall sound 684
Sweet are the *harps* in golden music 349
Sweet *harps* they hold 117
Then, with golden *harps* we'll sing 673
What ringing of a thousand *harps* 1836

HARSHNESS

No *harshness* hast thou 828

HARVEST

"Almost persuaded," *harvest* is past 85
By and by the *harvest* 1771
Earth's broad *harvest* whitens 409
Lord of *harvest,* grant that we 359
Lord of *harvest,* let there be 1783
Mighty shall the *harvest* be 1783
O thou who art Lord of the *harvest* 1298
Of the holy *harvest* field 76
Oft his *harvest* reapeth 1668
The *harvest* eyes only can gather 1298
The *harvest* is certainly coming 1770
The *harvest* is passing away 2293
The *harvest,* love's new day 191
The *harvest* waves in the breezy 1929
Thine be the *harvest* by and by 1169
Thine is the *harvest,* thine the seed 1146
Waiting for the *harvest,* and the time 1771

HARVESTS

Not alone for bounteous *harvests* 1280
Where *harvests* ripen, thou art there 1439

HASTE

And, Lord, *haste* the day 2249
Christians, *haste* your vows to pay 288
Haste, haste to bring him laud 2215
Haste, let us lay our gifts before 2200
Haste the Fount of Life to meet 1766
Haste the joyous jubilee 280
Haste thee away, why wilt thou stay 353
Haste, then, my brother, no time 2068
Haste, then, on from grace 980
Haste to prepare the way 982
Haste to the reaping 705
Haste to your heavenly Father's throne 777
Haste with joy our vows to pay 288
Haste with joy to preach the word 141
Then *haste,* my soul, the song 770
We *haste* to Zion's hill 786

HASTEN

And *hasten,* Lord, that perfect day 520
And *hasten* to thy glorious day 499
Come, then let us *hasten* yonder 52
Early *hasten* to the tomb 552
Hasten away while in sorrow 1972
"*Hasten,* mortals, and adore him 684
Hasten now, his word obey 692
Hasten so glad and free 804
Hasten the joyful day 1332
Hasten to Bethlehem's stall 302
I will *hasten* to him 804
May we *hasten* on 1680
O *hasten* and take control 1208
Savior, *hasten* thine appearing 673
The welcome dawn, will *hasten* on 1
Then *hasten* for time is fast speeding 1925
With such I *hasten* to the place 1806

HASTING

Hasting from afar 517

HATE

And, armed with cruel *hate* 12
And *hate* what we deplore 1184
"For *hate* is strong, and mocks 840
I *hate* the sins that made thee mourn 1347
I *hate* the work of sinners 1557
Nor *hate,* nor pride's caprice 2134
Our *hate* and want of charity 2122
Some will *hate* thee, some will love 367
Stern in their *hate,* oppose 1156
Where *hate* and lust and falsehood 1549

HATES

From war's embattled *hates* 1916

HATH

He *hath* the words of life 804
It *hath* no need of suns 1965

HATRED

And ev'ry *hatred* slain 1930
Free from all *hatred,* sin, and strife 1670
Let *hatred* and tormenting fear 1646

More and more must *hatred* cease 1069
We would be one in *hatred* of all 421
When shall all *hatred* cease 2073

HATREDS

And human *hatreds* flee before 138

HAUNTED

Prayerless, anxious, vainly *haunted* 2224

HAUNTS

In *haunts* of wretchedness and need 2270

HAVE

All I am, or *have*, or hope 259
All I *have* I bring to Jesus 1688
All that I *have* and am 291, 855, 920
All that I *have* is now no longer 855
All that I *have*, or am, or hope 139
All that we *have* is thine 2167
All that we *have* we hither bring 1984
All we *have* to offer 1680
And I shall *have* my song to sing 882
And there *have* I, as vile as he 1961
But he will *have* a right 2290
But what *have* I, a little child 1928
For we *have* no hope nor Savior 42
Have God to be his Guide 704
I *have* a Christ who satisfies 832
I *have* a Father who hears (warns) 831
I *have* a home prepared for me 832
I *have* a Master so gentle 831
I *have* a Savior who keeps 831
I *have* a Shepherd who leads (seeks) 831
I *have* a witness bright 832
I *have* believed him 831
I *have* no earthly store 869
I *have* no help but thine 727
I *have* the smiling of his face 564
I shall not *have* to go alone 867
I would not *have* the restless will 443
Let him *have* his way with thee 2324
Let me *have* thy loving mind 523
Must I *have* a heart of shame 1710
They *have* their day, and cease 1797
They that *have* my spirit 983
Thou canst *have* the crown abiding 175
Though you *have* only a smile 907
We *have* but faith, we cannot 1797
We *have* no refuge, none on earth 1289
We shall *have* thy fellowship 1919
Whate'er we *have*, whate'er we are 200
Whom *have* I in the heavens 2054
Why should I *have* a care 2294
Would we *have* one sorrow less 2089
Yes, thou shalt surely *have* my heart 722
You *have* the gospel with others 908

HAVEN

Down to the *haven* call your 1550
Into its long-sought *haven* 180
So to the *haven* he them brings 773
That *haven* of repose to find 97
The *haven* is not far away 2146
The "*Haven* of Rest" is my Lord 1257
You from the *haven* under 1550

HEAD

All glory to our risen *Head* 79
And following our triumphant *Head* 97
Calmly, with reverend grace, thy *head* inclining 98
Head of thy church beneath 1579
His *head* with radiant glories 1201
If Christ, my *Head* and Master 898
Lay but my fainting *head* 98
Light's all lovely fountain *head* 1516
Low lies his *head* with the beasts 254
My *head* thou dost with oil 1904
O bleeding *head!* so wounded 1476
O Christ, the church's *head* 1175
Our exalted *Head* to be 664
Thou, our *Head*, who throned 1760
Till soon it raised its *head* 11
Up unto thee, our living *Head* 1029
While softly on my *head* thy 2020
Would he devote that sacred *Head* 38

HEADS

And on their *heads* are crowns of gold 117
"Lift up your *heads* 1366
The *heads* that guide endue 1441
While our *heads* in prayer 759
Will their *heads* before him wave 76

HEAL

For thou alone canst *heal* 392
Heal every wound 311
Heal my wounded, bleeding heart 745
Heal my wounded, broken spirit 1607
Heal our differences of old 1182
Heal our wounds, our strength 342
Heal our wrongs and help 1760
Heal the heart broken by sorrow 705
Heal the sick, and lead the blind 994
Heal the sick, the captive free 1181
Heal the wounded of its pain 744
Heal their diseases 458
Heal thou sin's every smart 1828
Heal thou the sickness 650
None else could *heal* all our souls' 2000
Where'er they *heal* the maimed 471
Whom Christ doth *heal* 278

HEALED

And, *healed* of our diseases 515
And, when bleeding, *healed* thy wound 672
Come and be *healed* at the fountain 353
For he *healed* their sick at even 2254
He *healed* the broken-hearted 1556
Thy cruel wounds my own have *healed* 60

HEALING

The *healing* of his seamless dress 2181
With *healing* and hope for my 1868

HEALS

He *heals* all my diseases 854
Heals his wounds 794

HEALTH

And his saving *health* proclaim 357
And thy saving *health* extend 582
For *health* and strength thy mercy 1518
For *health* preserved, for strength 1807
Health to the sick in mind 2051
His saving *health* abroad 1486
My *health,* and friends, and parents 1141
Our *health* while we are living 283
That so what *health* and strength 576
Thou art my *health,* my joy 1284
Thou art our *health* and salvation 584
Thy saving *health* to us afford 587

HEAP

Heap on his sacred altar 1734

HEAR

All that fear God, come, *hear* 50
All ye who *hear,* now to his temple 1637
Almighty Father, *hear* our cry 314
America, God *hear* the prayer 1608
And *hear* it still from day to day 303
And *hear* me when I call 176
And *hear* the angels sing 948
And *hear* the birds sing sweetly 1437
And *hear* the blood speak, that hath 73
And *hear* the brook, and feel 1437
And *hear* the Judge pronounce our name 1111
And *hear* thee inly speak 1824
And *hear* us while we pray 188, 1927
And it thou art well-pleased to *hear* 329
And Jesus, listening, can *hear* 1980
And yet I *hear* a voice that bids 2201
But *hear* the angels' warning 247
But *hear* us from thy lofty throne 648
But now I *hear* thee and rejoice 1140
But thou wilt *hear* my cry 1376
Can they *hear* without a preacher 1136
Dids't *hear* thy perfect glory sung 9
Don't you *hear* the angels singing 1991
Don't you *hear* the bells now 1991
Dost thou *hear* him say 680
Father and Redeemer, *hear* 492
First let me *hear* how the children 1831
First let me *hear,* then sing to thee 604
Happy all who *hear* the message 369
Hark! we *hear* a distant music 1993
He can *hear* the great petition 561
Hear a far voice calling 939
Hear a voice saying: "I know you not" 1758
Hear and bless our prayers 220
Hear and heal me now, I pray 717
Hear and heed our humble cry 1179
Hear and receive thy church's 1162
Hear, for Jesus intercedes 2121
Hear, forgive and save 589
Hear him, ye deaf! his praise 1351
Hear his pledge of coming aid 276
Hear his loving voice calling still 565
Hear his soul-burdened plea 1268
Hear in this solemn evening hour 136
Hear me, and from thy dwelling place 1002
Hear me, blest Savior, when I call 1002
Hear me, for thy Spirit pleads 2121
Hear my cry, my King and God 710
Hear my humble cry 1607
Hear my loud cry, my King 527
Hear my solemn vow 225
Hear now his loving call 348
Hear, O Christ, my heart's petition 1688
Hear, O Christ, the praises 563
Hear, O *hear* him calling 565
Hear, O *hear* me, humbly crying 1516
Hear, O *hear* our supplication 743
Hear, O *hear* us, when we pray 1683
Hear, O Lord, our litany 416
Hear our cry 929
Hear our song of thankfulness 492
Hear the Bride saying, "no longer 807
Hear the cry thy people raises 220
Hear the glad message, why will 1605
Hear the harps resounding 600
Hear the hymn ascending 600
Hear the melody ringing 850
Hear the news of Jesus' birth 1100
Hear the prayer our hearts uplift 538
Hear the trumpet blow 736
Hear the trusty Pilot calling 1642
Hear the victors who o'ercame 295
Hear the voice that entreats you 2058
Hear their sighs and count 1775
Hear them while they make their moan 488
Hear then in love, O Lord 2260
Hear thou our prayer, the spoken and 436
Hear thou the prayer I make 1220
Hear thou the songs and prayers 1384
Hear thou thy servants when they call 372
Hear thy children's cry 964, 999
Hear us, for these our squadrons 595
Hear us from thy bright abode 1159
Hear us from thy throne 2009
Hear us, Godhead infinite 470
Hear us, holy Jesu 962
Hear us, holy Jesus 1009
Hear us Jesus, as we meet 2047
Hear us now, and hear us then 1161
Hear us, O Lord, on thy providence 1611
Hear us, we humbly pray 2051
Hear us when we call 1769
Hear we no beat of drums 732
Hear we not thy golden bells 2018
Hear we the Shepherd's voice 682
"*Hear* what the Lord hath done for me" 2221
Hear, while I lift imploring hands 1455
Hear you now his loving 1996
I can *hear* the voice of Jesus 805
I can *hear* their triumph-song 507
I *hear,* and bow me to the rod 2202
I *hear* far voices out of darkness 2248
I *hear* his voice of cheer 874
I *hear* it from yon cross 1284
I *hear* my people crying 1943

I *hear* once more the voice of Christ 37
I *hear* the blessed Savior call 888
I *hear* the gathering sound 1914
I *hear* the noise of wings 1247
I *hear* the rolling thunder 1437
I *hear* thee, and I answer 1533
I *hear* thy summons to that distant 1533
I *hear* thy whisper in my heart 333
I shall *hear* their song of love 1499
Jesu, *hear* and save 1161
Jesus, *hear* and save 589
Let him often *hear* your voice 2268
Let me *hear* thee softly speaking 1672
Let none *hear* you idly saying 679
Let them *hear* thy tender call 488
Lord, I was deaf; I could not *hear* 1140
Lord, thou shalt early *hear* my voice 527
May *hear*, so calm and plain 1854
May I *hear* him say, "Well done" 1710
May I *hear* thee say to me 1007
Most beautiful I *hear* 13
Now *hear* me while I pray 1227
Now ye *hear* of endless bliss 625
O *hear* and heed the prophet's cry 2155
O *hear* his sweet call 504
O *hear* his tender pleading 2280
O *hear* my earnest cry 1455
O *hear* our call 1175
O *hear* our cry, good Christian 149
O *hear* our urgent cry 490
O *hear* the angel voices 1399
O *hear* the angels sing 796
O *hear* the voice of Jesus 1867
O *hear* us for our native land 1185
O *hear* us, for to thee we cry 1371
O *hear* us when we cry to thee 418
O *hear* ye brave, the sound that moves 516
O let me *hear* thee speaking 1408
O may we ever *hear* thy voice 2025
O might I *hear* thy heavenly tongue 190
O that I could *hear* him saying 805
Only let me *hear* thy call 997
Pray we that thou wilt *hear* us 92
Savior, let them *hear* thee 1703
Savior, may we *hear* thy call 970
Shall we *hear* a welcome 2297
Somehow I *hear* him gently call 1756
Soon shall ye *hear* him say 147
Still *hear* and do thy sovereign will 1105
Still wilt not *hear* thine inner God 2130
Surely he will *hear* my call 1218
That I may *hear* thee whisper, "Child 387
The Lord me will not *hear* 50
Thou who wilt *hear* our prayer 1373
'Tis thy Savior, *hear* his word 672
We faintly *hear*, we dimly see 1428
We *hear*, and henceforth heed 1819
We *hear* it each and all 956
We *hear*, O Lord; thy truth reveal 1094
We *hear* that Spirit's call 197
We *hear* the call; in dreams 1496
We *hear* the Christmas angels 1426
We *hear* the throb of surging 1467
We *hear* the words so gently spoken 1316
We *hear* thy call 917, 2181
We *hear* thy true voice leading 1880
We *hear* thy word 591
We *hear* within, the solemn voice 1539
We shall *hear* the wondrous strain 2191
We soon shall *hear* the archangel's 1653
When they *hear* the battle-cry 2264
Whene'er we *hear* that glorious word 428
While I *hear* him say to me 259
Wilt *hear* us when we pray 121
Wilt thou not *hear* us while we 2030
Ye *hear* his words so blest 70

HEARD

As who had *heard* God's message 1532
Be there *heard* the Christmas anthem 369
But surely God hath *heard* my voice 50
But truly, God has *heard* my voice 361
Hast thou not *heard* 685
Have you *heard* the Master's call 695
Have *heard* and known his voice 303
He *heard* me when I cried 1455
Heard him pray, "Forgive them 1498
Heard him yield his soul to God 1263
Heard me pray 415
Heard the angels singing 524
Heard the story 945
I have *heard* thine accent 798
I *heard* my mother kindly say 870
Is *heard* the cry of anguish 923
One *heard* him calling long ago 196
She *heard* her own name spoken 626
The cries of clashing creeds are *heard* 14
Thou hast *heard* me, light is 1703
Till I *heard* a sweet voice 1257
Till late I *heard* my Savior say 1001
We have *heard* the Macedonian call 1985
Where only Christ is *heard* 1350
Who have never even *heard* 1570
Who *heard* the angelic herald's 298

HEARDST

Thou *heardst*, well pleased, the song 1354

HEARER

O thou that *hearer* art of prayer 1631

HEAREST

Thou *hearest* these, the good 1386

HEARETH

Knowing he ever *heareth* my prayer 2148
Whosoever *heareth*, speed the news 1833

HEARKEN

And *hearken* to his word 1547
And *hearken* to thy 1188
At first I would not *hearken* 892
He will *hearken*, he will save 271
Hearken from thy throne on high 1179
That thou may'st *hearken* to my speech 1135
Would not *hearken* to his calls 395

HEARS

God *hears* thy sighs 536
He *hears* and answers prayer 561
He *hears* our plea 791
He *hears* your silent heartful call 2338
Hears thy burdened sigh 987
Hears thy feeblest prayer 987
If he *hears* the raven's cry 1218
The Father *hears* him pray 113
Who *hears* our solemn vow 329
Who *hears* us sing today 626
Zion *hears* the watchmen 2149

HEAR'ST

Thou who *hear'st* each contrite 442

HEART

A broken and a contrite *heart* 31
A broken contrite *heart* 1171
A broken *heart*, a fount 1333
A broken *heart* love's cradle is 1333
A *heart* in every thought renewed 1350
A *heart* from sin, set free 1350
A *heart* resigned, submissive 1350
A *heart* that always feels thy blood 1350
A *heart* that still moves 797
A humble, lowly, contrite *heart* 1350
A life-revering *heart* within 1508
A lowly *heart*, that waits 797
A new and contrite *heart* 75
A wonderful song into my *heart* 25
Ah! sense-bound *heart* and blind 2044
All his *heart* went out to bless 1789
And all her *heart* with joy 2149
All my *heart* to him I give 891
An open *heart* and ear 1094
An open *heart* and hand 14
And a *heart* at leisure from itself 443
And all my *heart* is love 1021
And all the windows of my *heart* 39
And all thy *heart* be filled with 1821
And all ye men of tender *heart* 41
And clean of *heart*, and strong 1608
And every *heart* adore him 1968
And every *heart* be love 2106
And from my stricken *heart* with tears 203
And from thy *heart*, a token, streams 2021
And *heart* that kindled at the zeal 1491
And I my *heart* the closer lock 558
And if my *heart* and flesh are weak 848
And in my *heart* I feel the thrill 2
And in our secret *heart* we name 121
And in your *heart* rings heaven's song 1640
And lest my *heart* should change 434
And let the *heart* of every one 533
And my drooping *heart* he cheers 942
And my *heart* has been filled 864
And my *heart* has slowly trusted 223
And my *heart* shall rejoice 2026
And my *heart* within overflows 1501
And my wistful *heart* said 1498
And O, his *heart* that holds me 818
And of his *heart* the purposes 2329
And pure in *heart*, behold thy beauty 1423
And sad was my *heart*, for I knew 1941
And so my *heart* shall e'er contend 1915
And still his great *heart* yearneth 1556
And the *heart* faint beneath 1794
And the *heart* of the eternal 1767, 1999
And then new *heart* springs up 856
And there, to cleanse the *heart* of man 1921
And tho' my *heart* grows weary 874
And while my *heart* exults with joy 1455
And wild *heart* all aflame 818
And with my *heart*, my voice 1362
And yet to have a purer *heart* 1582
Art greater than our *heart* 1177
As long as this poor *heart* shall beat 23
Be he of every *heart* the Light 1884
Be joyful in the Lord, my *heart* 1729
Because of this my *heart* is glad 570
Before my sinful *heart* was stirred 926
Beneath it the *heart* is still 1583
Bringing to my *heart* pain and woe 214
But above all, the *heart* must bear 1062
But now from the *heart* of joy 613
But oh, this faithless *heart* of mine 1318
But thou my *heart*, awake thee 1297
Calls my *heart* to be his own 53
Come to my *heart*, O thou wonderful 326
Come to my sad, weary *heart* 1742
Come when your *heart* is distrest 1331
Create a clean *heart*, Lord renew 31
Do not let your *heart* be troubled 1270
Down in the human *heart* 1655
Earnest *heart* service give 463
Envious of *heart*, blind-eyed 438
Ever in thy *heart* to stay 963
Ever to thee my *heart* still 1254
Evermore in *heart* and mind 64
Every *heart* be quaking 1004
Every *heart* be thine alone 581
Every *heart* enthrone him 357
For every thirsty, longing *heart* 1924
For heathen *heart* that puts her trust 583
For my *heart* was full of sin 1573
For of my *heart* God is the strength 2054
For once my *heart* was poor 303
For the *heart* and mind's delight 484
For thee alone my *heart* would beat 2302
For within his *heart* of love 2255
For you his *heart* is yearning 2280
Forever on thy burdened *heart* 2217
From all my *heart*, while I may live 123
From *heart* to heart the bright hope 2030
Gracious God, my *heart* renew 554
He to every *heart* brings cheer 1726
He whose *heart* was broken 3
Heart and voice to thee we raise 597
Heart in *heart*, as hand in hand 555, 972
Heart of my own *heart*, whatever befall 177
Here is my *heart!* Commended to thy 724
Here is my *heart!* O Spirit make it 724
Here is my *heart!* Surrendered full 724
Here is my *heart!* Though it be hard 724
Here may my *heart* in peaceful rest 2096
Here's my *heart*, O take and seal it 340

High on his *heart* he will bear it 2322
His evil *heart,* his greed and hate 1381
His father *heart* is good 1896
His *heart* is made of tenderness 2305
His *heart* is touched with 401
His *heart* went out to you 2242
His loving Father *heart* will never 1896
Holy Ghost, each *heart* be filling 446
How my full *heart* will praise him 2246
How my glad *heart* yearns and my 1954
How the *heart* yearningly turns 2136
If in my *heart* I sin regard 50, 361
If in your *heart* you would know 907
If thou, O *heart,* but give thy youth 2226
If you would his *heart* rejoice 2268
If your *heart* keeps right 903
In every *heart* and brain shall 2003
In *heart* and mind ascend 1325
In him rejoice with *heart* and voice 6
"In my *heart* I will enthrone him 1703
In my *heart* there rings a melody 833
In the *heart* he implanteth a song 1976
In whose *heart* are thy ways 783
In your *heart* enthrone him 143
Joining *heart* to *heart* with others 1182
Let all, with *heart* and voice 304
Let but my fainting *heart* be blest 1231
Let each *heart* repeat the strain 280
Let every *heart* leap forth 347
Let ev'ry *heart* obey thy will 49
Let every *heart* prepare him room 1039
Let me with my *heart* today 1085
Let my contrite *heart* rejoice 554
Let my glad *heart,* while it sings 449
Let my *heart* be all thine own 998
Let my youthful *heart* be thine 1690
"Let not your *heart* be troubled" 2296
Let thy *heart* forever be 1766
Long my *heart* has sighed for thee 800
Long my *heart* hath panted 1004
Low in the *heart* faith singeth 464
Making my *heart* in its sorrow 1742
Many dear to my *heart,* over there 1503
May every *heart* confess 1409
Must I have a *heart* of shame 1710
My bounding *heart* shall own 1824
My ever-grateful *heart,* O Lord 2223
My grateful *heart* inspires my tongue 2238
My *heart* alive to keep 1444
My *heart* an altar, and thy 1778
My *heart* and life to him belong 1907
My *heart* be daily nearer thee 1407
My *heart* doth me instruct 570
My *heart* for gladness springs 1723
My *heart* for very joy doth leap 34, 528
My *heart* fulfil its vow 1689
My *heart* has no desire to stay 915
My *heart* I yield without delay 558
My *heart* incline thou not 1433
My *heart* is at the secret source 1242
My *heart* is dead within 869
My *heart* is fixed, no fears 2016
My *heart* is in thy care 1242
My *heart* is pained, nor can it 2033
My *heart* is resting, O my God 1242
My *heart* is so happy 1926
My *heart* is sometimes heavy but 2108
My *heart* is weak and poor 1202
My *heart* may low be laid 921
My *heart,* my life, my all 1822
My *heart* now longs and yearns to go 686
My *heart* o'erflows, for I love him 2272
My *heart* rejoice! my lips, sing 1422
My *heart* restores its borrowed ray 1465
My *heart* shall triumph in 1811
My *heart* to thee entwine 1027
My *heart* unto thy testimonies 1826
My *heart* was free 94
My *heart* was pierced to the core 825
My *heart* with joy is singing 2109
My *heart* with rapture thrills 1225
My *heart* within me thrills 1224
My *heart* yet fearless is 1903
My very *heart* and flesh cry out 783
Near to the *heart* of God 1969
Nearer to thy *heart* of love 1264
No *heart* so dead, but his touch 829
No human *heart* can know 252
No human *heart* could enter 820
No longer then my *heart* shall mourn 1021
No wider than the *heart* is wide 1358
Nor is the least a cheerful *heart* 2223
Nor let thy faithless *heart* despise 1842
Nor yet the haughty *heart* 1557
Not e'en the praising *heart* 478
Now let every *heart* be fed 1028
Now, Lord, let ev'ry waiting *heart* 1031
O deep within my *heart* now shine 1470
O for a *heart* that never sins 1920
O how my *heart* is tempted 865
O let our *heart* and mind 97
O Lord, my God, with all my *heart* 54
O my *heart* in tune be found 184
O my longing *heart* is there 913
O to that *heart* draw nigh 75
Often has my *heart* gone astray 214
On him my *heart* relied 1455
On thee alone their *heart* relies 1432
Opens to you the sacred *heart* 75
Or how his *heart* upon the cross 817
Out of the *heart* of the Father above 326
Over the *heart* of the mourner 181
Over the *heart* of the weary 181
Patient O *heart,* though heavy be 464
Pure in *heart* I still would be 1218
Pure in *heart* may we abide 992
Shrouding *heart* and home 449
So having in each *heart* thy word 1294
So let my *heart* and voice 890
Soon thy *heart* be cold and silent 692
Still be the lone *heart* of anguish 1098
Still to shield this *heart* 1055
Strong in *heart,* and hand, and brain 485
That e'er my *heart* with joy 1569
That *heart* to *heart* more closely 1402
The contrite *heart* 651, 1964
The *heart* can push the sea 1358
The *heart* of all these springs 2183

The *heart* of God revealed 2022
The *heart* that bled and broke 1467
The saddened *heart,* the restless 2029
Then shall my *heart* from earth 2033
There in the *heart* of the wildwood 946
There let my weary *heart* 872
There to my *heart* was the blood 402
This *heart* of mine renew 724
Thou, and thou only, first in my *heart* 177
Though into one *heart* alone may fall 399
Thy *heart* has never known recoil 2270
Thy Spirit touching *heart* and 1169
Thy tender *heart,* redemptive love 1356
'Tis thine, to cleanse the *heart* 315
To come to him now with thy sin-burdened *heart* 1542
To every *heart* of grief and care 239
To lift the *heart* to God above 201
To make thy *heart* his lowly 173
To my *heart,* O enter thou 1588
To the Savior's *heart* I flee 51
To thee my *heart* and soul belong 1002
Until my *heart* is pure 250
Until my very *heart* o'erflow 1170
Upon my *heart,* bestowed by thee 526
We lay it not to *heart* 19
Weary, aching *heart* 352
Weary was our *heart* with waiting 1993
Well may this glowing *heart* 1392
What has thy *heart* decided 1584
What if the poor *heart* complaineth 1098
When *heart* doth fail 168
When on my aching burdened *heart* 1509
When the *heart* by sorrow tried 2253
When the *heart* grows sick with 1957
When the sad *heart* is weary 349
When thy *heart* enfolds a brother 2263
When thy *heart* is filled with fear 63
When thy *heart* is wounded 987
When your *heart* is full of fear 2268
Where every humble, contrite *heart* 927
Where he is in the *heart* 1515
Where'er the gentle *heart* finds 1515
Where'er the *heart* forsook 1515
Which from thy *heart* doth flow 75
While my *heart* thy word obeys 780
While the *heart* is young 1706
While yet the *heart* is young 1706
Whose *heart* is true within 772
Whose *heart* with pity still 1290
Whose secret *heart,* with influence 267
Why should my *heart* be lonely 2296
With a child's glad *heart* of love 1687
With a glad *heart* and free 1144
With a *heart* most kind 3
With a lightened *heart* on the road 864
With a sympathizing *heart* 2093
With all my *heart* I come 1045
With *heart* and voice we all 21
With *heart* content 904
With *heart* sincere and perfect 1557
With humble *heart* and bending 640
With Lincoln's *heart,* and Lincoln's 1608
With longing all my *heart* is 1571
With melting *heart,* and laden 192
With their whole *heart* and mind 212
Within my *heart* appear 306
Within my *heart* holds constant 1297
Within my *heart,* speak, Lord 1444
Within my *heart* thy love beget 838
Within our *heart* of hearts 2044
Would ye his *heart* rejoice 682
Yea, even with my whole *heart* 1826
Yea, only as the *heart* is clean 1582
Yet has my *heart* no rest 1259
Yet let my full *heart* what 2201
Yet to each loving *heart* how 1155
Your *heart* shall live forever 360
Your *heart* shall live, ye saints 2078

HEART-ACHE

Never a *heart-ache* and never a 407

HEART-CRY

This is my *heart-cry* 1829

HEARTH

Every *hearth* is aflame, and 1995
Love deepens round the *hearth* 40
Of every *hearth* to make a home 325

HEARTHS

Like *hearths* of comfort, eager 385

HEARTS

Across our *hearts* are written 2173
All *hearts* are knit in holy love 1369
All *hearts* beat as one 1768
All our *hearts* to be thine own 144
And all, with *hearts* of gladness 1859
And eager *hearts* awoke to greet 1652
And faithful are the gentle *hearts* 325
And faithful *hearts* are raised on high 1543
And *hearts* creative bridge 2198
And *hearts* in worship blend 1529
And hence with grateful *hearts* 67
And if our *hearts* and flesh are weak 240
And in our *hearts* be love 1301
And in our *hearts* thy work begin 1402
And in their *hearts* thy ways 782
And kindling *hearts* that burn 1155
And loving *hearts* without alloy 1478
And only our *hearts* can enfold 1298
And our frozen *hearts* to glow 1092
And our *hearts* are cold 1066
And our *hearts* are made to bleed 2127
And questing *hearts* that long 1368
And saddened *hearts* rejoice 2273
And seeking thee, their *hearts* 1405
And simple *hearts* without alloy 1812
And soon their *hearts* began to burn 975
And the *hearts* of men are stirring 1993
And their glad *hearts* within their bosoms 298
And then with *hearts* unlifted 149
And thousand *hearts* ascending 1911
And when our *hearts* are cold 1396
And while in thee our *hearts* rejoice 2027
And with *hearts* united take 256

But all their *hearts* are one 671
But lonely *hearts* can rest in thee 2171
Cheerless though our *hearts* may be 1100
Come, gracious Lord, our *hearts* renew 1026
Come in humble *hearts* to dwell 1272
Come to our *hearts* tonight 723
Do thou our inmost *hearts* possess 1037
Foolish *hearts,* why will ye wander 1767
For all men's *hearts* were opened 2135
For *hearts* aflame to serve 593
For *hearts* that ache, the angels 2207
For, if their *hearts* to me 2245
Fresh *hearts* to trust and love 1166
Glad *hearts* to thee we bring 332
Gladly our *hearts* to thee in praise 454
Grateful *hearts* in hymns of praise 1113
Happy *hearts* and voices gladden 409
Happy *hearts* to him were dear 2255
He is sifting out the *hearts* of men 1215
Hearts all pure and free from sin 1173
Hearts and minds and hands 101
Hearts and voices raising praises 1680
Hearts are light that once were 1305
Hearts around thee sink 294
Hearts at peace that know 1796
Hearts break with burdens 705
Hearts grow faint and hopes 755
Hearts now cold again will love 1738
Hearts of one accord 501
Hearts of the people mourn 220
Hearts that far from thee were 1179
Hearts too unspoiled for gain 2182
Hearts unfold like flow'rs 1040
Hearts will be happier 1750
Here to our waiting *hearts* proclaim 1032
Here with *hearts* rejoicing 256
Human *hearts* in thee would rest 1686
Hungry *hearts* with good supplies 1622
If in our *hearts* there is naught 2241
If thou our *hearts* will raise 33
In faithful *hearts* forever 2076
In *hearts,* and lips, and hands 2183
In him shall true *hearts* 919
In our *hearts* keep watch 486
In our *hearts* thou'rt ever near 579
In our *hearts* thy love increase 1813
In whom all *hearts* find rest 419
Jesus, may our *hearts* be burning 1005
Let all our *hearts* agree 1029
Let anxious *hearts* grow quiet 1359
Let *hearts* downcast 1083
Let loving *hearts* enthrone him 2215
Let not our *hearts* be desolate 266
Let not our slothful *hearts* refuse 2220
Let our *hearts* and souls be stirred 220
Let the tender *hearts* be glad 2007
Let your drooping *hearts* be glad 1560
Let your *hearts* be true and humble 363
Lift up our *hearts,* O King of kings 82
"Lift up your *hearts* 1366
Little *hearts* are praying 1102
Little *hearts* may love thee well 962
Lo! in our *hearts* shines forth 1443
Lord, in our *hearts* more richly 1952
Lord, may our *hearts* retain thee 1415
May all our *hearts* in one agree 1809
May *hearts* of stone here learn 2107
May our *hearts* thy love confess 1120
May struggling *hearts* that seek 32
May these cold *hearts* of ours 923
Men's *hearts* failing them for fear 296
No longer our *hearts* feel the thrill 2055
No! While our *hearts* are tender 2230
Now in our longing *hearts* 723
Now upon our *hearts* descend 759
O *hearts* our bruised and dead 2167
O *hearts* that are weary and sinful 1926
O how our *hearts* beat high 428
O may our *hearts* his presence feel 642
O may our *hearts* to him 1883
O sorr'wing *hearts* of slaves 2183
O true *hearts* have gone forth 1987
O what can little *hearts* do 1536
O'er all faithful *hearts* who on thee 744
On the dawn your *hearts* be setting 36
Only in stubborn *hearts* and wills 2228
Our barren *hearts* make fruitful 1952
Our happy *hearts* give back your chime 1661
Our *hearts* are forever repeating 1298
Our *hearts* be kind 1934
Our *hearts* be pure from evil 1854
Our *hearts* be ruled 84
Our *hearts* have felt the rapture 2061
Our *hearts* his love to feel 1398
Our *hearts,* if God we seek to know 327
Our *hearts* in true devotion bow 1149
Our *hearts* receive thy gracious word 2197
Our *hearts* rejoice anew 1418
Our *hearts* responsive ring 138
Our *hearts* still whispering 1459
Our *hearts* upleap in gladness 1874
Our *hearts* unite in daring 309
Our *hearts* were filled with sadness 350
Our *hearts* with heavenly love inspire 375
Our *hearts* with sighing wake 247
Our *hearts* would own, with saints 300
Rebel *hearts* for Christ ye tame 275
Shall our *hearts* forget his promise 77
Soon our happy *hearts* will quiver 1711
Still in our *hearts* we dwell 751
Still to this our *hearts* must tend 1271
Ten thousand *hearts* are bounding 1320
That here our *hearts* may worship 2165
That in our darkened *hearts* thy grace 58
That in our *hearts,* from this good 1402
That in our *hearts* sweet thoughts 1633
That our weak *hearts* no more 459
That we, with our *hearts* in heaven 76
That with *hearts* by thee made brave 357
The bruised and broken *hearts* to win 1702
The *hearts* that seek thee, lead 1317
The mournful, broken *hearts* 1351
The weary *hearts* are sighing 149
Their *hearts* shall burn within 2069
Thou, Lord, of all our *hearts* 1291
Though our *hearts* from care are free 1100
Thy children's *hearts* made purer 2086
To God your *hearts* and voices 1493

To hear what to our *hearts* there might 1094
To thee our humble *hearts* aspire 146
To thee with longing *hearts* 502
To write upon the *hearts* of men 309
Unto troubled *hearts* give peace 2227
We with grateful *hearts* would gather 144
When our *hearts* are sad with 1979
When our *hearts* lowly bend 2093
When their *hearts* are lifted high 2264
Where human *hearts* by bitterness 422
While cloistered *hearts* are longing 1880
While our *hearts,* with deep devotion 1159
While remembering *hearts* thou 2018
While we raise our *hearts* in love 105
Whose *hearts* beat time to music 2162
Whose *hearts* have Christ confessed 666
With ever joyful *hearts* 1299
With glowing *hearts* by his cradle 1399
With grateful *hearts,* O God, to thee 902
With grateful *hearts* rejoice 1334
With grateful *hearts* the past 643
With *hearts* all unafraid 191
With *hearts* to thee more wholly 1432
With joyful *hearts* and voices 1734
With longing *hearts* we turn to thee 384
With steadfast *hearts* seek ye 533
With those whose *hearts* are breaking 1329
With willing *hearts* we tread 404
Within are *hearts* sore burdened 1604
Within our passioned *hearts* 1072
Yet all the while, though *hearts* 1088
Yet with *hearts* bowed down 753
Young *hearts,* if God his Spirit send 1536
Your *hearts* lay down before him 1734

HEAT

From the burning of the noontide *heat* 203
Heat was in the very sod 627
In the *heat* and stress of duty 331
The gracious light and *heat* 7
Though in desert *heat* it cower 2319

HEATED

When *heated* in the chase 125

HEATHEN

O soon may the *heathen* 2245
Say to the *heathen* from thy throne 116

HEAVEN

A dear one in *heaven* 18
All in *heaven* above adore thee 746
And Christ, our Lord, by *heaven* 1487
And *heaven* and earth 1095
And *heaven* and nature sing 1039
And *heaven* gained, I'll gaze 915
And *heaven* is all possessed 548
And *heaven* itself more near 33
And *heaven,* the heart's true home 670
And now to *heaven* ascended 283
And of *heaven* where he is gone 1118
And then to *heav'n* again returned 1290
As in *heaven,* on earth adored 1625
As in *heaven* thy will be done 1182
Bending from high *heaven* down 1665
But *heaven* is nearer, and Christ 1578
But *heaven* shines clearer 1578
Christ, by highest *heaven* adored 675
For as high as is the *heaven* 1472
For where *heaven* is but once 788
For without thee, even *heaven,* every 2319
From God the Lord, who *heaven* 2139
From *heaven* he came and sought her 1845
God and *heaven* are still my own 980
Heaven above is softer blue 1195
Heaven and earth, and all creation 1626
Heaven and earth are full of thy glory 750
Heaven and earth are praising thee 382
Heaven and earth are telling 1792
Heav'n and earth at last remove 2341
Heaven and earth his praises sing 684
Heaven and earth may fade 1195
Heaven and earth must pass 1762
Heaven and earth shall flee 933
Heav'n and earth, the surging sea 1213
Heaven and earth with loud 1126
Heaven and earth, your praises bring 543
Heav'n is bright above 409
Heaven is here, where misery lightened 716
Heaven is ringing, earth is singing 208
Heav'n is still with anthems 1178
Heaven is still with glory ringing 253
Heaven is touching earth with rest 382
Heaven is with thy glory ringing 1673
Heaven is won today 2204
Heaven itself without thee 1034
Heaven shall triumph in the sight 2342
Heaven shames thee with its glorious 133
Heaven will bring me sweeter rest 980
Heaven will the mysteries 1282
Heaven with hallelujahs rang 1762
Heaven with hosanna rings 1704
Heaven with joy and holy longing 282
Heaven with the echo shall resound 631
High *heaven* that heard the solemn 1392
Him though highest *heaven* receives 655
Him whom *heaven* and earth adore 129
In *heaven* to see thy face 2178
It is *heaven* just to know that Jesus 623
It is *heaven* where thou art 369
Leading to *heaven* on high 729
Let *heaven* above his grace 2078
Let *heaven* and earth and rocks 237, 1677
Let *heaven* rejoice, let earth 2014
Like the *heaven* above 1101
Many are sighing for *heaven* 1600
Most of all that out from *heaven* 1158
Nor *heaven* have I, nor place 1277
Nothing left but *heaven* and prayer 755
Now in *heaven* exalted high 1203
O God in *heaven,* hear 490
O yes, 'twill be *heaven* to see him 2212
Of *heaven* the sign, of earth 1810
Once *heaven* seemed a far-off place 1722
Our God, *heaven* cannot hold him 933
Over *heaven* his throne 1624
Pleading in *heaven* for me 1517
That *heaven* may come to earth 454

That *heaven* so bright and fair 118
That in *heaven* he may meet me 411
That thee in thy new *heaven* 1146
That we, to *heaven* ascended 1317
The *heaven* prepared for me 779
The *heaven* that hides him 96
The Lord from *heaven* be kind 540
There a *heaven* on earth must be 1588
There to see *heaven* descend to 302
There's a little bit of *heaven* 1957
This is *heaven,* its peace, its 716
Thou in *heaven* shalt hear 297
Till each in *heaven* appears 1167
Till glorious from thy *heaven* 2270
Till *heaven* and earth re-echo 1556
Till *heaven* on high rejoices 1320
Till in *heaven* our souls repose 1744
Till in *heaven* we take our place 1190
Till in *heaven,* ye sing before him 684
'Tis *heaven* my Jesus here to know 1722
'Tis *heaven* below my Redeemer 1741
'Tis *heaven* to know my sins forgiven 1722
To *heaven* I'll follow Jesus 1949
To *heaven,* the place of his abode 1201
To know he is with me is *heaven* 623
To walk with thee is *heaven* 240
When *heaven* and earth out of darkness 748
When *heaven* and earth shall pass 1290
Where Jesus is, 'tis *heaven* there 1722
While *heaven* the note prolongs 682
Whom have I in *heaven* but thee 998
Whom have I, Lord, in *heaven* but thee 932
Whom *heaven* and earth cannot contain 1188
Whom in *heaven* but thee 1607
Whom the *heaven* of heavens obeys 356
Wooing us to *heaven* 1732

HEAVENS

Above the highest *heavens* thou 2038
And higher than the *heavens* 1556
And spangled *heavens,* a shining 1932
Beneath the spreading *heavens* 1759
From the still *heavens* 1852
God will make new *heavens* 1362
High as the *heavens* our voices 184
High o'er all the *heavens* he 394
Higher than the *heavens* his throne 665
Higher than the highest *heavens* 1498
Like the arching of the *heavens* 606, 615
Now let all the *heavens* adore 2149
Now let the *heavens* be joyful 1854
On thee for whom the *heavens* 67
Over the *heavens* he spreads his 2307
The *heavens* are not too high 1062
The *heavens* declare his glory 1485
The *heavens* have told his 1889
The *heavens* shall express 619
The *heavens* with joy receive 1883
The opening *heavens* round me 1240
Thou from the *heavens* didst send 1164
Though the *heavens* shall melt away 276
Through thee the *heavens* are 414
Thy starry *heavens* reveal 2303
'Till thy reflected *heavens* 1359
When the *heavens* seem to frown 169
Ye *heav'ns,* reflect it to the ground 1308
Yet he whom *heavens* cannot 263
Yet to view the *heavens* he 665

HEAVENWARD

Rather may we *heavenward* rise 233

HEAVY-LADEN

"Come unto me, all *heavy-laden*" 1316
When the *heavy-laden* cast all 2260

HEED

And *heed* thy brother's call 156
He will *heed* your supplication 561
Heed not its slander and scorn 1098
Heed not its voices calling 1193
Heed not the treacherous voices 548
Heed not when they flatter 1668
Heed what he sayeth 804
Heed ye the steward's call 682
O will you not *heed* him 1925
We *heed,* O Lord, thy summons 1943
Where we *heed* the voice of duty 716
Will you *heed* the call 3

HEIGHT

Colorado's lofty *height* 518
From that *height* which knows 743
His own son from heaven's *height* 126
In the *height* of heaven above 217
Neither in *height* nor depth 1318
On Zion's sacred *height* 1864
That to perfection's sacred *height* 459
'Till o'er the *height* the morning 1

HEIGHTS

Higher than the *heights* above 672
New *heights* I'm gaining every day 915
O ye *heights* of heaven adore him 1558
Of *heights* and depths of mercy 1556
The *heights* of hills are his 1335
What *heights* of joy 737
When over dizzy *heights* we go 2029

HEIR

An *heir* to a mansion, a robe 1229
And *heir* to a mansion preparing 1648
And he's an *heir* of heav'n 792
Heir of salvation, purchase 213

HEIRS

Heirs of his wondrous salvation 263
Heirs of the Father, at the throne 1670
Heirs of their great heritage 485
Making us *heirs* of his kingdom 263

HELD

All, all are thine, and *held* 1429
Because I *held* upon a selfish road 183
Held by love, to peace I win 2224
Held in thy law, I stand 856

HELL

Alleluia! *Hell* is vanquished	669
Hell and the grave combined	237
Hell builds her palaces of state	1440
Of *hell* subdued, and peace	1035
There, if in *hell* I lie	1452
Though *hell* assail us	291
To rescue me from *hell*	2077
To turn aside from thee is *hell*	240

HELMET

Our *helmet* is his salvation	2180
Salvation's *helmet* on each head	413

HELP

A present *help* is he	917, 2181
All my *help* from thee I bring	994
An ever-present *help* and stay	1729
And God himself doth *help*	546
And *help* divine implore	1256
And *help* in ev'ry whelming flood	1915
And *help* in thee we found	648
And *help* me still to say	1245
And *help* our misery	2071
And *help* their weakness	718
And *help* us heed	383
And *help* us live daily in true	959
And *help* us, this and every day	1273
And *help* us when we pray	648
And still he doth his *help*	93
And with thy *help*, O Lord, our battles	2188
As we thy *help* have sought	1175
Be thou my *help* when troubles	2103
But *help* thy foolish ones	1797
But our *help* is near	736
But that Jesus will *help*	1976
By just a little *help* from you	400
"Come over and *help* us," they cry	509
For God will be her early *help*	571
For thou my *help* hast been	1172
He did me *help* afford	857
He'll *help* us clear	19
Help all the nations, near and far	1381
Help and comfort give you to	2265
Help and keep us to the end	480
Help can only come from thee	1603
Help him the wand'ring ones to find	681
Help me bear the strain of toil	1466
Help me each day, on life's	1152
Help me every day to be	1304
Help me, I pray	691
Help me, oppressed by things	390
Help me the cross to bear	1689
Help me the first approach to feel	889
Help me the lost to win	1774
Help me the slow of heart	1466
Help me throughout life's changing	1400
Help me, thus on thee depending	1583
Help me thy will to do	265
Help me to throw out the old life-line	529
Help me to labor earnestly	1128
Help me to sacrifice myself	1128
Help me to tear it from thy throne	1347
Help me to watch and pray	4
Help me walk from day to day	986
Help my unbelief	1607
Help, O *help* us to endure	492
Help of the helpless	27
Help those who are weak	1820
Help thou dost not disdain	1715
Help thy vain worlds to hear	1797
Help to chant Immanuel's praise	659
Help to sing our Savior's merits	659
Help to rear its shining ramparts	656
Help us all to do our best	1022
Help us by thy spirit's pleading	220
Help us, dear Lord, our cross to bear	235
Help us in thought and word	1396
Help us to be faithful to thee	1372
Help us to pass it on	1353
Help us unto thee to pray	1173
Help us know thy grace and power	579
Help us, Lord, to lift our eyes	742
Help us now, each moment	1158
Help us one and all	1769
Help us our battle for the right	422
Help us, that with eager mind	930
Help us thy name to sing	338
Help us through good report	1119
Help us thy likeness to show	1694
Help us to do the things we should	468
Help us to feed upon thy word	397
Help us to help each other	1029
Help us to look to that bright place	1918
Help us to know thou keepest	383
Help us to praise	338
Help us to see in all that lives	1508
Help us to serve our brethren	456
Help us to serve thee	705
Help us to shed abroad thy deathless	1819
Help us to stand where thou hast	2277
Help us, too, in sport	930
Help us to spread thy gracious	419
Help us while we sing	757
Help your fallen brother rise	1955
Hither by thy *help* I'm come	340
Holy Spirit, *help* us daily by	757
Holy Zion's *help* forever	281
I *help* from him obtained	1455
I will *help* and strengthen	1786
Lord, *help* us, and inspire	1609
Lord, thou cans't *help* when earthly	1162
May we, where *help* is needed	1371
My *help* is from the Lord above	885
"My *help* is sure"	564
No one else your *help* provides	1766
No other *help* I know	444
None can *help* you but Jesus only	111
O *help* thy children when they call	445
O *help* us, Jesu, from on high	1396
O *help* us stand unswerving	1549
O *help* us so to live and die	1396
O *help* us, through the prayer of faith	1396
O *help* us to see 'tis only	916
O *help* us when our spirits bleed	1396
O who will *help* us to garner in	1540

On thy higher *help* relying 2047
One who can *help* my burdens 865
Or *help* one fainting robin 899
Ready to *help* me 1047
Savior, *help* me or I die 269
The *help* of all who find 874
The orphan's *help* is he 1394
Their *help* Omnipotence 767
There was no *help* in earth below 2316
Thou cans't *help* their load 294
To *help* me on to God 87
To their *help* thy Spirit send 2264
Trusting in thy *help* alone 711
When all human *help* is vain 993
When no other *help* is near 2268
When nothing else could *help* 891
Will you *help* the trembling 251
Wonderful *help* for the work 2314
You can *help* them at your door 679

HELPED

Who *helped* the right, and fought 1296
Yes, hitherto hast *helped* me 2035

HELPER

And where there is a *helper* 1252
Be thou our *helper,* ever near 1905
Be thou our *helper* in the strife 161
Greater than our *Helper* 922
Must be a *helper* too 1252
Our *helper* he, amid the flood 12
When there is no *helper* near 63

HELPERS

When other *helpers* fail, and comforts 27
Who will be his *helpers* 2287

HELPEST

And *helpest* them to render 1089

HELPETH

That *helpeth* others to be strong 576

HELPLESS

And *helpless* and defiled 1830
Be to the *helpless* a helper 1601
Help of the *helpless,* O abide 27

HELPLESSNESS

From tender childhood's *helplessness* 2270

HELPS

He *helps* the needy and regards 2078
He *helps* the stranger in 911

HERALD

Let the Savior's *herald* go 1747
That we may *herald* his praises 263
When Christ the *herald* comes 732
While we *herald* the tidings 2113

HERALDS

As *heralds,* speed us on our way 1169
One of his *heralds,* yes, I would 1831
The *heralds* of thy wondrous grace 1702
Thy *heralds* brought glad tidings 2072
What are they but the *heralds* 1391

HERB

As on drooping *herb* and flower 966, 1012

HERDSMEN

Thanks, good *herdsmen,* true your story 1718

HERESIES

By *heresies* distressed 1845

HERITAGE

Around us lies the *heritage* 46
I have a *heritage* of joy 1242
On me the *heritage* conferred 1376
On me their *heritage* conferred 1134
Their *heritage* a sunless day 2267
Thy *heritage* shall still remain 1935

HEROES

For all *heroes* of the Spirit 1280
Heroes for it died 501
O beautiful for *heroes* proved 1311
The *heroes* that had lost the day 2182
Till among the *heroes,* we are heroes 1205

HID

And *hid* thy power divine 2168
From him he has not *hid* his face 72
Hid in flesh from fleshly sight 1095
Is *hid* from mortal eyes 194

HIDDEN

Have I *hidden* in thee, O Thou 1477
Hidden in human wretchedness 385
Hidden in the hollow 1091
Hidden in the Savior's side 2261
Hidden in thy wounded side 963
Hidden with Christ who is our life 1670
Though *hidden* to the view 14
Though *hidden* yet from all our eyes 473
With thee is *hidden* still their life 590

HIDE

From thee, O Lord, I cannot *hide* 1438
He will *hide* me, he will 2257
Hide me, O my Savior, hide 994
Hide not thy face from me 2078
Hide within thy heart his word 295
In thee forever may they *hide* 1370
In thee, O Lord, I *hide* me 772
Jesus, our Savior, *hide* us 1850
Let me *hide* myself in thee 1671
O *hide* them and preserve them 460
There will I *hide* till life's trials 2136
Thus might I *hide* my blushing 38
Thy face *hide* from my sin 31
Well might the sun in darkness *hide* 38
You cannot *hide* from God 2338

HIDES

And *hides* our life above 93
He *hides* himself within the love 1891
The heaven that *hides* him from 96

HIDETH

He *hideth* my soul in the cleft 24

HIDING-PLACE

My Savior and my *hiding-place* 858
None other *hiding-place* from guilt 1277
Thou art my *hiding-place* 1314

HIE

Hie thee to thy quiet home 2154

HIGH

Let *high* and lowly, young and old 2328

HIGHLANDS

Over the *highlands* of glory 181

HIGH PRIEST

Thou art the great *High Priest* 1715

HIGHWAY

And by the broad *highway* 2195
The King's *highway* of holiness 1001

HIGHWAYS

Afoot on dusty *highways* 762

HILL

And in thy high and holy *hill* 2311
Hill and vale, and tree and 484
Hill of Calvary, I go 2247
Moving on to Zion's *hill* 966, 1012
O Christ, the Lord of *hill* and plain 81
On every *hill*, a beacon light 1469
On the wintry *hill* 940
On yonder *hill* of Calvary 1568
Or Zion's fruitful *hill* 771
The *hill* of Zion yields 351
The Lord from out his holy *hill* 1430
Turning to thy holy *hill* 589
Up to the *hill* of God, they'll say 198

HILLS

All the *hills* were ringing 524
And far on the *hills* by feet untrod 1929
And joyful are the *hills* 2081
And let our *hills* and valleys 1185
And lo! already on the *hills* 2075
And the *hills* bow down to greet 363
Before the *hills* in order stood 1375
For wooded *hills* in verdure 1779
Hills and valleys voice their 1975
Let the *hills* be joyful before him 747
Likewise the little *hills* the same 1454
'Mid silent *hills*, beneath fresh 2291
On the *hills* of thy beauty 236
On your far *hills*, long cold 733
O'er these dark *hills* of time 5
Over the *hills* and the valleys 1981
Shaking the *hills* with power 90
So, o'er the *hills* of life 732
The answering *hills* of Palestine 272
The *hills* leap up in gladness 1734
The *hills* take up the song 516
The *hills* with joy are ringing 2120
The *hills* with thunder shake 247
The lofty *hills* brought low 1998
There are so many *hills* to climb 1922
These *hills* he toiled over 236
Though *hills* amidst the seas be cast 571
Though the *hills* be steep 1044
Till these eternal *hills* remove 1354
Till to thy far *hills* we rise 1158
Unshaken as eternal *hills* 1539
Up to the *hills* where Christ 1143
Where from flowery *hills* 1837
Ye *hills* and valleys lift your 2328

HILLSIDE

Upon the breezy *hillside* 2195

HILLTOP

While ever on the *hilltop* 1549

HINDER

That *hinder* to enthrone thee 284

HINDRANCES

Yet *hindrances* strew all the way 2033

HOARDS

Wiser than the miser's *hoards* 2007

HOBGOBLIN

Hobgoblin nor foul fiend 2290

HOLD

And *hold* me lest I fall 176
Christ of Calvary, *hold* their hands 488
Christ will *hold* me fast 2232
Closer *hold* his nail-pierced hand 398
He will *hold* me fast 2232
Hold fast his simple way 377
Hold fast the truth that you have heard 547
Hold fast thy loyalty and know 2226
Hold me with thy powerful hand 652
Hold o'er my being absolute sway 691
"*Hold* the fort, for I am coming" 736
Hold the gospel banner high 1788
Hold thee in full survey 154
Hold thou full sway 1819
Hold thou my trembling hand 178
Hold thou thy cross before 27
Hold up my goings, Lord 1135
Hold up to earth the torch 703
Hold us in honor, truth 1165
Hold us who wait before thee 1969
If I still *hold* closely to him 119
If we but *hold* to thee 205
It will surely *hold* in the floods 2298
It will surely *hold* in the straits 2298
Let all who *hold* this faith 2090

O *hold* thy hands above me 1297
Then *hold* thee still, my heart 1283
We *hold* ourselves for thee 309
Whom still I *hold* but cannot see 333

HOLDER

O *Holder* of the keys of death 590

HOLDETH

And he *holdeth* our crowns 896
He *holdeth* me up, and I shall not 24
He *holdeth* the wealth of the world 1229

HOLDS

And it *holds,* my anchor holds 2056
He *holds* me with his arm 1756
He *holds* the key 1282
It *holds* the fainting spirit up 2192
Which *holds* me evermore 303
Who *holds* all men and nations 2165
Who safely *holds* our soul in life 361

HOLD'ST

Thou *hold'st* us still in thine 2029

HOLIDAYS

And our happy *holidays* 273

HOLINESS

And *holiness* forever, Lord 598, 1886
And *Holiness* shall whisper 1057
Holiness I crave from thee 1835

HOLLOW

And in the roof-tree's *hollow* 1724
In the *hollow* of his hand 1674

HOLY

All that is not *holy* 143
Be silent, be silent, for *holy* 172
O for that *holy* dawning 1
Only thou art *holy,* there is none 749
That *holy* I may be 135

HOMAGE

And *homage* to their king 1625
Here our humblest *homage* pay we 1126
Homage of each humble heart 753
I may meet *homage* give 1423
Offering *homage* glad and true 412
Ours the *homage,* thine the gift 1665
To thee its humble *homage* raise 2117
To thee their *homage* show 671

HOME

A *home* by thee made happy 1344
A *home* in heaven above 348
A *home* where changes never come 1531
A *home* with the pure and blest 1411
A *home* within the wilderness 203
Afar from *home,* through gain 2291
And from thy celestial *home* 342
And *home* rejoicing brought me 1876
And in a fairer, happier *home* 1480
And our eternal *home* 1375
And then go *home* my crown 1223
Anywhere with Jesus will be *home* 108
At *home,* abroad, where'er 1906
But in Bethlehem's *home* was 2026
But when *home* our souls are 1581
Come *home* and thou shalt 158
"Come *home,* come home 1743
E'en now to their eternal *home* 1067
For *home* where our affection 481
For *home* with its gladness 2194
For I am nearer *home* today 1580
For the *home* and for the cheer 273
For the *home,* the church, the school 1280
Gathering *home,* gathering home 2004, 2145
Happy the *home* where Jesus' name 667
Here in earth's *home* preparing 1457
His bright *home* preparing 622
Home closer draws her circle 2097
Home of my soul, how near 494
Home of the pure and blest 181
Home of the stranger 1656
Home to the realms above 180
Home, weary wanderers, home 326
I'll soon be at *home* over there 1503
I'm going *home* to die no more 1243
I'm going *home* to glory 1500
I'm nearer *home* to day 1580
In a better *home* above 555
In our eternal *home* 347
In our *home* beyond the sky 78
In the Father's *home* above are 1945
In the *home* and in the throng 411
It was thine only *home* 1528
Let Israel, *home* returning 1497
Lord, in that *home* with thee 2020
My *home* is brighter far than Sharon's 799
My *home* is far away 799
My *home* shall thy pavilion 1134
No *home* on earth is like it 1988
Now I am coming *home* 977
O happy *home* where each one serves 1393
O happy *home,* where every wounded 1393
O happy *home,* where little ones are 1393
O happy *home,* where two in heart 1393
O that *home* of the soul 896
Of every *home* a heaven 325
Of every *home* the Guest 1884
Our endless *home* shall be 277
Our heart's true *home,* when all 586
Our spirit's *home* with joy 1329
Ready for the soul's bright *home* 2241
Straight to my *home* above I travel 1245
Telling to us in our distant *home* 1984
That unchangeable *home* is for 896
The common *home* of rich and poor 2142
The faraway *home* of the soul 896
The *home* above together share 870
The *home* of God's elect 489, 961
The *home* of the soul is with God 2271
The sweeter is *home* to me 1913
Then at last go *home* to thee 448
There is a *home* at the end 829

There is the *home* of my Savior 181
There's a bright *home* above 1338
There's a *home* for little children 1988
This *home* made ready for its Guest 1528
This *home* we consecrate today 1528
Thy everlasting *home* of peace 1393
Till in the *home* of heaven we find 721
Till we are gathered to thy *home* 29
To his humble *home* 517
To my eternal *home* 1097
To see thee in each quiet *home* 1384
To that dear *home* where there will be 1939
We are traveling *home* to God 277
Welcome back to *home* 939
When *home* is entered, not a load 1274
When the *home* of the faithful our 2113

HOMES

And *homes* are bare and cold 2167
Christ to their *homes* giveth 666
For our *homes* and every good 518
For peaceful *homes* and healthful 1439
Glad are the *homes* that sorrows 349
Homes crowned with beauty 560
Homes that are free from 560
Homes that are joyous 560
Homes where the altar fires burn 560
Homes where the children are led 560
Homes where the father is true 560
Homes where the Lord is an honored 560
Homes where the Master's will 560
Homes where the mother in queenly 560
In *homes* where childhood tender 923
Lord, let us in our *homes* agree 667
'Mid the *homes* of want 1747
Or in *homes* of the poor and lowly 1815
Our *homes* and all we love 2303
Rude the *homes* which they upraised 1553
That through our *homes* doth move 1457
They are the *homes* where he 263
Through the *homes* in every nation 634

HOMELAND

Awaiting in the *homeland* 2096
In that fair *homeland* we'll know 207

HOME-LIGHTS

When *home-lights* we see shining 2225

HOMESTEADS

And the *homesteads* and 1042

HONEY

Than *honey*, honey from the comb 618
The *honey* of all these flow'rs 2183

HONOR

All *honor* and blessing with 2330
All *honor* be to Jesus 283
And be with *honor* crowned 2331
And *honor* all his laws 914
Bringing *honor* to thy name 461
Come, and now *honor* thy word 1981
Great *honor* is before his face 1486
Honor, glory, might, and merit 101
"*Honor*, riches, power, dominion" 543
Honor them, the faithful few 1788
Jesus is worthy to receive *honor* 323
Nor could all wordly *honor* give 1241
Of tarnished *honor*, falsely strong 82, 1079
Sing forth the *honor* of his name 50
That to thine *honor*, Lord 1301
Thee will I *honor* 427
Unto great *honor*, glory 1873
We will, for *honor* of thy name 1608
With *honor* thou hast crowned 1450

HONORS

All grateful *honors* paid on earth 2106
For she *honors* on his throne 1213
To royal *honors* raised our head 2106
We sacred *honors* pay 237

HOPE

A *hope* so great 194
A *hope* that triumphs over death 1038
All we *hope* to be 1680
And *hope*, and joy, and peace 1078
And *hope*, and praise, and love 1980, 2001
And *hope* in him through all 904
And *hope* that never yields 1859
And *hope* to see thee soon 869
And humbly *hope* for more 767
And I *hope*, by thy good pleasure 340
And its *hope* is abiding and sure 1115
And patient *hope* is crowned 1959
And they who dearest *hope* 1511
And to one *hope* she presses 1845
And who in *hope* to Christ 1621
And with a *hope* more sweet 683
Bright with *hope* is burning 52
Come, O thou blest *hope* 1742
For bright *hope* is uplifting 1505
For *hope* regained 1807
For on his coming the *hope* of salvation 1617
For the new *hope* that shines on 2162
For thee, not without *hope*, I mourn 2202
Full of *hope* and promise sweet 238
He then is all my *hope* and stay 1244
High *hope* is yours today 2340
His people's *hope* 1869
Hope and be undismayed 536
Hope and desire for noble lives 1374
Hope and faith and love rise 1295
Hope, as an anchor so steadfast 1742
Hope be emptied in delight 636, 1192
Hope fails us otherwise 2171
Hope for the sunshine tomorrow 1742
Hope is not gone 922
Hope of all the earth thou art 343, 658
Hope of earth and joy of heav'n 1817
Hope of the dreary 1656
Hope of the hopeless, my Savior 1575
Hope of the penitent 355
Hope smiles, reviving round 1924
Hope soars beyond death 1238

Hope soon change to glad fruition 980
Hope still, and thou shalt sing 125
Hope with a gentle persuasion 1742
How firm our *hope* and comfort 1065
How joyful is the *hope* that lingers 2301
I have no *hope* beside 2046
I *hope* to see my Pilot face to face 1802
If *hope* but light the water's crest 826
If we have not *hope* in thee 42
In cheerful *hope,* with heart 904
In flaming *hope* they sing 1604
In glorious *hope,* their proud 1532
In *hope,* against all human hope 453
In *hope* that sends a shining ray 1466
In whom none *hope* in vain 2171
Jesus is my *hope* and trust 991
Let Israel *hope* in the Lord 1129
Let us *hope,* let us watch 2113
My fainting *hope* relies 392
My *hope* burns low 1277
My *hope* I cannot measure 921
My *hope* is fixed above 1016
My *hope* is in his word 1129
My *hope,* my salvation, my all 1512
My *hope* of heav'n, I find in thee 2087
My steadfast *hope* shall not remove 2295
No *hope* within 2316
No, let a new and better *hope* 2177
None other *hope* in heaven 1277
Nor from my *hope* remove 1003
Nor let my *hope* be lost 914
Not for the *hope* of gaining 1235
O *Hope* of every contrite heart 1019
O our only *Hope* and Guide 966, 1012
O what a blessed *hope* is ours 779
Of patient *hope* and quiet 1473
On thee alone my *hope* relies 2244
On thee, and thee alone, our *hope* 404
On thee my *hope* relies 2119
One *hope,* one faith, one love restore 496
One the *hope* our God inspires 2067
Only *Hope* of human race 538
Our *hope* for years to come 1375
Our *hope* is in no other 828
Our *hope* till his coming again 2194
Our *hope* when autumn winds 1146
Our only *hope* the Crucified 479
Safe in *hope,* thy spirit in me 2224
So far exceeding *hope* or thought 1002
So let us *hope,* when faith 2332
Stirring *hope,* dispelling fear 742
Sweet is the *hope* and its power 1763
The *hope* in which ye yearn 1391
The *hope* like the years decay 1411
The *hope* of all the years 2074
The *hope* of all who seek him 874
The *hope* of heaven's eternal days 100
The *hope* that shines eternal 1474
The sinner's *hope* let men deride 2192
Then may we *hope,* the angelic 298
There's *hope* only promised today 1925
This all my *hope,* and all my plea 493
This *hope* our Master bare 1727
This *hope* shall last 573
This is all my *hope* and peace 2214
Thou art the *hope* remaining 573
Thou *Hope* of sinners here 75
Though *hope* no brightening gleam 133
Through high *hope* to impart 120
Thy *hope,* thy chief delight 201
Till *hope* in full fruition 493
To perfect *hope* and peace 839
To signal *hope* and set us free 1168
Vainly we *hope* for the harvest-tide 574
Watching long in *hope* and fear 103
We *hope* in glory to appear 2090
What do you *hope,* dear brother 2293
Whate'er we *hope,* by faith we have 146
When *hope* is waning 922
When *hope* within me dies 2296
When our *hope* was high 925
Where at last we *hope* to meet 929
Whispering *hope,* O how welcome 1742
Whose *hope* upon the Lord doth rest 1394
With humble *hope* attend thy will 392
With that blessed *hope* before us 280
Without a *hope* besides I flee 2103

HOPED

All you had *hoped* for, all you had 1532

HOPES

All her *hopes* my spirit 1814
All my *hopes* have been raised 802
All thy *hopes* to scatter 1668
And our lost *hopes* restore 128
And with *hopes* of endless glory 2279
As earthly *hopes* remove 205
Fresh *hopes* have wakened 1131
Hopes deceive and fears annoy 934
My *hopes* all shattered seem to be 824
On this alone my *hopes* depend 1517
Other *hopes* may swiftly pass 2057
Our many *hopes* and fears 121
The common *hopes* that make us 2160
The highest *hopes* we cherish 1920
The *hopes* and fears of all the years 1426
The *hopes* that lead us onward 185
The *hopes* that soothe 1146
Then their sinking *hopes* sustain 1775
Though my earthly *hopes* are 1643
Thy *hopes* the God of grace shall 1700
To brighter *hopes* and kindlier 82
To cast our *hopes,* to fix 1171
What mighty *hopes* are in our 1217
When fond *hopes* fail, and skies 464
When thy secret *hopes* have perished 1642
Where our earliest *hopes* began 1271
Why *hopes* are crushed, and castles 1282
With *hopes* of future glory chase 1927

HOSANNA

And loud *hosanna* sing 1507
Hosanna in the highest 48
"*Hosanna,* Lord!" thine angels cry 764
"*Hosanna,* Lord!" thy saints reply 764
Hosanna to th' anointed King 2014
Hosanna we sing, for he bends his ear 765

HOSANNAS

And glad *hosannas* bring 1485
And loud *hosannas* shall proclaim 237
And loud *hosannas* sing 48
Glad *hosannas,* glad hosannas 208
He is coming with loud *hosannas* 699
Hosannas languish on our tongues 318
Made sweet *hosannas* ring 44
Sweet *hosannas,* sweet hosannas 1099
With glad *hosannas* ring 237
With your glad *hosannas* make 1833

HOST

A mighty *host,* by thee redeemed 1507
Against me though an *host* encamp 1903
And all the twinkling, starry *host* 427
And ever with the heavenly *host* 307
Christ hath our *host* surrounded 283
Heaven's *host* their noblest praises 1105
His sacramental *host* 1081
Lo! the angelic *host* rejoices 684
Part of his *host* have crossed 324, 1067
Satan and his *host* defy 1788
The angel *host* on high 28
The whole triumphant *host* 1864
Thy ransomed *host* in glory 1880
Till Satan's *host* is vanquished 548
Till, with all the angel *host* 357
Who for God had been a *host* 1788

HOSTEL

The *hostel* rang with song 918

HOSTS

All the heavenly *hosts* adore thee 659
All the *hosts* of light 143
And Satan's *hosts* he hath confounded 1080
And the *hosts* of sin withstand 2064
Angel *hosts* his praises sing 1558
Angelic *hosts* to him accord 2328
Come, O Lord of *Hosts,* today 281
Conqu'ring *hosts* with banners 1109
For all the *hosts* of heaven 2168
From whom all *hosts* of angels 1378
Heavenly *hosts* sing hallelujah 1720
His angel *hosts* attend ye 1309
Hosts advancing to the fray 2157
Hosts of evil 'round us 580
Hosts on high, his power 1626
Israel's *hosts* triumphant go 142
Let all the *hosts* of earth and sky 2328
No longer *hosts* encountering hosts 198
Not all the *hosts* above 150
Lord God of *Hosts,* be with us yet 583
Lord God of *Hosts,* that reign'st 782
Of *hosts* he is the Lord 2137
So sang his *hosts* 1366
Sing on, heaven's *hosts* 1366
Strong in the Lord of *Hosts* 1746
The *hosts* of God encamp 2060
The *hosts* of sin are pressing hard 1256
The *hosts* of sin are vanquished 1418
The Lord of *Hosts,* and none 2327
The Lord of *Hosts* is marching on 1860
The ransomed *hosts* surround 49
Though *hosts* encamp around me 567
Though mighty *hosts* of cruel foes 153
Till amid the *hosts* of light 1271
Unnumbered *hosts* are telling 1464
We are the *hosts* of those who swear 2285
Which *hosts* of angels chanted 298
While *hosts* cry, hosanna 953
With the countless *hosts* of light 131
With thine angel *hosts* we cry 1673

HOUR

And from his *hour* of darkness draw 1522
And *hour* by hour fresh lips 1856
And in this *hour* of quietness 944
And let us not for one short *hour* 1291
And may that *hour,* O faithful Guide 845
And the *hour* has come to die 1642
And when my dying *hour* draws near 1517
At the blessed *hour* of prayer 2093
Be this thy mighty *hour* 312
Blessed *hour* of prayer 2093
But at the *hour* appointed 283
But in the *hour* of grief or pain 1348
By thy lonely *hour* of prayer 269
Come in this most solemn *hour* 760
Comes the Lord when strikes the *hour* 36
E'en the *hour* that darkest seemeth 566
Every *hour* I need thee 868
Filling this hallowed *hour* with joy 723
For one brief *hour* of prayer 199
I need thy presence every passing *hour* 27
I shall in Christ, in that glad *hour* 453
In earth's last *hour* of fleeting 1424
In sorrow's lone *hour* 1477
In temptation's *hour* 143
In the last sad *hour,* as I stand 1954
In the solemn *hour* of dying 993
Let this my every *hour* employ 1824
Nor 'til that *hour* shall God's whole 2130
Now, in this the accepted *hour* 538
Now, O Lord, this very *hour* 717
O in that *hour,* fairer than daylight 1793
O may this *hour* be one of beginning 529
Secure against the threatening *hour* 572
Strength to serve thee, *hour* by hour 42
Such is the Christian's parting *hour* 793
Temptation's *hour* shall lose its power 2289
That as we share this *hour* 86
That in each *hour* of sore distress 822
The *hour* I first believed 88
The *hour* is come again 1914
There's not an *hour* that he 2000
This is the earth's darkest *hour* 86
This is the *hour* of banquet 727
Thou hast but an *hour* to fight 2157
Till in life's latest *hour* I bow 1392
Till that *hour* the Shepherd 990
To bring at last the glorious *hour* 1168
To weary ones in needful *hour* 1170
Waiting, only waiting, till the *hour* 1264
We are watching for the *hour* 2158
When hearing of that awful *hour* 206

When in that sad *hour* 2258
When in the solemn *hour* of death 1509
Why, Jesus, in thy dying *hour* 1482

HOURS

And all three *hours* his silence 1333
And as our *hours* begin with thee 1934
And as the *hours* swing open 564
And changeful *hours* bring sun 21
And in *hours* of deep disaster 461
And lonely *hours* of pain 434
For all its sorrowing *hours* 2030
For *hours* of cheer where friendship's 1329
For the nurturing *hours* 409
Hours and passing moments 2204
In happy *hours* of singing 1252
In *hours* of weakness be thou nigh 650
In silent *hours* of care 1252
In the many *hours* of sickness 993
Its *hours* too swiftly fly 322
Lord, though these *hours* of praise 1175
Precious *hours* in folly spent 1179
Silent through those three dread *hours* 2059
The brief *hours* are not lost 362
The Lord be with us through the *hours* 1884
These golden *hours,* these opening 21
Through the *hours* in darkness 1672
Through the silent *hours* of night 632
What peaceful *hours* I once enjoyed 1347
While the *hours* in order flow 1301

HOUSE

A *house* not made with hands 1539
And for the *house* of God our Lord 843
And in God's *house* forevermore 1904
And in the little flat-roofed *house* 145
And, joyful in the *house* of God 540
And to his *house* we'll go 198
Anywhere with Jesus is a *house* 108
Blest are they in thy *house* 783
But I into thy *house* will come 527, 1176
"Come, in the *house* of God appear 540
Come then, O *house* of Jacob 198
Ere we from thy *house* depart 753
Except the *house* be built 456
For thee this *house* of praise 502
For this thy *house* we praise thee 1529
Happy, who in thy *house* reside 782
Here in thy *house* I give to thee 361
My Father's *house* above 66
In the *house* of God abiding 78
It is a treasure *house* of gold 2087
It is the *house* of prayer 2178
It was thy Father's *house,* more great 1528
My Father's *house* is built on high 1243
My Father's *house* of light 827
My Father's *house* on high 494
Nearer my Father's *house* 1580
O *house* not made with hands 1404
O let this *house* be thy abode 114
That in this *house* have called 1679
The Father's *house* is mansioned 2163
The *house* of thine abode 859
This *house* to glorify 1175
This *house* we dedicate to thee 2107
Thy *house* becometh well 598
We are God's *house* of living 263
Within his *house,* the house of prayer 2219
Within thy holy *house* once more 1436
Within thy *house* will I abide 1376

HOUSES

And where the tall dark *houses* 2195

HOVERS

Hovers the gleam 1550

HUE

Death's pallid *hue* come o'er thee 1476

HUMANITY

Let broad *humanity* have birth 1072
To thee our full *humanity* 240

HUMBLED

And *humbled* all our pride 361
Humbled for a season 143
Humbled to a mortal child 1161

HUMBLENESS

And worship him in *humbleness* 41

HUMBLING

Humbling thyself to death on Calvary 58

HUMILITY

And in great *humility* 2026
In meek *humility* this will I do 30
So glorious in *humility* 769

HUNG

Of him who *hung* upon the tree 1487
When Jesus *hung* upon the tree 1968
Where he *hung,* the dying Lord 140, 1263

HUNGER

Hunger and thirst are felt 774
O happy, if ye *hunger* as Jesus 1391

HUNGERS

And *hungers* for the truth thou dost 1474

HUNGRY

Let the *hungry* be fed 2113
When the *hungry* craveth food 2260
Who to the *hungry* giveth food 1394

HURT

And every *hurt* be healed 2075
Though to his *hurt* he swear 2311

HUSH

And *hush* the tempest into peace 2325
Hush, be every murmur dumb 2089
Hush my spirit into peace 1644
Hush the storm of human passion 2049

Hush the storm of strife and passion 1760
O *hush* the noise, ye men of strife 948
The solemn *hush* of nature 1793
Thou canst *hush* the ocean wild 1007
There's a *hush* of expectation 1993
To *hush* to peace the strife 120
When across my *hush* of wonder 730

HUSHED

And *hushed* the wind 1831
And *hushed* their raging 418
Hushed are the sheep-bells 1611
Hushed be the accents of sorrow 660
Hushed is every doubt 1237

HYMN

The *hymn* of praise for ever 1366

HYMNS

And *hymns* of glory sing 337
And we must *hymns* of welcome 1842
Choral *hymns* addressing 1792
Her *hymns* of love and praise 859
Hymns of adoration sing 1619
Hymns of glory and of praise 142
Hymns of praise then let us 971
Let *hymns* of praise his triumph 1937
Let our vesper *hymns* be blending 1295
Little *hymns* thy praises swell 962
Once more to thee our *hymns* 186
Therefore in our *hymns* we pray 78
They sang their *hymns* of praise 44
To thankful *hymns* of joy 125
To thee our morning *hymns* 1856
Where *hymns* of gladness cheer 716

I

ICE

From our northland's *ice* and snow 518

IDEALS

The lost *ideals* of other days 1821

IDLED

I *idled* about without purpose 1941

ILL

He'll help us clear from all the *ill* 19
No *ill* can harm me 1674
Secure whatever *ill* betide 1905
The *ill* is only what he deems 1112
The *ill* that I this day have done 59

ILLS

And *ills* I cannot flee 1509
Ills have no weight and tears 27
Life's *ills* without, sin's strife 1978
Of mortal *ills* prevailing 12

ILLUMINATE

Illuminate my soul 1021

ILLUMINED

Illumined by the glory of thy face 1287

ILLUMINING

Of thy divine *illumining* 1088

IMAGE

Dark, till in me thine *image* 1018
For by thy transforming *image* 978
In thine *image*, pure renew me 798
The brightest *image* of his grace 1308
The Father's *Image* bright 559
Thine *image* and thyself are there 591
Till thine *image* it restore 219
True *image* of the Infinite 2022
When in thine *image* I shall stand 1413

IMITATE

And *imitate* the blessed throng 1809

IMMORTALITY

Our *immortality* endures 911

IMMORTALS

But beautiful as songs of the *immortals* 37
There to dwell with the *immortals* 1991

IMPART

Glorious Lord, thyself *impart* 220
In love to us *impart* 28
The precious things thou dost *impart* 1170
Wilt thou *impart* to every heart 1417

IMPARTS

Jesus thy Son to us *imparts* 469
So God *imparts* to human hearts 1426

IMPATIENT

Because I was *impatient*, would not wait 183

IMPLANT

Implant, and root it deep 2202

IMPLORE

And saving grace *implore* 1175
Gracious Savior! we *implore* thee 1813

IMPRESS

Impress thine image on our heart 793

IMPRISON

Imprison me within thine arms 1202

IMPROVE

Improve thy talent with due care 152

INARMED

Inarmed shall live as comrades 2003

INCARNATE

Of his *incarnate* Lord 91

INCARNATION

For me, kind Jesus, was thy *incarnation* 35

INCENSE

And let the *incense* of our prayers 1927
As *incense* let my prayer 1433
Incense owns a Deity nigh 2196
To rise like *incense*, each to thee 520

Unto him, like *incense* 1110
With *incense* go from Rome 90

INCESSANT

Incessant we shall sing 298

INCLINE

And *incline* our hearts to keep 1133
Incline our hearts with godly fear 1595
Incline to me a gracious ear 1434
"*Incline* your heart and come 2155
To me *incline* thine ear 1135

INCLINED

And he at length *inclined* to me 887

INCLINES

He *inclines* a gracious ear 1837

INCLUDED

"Jesus *included* me too" 807

INCREASE

Increase in us the kindled fire 146
Increase it, Lord, that at thy call 2122
Increase my courage, Lord 87
Increase our joy, uphold us 1873
May fellowship *increase* 56
More of his kingdom's sure *increase* 1216
O Lord, *increase* our faith and love 2221
Victorious in its bright *increase* 1091

INDIGNATION

Thine *indignation* cause to cease 587

INDULGE

Indulge me but in this 1332

INEFFABLE

Before the *Ineffable* appear 420

INFANT

As thou wast once an *infant* 1406
But God from *infant* tongues 28
Holy *infant* so tender and mild 1720
The seeming *infant* of a day 9

INFLAME

And seeking thee, itself *inflame* 1409
Inflame, we pray, our inmost hearts 1403

INFLICTS

Inflicts a deeper wrong 240

INFLUENCE

Humble though our *influence* be 634
Who dost by hidden *influence* 414

INFORM

Thou only can'st *inform* 2023

INHABITANTS

Let all the world's *inhabitants* 2329

INHABITEST

Inhabitest the humble mind 1032

INHERIT

Let us all in thee *inherit* 1190

INHERITANCE

And may with thine *inheritance* 532
The bright *inheritance* of saints 494
Thou mine *inheritance*, now and always 177
To an *inheritance* divine 231
Yea, the *inheritance* I got 570

INIQUITY

Ah! mine *iniquity* crimson 1276
Blot out all mine *iniquity* 31
Do no *iniquity* 212
From mine *iniquity* 31

INIQUITIES

All mine *iniquities* blot out 31
All thine *iniquities* who doth 1513
And from all his *iniquities* 1129
Iniquities I must confess 1631

INNOCENCE

Go forth from *innocence* of youth 546

INSCRIBED

Inscribed upon the Cross we see 2192

INSPIRE

Inspire our wills to speed 1595
Inspire thy heralds of good news 419
Inspire us still 588

INSPIRES

Inspires us with the thought 1945

INSTINCT

The *instinct* that can tell that God 2321

INSTRUCT

Instruct our lips to speak 84

INSTRUCTOR

Divine *Instructor*, gracious Lord 787
Divine *Instructor*, heavenly Lord 457

INSTRUMENT

On a ten-stringed *instrument* 2112

INSTRUMENTS

While *instruments* of loftier sound 55

INTENT

Intent on pleasing thee 443

INTERPOSED

Interposed his precious blood 340

INTERPRETED
Interpreted by love 386

INTERPRETER
God is his own *Interpreter* 577

INTERCEDE
For me to *intercede* 113

INTERCEDING
Ever for us *interceding* 659

INTERCESSION
Who made *intercession,* "My father 73

INTERCESSOR
Intercessor, Friend of sinners 77
O *Intercessor,* who art ever living 1545

INTERCOURSE
In *intercourse* at hearth or board 478
Secret *intercourse* with God 752

INTEREST
An *interest* in the Savior's blood 94

INTRODUCED
Blest Savior, *introduced* by thee 154

INVITATION
The *invitation* is to all 336
The pressing *invitation* is that you 1337

INVITES
And then *invites* us thus to feast 722
And today he *invites* you to come 1115
Jesus *invites* you here 85
Ye hear how kindly he *invites* 75

INVOKED
When *invoked* by priest and seer 611

INVOLVED
Involved in shadows 1059

IRE
In *ire* and exultation 1365

ISLES
Isles of the sea where darkness 1366
Isles of the southern seas 733
Savior, lo! the *isles* are waiting 1686
The *isles* are waiting for thy word 1467
Ye *isles,* give ear to me 574

ISSUE
The *issue* can we know 90

J

JACKET

God in a workman's *jacket* 2262

JERUSALEM

And was *Jerusalem* builded there 95
Till we have built *Jerusalem* 95
True *Jerusalem* and free 78

JEST

A *jest* and byword are they grown 473

JEWELS

All his *jewels,* precious jewels 2229
And *jewels* rich and rare 2085
And shining *jewels* cover the heavens 1297
Are the *jewels,* precious jewels 2229
Brighter than royal *jewels* 638
Nor the glittering *jewels* of time 871
What are they but his *jewels* 1391

JOIN

And *join* the chorus of the skies 1514
Gladly *join* our song 61
I *join* the heavenly lays 1864
I will *join* the saints and 1847
If you would *join* the glad songs 905
Join all my powers to praise 1897
Join all ye bright celestial choirs 1895
Join all your sacred powers 1122
Join in a song with sweet accord 351
Join in the praise with the blood-bought 1758
Join me in glad adoration 1637
Join our happy throng 1586
Join our praying Pattern 752
Join the angel song 1211
Join the everlasting song 47
Join the triumph of the skies 675
Join the war, and face the foe 1560
Join with all nature in manifold 647
Join with men and angels 1833
Join with the ransomed his praises 2235
Let all within me *join* 1315
Shall *join* our souls to thee 767
The Gentile and the Jew shall *join* 209
'Till we *join* the church above 1676
To *join* with these today 33
Until we *join* the church above 15
Up and *join* the royal army 2159
We shall *join* the endless chorus 1738
We, thy children, *join* the chorus 208
We'll *join* the everlasting song 47
When I shall *join* them, my 2235
Whom thou forevermore dost *join* 1473

JOINED

And *joined* them as they walked 975
I *joined* the mockery 873
Inseparably *joined* in heart 97
Joined in one spirit 230
Lord, I have *joined* in the hateful 1015

JOINS

He *joins* the faithful host 620
He *joins* the glorious host (martyr) 620
He *joins* the noble (sacred) host 620

JOURNEY

All along my pilgrim *journey* 2042
And like thee, all my *journey* run 769
As they *journey* homeward 517
As they onward *journey* 1110
As ye *journey,* sweetly sing 277
Happy, how happy our *journey* 2129
Her *journey* not yet done 432
On all the *journey* of our life 1401
Only with thee we *journey* 1059
They *journey* on from strength to 782
We are going on a *journey* 2284
We *journey* in its light 1057
We *journey* to a city 2172
We *journey* to a country 2172
Where'er I *journey* thou art there 815
While on my *journey* here below 482

JOURNEYED

Journeyed oft with weary feet 521

JOURNEYS

And he who *journeys* in them 2193
Faith's *journeys* end in welcome 670

JOY

A *joy* no language measures 1377
All hail, with *joy* we greet thee 48
An Easter of unending *joy* 1187

And hitherto hast *joy* supplied 2035
And in their *joy* rejoice 532
And is there a *joy* which thou 1583
And it shall be thy *joy* and crown 477
And *joy*, and strength and power 1183
And *joy* eternal find 1597
And *joy* from heart to heart 792
And *joy* in every trace 1324
And *joy* in heavenly greeting 642
And *joy* shall be expressed 570
And *joy* succeeds to pain 2171
And *joy* to see the cheerful light 2332
And *joy* with suffering blent 2077
And *joy* within thee wait 786
And *joy* without a tear 1223
And the *joy* he bestows 2266
And the *joy* of our Lord to be 1338
And the *joy* of thy salvation 1603
And the *joy* set before him 2063
And the *joy* we share as we tarry 819
And there forever sharing its *joy* 1457
And with *joy* our eyes 507
And with *joy* the owner 1198
And with *joy* we shall gather 699
Are you longing for *joy* 180
As here with *joy* this stone 1427
As with *joy* they hailed 129
Beaming with *joy* and gladness 180
Beyond my highest *joy* 859
Boundless their *joy* above 1537
But O the *joy* when I awake 1749
Daily *joy* its truths afford 780
Each *joy* and each sorrow to share 701
Earthly *joy* for them is past 555
Emmanuel, our *joy* unending 1316
Ever new that *joy* shall be 1687
Every *joy* or trial falleth 1091
For all the *joy* of morning light 1228
For summer *joy* in field 1938
For the *joy* of ear and eye 484
For the *joy* of human love 484
For very *joy* it laughs and sings 1723
His *joy* shines forth 120
His *joy* will gladden every day 2269
How great the *joy* that thou 1002
How sure is *joy*, for all who turn 1389
I *joy* to call thee mine 1475
If *joy* shall at thy bidding fly 1119
In *joy*, in grief through life 1689
In *joy* or in sorrow 1820
In *joy* or sorrow Christ is all 906
In the *joy* of what thou art 978
In thy *joy*, O let thy brother 2263
It will *joy* and comfort give you 1817
Jesu(s) our only *Joy* be thou 1019
Joy amid the darkest night 1973
Joy and rapture ev'rywhere 2191
Joy and sorrow interwoven 1643
Joy and warmth will follow 1305
Joy attend us in believing 519
Joy awaits me in the morning 1044
Joy, behold the Savior 474
Joy breaks in song from her jubilant 601
Joy for all his children willed 1066
Joy in each amazing token 282
Joy is like restless day 821
Joy, joy, for Christ is born 2215
Joy like a river around me 2222
Joy of every longing heart 343
Joy of heaven, to earth come down 1190
Joy of the desolate 355
Joy of the sad 1656
Joy that fills the heart 1973
Joy that never shall depart 1973
Joy that throbs within my heart 1973
Joy that triumphs over pain 1973
Joy—the message hear 474
Joy to find in every station 980
Joy to my heart 'twill bring 982
Joy to our hearts, and faith 1873
Joy to the lands that in darkness 660
Joy to you he will restore 1885
May the *joy* of thy salvation 741
My *joy* doth ev'ry bound exceed 2302
My *joy* in grief, my shield 2034
My *joy* is in thy beauty 2119
Nearer the *joy* I long to share 1267
Now with *joy* is ringing 52
O *joy*, all joys beyond 1959
O *joy*, for all its former woes 1836
O *joy* of all the meek 1019
O *joy* that seekest me through pain 1465
O *joy* to the victor 1987
O Lord of *joy* and hope 1491
O the *joy* of full salvation 1688
O the *joy* that waits you 1997
O the *joy* to see thee reigning 2018
O 'twere not in *joy* to charm me 980
O what *joy* it will be when his face 809
O what *joy!* mortal tongue 1751
O what *joy* the sight affords 1117
O with what *joy* they my heart 807
O with what *joy* they went away 136
Of *joy* that hath no ending 350
Of the blessed *joy* he brings 1583
Once earthly *joy* I craved 1220
One in *joy*, and light, and love 582
One in the *joy* of work well done 1453
One with the *joy* that breaketh 421
Our *joy* that hath no end 1854
Shall be the *joy* of all the earth 513
So may we with holy *joy* 129
Still let new *joy* be given 1863
That it might be our highest *joy* 1468
The *joy* of all below 1869
The *joy* of all the lands 646
The *joy* of all who dwell above 1869
The *joy* of his blessed presence 1950
The *joy* of life, the fire of love 316
The *joy* of more abundant life 2277
The *joy* of salvation 931
The *joy* of spring, the hush 2277
The *joy* of summer and of spring 1461
The *joy* of the reaper to share 1098
The *joy* of thine abode 2178
Their *joy*, the joy of heaven 1869
Their *joy* unto their Lord 2164
There is *joy* for all the members 1767

There is *joy* for the taking 903
There is *joy* today for a soul 1664
There is *joy* to tell the story 943
There will be *joy* in the golden 1750
There with *joy* thy praises render 394
There's *joy* and peace in my soul 1016
Thou art my *joy,* thou my new 123
Through *joy* or sorrow, as thou deemest 1059
Thy *joy* crown all our days 1313
Thy *joy* supreme what words 1424
Thy *joy,* thy tender fatherhood 67
Thy *joy* to do the Father's will 550
Thy salvation's *joy* impart 554
Till morning's *joy* shall end 670
'Tis the *joy* of Christ, my Savior 1973
To God, my chiefest *joy* 1483
To *joy* and gladness wake us 1402
To *joy* celestial rise 324
True *joy* in heavenly things 1480
True *joy* on earth below 348
'Twill be my *joy* through the ages 881
Unto *joy* or sorrow grown 359
What a *joy* 'twill be, her dear face 2066
What a *joy* 'twill be when I wake 1044
What *joy* shall fill my heart 1437
What *joy* the happy earth to greet 1863
What *joy* thy mandate to obey 391
What *joy* 'twill be, at set of sun 2281
What *joy* will be mine when his face 623
While we with *joy* beholding 1874
Who alike in *joy* and gladness 1516
With *joy* and peace thou shalt 1651
With *joy* I'll follow Jesus 1949
With *joy* my being thrills 1249
With *joy,* my soul, pray on 1639
With *joy* shall I lift up 1024
With *joy* the message to declare 1169
With *joy* the summons we obey 2304
With *joy* their faces shall be 1890
With *joy* their Lord surrounding 644
With *joy* we view the pleasing 2176
With what *joy* they hail 474
With your *joy* and sorrow 1210
Your Commander's *joy* to share 262

JOY-BELLS

Joy-bells ringing in your heart 2339

JOYLESS

Joyless is the day's return 292

JOYS

All our *joys* and all our groans 656
And all the *joys* I have 1201
And from earthly *joys* abstain 500
And *joys* that never cease 2178
And let your *joys* be known 351
And the *joys* of motherhood 238
And when the *joys* of sense 902
Are you grieving over *joys* 112
But all their *joys* are one 323
But lo! what sudden *joys* we see 697
Earthly *joys* are fleeting 1114
Earthly *joys,* our hearts beguiling 993
Earth's *joys* grow dim 27
For *joys* "laid up" above 1980, 2001
For the *joys* that most we cherish 929
Her *joys* and pleasures planned 145
In my dear *joys* have part 1142
In our *joys* and in our sorrows 970
Its *joys* have not been told 2172
Joys are his, serene and pure 1748
Joys that through all time abide 934
Mine to tell of *joys* to come 738
New *joys* may blossom to the end 1523
Of *joys* there is full store 570
Our *joys* go one by one 2171
Our *joys* scarce last the looking 960
Preparing us for *joys* above 1523
Surpassing all the *joys* we know 1409
The *joys* I feel, the bliss I share 1806
The *joys* of day are over 1851
The *joys* that cannot be expressed 305
These are the *joys* which satisfy 1038
Thy *joys* that I might see 960
Thy *joys* when shall I see 960
What *joys* await us there 961
What need have I to borrow the *joys* 2109
When the *joys* on earth are few 63
Whose *joys* eternal flow 2023

JUBILANT

All *jubilant* with song 961

JUBILATIONS

With glad *jubilations* 1768

JUBILEE

Still that *jubilee* of song 1272

JUDGE

And *judge* each rebel nation 2138
As *judge,* on clouds of light 1842
For thou, the righteous *judge* 2099
Great *Judge,* to thee our prayers 644
Jesus, the *Judge,* shall come 1653
Judge and Savior of our race 1145
Judge her not for fields unwon 1033
Judge her not for work undone 1033
Judge of angels and of men 1161
Judge of the nations, spare us yet 583
O *Judge* divine of human strife 1646
The *Judge* of all men doth appear 644
The *Judge* of all the earth is just 1893
The righteous *Judge* of judges 1378
Then God, the *Judge,* shall own my name 1226

JUDGES

Judges of his Israel 275

JUDGMENT

A Shelter from *judgment* 20
And he thy *judgment* shall bring 1708
Blessed are they that *judgment* 1340
Come with thy timeless *judgment* 1340

For *judgment* and salvation 2076
For *judgment* he displays 2312
For *judgment* sets his throne 1887, 1888
He *judgment* brings, and victory 733
In *judgment* therefore shall not 1841
On all, the *judgment* of the Cross 185
To *judgment* and to righteousness 2329
Warning of a *judgment* near 1033
Who righteous *judgment* executes 1394

JUDGMENTS

His *judgments* truth shall guide 198
It is not mine to question the *judgments* 954
Nor, from thy *judgments,* when 1873
The *judgments* of the Lord are true 618
The righteous *judgments* of his mouth 533
Thy *judgments* are a mighty deep 731, 2079
Thy *judgments* deep as floods 2080
Thy *judgments* right 1871
Thy righteous *judgments* I declare 789
When his righteous *judgments* come 1622

JUDGMENT-SEAT

Before the awful *judgment-seat* 1285

JUNGLES

Through *jungles,* sluggish seas 720

JUST

And 'tis prosperous to be *just* 1574
For all the *just* his word is sown 191
The *just* shall enter in 1484
The *just* shall flourish in his days 1454
The *just* who does his will 1857

JUSTICE

And *justice* from her heavenly 1901
And may thy *justice* still protect 2079
Forever firm, thy *justice* stands 731
God of *justice,* save the people 1280
Justice reigns supreme o'er all 656
Justice shall guard his throne 1917
Justice shall vanquish grief 1275
Justice thy diadem 1312
Justice to give each one 1888
Justice, to set us in his steps 909
Let *justice* and peace like a river 584
Let *justice* rule in all the earth 1930
Thy *justice* is like mountains 2080
Thy *justice* like mountains 916
When *justice* shall be clothed 2075
Where *justice* rules from shore 1165
While *justice,* temp'rance, truth 1739
With *justice* by and by 1

JUSTIFIED

And, *justified* by grace 2090
Justified in him are we 664
Rising, he *justified* freely 1575

K

KEEN

Keen was the trial once 1537

KEEP

All within *keep* silence 563
And as I *keep* close to his side 1958
And ever *keep* me close 973
And I shall *keep* it unto the end 1827
And *keep* his truth forevermore 1651
And *keep* it still awake 889
And *keep* me always loyal 920
And *keep* me pure within 178
And *keep* the portals of our hearts 1934
And *keep* them by thy watchful 81
And *keep* thy conscience pure 201
And *keep* us in his grace 1299
And *keep* us through life's wintry 2097
And will *keep* our hearts aglow 1955
But *keep* thy precepts still 459
Do thou, O Lord, *keep* watch 176
Ever *keep* the end in view 480
Father, *keep* this heart from straying 461
God *keep* you in his sight 1850
He will *keep* me 'til the river 895
He will *keep* on loving us 2055
He will *keep* the joy-bells 2339
He will *keep* you all the way 2283
He will *keep* you to the end 1996
Holy Spirit, *keep* us safe from sins 757
I could never *keep* my hold 2232
If I can *keep* one spirit singing 899
Keep by thy mighty hand 650
Keep conscience as the noontide 152
Keep far our foes 31
Keep from ill; from sin defend us 1683
Keep her faith in simple manhood 1280
Keep it long in the fire 1834
Keep love's tie unbroken, Lord 486
Keep me by thy saving grace 1612
Keep me close in touch 224
Keep me ever, by thy Spirit 606
Keep me from secret sin 1645
Keep me in the narrow way 637
Keep me, Lord, for well thou knowest 1055
Keep me, Lord, forever thine 637
Keep me, my God, from stain of sin 1128
Keep me, O keep me, King of 59
Keep me safe by thy dear side 448
Keep me trusting in thy word 2043
Keep my faith and courage strong 2043
Keep my heart unspoiled 461
Keep my thoughts pure, guide me 882
Keep, O keep, our children's face 1553
Keep, O keep them, in their weakness 741
Keep, O keep us, Savior dear 500
Keep, O Lord, our brothers safe 2274
Keep of my lips the door 1433
Keep our loved ones, now far absent 741
Keep the homeland in view 2271
Keep the light of hope eternal 1270
Keep them faithful to the end 2264
Keep them faithful unto death 760
Keep them in conscience free 1379
Keep them not away" 996
Keep them true-hearted 2291
Keep thou my feet 1053
Keep thou the faith, unstained 1784
Keep thou them in the hour of flight 490
Keep us all, in safety keep 1197
Keep us ever at thy side 966, 1012
Keep us evermore thine own 492
Keep us faithful 492
Keep us from all harm 290
Keep us from temptation, from evil 1594
Keep us in life, forgive our sins 1289
Keep us in the narrow way 129
Keep us in thy presence dear 930
Keep us, mighty Savior 256
Keep us on our guard 988
Keep us pure 492
Keep us true to thee, and wise 1158
Keep us, we pray thee, steadfast 1374
Keep your hand upon the throttle 1076
O Jesus, *keep* me in thy sight 1851
O *keep* me ever in thy love 790
O *keep* them, keep them, thou 460
O *keep* them undefiled 460
O *keep* us building, Master 2198
O *keep* us in the pathway their 487
Safely *keep*, while I sleep 415
So *keep* thy law shall I 1826
Spotless *keep* his fair abode 1835
Still *keep* me, guide me, love me 1128
Thee they ever *keep* in view 752
To guide and *keep* aright 1169

To *keep* us still thine own 267
To such as *keep* his covenant 1798
We *keep* the memory 266
We *keep* the sacred feast 927
We may *keep* the feast at last 538
Who would *keep* abreast of truth 1574
Why should I *keep* one precious thing 855
Would *keep* our inmost conscience pure 1300

KEEPER

Jehovah is himself thy *keeper* 2139
Thy faithful *Keeper* is the Lord 885

KEEPEST

Those thou *keepest* always see 739

KEEPETH

He *keepeth* me from day to day 847
He *keepeth* promises 573
Who *keepeth* Israel in his 2139

KEEPS

And *keeps* his courts below 1625
And *keeps* me singing along the way 1756
And now he *keeps* me by his power 834
And *keeps* my happy soul 2034
For he *keeps* both day and night 1674
He *keeps* me now from day to day 1907
He *keeps* on loving us still 2055
Keeps me singing as I go 2002
Still it *keeps* us 450

KEEP'ST

Thou *keep'st* thy chosen souls 1889

KEN

Beyond our *ken* thou shinest 1378

KEPT

Be ever *kept* in mind 329
For I'm *kept* from all danger 430
Has *kept* in deepest peace 462
Kept a sacred Lent for us 268
Kept by thy care 1939
Kept peaceful in the midst 1119
Kept the folded grave-clothes 2010
Still he *kept* a holy 268
Thou has *kept* thy pilgrim people 487
They have *kept* the faith with patience 1499
While I *kept* guilty silence 772
Zion, *kept* by pow'r divine 2341

KEY

Christ has the *key,* O death 498

KEYS

The *keys* of death and hell 1653

KILL

The body they may *kill* 12

KIND

Let me be *kind* in word and deed 1128

KINDLE

And *kindle* in our breasts 315
And *kindle* it, thy holy flame 306
And that shall *kindle* ours 318
Kindle a flame of sacred love 318, 1521
Kindle every high desire 761
Then *kindle* in us zeal 1401

KINDLED

Kindled by a spark of grace 1695
Kindled in some hearts it is 1696

KINDLES

Then *kindles* love divine 1405, 1409

KINDNESS

And *kindness* conquer wrong 384
And *kindness* dwell in human hearts 419
And *kindness* in our bosoms dwell 1119
Let me thy *kindness* know 2244
The weakest his *kindness* may claim 698
There's a *kindness* in his justice 1767, 1999
They who once his *kindness* prove 1581
To me in *kindness* come 1557
While *kindness* in his bosom 2133

KINDRED

From every *kindred,* every tongue 671
Let every *kindred,* every tribe 47
Let goods and *kindred* go 12
Let my *kindred,* Lord, of mine 2227
There my *kindred* and friends are 1503
Thy *kindred* and their graves may be 132

KINDREDS

All *kindreds* of the earth shall own 1858
All *kindreds* shall remember 360

KING

And Christ was *King* and Lord 2135
And let the *King* of Glory pass 1081
And now, O *King* eternal 1057
And to crown him *King* 1994
And to heaven's eternal *King* 357
And will this sovereign *King* 1897
But who is he that is the *King* 2327
Christ Jesus is *King* 1599
"Come, *King* of Grace" 312
Come quickly, *King of* Kings 1877
For God's a great God, and great *King* 1335
For lo, the *King* comes nigh 2137
From heaven's all-gracious *King* 948
God is *King,* in depth and height 610
Hail, thou *King* of victory 288
He is *King* on his throne 537
He with the *King* of Glory 1786
He's a *King* on a throne 1971
In Christ, our heavenly *King* 147
Jehovah as *King* is enthroned 537
Jesus Christ, the *King* of Glory 664
King battles still with king 592
King forever, ceasing never 2196
King of Glory now 143

King of Glory, reign forever 673
King of Grief, I watch with thee 2059
King of Kings, from heaven 521
King of Kings in heav'n we'll 1817
King of Kings, yet born of Mary 1060
King of Life, who hast created 1049
King of Mercy, thou hast saved 1049
King of our lives, by thy grace 2128
King of Righteousness and Peace 1073
King of the earth and air 1518
King triumphant, King victorious 1049
King within my conscience reign 761
Mighty *King*, thine arm revealing 2342
Now may the *King* descend 2203
O glorious *King*, we bless thee 1415
Our *King* to see, and oh, to be 2207
Our risen *King* and Savior 49
So thou art still our *King* 1448
The *King* in all his beauty 2172
The *King* in his glory hath chosen 2271
The *King* of all kingdoms 896
The *King* of Glory enters in 1080
The *King* of Glory is the King 2137
The *King* of Heaven, the glorious 1493
The *King* of Kings, and Lord 1869
The *King* of Kings confessing 1320
The *King* of Kings is drawing near 1082
The *King* of Kings, salvation brings 2215
The *King* of Kings with glory crown 535
The *King* of Love in triumph rides 510
The *King* shall come when morning 1877
The *King* who reigns in Salem's 198
The Lord is *King!* child of the dust 1893
The Lord is *King!* who, then, shall dare 1893
The Lord of Hosts, he is the *King* 1857
The Lord omnipotent is *King* 1893
The Lord our God is *King* of Kings 1334
Then before our *King* the foe 1994
This *King* my heart hath now 2140
This *King* of Love shall conquer 510
This, this, is Christ the *King* 2215
Thou art coming to a *King* 330
Thou art the *King* of Israel 44
Thou art the *King* of Mercy 828
Though now as *King* he reigneth 2230
'Tis the Lord, the *King* of Glory 2286
To Christ, your risen *King* 1083
To seek for a *King* was their intent 1861
To the *King* of Glory bring 543
Trying to follow our Savior and *King* 2129
Unto this *King* mine all 2140
When Christ, our *King*, in beauty comes 1877
When God, our *King* shall thither 1167
When the *King* commands the spirit 1991
Who is this glorious *King* that comes 1857
Who, O *King* of all creation 1213
Yielding henceforth to our glorious *King* 2128
Your God is *King;* your Father 1893
Your Lord and *King* adore 1653

KINGDOM

All *kingdom*, power and glory 360
And Christ's great *kingdom* shall come 2208
And in his *kingdom* I have a share 1756
As in thy heavenly *kingdom*, Lord 1406
Be the *kingdom* all thine own 227
Be the *kingdom* and dominion 1306
Come, God's own *kingdom*, and 466
For Christ's coming *kingdom* are you 112
For his the *kingdom*, his of right 1858
For the *kingdom* and the power 581
For the *kingdom* of darkness 2113
For thy *kingdom* makes us bold 1182
He that unto God's *kingdom* comes 1148
His *kingdom* cannot fail 1653
His *kingdom* is forever 12
His *kingdom* is glorious, and rules 2330
His *kingdom* stretch from shore 1008
His *kingdom* tarries long 1669
Kingdom without end 1833
Let thy *kingdom* come, O Lord 486
Let thy *kingdom* come, we pray thee 581
Marching upward to the *kingdom* 2159
May thy *kingdom* holy on earth 1594
Now thy gracious *kingdom* bring 343, 658
Ordaining, maintaining his *kingdom* 2166
Since the *kingdom* now is here 363
The *kingdom* is coming 509
The *kingdom* of love and light 2208
The *kingdom* shall be builded 781
The *kingdom* that I seek 2083
The *kingdom* yet to be 156
There of the *kingdom* learned 91
Thine is the *kingdom* and the power 1507
Thy *kingdom* come, O Lord, thy will 438
Thy *kingdom* hath none end at all 628
Thy *kingdom* shall inherit 2076
Thy *kingdom* stands and grows 1856
Till his *kingdom* come 1069
To seek the *kingdom* of thy peace 1124
Unto my *kingdom* ye may come 949
Whose are the *kingdom*, the crown 228
Within the *kingdom* of his might 1729
Would you in his *kingdom* find a place 2324

KINGDOMS

And the *kingdoms* of this world 676
For not like *kingdoms* of the world 1539
Kingdoms rise and wane 1586
Kingdoms wide that sit in 1593
Now the *kingdoms* of this world 2150
Till the *kingdoms* of the world 1747
To conquer the *kingdoms* of sin 509
When all its *kingdoms* shall his 1374

KINGS

Christ of *kings* the King 1034
Kings and priests henceforth forever 669
Kings bow before his throne 360
Kings came from far to gain 1253
Kings shall fall down before him 661
Kings shall render tribute 286
Let *kings* and people praise 1898
Not *kings* alone, but nations 2267
The *kings* of the east are riding 1878
Which *kings* and prophets waited for 768

KINSMAN

Kinsman of the King divine 1051

KISS

By *kiss* of child, and touch 604
With friendship's *kiss,* and loyal 1251

KISSED

A sunbeam *kissed* the hidden spot 11

KNEE

Bending low the *knee* 1680
Every *knee* shall bow 143
Every *knee* to him shall bow 1117
Full reverently upon their *knee* 1861
There to bend the *knee* before 129
Thou who at thy mother's *knee* 930
Till every *knee* shall worship 33

KNEEL

And while we *kneel* confessing 1853
Could we but *kneel,* and cast 1431
Kneel and pray 929
Kneel in awe and wonder 52
Lo, *kneel* where lies in manger bed 320
Lowly we *kneel* in prayer before 1473
To bless them as they *kneel* 1944
We *kneel* and adore thee 2188
We *kneel,* and all around us seems 1183
We *kneel* at close of day 188
We *kneel,* how weak; we rise 1183
When I *kneel* in prayer, and with thee 808
When they *kneel* before thee here 2264
Yea, let us *kneel* before the Lord 1334

KNEELING

Kneeling on the floor 1110

KNEES

All *knees* in lowly homage bow 372
All *knees* must bend 373
All *knees* must bow 1968
And on our *knees* before the Lord 1335
Nor my *knees* press Gethsemane's 236
On our *knees* we fall and pray 1145
To thee all *knees* are bent 92

KNELT

As he *knelt* 'neath the old olive trees 1268
But silent *knelt* the mother 1488
I *knelt* at my mother's side 2066
Jesus *knelt* on the ground 1268
Where Jesus *knelt* to share 386

KNEW

He *knew* his thorny crown would be 2242
I *knew* not of his love 303
I *knew* not what I did 497
Not as we *knew* them anymore 491
She *knew* her Lord had come 1713
This they *knew* the night they hailed 1075
Though he *knew* what it meant 2063
When I *knew* my sins forgiv'n 25
Who *knew* your need and saw your sin 549

KNIGHTS

The *knights* of service choose 309

KNIT

And *knit* our hearts in one 1403
God, *knit* thou sure the cord 813
Knit sundered hearts in one 244
O *knit* my thankful heart to thee 1025
That, closely *knit* in holy vow 1370

KNOCK

God calling yet! and shall he *knock* 558
Knock, and it shall be opened 111

KNOCKETH

He *knocketh* at our hearts' closed 1290

KNOCKING

O Jesus, thou art *knocking* 1414

KNOCKS

As he *knocks* and asks admission 692
He gently *knocks,* has knocked before 192

KNOW

All they, O Lord, that *know* thy name 1435
All who *know* thee bless 1073
Alone I *know* I can but fail 866
And I *know* he watches me 2296
And I *know* it's there to stay 833
And I *know* that thou art with me 2092
And *know* as we are known 15
And *know* how he doth bless 1261
And *know* not what they do 497
And *know* of his wonderful might 553
And *know* our prayer is heard 1029
And *know* that he dearly loves you 1754
And *know* that I share in his love 884
And *know* the ancient presence 1914
And *know* thou hear'st my prayers 1003
And *know* thy hidden name 1714
And *know* with assurance 1974
And make us *know* and choose 310
And may we *know,* Lord Jesus, the touch 515
And now I *know* it all 303
And surely thou dost *know* 973
And they that *know* thy name 1887, 1888
And though I *know* not why or how 13
And we who *know* how true thou art 785
And yet I *know* when these are past 847
And you will *know* him as never 2337
As yet we *know* thee but in part 1520
Blessed Jesus! would we *know* him 1577
But I *know* of a name 850
But I *know* whom I have believed 849
But O, I *know* my guide 822
But still we *know* the door once 1597
But this I *know,* all flesh 817
But this I *know,* he heals 817
But this I *know,* his praise 823
But this I *know,* on Calvary 823
But this I *know,* some happy day 823
But this I *know,* that he was born 817

But this I *know,* the skies will thrill 817
But this I *know,* when 'tis laid 847
But this I surely *know* 860
"Did ye not *know* it is my work 1468
Following him I *know* 981
For I *know* whate'er befall me 66
For O, I *know* he leadeth me 847
For those who *know* it best 862
For we *know* the Lord of Glory 1118
For we *know* thou guardest well 2275
For well we *know,* where'er they be 590
From those that *know* thee may thy love 2079
I am peaceful, for I *know* 2056
I *know* eternal life he giveth 852
I *know* he cares 401
I *know* he hears my praise 860
I *know* he loves me too 602
I *know* he loves them all 602
I *know* he'll come for me 823
I *know* he'll never send a load 1896
I *know* his name 914
I *know* his promise never faileth 852
I *know* I shall be happy 1949
I *know* I shall see him, shall 1741
I *know* I shall see in his beauty 1649
I *know* I'm in the Savior's hand 1907
I *know* I'm nearing the holy ranks 1247
I *know* in his word he hath promised 1922
I *know* my God is just 291
I *know* my Guide 1318
I *know* my Savior cares 401
I *know* not how, or when, or where 847
I *know* not how that Calvary's 846
I *know* not how that Joseph's tomb 846
I *know* not how the Spirit moves 849
I *know* not how this saving faith 849
I *know* not, O I know not 961
I *know* not what may soon betide 2295
I *know* not what of good or ill 849
I *know* not when my Lord may come 849
I *know* not where his islands lift 848, 2310
I *know* not which is best 979
I *know* of a Book (day, home, name) 850
I *know* that but in dying 1404
I *know* that God is good 2310
I *know* that he is leading (living) 874
I *know* that he is with me 134
I *know* that I shall not be left 2238
I *know* that Jesus liveth 852
I *know* that life he giveth 852
I *know* that safe with him 914
I *know* that some day when 871
I *know* that the light of his 1649
I *know* who standeth fast 853
I *know* who true remaineth 853
I may not *know* the way I go 822
I only *know* a living Christ 846
I only *know* he loves me 818
I only *know* I cannot drift 848, 2310
I only *know* its matchless love 846
I only *know* the Manger Child 846
I shall *know* him, I shall *know* him 2246
I shall *know* my Redeemer when 2246
I would be humble, for I *know* 897
I would *know* no will but thine 1690
Its saving power may *know* 83
Jesus we *know,* and he is on 1610
Know on earth thy blessing given 1553
Know that the Lord is God alone 184
Know that the Lord is God indeed 57
Know the blessing of his presence 969
Know thy certainty 978
Know what wealth of grace 978
Know ye not your Captain's 1560
Lead us to *know* the worth 56
Let all *know* thee, and obey thee 581
Let it *know* no revocation 1690
Let me *know* it is to me 1207
Let me *know* thy presence 2123
Lord, we *know* not how to go 1181
May they *know* this house their own 1567
Nor *know* to what high purpose thou 491
That we may *know* its depth 454
That we may *know* that thou 522
That we may *know* thy name 1149
That's why I *know* the old story 1971
Then I *know* the sins of earth beset 431
Then, Lord, shall I fully *know* 2261
Then may we *know,* earth's lesson 456
Then shall I *know* what means 1416
Then shall they *know,* they that love 666
Then shall we *know* and taste 305
Then we shall *know* and praise 315
There none shall *know* suffering 1870
There, we *know,* thy word believing 1691
They cannot, for I *know* 822
They *know* not that the Savior said 2245
They *know* not what they do 497
Till all shall *know* the loveliness 419
'Tis what I *know* of thee, my Lord 1284
To *know* that God is mine 1038
To *know* thee as thou art 28
Truly *know* that thou art mine 70
We *know* as surely as the bird 1294
We *know* no dawn but thine 311
We *know* no help but thee 1396
We *know* not what is coming 460
We *know* that all mountains 1372
We *know* that his heart 765
We *know* that those who enter 1597
We *know* that thou art strong 384
We *know* that thou art wise 384
We *know* thee truly but in this 1495
We *know* them living unto thee 590
We *know* thou wilt 713
We *know* thy cross is not a loss 1417
We *know* we at the end 707
We *know* we'll rise again 498
We *know* we've nothing worthy 1597
We *know* who giveth all 1938
We may not *know,* we cannot 1963
We shall *know* as we are known 2256
We shall *know* each other better 2256
We shall *know* no sin or sorrow 1991
We shall only *know* the blessing 1991
We, too, would *know* God's love 1591
We'll *know* why clouds instead 1282
Well I *know* the heart that 1643

Well we *know* his voice 983
What yet shall be I may not *know* 882
When shall we *know* thee as we ought 2170
When we *know* it comes from thee 144
When you *know* him, when you 2269
Who *know* and feel its power 1906
Who *know* his power, his grace 1105
Would you *know* the peace that comes 2324
Yet I *know* as I onward plod 729
You can *know* Jesus, but you must 2337
You'll *know* his way is always best 2269

KNOWEST, KNOW'ST

Come, thou who *knowest* what we need 383
For thou, who *knowest,* Lord, how soon 1236
Knowest all its truest need 1207
O Father, thou *know'st* he hath died 73
Thou *knowest,* Lord, man's sinful state 1381
Thou *knowest* my sitting down 1452
Thou *knowest* the way to bring me back 2202
Thou *knowest* our infirmity 161
Thou who *knowest* this our path 1796

KNOWETH

And *knoweth* more of all my needs 39
He *knoweth* best 847
He *knoweth* what is best 1283
Like the seed when no man *knoweth* 36

KNOWLEDGE

All our *knowledge,* sense, and sight 220
And our deeper *knowledge* 925
And thy *knowledge* fills the earth 2318
Beyond all *knowledge* and all thought 1461
For *knowledge* is of things we see 1797
His *knowledge* rules high over all 2338
How vast his *knowledge,* how profound 155
Knowledge, all things empty prove 636
Knowledge and faith and life 469
Knowledge thou has lent 2173
Knowledge we ask not 2173
Knowledge will come of his blessings 2337
Knowledge with its gladd'ning streams 1628
Let *knowledge* grow from more to more 1797
May *knowledge* of thy ways 2098
My *knowledge* of that life is small 1148
Nor do I for the *knowledge* pray 387
Such *knowledge* is too strange 1452
The *knowledge* of his covenant 2116
Thy *knowledge* is the only line 788
To give *knowledge* of salvation unto 215
When *knowledge,* hand in hand 2075

KNOWN

And be thou *known,* when fears 1318
Be *known* to us in breaking bread 1716
It is well *known* to thee 1452
Knowing as I am *known* 1452
Known long before conceived by me 2039
Since they have never, never *known* 420
Those who've never *known* thee 517
To thee are *known* its toils 2036
Where'er the Christ is *known* 1113
Ye who have *known* Jehovah's 778

KNOWS

A Savior who *knows* how to save 20
But Jesus *knows* and will provide 2295
But 'tis enough that Christ *knows* 1148
God *knows* the way, he holds 1282
God only *knows* the love of God 1458
He *knows* and tempers every wind 845
He *knows* he at the end 2290
He *knows* not where to flee 156
He *knows* our feeble frame 2305
He *knows* the clouds that would 845
He *knows* the pain of the heart 506
He *knows* the way 847
He *knows* the way he taketh 921
He *knows* thine hourly need 548
He *knows* what sore temptations 2305
He *knows* your thoughts that blight 2338
He *knows* your trials 378
Jesus *knows* all about our struggles 2000
Jesus *knows,* he knows 63
Jesus *knows* thy conflict 987
Knows he's neither wise nor strong 1647
Knows neither near nor far 96
Knows thine ev'ry care 987
Knows thy deep contrition 987
That *knows* not race nor station 1549
Who *knows* my heart's most secret 303
Yet who that *knows* the worth of prayer 2221

L

LABOR

All *labor* vainly done 240, 1428
"All ye that *labor* come to me 75
And *labor* on at thy command 499
And *labor* till the Master comes 2113
And *labor* up the heavenly hill 1142
And *labor* while 'tis day 1598
Blest *labor,* doubly blest 2147
But *labor* ends with sunset ray 2120
Come, all ye that *labor* 347
For it we must *labor* 501
He'll *labor* night and day 2290
I'll *labor* night and day 707
In our *labor,* rest more sweet 342
Labor ended, Jordan passed 119
Labor is rest, and pain is sweet 1824
Labor is sweet, for thou hast 1478
Labor well done shall receive 167
Let me *labor* till the ev'ning shadows 1710
Let us *labor* for the Master from 2259
Lo! from earth's imperfect *labor* 2275
May all our *labor,* crowned by 458
My daily *labor* to pursue 499
O happy, if ye *labor* as Jesus did 1391
That useful *labor* yet may build 1072
There is *labor* for all 2113
Thou who didst with Joseph *labor* 634
To *labor* and to love 201
Until we *labor* for those gifts 1386
When on the sweat of *labor* 2262
Where I may *labor* through life's short 955
With *labor* long have wrought 1175
Yea, let our hopeful *labor* be 1174

LABORED

We have *labored* here together 1499
We have *labored* side by side 1499

LABORERS

As *laborers* in thy vineyard 1166, 1344
Before his *laborers* lies 97
More *laborers* for the Lord 1496

LABORS

All *labors* past, O then may I 1027
And, when at last our earthly *labors* 712
And when our *labors* all are o'er 2325
E'en servile *labors* shine 1825
From all their *labors* now they rest 1108
Not the *labors* of my hands 1671
Our God, his *labors* but begun 1593
We, to their *labors* entering in 1496
Where all our *labors* end 97
Where in others' *labors* sharing 716

LACK

And they may *lack* their food 616
That we no *lack* of grace may 408

LADDER

Let Bethel's shining *ladder* rise 2291
What are they but the *ladder* 1391

LAID

And *laid* a silent loveliness 40
And *laid* his hands on each 949
And *laid* on me thine hand 1452
For he *laid* down the life which he 2063
Gentle Mary *laid* her Child 524
I *laid* me down and slept 1430
Is *laid* for your faith in his excellent 776
Jesus Christ *laid* down his life 1198
Laid down his life without murmur 531
Laid down his sweet head 159
Laid in a manger 1504
Laid in the tomb, to save both you 498
Laid the Son of Man his head 369
They have *laid* aside their armor 1499
They *laid* the Savior's body 626
Thou hast *laid* thy throne's foundation 610
'Twas *laid* before the world's 1290
Were you there when they *laid* him in 2206
When he *laid* down his life 1115

LAKE

Lake and mountain, field and fountain 208

LAMB

A follower of the *Lamb* 87
And on God's *Lamb* our guilt 2155
And to the *Lamb* that once was slain 671
And was the holy *Lamb* of God 95
But Christ, the heavenly *Lamb* 1279
Dear dying *Lamb,* thy precious blood 1961
Every *Lamb* is sprinkled 983

For the dear *Lamb* of God left his 1561
For the *Lamb* is all the light 938
If of this *Lamb* I nothing knew 1422
Is our Paschal *Lamb* today 287
Jesus, the *Lamb* of David's line 1670
Lamb of God, grant us thy peace 1028
Lamb of God, thy glory 1034
Lamb of God, to thee I cry 1761
Lamb of God, we bow before thee 597
Lamb upon the throne on high 597
Like a *lamb* he humbly yielded 1728
Lo! the *Lamb* so long expected 668
O *Lamb* of God, for sinners slain 316
O *Lamb* of God, I come 1046
O *Lamb* of God, we only know 1525
O *Lamb,* once slain 1366
Rejoicing in the *Lamb* of God 147
The *lamb* finds the good Shepherd's breast 179
"The *Lamb* for me was slain." 1422
The *Lamb* for sinners slain 512
The *Lamb* is the Light in the city 1946
The *Lamb* of God was slain 1351
The *Lamb* once slain 1366
The *lamb,* the linnet, and the hare 1103
The *Lamb* which dwells amidst 774
The *Lamb* who went before them 2172
Thou *Lamb* of God, enthroned on high 43
Thou, our Paschal *Lamb* indeed 287
Thy loving *lamb* to feed 2020
Till the *Lamb* of God may die 2059
To see the *Lamb* who died 1959
To the *Lamb* that once was slain 543
Where Christ, the *Lamb,* doth reign 1397
Worthy, O *Lamb* of God, art thou 2022
Worthy the *Lamb,* enthroned to reign 1366
"Worthy the *Lamb,*" let us reply 671
"Worthy the *Lamb* that died," they cry 671
Worthy the *Lamb* that once was slain 1704

LAMBS

And *lambs* for whom the Shepherd 2167
And wilful *lambs* that go astray 1928
For thee the *lambs* within her bosom 505
The happy *lambs* of Jesus 33
The *lambs* lie in his bosom 1928
While the *lambs* thy bosom share 1691

LAMENT

Through the rude wind's wild *lament* 627

LAMENTATION

Your *lamentation* then shall be 1337

LAMP

And every *lamp* more brightly burn 1453
And the *lamp* that gives light 130
Bright as a *lamp* its doctrines 787
Lo! a more heavenly *lamp* shines 1803
May her *lamp* of truth be bright 1033
My *lamp* all trimmed and burning 1749
The *lamp* was burning dim 797
This *lamp* shall guide our steps 787

LAMPS

Let all your *lamps* be bright 2331
Though *lamps* go out, and home 2174
Whose *lamps* are trimmed and burning 1597
Will our *lamps* be burning bright 2297
Your *lamps* with gladness take 2149

LAND

A *land* upon whose blissful shore 1965
All the *land* lies quiet 33
And all the *land* lies quiet 33
And every *land* is thine 419
And so in the *land* of the promise 871
And so thou in the *land* shalt 1707
And the beauteous *land* 1101
And through this desert *land* 1101
Anywhere with Jesus, over *land* and sea 108
For in that *land* of joy and song 2301
From *land* to *land* the love of Christ 1652
From New England's storied *land* 518
"From the *land* of hunger 939
From this broad *land* a mighty 1702
Going to a better *land* 2284
In all the *land,* one stedfast band 84
In England's green and pleasant *land* 95
In every *land* disciples meet 2174
In that beautiful *land* 896
In that lovely *land* of unclouded 1502
In the *land* of the east 1984
In the *land* of the unsetting sun 1751
In the *land* where there cometh no 1751
In the new *land,* wild and lonely 1553
In this free *land* by thee our lot 585
In this *land* of sin and woe 1612
It may be in the better *land* 1282
Land of the noble, free 1225
Land of the pilgrims' pride 1226
Land me safe on Canaan's side 652
Land where my fathers died 1226
Long may our *land* be bright 1226
Lord of every *land* and nation 1214
Marching to the promised *land* 2067
Not for this *land* alone 557
O be our *land* forever blest 1595
O blessed is that *land* of God 2120
O *land* of love, and joy, and 1965
O'er every *land* 1
O'er *land* and sea creeps on 1939
On *land* or sea, what matters where 1722
O the *land* of an unclouded day 1502
O the *land* of cloudless day 1502
Our *land* shall own thee Lord 515
Our *land* shall yield increase 909
Over *land* and sea, wherever 1994
Stalking through the *land* 1788
Then God upon our *land* 2099
Through her shall every *land* proclaim 2197
To a pleasant *land* he brings 1837
To Canaan's fair and happy *land* 1563
To ev'ry *land,* to ev'ry race 1368
To this fair *land* the Pilgrims trod 640
The dry *land* also from his hands 1335
The *land* of rest, the saints' delight 779

The *land* that knows no sea 1429
The *land* we love the most 1185
There is a *land* of peace 1959
This *land* we fondly call our own 640
Through the *land* of their sojourn 1894
Until in every *land* and clime 1507
While ev'ry *land* its joyous 1666

LANDS

All heathen *lands* and kingly 2045
And far to *lands* of pagan shame 1702
And distant *lands* and isles 671
Distant *lands* with one acclaim 275
Heathen *lands* shall see from far 479
In *lands* where shadows hide 1467
Lands of the East, awake 733
Lord of all *lands* and our own 596
Lord of the *lands*, make Canada 1165
Mine are all *lands* and seas 1224
O'er heathen *lands* afar 2073
So from all *lands* thy church 469
The *lands* so long enshrouded 149
Till all *lands* receive the witness 2318
Uprising from all *lands* today 82
While distant *lands* their tribute pay 2099

LANES

And where through *lanes* 2195
Glad for the country *lanes* 539
To learn the *lanes* of spirit more 1294

LANGUAGE

Bad *language* disdain 2336
No *language* my rapture can tell 1649
Nor into *language* break 1862
What *language* shall I borrow 1475

LANGUISH

As flesh and spirit *languish* 98
Say, why do I *languish* 795

LANTERN

A *lantern* to our footsteps 1544

LAP

On Mary's *lap* is sleeping 2215
When from her *lap* the holy Child 1186

LARCHES

Green now is on the *larches* 1725

LARK

The *lark* is in the sky 151

LAST

Last like the sun it shall 735
'Twill *last* while endless ages roll 1722

LAST-BORN

Last-born of the nations 709

LASTS

And *lasts* forevermore 1478

LAUD

And *laud* and magnify 1785
His *laud* and benediction 489
Laud and honor to the Father 217, 281
Laud him, ye stormy winds 2328
Laud, honor, might, to him alone 1366
Laud thy pow'r in exultation 1213
Yea, I will *laud* him until death 1621

LAUGHS

Laughs at impossibilities 453

LAUGHTER

O Christ, the *laughter* of holy white 1327

LAUNCH

Launch your vessel, and crowd 1550
We *launch* upon its depths 1919

LAUREL

Thine is the victor's *laurel* 489

LAURELS

So few bright *laurels* won 1849

LAW

All the *law* of love fulfilling 2047
Be my *Law*, and I shall be 761
Come, then, *Law* divine 294
From thy *law*, with thee to guide 780
O thou from whose unfathomed *law* 40
The *law* of love fulfilling 1402
Thine is Judea's *law* with love 522
Thy *law* is there 591
To live by thy free *law* 456
Who in the Lord's most holy *law* 212

LAWS

But to live out the *laws* of Christ 603
If done t'obey thy *laws* 1825
Laws divine to them were spoken 611
Laws, freedom, truth 1354
Laws which never shall be broken 1626
Thy *laws* are pure 1871
Whose *laws* are love 1397
Until the *laws* of Christ become 603

LAY

And *lay* at Jesus' feet 1949
And *lay* my finger on thy heart 1358
Down we *lay* the heavy burden 662
He *lay* a captive bound 283
Here would I *lay* aside 727
I *lay* in dust life's glory 1465
I *lay* my griefs on Jesus 854
I *lay* my wants on Jesus 854
I shall *lay* me down in peace 810
I will both *lay* me down 526
I'll *lay* my honors down 154
Lay down the burden and the care 455
Lay down, thou weary one, lay down 842
Lay hold on life, and it shall be 477
Lay no trophy at his feet 1222
Lay the hosts of error low 262
Lay their honors down and worship 1006

Lay up thy treasures there 1193
Lay upon God's altar 1565
Lay we ev'ry burden down 1711
Lay your sins and cares 344
Long *lay* the world in sin and error 1399
Lord, behold, we *lay* our passions 405
Meek and lowly *lay* 517
Nor *lay* thine armor down 1256
Nor when I'll *lay* my burden down 823
Now we *lay* us down to rest 2062
There he *lay*, the Undefiled 524
Thine own before thy feet we *lay* 67
Thou *lay* the work he gave thee 1177
Thou shalt *lay* the burden down 71
We *lay* it before thee, we kneel 2188
We *lay* it not to heart 19
When I shall *lay* my armor by 1421

LAYS

Mild he *lays* his glory by 675
That *lays* upon the altar the dearest 886

LEAD

Again to *lead* us forward 1549
And do thou *lead* me in thy 1719, 2116
And *lead* me by thy grace 1228
And *lead* me on until earth's joys 1818
And *lead* me to thy holy hill 1519
And *lead* the lost to life 228
And *lead* the world-triumph 709
And *lead* thee in the path whose 2226
And *lead* them in thy ways 1123
And *lead* them to the truth 2098
And *lead* through death to realms 1078
And *lead* to endless day 861
And *lead* to the other shore 2066
And *lead* to victory o'er the grave 1823
And *lead* us in the paths of peace 1595
And *lead* us in those paths 1776
Come, *lead* me unto thee 1462
Do thou me *lead* unto the Rock 1357
For God will *lead* through darkened 824
Gently *lead* me all the way 1682
Gently *lead* us by the hand 755
Gently, Lord, *lead* thou our mothers 1014
He will kindly *lead* me 900
He will *lead* me safely in 403
He will *lead* me where no tears 2246
He will *lead* thee by the hand 276
He'll *lead* us at last to his 1909
If they *lead* through the temple 1815
If thou *lead* us through rough 988
Lead forth my soul, O Christ 406
Lead forth this age in love's large 1445
Lead lives of love, that others who 1548
Lead me all my journey through 652
Lead me by thine own hand 2083
Lead me, for I trust thee 224
Lead me gently, gently, as I go 1684
Lead me, O Lord, till perfect day 821
Lead me through the vale 2042
Lead me to Calvary 1050
Lead me to Christ, the living way 319
Lead me to God, my final rest 319
Lead me to heav'n above 1585
Lead me to holiness, the road 319
Lead me to the Lamb of God 637
Lead, O *lead* me into light 1703
Lead on, O Cross of martyr faith 507
Lead on, O God of might 1057
Lead on, O Love and Mercy 1505
Lead on till peace eternal 1505
Lead onward to the perfect day 456
Lead their praises 2333
Lead them safely by the hand 1775
Lead thou me on 1053
Lead us all our days 966, 1012
Lead us all with hearts aflame 2141
Lead us by faith to hope's 586
Lead us by thy pierced hand 1028
Lead us daily nearer thee 442
Lead us from night 585
Lead us from sin and night 26
Lead us, O Christ, our life-work 1918
Lead us, O Father, to thy heavenly 1059
Lead us on our journey 964, 999
Lead us on our way to heaven 1118
Lead us on to great endeavor 470
Lead us on victorious over 256
Lead us, send us, bless us 695
Lead us through Christ, the true 1059
Lead us through the vale of tears 966, 1012
Lead us to Christ, the living way 310
Lead us to heaven, that we may share 310
Lead us to holiness, the road 310
Lead us to know the worth 56
Lead us to our Sabbath rest 1022
Lead us to the Crucified 759
Lead us to the feast of love 759
Let him *lead* me where he will 863
Lord, *lead* me on to higher ground 915
Lord, *lead* me to some soul 1152
Lord, *lead* me up the mountain side 915
May it *lead* us, Lord, to render 243
Now *lead* us into truth 1526
O *lead* me, if in sin I stray 1438
O *lead* me, Lord, that I may lead 1170
O *lead* us safely on 1977
O let them *lead* me 1701
O may we *lead* the pilgrim's life 1119
Or *lead* one groping pilgrim 899
Safely he would *lead* thee 987
Savior, *lead* me, till at last 1682
So *lead* us then, though suffering's 1948
That *lead* our wandering feet 1424
Then *lead* me on the Rock 1134, 1376
They had never been able to *lead* 2063
Thou alone shalt *lead* 811
Thou wilt *lead* me all the way 969
Though they *lead* o'er the cold, dark 1815
To *lead* them to the right 156
To *lead* us from ourselves to thee 67
To light and *lead* our nation 923
'Twill *lead* me in love to 1868
Where I *lead* to follow me 126
Wheresoe'er the truth will *lead* 64
You can *lead* the little children 679

LEADER

And they who with their *Leader* 961
Be the *Leader* of our life 127
Christ, our *Leader,* walks beside us 2284
Heav'nly *Leader,* still direct us 989
Only thou our *Leader* be 277
Our faithful *Leader* to the end 2118
Our glorious *Leader* claims 530
Our *Leader* all controls 1320
The Lord himself thy *leader* 548
Thou my *Leader* and Defender 1688

LEADERS

Triumphant *leaders* in the war 1859

LEADEST

And *leadest* now the selfsame 1948
Thou *leadest* me by unsought ways 856
Where thou *leadest* we would go 1197

LEADETH

And *leadeth* them tenderly home 698
He *leadeth* me the quiet waters 1904
He *leadeth* my soul where the still 1894
It *leadeth* wise men from afar 2086
Since God through Jordan *leadeth* me 702
Since 'tis my God that *leadeth* me 702
Wherever he *leadeth* me 1822

LEADING

Westward *leading,* still proceeding 2196

LEADINGS

It is but mine to follow the *leadings* 954

LEADS

All that *leads* us up to thee 1158
And he *leads* his children on 1572
And *leads* me on the homeward way 1907
And *leads* men in the paths 1614
And *leads* the conquering line 2294
And *leads* the faithful to the light 1948
Anywhere he *leads* me in this world 108
Christ *leads* me through no 1148
Everywhere he *leads* me I would 403
For he *leads* and guides me 1907
He *leads* and guides me all 482
He safely *leads* my soul along 153
He *leads* us through this hallowed 2016
Jehovah *leads* and vict'ry will 1860
Leads forth in beauty 585
Leads them where the precious 356
That *leads* to light and day 432
That *leads* you into rest 308
The other *leads* us safe and slow 2029
Though sometimes he *leads* through 2002
Where he *leads* I'll follow 1804
Where he *leads* me I will follow 814
Where he *leads* so tenderly 51
Where he *leads* us we can never 2159
Wherever he *leads* I'll go 1822
While he *leads* I cannot fall 1721
Winding or straight, it *leads* 2083

LEAGUES

But more for *leagues* of open sea 2185

LEAN

And *lean* for succor on his breast 1421
But wholly *lean* on Jesus' name 1244
Lean on my breast 836
Lean on the arm of thy Lord 1269
Lean on thy Guide 477
Lean thou only on his Word 276
Lean thou strong upon his Word 276
Lean, weary one, upon his breast 168
Nor ever shall, until they *lean* 1236
Wholly *lean* upon him, then 169

LEANING

Leaning upon him, how sweet 1678

LEAP

And *leap,* ye lame, for joy 1351
My heart for every joy doth *leap* 34

LEARN

And *learn* of thee, the lowly one 769
And *learn* the height, and breadth 305
And *learn* to know and fear 2203
And *learn* to love, dear Lord 2122
And let those *learn,* who here 1899
But *learn* what God is like 617, 2321
Can *learn* to read God's holy book 1536
From thee we *learn* what love is 1490
Here I *learn* of full salvation 431
It is then we *learn* the fullness 662
Learn his law and accept 1706
Learn his name to magnify 684
Learn of him to bear the cross 552
Learn of Jesus Christ to pray 552
Learn thy love while gazing 1271
Learn to say with all your heart 273
Let us *learn* the wondrous story 684
More about Jesus let me *learn* 1216
O shall we never *learn* the truth 1609
Shall *learn* in thy way to abide 2277
That we may *learn* his goodness 2165
Then *learn* to scorn the praise 2321
When we *learn* and when we pray 962, 1009
Who *learn* of thee the truth 1526
You'll *learn* some new thing 130

LEARNED

For I've *learned* the wondrous secret 1973
I'm so glad I *learned* to trust thee 2092
Learned to hearken and obey 930
Nor *learned* thy wisdom, grace 2170
When the *learned* and the high 2260

LEARNER

Lowly and humble, a *learner* of thee 326
There a humble *learner* would I choose 141

LEARNS

That *learns* to value beauty 1549

LEAVE

All I *leave* to follow thee 1688
And gladly *leave* to him the rest 2269
And I *leave* them there 1471
And *leave* his dark abode 237
And *leave* the rest to him 1292
And *leave* the world behind 1038
And *leave* your sheep 320
And peaceful *leave* before thy feet 643
And whene'er you *leave* the silence 942
As we *leave* thy holy place 1153
But thou wilt never *leave* me 820, 2119
Come, and *leave* me never 740
"Come, *leave* the world, and give 724
He never will *leave* nor forsake 698
He will never, never *leave* me 834
He will not *leave* you 1331
I will *leave* all and follow 196
I will *leave* them all there 1982
Leave, ah leave me, not alone 994
Leave all things to a Father's will 1431
Leave him no room to enter 534
Leave it to him, our Lord 473
Leave me alone no more 1208
Leave me not, but ever love 415
Leave not its tenant when its walls 2248
Leave the gloomy haunts 394
Leave the path where now they 2043
Leave the wreck, and in him trusting 474
Leave their royal halls 1110
Leave this vain world and follow 196
Leave to God the coming days 1606
Leave to his sovereign sway 536
Leave us not to doubt 755
Leave we now thy servant 1303
Leave your burden at the place 2252
My God, to thee, I *leave* the rest 1231
Never *leave* me, nor forsake me 973
Never *leave* them till thy face 1775
Never *leave* us nor forsake 966
Nor *leave* him thus alone 957
Nor *leave* my sinful heart 1434
Nor to vainglorying *leave* 1873
Nor will *leave* the desolate 327
Now behind we *leave* the past 64
Or *leave* thy work undone 2072
Prone to *leave* the God I love 340
Thou mightst *leave* me, but the rather 1138
Thou wilt not *leave* us in the dust 1797
Though I oft *leave* the way he 1915
To thee we *leave* them, Lord 590
We would not *leave* thee, though 1177
We'll never *leave* our safe retreat 1905
When we are strong, Lord, *leave* us not 586
Who will *leave* the world's side 2287

LEAVEN

E'en now a false and worldly *leaven* 1915

LEAVES

And green its *leaves* abide 1841
Green were the *leaves* hanging 946
Is still with thee nor *leaves* thy 1881
Leaves are opening wide 61
Leaves, dainty-green their coverings 1293
Leaves on every bough 2204
The little gray *leaves* were kind 947

LEAVETH

Leaveth not in useless silence 2275

LEAVING

Gladly *leaving* all below 277
Leaving all behind us 1680

LED

And *led* the tyrant Death in chains 697
And *led* thee to a cruel death 965
Be not *led* astray 2153
Evermore be *led* to thee 129
How Moses *led* his people 2179
Jesus *led* me all the way 66
Led by grace that love to know 1195
Led by the light of faith (the star) 1399
Led by the Master, that soul 1600
Led by the Spirit 804
Led by thee from earth 2009
Led in paths of light 2129
Mary, *led* by heav'nly grace 141
O holy Father, who hast *led* thy children 92
That he *led* us in his perfect way 169
Thou hast *led* us into rest 597
Thou hast, O Savior, *led* the way 1948
Thus *led* by his Spirit 1820
Till, *led* by thy free spirit 1217
Which *led* the wise men from the east 1650
Who hast *led* them safe through all 1612

LEFT

And I am *left* alone with thee 333
And *left* his nets to follow thee 2189
And *left* my brother wounded 183
And *left* the lonesome place 1877
And straightway *left* all things 196
And thou hast *left* them to their own 2239
And when he *left* his faithful friends 145
Are we *left* in sorrow now 77
At which he *left* his earthly all 196
But they have *left* an aching void 1347
Christ has *left* his throne of glory 1180
For me he *left* his throne above 1534
Hast thou *left* aught for me 827
How he *left* his home in glory 895
I *left,* I *left* it all for thee 827
Jesus *left* heaven my Savior to be 1971
Left alone with human sin 2059
Left for us his Father's home 1728
Lord, I have *left* thee 256
Not *left* to lie like fallen tree 590
Often have we *left* thee 256
The Lord who *left* the heavens 229
They *left* me orphaned 878
"Though thou hast *left* me 1015

LEGION

A *legion* of angels shall carry me 871

LEGIONS

Angelic *legions* guard him home 697
But Christ their *legions* hath dispersed 79, 1937
His *legions* are scattered 1599
Whom angelic *legions* serve 563

LEND

Mary, Joseph *lend* your aid 105
O Master, *lend* us sight to see 2198

LENDS

And *lends* the right a hand 1880

LENGTHEN

When the evening shadows *lengthen* 71

LENGTHENS

Who kindly *lengthens* out our days 1733

LEPER

The *leper* with his tainted life 2008

LESS

"Less of self, and more of thee!" 1498

LESSON

And the burden, and the *lesson* 62
Learning life's great *lesson* 1264
Learning wisdom's *lesson* 141
O to learn this *lesson* well 380
Sweeter *lesson* cannot be 1687

LESSONS

For the *lessons* of our youth 273
O how precious are the *lessons* 942
Sweet indeed have been the *lessons* 835

LETTERS

Its *letters* flame 850

LIBERTY

But in the end, to *liberty* 361
Equal in *liberty* 601
Thy *liberty* in law 1311
Your *liberty* receive 241

LIE

And here I will unwearied *lie* 444
From every *lie* set free 1373
How canst thou *lie* asleep 1208
Let him no more *lie* down in sin 1801
O to *lie* forever here 1195
Prostrate *lie* with deepest reverence 600

LIES

Around us *lies* the heritage 46
From *lies* of tongue and pen 1365
'Gainst *lies*, and lusts, and wrongs 1204
Lies the "city four-square," 938
Low *lies* man's pride and 1652
Still in thee *lies* purest pleasure 1004
Where *lies* our path? We seek 1951

LIETH

Far, far away it *lieth* 2172
The blessed Christ Child *lieth* there 528

LIFE

A *life* for all eternity 60
A *life* of service, death of shame 1534
A *life* that like a river flows 1349
A new *life* to begin 1442
A Shepherd who giveth his *life* 20
Ah no! till *life* itself depart 1514
And *life* is larger for thy law 300
All my *life* thou shalt control 223
All my *life* was wrecked by sin 2002
All other *life* is short and vain 703
All that hath *life* and breath 1627, 1637
All through *life* he will not leave 1577
All through the *life* that's mortal 2251
All thy *life* was prayer and love 752
Alone, his *life* he gave 957
And all my *life* sustaineth 2216
And all of *life* grows holy 1880
And endless *life* are given 1875
And every *life* shall be a song 2003
And for her *life* he died 1845
And for the *life* ineffable 1291
And for thy *life* gave up his own 1514
And have imperfect *life* to offer thee 183
And human *life* become divine 2142
And *life* and everlasting joys 457
And *life*, and health, and bliss 1924
And *life* and mortal powers shall fail 153
And *life*, brief life, is speeding 1952
And *life* eternal gain 494
And *life* for them is *life* indeed 491
And *life* in us renew 587
And *life* to joy awakes 1877
And *life* was a merry chime 2272
And lift us to a nobler *life* 82
And on *life*, while life shall last 357
And this mortal *life* is o'er 2019
And though they take our *life* 19
And through all *life*, forever 2303
And through thy *life*, so radiant 1490
And thy *life* and resurrection 1075
Be this, while *life* is mine 2243
Be thou for us in *life* our Daily Bread 586
Be thou my *life* and aim 1407
Be thou our true, our inward *life* 161
Be thou through *life*, our Strength 1939
Beautiful *life* that has no end 981
Beautiful *life* with such a friend 981
Because of *life* the fountain pure 2080
But all my *life*, in every step 478
But in thy *life* the law 1226
But *life* began to darken 892
But woke to *life* and hope 11
Calling back to *life* from death 521
Comes the *life* eternal here 36
Dying, to new *life* restore me 1516
Each loving *life* a psalm 1319
Enfolding *Life*, bear on thy wing 1355
Eternal *life* above 120

Eternal *life* and joy 799
Eternal *life,* eternal joy 799
Evermore their *life* abides 485
For Christ to *life* is risen 1724
For they eternal *life* shall win 1493
Freshening *life* in vale and lea 331
From him my *life* and all things 1621
God make my *life* a little (flower, song, staff) 576
He is of *life* the way 1418
Healing and *life* for all earth's 2135
Here of *life* the fountain flows 1588
His daily *life* he gave 145
His *life* had also its sorrow sore 1249
His *life* of truth 1366
His *life* within the keen air 2097
How happy then my *life* shall be 1248
How he his *life* should frame 618
How joyful *life* might be 1442
I that *life* to thee resign 1690
If *life* be long, I shall be glad 1148
If on *life,* serene and fair 449
If such a *life* of joy can crown 844
In all *life* thou livest 916
In all thy changing *life* I'll be 836
In *life,* in death, O Lord, abide 27
In *life* where sin denied 1124
In my *life* his plan fulfil 758
Is not our *life* with hourly mercies 435
Is your *life* darkened by hopes 907
Is your *life* just a tangle 903
Jesus shall my yielded *life* 1573
Lamenting all my sinful *life* 1456
Let us all thy *life* receive 1190
Let your *life* speak well of Jesus 2339
Life and health and peace 1813
Life, and joy, and peace imparts 521
Life and light, and love immortal 2224
Life and love in every place 990
Life and peace to me impart 637
Life and salvation therefore go 433
Life at his hands, shall receive 353
Life beckons us and learning 1951
Life deriving from his death 1813
Life eternal we have won 480
Life finds its brotherhood 334
Life from the dead is in that word 494
Life, full and free, before you 2340
Life has lost its shadows 1680
Life is brief 2299
Life is dark without thee 1800
Life is death, if severed 1034
Life is given through thy name 659
Life is naught without thee 2010
Life is waning, life is brief 2299
Life, light, and joy it still imparts 787
Life like a fountain 731
Life, love and joy 572
Life nor death can part us 258
Life nor death, nor powers 992
Life of our *life,* our praise 1163
Life of the dead 1656
Life offers many an easy prize 2340
Life seems a seething waste 383
Life shall not end the strain 304
Life through thy death restore 1415
Life will overflow 1210
Life with an ampler air 120
Life with its way before us lies 472
Life with trials hard may press me 980
Life would be worthless without him 506
Lifting my *life* till it rises above 326
Living with Jesus a new *life* divine 407
Long *life* thou to the king 1134
Lord of *life,* and light, and glory 1159
Lord of *life,* and truth, and right 1211
Lord of *Life,* be ours thy crown 2253
Lord of *Life,* beneath the dome 382
Lord of my *life,* I come 1045
Lord, thou art *life,* though I be dead 1277
Making all *life* new and free 331
Making this earthly *life* full 721
Man's *life,* begun so lowly 1879
May our quiet home *life* be 634
May they now, till *life* shall end 760
May we this *life* improve 2176
Meeting *life* with steadfast face 930
Mine the *life* won, through thine 2201
More than *life* to me 1607
My *life* and all its ransomed powers 150
My *life* in thee, thy life 979, 1250
My *life* is "Hidden with Christ 729
My *life,* my friends, my soul 1260
My *life* to give, my vows 1045
My *life* will still be filled with praise 824
Nearer, still nearer, while *life* 1266
New *life* in me he can engender 2140
Nor *life* nor death can part 230
Not *life,* or death, with all their 2199
Now may thy *life* to us descending 1316
O by thy *life* laid down 1920
O fuller, sweeter is that *life* 491
O Jesu, be our *life* like thine 2147
O let my *life* be given 2077
O *Life,* the Well that ever flows 1424
O Lord of *life,* and glory 1475
O Lord of *Life,* our hopes fulfil 1872
O Lord of *Life,* to thee we kneel 1608
O perfect *Life,* be thou their full 1473
O that my *life* might magnify 890
O thou who art the *Life* and Light 1507
O thou whose *life* and words were one 1527
Of the *life* of one who came 521
One less of *life* for me 1578
Or of the *life* he died for them 1551
Our *life* and peace to bring 229
Our *life* in Christ concealed 779
Our *life* is but an autumn sun 1918
Our *life* to live, our death 1461
Our *life* when we shall die 283
Our *life,* while thou preservest 767
Our *life* would welcome thy control 784
Our throbbing *life* is full of thee 1163
Out of my *life* may Jesus shine 1601
Pure in *life* and heart and mind 1120
So let thy *life* our pattern 1119
So *life* and light and love came 1571
So must this fleeting *life* of ours 1598

So shall our *life* of faith be full 721
So, when our *life* is clouded o'er 475
So, when this *life* is ended 1552
Springing into *life* and gladness 1041
Still let new *life* and strength 1863
Surely his *life* will never cease 1753
That by thy *life* our vows are fed 725
That in our daily *life* may flame 204
That *life* to win 2023
That ours might be thy perfect *life* 1482
That thou thy *life* didst dedicate 2302
That through its *life* thy life 1844
That when this *life* is past 1150
The *life* above, when this is past 703
The *life* divine to show to man 9, 706
The *life* everlasting if ye would obtain 18
The *life* of my delights 1240
The *life* that knows no ending 252
The *life* that maketh all things 2030
The *life* that so was given 2021
The *life* that thou alone canst give 1323
The Lord of *Life* hath victory 1803
The new-born *life* how glad 1863
The tearless *life* is there 252
Then forth to *life,* O child of earth 546
Then from our *life* unto others 1694
Then *life* shall be thy service 1230
Then to *life* I turn again 2247
Then when all of *life* is over 2259
Then with new *life,* forth from the tomb 498
There is *life* at this moment for thee 1974
There is *life* for a look at the 1974
There's *life* in that cross 2
Thine is the mystic *life* great India 522
This mortal *life* also 12
Thou art the *life,* by which 828
Thou art the *Life;* the rending 2023
Thou my *life,* my God, my all 1644
Thou, of *life* the Author 2204
Thou of *life* the Fountain art 994
Thou the *Life,* the Truth 2009
Though *life* is past, this hope 573
Through all our *life* be near us 1299
Through all our *life,* in death's last 1518
Through the *life* of him who died 245
Thy death O Christ, means *life* 60
Thy *life* in me 979
Thy *life* is in the quickening air 591
Thy *life* is still a summons 1549
Thy *life* my death efface 1407
Thy *life* our code 300
Thy *life* the bond of fellowship 1526
Thy present *life* through all doth flow 591
Till our *life* on earth is done 962
Till this fleeting, fleeting *life* 1684
'Tis *life,* and health, and peace 1351
'Tis ne'er too late, while *life* shall last 1442
To all, *life* thou givest 916
To blessed *life* thou openest mine eyes 123
To die in thee is *life* 979, 1250
To know thee is eternal *life* 1646
To "*life*" and peace within the fold 1097
To pour fresh *life* in every part 315
To see thee in each human *life* 1384
To share in *life* eternal 1879
Trusting him while *life* shall last 1721
We our *life* in him will find 64
What though thy *life* may be drear 1269
Whate'er in *life* shall be their share 1370
When *life* anew pours out its wine 204
When *life* is over and daylight 2235
When *life* on earth is ended 2216
When my *life* on earth shall end 2227
Where a *life* is spent in service 299
Which neither *life* nor death can part 1350
While o'er my *life* his strong 1627
Who, by his perfect *life* of love 466
Who is *life* in life to me 131
Who *life* and soul hath given me 1627
Who through *life* has been my Guide 66
Whose *life* and death reveal thy face 419
Whose *life,* like light, is freely 2028
Will make a better *life* 10
With *life* itself I'll freely part 722
Yea, evermore, in *life* and death 1187
Yea, *life* is short, though far we roam 725
Yea, through *life,* death, through sorrow 683
Yes, thou art still the *Life* 1511

LIFE-BLOOD

But with thine own *life-blood* 2287
E'en while his *life-blood* flowed 2144
His *life-blood* shed for us 266
O could my *life-blood* as it races 23

LIFE-BOAT

And out with the *life-boat* 2068

LIFT

And *lift* his head in glory 2138
And *lift* my prayer to thee 1436
And *lift* our hearts and voices 1464
And *lift* the spirit's sword 2028
And *lift* to heaven the voice 1116
And *lift* us to a holier life 1079
And *lift* us to a nobler life 82
Come, *lift* your hearts on high 304
Ever *lift* thy face upon me 978
God shall *lift* up thy head 536
He will *lift* you by his love 891
Heavenward *lift* thy soul's regard 1748
I *lift* my heart to thee 1509, 1851
I *lift* my soul to thee 2244
Joyfully we *lift* to thee 208
Lift eager hands as here 1361
Lift from this and every nation 470
Lift high his royal banner 1786
Lift high the blood-red flag 826
Lift high the Cross of Christ 958, 1669
Lift high the fallen standard 1328
Lift his banner high, wave it 2159
Lift my earth-bound longings 1471
Lift my heart to things above 758
Lift our contrite hearts to thee 1553
Lift the nations from the shadows 1160
Lift their hands in thanks to God 518
Lift thou thy world, O Christ 406

Lift up a living nation 1365
Lift up our hearts, O King 82
Lift up our hearts to seek 2013
Lift up the cross for Jesus 1945
Lift up the everlasting gates 778
Lift up the fallen 1655
Lift up thine eyes, and seek 477
Lift up your hands the Lord 193
Lift up your heads, ye gates 1857
Lift up your heart 1653
Lift up your hearts in jubilant 1652
Lift up your voice 1653
Lift up your voice and sing 874
Lift up your voice, and with us 41
Lift up your voice with one 193
Lift us to high resolve 1943
Lift us to the joy divine 1040
Lift we hearts and voices 1205
Lift we up our eyes to thee 1084
Lift we up our hearts, O Lord 127
Lift ye then your voices 544
Lift your heads, eternal gates 655
Lord, *lift* me up and let me stand 915
Lord, *lift* on us alway 526
May *lift* our souls on high 55
No one to *lift* them from sin 705
Now *lift* your hearts, your voices 2332
O *lift* the veil, if veil 89
Shall *lift* the joyful sound 28
Still *lift* your standard high 1654
The Lord *lift* up his countenance 1885
To thee *lift* up mine eye 1143
To thee we *lift* our hearts and pray 2028
To thee we *lift* our hearts in praise 191, 1445
To thee we *lift* our prayer 75
We *lift* glad eyes to our 1287
We *lift* our hearts and voices 708
We *lift* our hearts in praise 1313
We *lift* our hearts to God on high 1300
We *lift* our spirits as to God 1329
We *lift* up hands of prayer 514
We *lift* up our voices tremblingly 2004
We'll *lift* to thee, with grateful hearts 1939
When we *lift* our hearts to thee 589

LIFTED

I've been *lifted* up, and from sin 802
Jesus *lifted* me, when he 1501
Lifted high amid the ages 950
Lifted up was he to die 1203
They *lifted* up their voice 598, 1886

LIFTS

And *lifts* his brother's load 1880
And *lifts* his soul on high 414
And *lifts* the burden from the heavy 817
He *lifts* his helpless hands 156
While he *lifts* his hands 1697
Who *lifts* above the nation 1549

LIGHT

A burning, and a shining *light* 2239
A heavenly *light* may flash 737
A *light* to my path alway 2084
A *light* to shine upon the road 1347
A triple *light* was given 1341
All the *light* of sacred story 934
And by the *light* of that same star 1861
And everlasting *light,* its glory throws 1959
And from it love's pure *light* 29
And God himself is *Light* 2151
And in its sevenfold *light* 1810
And in that *Light* of life I'll walk 842
And in that purest *light* of thine 2080
And in thy *light* our souls 731
And let thy glorious *light* 306
And *light* and beauty brings 1877
And *light* is beaming from the radiant 148
And *light* of knowledge in their eyes 2003
And *light* triumphant breaks 1877
And like unto the *light,* he shall 1708
And still that *light* she lifteth 1544
And the *light* on my path 1847
And walking in the *light* of God 198
And when the *Light* of heaven fills 134
And when with morning *light* 1939
As the *Light* of *Light* descendeth 1060
Be thou my *Light,* be thou my guide 319
Be thou my *Light,* be thou my Way 1519
Be thou the perfect *Light* 463
Because that *light* hath on thee shone 2151
Blessed heavenly *Light,* shining 1672
But 'mid the *light* declining 1853
But the *light* of the better life resteth 1098
But this shall *light* me through 1284
By the *light* of burning martyrs 1574
Come, *Light* serene and still 311
Come to the *Light,* 'tis shining 1946
Dost life and *light* restore 86
Dwelling in *light* supernal 642
Everlasting *light* shines o'er it 656
First-born *light* in gloom 1195
For all the blessings of the *light* 59
For Christ Jesus, the *Light* of the world 1956
For Jesus is my *Light* 1980
For Jesus, our *Light,* our 2194
For the old *light* that gleams 2162
From shades of night he calls the *light* 6
God, thine everlasting *Light* 2341
God's *light* to earth thou bringest 1490
Happy *light* is flowing 1800
He is the *Light,* in him is no darkness 2152
He will give the *light* we need 64
Heav'n's *Light* came beaming 1504
Holy *Light,* that knows no shading 1084
I have *light* in my soul for which 2211
I may of endless *light* partake 152, 545
In its constant *light* I go 780
In its *light* and power 143
In *light,* in hope, in happiness 1363
In *light* inaccessible 916
In morning *light,* in eventide 1363
In the full *light* of day they saw 197
In the *light* of that star lie the ages 1995
In thee alone is *light* 2171
Into the *light* that nevermore 1532

Is coming with orient *light* 1095
It gives a *light* to every age 7
It is a never failing *light* 2087
Its *light* we may borrow 1750
Let them have the glorious *light* 1554
Let there be *light* 2051
Let there be *light* again 1340
Let there be *light* today 2013
Let thy clear *light* forever shine 390
Let thy *light* within me shine 637
Light and life art thou within 717
Light and life to all he brings 675
Light and love upon my way 934
Light by night and shade by day 541
Light for the just is sown 1889
Light for the path of life 1130
Light from heaven he will surely 1048
Light I never saw before 1703
Light is breaking, *light* I never 1703
Light of all eternal days 227
Light of all souls, from thee we seek 596
Light of knowledge, ever burning 242
Light of life, all health 1084
Light of life, in childhood's 1084
Light of life, shine o'er us 1800
Light of life, so sweetly gleaming 1084
Light of life, that knows no fading 1084
Light of life, that knows no setting 1084
Light of *light* from God 220
Light of the glad 1656
Light of the straying 355
Light of the village life 2200
Light of the world, before thee 1089
Light of the world, illumine 1089
Light of the world, through whom 454
Light of the world, thy beauty 1089
Light of the world, undimming 1087
Light that ever shall endure 1748
Light that guides us back to thee 742
Light the way of true salvation 219
Light to our blindness, O be thou 438
Light to the eyes impart 618
Light up ev'ry dark recess 756
Light up our way, lead forth 191, 1445
Light up this house with glory 1090
Light up thy Word, the fettered page 191, 1445
Lord and *light* of every age 485
May *light* upon me shine 2085
Melting in the *light* of day 1192
Mid all its *light* his eyes were dim 785
More *light* than we can dream 377
Morning *light* breaks in eastern sky 982
My *Light* and my Life-giver 2216
My *light* in Satan's darkest hour 2034
New *Light* and joy he lendeth 1552
New *light* to lead through shrouding 2069
Now gently *light*, a glorious crown 2228
O gentle Jesu, be our *Light* 1812
O gentle Jesus, be our *light* 1478
O God, our *Light*, to thee 32
O Jesu, *Light* of all below 1405
O Jesus, *Light* of all below 1409
O *Light* all *light* transcending 1850
O *light* of *light;* within us dwell 1445
O *light* of our dark sky 1544
O *light* that followest all my way 1465
O Lord of *Light*, all worshiped thee 2082
O may its *light* shine through 2086
O uncreated *Light* of *Light* 1934
Of *light* that shineth more 191, 1445
One the *light* of God's own presence 2067
Our *light* and our defense 1167
Our *light*, our life, our love 1160
Pure the *light* within 1680
Savior, be my *light* 1672
Shedding *light* that none can 242
So purer *light* shall mark the road 1347
Son of God, love's pure *light* 1720
Soon for us the *light* of day 1745
Stepping in the *light* 2129
Sweetly the *Light* has dawned upon 1946
That he, the uncreated *Light* 1301
That the *light* of the glorious gospel 574
The clear *light* of heaven streams out 1095
The gracious *light* and heat 7
The *light* and darkness are of his 1289
The *light* and flame of youth 613
The *light* is fading from the western 1852
The *light* of his love shineth 1848
The *light* of life eternal 137
The *Light* of the world is Jesus 1946
The *light* of this life shall be darkened 1098
The *light* of truth to me display 319
The *light* of truth to us display 310
The *light* streams from his Cross 185
The *light* that shone on Bethlehem 1487
The *light*, the oil, the robes 1597
The *light* we walk in darkens 2183
The Lord hath yet more *light* 2177
The morn of *light*, is here 33
The morning *light*, the lily white 2012
The people's everlasting *light* 322
The very *light* of our new day 1318
Then the clearer immortal *light* 1913
There's a *light* in the valley of death 2211
Thine was the *light* that cheered 1692
Thou *Light* of all times and hearts 1088
Thou *Light* of men 1023
Thy gospel *light* forever shine 2142
Thy *Light* is come 542
Thy *light*, so glad and golden 1089
Till they inward *light* 292
To be a *light* to lighten 1154
To give *light* to them that sit 215
To kindle so a growing *light* 1410
To *light* and life the soul 462
True *Light* of life, all joy 1087
True *Light* that lightenest all 1592
Unholy *light* casts on the dear place 383
Unresting, unhasting and silent as *light* 916
What *light* shall be their perfect guide 789
Where gospel *light* is glowing 1341
Where *light*, and life, and joy 1918
Where thou, eternal *Light* of light 1918
Where thy pure *light* may shine 1175

Whose *light* grows never pale 1377
Will *light* the shadows 1352
With *light* and comfort 310
With *light* and life since Eden's 92
With *light* and love divine 1374
With *light* and mirth 120
With the morning *light,* O Lord 710
Wondrous *Light* that led them 517

LIGHTED

All *lighted* with the glory 1597

LIGHTEN

And *lighten* with celestial fire 313
Ever now to *lighten* nations from afar 517
Lighten our darkness, and banish 1611
Shall *lighten* every land 198

LIGHTENS

Lightens the dark that round us 1353

LIGHTEST

Who *lightest* every earnest mind 419

LIGHT-HOUSE

Strong-founded like a *light-house* 1784

LIGHTNINGS

Lightnings thy sword 612
When *lightnings* flash and storm winds 591
Ye *lightnings,* wildly bright 1936

LIGHTS

And our *lights* be clear and steady 2297
And the *lights* of men are paling 1993
But where it *lights,* the favored place 1960
Let the lower *lights* be burning 255
Lights up the languor of his breast 793
Lights who lighten every land 275
The *lights* of evening round us 653
They are but broken *lights* 1797
True *lights* to lighten every land 1859
Ye *lights* of evening, find a voice 41

LIGHT-YEARS

Where *light-years* frame the Pleiades 96

LIKE

I should *like* to have been with them 884
Would you *like* to know the sweetness 942

LIKENESS

And with thy *likeness,* when I wake 1135
In his *likeness* I shall soon 2057
In his own *likeness* we shall then awake 16
In human *likeness* dwelt 2334
There in his *likeness* joyful 747
Thy perfect *likeness* wear 234, 1805

LILIES

And *lilies* cheer us 1727
Here the white *lilies* shine like stars 279

LILY

And the sweet meadow-side *lily* 1831
He's fairer than the *lily,* brighter 2108
How sweet the *lily* grows 267
The *Lily* of the Valley, in him alone 834

LIMB

In active *limb,* and muscle tense 882
Sturdy of *limb,* with bounding health 588

LIMIT

So to the land's last *limit* 1550

LIMITS

Its own appointed *limits* keep 81

LINE

Greatest of the prophets' *line* 1051

LINEAGE

Of Jesse's *lineage* coming 1107

LINES

None its *lines* of woe can 2059
Unto me happily the *lines* 570

LINGER

All who *linger,* all who fall 1735
And *linger,* shivering on the brink 1966
Linger near his mercy-seat 276
Linger, O blessed Redeemer 1208
One moment will not *linger* 19
Why should we *linger* and heed not 1743

LINGERING

Angels are *ling'ring* near 85
Here *lingering* still, we ask 100

LINGERS

Although he *lingers* long 1283

LINK

We *link* them to the work 1382

LINKED

Linked in bonds of common service 1760

LINKS

All the loving *links* that bind us 1955

LINTEL

And be the *lintel* blest 210

LION

No *lion* can him fright 2290
There's Judah's *Lion,* and the Lamb 91

LIONS

The *lions* that devour 90
The *lion's* young may hungry be 616

LIP

No *lip* to fawn, no hand to beg 1281
Not for the *lip* of praise alone 478
That parched, dry *lip* 734
Then the cool *lip* its thirst 1352

LIPS

A thousand *lips* to sing thy praise 23
And bitter *lips* in blind despair 1397
And from his *lips* salvation 2133
And *lips* that we might tell 68
And of my *lips* keep thou 1434
And when these failing *lips* grow 30
Both with *lips* and hearts 633
From *lips* of suffering sisters 149
From the *lips* of sinners 143
Hark, his gracious *lips* bestow 655
His *lips* with grace o'erflow 1201
If thou our *lips* wilt open 33
Instruct our *lips* to speak 84
Just to learn from his *lips* 1989
Lips, that while thy praises 1179
Little *lips* that thou hast made 1570
Little *lips* thy love may tell 962
May faithful *lips*, with trumpet 2107
May our *lips* and lives agree 1120
My *lips* no more can silence 34
My *lips* no more their silence 528
My *lips* thee praise shall give 1172
My *lips* thine eager praises 1140
O *lips* divine, that taught 1491
O what can little *lips* do 1536
Our *lips* and lives shall gladly 1733
The little *lips* can praise 1536
Thy *lips* refrain from speaking 1320
To touch our *lips*, our minds 1785
To whom the *lips* of children 44
Whene'er our *lips* are silent 1535

LIST

Jesus is pleading, O *list* to his 985
List to his loving words 1804
List to the peace-speaking voice 353
List to what the spirit saith 175
Then *list* to the note of this solemn refrain 18

LISTEN

And *listen* as we pray 1529
Do not us *listen* vainly 214
Listen now while we repeat it 996
Listen, O ye weary 940
Listen to a little child 976
Listen to my evening prayer 1013
Listen to our humble cry 233
Listen to the wondrous story 684
Listen while we sing 1680
O *listen*, my boy, while I say 130
Savior, *listen* while I pray 1304
Shall we *listen* to their voices 1712
The Holy Spirit from on high will *listen* 1964
When God the Lord will *listen* 1

LISTENING

I am *list'ning*, Lord, for thee 1207

LISTENS

O how patiently he *listens* 942

LISTETH

Whose quick'ning Spirit where it *listeth* 422

LIT

Lit by my Savior, eternity's Star 2314
That *lit* thy lonely pathway 769

LITANIES

There are the lovely *litanies* 14

LITTLE

He was *little*, weak, and helpless 1572

LIVE

All they that seek the Lord shall *live* 72
All who *live* in love are thine 1040
And ever *live* to thee 1482
And I *live* for Jesus only 1573
And if to *live* or die 1250
And let me *live*, blest Jesus 1910
And *live* as now he lives 260
And *live* for evermore 1935
And *live* for him who died 336
And *live* in truth before thee 2303
And *live* no more to die 391
And *live* on God's delight 120
And *live* this short, revolving day 2176
And now I *live* in him 842
And we shall *live* in thee 1373
As in thy sight to *live* 4
Be by all that *live* adored 582
But *live* thy life divine 1386
But *live* with thee the perfect 250
But there they *live* in such delight 960
By thee may I strongly *live* 761
Can *live*, and look on thee 420
Dear Lord, and shall we ever *live* 318
Doth *live* and reign eternally 314
For without thee I cannot *live* 1801
God's children cannot *live* 2
I cannot *live* from his presence 829
I shall not *live* in vain 899
I, while I *live*, will call 857
I would *live* ever in the light 1045
I'll *live* for him who died 1248
In his presence daily *live* 70
In thee I *live*, in thee I shall 123
In thee to *live* and die 91
It will *live* and shine 656
Let me *live* to thee alone 998
Let us *live* and labor 925
Live for Jesus ev'ry day 2339
Live! for the truth is living 2183
Live thy creed 703
Live thyself within my heart 523
Live to him, thyself denying 2153
"Lord, while I *live* let me not 2143
May I *live* upon thy smiles 1647
May we *live* in holiness 744
May we *live* to thee alone 1179
May we *live* with thee forever 929
Nearer to thee would *live* 463
Now in thee only, do I *live* 60
O *live* in us, so may the sons 1474
O may we ever with thee *live* 1439
Our Lord doth *live* 498
That we may *live*, and sing 79, 1937

That we may *live* the life of love 1291
That we may *live* to glorify 465
The gift of life to all who *live* 82
Then *live* for Christ both day 2281
Then *live* with him on high 1030
Thine would I *live,* thine 1137
Thus would I *live,* yet now 1940
'Tis to my Savior I would *live* 1241
To *live* with thee 158
We *live* thy life 784
We shall *live* in heaven with 1173
We would not *live* by bread 1716
Whether to *live* or die 979
While I *live* by faith and do 834
Who died that we might *live* 82
Who does not *live* serenely 1359
Would you *live* daily his praises 2323
Would you *live* in the light 694

LIVED

And that he *lived* at Nazareth 817
As thou hast *lived,* so would we 726
As thou, Lord, hast *lived* for others 1760
Bravely he *lived* to shield the right 1753
Christ *lived,* and loved and loves 1593
In quiet Galilee, he *lived* 145
Jesus hath *lived,* hath died 1024
They *lived* not only in ages past 875
When he *lived* on earth 1581
When he *lived* with mortals 1099
Who have *lived* to do thy will 485
Who *lived* and died for sinful 2179

LIVES

All our *lives* are building stones 656
All whose *lives* have blest us 657
And ever in our *lives* express 1405, 1409
And he *lives* to intercede 2268
And our *lives* would be all sunshine 1999
As *lives* the flower within the seed 1571
Christ Jesus *lives* today 874
Finding their *lives* in thee 1474
For *lives* bereft of purpose 189
For our *lives* but just begun 273
For their *lives* are precious 286
He ever *lives* above 113
He *lives* for evermore 260
He *lives* forever with his saints 1200
He *lives,* he *lives,* Christ Jesus 874
He *lives,* our Lord who once 260
He *lives* that I may also live 851
He *lives* that I may honor give 851
He *lives,* the sinner's cause 1895
He *lives* to bless them and defend 426
He *lives,* to die no more 1895
He *lives* to save us all 626
He *lives* triumphant o'er the grave 851
He *lives* within my heart 874
In our *lives* to show him 357
In purer *lives* thy service find 386
Jesus *lives* and every grace 990
Jesus *lives,* by this we know 992
Jesus *lives!* For us he died 992
Jesus *lives!* Henceforth is death 992
Jesus *lives!* Our hearts know well 992
Jesus *lives!* To him the throne 992
Little *lives* may be divine 962
Lives again in better guise 1075
Lives but in its own excess 483
Lives in glory now on high 287
May our *lives* his image bear 519
May with our *lives* give thanks 171
Now he *lives,* no more to die 288
Our *lives* are judged today 185
Our *lives* expand beneath his hand 2100
Our risen *lives,* O Christ, receive 391
Pure is all that *lives* with thee 610
Shaping our *lives* by his blessed 2129
"Sire, he *lives* a good league hence 627
Something *lives* in every hue 1195
Still for us he *lives* and pleads 480
Then, arising, *lives* forever 356
This mighty God forever *lives* 2313
Until our *lives* are perfected 1059
Upward we reach, whose *lives* 162
Where human *lives* are thronging 1880
Young *lives* like yours he needs 2340

LIVETH

For her Lord now *liveth* 2010
He *liveth* longest who can tell 703
Jesus ever *liveth* 622
Lord who *liveth,* youth undying 1796
Now Christ *liveth* in me 1571
'Tis the God who ever *liveth* 2288
Who *liveth,* and was dead 91

LIVING

Or in *living* or in dying 2065
To be *living* is sublime 2157

LOAD

And ye, beneath life's crushing *load* 948
Beneath its *load* of condemnation 724
Bowed down beneath a *load* of sin 109
E'en to the last,
beneath our sorrows' load 98
Sharing all my *load* 1000
Thy heavy *load* my arm upbears 836
To ease their *load* 883
Who, beneath some *load* of grief 400

LOADS

And *loads* to lift 174
What food luxurious *loads* the board 89

LODGING

Cold and bare the *lodging* 803

LONE

To tend the *lone* and fatherless 2167

LONELINESS

Loneliness changed to reunion 1763
The *loneliness,* the weariness 944

LONENESS

And soon in solemn *loneness* 820

LONG

And *long* to feast upon thee still 1023
And we *long* to do thy will 589
Apart from thee I *long* and thirst 1436
But I *long* to meet my Savior 2246
But I *long* to rise in the arms 808
But O we *long* to know 2178
For thee I *long*, for love divine 1458
I *long* for the fragrant flow'rs 1913
I *long* to be like Jesus 854
I *long* to be with Jesus 854
I *long* to know thy will 1829
I *long* to make thy words my own 838
I *long* to scale the utmost height 915
I *long* to see thy face 573
Jesus, I *long*, I *long* to be 529
Thou dost *long* for rest 1766
'Twill but make me *long* for home 2257
We *long* to be near him 1909
Why what we *long* for most of all 1282
Yet I *long* to prove and show 997, 998
Yet *long* these multitudes to see 2270

LONGED

And feebly *longed* thy face 2170
If I have *longed* for shelter 901
Longed for the love of human friend 1527

LONGING

Your Savior is *longing* to bless 2293

LONGINGS

Thus my *longings*, heav'nward 1583

LONGS

And *longs* to bind God's children 1549
And *longs* to join the ransomed 1404
And *longs* to reach her crown 432
He *longs* to save thee 1577
So *longs* my soul, O God, for thee 125
Who *longs* to love and bless 149

LOOK

Ah! *look* how patiently he hangs 1333
And all who *look* for Jesus 1988
And never *look* in vain 856
And only *look* on us as found in him 99
By thy *look* of love directed 633
Forward we *look*, nor fear 162
Helpless, *look* to thee for grace 1671
I *look* at heaven and long to enter 2201
I would *look* up, and laugh 897
If we *look* to the Cross blest 1956
Inward we *look* and marvel at thy power 162
Lamb of God, I *look* to thee 523
Look above and dry thy tears 2126
Look away to Jesus 1114
Look down from heaven in love 2131
Look down from the sky 159
Look down on all earth's
  sin and strife 82, 1079
Look down on thy creation 1373
Look down with sad and wondering 1660
Look ever to Jesus, he will 2336
Look for storms of wind and rain 1076
Look from heaven and save 589
Look in gladness on high 568
Look, my soul, be still 1554
Look now! for glad and golden 948
Look on him we pierced 339
Look on him whom once they 2342
Look on the anguish, the sorrow 607
Look on the heart by sorrow broken 246
Look on the side that is brightest 1269
Look on the tears by sinners shed 246
Look on thy children from on high 188, 1927
Look on thy hands and read it there 333
Look on us with loving eye 962
Look to God in faith, he will 2094
Look to the Lamb of God 906
Look unto me, thy morn shall rise 842
"*Look* unto me, ye people 2058
Look up and let Jesus 931
Look up, the victor's crown 1204
Look up! thou'lt reach that blest abode 1531
Look up to him, he's always near 1640
Look up, ye saints of God 1959
Look upon a little child 523
Look upward to the skies 1391
Lord, *look* with grace on me 2302
Nor behind thee *look* 1866
O Father, *look* from heaven and bless 471
O *look* on me, and by thy saving 1239
One *look* from thee would give me 1395
Savior *look* with pitying eye 269
The longer you *look* at the depths 1338
Then *look*, sinner, *look* unto him 1974
Upward we *look*, where march the stars 162
We *look* to thee, heed thou our plea 1417
When I *look* down from lofty mountain 1437
When I *look* up unto the heavens 775
When unto thee I *look* and pray 1434
When you *look* at others with 2265
While we *look* up with filial fear 364
Who *look* to him shall walk 1890
With a *look* recall 937
Yet I *look* on, beyond earth's 1254
Yet who dost *look* in mercy 1505

LOOKED

I *looked* to Jesus and I found 842
Looked down where he lay 159
Looked on us tenderly 705
They *looked* to him,
  and lightened were 616, 1902
They *looked* up and saw a star 1861
To thee we *looked*, to thee we cried 648
When he *looked* with pleading eyes 696
Yet none there were who *looked* 918

LOOKING

And *looking* for our Lord 2037
By *looking* to Jesus 1820

LOOKS

And earth itself *looks* fairer 33
He *looks!* and ten thousands of angels 1512
He *looks* down from heaven 968
High *looks* I will not suffer 1557
Life's common *looks* and tones 478
Who *looks* in love to Christ 2289
Who *looks* to him with lively faith 128

LOOM

Thine is the *loom,* the forge, the mart 199

LOOMS

Behold, there *looms* the mystery 46

LOOSE

Loose from their chains the captives 244
Loose our captive chains 964
We *loose* wild tongues that have not 583

LOOSED

He hath *loosed* the fateful 1215

LORD

And Christ is *Lord* indeed 1786
But yet the *Lord,* that is on high 1886
Come bow before the *Lord* 337
Jesus who art the *Lord* of all 1037
Lord, grant that we aright 1052
Lord, I want to be like Jesus 1139
Lord, I want to be more 1139
Lord of every grateful creature 2308
Lord of seas uncharted 2274
Lord, we are few, but thou art 1032
My dear almighty *Lord* 1035
O suffering *Lord* on Calvary 1417
On thee our *Lord* victorious 1341
The *Lord* is never far away 1729
The *Lord* of hosts, and none 2327
Thou art our holy *Lord* 1715
'Tis the *Lord* of all creation 2288
What will it be, O *Lord* 1805
When the *Lord* of Love was born 2306
Where the *Lord* of Love was born 2306
Yea, gracious is our *Lord* 857

LORDS

Lord of *Lords,* in human vesture 1060
Other *lords* have long held sway 998
When *lords* and kings are known no more 535

LORE

And all the *lore* its scholars 1960

LOSE

He will not *lose* one soul 291
I can never, never *lose* my way 1684
Lose the way to endless rest 233
We *lose* him not, unsought 1891
We *lose* ourselves in heaven 1801
We *lose* the duty in the joy 1810
We shall *lose* our care and sorrow 1738

LOSS

And count all else as *loss* 84
In each *loss* or triumph 501
Though the *loss* sustained our spirits 1771

LOST

And *lost* I am, till thou art mine 1018
And much will be *lost* should 1540
And some have *lost* the love 136
And the *lost* are found 2007
And then she *lost* her care 626
And we had *lost* our way 350
Be *lost* in silence and forgot 209
How the *lost* may be restored 287
I have *lost* my load at the foot 864
I once was *lost,* but now am 88
I was *lost,* but Jesus found me 895
I was *lost* in sin, for the world 802
If you're *lost* in sin, all is dark 2258
Lost for the lack of the help 705
Lost in darkness, far from love's 1048
Lost in the maze of purposes 422
Lost in this dawning light 425
Lost in wonder, love, and praise 1190
Once I was *lost* upon the plains 624
Reaching to all the *lost* 2315
Seeking the *lost* 326
Their *lost* Messiah see 1497
To God the *lost* to bring 2167
To save the *lost* in Christ's dear name 1440
To the *lost* as you journey 111
You are not *lost* from his sight 1754

LOT

And though it be my *lot* to bear 954
Be faithful, ever faithful,
where'er thy *lot* 1784
Be mine a happier *lot* to own 1243
Happy Zion, what a favored *lot* 2341
Sad were our *lot,* evil this earth 666
Should our *lot* be hard 988
The *lot* that fallen is to me 570
There, there is the worthiest *lot* 1583
Whatever my *lot,* thou hast taught 2249

LOVE

A *love* by thee kept true 1344
Again let *love* be crowned 1313
All his *love* confessing 357
All in vain if *love* I need 636
All meaner *love* is perishable 1284
All that childlike *love* can render 753
All the *love* of Jesus learn 1303
All who *love* and fear thy name 1213
Almighty *Love,* by thy mysterious 1165
And a purer *love* attaining 140
And all his boundless *love* proclaim 1308
And all his wondrous *love* abuse 2218
And all thy *love* to me 1141
And by *love* inflamed, arise 1566
And cans't thou e'er such *love* forget 1514
And, from *love* the "good work" done 141
And happy they that *love* the way 1167

And his *love* is now my happy song 1907
And his *love* made them strong 875
And his *love* with gladness sing 1272
And how that *love* was shown 826
And I *love* that old Cross 1561
And *love*, and life, and rest 489
And *love* beyond degree 38
And *love* fills every breast 667
And *love* him more in heaven 1962
And *love* is marching on 507
And *love* it more and more 2309
And *love* its Galilee 917, 2181
And *love*, joy, hope like flowers 661
And *love* lights up our mortal 314
And *love* like that which thou 1410
And *love* of Christ in perfect 1859
And *love* shall cast out fear 490
And *love* so deep and fervent 1849
And *love* supreme remain 1930
And *love*, that soul through me 1152
And *love* the faithless sinner 2202
And *love* thee daily better 244
And *love* this sight so fair 1960
And *love* thy holy Word the more 1389
And *love* to all men 'neath the sun 445
And *love* to all will reign 667
And *love* to man, and God 2326
And our *love* his gifts excite 1178
And our *love* to thee grow cold 589
And out of *love* supernal hast offered 2021
And perfect *love* and friendship 232
And so our feeble *love* is fed 266
And still his *love* he giveth 1883
And that *love* so deep, so moving 450
And the best is *love* 636
And the Father's boundless *love* 1209
And this *love* to those around 2339
And those that *love* the shade 2250
And thou hast said, I *love* 114
And thou in *love* shalt reign 1507
And thy exceeding *love* 1479
And thy *love* exceeding great 2018
And thy *love* so pure, so changeless 978
And thy *love* the flame 1778
And they that *love* his name 2078
And we must *love* him too 1963
And what we *love* we yet shall be 370
And where his *love* resolves to bless 1897
And where they *love* each other 1252
And wilt thou thus his *love* 1343
And with true *love* and brotherhood 599
And yet God's *love* is not 2097
Be *love* the power 2100
Because *love* has been lavished 182
Because we *love* thee and thy work 2088
Beloved, let us *love* 202
Blest Savior, then, in *love* 1227
Breathing that *love* as heaven's own 1284
But by his *love* and mercy 2061
But for that *love* which died 1978
But *love* shall never fail 2175
But tender *love* and healing 2147
But yet in *love* he sought me 1876
By gentle *love* thy Cross 1286
By his *love* my will subdued 1218
By the *love* that passeth knowledge 1160
Can a Father's *love* refuse 449
Can *love* their Maker, Savior, Friend 1536
Close to us in the Christ we *love* 1380
Cold is our *love*, Lord 1014
Come, as thou didst of old in *love* 1609
Come, in thy *love* to dwell 455
Could ne'er his *love* repay 150
Deeper the *love* my soul desires 1267
Did e'er such *love* and sorrow 2236
Do thou in *love* sustain us 43
Dost thou *love* the Lord, all else 1838
Drawn from earth to *love* thee solely 220
Eternal *Love*, in thee we rest 1461
Eternal *Love*, with them abide 1370
Even so I *love* thee, and will love 1235
Faithful are these who *love* the truth 325
For all we *love*, the poor, the sad 1478, 1812
For in *love* and not in anger 2257
For *love* and for hope that no power 423
For *love* like this, O may our song 2117
For *love* of thine which never tires 481
For *love* to answer every call 1346
For mother's *love*, and father's care 1346
For my *love* is often cold 2232
For the Lord of *Love* is born 2306
For the *love* of Christ constraining 487
For the *love* of God is broader 1767, 1999
For the *love* that brought them 409
For the *love* that met us here 273
For the *love* which from our birth 484
For thy *love* has said to me 972
For thy *love* is before mine eyes 1043
For very *love*, beholding 489
From *love* of pleasure, lust of gold 189
Full of wondrous *love* is he 2233
God of *love*, protect and save 1603
God of *love*, to mine attend 2121
God of *love*, we pray for these 488
God's *love* to earth thou bringest 1490
God's wondrous *love* in saving 298
God's wondrous *love* to man" 149
Great *love* of God, come in 1463
Happy in thy precious *love* 1197
He in *love* has come 474
He is *love* beyond a brother's 1581
He is *love*, he is love 1191, 1615
He will *love* me dearly 900
Hence God this generous *love* 2334
Here's *love* and grief beyond degree 697
Him to *love* and him obey 223
His all-redeeming *love* 113
His great *love* proclaim 1707
His is *love* beyond a brother's 1577
His *love* alone can give us peace 2135
His *love* and light fill all my soul 1578
His *love* can fill your soul 2324
His *love* can never fail 822
His *love* eluded still 878
His *love* foretells thy trials 548
His *love* in me forever liveth 1915

His *love* is all-availing 2216
His *love* is ever flowing 2109
His *love* is far greater than mortals 2055
His *love* is the theme of my song 1649
His *love* laid hold on me 1322
His *love* shall be the guide 377
His *love* shall ne'er grow cold 348
His *love* shall never end 304
His *love* shall protect you, his Spirit 1542
His *love* thy joy increase 567
His *love* to all proclaim 1485
His *love* will cheer and fill 906
His pardoning *love* will shed 1964
His perfect salvation, his wonderful *love* 24
His wondrous *love* confess 1636
How he can *love* such a sinner 1971
How can I *love* thee as I ought 1002
How great thy *love* appears 265
How oft of faithful *love* my lips 1251
How shall I *love* that word 494
How shall we *love* thee, holy 438
I am resting in his *love* 562
I *love* by faith to take a view 861
I *love* his name (word) 1897
I *love* its music to repeat 1912
I *love* the blessed Savior's name 1867
I *love* the Christ who all my burdens 2108
I *love* the Christ who died 833
I *love* the Cross of Jesus 872
I *love* the name of him whose 1912
I *love* the name of Jesus 854, 1867
I *love* thee because thou hast first 1246
I *love* thee, dearest Lord 1020
I *love* thee for wearing the thorns 1246
I *love* thee in the loveliness 1863
I *love* thee, Lord Jesus 159
I *love* thy church, O God 859
I *love* thy rock and rills 1225
I *love* to sing its worth 1967
I *love* to stand within its walls 1809
I *love* to think on mercies past 861
I *love* to tread the hallowed courts 1809
I shall give *love* to those in need 182
I will ever *love* and trust him 70
I will *love* thee forever, grieve thee 1199
I will *love* thee in life, I will love 1246
I will *love* thee more and more 758
I will *love* thee to the end 758
I will *love* thee without end 1814
I would be ever singing the *love* 638
I would in thy *love* abide 1682
If I *love* him, when I die 995
If our *love* were but more simple 1999
If we *love* not the world 438
If you *love* him why not serve 2156
In a *love* which cannot cease 1195
In God alone hath *love* its true abode 202
In God's *love* abiding I have joy 1565
In him the *love* of God is shown 377
In his boundless *love* and mercy 894
In his *love* for all his people 936
In his *love* to share 928
In Jesus' *love* reposing 137
In *love* and pity infinite 1371
In *love* he lifted me 926
In *love* I will follow thee 1583
In *love* my soul would bow 1689
In our *love* for one another 936
In self-forgetting *love* 15
In thy blest *love* I rest 979, 1250
In thy dear *love* confiding 1476
In thy dying *love* for man 798
In thy great *love* its life prolong 2011
In thy *love* look down 741
Jesus for thy *love* most tender 144
Jesus' *love* is sweeter 1556
Jesus' *love* the nations fires 1695
Just as I am, thy *love* unknown 1046
Large as thy *love* for evermore 2142
Larger, as *love* to reverent eyes 1523
Learning how to *love* from thee 1687
Let all that *love* thy name rejoice 527, 1176
Let *love* abound 2100
Let *love* awake, and pay 1940
Let *love* more fervent glow 2134
Let *love* of Christ attend 471
Let me in thy *love* abide 448
Let me *love* and cling to thee 1138
Let me *love* thee more and more 1684
Let them that *love* thee and thy peace 843
Let thy *love* and matchless grace 2043
Let us each, thy *love* possessing 1125
Let us *love* and pray for sinners 251
Let us *love* each other too 251
Let us *love* our God supremely 251
Let us not thy *love* forego 1145
Looking then for deathless *love* 555
Lord, I *love* to worship there 2121
Lord Jesus, who dost *love* me 1297
Lord, thy *love* at last hath 1498
Love all lovely, Love Divine 1189
Love and grief my heart dividing 1813
Love and mercy found me 986
Love and peace they taste 677
Love and praise to Christ belong 1510
Love and watch that lowly maiden 1572
Love as the Master loved you 1601
Love at last has won 1198
Love be yours and love be mine 1189
Love bridged the gulf 'twixt me 2316
Love brings the glorious fullness in 575
Love brought my Savior here to die 2316
Love can make your dwelling 940
Love eternal, free and boundless 356
Love for plea and gift 1189
Love found a way that could 2316
Love found a way to redeem 2316
Love him, love him, all ye little 1191, 1615
Love in all I see 1643
Love in heaven will shine 636, 1192
Love in loving finds employ 1687
Love in that story so tender 1832
Love is kind and suffers long 636
Love is king forever 940
Love is king where he doth reign 1211
Love is meek and thinks no wrong 636, 1192

Love is the golden chain 792
Love is the theme, love is supreme 1559
Love lifted me 891
Love lifted me from depths 2316
Love makes angel music 940
Love makes labor lighter 2124
Love not the world but rather 1193
Love not the world that passes 1193
Love not the world, "this present 1193
Love of God, and love of neighbor 1796
Love of God, so pure 1138
Love of God, unspent and free 1077
Love of Jesus in its fullness 2339
Love of the Holy Ghost 1463
Love of the living God 1463
Love one another more 1175
Love only waits to forgive 326
Love opened wide the gates 2316
Love paid the ransom for me 1832
Love sent my Lord to the Cross 2316
Love shall be our token 1189
Love shall tread out the baleful 1319
Love so amazing, so divine 2236
Love so mighty 891
Love than death itself 1192
Love, that bled upon the tree 442
Love, that caused us first to be 442
Love that draws us lovingly 442
Love that meets our hearts 1158
Love the Lord, and do your part 273
Love thee more dearly 379
Love thee with unsinning heart 2261
Love this Friend: he longs to save 1577
Love to death consigned him 990
Love to God and all men 1189
Love to God and man displaying 519
Love to serve them faithfully 974
Love to the loveless shown 1255
Love triumphant still in death 2247
Love unbounded, wonderful 1616
Love was born at Christmas 1189
Love which bore the Cross 1271
Love will always with us stay 1192
Love will ever with us stay 636
Love with every passion blending 1058
May all its *love* and yearning 724
May in *love* be still increasing 1402
May *love* alone for wrong atone 1165
May they *love* and may they praise 741
May thy *love* with tender 966, 1012
May thy tender *love* to me 1684
Meet for him whose *love* espoused 217
"Mine is an unchanging *love* 672
Mine is *love* unchanging 939
Mine to show a Savior's *love* 738
More of his *love* to others 1219
More of his *love* who died for me 1216
More of thy *love* and truth 1284
More of thy *love* I'd have 463
My Lord, my *Love,* is crucified 1460
My *Love,* the Crucified, hath sprung 2015
My Savior's *love* makes all scenes 867
Naught else is worthy his *love* 531
No! thy *love* hath conquered 1471
Nor why unworthy, Christ in *love* 849
Nor yet because who *love* thee not 1235
Not for more *love* our craving 385
Nothing but *love* shall I receive 1001
Nothing from thy *love* shall sever 673
O awful *love,* which found no room 1124
O by that *love* which every love 435
O by thy *love* and anguish 1920
O Christ, thy *love* is mighty 1874
O for the wonderful *love* he has 1743
O generous *love!* that he who smote 1630
O God of *love* whose spirit 419
O how I *love* him, Savior 2144
O how I *love* Jesus 1967
O Lamb of God, whose *love* is light 247
O let his *love* your hearts constrain 336
O *love,* all thought surpassing 1464
O *love* divine and gentle 1457
O *Love,* divine and true 497
O *Love,* how gracious is thy way 1025
O *Love,* most patient, give 734
O *Love* of God most free
(kind, strong, wise) 2029
O *Love* of God our shield and stay 1461
O *love* that casts out sin 1463
O *Love* that now extendeth 1464
O *Love* that our redemption 1464
O *love* that passeth knowledge 1414
O *love* whose beams have shone 1464
O may I *love* thy precious Word 2085
O may my *love* to thee, pure, warm 1227
O may this glorious, matchless *love* 641
O may thy *love* possess me 1025
O may thy mighty *love* prevail 965
O may we *love* the house of God 1432
O that fervent *love* today 1566
O that thy *love* were by all adored 529
O the *love* that drew salvation's plan 2335
O the *love* that in thy kingdom 2019
O thou whose *love* provideth 2119
O Trinity of *love* and power 81, 418
O 'twas *love,* 'twas wondrous 575
O what wonderful *love* 802
O wide-embracing, wondrous *love* 1461
O will you not *love* him today 1925
O wisest *love!* that flesh 1630
O wondrous *love,* that he should leave 1534
O wondrous *love!* To bleed and die 109
O wondrous *love,* to die for me 825
O wondrous *love* to you and me 2242
Of God's own *love* his dear 1316
Of Jesus and his *love* 1830
Of *love* as boundless as the sea 1534
Of *love* so free and boundless 350
Of *love* which cannot cease 350
Of simple cares and *love* 107
Of strong, deep *love* to thee 1849
On our Father's *love* relying 2065
One in *love* and one in thee 42
One in our *love* of all things sweet 421
Once again in *love* draw near 760
Only his great eternal *love* 1249

Only, O Lord, in thy dear *love* 1273
Our *love,* as low or pure 185
Our *love* so faint, so cold 318
Out of myself to dwell in thy *love* 1602
Perfect *love,* bereft of fear 294
Pure, unbounded *love* thou art 1190
Pure, universal *love* thou art 333
Radiant with the *love* of God 716
Ready to *love* and work 466
Redeeming *love* has been my theme 1961
Resting in the shelter of his *love* 562
Round thee in *love* we draw 1312
Should I not *love* thee well 1235
Simply resting in thy *love* 1085
Since better is thy *love* than life 1172
So generous was his *love* 128
So God's *love* is reaching 61
So let the *love* of Jesus come 151
So marvelous the *love* 2168
So that when thy *love* shall call us 1125
Somehow his *love* will never let me go 1756
Son of God, whose *love* has bound us 470
Springing from eternal *love* 541
Still he doth *love* me wherever 806
Still thy dear *love* doth gladden 815
Stronger his *love* than death or hell 1458
Such *love* and meekness so divine 1226
Such *love* constrains me 1104
Sure, there was never *love* so free 722
Surely his *love* will bless it 1773
Sweet is the tender *love* Jesus 1804
Sweeter far than any *love* 1804
Telling of a *love* unchanging 1096
That boundless *love* itself that gives 2115
That I may *love* what thou dost love 250
That *love* which wept with woe 1978
That theirs may be the
love which knows 1473
That we may *love* not doctrines 317
The Christ-like *love* of neighbor 923
The Father's *love* revealing 726
The Lord doth dearly *love* all those 1394
The Lord of *Love* was standing 878
The *love* divine which made us thine 706
The *love* of Christ constraineth 1906
The *love* of Christ to me 1458
The *love* of God to me 575
The *love* of Jesus, what it is 1019
The *love* that asks no questions 886
The *love* that casteth out 1072
The *love* that made them strong 434
The *love* that makes undaunted 886
The *love* that never falters 886
The *love* that pays the price 886
The *love* that seeks no gain 1474
The *love* that sends the showers 1853
The *love* that shines serene 1146
The *love* that stands the test 886
The *love* that through all troubles 1391
The *love* that yearns to see thee 1474
The *love,* the work that bless 596
The *love* unbought is all thine 1479
The *love,* which bore the greater load 1978
The Savior God in *love* draws nigh 173
The Savior's *love* revealing 1962
Thee may we *love* alone 1405, 1409
Thee shall I *love* in endless 1953
Thee will I *love* beneath thy 1953
Thee will I *love,* my joy 1953
Thee will I *love,* my Lord 1953
Thee will I *love,* till sacred 1953
Thee will I *love* with all 1953
Them who *love,* by thy sore 1049
Then be his *love* in Christ 1785
Then in wondrous *love,* and tender 259
There by his *love* o'er-shaded 1675
There thy *love* and mercy 1553
There's a little of his *love* 1957
There's *love,* and life, and lasting 1322
They *love* to sing to God, their King 28
This *love* beyond all measure 22
This was boundless *love* indeed 1581
This wondrous *love* enfolds 150
Those who *love* the Father 1004
Thou all-sufficient *Love* Divine 2034
Thou wilt *love* me to the end 1304
Though unseen, I *love* the Savior 1510
Thy living *love* send down 1699
Thy *love* alone can break the spell 1440
Thy *love* and favor kept to us 92
Thy *love* and light to show 515
Thy *love* divine hath led us 585
Thy *love* has brought me 60
Thy *love* has veiled thy glory 2168
Thy *love* hath blessed the wide world's 92
Thy *love* is in the sunshine glow 591
Thy *love* is law, thy law is love 1360
Thy *love* my heart sustaineth 1419
Thy *love,* not mine, bids fear 1284
Thy *love* the law that rules 1526
Thy *love* to all abound 1313
Thy *love* to me I ill could spare 883
Thy *love* to tell, thy praise to show 1170
Thy *love* we plead, our faith 944
Thy *love* we praise which knows 708
Thy *love* will bless the pure 1424
Thy perfect *love* cast out all fear 2142
Thy wondrous *love* adore 1405
Thy wondrous *love* declare 1689
Till broken *love* be whole 2273
Till the *love* of God 1069
Till thou thy perfect *love* impart 1714
Tis his wonderful, wonderful *love* 1559
Tis redeeming *love* in Christ 1573
To bless the *love* of God above 6
To show God's *love* aright 1107
To show thy *love* by morning 1811
To sing his *love* and mercy 860
To thee in reverent *love,* our 92
To thee my *love* grows ever 1254
To thee, whose faithful *love* 2118
To us thy pardoning *love* 452
Trusting thy *love* and thy grace 584
'Twas *love* that held him 2242
'Twas *Love* that opened wide 1194
'Twas wondrous *love* which led 1556

Us warmly in thy *love* enfold 2097
Waiting 'til *love* can raise 2198
We *love* him and seek him 1909
We *love* not world but 1916
We *love* th' example 404
We *love* the word of life 2178
We *love* thy Cross, the shame 316
We *love* thy laws (name) 316
We *love* thy mercies 586
We *love* thy name, we heed 1163
We *love* to hear of thee 2025
We *love* to sing below 2178
We thy *love* and grace proclaim 227
We will *love* both friend and foe 428
We will *love* thee as we ought 1581
What *love* through all his actions 2132
What patient *love* was seen 2217
What thy *love* can do to men 1092
When Christians *love* and live 1579
When *love* and law are one 2098
When *love* in one delightful 792
When my *love* for man grows 2247
When the Lord of *Love* was born 2306
When thy *love* our hearts shall 589
Where perfect *love* shall cast 1424
Where the Lord of *Love* was born 2306
While *love*, almighty love, is near 274
Who from his *love* can sever 2136
Who his pard'ning *love* would know 25
Who *love* deceit and violence 1261
Who *love* the blessed Savior 1988
Who would not *love* thee with 1367
Whom *love*, and love alone 419
Whom *love* led on to mortal pain 1417
Whose *love* will never die 1988
Will *love* thy truth 1
With *love* like thine, confessing 300
With *love* so faithful and so deep 303
With *love* that conquers fear 434
With *love* they keep perpetual tryst 491
"With *love* to man this cup 2133
With patient, uncomplaining *love* 1400
With spotless *love* and lowly fear 417
With that pure *love* of thine 559
With the *love* of Jesus beaming 1084
With them thy *love* to own 437
With thy *love* enfold us 451
With thy *love* my bosom fill 1761
Why should we *love* the dreary night 196
Wonderful *love* of the heart that was 623
Wond'ring at the *love* that crowned us 1510
Wondrous in redeeming *love* 1622
Yea, *love* with thee shall make 1651
Yet dearer is thy *love* I share 883
Yet I *love* thee, and adore 672
Yet I may *love* thee too 1234
You'll *love* him just as others do 2269

LOVE-BEAMS

His *love-beams* from heaven 871

LOVED

And *loved* his name below 1988
Be with thine own, thy *loved*, who stand 495
But as thyself hast *loved* me 1235
But he *loved* me so, would not 1501
"For God so *loved* the world that 1866
For he whom Jesus *loved* hath 1319
Glory be to him who *loved* us 543
"Glory unto him who *loved* us 669
God so *loved* us 450
He *loved* thee well, and calmly said 785
He *loved* us from the first of time 1064
He *loved* us to the last 1064
His *loved* and his own 2229
I *loved* the garish day 1053
I *loved* to choose and see my path 1053
If ever I *loved* thee, my Jesus 1246
Living, he *loved* me 1575
Loved thy day, revered thy name 1553
Loving him who first *loved* me 1687
O dearly, dearly has he *loved* 1963
So *loved* he the world that he gave 2102
They *loved* their Lord, so dear 875
Thou hast *loved* us, love us still 1683
We have not *loved* thee as we ought 2170
Which I have *loved* long since 1053
Who *loved* to do his Father's will 2161

LOVE-LIGHT

All in the *love-light* of Jesus' 1831
Then will this *love-light* of thy 1287

LOVELINESS

And laid a silent *loveliness* 40
O what alluring *loveliness* is found 16

LOVER

Lover of children, boyhood's 1491
Lover of men, O hear my call 1851
Lover of souls, from ill 2015
The *lover* of the pure 283

LOVERS

The *lovers* of all holy things 1291

LOVES

Ah, who that *loves* can love 1555
Because he *loves* me so 860
Because he *loves* the little things 602
For my Savior *loves* me so 2232
He calls you, for he *loves* you 3
He ever *loves* and cares 865
He *loves* and remembers his children 553
He *loves* ev'ryone, he loves you 1754
He *loves* me too 602
He *loves* me too well, to forsake 1922
I am so glad that Jesus *loves* me 806
If God so *loves* the little birds 602
If he so *loves* the little flowers 602
Jesus Christ, who *loves* me so 424
Jesus *loves* me, he will stay 995
Jesus *loves* me, loves me still 995
Jesus *loves* the children 928
Jesus *loves* to answer prayer 330
Loves the little lilies 928
O how he *loves* 1577
Somehow he *loves* me better 1756

Still he *loves* the earth he leaves 655
This is the dearest, that Jesus *loves* me 806
To know that he *loves* me 623
Yet *loves* me without end 303

LOVEST

Thou Christ who *lovest* field 2277

LOVETH

And he who *loveth* not abides unblest 202
And he who *loveth* not dwelleth in night 202
He *loveth* righteousness 1261

LOVING

He is tender and *loving* 1982
Ineffable in *loving* 1378
Loving and kind art thou 1276

LOVINGKINDNESS

For thy *lovingkindness* makes us 1800
His *lovingkindness* changes not 153
His *lovingkindness* in the skies 153
His *lovingkindness,* O how free 153
His *lovingkindness,* O how great 153
His *lovingkindness,* sing in death 153
O how great thy *lovingkindness* 978
Showing forth thy *lovingkindness* 951
The *lovingkindness* of my God 1436
The *lovingkindness* of the Lord 2329
Thy *lovingkindness* show 265
Thy *lovingkindness* to show forth 2112
Thy wondrous *lovingkindness* show 1135
Who thee with *lovingkindness* doth 1513

LOVINGKINDESSES

And *lovingkindnesses,* for they 1719

LOV'ST

Who, loving, *lov'st* them to the end 1517

LOWERS

O God, whilst evil *lowers* 923

LOWLINESS

And *lowliness* become mine inner 306
Thou cam'st to us in *lowliness* of thought 58
True *lowliness* of heart 306

LOYAL

Loyal ever to the Master 398

LOYALTY

May *loyalty,* sacrifice, courage 1372
'Tis *loyalty, loyalty, loyalty,* to Christ 516

LULL

Or *lull* the drowsy glade 2250

LULLED

Lulled be your restless waves 733

LURE

Lure the sad and weary
to our home above 163
The *lure* of gold we feel 1951
Till the *lure* of sense be vanquished 1049

LUST

By *lust,* and shame, and guilt 724
While *lust* and greed for gain 1397

LUSTER

And as the rainbow *luster* falls 437
And the *luster* of his kindly 2246
Shedding its *luster* on our darkened 1443
The *luster* of thy cross 84
With *luster* shining more and more 1132

LUSTS

What *lusts* and fears within 1419

M

MADE

And he has *made* me glad 842
And *made* a mighty noise 598
And *made* his Cross the Victor's 1080
And *made* us kings and priests 1108
And *made* us priests to God 2106
And now *made* willing to return 2202
And steadfast *made* my way 887
And thou hast *made* each step 447
And thou hast *made* him, thou art 1797
And ye that have *made* him your choice 164
For God of Zion hath *made* choice 2205
For thou hast *made* and dowered me 882
For thou hast *made* them glad 410
God hath *made* his saints victorious 1626
God *made* the little birds and flowers 602
God who *made* the grass
(sun, all things) 614
He *made* me ev'ry whit whole 1016
He *made* me pure within 1016
He *made* its waves and tides 1334
He *made* the lame to run 1255
He *made* the shining worlds 1061
He *made* the sky and earth 911
He *made* them every one 68
He *made* them his very own 881
He *made* them like snow 122
How hast thou *made* thee weak 528
"I with my chosen one have *made* 619
If you would be *made* pure 2338
In suffering thou hast *made* us one 596
It is he that hath *made* us 1310
Lord, thou hast *made* the blind 1140
Made holy by the might of love 507
Made of one blood 601
Made the glorious marvel 1036
Made us kings with him to reign 543
Made us of clay, and formed us men 184
Made you with himself to live 1736
Of one hast thou not *made* 1381
That hath *made* heaven and earth 1861
That he who *made* all nations 1551
That *made* the whole creation groan 373
The Lord God *made* them all 68
Thou hast *made* my life victorious 951
Thou hast *made* us free 2287
Thou who hast *made* my home of life 2248
Thy word *made* flesh, and in a manger 438
Till thou hast *made* us free 1029
Who hath *made* all things well 68
Who *made* complete
atonement on Calvary 139
Who *made* the earth and heavens high 1394
Who *made* the swelling deep 1394

MADEST

Thou *madest* man, he knows not why 1797

MAD'ST

Thou *mad'st* us kings and priests 671

MAGI

Come in, ye *magi* 320

MAGNIFY

And *magnify* the wondrous grace 1339
And *magnify* thy grace 434
Magnify them all in me 1138
O *magnify* the Lord with me 1890, 2060
We *magnify* thy holy name 2027

MAID

Mary, the pure and lowly *maid* 1632

MAIL

Strong *mail* of craft and power 19

MAIMED

Maimed and sick with sin 279

MAINTAIN

Maintain the glory of his Cross 914

MAJESTIES

For purple mountain *majesties* 1311

MAJESTY

But here in present *majesty* 1872
By thy glorious *majesty* 1761
Come thou glorious *Majesty* 1085
He who in *majesty* all things 1621
His *majesty* adored 231
Let his glorious *majesty* 1766
Like her, whom heaven's own *majesty* 1632
Majesty combined with meekness 1073

The *majesty* of law 1312
Thy *majesty* and greatness 2081
Thy *majesty* how bright 1234
Thy sovereign *majesty* 338
To him all *majesty* ascribe 47

MAKE

And didst *make* forever thine 1196
And glorious *make* his praise 50
And he will *make* it plain 577
And let us freely *make* him 347
And *make* a joyful noise 1335
And *make* a thousand hearts 1032
And *make* his path to know 2116
And *make* his pathway bright 2085
And *make* it live again 1609
And *make* me all like thee 1714
And *make* me love thee as I ought 1778
And *make* me pure within 1150, 2046
And *make* my heart a house of 2202
And *make* our life a daily psalm 1592
And *make* our lives thy royal 2024
And *make* our lukewarm hearts 1478, 1812
And *make* our secret soul to be 764
And *make* our spirits glad 1535
And *make* the broad earth thine 321
And *make* the nations one 2074
And *make* the sacrifice complete 1521
And *make* thee there an altar 1470
And *make* them know with joyful 1360
And *make* this house thy home 1776
And *make* thy people hear 1659
And *make* thy people one 1401
And *make* thy servants' hearts 307
And *make* thy sinful children 206
And *make* thy willing people 312
And *make* thy word my guide 1871
And *make* to us the Godhead 1777
And *make* us blest 311
And *make* us brave and full of 185
And *make* us one in thee with God 1130
And *make* us souls that 1780
And *make* us strong in faith 1810
And *make* us temples worthy 375
And *make* us to go on to know 2177
And *make* us wise in knowing 2170
And me to walk doth *make* 1904
And thou wilt *make* me ever live 1376
Come, *make* your wants 1893
Do thou *make* haste to me 1433
Do thou *make* whole again 388
For God doth *make* his world 1803
For he the same did *make* 1335
For she can *make* thee inly right 2226
God will *make* new heavens 1362
He will *make* for you a feast 1996
He will *make* good his right 707
He will *make* his kingdom glorious 2342
He will *make* our pathway clear 480
He yet shall *make* thee blest 1700
Him therefore famous *make* 1898
How can I *make* a lesser sacrifice 888
I will *make* my prayer to thee 710
I will *make* thy praises known 1376
Lord, *make* him thy great battle 2050
Lord, *make* it bloom 2086
Lord, *make* these faithless hearts 1431
Lord, *make* these moments blest 2203
Lord, *make* thou the answer clear 529
Lord, *make* us pure, enrich our life 2122
Make a Christmas in my heart 369
Make a heaven of my manger 369
Make a lost world thy home 1776
Make all my soul athirst for thee 734
Make all our moments calm 1023
Make and keep me pure within 994
Make Christ your Savior-King 2340
Make clear our eyes to see 1916
Make conflicts everywhere to cease 384
Make each heart thy happy home 760
Make each one nobler 594
Make each throbbing heart-beat 2123
Make every burden light 723
Make every one a member true 1379
Make every path of duty 1143
Make forgiveness feel so sweet 2261
Make friends of God's children 1820
Make haste to heal these hearts 2270
Make her in holiness excel 2304
Make here a spring of friendship 1527
Make it a temple set apart 1082
Make it one with the flame 1834
Make Jesus your friend ere 430
Make known to every heart 1551
Make manifest in this dread time 645
Make me a blessing 1601
Make me as a weaned child 1647
Make me burn thy love to know 1566
Make me crystal pure 606, 615
Make me gentle as a dove 1218
Make me glad and free 615
Make me in thy royal palace 754
Make me know that thou canst save 448
Make me like thee 1910
Make me, Lord, in work and play 976
Make me, Lord, obedient, mild 976
Make me lovely too 615
Make me, Savior, what thou art 523
Make me, Savior, wholly thine 70
Make me steadfast, wise 448
Make me strong and sure 606, 615
Make me teachable and mild 1647
Make me thy life to share 1027
Make music on the air 272
Make my heart anew 606, 615
Make my heart thy throne 2123
Make my spirit right and true 554
Make no delay, but take your lamps 1597
Make, O Lord, our children shine 1073
Make of my troubles quickly 865
Make our earth an Eden 1101
Make our enlarged souls possess 305
Make our faith strong 1715
Make our hearts thy habitation 743
Make pure the heart's desire 1401
Make pure thy children's erring 1495
Make sin's destruction surer 2086
Make somebody happy today 907

Make straight all the crooked places 1998
Make straight the highway 720
Make strong our faith 1149
Make the blind to see 2049
Make the glorious tidings known 1994
Make the rougher places plain 363
Make the withered trees to grow 1092
Make thee a bed, soft, undefiled 513, 528
Make them a royal priesthood 1166, 1344
Make them apostles 594
Make them from self to cease 1431
Make them show forth thy praise 388
Make them subject to thy reign 2342
Make this a home for men, and guide 1527
Make this poor self grow less 1407
Make this thy holy shrine 1175
Make thou thy flame in us 408
Make thy servants strong 1049
Make thy Spirit's help so meet 2261
Make thy temple in each breast 346
Make thy way plain before 1054
Make us brave in self-denial 988
Make us brave without a fear 1009
Make us contrite, pure and lowly 1685
Make us each a holy child 962
Make us eternal truths receive 375
Make us for awhile forego 346
Make us happy, full of cheer 1009
Make us hate and shun the ill 1120
Make us, Lord, like him to be 1051
Make us more like Jesus 757
Make us more than conqu'rors 2010
Make us one, we now implore 1182
Make us patient and enduring 989
Make us patient, gentle, kind 1120
Make us resolute to do 1120
Make us responsive to thy will 1163
Make us thine own from this hour 1694
Make us thy blest sanctuary 563
Make us thy ministers of life 1072
Make us thy sorrow feel 86
Make us unworthy here 1177
Make wars throughout the world 1369
Make ye straight what long was 363
Make you his service your 2060
Now *make* in us thy dwelling 1853
Now *make* us strong, we need 447
Now, O now, *make* him your choice 1996
O could we *make* our doubts 1966
O *make* but trial of his love 2060
O *make* me clean 1582
O *make* me daily, through thy grace 1407
O *make* me love thee more and more 1002
O *make* me thine forever 1475
O *make* me thine indeed 868
O *make* my heart thy throne 920
O *make* that blessing mine 1349
O *make* the nations understand 384
O *make* thy church, dear Savior 1544
O *make* thy rest within my 1910
O *make* us worthy, gracious Lord 1482
O Savior, *make* thy presence 785
Of this I *make* my boast 898
One *make* us all, true comrades 1130
Or *make* his love decay 1064
Receptive *make* our spirits 1359
So do thou *make* us glad 1541
Steadfast *make* my willing heart 554
That I may *make* my life today 1345
Thou can'st *make* the blind to see 1138
Thou didst for me *make* thy bed 1199
Thou didst *make* them, thine are 488
Thou dost *make* my courage stand 2224
Thou, Lord, didst *make* all for thy 469
'Tis thou alone canst *make* me 1018
Trusting thee to *make* me holy 811
We *make* this great memorial 2168
We must *make* the run successful 1076
What can *make* me whole again 2214
Which *make* the spirit mount 1038
Who shall *make* me dismayed 1903
Will *make* a better life 10
Willing to take you and *make* you 569
Without our aid thou did us *make* 57
Would you have him *make* you free 2324

MAKER

God's their only *Maker* 1305
Its *Maker* and its King 965
Maker, and Monarch, and Savior 1199
Maker of all, above, below 591
Maker of men, our purpose seal 1608
Maker, Teacher, infinite 1161
O God, thou art the *Maker* 1378
On God, our *Maker,* calling 1843
Our *Maker,* Defender, Redeemer 1546
When Christ, the mighty *Maker,* died 38

MAKES

And all that *makes* the day 468
And *makes* a heaven above 1090
And *makes* all within me 795
And *makes* his law his chief 773
And *makes* my joy complete 1201
And *makes* our task his own 2160
And *makes* the little band complete 1809
And *makes* the nations prove 1039
And *makes* the simple wise 618
And *makes* the singer glad 576
And *makes* their lives his own 666
And *makes* your Master his great 733
As *makes* a world of darkness 7, 1933
"Christ Jesus *makes* thee whole" 1830
Ev'ry one who *makes* request 561
He *makes* green things grow 1620
He *makes* me down to lie 1904
He *makes* me triumph over death 1201
He *makes* the grass the mountains 2307
He *makes* the sinner sad 786
It *makes* my joys full 1912
It *makes* the coward spirit 2192
It *makes* the wounded spirit 794
Makes brighter her halls 1440
Makes the trusting hearts his home 1041
That *makes* thy kingdom come 1166
Till our God *makes* all things new 251
'Tis he that *makes* me strong 858

What *makes* this rage and spite 1255
Who *makes* the woeful heart to sing 427

MAKEST

Thou, Lord, only that *makest* me 1054
Thou *makest,* Lord, the evening 1852

MAKING

Thou art in the *making* still 370

MAK'ST

And *mak'st* approach to thee 1631
And *mak'st* it soft with plenteous 410
Thou *mak'st* it rich to grow 410

MALADIES

My sinful *maladies* remove 319

MALICE

From all *malice* and unkindness 993

MAN

A mortal *man* ashamed of thee 967
And every *man* decideth the way 2101
And everywhere that *man* can be 877
And *man,* at war with man 948
And *man* can on and dare 1727
And *man* goes forward proud 1593
And *man* is blessed evermore 625
And *man* shall rule the world 1443
And *man,* thy marvel seeing 1843
And neither *man* nor work 396
And the unrighteous *man* his 2155
Blest is the *man* whose strength thou art 783
But to every *man* there openeth 2101
But where Lord and *man* both in one 1583
By serving *man,* God's will 456
Did the Lord a *man* become 1814
For Lord, unto the righteous *man* 527
For *man* shall be at one with God 2003
For *man,* the creature's sin 38
Frail *man,* his days are like the grass 1798
God is not *man,* to be deceiving 1896
God to *man* his blessing give 582
Happy the *man* whose hopes rely 911
How *man* may triumph over death 422
If I were a wise *man* 933
In all that thou dost *man* entail 2277
Like them, let *man,* the throne 55
Man can triumph over death 738
Man, created in thine image 579
Man decays and ages move 566
Man exalted to the sky 1761
Man fain the lightning would appease 1088
Man hath defied thee 1088
Man lives not for himself alone 456
"*Man* liveth not by bread alone" 161
Man may trouble and distress 980
Man redeemed, his sins forgiven 684
Man shall love man, with heart 2003
Man to God devoted live 582
Man to God hath reconciled 288
Man whom thou hast richly dowered 2308
Man with God is on the throne 1697
May *man* enthrone thee, Prince 371
No *man* can truly say that Jesus 1777
No *Man* of Sorrows stands 2147
Nor only as a *man* appears 2334
Now each *man* to his post 620
Now for *man* the noblest tree 1728
O Savior Christ, thou, too, art *man* 136
O thou, of God and *man* the Son 427
O what is *man,* I cry 1450
O what is *man,* in thy regard 1450
On *man* thy wisdom hath bestowed 1450
Pride of *man,* and earthly glory 53
Rejoicing as a *man* of strength 1862
Since every *man* has been blood 1224
Since, then, no *man* can help 1621
That *man* is truly blest 782
That *man* to judge thee hath 35
The *Man* of love, the Crucified 1893
The *man* that seeks thy peace 786
The *man* that walketh uprightly 2311
The *man,* the Christ, the soldier 818
The *man* whose heart is froward 1557
The Master's *man* is there 1252
The new *man* all put on 1842
The old *man,* all be put away 1842
The old *man,* meek and mild 797
Thee as *Man* for sinners slain 1686
Then it is the brave *man* 1574
This poor *man* cried, God heard 616, 1902
To *man* the promised peace 559
Very *Man,* though God-begotten 634
What *man* is he that fears 2116
What *man* is he that life 1321
What *man* shall stand before 1857
When a poor *man* came in sight 627
When *man* shall use for peace 1916
When the *man* of toil, and care 2260
When the proud *man* from his pride 2260
Where thou art not, *man* hath naught 342
Wherever *man* is found 1156
Who is this, a *man* of sorrows 2288
Who unto *man* his Son 34, 513
Would *man* but wake from out 2130

MANE

The lion's gory *mane* 1931

MANGER

A *manger* was his cradling place 1253
And he is in the *manger* now 625
And in a *manger* laid 2282
A *manger,* stall, and swaddling clothes 559
As the *manger* bed where our Savior lies 1095
At that *manger,* rude and bare 129
Coldly in a *manger* laid 2288
Down in a lowly *manger* 551
For the *manger* of Bethlehem 1995
From his poor *manger* to his bitter Cross 298
Hark! a voice from yonder *manger* 52
In his *manger* cradle 940
See him in a *manger* laid 105

There is a *manger* on the hay 2300
Thou who in a *manger* 517
To that lowly *manger* bed 129
When Bethlehem's *manger* was his only 817
When in *manger* rude he lay 412
Who didst in a *manger* lie 1009
Who is it in yon *manger* lies 528

MANHOOD

And *manhood* found its chief delight 1442
The highest, holiest *manhood* 1297
What God in *Manhood* bore 197

MANIFEST

Manifest thyself to me 1761

MANIFESTS

Manifests his pard'ning favor 1510
That *manifests* the Savior's power 132
To whom he *manifests* his love 1869

MANKIND

All *mankind* is nobled through 1075
Broken for *mankind* 3
Mankind shall then be truly free 428
O holy Savior of *mankind,* ride 1507
O now to all *mankind* 2051
Of all *mankind* the Servant 1491
Of *mankind* the life and light 1161
Still let *mankind* thy blessings 1781
To all *mankind* good will: "Glory 1113

MANNA

Brethren pray, and holy *manna* 251
Daily *manna* still provide you 556
For thy *manna* we are pining 219
I'm feasting on the *manna* 431
Life–imparting, heavenly *manna* 1126
Manna feeds them from the skies 1612
O *manna* from above 1317
Thy hungering ones with *manna* 1170
Thy *manna,* Lord, before me 2140
'Tis *manna* to my hungry soul 2087
'Tis *manna* to the hungry soul 794
With his heav'nly *manna* feeding 65
With his *manna* he my hungry 1834
With *manna* in the wilderness 1716

MANNER

When he, in wondrous *manner* 534

MANSION

A heavenly *mansion* near 1243
A *mansion* with the blest 252
O one, O only *mansion* 489
That heavenly *mansion* shall be mine 1243
Wonderful *mansion* that shineth 2314

MANSIONS

Back to the heav'nly *mansions* hasting 2137
In *mansions* of glory and endless 1246
In the *mansions* bright and blessed 1731
Large are the *mansions* in thy Father's 349
The *mansions* rise beyond the skies 2207
Up to the beautiful *mansions* 2145
Within thy *mansions* we have all 522

MANTLE

Elijah's *mantle* o'er Elisha 594

MANY

Where the *many* toil together 2006
Where the *many* work together 2017

MAPLES

Let *maples,* birches, willows 2082

MARCH

Ever singing, *march* we onward 1040
March, in heavenly armor clad 1560
March on, O soul, march on 1204
March on, O youth of God 115
March we forth in the strength 574
May *march* with thee to smite 1373
One the *march* in God begun 2067
Still *march* in firm array 1654
Then onward we *march,* our arms 2180
We *march* with thee where martyrs 309
We *march* right onward to a crown 264
When the *march* is over 256
Where *march* the stars and sun 162
Who *march* 'neath Christ's banner 1909
With thee we *march,* O Master 510

MARCHING

Our God is *marching* on 1215
We're *marching* through Emmanuel's 351

MARGIN

On the *margin* of the river 1711
While others to the *margin* come 1067

MARINER

Mariner beware 1114

MARK

And *mark* her bulwarks well 646
Mark all her bulwarks 2312
"*Mark* my foot-steps, my good page 627
Mark the sea-bird wildly 568
Mark that miracle of time 552
Mark the first signal 2331
Mark well the perfect, upright 1935
Still they *mark* each warrior's way 295
We *mark* her goodly battlements 1539

MARKED

And *marked* the door with blood 1194
Have *marked* my erring track 39
They *marked* the footsteps that he 530

MARKETS

In our busy *markets* 2300

MARKS

Hath he *marks* to lead me 119

MARRED

And *marred* the pattern drawn 183
Though *marred* with earthly 1849

MARROW

Even as with *marrow* and 1172

MARSHAL

O *marshal* us, the sons of sires 1916

MART

And crowded *mart* and streets 1604
In crowded *mart,* by stream 1116
In *mart,* and court, and parliament 1507

MARTS

While in the *marts* of labor 923

MARTYR

The *martyr* first, whose eagle eye 1931
Though I as a *martyr* bleed 636

MARTYR-BAND

Firm as a *martyr-band* 1156

MARTYRS

And the blessed *martyrs* follow 746
Jewish *martyrs* gladly died 1196
Martyrs testified 501

MARVEL

I *marvel* that he would descend 880
Inward we look, and *marvel* 162
The *marvel* of Emmaus road 2069
We *marvel* at the purpose that 1549

MARVELED

And *marveled* at the radiance 2193

MARVELS

The *marvels* he hath wrought 537
The *marvels* of his might 1552
These *marvels* sweeter far to trace 1863

MASTER

Ah! Who shall thus the *Master* 1285
And how the *Master,* ready 1831
And the *Master* calls for you 679
But Jesus for our *Master* own 317
But the *Master* of the sea 891
But thou, O Christ, art *Master* 1951
Christ, the royal *Master* 1586
Doth the *Master* wait to bless 521
For he, who is our *Master* 1252
Hark! 'tis the *Master* speaks to 681
He is coming, our Lord and *Master* 699
He is my *Master,* Lord, and King 1822
He's the *Master* of the sea 891
Jesus, *Master,* wilt thou use 997
Let us be useful, dear *Master* 1694
Loud and long the *Master* calleth 679
Master, at thy foot-stool 695
Master, let it now be heard 1207
Master, speak, for O thou knowest 1207
Master speak, O speak to me 1207
Master speak, though least and lowest 1207
Master, the terror is over 1208
Master, thou wilt keep us 2287
Master, with anguish of spirit 1208
My gracious *Master* and my God 1351
My *Master* was a comrade 1252
My *Master* was a helper 1252
O Lord and *Master* of us all 2181
O *Master,* from the mountain side 2270
O *Master* of abundant life 1417
So very rich my *Master* was 1253
Someone's betraying his *Master* 1757
Sowing for the *Master* 1771
The *Master* hath called us 1909
The *Master* of the centuries 816
Thee, my *Master* and my Friend 2018
Thee my new *Master* now I call 1137
'Tis the *Master* calleth, now the voice 1997
Whither the *Master* has entered 1742
With thee, O *Master,* let me live 1466

MASTER-BUILDERS

By wise *master-builders* squared 1567

MATE

O poor man's *Mate,* our lowliest 1491

MATTER

'Twill *matter* to me but little 1411

MATTERS

It *matters* not what foes intend 1723
What *matters* where on earth 1722

MAY

May it guide us still to thee 950
May that sacred emblem be 950

MAZE

That since this *maze* of life 2039
While life's dark *maze* I tread 1227

MEAD

Or the dewy *mead* 983

MEADOW

Holy the *meadow* where thy feet 385

MEADOWS

Fair are the *meadows* 427
Long ago, to lonely *meadows* 1100
O'er the still *meadows* the night 1611
Out in the sunny *meadows* 2195
The *meadows* where we play 68

MEANETH

Hearken, what *meaneth* the sudden 984
"Whosoever" surely *meaneth* me 802

MEANING

His *meaning* still is love 133
The *meaning* and the mystery of 191, 1445

The *meaning* of our eager strife 185
The *meaning* of thy chastening hand 189

MEANS

All *means* are thine 534
For *means* of grace and hopes 1439
What *means* this ether ranger 1878
What *means* this strange commotion 2218

MEASURE

None can *measure* out thy patience 711
The *measure* and the pledge of love 2192
This love, beyond all *measure* 22
We *measure* gain and loss 185

MEDIATION

While thy blessed *mediation* 1073

MEDICINE

And *medicine* in sickness 489
The *medicine* of my broken heart 2034

MEDITATE

And when on thee I *meditate* 1172

MEDITATES

And *meditates* on his law day 1841

MEDITATION

My *meditation* weigh 527

MEDITATIONS

And joyful *meditations* fill 1436

MEEK

For all the *meek* thou wilt provide 72
Meek to suffer, strong to save 1761
The *meek* and poor of spirit 2076
The *meek* in judgment he shall 2116
The *meek* shall hear with joy 1902
The *meek* shall hear with joyfulness 616
Thou to the *meek* and lowly 1378
To the *meek*, and the lowly, and 236
While all the *meek* rejoice 1890

MEEKNESS

Holy Savior, who in *meekness* 718
In our *meekness* to be wise 2255
More of his *meekness*, more humility 1219

MEET

All *meet* thee in the blessed home 1393
And now we *meet* again 206
But to *meet* him empty-handed 1222
Come down and *meet* us now 329
He'll *meet* thee while yet on the way 1494
I *meet*, along the crowded way 1410
I'll *meet* that dear one there 1152
I shall *meet* him in glory 623
In Christ now *meet* both East 919
Life's tumult we must *meet* again 32
Lord, *meet* us by the way 1171, 1506
Meet at my table, and record 2132
Meet him in the evening 1210
Meet him in the noon-tide 1210
Meet him now with consecration 1726
Meet him on our hillsides 2300
Meet him there tomorrow 1210
Meet upon his brow 143
Meet with the blood-bought throng 2325
Now shall *meet* him in the air 1106
Oft as they *meet* for worship here 540
One in thee together *meet* 2047
Or "*meet* him in the air" 849
Shall we *meet* and cast the anchor 1712
Shall we *meet* in that blest 1712
Shall we *meet* in yonder city 1712
Shall we *meet* with Christ 1712
Shall we *meet* with many 1712
Soon we shall *meet* him face to face 1670
That he can *meet* their need 549
That he should let us *meet* 2061
Then shall we *meet* to part no more 2325
There those who *meet* shall part no 1965
There we shall *meet*, from every clime 1254
There we shall *meet*, in answer 1254
There we shall *meet* in joyous 1254
There you'll *meet* the Superintendent 1076
Thrice happy they who *meet* above 771
Thy Holy Spirit, *meet* with those 2052
To *meet* him in clouds of the sky 24
To *meet* the dawning day 301
We *meet*, as in that upper room 335
We *meet* on earth for thy dear 1031
We *meet* the grace to take 1031
We *meet* with one accord 1132
We shall *meet* on that beautiful shore 1992
We shall *meet* our King eternal 1738
We shall *meet* our loved and own 2191
Whatever I may *meet* 1949
When we *meet* to praise and pray 1272
Why didst thou *meet* the tempter's 1482
You can *meet* them in school 875
You may *meet* with misfortunes 130
You may *meet* your Savior 2252
You will *meet* with trials as 2339

MEETING

Joyful, joyful will the *meeting* be 347
O there'll be a glorious *meeting* 2297

MEETS

And *meets* him with his might 1784
But *meets* the foeman face to face 1784
He *meets* us, while to him we 1661
It *meets* his tender view 602
Lo, Jesus *meets* thee, risen from 2010
Meets, supplies my every need 978
There the Savior *meets* his loved ones 2275
Therefore still he *meets* our needs 990

MELODIES

Melodies sweet for Christ our King 1670
The holy *melodies* of love arise 37

MELODY

A *melody* of love 604
And grave sweet *melody* 2112

And the *melody* that he gave 819
In our choicest *melody* 101
Our *melody* we raise 44
The sweetest *melody* he gave to me 25
There never was a sweeter *melody* 833
'Tis a *melody* divine 25
'Tis a *melody* of love 833

MELT

And *melt* in fires of love 2098
And *melt* mine eyes to tears 38
Holy Spirit, *melt*, refine it 461
Melt my heart and fill my life 1056
Melt my stony heart 1000
Melt the clouds of sin 1040
Melt the cold with fire 744
Melt the frozen, warm the chill 342
Shall *melt* away, and droop 157

MEMBERS

And his true *members* all unite 1842
Members united in that mystic 2278
On all her *members* breathe 1579
Through its *members* world-wide may 634

MEMORIALS

Sweet *memorials*—till the Lord 2089

MEMORIES

And its *mem'ries* sweet, so with joy 2066
Grand *memories* on thee shine 1312
That holy *mem'ries* of thy Cross 235
Where the holiest of *memories* pilgrim-like 236

MEMORY

And mind and *memory* flee 30
How sweet their *memory* still 1347
In *mem'ry*, Lord, of thee 234, 1805
Nor can the *memory* find 1019
Sad *memory* weaves no veil 1285
Tranquil *memory* to the dead 1606
True *memory* of thee 204
Your *memory* hallowed in the land 1532

MEN

A million murdered *men* 2285
All *men* in his name befriending 584
All *men* shall be blest 286
All *men* the whole world through 14
And all *men* are my kin 1224
And all *men* learn thy love 1529
And all *men* see thy light 1442
And *men* and angels sing before 2149
And *men* are timid grown 2226
And *men* may see thy grace 1123
And seeking *men* unto him 2086
And the *men* go forth to reap 1929
And then, by *men* and angels 2072
As *men* of old have sung 1107
Be ye as *men* that wait 682
Bidding all *men* to repentance 363
But *men* made strange, and none 1255
Can we to *men* benighted 512
Come the wise *men* on their way 299
For *men* transformed to meet 2040
For *men* who gird the world 2040
From proud *men* thy servant hide 730
Hark, how from *men* whose lives 1397
Here may our fellow *men* be shown 1527
It comely is and right that upright *men* 2329
Let all *men* praise thy name 1123
Let all *men* worship thee 1123
Let *men* their songs employ 1039
Like those strong *men* of old 1204
Lord of *men* as well as angels 1214
Making all *men* a brotherhood 1275
Many mighty *men* are lost 1788
Men and humble beasts with them 609
Men he raises from the dust 991
Men in whose ears his sweet 1702
Men look for God and fancy 1698
Men lost and dying, souls 1829
Men scorn thy sacred name 2073
Men shall be blest in him 735, 1454
Men shall forsake their fear 284
Men who are lost and constantly sinning 529
Mighty *men* around us falling 736
Nor *men* their brothers harm 1930
Now from all *men* be outpoured 1936
O happy *men* that pay 1167
O that *men* to the Lord 773
O that *men* would praise the Lord 1837
On! for Christ at least be *men* 2157
Only righteous *men* and women dwell 656
Set all *men* free 1366
Show dying *men* thy shining face 383
So that sinful *men* and women 2254
Still let *men* see heaven's opened door 2291
Strong *men* and maidens fair 1654
Strong *men* who fall to rise 1593
That all *men* everywhere 23, 799
That all *men* thy love may see 1474
That *men* may find through thee 1474
That *men* may hear the grateful song 1729
The Lord of *men* and angels 763
The *men* of grace have found 351
The *men* in air who closer bring 1355
The *men* who would be like him 1252
The wise *men* had a star 1928
Therefore, Christian *men*, be sure 627
These and all *men* in thy sight 416
Thou hast thy young *men* at the war 396
Though *men* by men deceived 853
Three wise *men* bearing gifts 918
Three wise *men* came from country far 1861
Through thee, enslaved *men* find 1658
Till *men* at last shall ring the bells 1507
Till *men* in all thy countryside 2277
Till *men* of him new-born 120
To blind *men* send the light 156
To him all *men* shall bow 1945
To sinful *men* thy justice 1368
When all *men* find thy liberty 1168
Where'er *men* own his sway 284
Which *men* divide with men 204
While *men* are like a cradle 1915

Wise *men* are we kneeling 1717
Wise *men,* guided by a star 609
Wise *men* in their wisdom 517
Wise *men* sought and found him 524
Ye that are *men,* now serve him 1786

MEND

God *mend* thine every flaw 1391

MENTION

The *mention* of thy glory 489

MERCY

After thy *mercy* think on me 1719, 2116
And all the tender *mercy* he hath 1634
And by thy *mercy* thou art mine 60
And he whose *mercy* ruled 6
And in thy *mercy* heal us all 136
And let me still thy *mercy* prove 790
And let thy *mercy* bless thy servant 1423
And *mercy* more than life 1311
And *mercy* while we live 1930
And yet his *mercy* condescends 150
Be his abounding *mercy* praised 231
Be silent, be silent, his *mercy* record 172
But his *mercy* waneth never 566
But that God can in *mercy* pardon 1976
But thy *mercy,* ever-flowing 754
Father of *mercy,* from thy watch 436
For *mercy,* Lord, is all my suit 1456
For *mercy* shall be built 619
For the Lord is gracious, his *mercy* 1310
For thy *mercy,* Lord, I wait 629
God of all *mercy,* for pardon 584
God's free *mercy* streameth 1800
Have *mercy* on us, Jesus 43
Have *mercy* upon me 31
Have *mercy* upon us 1326
His *mercy* is forever sure 57
His *mercy* lasts always 1484
His *mercy* lifts me when I fall 1756
His *mercy* saved our souls 2090
His *mercy* the whole earth doth 2155
His tender *mercy* doth endure 532
His wondrous *mercy* forth-telling 263
How great is thy *mercy* and goodness 2194
How vast the *mercy* and the love 965
If, in *mercy,* thou wilt spare 449
In *mercy* hear my prayer 2078
In *mercy* hear thy hungry children's 712
In *mercy,* Lord, bestow on me 1964
In *mercy,* Lord, incline 2099
In *mercy* to our weakness 2168
In tender *mercy* turn thou 2078
Is the *mercy* he will show 1472
It is that *mercy* never-ending 1290
Jesus, in *mercy* bring us 489, 961
Let all thy *mercy* on our souls 465
Let *mercy* everywhere increase 384
Let thy *mercy* light on me 1138
Let thy *mercy* show thy power 538
Lord, thy *mercy* still entreating 1179
Matchless in his *mercy* 1210
Mercy and truth are all his ways 535
Mercy, good Lord, mercy I ask 1456
Mercy had saved me 1262
Mercy invites to heavenly joys 1924
Mercy is pleading today 353
Mercy now, O Lord, I plead 717
Mercy still reserved for me 395
Mercy there was great, and grace 2335
Mercy thy days shall lengthen 567
Nor God's *mercy* stifle 1668
O boundless *Mercy,* pardoning all 186
O by each *mercy* sent us 1953
O let thy *mercy* make us glad 1478, 1812
O thou whose *mercy* found me 2119
On them let thy *mercy* shine 488
On thy *mercy* I rely 1682
On us thy *mercy* lighten 1377
Requiring *mercy* for my sin 1456
Savior, from thy *mercy* flow 1173
Speechless, I thy *mercy* trust 554
Still by constant *mercy* fed 380
Such *mercy,* such love 880
That *mercy* crowns it 643
Then in *mercy,* Lord, draw near 1775
Then let thy *mercy* spare 648
There is *mercy* with the Savior 1999
There's *mercy* with the Lord 308
Thou dost us here in *mercy* 200
Thou hast *mercy* to relieve us 1683
Though *mercy* long delay 1171
Thy everlasting *mercy* 1327
Thy *mercy,* highest heaven 1362
Thy *mercy* on thy people, Lord 583
Thy *mercy* sought me 60
Thy *mercy* to implore 244
Thy *mercy* will not fail me 1297
Thy *mercy* will not fail us 2072
Thy sure *mercy* ever kind 45
'Tis *mercy* all, that thou hast 2033
To perform the *mercy* promised 215
To whom the Lord in *mercy* 772
Whose blood-bought *mercy* frees us 1320
Widely as his *mercy* flows 1618
With his *mercy* he may shield us 668
With *mercy* and with judgment 1923
Wonderful *mercy,* wonderful love 2314
Wonderful, wonderful *mercy* I sing 2314

MERCY-DROPS

Mercy-drops round us are falling 1981

MERCY-SEAT

At the blessed *mercy-seat* 759
Come to the *mercy-seat* 355
How beautiful thy *mercy-seat* 1234
Nearer the Christian's *mercy-seat* 1267
O'er the blest *mercy-seat* 1689
Pleading at thy *mercy-seat* 589
Thy *mercy-seat* is open still 392

MERIT

All the Savior's dying *merit* 339
By thine all-sufficient *merit* 343, 658
O for the priceless *merit* 1325
Trusting only in thy *merit* 1607

MERITS

And in his *merits* thou 348
By thy *merits* we find favor 659
Thine all the *merits,* mine the great 2201

MESSAGE

A *message* angels fain would sing 799
Always the same sweet *message* 2195
And for your *message* millions wait 1469
And let not this *message* to you 18
Blest in the *message* Gabriel 1865
Comes this *message* sweet to me 1096
Dearer far than any *message* 1804
Forth with thy *message* send us 515
Message of salvation 1180
My *message* as from God receive 336
Proclaims from heaven the *message* free 9
The clearer *message* from above 2027
This is the *message* that I bring 799
This *message,* blessed Savior, to her 2237
To bear the *message* which they bring 1113
To the *message* of thy birth 369
We've a *message* to give to the nations 2208
Wonderful *message* that cannot grow 1972

MESSAGES

His *messages* of love to bear 1893

MESSENGER

A *messenger* from heaven sent 547

MESSENGERS

Messengers of truth to be 126

MESSIAH

Thine own *Messiah* reigns 1666

MET

And *met* us face to face 2163
And *met* within thy holy place 199
Met together Death and Life 288
They *met* the tyrant's brandished 1931
Thou who, sinless *met* the tempter 2049

MIDDAY

It may be at *midday* 953

MIDNIGHT

Dark, dark hath been the *midnight* 1923
Lo! at *midnight,* who is he 2286
Midnight hears the welcome voices 2149
Our *midnight* is thy smile 1155
'Tis *midnight,* and for others' guilt 2091
'Tis *midnight,* and from all removed 2091
'Tis *midnight,* and from heavenly plains 2091
'Tis *midnight,* in the garden now 2091
When the dark *midnight* is over 1742

MIDST

Since God is in the *midst* of her 571

MIGHT

All *might* and majesty are thine 1864
And reveal her ancient *might* 1069
And wondrous is his *might* 1636
Be strong, and in his *might* 1860
But only in thy *might* 1169
By the Spirit's *might* 925
For the *might* of thine arm we bless thee 487
God of our youth, be thou our *might* 588
He, with all-commanding *might* 1074
His *might* thy heart shall strengthen 567
In the *might* of God arrayed 1747
Is more of *might* by far 598, 1886
Learning all the *might* that lies 2247
Lest the *might* of fierce temptation 1049
No human *might,* no earthly pride 1636
O measureless *Might,* ineffable Love 1546
O Wind of heaven, by thy *might* 81
One in *might,* and one in glory 281
The *might* of his Spirit 423
Thine ancient *might* did break 593
Thy *might* in us to dwell 312
Till in its *might* it is akin to pain 1254
Unthinkable in *might* 1378
Whose *might* they own 1865
With his *might* will Christ 2096
With *might* thou strengthenest me 1462

MILK

With *milk* and honey blest 961

MILLIONS

And *millions* more, still on the way 1875
China's *millions* join the strains 1070
Earth's *millions,* swarming like an angry 2135
I'll shout with the *millions* on high 24
Millions in darkness are needing 1972
Millions of souls forever may 433
Millions yet have never heard 1136
While *millions* without number 1485

MILLS

Among these dark satanic *mills* 95

MIND

A ready *mind* to understand 189
Already in the *mind* of God 1397
And a *mind* to blend with 443
And innocent the *mind* 1934
And let that *mind* which was 2334
And *mind* equipped 603
And when we find thy blessed *mind* 84
And your *mind* grows dizzy 1754
Let this *mind* be in us which was 58
Man's *mind* and heart make free 1830
May erring *minds* that worship 1530
May the *mind* be humbled 925
My *mind,* O Lord, is thine to keep 1844
Nor *mind* thy brightness comprehend 1423
O *Mind* of God incarnate 1490
Our *mind* illume, disperse 1163
Pure was the *mind* of Christ 1804
That *mind* and soul, according 1797
The humbled *mind* bestow 393
The *mind,* O Lord, is ours to keep 1844
The same in *mind* and heart 230

Though my *mind* great wisdom 461
True in *mind,* and pure 930
When we his *mind* obey 377
Whose *mind* is dim 420
Whose *mind* is stayed on thee 2053
With confident and humble *mind* 1238
You must *mind* and bear the image 942

MINDS

And *minds* that comprehend 2165
Our *minds* from bondage free 315
Unto our *minds* give freedom 1873

MINES

Deep in unfathomable *mines* 577

MINGLES

Hark, it *mingles* with the raptures 669

MINISTER

Joyfully *minister* that gift 454
O may we *minister* to them 503
To *minister* to men 547

MINISTERED

Such as *ministered* to thee 500

MINISTERS

Ye *ministers,* that do fulfil 1547

MINISTRIES

And by thy Spirit's *ministries* 2107
And still their silent *ministries* 2163
The wiser *ministries* of love 2027

MINSTRELSY

Then all *minstrelsy* 1034

MIRACLE

This God-like *miracle* of grace 641

MIRRORED

For *mirrored* in its depths 1582

MIRRORS

Mirrors back his beauty 1305

MIRTH

And *mirth* that has no bitter 445
Him serve with *mirth,* his praise forth tell 57
While angels sing with tender *mirth* 34

MISCHIEF

From tainting *mischief* keep them 99

MISDEEDS

Our *misdeeds* to thee confessing 1179

MISERY

O the *misery* my sin has caused 977

MISS

Let us not *miss* the accepted hour 2228
Nor *miss* our providential way 274

MISSION

And may its *mission* ever be 2107
Unto your *mission* be true 1601

MIST

Beyond the *mist* I fain would rise 915
From the *mist* his brightness 566

MISTRUST

And fainting, I *mistrust* thy grace 1517
Too long *mistrust* and fear 1609

MISTS

And the *mists* have rolled away 2256
Lifting the raveled *mists* 1780
'Mid *mists,* and rocks, and 1544
Mists fold away 732
The *mists* of earth away 240
The *mists* of error and of vice 2176
When in *mists* obscuring, siren 2274
When the *mists* of doubts and passion 1603

MISUSINGS

Look not on our *misusings* of thy grace 99

MIXED

Our sweet is *mixed* with bitter 960

MOAN

The *moan* of pain, the futile cry 1467

MOCK

We *mock* thee when we do not 1797

MOCKED

And *mocked* me as I wailed 1322
And *mocked* the cross and flame 1931
And *mocked* thy saving kingship 1124
As if I *mocked* alone 873
Mocked, imprisoned, stoned, tormented 677

MOLD

And *mold* them to thy will 459
Mold me and make me 691
Mold my life, and use me 2123
Mold them, Father, kind and good 2227

MOLEST

No powers of darkness me *molest* 59
Nothing can *molest* or turn 1808

MOMENT

And every *moment* watch and pray 499
And from this *moment,* live or die 1144
Come thou, this *moment* 336
Each *moment* with its good 1939
Listening every *moment* to the Spirit's 1790
Moment by moment, he thinks 407
Moment by moment I'm kept 407

Moment by moment I'm under 407
Moment by moment I've life from 407
Moment by moment, O Lord 407
Never a *moment* that he forgets 829
One *moment* will not linger 19
Serving him *moment* by moment 1030
Soon the *moment* of grace is past 158
That *moment* Amalek prevailed 2221
That *moment* from Jesus a pardon 2101
This *moment* we share 172
Walking each *moment* close by 2148
When each *moment* so madly is 1208
When will the *moment* come 1421
Will you this *moment* his grace 1206

MOMENTS

And, as the *moments* fly 1345
Precious *moments* idly wasted 1179
So the little *moments* 1101
The *moments* are passing 1743
The *moments* fly apace 1584
Trusting as the *moments* fly 1721
When the peaceful, happy *moments* 2001
While swift the *moments* fly 2301
Will brighten the *moments* of earth's 10

MONARCH

As *monarch,* but the humble child 373
Monarch of all things, fit us 467
What are the *monarch,* his court 1538

MONARCHS

And earthly *monarchs* clamor forth 49
Ye *monarchs,* wait his nod 1900

MONEY

All your *money,* talents, time 259
Money cannot buy your reward 2265

MONTHS

Months in due succession 2204

MOODS

For beauty's benedictive *moods* 1779

MOON

Fairer than the silver *moon* 742
He shall, while doth the *moon* 1454
Moon and stars the strains prolong 1975
Moon and stars with silvery light 715
No *moon* shall harm thee 2139
The *moon* and stars ordained 1450
The *moon* and stars their Maker's name 2250
The *moon* shines full at his command 877
The *moon* takes up the wondrous tale 1932
The silver *moon,* the golden sun 2294
Thou silver *moon* with softer gleam 41
Unto the *moon* and to the stars 775

MOONLIGHT

Fairer still the *moonlight* 427

MOOR

O'er *moor* and fen, o'er crag 1053
Seeking them o'er *moor* and fen 1735

MOORINGS

And *moorings* safe in waters still 2185

MORN

A happy *morn* will dawn for you 2269
And every *morn* anew his goodness 573
And from *morn* to set of sun 746
And with the *morn* those angel faces 1053
At *morn* and eve thy radiance 1424
His coming like the *morn* shall be 327
Morn to darkest night succeeds 990
O brighter than that glorious *morn* 1877
O brighter than the rising *morn* 1877
That *morn* shall tearless be 1465
The fair, sweet *morn* awakes 1923
The *morn* shall break; the dawn 1860
The summer *morn* I've sighed for 1923
Thou rising *morn,* in praise rejoice 41
Upon this happy *morn* the Lord of Life 1704
While this *morn* of joy and love 662

MORNING

A *morning* promised long 1
And the *morning* breaks, eternal 2259
And when the *morning* breaks 591
As some sweet summer *morning* 1849
As to each new-born *morning* 1793
At *morning,* at noon, and 2084
Each *morning* thou art nearer 2146
Early in the *morning,* our song 749
Fair as the *morning,* looking 1605
Fairer than *morning,* lovelier 1793
For the *morning* seems to dawn 2154
From *morning* till ev'ning glad carols 931
Good *morning,* up there, where Christ 2225
Good *morning,* up there, where cometh 2225
Heaven's *morning* breaks 27
How sweet on a clear, Sabbath *morning* 1986
In the dawning of the *morning* 2256
In the glad *morning* of my day 1044
Let eternal *morning* rise 382
Let thy glorious *morning* dawn 1554
Lo, the *morning* breaketh 1833
May the *morning* chase the night 1554
May when life's great *morning* 2275
More than they that for *morning* 1129
Morning by morning new mercies 647
Morning, evening, bless his name 1211
Morning soon will dawn 922
O blessed Easter *morning* 1418
O bright and happy *morning* 1418
O gladsome Easter *morning* 1418
Of that swift-speeding *morning* 137
Oh for that glad *morning* when 1264
On that bright and cloudless *morning* 2259
So shall it be at last,
in that bright *morning* 1793
Some bright (glad) *morning* 167
Sowing in the *morning* 1693

Still in the *morning* mending 751
The *morning* breaks, the shadows flee 333
The *morning* draweth nigh 1
The *morning* shall awaken 252
Thou art fairer than the *morning* 2019
Thou art our *Morning* and our *Sun* 1380
Till *morning* cometh, watch 1289
'Tis thine own third *morning* 2204
When in the *morning* unto thee 1434
When *morning* bright breaks through 1818
When *morning* dawns, farewell 16
When *morning* lifts the veil 586
When the bright and glorious *morning* 2246
With the early *morning* rays 966

MORNINGS

Mornings of joy give for evenings of 2322

MORNS

The radiant *morns* unfold 40

MORROW

A brighter *morrow* dawned 368
The *morrow* let bring what it may 1542
There is a *morrow* for thee 1269

MORROWS

Coming *morrows* we may never 929

MORTAL

No *mortal* can with him compare 1201
No *mortal* so happy as I 795

MORTALITY

Farewell, *mortality* 425

MORTALS

But timorous *mortals* start 1966
But, while *mortals* rise and perish 1618
Christ, awhile to *mortals* given 655
For *mortals* and for sinners 252
Giving needy *mortals* health 1006
Let *mortals*, too, upraise 2243
Mortals, give thanks and sing 1653
Mortals join the mighty chorus 1040
While *mortals* sleep, the angels 1426

MOTHER

Ah! ah! beautiful is the *mother* 257
Alleluia, joyful *mother* 78
As a *mother* stills her child 1007
But his *mother* only 933
How blest that *mother*, in whose shrine 1865
"Like as a *mother*," grant, O God 1093
Mary was that *mother* mild 1572
My *mother* dear, in humble prayer 870
No *mother*, e'er so mild 1234
Now was she, that *mother* blessed 140
'Round yon Virgin, *mother* and child 1720
The *mother* who bore you loves you less 1338
Where a *mother* laid her Baby 1572
Who, of Christ's dear *mother* thinking 1263
Who, on Christ's
dear *mother* gazing (thinking 140
Who upon that *mother* gazing 1263

MOTHERS

He patient is, as *mothers* are 1093
It was good for our *mothers* 2095
Mothers cease their own to cherish 2341
The *mothers* brought their little ones 505
The *mothers* from a village 949
When the anxious *mothers* 1099

MOTION

The Lord of every *motion* there 2033
The *motion* of a hidden fire 1641

MOTIVE

Through mortal *motive*, scheme and 67

MOUNT

Beneath that *mount* another scene 2147
Let Zion's *mount* rejoice 2312
Nightly to the *mount* repair 752
The *mount* on which I'm standing 853
Then shall I *mount* and soar away 153
Then shall they *mount* as eagle's 595
We'll *mount* aloft to thine abode 157
Yonder on Calvary's *mount* 1206

MOUNTAIN

A *mountain* that shall fill the earth 1539
And to your *mountain* flee 1261
Calling from Calvary's *mountain* 2317
Calvary's mournful *mountain* climb 552
Far over the *mountain* and through 1909
From thee, like Pisgah's *mountain* 1341
High on yon celestial *mountain* 356
I'm living on the *mountain* 431
Mighty *mountains*, purple-breasted 104
On the *mountain* I have seen him 835
Over *mountain*, plain or sea 686
The purple-headed *mountain* 68
Upon a *mountain* builded high 2197
Upon the highest *mountain* 1945
Which Christ upon the *mountain* shows 1543
Ye shall not, in the *mountain* pine 1900

MOUNTAINS

And all through the *mountains* 1983
And as the *mountains* high 2079
And the *mountains* in reply 105
As *mountains* their foundations 731
Away on the *mountains* wild 1983
Before him *mountains* melt 1889
Before him on the *mountains* 661
Before the *mountains* had their birth 1174
Cold *mountains* and the midnight 1226
Here let the *mountains* thunder 1936
His *mountains* lift their solemn 1899
Let *mountains* from their seats 572
Let the *mountains* tremble at his word 747
Out on the *mountains* wild and high 681
Over the *mountains*, through the deep 2152

The lofty *mountains* shall bring forth 1454
The *mountains* are his own 1334
Though *mountains* fall and earth's 1896
Walk upon England's *mountains* green 95

MOUNTAINSIDE

From every *mountainside* let freedom 1225

MOUNTAINTOP

Then let me on the *mountaintop* 1714

MOUNTAINTOPS

Loud from the *mountaintops* echoes 660

MOUNTS

He *mounts* up through the sky 2137
Life *mounts* in every throbbing vein 40

MOURN

And they who *mourn*
and they who fear 1530, 2052
Mourn with our mourning land 648
Now we *mourn* our stubborn pride 442
That they who *mourn* shall blessed be 374
Though we may *mourn* those in life 1737
We would not *mourn* them, for we go 2199

MOURNED

And *mourned* because I found it not 1001

MOURNING

Mourning 'neath their sorrow's load 363
Once they were *mourning* here 530

MOUSE

The *mouse,* the coney, hear our prayer 1103

MOUTH

And with my *mouth* I shall 619
By the *mouth* of many messengers 574
From infants' and from sucklings' *mouth* 775
I with my *mouth* unto him cried 50
My *mouth* his praises shall express 1890
Our *mouth* shall show thy praise 33
Then shall my *mouth* with joyful lips 1172
Therefore my *mouth* and lips I'll frame 628

MOVE

And ever *move* toward thee 1029
And ever towards each other *move* 1029
And may thy Holy Spirit *move* 1371
And *move* and march wherever 285
And *move* within us while we pray 1318
At thy bidding may I *move* 1687
For how can I *move* onward one step 1818
Forward again we
move at thy command 1443
Him, in whom they *move* 1625
In our ranks you *move* united 62
It cannot freely *move* 1202
Just to simply *move* in the conscious 1643
Move among us, still defying 1796
Move me, draw me, win me 740
Move o'er the waters' face 2051
Move the faithful spirits 501
Move we on together 501
Move with one impulse every mind 1132
None can *move* us from thy presence 42
None of these shall *move* me 431
Onward we *move,* relying on thy care 162
Till we unerring *move* at length 1294
We'll *move* at his command 516
With growing ardor onward *move* 685

MOVED

He holdeth me up, and
I shall not be *moved* 24
He *moved* my soul to seek him 879
Her father's God before her *moved* 2239
I shall not *moved* be 570, 1258
Moved by thy divine compassion 1510
Moved the Lord of Life to die 356
Which *moved* ere form was made 438

MOVES

He *moves,* and there is power 120
Moves my will, directs my way 450

MOVEST

Who *movest* planets in their turn 371

MOVING

Moving yet and never stopping 62

MULTITUDE

And of that shouting *multitude* 873
Multitude which none can number 677
Till the *multitude* make virtue 1574

MULTITUDES

Multitudes, whom thou art seeking 1703

MURDERER

A *murderer* they save 1255

MURMUR

I will not *murmur,* Lord, nor fear 893
Nor ever *murmur* nor repine 702
Or *murmur* at his wise decrees 1893
That will not *murmur* nor complain 1348
To bear without a *murmur* 1556

MURMURS

The *murmurs* of self will 1408

MUSIC

A distant *music* mingles with 1604
And mightier *music* thrill 2003
And still their heavenly *music* 948
And sweeter than *music* his voice 795
And the *music* of their glad amen 1242
Heaven's *music* chimes the glad 1238
Is it the *music* of his peoples' prayer 683
Its *music* dried the falling tear 1912
Its *music* rolls along 516
Joyful *music* leads us sunward 1040

Let *music* swell the breeze 1225
Let not the *music* that is in us 649
Like heav'nly *music* swells 22
Lord, while the *music* round us 55
Make *music* for the Lord to hear 41
O the joyful *music*, all in chorus 1205
Sweet *music* fills the world 55
Sweeter far than *music* 1034
The *music* of the gospel leads 670
The *music* of the heart 1625
There from the *music* round about 2248
There's *music* in my soul today 1980, 2001
'Tis *music* in my ear 13
'Tis *music* to the sinner's ears 1351
We, in thine angels' *music* 1592
When, amid the *music* 1114
Where the *music* of the ransomed 1712
Whose *music* like a mighty wind 1296
With the sweetest *music* from the harp 163

MYRIADS

And *myriads* wait for his word 1512

MYRRH

And *myrrh* their texture fills 1249
Myrrh from the forest, or gold 254
Myrrh is mine, its bitter perfume 2196

MYSTERIES

But the high *mysteries* of thy name 2022
The *mysteries* sublime 91
The unveiled *mysteries* of God 197

MYSTERY

Behold, there looms the *mystery* 46
By the holy *mystery* 1761
By this great vision's *mystery* 1543
O who has this *mystery* sounded 1617
Wondrous *mystery* of the soil 1665

N

NAIL

Can I *nail* him to the cross 1709
Can I *nail* them once again 1709
Nail my affections to the Cross 1519

NAILED

And *nailed* thee to the Tree 1415
For in Jesus, my Lord, were they *nailed* 1982
I *nailed* him to the tree 873
Nailed to the cross, by the world 623
Nailed to the cross, in pain and agony 498
They are *nailed* to the Cross 1982
They *nailed* him naked to a Cross 1253
They *nailed* my Lord upon the tree 1568
Unto him who was *nailed* 1974
Were you there when they *nailed* him 2206

NAILS

By sharp *nails* fastened to the tree 206
Those cruel *nails,* O Savior 497

NAKED

And *naked* to thy glance 240

NAME

A *name* most sweet in heaven 1968
And here thy *name,* O God of love 1354
And his marvellous *name* 850
And his *name* you will adore 1996
And in his *name* their trust 887
And on God's *name* will call 910
And some day at his *name* 13
And the *name* of Jehovah exalted 2113
And the *name* of our Master all nations 1987
And the same dear *name* 850
And to thy *name,* O thou most 2112
At the *name* of Jesus bowing 1817
At thy great *name* exalted 373
Be his *name* adored 1070
By thy best *name* of Comforter 1318
Christ Jesus is his *name* 19
Eternal glory to thy *name* 49
Ever and forever shall his *name* endure 286
Ever, Lord, thy *name* be known 1567
Every precious *name* in one 1814
Far as thy *name* is known 2312
For awful is his *name* 2331
For the *name* of God is excellent 1624
Forever be thy *name* adored 457
God's *name* hold in reverence 2336
Hallowed be his *name* beneath 1625
His glorious *name* in every land 1860
His *name* dispels my guilt 1867
His *name,* forever shall endure 1454
His *name* is all my boast 914
His *name,* like sweet perfume 1008
His *name* salutes my listening ear 2117
His *name* shall be the Prince 1917
His *name* shall cheer and warm 1514
His *name* shall stand for ever 661
His *name* to glorify 19
His *name?* We call his name Jesus 1754
His *name* yields the richest perfume 795
Hosanna to th' eternal *name* 1308
I in thy *name* will lift my hands 1172
In our Leader's *name* we'll triumph 736
In the *name* of Christ 1069
In thy *name* we assert our right 1281
Jehovah's *name* to bless 193
"Jesus," O, how sweet the *name* 1912
Jesus, the *name* that charms our fears 1351
Jesus, the *name* to sinners 1017
Just and holy is thy *name* 994
Let the Redeemer's *name* be sung 508
Let us his *name* together 616, 1902
Let us to praise his *name* agree 1890
May they all, thy *name* confessing 718
My *name* is written on his hands 1131
Name them one by one 2265
No music's like thy charming *name* 2025
No other *name* but Jesus 1867
No other *name* I plead 2046
No other *name* thrills the joy-chords 506
None other *name* for me 1322
Nor *name,* nor form, nor ritual 1428
Now gladly trusting in his *name* 1016
Now thy *name* alone to bear 998
O by that *name,* in whom all fullness 435
O let God's *name* be praised 1898
O magnify the precious *name* of Jesus 2315
O *name* of might and favor 1481
O the precious *name* of Jesus 1817
On God's *name* will I call 910
On thy *name* we humbly call 1179
One holy *name* she blesses 1845

One Lord, whose glorious *name* 2134
One *name* we bear, one bread 335
Praise, laud and bless his *name* 57
Sing to his *name* 1366
Such is the precious *name* 13
Sweetest *name* I know 2002
Sweetest *name* on mortal tongue 1867, 1968
That in the *name* of Jesus 90
That *name* hath brought salvation 1415
That *name* I fondly love 1912
That *name* in life our stay 1415
That *name* to us is Love 661
That we thy *name* may hallow 1952
The Lord is his *name* 2322
The mighty God was still his *name* 9
The *name* all-victorious of Jesus 2330
The *name* before his wondrous birth 1968
The *name* of God exalted be 2328
The *name* of him whose death 13
Their *name* an everlasting name 1869
Then to thy *name* be glory given 645
There is no other *name* like Jesus 13
These, in the *name* of Jesus 90
They in thy *name* shall all the day 1390
This *name* all others shall survive 1514
Thus thy glorious *name* confessing 1178, 1673
Thy gracious *name* we sing 1415
Thy great *name* we praise 916
Thy holy *name* be blest 1228
Thy mighty *name* salvation is 2034
Thy *name* be ever praised 2166
Thy *name* be glorified 265
Thy *name* be known through every 1165
Thy *name* can save 1948
Thy *name* I love 1225
Thy *name* is life, and health 1031
Thy *name* is Love, I hear it 1284
Thy *name* makes free 1948
Thy *name* proclaimed by every lip 1526
Thy *name* salvation is 1031
Thy *name* shall glorify 54
Thy *name* to glorify 265
Thy *name*, we bless, almighty God 640
Thy new, blest *name* of Love 1350
Thy saving *name* is given 240
Till his *name*, by all confessed 357
To bless his holy *name* unite 193
To magnify his holy *name* 628
To me, with thy dear *name*, are given 2034
To praise thy *name*, give thanks 1811
To receive a *name* 143
Truly Jerusalem *name* we that shore 1538
Unite my heart, that I thy *name* 54
Unto thy *name* always 54
Upon the *name* of God the Lord 857
Were we but two his *name* to tell 263
Whate'er our *name* or sign 917, 1428
Where'er thy *name*, O God, is known 2313
Who in the Lord's *name* cometh 44
Whose the *name* I glory in 131
Yea God, my God, thy *name* 1483

NAMES

All other *names* above 1481
In varied *names* we stretch 522
Whose *names* thou wilt thyself 503
Whose *names* thy book enrolls 1442
Wondering if our *names* are there 755

NATION

A *nation* in a day 1911
At last every *nation*, the Lord 509
Be ours a *nation* evermore 1165
In every tongue and *nation* 33
Jesus, out of every *nation* 77
Let every *nation* now behold 768
Nation by *nation* still goes 438
Nation with *nation*, land with 2003
Our plenteous *nation* still in power 1873
Still to this most favored *nation* 1159
'Till each remotest *nation* 512
To Christ shall every *nation* bow 1081
To heal his ancient *nation* 1497
While every *nation*, every shore 572
With him the *nation* bows before 1873

NATIONS

All *nations* fear his name 1061
All *nations* shall adore him 661
All *nations* shall him call 1454
All *nations* to thy throne shall throng 2197
All the *nations* gather, gather in 409
All the world's *nations* through 126
Among the *nations*, he shall judge 198
And all *nations* hail him 286
And may the *nations* see 557
And *nations* bow to thy command 1026
And *nations*, crowding to be born 479
Be it to the *nations* told 1686
Calling the *nations* to glad federation 601
For all the *nations*, tongues and climes 2177
Hark! the waking up of *nations* 2157
Joyful, all ye *nations*, rise 675
Let all the *nations* fear him 1485
Let all the *nations* know 241
Let differing *nations* join 2099
Let the *nations* now rejoice 2169
Let the *nations* shout and sing 582
Lord of the *nations*, thus to thee 1185
Nations afar, in ignorance deep 1366
Nations beheld their coming Lord 1366
Nations come, your voices raise 1211
Nations now from God estranged 2342
Nations serve our King 286
O *nations* all! O nations all 210
Of *nations* in commotion 1911
O'er all *nations*, God alone 665
On the *nations* sunk in night 275
Over *nations* hold thy sway 2227
The gathering *nations* come 1917
The *nations* all possess 1901
The *nations* growing kinder 90
The *nations* thou wilt judge 1123
Then *nations* shall rejoice 1401
Till Christ has all the *nations* blest 1871
Till the *nations* far and near 1783
To bear before the *nations* 1544
To this the joyful *nations* round 198

To you and all the *nations* 298
Two *nations,* great and free 2134
We've a Savior to show to the *nations* 2208
When the *nations*
of the world shall worship 547
When the ransomed *nations* fall 748
Who hast the *nations* in thy heart 1467
Ye *nations* all be still 796
Ye *nations* bend, in reverence bend 1900
Ye *nations,* bow with sacred joy 184

NATURE

All my *nature* refine 1068
All *nature* joins in singing 2081
All *nature* joins to sing the triumph song 148
All *nature* shows thy boundless love 2117
All *nature* sings, and round me 2012
And all *nature* rising break 2299
How beauteous *nature* now 2176
In all that *nature* hath supplied 1363
My sinful *nature* thou canst 1829
Thy *nature,* and thy name is Love 333
Thy *nature,* gracious Lord, impart 1350
Till o'er our ransomed *nature* 512
When *nature* fails, and day 2223

NAUGHT

And *naught* can satisfy 1436
I'm rich with *naught* beside 1112
Let there be *naught* unfinished, broken 649
Naught as an offering to Jesus 1266
Naught be all else to me,
save that thou art 177
Naught can harm his Father's child 2257
Naught that is good will he 1640
Naught today my soul shall move 1085
Naught withholding, freely yielding 579
O *naught* of gloom and naught 1810
There, where *naught* our hearts 1738
To know that *naught* in man can tell 100

NAVIES

Far-called our *navies* melt away 583

NEAR

Be thou forever *near* me 1408
When at last I *near* the shore 1007

NEARNESS

In *nearness* shall thy voice be 1318

NEED

All I *need* to cleanse and make 834
All my *need* divinest 740
All that we *need* to do 539
All you may *need* he will provide 168
All you *need* I will surely give you 52
An equal *need* of kindly thought 1410
And *need* some deep revealing 447
And that, beyond my *need,* is meat 883
And thou art all I *need* 2046
Both *need* and want will by him 506
But I *need* thee, greatly need 766
But just my own exceeding *need* 1479
Ev'ry *need* he can fully supply 111
For I *need* thee, from life's 973
I *need* his wide forgiveness 497
I *need* not fear though dark 867
I *need* not tell thee who I am 333
I *need* the love of Jesus 869
I *need* thee, O I need thee 868
I *need* thy presence every passing 27
Is to feel your *need* of him 358
Jesus every *need* supplying 2065
Just when I *need* him most 1047
Much we *need* thy tender care 1683
Need him in the sunshine hour 866
Need him when the storm clouds 866
Nor do I *need* another arm 727
Nor less the *need* of armor 908
Nor *need* each other's name to know 1410
Nor *need* our voices ascend 713
Now ye *need* not fear the grave 625
O God, we *need* thee all our days 1356
Our *need* is to be still 1359
Our utmost, sorest *need* 1810
The *need* I gladly own 866
The *need* will soon be past 1479
The Savior whom we sorely *need* 1168
The weary *need* of sleep's deep 2048
There they *need* no sunshine 938
They *need* him 908
Thy children's *need* thou knowest 534
Thy Holy Spirit, when they *need* 1520
We *need* a patient guide 1942
We *need* the comrade heart 1942
When we *need* relief from an inner 988
When you *need* his strong right hand 2268
Where they *need* no star to guide 129
Who at my *need* his life did 1255
Who has the *need* of help from me 182

NEEDED

All I have *needed* thy hand 647

NEEDEST

Lord, thou *needest* not, I know 997, 998
Nevermore thou *needest* seek me 2006

NEEDS

And knoweth more of all my *needs* 39
But the pow'r of God she *needs* 1069
He's all that it *needs* and more 1950
Somebody else *needs* him 908
Somebody *needs* your love 1600
With all my *needs* I e'er to him 2096

NEEDY

When the *needy* seek him 285

NEGLECT

Through thy *neglect,* unfit to see 1551

NEGLECTED

Have *neglected* and delayed 442
The heart's *neglected* duty brings 1292

NEIGHBOR

Nor yet against his *neighbor* 2311

NEIGHBORS

Let all your *neighbors* see 549
True *neighbors* would we be 1930

NERVE

Holy strivings *nerve* and strengthen 71
Let every *nerve* and sinew 2157

NERVED

And *nerved* his will 196

NERVES

And *nerves* the feeble arm 2192

NEUTRAL

Neutral you cannot be 984

NEWBORN

Newborn to freedom and knowledge 601

NEWS

And of the *news* that came 1487
Blessed *news* of free salvation 1866
Blessed *news* to you and me 1866
By thee the joyful *news* 1035
The joyful *news* of sins forgiven 1035
The *news* of heavenly grace 241
'Tis yours to make
the good *news* known 1469
To bring good *news* to souls 1702
To you the joyous *news* we bring 918

NIGHT

A little nearer every *night* 2048
And as this gloomy *night* 2332
And *night* and day thy power 1871
And *night* in turn is drawing on 1300
And *night* is turned to day 284
And *night* to night doth knowledge 1862
And *night* to night proclaim 40
And *night* will soon be here 178
And soon the *night* of weeping 1845
And the *night* of fear and sorrow 1603
And there is "no *night* there" 938
And thus that dark betrayal *night* 266
As through the *night* they vigil keep 2306
Be ever watchful, *night* and day 1188
But *night* doth shine as day 1452
By *night*, Arabia's crimsoned sands 2239
By *night* the silver harvest 712
By thy *night* of agony 1145
Chasing far the silent *night* 976
Dark the *night* of sin has 255
Dark though the *night*, joy cometh 464
E'en though the *night* be dark within 1808
Ere the *night* of death o'ertake 1222
Fearful *night* without a dawn 2319
For all too soon the *night* 1598
For long hath been our sorrow's *night* 1174
Hark! through the silent *night* 559
In the dark *night* of mortal 422
In the *night*, that solemn night 2297
It is good when *night* is falling 951
It is not *night* if thou be near 1801
It is the *night* of the dear Savior's 1399
Let us as *night* is falling 1843
Long hath the *night* of sorrow 327
Lord of the *night*, let thine angels 1611
More than from those of *night* 462
Ne'er a *night* there can be 1870
Night and noonlight 104
Night and stars, in God rejoice 1071
Night has passed, and they have entered 2275
Night is drawing nigh 1302
Night repeats the wondrous song 1975
Night shall end in day 293
Night to day shall then be changed 2342
Night visits not thy sky 1087
Night will be changed to the 1763
No *night* in the year 1095
No *night* so dark but his love 2000
Nor how dark was the *night* 1983
O *night* divine, O night when 1399
O thou, who, sorrowing in the *night* 1527
On a cold winter's *night* that was 1861
Singing sweetly through the *night* 105
Sire, the *night* is darker now 627
Stormy all the *night* 352
Stumbling and falling in disastrous *night* 1511
That *night* in which he was betrayed 2133
That *night* the apostles met 1493
The dark *night* is ending and 1768
The darkest *night* is full of light 1462
The long, dark *night* is past 149
The long *night* of weeping is now 1599
The Lord be with us till the *night* 1884
The *night* approaches too 958
The *night* has lingered long 247
The *night* is dark and I am far 1053
The *night* is black 2044
The *night* of fear has passed away 1661
The *night* of grief is ended 1418
The world's dark *night* is hastening on 550
Then surely shall the very *night* 1452
Then when the *night* is upon us 1742
There is never a *night* so long 1976
There is no *night* can fright 1533
This *night* of sin will soon be gone 1639
Though the *night* be dark and 1681
Though the *night* be lone and 1044
Though the *night* deepens and tempest 2136
Till in the *night* of hate and war 1124
Till through the deep Judean *night* 1366
To you, this *night*, is born a child 513
What so withered is at *night* 1598
When in the *night* I sleepless 59
When through the *night* the furnace 2262
Who all *night* long unwearied 152
Wild the *night* on Galilee 521
With thee all *night* I mean 333
Ye that are standing *night* by 193

NIGHT CLOUDS

The *night clouds* have flown 1855

NIGHT WATCHES

Through the long *night-watches* 1302

NOISE

Above the *noise* of selfish strife 2270
Lest your *noise* should waken Jesus 257
Loud as many waters' *noise* 2261
Than *noise* of many waters is 598, 1886
With joyful *noise* let us the Rock 1335

NOISES

Within were *noises* multitudinous 2135

NOON

Come to me in the sultry *noon* 345
Its glorious *noon* how quickly past 1918

NOONDAY

At *noonday* trod the market place 389

NOONTIDE

Our *noontide* is thy gracious 1155
Sowing in the *noontide* 1693, 1771
Sweet is thy *noontide* calm 181

NORTH

Lo, from the *north* we come 733
Till *north* and south the kingdoms 1906
To *north* and south, to east and west 1469

NOTE

Sweetest *note* in seraph song 1867, 1968
That endless *note* shall never die 1914
That *note* shall soar from every living 1914
Triumphantly in wondrous *note* 1670

NOTES

Bearing *notes* of perfect pardon 1866
He *notes* your footsteps ere 2338
Its *notes* proclaimed sweet peace 1113
Let the *notes* of holy mirth 1070
O grant its rich and swelling *notes* 55
Their *notes* let all things 1854
To *notes* almost divine 190
With them to raise our *notes* 437

NOTETH

He who *noteth* every tear 2258

NOTHING

And *nothing* can I lack 921
Forgetting in *nothing* his blessing 1820
For *nothing* changes here 921
For *nothing* good have I 837
I *nothing* lack if I am his 1876
Nearer, still nearer, *nothing* 1266
Nothing but the blood of Jesus 2214
Nothing can for sin atone 2214
Nothing can our peace destroy 1058
Nothing can terrify 2020
Nothing can thy power withstand 1197
Nothing desire, or seek, but 1025
Nothing in my hand I bring 1671
Nothing so small can be 1825
O Jesus, *nothing* may I see 1025
Pleading *nothing* but the blood 977
So I can *nothing* lack 1928
That I am *nothing*, thou art 1407
To you is it *nothing* that Jesus 73

NOTHINGNESS

And seem toward *nothingness* to dare 1294

NOTIONS

By *notions* of our day and sect 2177

NOURISHED

Nourished by thy boundless 951

NOWELLS

Nowells ringing 945

NUMBER

In *number*, weight, and measure 1367
'Twas not their *number*,
nor their strength 1448

NUMBERED

Numbered with the malefactors 2288

NUMBERS

Vast *numbers* of angels the shepherds 1650

NURTURE

Vinedresser's *nurture* and care 1098

O

OAK

Cringing before the riven *oak* 1088

OAKS

Let *oaks* and elms take up 2082

OARS

Oars labored heavily 476

OATH

His *oath,* his covenant, his blood 1244
I on his *oath* depend 1864
To perform the *oath* which he sware 215

OBEDIENCE

In *obedience* all her joy 1687
With *obedience* glad and steady 1207

OBEDIENT

Obedient to thy high commands 728
Obedient to thy will 1872

OBEY

And to *obey* thee first of all 797
And we just *obey* and trust 1041
Gladly then shall I *obey* 1690
Let every *heart* obey thy will 49
May those *obey* the rule of heaven 1921
Obey thy sovereign word 515
Or *obey* your Lord's command 398
Swift and fearless to *obey* 485
That all who will *obey,* with him 799
That all who would *obey* 1490
They all shall sweetly *obey* 1208
Ye who *obey* what he commands 1547

OBJECT

One the *object* of our journey 2067

OBJECTS

Happy *objects* of thy grace 673

OBLATION

And thy life's *oblation* 35

OBSTRUCTION

Always mindful of *obstruction* 1076

OBTAIN

The life everlasting if ye would *obtain* 18
We shall *obtain* delivering grace 2305

OBTAINED

That have *obtained* the prize 324

OCCASIONS

New *occasions* teach new duties 1574

OCEAN

An *ocean* without shore 1377
For me the *ocean* of his love 1534
From *ocean* unto ocean 515
In the *ocean* of thy love we soon 1919
Loud may the troubled *ocean* roar 572
Ocean hoary, tell his glory 104
On a wild and stormy *ocean* 474
That *ocean* unexplored 2177
The rolling *ocean,* rocked with storms 1899
Till in the *ocean* of thy love 1801
When walking on life's *ocean* 2251

OCEAN FLOODS

Ocean-floods have lift their roar 610

OCEANS

Oceans, chant the rapture 258

ODOR

An *odor* of a sweet perfume 2070

ODORS

Odors of Edom and offerings 254
When mingling *odors* breathe 771

O'ERCOME

O'ercome the world's allurements 465
Ye may *o'ercome* through Christ 1746

O'ERCOMETH

He that *o'ercometh,* Lord, with thee 2050
To him that *o'ercometh* God giveth 2336

O'ERTAKEN

That hath us now *o'ertaken* 19

O'ERTHROW

O'erthrow them all, that they may 405

OFFENCES

All *offences* purge away 359

OFFEND

Lest I *offend* some other 901
That I *offend* not thee 270

OFFENDER

The vilest *offender* who truly 2102

OFFER

All our living we may *offer* 639
And *offer* all my works to thee 499
Ere we can *offer* our complaints 572
Here, great God, today we *offer* 101
Lord of all gifts, to *offer* thee 67
May we *offer* for thy service 579
Offer incense, pray and be 1838
Offer ourselves, Lord, souls and 2278
Offer pardon and peace to all 1732
Offer thy life on the altar 1098
Offer ye your praises meet 288
Singing, we *offer* prayer 467
Vainly we *offer* each ample 254
We *offer* thee our youth 84

OFFERED

And *offered* there in his presence 1861
And unto him *offered* myrrh 1650
'Tis *offered* now, O Lord, to thee 724

OFFERETH

This to thee he *offereth* 175

OFFERING

An *offering* and a sacrifice 420
An *offering* of love I render 724
And a golden *off'ring* at the cross 1985
No *offering* of my own I have 2310
She makes the same pure *offering* 33
Some *offering* bring thee now 1689
The only *offering* perfect in thine eyes 99
What shall my *offering* be 2219

OFFERINGS

Bringing all our *offerings* meet 2047
Ever bringing *offerings* meet 2047
Offerings bring, and serve with 1570
Offerings of praise and prayer 753
Our willing *offerings* brought 1175
So with meetest *offerings* 1110
These are the *offerings* to lay 2322

OFFERS

He *offers* free to all 575
He *offers* thee full restoration 1494
Now our great Elijah *offers* 1697
Offers help in time of need 480
Offers you pardon and peace 1617

OFFICE

Each in his *office* wait 2331

OFFSPRING

Thine let our *offspring* be 1696

OIL

If our *oil* we hope to borrow 2297

OINTMENT

'Tis like the precious *ointment* 771

OLIVE

Bearing the *olive*, hers be the blessing 601

OLIVES

But the *olives* they were not 947
Thine *olives* of Gethsemane 2082

OMISSION

O may the least *omission* pain 889

OMNIPOTENT

Omnipotent to save 1064

ONE

And ev'ry *one* who seeks 2085
And freely with that Blessed *One* 1439
And no *one* may rest till the "harvest 1540
And *one* our Lord and King 325
But *one* was out on the hills away 1983
Christ the blessed *One* gives to all 1732
"Come to me," saith *One*, "and coming 119
Each *one*, like the falling leaf 2299
For every *one* is happy 1988
For this shall every godly *one* 1314
Kind to the erring *one* 1804
Let him in, the Holy *One* 1996
May they in thee be *one* 1370
My *One* and my All, and my Joy 1583
No *one* but Jesus ever loved so 2144
No *one* so loving 2148
No other *one* can cheer me 981
O favored *one*, who, 'ere he knew 2189
One by one, we leave behind us 1955
One by one we'll gain the portals 1991
One here will constant be 2290
One in charity 1586
One in hope, in doctrine 1586
One in the bond of peace 2074
One in the freedom of the truth 2030
One in the holy fellowship 2028
One in the larger thought 2030
One in the love that suffers 2028
One in the joy of paths 2030
One in the patient company 2028
One in the soul's perennial 2030
One in the truth that makes men 2028
One in the vision of thy peace 2028
One in truth and charity 1033
One with thyself, may every eye 2217
Onward ever, each new *one* 2299
Some *one* distressed may listen 1773

Some *one* will gladly hear 1773
That each be *one* with other 2175
That lofty *One,* before whose throne 1964
The Holy *One,* the Son of God 1964
The loved *One* on the Cross 1425
The *One* who for sinners died 2066
There is never a wand'ring *one* 1976
There's no *one* to save you but Jesus 2293
There is *One* sustaining 922
There is *One* who waits your heavy load 2252
Thy little *one* doth keep 1910
'Tis not each *one* is called 1987
Yet *one* came down from heaven's 1425
Yet *one* o'er all the earth 1845

ONES

All the pure *ones,* all the bright ones 2229
And burdened *ones,* where'er he came 2218
And faithful *ones* are crowned 1027
And the little *ones* he blessed 1099
And though brave *ones* have fallen 1987
Bearing the loved *ones* over the tide 1605
Dear *ones* in glory, looking 1605
Earth's burdened *ones* find welcome 1658
For loved *ones* you may intercede 1640
For weary *ones* who seek 2069
He is gently calling little *ones* 900
Let my near and dear *ones* be 1304
"Let the little *ones* come unto me" 884
Like thy blessed *ones* above 1197
Little *ones* be wholly thine 962
Little *ones* to him belong 995
Little *ones* we bring to thee 974
Living *ones* changed to his image 1763
Looking for lost *ones* straying 1605
Loved *ones* are waiting, looking 1605
Now, these little *ones* receiving 1691
O happy *ones* and holy 1845
O the dear *ones* in glory, how they beckon 2246
Only little *ones* are we 581
Sad *ones* or bright ones 1831
Sleeping *ones* raised in a moment 1763
Softly may weary *ones* rest from 1611
The blessed *ones* repeat through 1936
The people's poor *ones* he shall 1454
Then with loved *ones* gone on before 1847
Those endless Sabbaths the blessed *ones* 1538
Thy holy *ones,* behold they come 1247
Watching for dear *ones* waiting 1605
When his chosen *ones* shall gather to 2259
When the weary *ones* we love 2089
While as ransomed *ones* we sing 1994
With our sainted *ones* in glory 486

ONWARD

Leading *onward,* beaming bright 129

OPED

He has *oped* the heavenly door 625

OPEN

And *open* all our eyes 315
I *open* to the day 39
If thou our lips wilt *open* 33
Open blest mercy's gate 435
Open heaven's door 988
Open my ears that I may hear 1587
Open my heart, and let me 1587
Open my mouth and let me bear 1587
Open now the crystal fountain 652
Open now to him your heart 1996
Open our ears to hear 2228
Open thine arms and take me 1018, 2202
Open thou mine eyes to see 997, 998
Open thou our ears and heart 220
Open wide, O God, thy doors 1567
Shall *open* to our sight 194
Then *open* thou our eyes 335
We cannot *open* a door of prayer 884

OPENED

And *opened* heaven for our 1692
And *opened* the life-gate 2102
Christ hath *opened* Paradise 289
He hath *opened* heaven's gate 700
He *opened* up its treasure store 1907
Jesus *opened* up the way 977
Opened for the King 622
Opened wide the gate to God 1644
Thou hast *opened* Paradise 142

OPENETH

Openeth to me heaven again 1735

OPENS

Each little flower that *opens* 68
He *opens* wide the heav'nly 1661
Opens to you his sacred heart 75
Which *opens* into light 39

OPES

That when my Savior *opes* the gate 1749

OPPOSED

Though *opposed* by many a foe 1560

OPPOSITION

In the midst of *opposition* 1775

OPPRESS

Or guilt the soul *oppress* 75

OPPRESSED

Be thou to the *oppressed* 1312
Let the *oppressed* a strong friend 378
Oppressed so hard they could not 2240
Oppressed with various ills, draw near 136

OPPRESSION

Oppression, lust, and crime 2073

OPPREST

Waiting on Jesus when I'm *opprest* 2148

ORB

And heaven's whole *orb* with hallelujahs 298

ORCHARDS

Behold, the bending *orchards* 1952

ORDAINS

Thou dost whate'er thy will *ordains* 43

ORDAINEST

King who *ordainest* thunder 608

ORDER

Order thou our ways 988
The marching *order* sound 1945

ORDERED

Thou hast *ordered* all my goings 415

ORDERS

All the heavenly *orders* 143
Marching *orders* may divide us 366

ORGAN

Let the *organ* thunder 2141
The blast of war's great *organ* 37
We bid the pealing *organ* wait 55

ORIGINAL

Their great *Original* proclaim 1932

ORPHAN

When the *orphan* brings to thee 2260

ORPHANS

Alleluia! not as *orphans* 77
Orphans no longer fatherless 1836

OTHER

There was no *other* good enough 1963
Though from each *other* far we be 2291
You've no *other*,
such a friend and brother 112

OTHERS

And *others* worship here in turn 186
Do *others* see Jesus in you 2281
Let *others* see Jesus in you 2281
Others near by you may be 907
Others will trust him if only 1601
So may we for *others* live 1760
That *others* who behold your life 1548
Till *others* catch the living flame 314
To be to *others* kind and good 468
While on *others* thou art calling 1607
While *others* bear their burdens 954

OUTCAST

All the *outcast* thronged to hear 2255
By thee the *outcast* and the poor 58
To the *outcast* and forlorn 1747

OUTCASTS

To lead his *outcasts* home 1497

OUTLIVE

Lord, let me never, never *outlive* 1475
Will Christ *outlive* Mohammed 90

OUTPASS

Shall far *outpass* the power 306

OUTWEIGHS

But it ne'er *outweighs* his grace 1848

OVERBORNE

Why are we ever *overborne* 1183

OVERBRIM

Overbrim and overflow 483

OVERCAME

He who *overcame* our enemy 1080

OVERCOME

And being thine, will *overcome* 1948
For thou hast *overcome* with 1692
Overcome thy fears 987

OVERCOMETH

To him that *overcometh* 1786

OVERPOWER

Not they can *overpower* us 19

OVERTHROW

Overthrow the hosts of sin 1033
Will *overthrow* the wrong 1

OVERWHELM

They shall not *overwhelm* his soul 1314

OWE

All to him I *owe* 837
All to thee, our God, we *owe* 1628
O Son of God, I *owe* to thee 60
Owe we our humble thanks 1633
The debt of love I *owe* 38
This do I *owe,* nor can I e'er repay him 139
To him I *owe* my life 1201
To thee we *owe* the peace
that still prevails 92
We *owe* thee thankfulness and praise 1439

OWN

And *own* how dreadful is this place 1105
And *own* thee as their King 1086
And *own* thee King forevermore 372
And *own* thy sovereign right 1137
And *own* your gracious God 337
And thou shalt *own* thy darkness 2151
At last I *own* it cannot be 1018
Blest are all that *own* thy reign 1073
But dim or clear, we *own* in thee 1428
Father, I *own* thy love alone 1910
Him alone God we *own* 600
I *own* no other Master 1104
If only thou wilt *own* it 1906

In thee alone, dear Lord, we *own* 2289
Now I gladly *own* him as 2335
Own and kiss the chastening rod 2342
Own his right to every service 2339
Own his title, praise his name 1117
Shall *own* him Lord and King 33
So shalt thou, wondering, *own* his way 536
Then will he *own* his servant's name 914
To thee we *own* allegiance 454
We *own* thy sway 917, 1428, 2181
We'll *own* the favoring gale 902
When all shall *own* the Master's sway 156

OWNED

For thou hast *owned* my cause 1430
But when I *owned* my trespass 772

OWNERSHIP

Ours are they by an *ownership* 2163

OWNS

And *owns* her Maker good 2250
He *owns* me for his child 113
He *owns* the ransom and forgives 209

OX

Ox and ass before him bow 625

OXEN

Oxen lowing 945
Where the *oxen* had been fed 369
With the *oxen* standing by 1572

P

PAGE

Beyond the sacred *page* 249
Deep in the prophet's sacred *page* 1366
"Hither, *page,* and stand by me 627
Page and monarch, forth they went 627
The fettered *page* from killing 191, 1445
Then on memory's *page* I can 2066

PAGES

And in their sacred *pages* still 197
Are *pages* in that book, to show 1960
Its *pages* teem with sacred lore 2087
O may these heavenly *pages* be 457

PAID

He *paid* the great price 122
Jesus *paid* the price 1198, 1564
Paid the debt and made me free 894
Your debt he hath *paid* 73

PAIN

A *pain* to feel it near 889
And *pain* for him is sweet 1578
And *pain* I need not fear 1949
And thinking of our Savior's *pain* 206
But thine the deadly *pain* 1475
Great the *pain* and loss 1198
If worn with *pain,* disease, and grief 1509
In all my *pain* and misery 1150
In *pain,* and want, and weariness 1363
Learning then, in *pain* and loss 555
Naught but *pain* and sorrow 977
No *pain,* no sickness, and no weeping 1274
Nor *pain* nor death can enter there 1243
O what needless *pain* we bear 2210
Pain and loss are but the shadow 264
Pain and tribulation bore 217
Pain may rack this earthly 2057
Strong with thee to suffer *pain* 500
There'll be no *pain,* no death 16
Though *pain* and passion may 2003
Through *pain* and trouble thou hast 361
Thy *pain* close cherished 534
To bear an untried *pain* 240
Transient *pain* may be but a way 988
What *pain,* what labor, to secure 444
Whate'er the *pain* and shame may 189
When in mortal *pain* we lie 739
Where *pain* and sorrow daily come 374
While in our mortal *pain* 1715
Who *pain* didst undergo 828
Ye who long *pain* and sorrow bear 41

PAINED

Pained thy Father-heart today 2227

PAINS

And *pains,* the groans, and griefs 1111
But more than *pains* that wracked 734
But the *pains* which he endured 971
By thy *pains* and consolations 1686
For indeed no *pains* he spares 1668
O in what divers *pains* they met 136
Remember thee in all thy *pains* 30
The *pains* of death took hold 857

PAINTS

He *paints* the lily of the field 602

PALACE

And never a *palace* shone half 1095
That his *palace* should be decked 217
They're building a *palace* for me 1229
We are going to his *palace* 2284

PALACES

And ever may thy *palaces* 843
Her *palaces* survey 2312
Out of the ivory *palaces* 1249
The Lord within her *palaces* 646
Zion in all thy *palaces* 540

PALL

One night will spread its *pall* 56

PALM

And then the victor's *palm* 2172
And victor's *palm* I wave 1411
The *palm* of victory thine 1086
'Tis no *palm* of fading leaves 1748

PALMS

Beneath the Indian *palms* 33
Holding *palms* of victory in their hands 677
Now, with triumphal *palms,* they stand 774

Palms of triumph in their hand 669
We wave our *palms* before thee 48
With *palms* before thee went 44

PANG

And with a *pang* more thrilling 683

PANGS

All fiery *pangs* on battlefields 734
By thy *pangs,* to us unknown 1761
O the *pangs* his soul sustained 552
Pangs, not his own, his spotless 426

PANTS

It *pants* for thee 1519
Pants for thee each mortal 1686

PARACLETE

Paraclete, and Heavenly Guest 597

PARADISE

Not *paradise,* with all its joys 1875

PARDON

And come for the *pardon* God cannot 73
And he will abundantly *pardon* 2155
And *pardon* abundant and free 1494
And *pardon* o'er our sinful spirits 29
Come to Christ, and *pardon* take 2283
For my *pardon* this I see 2214
For *pardon,* and for charity 594
For *pardon* and peace we implore 584
For the *pardon* of sin is the crown 1338
I am trusting thee for *pardon* 811
Jesus will freely *pardon* 2280
Like him, with *pardon* on his tongue 1931
My *pardon* and my love 827
Pardon all our past transgressions 711
Pardon, and holiness, and heaven 146
Pardon and peace to dying men 1875
Pardon, bestowed through Jesus' blood 641
Pardon each infirmity, open 1745
Pardon for all flows from his side 1460
Pardon for sin, and a peace 647
Pardon for sins of deepest dye 641
Pardon for you and for me 1743
Pardon from an offended God 641
Pardon my iniquity 629
Pardon our offences 964, 999
Pardon our weakness, and blot 1757
Pardon, peace, and joy are found 1559
Pardon that brings the rebel nigh 641
Pardon there was multiplied 2335
Pardon thou and save us 256
Pardon thou each deed unholy 1685
Thy broken heart, my *pardon* 60
Thy *pardon* and thy love 2077
Thy *pardon* grant, thy peace 1509
Thy *pardon,* Lord, for war's dark 1916
To find their *pardon* and their joy 1545
To *pardon* and endure 201
Whispering of *pardon* and 1678
Willing to *pardon* and cleanse 569

PARDONED

By it I have been *pardoned* 2315
Pardoned—it shall suffice 2143

PARDONING

Who is a *pardoning* God like thee 641

PARDONS

And *pardons* me all my sin 876
Fear not, he *pardons* all 133

PARENTS

And *parents* hold him dear 667

PART

And I, my tuneful *part* 1362
And grant us nevermore to *part* 99
And *part* is crossing now 324
And *part* is yet to win 325
And *part* them, Lord, to each and all 520
As though we ne'er should *part* 133
Be mine this better *part* 1458
Eager to play the hero's *part* 588
Let us do our *part* ere day is done 400
Part of the battlefield is won 325
So shall no *part* of day or night 478
Until this earthly *part* of me 250
Who the Lord and me shall *part* 1195

PARTAKE

All may of thee *partake* 1825
All *partake* the glorious bliss 1695
Let all *partake* the sacred draught 2133

PARTAKERS

Partakers of the Savior's grace 230
Partakers of thy grace 503

PARTAKES

Partakes one holy food 1845
Thrice happy he who here *partakes* 1232

PARTED

And those long *parted* meet again 1965

PARTING

How tearful the *parting* from faces 1926

PARTINGS

A few more *partings* o'er 5

PARTNER

Partner of my throne shalt be 672

PARTNERS

Partners of thy endless reign 655

PASS

And when I *pass* death's portal 2251
But *pass* not from us 1592
Do not *pass* me by 1607
Do we *pass* that cross 1005
Ere it wholly *pass* away 1145
It shall never *pass* away 938

It will *pass* into the splendors 656
Let them not *pass,* like weeds 2267
Lord, we would *pass* from hours 2147
No longer *pass* thee by 1415
O thou who dids't *pass* through 2004
Pass from my heart away 425
Pass me not 1138
Pass on and carry swift the news 720
Pass on the torch, pass on the flame 1608
Pass the stars, the day, the night 382
Pass the word along 1769
Pass we thus our happy days 752
So when I *pass* earth's gloomy vale 153
Soon will *pass* God's day of grace 692
Swift shall *pass* thy pilgrim 980
They *pass* through Baca's thirsty vale 782
Though we *pass* through tribulation 2065
We safely *pass* where thou 1078
We shall *pass* inside the gate 2191
When thou dids't *pass* the temple gate 1528
When upward we *pass* to his kingdom 2225
Who *pass* unheeding by 86

PASSED

But while I *passed* my Savior by 1322
Passed the sharp and piercing 1263
Splendid you *passed,* the great 1532
They *passed* and gave no sign 2182

PASSES

"Jesus of Nazareth *passes* by" 2218

PASSETH

Behold, the Master *passeth* by 196
For it *passeth* human measure 1573

PASSING

Passing from you and from me 1743
Passing soon and little worth 1748

PASSION

A *passion* to save the lost 529
All his wonderful *passion* and purity 1068
And the *passion* that he bore 700
And thy bitter *passion* 35
How shall this *passion* for souls be mine 529
In this thy bitter *passion* 1476
May our life-long *passion* 925
My *passion* and my love 1407
Now, vengeful *passion,* cease 2134
One holy *passion* filling all 1778
The *passion* of thy heart 204
To thee, before thy *passion* 44
True Recorder of his *passion* 339
We set the *passion* of thy Son, our Lord 99
While *passion* stains and folly 1059
Would you be free from your *passion* 2323

PASSIONS

And let our sinful *passions* reign 206
Dark *passions* subdue 2336
From earth-born *passions* set me 1150
May earth-born *passions* die 55
Till earthly *passions* turn 306

PASSIONTIDE

And through thy *passiontide* 1187

PAST

Ah, the *past* is dark behind us 1760
And forgetting all the *past* 492
From the dim *past* and present clear 604
God of the *past,* our times are in thy hand 586
In all the *past,* through all our hopes 586
The *past* he leaves behind 377
Through all the *past* thy truth 1595
Tis ne'er too late to leave the *past* 1442

PASTIMES

And our playful *pastimes* 757

PASTURE

And in the quiet *pasture* 2195
Never, from thy *pasture* roving 1691

PASTURES

And through the green *pastures* 1909
And where the verdant *pastures* 1876
Green *pastures* are before me 921
In *pastures* fair above 33
In *pastures* of peace he'll lead 1998
In the green *pastures* low 2020
In thy pleasant *pastures* feed us 1683
Nor let me from his *pastures* stray 319
Nor let us from his *pastures* stray 310
Not forever in green *pastures* 441
On England's pleasant *pastures* seen 95
The *pastures* of the blessed 961
The verdant green *pastures* so useful 959
To *pastures* green he'll lead 774

PATH

All the *path* which thou shalt tread 63
And dark is his *path* on the wings 1546
And rough seems the *path* to the goal 1489
And the *path* to the Cross 1982
And thine shall be a *path* 2151
Around the *path* I tread 176
Brightening all the *path* we tread 2067
But the *path* of that lone Galilean 1922
By the *path* his love will show 555
Christ is the *Path,* and Christ 477
Each *path,* by which in eager strife 1384
From the *path* of love and duty 1055
From the *path* of sin I turn 977
In the straight narrow *path* 463
In thy law's *path* make me to go 1826
Keep on praying when the *path* 1048
Mine be the *path* thy feet have trod 2326
My *path* to life is free 921
My *path* is lone, and weary are my feet 1395
No *path* we shun, no darkness 1459
No smoother is the ancient *path* 432
O how bright the *path* grows 2209
O'er life's *path* thy radiance 758
Oft on my *path* falls golden light 867
Our footworn *path* is fresh 1380

Path of the lowly 1656
Praying if the *path* be drear 1721
The *path* I take is known 2103
The *path* leads us on to the mansions 1909
The *path* of life thou showest me 2238
The *path* of prayer thyself 1506
The *path* of prayer thyself hast trod 1641
The *path* that the Savior trod 864
The *path* your Savior trod 1959
The upward *path* is smooth 201
Though by the *path* he leadeth 2296
Though sometimes the *path* seems rough 2002
Though dark my *path*, and sad my lot 1231
Though thy *path* is dark as night 367
Through each perplexing *path* 1364
Treading the *path* that Jesus trod 729
When dangers fierce your *path* assail 168
Whose *path* is in the sea 1385
Yes, on through life's long *path* 1654

PATHS

And all her *paths* are peace 886
From *paths* where hide the lures 2270
From the *paths* of virtue 1101
In *paths* of duty follow thee 235
In *paths* of life to go 1438
In *paths* of peace all lighted 1852
Into *paths* of sin have strayed 442
Joyful to follow thee through *paths* 406
O'er *paths* that are lonely its 1855
Sorrow's *paths* I often tread 895
The *paths* of peace have trod 267
The whole *paths* of the Lord 2116
There may be now in the *paths* 955
Through *paths* unknown we follow 586
Thy *paths* drop fatness still 410
Thy *paths*, O teach thou me 1719, 2116
Thy *paths* our chosen way 585
Thy truth's *paths* I have trod 1043
'Tis not from earthly *paths* 279
Undaunted in the *paths* of right 1700
When in slippery *paths* you stand 2268
When on willful *paths* we wander 1066
When *paths* are plain, and skies 1370

PATHWAY

But the steep and rugged *pathway* 441
Chasing from life's *pathway* sorrow's 163
Knowing that life's checkered *pathway* 1643
Man's *pathway* trod, 'mid pain 2218
Marching down the rough *pathway* 430
So shall our *pathway* lead 1401
This is the *pathway* of blessing 1104
Though rough and steep our *pathway* 1794

PATIENCE

And wait with *patience* for the morn 16
And with *patience* run the race 756
But strong in faith, in *patience* wait 266
By thy *patience* and thy courage 1022
His *patience* in pain 423
In lowly *patience* waiting to pass 1414
Joyful *patience* can endure 2018
My *patience* oft is failing 2216
Patience to watch and wait 1171
Patience untiring, and courage 578
With steadfast *patience* arm my breast 417

PATIENT

Patient, kind in all you do 273

PATRIOTS

For all the *patriots* win, and poets 2162
These are the *patriots* nations need 603

PATTERN

Be thou my *pattern;* make me 1226
For he is our childhood's *pattern* 1572
For his own *pattern* given 530
Thou art my *pattern* day unto 1829

PATTERNS

We but poorest *patterns* are 1305

PAUSE

Now they *pause*, where they have drifted 610
Pause, ere you answer 2

PAUSETH

He *pauseth* at our threshold 2218

PAVEMENT

The *pavement* of sapphire 1095

PAVILION

For he in his *pavilion* shall 1903

PAVILIONED

Pavilioned in splendor 1546
So at length, in thee *pavilioned* 730

PAY

And *pay* a grateful song of praise 2332
And *pay* the solemn vows I made 361
I'll *pay* my vows now to the Lord 910
Since I cannot *pay* thee 35

PEACE

A yearning for a deeper *peace* 1236
And a *peace* that endureth 647
And a *peace* that from you never 2339
And blessed *peace* to cheer us 1299
And his *peace* to every nation 1726
And in thy perfect *peace* may 2098
And *peace* abound below 1917
And *peace* shall reign on earth 43
And *peace* that passeth all 1713
And *peace* to men on earth 1426
And the *peace* of Israel 238
And then the *peace* so lasting 1849
Are at *peace* on this night 1095
As with his *peace* he graced 817
At *peace* with him wherever 139
Back to *peace* and purity 742
Bringing *peace* on land and sea 331
But *peace* divine like quiet night 821

Can lasting *peace* arise 384
Come, Blessed *Peace* as when 334
Come, *Peace* of God, and rule 334
For *peace* on earth, both far and near 481
For the *peace* of God's evangel 487
For there the *peace* of God came 2306
God is now willing to give you his *peace* 569
Great *peace* may I attain 1422
Heavenly *peace,* divinest comfort 66
Heaven's *peace* will enter in 1270
His *peace* will hallow all 2269
How lovely the *peace* with the 2271
I am resting tonight in this wonderful *peace* 430
I, ere I sleep, at *peace* 59
I have blessed *peace* with my Lord 2209
I have *peace* and joy that nothing 801
In Jesus for *peace* I abide 1958
In *peace* of home and friends 604
In *peace* that only thou canst give 1466
In sacred *peace* our souls abide 572
Indwelling *peace* thou canst impart 1349
Inward *peace,* and inward might 36
Jehovah with *peace* ever blesseth 537
Let *peace,* O Lord, thy peace 1927
Let *peace* within her walls 2304
Let thy *peace* be my bliss 415
May *peace* and concord ever be 1809
May *peace* attend thy gate 786
My *peace* is in thy favor 2119
No *peace* my wandering soul 2033
Now let thy *peace* possessed 455
Now thy perfect *peace* impart 1644
O may we dwell in *peace* 56
O the *peace* of love divine 1688
O this full and perfect *peace* 1195
O thou, who hast our *peace* restored 43
O what *peace* we often forfeit 2210
O wondrous *peace,* in thought 100
Of abiding *peace* within 912
Of *peace* on earth, good will 840
Our *peace* is ever in thy will 1217
Our *peace,* our consolation 1415
Peace and health and every 1159
Peace and joy you shall receive 2283
Peace and love and joy 1402
Peace and plenty for us wait 2191
Peace at the last is all our need 1692
"*Peace,* be still!" 475, 1208
"*Peace* be to you this evening 2048
Peace from God through endless day 519
Peace from our God, so rich 1670
Peace I ask, but peace must be 1644
Peace in our hearts, our evil 1162
Peace in our time, O Lord 1609
Peace in thy church, where brothers 1162
Peace is on the world abroad 1744
Peace is there that knows no 934
Peace is won for aye 2153
"*Peace,* it is I." 476
Peace of the dying 1656
Peace on earth, and mercy mild 675
Peace on earth bringing 302
"*Peace* on earth, good will from 684
"*Peace* on the earth, good will 948
Peace out of harrowed lives 1275
Peace, prosperity, and health 1628
Peace rolling in like the waves 2314
Peace shall be his portion 629
Peace shall follow battle 293
Peace surely based upon thy will 1609
Peace takes the hand of care 2171
Peace that shall crown a glad 1609
Peace thy panting soul now 1766
Peace to our brethren give 1121
Peace to the nations, and praise 607
Peace to this sacred house 786
Peace upon earth, and mutual 298
Peace when deep griefs o'erflow 311
Peace when the world its busy 1162
"Perfect *peace*—God will give 1096
Purchasing *peace* and heaven 2315
Resting in him, his *peace* and joy 1634
Seeking in *peace* and contentment 946
Shall come the boon of *peace* 46
So shall we have *peace* divine 500
Speak *peace* to every breast 33
Speaking *peace* to me 1041
Sweet *peace,* the gift of God's love 1958
Sweet *peace* thy promises 572
That *peace* may reign for aye 2100
The fruits of *peace* and joy 83
The *peace* he did leave 73
The *peace* of man, the peace of 210
The *peace* that dwelleth 1530
The *peace,* the joy I sought so long 1322
Their *peace* our heritage 1646
Then all is *peace* and light 1276
Then in believing, thy *peace* 60
"There is no *peace* on earth," I said 840
There is perfect *peace* though the 1979
There's nothing but *peace* 1958
Thou, the *Peace* that passeth 1022
Thy *peace* impart 1509
Thy *peace,* O God, send down 1699
Thy *peace* our spirits fill 2013
'Tis the holy *peace* of God 1744
To live at *peace* with every man 1930
To venture all that *peace* 1916
Unchanging *Peace,* mid storm 414
What are the *peace* and the joy 1538
What *peace* of mind 1237
When *peace* shall over all the earth 948
Where all is *peace,* and joy 118
With *peace* he crowns my head 851
With *peace* our borders bless 1185

PEACEMAKER

Peacemaker, Christ, whose living 1275

PEACEMAKERS

Hers be the blessing the *peacemakers* 601

PEAKS

Ere mountain *peaks* in oceans 725
Peaks, cloud-cleaving 104

PEAL

Peal out the watchword 2128

PEALED

Then *pealed* the bells more loud 840

PEALING

Nearer yet and nearer *pealing* 678

PEALS

In distant *peals* it dies 1900
Peals forth in joy man's old 2130
Peals like a trumpet promise 2262

PEARL

Of one *pearl* each shining portal 2149
Thou priceless *Pearl* for all 1424

PEASANT

Yonder, *peasant,* who is he 627

PENITENCE

If they will humbly in *penitence* 506
True *penitence* impart 1184

PENITENT

How the *penitent* forgiven 287
While like a *penitent* I stand 1279

PENITENTS

There the *penitents* that turn 1303

PENT

Pent be each warring breeze 733

PEOPLE

A newborn *people* may we rise 189
A ransomed *people,* strong and free 2291
All his *people* have been dearly 1922
All the *people,* great and small 2227
Amid thy *people,* songs of praise 72
And all Christ's *people* praise 952
And the *people* cry with wonder 2254
And the *people* knew his presence 2254
And to thy *people* be thou near 1188
And what the *people* do devise 2329
And where his loving *people* meet 96
And with his *people* I will meet 2219
Before his *people* all 910
Christ, thy ransomed *people* feed 287
Come, and thy *people* bless 338
Come like the *people* of his choice 337
God of thy *people,* hear us cry 593
Hear thy *people* as they pray 281
His *people* they, and he 1111
Jewish *people,* wandering far 1196
Let all the *people* praise 1123
Let all the *people* worship thee 640
Let his ransomed *people* raise 1622
Let my *people* go 2240
Let the *people* praise his name 518
Let the *people* praise thee, Lord 582
Let the *people* rejoice 2102
Long ago the *people* wondered 2254
Of *people* every tribe 1486
On thee thy *people* call 1320
On thy *people* pour thy power 580
Onward, then, ye *people* 1586
Our *people* drift and die 1365
People and realms of every tongue 1008
Sion's *people* tell his praises 356
So shall thy *people,* with thankful 607
That so thy *people* may rejoice 587
The *people* ceased to die 128
The *people* dwell in day 1917
The *people,* Lord, the people 2267
The *people* of the Hebrews 44
The *people* thronged about him 1556
Then among thy ransomed *people* 2158
Thy faithful *people* cry with one 405
Thy *people* lift their hearts 1165
Thy *people,* Lord, are singing night 2186
Thy *people* shall commemorate 1451
To draw thy *people* nigh 124
To thy *people* give the power 470
We are his *people,* and the sheep 1310
When *people* and the kingdoms do 2045
Where thy *people,* fully blest 966, 1012
With all the listening *people* gathered 2200
Ye *people,* place your confidence 1258
Zion's *people* tell his praises 356

PEOPLES

Among the *peoples* everywhere 1887, 1888
God of all *peoples,* let justice 584
Peoples of every name 1224
Peoples, kings, dominions 1049
That all of the world's great *peoples* 2208
The eager *peoples* flocking to be free 593
The *peoples* hunger for thee, Lord 1467
To all the *peoples,* peace 1609
To calm the raging *peoples* 2081

PERFECT

Perfect it in thy love 469

PERFECTED

Perfected in him I am 800

PERFECTIONS

Jesus, all *perfections* 1034

PERFECTNESS

But there are *perfectness* and peace 1920

PERFORMED

O who is like to thee, who hast *performed* 1387

PERFUME

Myrrh is mine, its bitter *perfume* 2196
Pouring *perfume* rare 141
With *perfume* and oil thou 1894

PERFUMES

Perfumes each lily bell 602

PERIL

For those in *peril* on the sea 418
From every *peril*, in the air 81
From every *peril*, on the land 81
In *peril* come thyself more near 495
Peril was nigh 476

PERILS

And the unseen *perils* compass 2274
From *perils* of the wind and wave 650
How many are the *perils* 1851
In *perils* of the common life 514
In *perils* of the sea 514
New *perils* past, new sins 1273
Perils lurk within the deep 2056
Through all the *perils* of our way 1461
When life's *perils* thick beset 556
When *perils* o'ertake us, escape 2188

PERIOD

Each future *period* that will bless 1064
Through every *period* of my life 2223

PERISH

All that is old doth *perish* 1948
And I *perish*, I perish, dear Master 1208
And *perish* in the general fire 1514
For none can *perish* there 109
For ever *perish* shall 2054
Perish all that fears the light 367
Perish every fond ambition 980
Perish policy and cunning 1171
Perish self in thy pure fire 761
Should not *perish* 22
We *perish* if we cease from prayer 1171, 1506

PERMIT

Not lightly does the Lord *permit* 2219
Permit no flower in thy view 2086
"*Permit* them to approach," He cries 1696

PERSON

God in the *person* of his Son 1308

PERSONS

With *persons* vain I have not sat 1043

PERSUADED

"Almost *persuaded*," Come, come 85
Almost *persuaded* now to trust 1740
And am *persuaded* that he is able 849

PERVERSE

If I have been *perverse*, or hard 901

PESTILENCE

From the noisome *pestilence* 271
Nor *pestilence* that walks by night 1908

PETITION

Yet, a great *petition* bringing 581
Your *petition* he will heed 2252

PETITIONS

Large *petitions* with thee bring 330

PHRASE

In differing *phrase* we pray 1428

PICK

Holding his *pick* more splendid 2262

PICTURE

It is the heaven-drawn *picture* 1544

PICTURES

He's all my fancy *pictures* 2108

PIECE

Each *piece* put on with prayer 1786

PIECES

And those shall he in *pieces* break 1454

PIERCE

Pierce the clouds of sinful night 743
Pierce the gloom of sin and grief 292
Pierce through the creeds 377

PIERCED

Pierced and nailed him to the tree 1106
Pierced by anguish so amazing 140
"They are *pierced* tonight by many 1983
Were *pierced* and wounded through and through 206

PILGRIM

Faint and weary, *pilgrim*, cheer thee 568
I'm a *pilgrim*, going home 810
I'm but a little *pilgrim* 1949
Pilgrim through this barren land 652
Then like a little *pilgrim* 1949
Weary *pilgrim*, welcome home 1076
Where every little *pilgrim* 1988

PILGRIMAGE

And through all life's *pilgrimage* 1583
Blest is the *pilgrimage* to heaven 2048
Soon our *pilgrimage* will cease 1711
Through thy *pilgrimage*, guard 2153
When this *pilgrimage* is o'er 2043
Who through this weary *pilgrimage* 1364

PILGRIMS

Inviting *pilgrims* as they pass 1970
Pilgrims here on earth, and strangers 2062
Pilgrims in a desert land 755
Pilgrims, may we travel with you 2284
Singing to welcome the *pilgrims* 670
Ye *pilgrims* on the road 147

PILLAGE

The soldiers' revels in the midst of *pillage* 37

PILLAR

Pillar of fire, through watches 1052
The flaming *pillar* leading on 1443

PILLARED

And in his *pillared* singing 818

PILLARS

And all the *pillars* fail 1261

PILLOW

My *pillow* on thy breast 2119
No downy *pillow* under his head 1199
Pillow, where lying, love rests 1656

PILLOWED

Pillowed on the loving breast 1195

PILOT

A *Pilot* who bringeth all vessels to land 20
A *Pilot* who knoweth the dangers at hand 20
Be our sure unerring *Pilot* 1603
Be thou their *Pilot* through the great 595
Good *Pilot* of the awful main 650
Great *Pilot* of my onward way 826
My *Pilot* knows the way 2234
My *Pilot* of the sea will one day 2234
My *Pilot* will be there 2234
Safe *Pilot* all who seek to find 1355
Strong *Pilot,* who at midnight hour 389
The Christ will our *Pilot* be 2190
Their *Pilot* be, by day, by night 490
Who will our *Pilot* be 2190

PINE

Beneath the *pine* or palm 1576

PINION

Far as the eagle's *pinion* 661

PINIONS

His outspread *pinions* shall thee hide 1908
I'm resting 'neath his mighty *pinions* 1896

PIONEER

Pioneer of boundless life 2100

PIONEERS

Pioneers! O Pioneers 62

PITCH

Yet nightly *pitch* my moving tent 494

PITIED

Pitied our sorrows 705

PITIFUL

Thou art *pitiful* and kind 523

PITY

All *pity,* care, and love 520
Amazing *pity,* grace unknown 38
And Christ-like tender *pity* 1505
Full of *pity* joined with power 357
In *pity* angels beheld him 881
In *pity* now thy servants bless 1174
Like *pity* shows the Lord 1798
Like the *pity* of a father 1472
Pity and heal my sinsick soul 1018
Pity and patience, still the 385
Pity incarnate for me has bled 1015
Pity my simplicity 523
Pity us and help our 929
The Lord in *pity* lingers still 1343
Thy *pity* without end 1475
Till through our *pity* and our shame 86
When I let the Savior's *pity* 1498
Where *pity* dwells, the peace of God 1319

PLACE

A *place* in this sanctified throng 2293
A *place* that is filled with his 1751
A *place* where all is joy 1969
A *place* where sin cannot molest 1969
A *place* where we our Savior meet 1969
And every *place* is hallowed 1032
And from that *place* where 1898
And in earth's darkest *place* 2051
And of the *place* where once it was 1798
And that I in his holy *place* 1903
At the *place* of prayer, in that little 2066
Be it ever so humble, there's no *place* 1212
Bowing toward thy holy *place* 710
Each *place* is home to them who pray 113
Even of thy holy *place* 1631
From *place* to place, his holy 2218
Happy, how happy, our *place* at his side 2129
He from his holy *place* looked 2045
His dwelling *place,* how fair 1061
How sweet within thy holy *place* 1432
I have no *place,* no shelter 1395
In every *place* to bring them in 1702
In my *place* condemned he stood 1203
Lord be a *place,* a portion, mine 2332
May I *place* mine 285
Mindful of thy *place* above 752
No lovelier *place* in the dale 1986
No *place* can part, nor hour 436
Not a *place* that he can enter 692
Not here is my *place* of rest 1411
Now for us a *place* prepareth 2288
O, how blessed is this *place* 1588
Place in my hands the wonderful key 1587
Place in the Lord reliance 567
Place your hand in the nail-scarred 694
The highest *place* that heaven 1869
The holy *place* wherein the Lord 571
The *place* of all on earth most 511
There is a *place* of comfort sweet 1969
There is a *place* of full release 1969
There is a *place* where Jesus sheds 511
There is a *place* where spirits blend 511
There is no *place* where earth's 1767
There thou dost our *place* prepare 659
There's a *place* of perfect rest 2252
There's a *place* that is wondrously fair 1989
Thy *place* is everywhere 788
Unto that *place* the tribes go up 843

We *place* within thy shrine 642
Who will *place* me on his right 131
Yea, in his *place* of holiness 193
Yea, in that *place* I do delight 1043
Zion, thrice happy *place* 86

PLACES

And in high *places* of the field 2050
Come to your *places* at the feast 1875
From earth's dark, cruel *places* 149
In their *places* now compacted 217
Making life's desert *places* bloom 1352

PLACETH

But *placeth* his delight 1841

PLAGUE

Nor *plague* approach thy guarded 1908

PLAGUES

Nor *plagues* that waste at noonday 1908
When fearful *plagues* around 1908

PLAIN

Across the sunswept *plain* 2285
From many a palmy *plain* 512

PLAINS

Above its sad and lowly *plains* 948
All o'er the wide-extended *plains* 1563
All the *plains* were lit that night 524

PLAN

God's perfect *plan* I cannot see 824
Let thy *plan* reveal the life 2198
Those who *plan* some evil 1302

PLANE

From the low *plane* of mortal toys 2203
Now on a higher *plane* I dwell 926

PLANETS

And all the *planets* in their turn 1932
And *planets* burn away 1361
Than *planets* sunward hurled 170
The *planets* glittering on 1936

PLANS

How splendid are the *plans* 1658
Oft our cherished *plans* have failed 2127
Plans and my thoughts 714
The *plans* that failed, alike were 1852

PLANT

All that may *plant* man's lordship 2003
And *plant* the Rose of Sharon 2325
Here *plant* thy throne, and here 502
Plant holy fear in every heart 310
Plant holy fear within my heart 319
Plant my feet on higher ground 915
The rising *plant* destroy 83
There's not a *plant* or flower below 877

PLANTED

But where the Lord has *planted* 1038
Planted here below 928
Planted in thy dwelling place 951

PLANTS

He *plants* his footsteps in the seal 577
Now he *plants* the tribes of Israel 1697
Olive *plants,* in strength and beauty 238

PLAUDIT

With the hearty, joyous *plaudit* 1076

PLAY

And *play* with loud noise 2329
And so the west winds *play* 39
At *play* when work was done 145
Nor let thou life's delightful *play* 1495
The meadows where we *play* 68
Will ye *play* then? will ye dally 2157

PLEA

Constant abiding, this is my *plea* 1829
Even then this shall be all my *plea* 1024
For my cleansing, this my *plea* 2214
Hast an unfailing *plea* 348
His death is my *plea* 73
The sinner's perfect *plea* 869
This is my earnest *plea* 1152, 1220
This, O Lord, is all my *plea* 222
With humble *plea* on thee we call 1381

PLEAD

Alone with God, didst *plead* for me 123
And *plead* his love for love 2310
And *plead* their cause in heaven 426
And *plead* thy death and passion 2168
And *plead* to be forgiven 1119
Earth's Redeemer, *plead* for me 77
For thine own dost ever *plead* 1760
Jesus, *plead* for me 937
Let us not *plead* thy love in vain 650
Lo, we *plead* thy promise now 538
Might *plead* thy gracious name 109
Nor for ourselves alone we *plead* 1442
O *plead* the truth, and make reply 1318
O *plead* with him now to come 2272
Plead with them earnestly 1655
Plead with them gently 1655
That thou wilt *plead* for me 1517
Then, Savior, *plead* for me 1517
They strongly *plead* for me 113
We humbly *plead* before thee 515
We *plead* for his blessing and trust 1909
We *plead* that all thy grace 1381
We *plead* the promise of thy word 1524

PLEADING

He's tenderly *pleading* with thee 1542
Pleading for you and for me 1743

PLEADINGS

And thy Savior's *pleadings* cease 692

PLEADS

And having with us him that *pleads* 99
And *pleads* our cause at God's 1064
And now he *pleads* our cause 1704
He *pleads* before the mercy-seat 173
He *pleads* with God; he pleads for thee 173
He *pleads* with you now to be 1925
Now he *pleads* for us above 357
Pleads for us, and hears our cry 287
Pleads the merit of his blood 358
While he so gently, so tenderly *pleads* 1542

PLEASANT

December's as *pleasant* as May 795

PLEASE

And let nothing ever *please* us 1118

PLEASED

And it *pleased* his gracious ear 1099
Be *pleased* to use it as thine own 2088
Pleased as man with men to dwell 675
Pleased with all that pleases thee 1647

PLEASES

Without him all that *pleases* 898

PLEASURE

For selfish *pleasure* we have sought 1518
For thy *pleasure* didst design 101
In our *pleasure* and our glee 1173
My all to his *pleasure* resigned 795
O what *pleasure* 2032
Our *pleasure* is but pain 960
Pleasure that can never cloy 1058
Shall I for *pleasure* live, or shrink 1251
Such *pleasure* and such play 960
Such *pleasure* as below 252
'Tis the Father's *pleasure* 143
To take whate'er thy Father's *pleasure* 904
When drooping *pleasure* turns to grief 1459
Where rivers of *pleasure* I see 24

PLEASURES

All earth's flowing *pleasures* 1034
All of its *pleasures,* pomp 1266
All our *pleasures* here below 1173
All worldly *pleasures* leave behind 158
And *pleasures* banish pain 1966
And *pleasures* evermore 2238
Do earth *pleasures* so enthrall 1709
Earth's *pleasures* shall I still hold dear 558
Its *pleasures* quickly die 1193
No *pleasures* of Egypt shall draw 871
Only true *pleasures* in Jesus 506
Pleasures of the world grow dim 2
Pleasures, riches, all must flee 1688
Should earthly *pleasures* wane 434
The fairest *pleasures* of the world 2
The *pleasures* lost I sadly 1322
With its witching *pleasures* 937

PLEDGE

But more for *pledge* of what remains 2185
By this *pledge* that thou dost love us 486
Take this *pledge* of mine and seal it 225
We *pledge* our loyalty 1951
We *pledge* the Lord anew 138

PLENTY

All the *plenty* summer pours 1628
Our *plenty,* wealth, prosperity 92
Plenty for pleasure 705
With *plenty* and with peace 1734

PLOW

For them we *plow* the land 712
O Christ, the *plow* 1327

PLOWSHARE

To *plowshare* beat their swords 284

PLOWSHARES

To *plowshares* men shall beat their swords 198

PLUCK

None can *pluck* us from thy hand 1197
Who shall *pluck* you from his hand 356

PLUCKED

Plucked from the destroyer's hand 1837

PLUNGE

Plunge in then, my brother 17
Plunge in today, and be made 402
Plunge then into the crimson flood 308

PLUNGED

I *plunged* in that river 17

POET

Hebrew *poet,* priest, and seer 1196

POETS

Poets sung its glory 501

POINT

And *point* me to the skies 27
If thou will *point* the way and remain 1372
I'll *point* to thy redeeming blood 1001

POINTS

And he *points* the way to the realms 1500
Anywhere with Jesus when he *points* the way 108
Christ *points* the harder way 2340
Points to the wounded feet and side 89
Who *points* the clouds their course 365

POLE

From *pole* to pole, that wars 376

POMP

In lowly *pomp* ride on 1660
In *pomp* of triumph Christ 1078
Lo, all our *pomp* of yesterday 583
Not the *pomp* of earth 1069
Upon its *pomp* and glitter 1193

PONDER

And on his doing *ponder* 534
Like Mary, let us *ponder* 298
Ponder nothing earthly minded 1060

POOL

And by each reedy *pool* 2195

POOR

And the *poor* a friend 2260
And with the *poor* he broke 1253
For the *poor* and needy 1787
God of the *poor* and weak, to our prayers 584
Her *poor* with bread will satisfy 2205
Poor though I be and weak 478
The humble *poor* believe 1351
The *poor* and them that mourn 278
Though so *poor* by Galilee 521
Thy *poor* with uprightness 1454
Till the *poor* have breathing-space 2007
With the *poor* and mean and lowly 1572

PORTAL

O heaven's *portal*, Zion fair 1569
Straight is the *portal* 2

PORTALS

And the *portals* high are lifted 1697
And through its *portals* gleaming 1962
Heav'nly *portals* loud with hosannas 1616
No longer from its brazen *portals* 37
Through the bright and shining *portals* 1055
Thy *portals* they are golden 1404
When at the golden *portals* I am 1808
Within its *portals*, fadeless joys 16

PORTENTS

No *portents* now their foes amaze 2239

PORTION

And him my only *portion* make 1864
And *portion* sure forever 2054
But if it be my *portion* 954
For thou art my *portion*, O Lord 2084
My *portion* in the land of life 2103
This only *portion*, Lord, be mine 1458
"Thou art my *portion*," saith my soul 1242
Though her *portion* be the scaffold 1574
Thy better *portion* trace 1667
When Jesus is my *portion* 2296

POSSESS

All that I *possess* to him 801
And *possess*, in sweet communion 1209
Our Lord shall *possess* them 509
Possess these hearts so lowly 1853
That, under thee, we may *possess* 445
Towards thee longing doth *possess* me 1470
We'll soon *possess* the land 516

POSSESSED

Of the full Deity *possessed* 2022

POSSESSING

With thee we are *possessing* 26

POSTERITY

And his *posterity* shall flourish 2116
To them and their *posterity* 2060

POTENCIES

For childhood's luring *potencies* 1779

POTTER

Thou art the *Potter*, I am the clay 691

POUR

And *pour* contempt on all my pride 2236
Before him *pour* ye out 1258
But the Lord will shortly *pour* 1695
Come, *pour* thy joys on human 375
Go, *pour* in the oil and the wine 1098
I will not *pour* out on thee 259
Meekly *pour* our thankful lay 45
They *pour* effectual prayers 113
O *pour* them from above 520
O *pour* thy grace upon us 1952
Pour down the riches of thy 1002
Pour down thy fire in us to glow 312
Pour down thy grace in cheering 770
Pour out thy soul for them 1551
Pour out upon us thine abiding 454
Pour upon us of thy fullness 677

POURED

And *poured* forth cries and tears 530
Poured for me the lifeblood 544
Poured out his life for us 705

POURS

The Lord *pours* eyesight on the blind 911

POWER

A mightier *power* and stronger 2005
All *power* and glory be 1485
All *power* in earth, all power 472
All *power* is given unto me 433
Almighty *Power* that made us 713
Almighty, thy *power* hath founded 1546
And Christ, with love's persuasive *power* 1427
And every *power* find sweet 1811
And his anointed's *power* 1455
And in his mighty *power* 1746
And Satan's *power* is burst 49
And still its *power* shall onward 1354
Bid the *power* of sin depart 222
But for more *power* to love 385
But God's *power*, hour by hour 53
By its transforming *power* 2315
By thy *power* all things are made 579
By thy *power* the lost to save 269
Come with soul converting *power* 1703
Come, with thy Spirit and thy *power* 502
Coming in *power* and love to reign 982

Daily *power* to conquer sin 760
Fill me with thy love and *power* 502
From sin's *power* do thou 142
From the hardening *power* of sin 993
God's great *power* shall win all 428
His craft and *power* are great 12
His *power* alone can cleanse the world 2135
His *power* can make you what you 2324
His *power* he will bestow 111
His *power* increasing still 1917
His *power* is from above 510
His saving *power* this very hour 1713
His sovereign *power* our bodies 328
His sovereign *power*, without our aid 184
His the *power* and glory 1833
His triumphant *power* I'll tell 894
How sin's *power* to overthrow 268
I am trusting thee for *power* 811
I shall his *power* adore 1864
In all his *power* and love 1940
In *power* and might excelling 1883
In *power* to do, and grace to bear 1370
Its saving *power* may know 83
Let no ill *power* find place 1944
Letting thine all-pervading *power* 1780
Lord be ours thy *power* to keep 2255
May thy tender mercy's healing *power* 1006
Mere human *power* shall fast decay 685
Messiah's *power* shall be revealed 114
My *power* is faint and low 1202
No *power* can take me out of his care 1756
O for thy mighty *power* 723
O mighty God, thy matchless *power* 157
Of his redeeming *power* 93
One in the *power* that makes thy children 421
Perfect in *power*, in love 749
Power, all power, surely is thine 691
Power and blessing grant us 458
Power and glory unto the Lord 1616
Power and service be our prize 1158
Power his image to retrieve 752
Power in prayer, Lord, power 1829
Power, like thee, our Lord, to live 752
Power to cleanse and make me 1573
Power to lift my head 223
Power to pray and power to do 1829
Power with men, and power 1829
Saints by the *power* of God are kept 231
So long thy *power* hath blest me 1053
So secure that no *power* can mine it 430
That I thy *power* may behold 1172
That *power* by which our Shepherd 459
That we to sin's dark *power* are dead 391
The *power* and pomp of nations 1998
The *power* of Satan breaking 248
The *power* which crucified thee 1124
The saving *power* impart 1777
The tempter's *power* withstand 515
There is *power*, power, wonder-working 2323
There is thy *power* 591
There's *power* in the blood 2323
Thine is the *power*, behold 1035
Thine is the *power*, be thine 469
Thine is the quickening *power* 92
Thine, O God, to give the *power* 36
Thine the *power* to guide and save 1075
Though ruthless *power* may 309
Through thy great *power* 50
Thy boundless *power* o'er all things 43
Thy gracious *power* shall hold me 2016
Thy *power* alone can break 1609
Thy *power* and love must still 1238
Thy *power* hath cleansed 60
Thy *power* my strength and fortress 417
Thy *power*, O Lord, can give 465
Thy *power* throughout the universe 1437
Thy *power* to bless what seraph 1424
Thy *power* to give 1175
Thy Spirit's ceaseless, brooding *power* 1467
To him be *power* divine ascribed 671
To me thy *power* impart 889
To save us all from Satan's *power* 599
To thee, whose faithful *power* 2118
To us thy quickening *power* extend 452
To whom the *power* is given 325
What God's almighty *power* hath made 1729
What *power* thy depths can fathom 1464
Where in eternal *power* and might 2316
While we trust thy love and *power* 42
Whose *power* a sceptor sways 376
With pentecostal *power* we shall 1401
With th' eternal *power* I hide 2224

POWERS

All my *powers* to thee surrender 1690
All the *powers* of music bring 1625
And all our consecrated *powers* 1733
And o'er the vanquished *powers* 82
Hell's fierce *powers* beneath 142
How the *powers* of darkness 293
Let adverse *powers* 116
Let all the *powers* within me join 209
May all my *powers* to thee aspire 631
No *powers* of darkness me molest 59
O may it all my *powers* engage 4
That all my *powers* with all their might 152, 545, 1953
That the *powers* of hell may vanish 1060
That word above all earthly *powers* 12
The *powers* of death have done 79, 1937
The subtle *powers* of darkness 1328
There no more the *powers* of hell 1303
These opening *powers* 21
To God the *powers* that dwell 55
We, with all the *powers* we have 357
When *powers* of earth and hell arose 2132
When the *powers* of sin would 1979
With all our *powers*, thy praise 314
With nobler *powers* conferred 2177
Wrestling with the evil *powers* 2059

PRACTISE

And *practise* all that we believe 375

PRAIRIES

Our *prairies* and our mountains 515

PRAISE

A thousand lips to sing thy *praise* 23
All *praise* and honor, glory, power 1427
All *praise* and thanks to God 1299
All *praise,* O risen Lord, we give 1037
All *praise* to God the Father's name 965
All *praise* to him belongs 1733
All *praise* to thee who art 965
All *praise* we would render 916
And evermore thy *praise* proclaim 1451
And in all our *praise* to thee 1120
And in thy *praise* will sing 1235
And *praise,* and work, and rest 491
And *praise* him by and by 320
And *praise* him with the seraphim 1
And *praise* shall tune the trembling 1700
And *praise* surround the throne 2014
And *praise* the Lord, who now as then 1296
And *praise* thee as long as thou 1246
And we *praise* thee for joy 423
At all times *praise* the Lord 133
Be *praise* and worship paid 265
Be thine the *praise* 469
But *praise* thee more for soil 2185
Ever *praise* him 2328
From angels *praise* 1366
Clad is the *praise,* sweet are the songs 666
Glad *praise* from air and land 81
God the One, all *praise* to thee 538
God's wondrous *praise* declare 1654
High *praise* to the eternal King 152
His endless *praise* proclaim 147
His *praise* all people sing 661
His *praise* all the day long 1741
His *praise* I long to speak 932
His *praise* may thither fly 1062
His *praise* my mouth shall still 616
His *praise* renew 573
His *praise* shall be recounted 360
His *praise* shall tune my voice 1759
How shall I *praise* thee who 2038
I *praise* him because he appointed 1741
I will *praise* and adore at the mercy seat 880
I will *praise* my dear Redeemer 894
I will *praise* the Lord in song 1500
If you are happy and *praise* fills 908
I'll *praise* thee as I ought 794
I'll *praise* thee early, Lord, and late 2302
I'll *praise* thee, from whose hands 2039
In whose sweet *praise* 1255
Jesus, be endless *praise* to thee 1024
Let me be a *praise* to thee 997
Let *praise* to thy Creator rise 1297
Let the Creator's *praise* arise 508
Let thy *praise* our tongues 1628
Lo! they *praise* and vanish 258
Lord, we *praise,* we worship thee 485
Merrily, cheerily, gladly *praise* thee 208
Now my evening *praise* I bring 1304
O may we ever *praise* him 763
O *praise* his name, he lifted 926
O *praise* our Redeemed, all mortals 1650
O *praise* the Lord for saving grace 870
O *praise* the name of Jesus 1912
O Zion, *praise* the Lord thy God 1636
Our prayer and *praise* and anthems 44
Praise and prayer are rising 258
Praise Christ, your risen Lord 1083
Praise Father, Son, and Holy Ghost 1613
Praise for all our work 1158
Praise for joys and sorrows 1158
Praise for the hope most glorious 2175
Praise for the joy of loving 2175
Praise for the sweetness 1221
Praise for the priceless blessing 2175
Praise for the singing 1221
Praise, glory, adoration 1320
Praise God, and on him cast 41
Praise God, for me the price 1422
Praise God, the Father of us all 1614
Praise him above, ye heavenly 1613
Praise him all creatures here below 1613
Praise him, all ye angels 1624
Praise him, all ye stars 1626
Praise him, angels in the height 1626
Praise him, clouds and vapors 1624
Praise him every tuneful string 1625
Praise him, field and flower 1620
Praise him for his grace and favor 1618
Praise him for his great salvation 1099
Praise him for his matchless power 1625
Praise him for his noble deeds 1625
Praise him for his precious 1099
Praise him for our harvest store 1619
Praise him, fowls and cattle 1624
Praise him from morn till fall of 1627
Praise him in the height 1624
Praise him, men and maidens 1624
Praise him, my soul, with sweet delight 155
Praise him, praise him all the day 1789
Praise him, praise him, shout aloud 747
Praise him, skies and water 1624
Praise him, stars and light 1624
Praise him, still the same forever 1618
Praise him that he gave the rain 1619
Praise him through time, till time 1131
Praise him till in heaven 1099
Praise him when drear and lone 133
Praise him when far away 133
Praise him when home is sweet 133
Praise him when joyful songs 133
Praise him when skies are bright 133
Praise him who by a simple flower 1633
Praise him who claims us 791
Praise him who is all praise above 155
Praise him who makes our life 1633
Praise him who pardons all 1634
Praise him who rules the nations 1614
Praise him who saved them from peril 607, 608
Praise him who will with glory 1634
Praise him, ye angels, praise him in 1635
Praise him, ye heavens with 1614
Praise him, your undying Friend 1099
Praise his mighty power 1620
Praise his name forever 600, 665

Praise his name for life and light 1606
Praise his name in all the earth 524
Praise his wonderful name 1268
Praise in the common words I speak 478
Praise is his gracious choice 304
Praise, laud and bless his name 57
Praise Love that maketh wars 1614
Praise shall employ my nobler 911
Praise the everlasting King 1618
Praise the God of our salvation 1626
Praise the high eternal One 1618
Praise the holy God of love 1625
Praise the Lord! for he hath spoken 1626
Praise the Lord for he is glorious 1626
Praise the Lord in every breath 1625
Praise the Lord, ye fountains 1624
Praise the mount, I'm fixed upon it 340
Praise the precious blood 544
Praise thee while life shall last 2302
Praise to God be ever given 563
Praise to God for hearing 1629
Praise to God for seeing 1629
Praise to Jesus while we play 1789
Praise to our victorious King 142
Praise to the Savior ascending 660
Praise to thy eternal merit 313
Praise we God, who hath inspired 242
Praise we the great of heart 1296
Praise we the peaceful men 1296
Praise we the wise and brave 1296
Praise where earth her bounty 1665
Praise with elation 1221
Praise with us the God of grace 1618
Praise ye him this happy day 1726
Praise ye Jehovah 1635
Praise ye Jehovah, Source of all 1634
Praise ye, praise ye God the Lord 104
Praise ye, the Father, God the Lord 1634
Praise ye, the Father, Son and 1635
Praise ye the God of death 1807
Praise ye the Lord for all his 1634
Praise ye the Lord, O let all that is 1637
Praise ye the Lord of life 1807
Praise ye the Lord, who o'er all things 1637
Praise ye the Savior, great is 1635
Praise ye the Son, who died 1634
Praise ye the sovereign Lord 2307
Praise ye the Spirit, Comforter 1635
Praise yet the Lord again 304
Risen Lord, all *praise* to thee 142
Shall thy *praise* unuttered lie 1214
Sing your Savior's worthy *praise* 277
So, *praise* the God of truth and grace 1571
That with purer, nobler *praise* 538
The *praise* of him who is thy God 125
Thee will I *praise,* for thou 1484
Then let all *praise* be given thee 86
Then *praise* the Lord with one accord 6
There also is thy *praise* proclaimed 2313
There shall I *praise* him with Eden's 2314
They shall thy *praise* proclaim 50
This to thy *praise,* O Lord, be sung 317
Though high above all *praise* 1785
Three persons *praise* we 45
Thus its *praise* creation brings 543
Thy name, thy *praise* we sing 48
Thy *praise* pursuing 1289
Thy *praise* resounds in grateful songs 770
Thy *praise* shall never, never fail 376
Thy *praise* shall sanctify our rest 1856
Thy *praise* shall sound
from shore to shore 508
Till I shall *praise* thee as I would 1288
Till we *praise* the Lord in his home 1979
To give to him the *praise* 1959
To God all *praise* and glory 1729
To join in holy *praise* and love 1809
To sing his *praise,* and do his will 117
To sing thy great Redeemer's *praise* 153
To thee all *praise* and glory be 1439
To thee all *praise* be due 1320
To thee I will give *praise* 54
To thee we *praise* and glory give 307
Too soon of *praise* we tire 1592
We *praise* thee and adore 91, 1632
We *praise* thee and confess thee 1481
We *praise* thee as the Lord 2277
We *praise* thee for Jesus, our Master 423
We *praise* thee for life's gathered gains 2185
We *praise* thee for the conflicts won 2185
We *praise* thee for the harbor's lee 2185
We *praise* thee for the radiance 1544
We *praise* thee for the surer 2027
We *praise* thee for thy mercies past 767
We *praise* thee, O God, for thy Spirit 2187
We *praise* thee with the glowing light 2186
We will ever *praise* thy love 450
We would *praise* thee, and surrender 144
We would *praise* thee every day 1197
We'll *praise* him who called us 2225
When his *praise* like the sea billows 809
When the *praise* of heaven I hear 2261
Where shall I my *praise* begin 1510
Who like me his *praise* should sing 1618
Who *praise* thee with a stammering 1105
Whose *praise* they swell 1865
With *praise* my mouth employ 1902
Yet shall thou *praise* him, when 464

PRAISED

God be *praised* for congregations 1182
"May Jesus Christ be *praised!*" 2243
The Lord is greatly to be *praised* 1451

PRAISES

Abba's *praises* we proclaim 597
And his sweet *praises* sing 1255
And never-ending *praises* give 72
And *praises* sing to God the King 1426
And *praises* throng to crown 1008
And *praises* to his holy name 2219
And thankful *praises* I will sing 2103
And with *praises* greet his love 369
And without *praises* die 1315
Ever his *praises* sing 891
Ever thus in God's high *praises* 1178

Glad be our *praises,* and 1611
Glad *praises* to thee we ever 959
God's *praises,* in their loving 1938
Happy, how happy the *praises* 2129
His *praises* proclaiming in song 164
His *praises* there may grow 1062
His *praises* we'll sing 1650
How can my *praises* ever find 2144
Let *praises* fill the sky 304
Low before him with our *praises* 1538
Never let his *praises* cease 1073
No, I must my *praises* bring 1814
Now thy grateful *praises* bring 715
O let its *praises* ever swell 1912
Praises and thanks we bring 261
Praises to thee joyfully 208
Praises voicing 945
Sing *praises* to their God 28
Singing his *praises,* gladly 2152
So I thy *praises* will make 1134
Such are the *praises,* God 1606
The *praises* of Jesus the angels 2330
The *praises* of my God shall 2060
The *praises* of redeeming love 298
The *praises* of thy royal name 1086
The *praises* of thy wonders 619
Their joyful *praises* bringing 2303
Thou didst accept their *praises* 44
Thy *praises,* Lord, I will resound 1362
Thy *praises* sound through every 2312
To Holy Ghost be *praises* 1341
To our Lord and Savior, *praises* 563
While with sweet, melodious *praises* 951

PRATTLE

When *prattle* and smile made home 2272

PRAY

All voices *pray* 92
And few there are who *pray* 1056
And *pray* for these before thee 1370
And *pray* God's peace to reign 1930
And *pray* that free from peril 1851
And *pray* that this may be our home 2142
And *pray* that thou still 2166
And *pray* that we may never dare 1522
And *pray* thee that offenceless 1851
And thus we *pray* in deed 1492
And will ever *pray* thee 35
Blind, we *pray* that we may see 442
Bound, we *pray* to be made free 442
But *pray* while kindred spirits 133
For I to thee will *pray* 527
For when I *pray,* before me 898
God be with them while they *pray* 555
Help me to watch and *pray* 4
I *pray* thee, from our hearts 828
I *pray* thee keep me thine 1251
I *pray* thee now that sinless 1851
I *pray* thee, Savior, keep me 855
More like Jesus when I *pray* 1218
O Lord, to thee we *pray* 1934
O thou must *pray* instead 534
Pray and fight, on Christ relying 2153
Pray and praise thee without ceasing 1190
Pray, and thy path shall be clear 1269
Pray for a thoughtful heart 133
Pray for Jerusalem 540
Pray, pray, be calm and still 1640
Pray, pray, for God understands 1640
Pray, pray for others' need 1640
Pray, pray though your eyes 1640
Pray, pray till faith grows 1640
Pray that help may be sent 49
Pray that Jerusalem may have 843
Pray the clouds away 1730
Shall *pray,* and pray aright 1171, 1506
Stained, we *pray* for sanctity 442
Then *pray* that your Savior 830
Therefore in our hymns we *pray* 78
Unto God *pray* without ceasing 561
Us now, we *pray,* O God, in anger 1873
We *pray* thee for all absent friends 121
We *pray* thee, God of love 121
We *pray* thee, hear us when we 373
We *pray* thee, Lord, arise 2073
We *pray* thou wilt fill us 1372
While to the Lord I *pray* 2219
While we *pray* for pardoning grace 1676
Will you *pray* with all your power 251

PRAYED

He *prayed* for them that did 1931
He *prayed* on the Tree 73
I was not ever thus, nor *prayed* 1053
Nor the thing *prayed* for come short 1538
There he *prayed* 'neath the old olive tree 1268
Till all who *prayed* and struggled 1505

PRAYEDST

Thou who *prayedst,* thou who 1760

PRAYER

All thine, are ours by *prayer* 1146
And fervent *prayer* ascend 1529
And *prayer,* by thee inspired 199
And *prayer* in endless praise 1714
And *prayer* will be answered 830
And to my *prayer* give ear 1135
And vesper hymn and vesper *prayer* 32
And watching unto *prayer* 1746
Anxious or troubled,
when with us is *prayer* 1183
Attending to my *prayer* 50
Be this the *prayer* of my last breath 1509
But *prayer* and tenderest pity 497
But *prayer* give life to all our 2147
Fasting with unceasing *prayer* 500
For her our *prayer* shall rise 557
For him shall endless *prayer* 1008
From his giving, *prayer* 2255
From out their tireless *prayer* 1353
God is now willing to answer your *prayer* 569
Hear thou the *prayer* thy servants 82
In all-prevailing *prayer* upon 1177
In ardent *prayer* and earnest 300
In humble *prayer* and fervent 1521

In the little children's *prayer* 936
Keep on praying, *prayer* is not 1048
Let thy *prayer* be in thy deed 294
My God, my God, my *prayer* doth thee 1239
My *prayer* has reached his ear 361
My *prayer* he will not hear 361
My *prayer* that riseth unto thee 1135
Nearer in *prayer* my hope 1267
Not for myself alone may my *prayer* 406
O may that holy *prayer* 1579
Of my *prayer* Hearer be 1407
Our *prayer* attend 338
Our *prayer* so languid 99
Prayer, and praising all men 2196
Prayer climbs the ladder Jacob saw 2221
Prayer is the contrite sinner's voice 1641
Prayer is the simplest form of speech 1641
Prayer makes the darkened cloud 2221
Prayer that the bond between them 2175
Prayer that the sweet surrender 2175
Prayer that thou wilt accomplish 2175
Prayer, the sublimest strains 1641
The needy's *prayer* he will not 2045
The *prayer* is accepted 73
The shout that every *prayer* 37
There's a mother's deep *prayer* 1995
This still its *prayer* shall be 1220
Thou to whom *prayer* did strength 1407
To be by *prayer* brought nigh 1872
To blend my pleading *prayer* 173
To thee we lift our *prayer* 75
Unto my *prayer* attend 1357
Watching, ever watching,
even unto *prayer* 1264
While in *prayer* we bowed 1179
Who turned not my *prayer* 50
With *prayer* and psalm they 1354
Your bitter *prayer* for pardon 2218

PRAYERS

Accept the *prayers* we bring 44
All the agonizing *prayers* 63
And *prayers* of glad thanksgiving 1591
And strong the *prayers* that bow the ear 666
By the *prayers* of faithful watchmen 1160
Dearer to God are the *prayers* 254
For her my *prayers* ascend 859
O let our *prayers* like incense rise 791
Offering *prayers* and praises 256
Our humble *prayers* implore 1364
Our *prayers* shall never cease 540
Prayers rise from hearts so dear 85
The *prayers* we raise 1342
There, when all our *prayers* are ended 929
Though faint my *prayers,* and cold 2295
Through him the first fond *prayers* 2181
To thee our *prayers* ascend 1386
When the *prayers* that they have prayed 2264
While the *prayers* of saints ascend 2121

PRAYEST

Be what thou *prayest* 703

PRAYING

For you I am *praying* 830

PRAYS

The suffering Savior *prays* alone 2091

PREACH

And *preach* thee, too, as love knows 428
If you cannot *preach* like Paul 679
Preach Christ in his wonderful 1770
Preach him to all, and cry in death 1017
Preach his gospel to our heart 339

PREACHER

Mighty *preacher,* by whose word 1051

PRECEPTS

His lofty *precepts* to translate 603
How kind his *precepts* 777
I will thy holy *precepts* make 270
Precepts and promises afford 1933
Sacred *precepts,* quickly broken 611
Thy *precepts* all respect 212
Upon thy *precepts* and thy ways 789

PRECIOUS

He is so *precious* to me 1741

PREPARATION

And may our *preparation* for 1529
Let this fleeting *preparation* 219

PREPARE

And O, thy servant, Lord, *prepare* 4
And thus *prepare* to meet thee 644
And, when to meet
thee we *prepare* 1171, 1506
But, above all, *prepare* thy heart 600
He shall *prepare* thy way 365
If the evil one *prepare* 963
If you would *prepare* 2258
Now *prepare* for God a way 363
O, *prepare* for him a throne 1726
Prepare across the earth the King's 720
Prepare in the desert a highway 1998
Prepare, my soul, to meet him 644
Prepare themselves to seek thee 33
Then, O my Lord, *prepare* 5
These, these *prepare* us for the night 420

PREPARED

And be by thee *prepared* 1291
God has *prepared* a rosy-tinted 1270
Prepared and mingled by thy 417
Then shall I be *prepared* to see 1910
Thou hast *prepared* the feast 1715
Which thou hast *prepared* before 1154

PREPARES

He that *prepares* this rich repast 722
Near himself *prepares* our place 655

PRESENCE

And all in Jesus' *presence* reign 1705
And ever in thy *presence* bright 437
And in his blissful *presence* 763
And in the *presence* of our Lord 393, 651
And in thy *presence* bow the head 2122
And in thy *presence* is no death 784
And in thy *presence* only 2168
And in thy *presence* rest 1019
And still he is nigh, his *presence* 2330
And with his glorious *presence* 779
And with thy *presence* blest 1476
As in thy *presence*, humbly I bow 691
Before his *presence* let us come 1334
But thy dear *presence* will not 1289
By this prevailing *presence* we 99
Come before his *presence* with our songs 1707
E'en though in thy *presence* thou grant 719
Forever with thy *presence* blest 114
From thy *presence* thus to win 1173
God's *presence* and his very self 1630
His living *presence* your being 2337
His *presence* calms my every fear 1756
His *presence* disperses my gloom 795
His *presence* doth forever 1896
His *presence* fills each heart 774
His *presence* is to men 120
His *presence* shall bless them 509
His *presence* sheds eternal day 644
In God's *presence* clouds will 1048
In his blessed *presence* live 891
In his dear *presence* finding 1849
In his *presence* daily live 70
In thy *presence* to abide 359
In thy pure *presence* kneeling 1849
Let me thy inner *presence* feel 1082
Let thy *presence* be their light 741
Let thy *presence*, great Redeemer 1603
Let us before his *presence* come 1335
Lord, thy *presence* let me see 176
Lord, thy *presence* on the deep 972
Lord, we thy *presence* seek 227
One unseen *Presence* she adores 1576
Only in thy *presence* 1034
Or from thy *presence* fly 1452
So shall his *presence* bless our 327
That I may in thy *presence* live 1323
There thy *presence* be confessed 346
Thou vailed *Presence* infinitely 2038
Thy own dear *presence* to cheer 647
Thy *presence* fills my solitude 856
Thy *presence* gives us childlike 2048
Thy *presence* here we own 2168
Thy *presence* in these sacred halls 1527
Thy *presence* is, my Lord 1444
Thy *presence* keeps my conscience 60
Thy *presence* now display 393, 651
Thy *presence* sweet communion 2174
Thy *presence* we have coldly 2170
Thy promised *presence* claim 1031
Thy soul-cheering *presence* restore 795
Waking or sleeping, thy *presence* my 177
What rejoicing in his *presence* 424
What will thy *presence* be 844
Where in his *presence* forever 829
Why hast thou me far from thy *presence* 1239

PRESENT

Be *present* as we worship 45
Be *present*, blessed Savior 1944
Be *present*, Holy Spirit 1944
Be *present*, O our Father 1944
Be thou, Lord, *present* in our hearts 1429
Before thee we *present* 44
Behold him *present* with his aid 572
But *present* still, though now unseen 2239
Christ, *present* them; God, receive 753
For thou, O Lord, art *present* there 1809
He will *present* them at the throne 1893
Here we *present* ourselves, our souls 466
Standing in the living *present* 1280
That were a *present* far too small 2236
We but *present* thee with thine own 1441

PRESERVE

Great God, *preserve* us in thy fear 640
Jehovah shall *preserve* thy going out 2139
Us and ours *preserve* from dangers 2062

PRESERVED

By thee *preserved* alive 587
Thus *preserved* from Satan's wiles 1647

PRESERVER

By thou my soul's *Preserver* 1851

PRESERVES

For God *preserves* the souls 2060

PRESERVEST

Lord, thou *preservest*
man and beast 2079, 2080

PRESS

And *press* the battle ere the night 413
And *press* with vigor on 154
Be a Christian! *press* on!
do not have any fears 130
But *press* to realms on high 4
Let us *press* on in patient 1794
Onward we *press* to make the vision 1443
Press on where he doth lead 377
Press onward then, though foes 1962
Press onward to the prize 1667
Press towards our glorious prize 492
Thus onward still we *press* 432
We shall *press* the sands of gold 2191
Weary, I know it, of the *press* 362

PRESSED

By Satan sorely *pressed* 109
Up, up, it *pressed* its way above 11
When *pressed* by the foe 1477

PRESSING

Pressing more closely to him 2129

PRETENDED

That man to judge thee, hath in hate *pretended* 35

PREVAIL

Shall thus *prevail* the tempter's 1440
Yet he may not *prevail* 176

PREVAILING

Of mortal ills *prevailing* 12

PREY

Let them be the lion's *prey* 1691
Satan's *prey* oft are they 1668
The *prey* of the cannon 709

PRICE

Praise God, for me the *price* he paid 1422
The *price* of redemption from sin 1868
To pay the *price* of sin 1963

PRIDE

Amid our *pride* and glory 1549
And all the nation's *pride*, o'erthrown 1124
And all the *pride* of sinful will 2198
And let thy foolish *pride* be still 1823
Be it thy *pride* to lift up 1312
For *pride* ambitious to succeed 189
From *pride* of place absolve 1943
From the *pride* that lurks within 993
He that is low no *pride* 704
Her *pride* is suffering 886
It was my *pride* and hardness 497
Our *pride* is dust, our vaunt 1124
Our *pride*, our Lord, disdained thee 1415
Our sinful *pride* to cure 559
Pride and sin lurk within 1668
Pride ruled my will 1053

PRIEST

A *Priest* and Victim, both in one 1488
And in our *Priest* we will 2025
And one was a *priest* 875
Christ the Victim, Christ the *Priest* 142
One *Priest* before the throne 1579
Our *Priest* in earth and heaven 1325
The great High *Priest* is with thee now 173
The *priest* of Israel slept 797

PRIESTS

Her *priests* I'll clothe with health 2205
O let thy *priests* be clothed 2205
Priests around his altar 466
Priests of God, now serving in 1838
That no *priests* give nor kings 2183
Vainly *priests* in hatred slew him 1075

PRINCE

"A *prince*," he said, "in Jewry!" 2141
And let the *prince* of ill 19
Come, *Prince* of Peace, and reign 284
Come, thou blessed *Prince* of Peace 280
Hail, the heaven-born *Prince* of Peace 675
Hail, thou *Prince* of Life adored 288
Lo, the *Prince* of common welfare 2017
More of his coming, *Prince* of Peace 1216
O holy Jesus, *Prince* of Peace 92
O *Prince* of Peace, thou bringer 1130
On, great *Prince*, assert thy right 1073
Prince and peasant, bond and free 485
Prince of Life, to thee I cry 1761
The ancient *prince* of hell 19
The bleeding *Prince* of life and peace 1460
The *Prince* is ever in them 961
The *prince* of darkness grim 12
The *Prince* of life they slay 1255
Thou *Prince* of life, arise 1449
Thou *Prince* of Peace, thou King 1366

PRINCES

For they the church's *princes* are 1859
Princes, who with Jesus dwell 275

PRINCIPALITIES

Principalities and powers 295

PRISON

When from this earthly *prison* 1243

PRISONER

The *prisoner* leaps to lose his chains 1008

PRISONS

And *prisons* would palaces prove 795

PRIVILEGE

No *privilege* so dear shall be 1237
What a *privilege* to carry 2210

PRIZE

As thou our *Prize* wilt be 965, 1019
Backward never looking till the *prize* 1680
I *prize* her heavenly ways 859
Lord, be mine this *prize* to win 1612
Onward to the *prize* before us 1731
Prize at the end 1656
Till the *prize* of God be won 1049
While others fought to win the *prize* 87

PROBLEMS

The *problems* of life will vanish 1950
When perplexing *problems* press 1210

PROCEED

O let us still *proceed* 97

PROCESSION

The brave *procession* of the spheres 46
We today's *procession* heading 62

PROCLAIM

Aloud *proclaim* his praise 361
And night to night *proclaim* 40
And there *proclaim*, my God, how 1437
Gladly *proclaim* the message 1773
His mighty deeds *proclaim* 33
Now *proclaim* Messiah's birth 103
One God of all *proclaim* 1328

Proclaim his sovereign power 148
Proclaim his wondrous works 533
Proclaim the day is near 2075
Proclaim the good Physician's 471
Proclaim the gospel tidings 1945
Proclaim the holy birth 1426
Proclaim this gospel grace 2155
Proclaim to a desolate people 1998
Proclaim to all his gracious Word 1469
Proclaim to every people, tongue 1551
Thou dost thy Lord *proclaim* 1705
Thus shall we best *proclaim* 1739

PROCLAIMED

The indwelling God *proclaimed* of old 591

PROCLAIMING

And all alike *proclaiming* 2072

PROCLAIMS

Proclaims from heaven the message 9, 706

PROCLAMATION

How sweet to hear the blessed *proclamation* 1808
Let the glorious *proclamation* 280

PRODIGAL

When the *prodigal* looks back 2260

PRODIGALS

Prodigals, confessing all 442

PROFESS

And then *profess* thy love 1142

PROFFERS

His coming *proffers* full salvation 1896

PROFIT

No *profit* canst thou gain 365
Their *profit* and their joy 1869
Yet is their *profit* small 19

PROLONG

Prolong for him your cheerful 328
Still *prolong* the brief, bright hour 727

PROMISE

And *promise,* in this sacred hour 329
Because thy *promise* I believe 1046
Claiming his *promise* to those who seek 2148
Every *promise* that you claim 2268
For the *promise* ever sure 1799
Fully trusting in thy precious *promise* 977
His *promise* ever standeth sure 1621
Just to rest upon his *promise* 2092
Leaning on thy *promise,* I go 214
Let this *promise* ring within thee 1642
Let this *promise* still be cherished 1642
Lo, the *promise* of a shower 1695
Never shall his *promise* fail 1626
Now we thy parting *promise* claim 764
O Father, who dost *promise* still 374
On his *promise,* we depend 480
Promise and command combining 754
Promise divine that never shall 2152
Resting on his *promise* 1787
Standing firmly on his *promise* God 2159
Still the *promise* lives unbroken 1096
That every *promise* is fulfilled 839
The *promise* of that faithful word 494
There's a *promise* that is sure and true 169
This is the *promise* of love 1981
Thy *promise* is for me 1003
Thy *promise* is fulfilled, and he 2189
Thy *promise* is my only plea 109
To see the *promise* of the day 720
Trusting, ever trusting, every *promise* 1264
Trusting the *promise,* "I will not 1808
We have Christ's own *promise* 1586
Whose *promise* shone with cheering 1632
With the bright *promise* of the glad 1352

PROMISED

A morning *promised* long 1
And, Jesus, I have *promised* 1408
Finding as he *promised,* perfect peace 1091
For he has kindly *promised* 860
He *promised* here to guide us 1535
He *promised* them he'd be, unseen 145
I *promised* her, before she died 2237
O Jesus, thou hast *promised* 1408
Perfect rest to me is *promised* 66
Promised for you and for me 1743
The Lord has *promised* good to me 88
The Savior *promised* long 674
This he has *promised* in his word 823
Thou has *promised* to receive us 1683
When will the *promise*d light arise 1026
Yet he has *promised* to be near 876

PROMISES

A thousand *promises* declare 2071
All his *promises* are true 480
All the *promises* do prevail 1554
And thy rich *promises* 868
His *promises* are sure 133, 1896
His *promises* like buds unfold 1640
I'm standing on the *promises* 1790
In the *promises* given his people 553
Promises in sorrow made 753
Thy *promises,* how firm they be 1065
Trusting his *promises,* now I am blest 1678
Whose *promises* prevail 853
Wonderful *promises,* meeting my need 2314

PROMISE-STRAIN

For once again the *promise-strain* 21

PROMISETH

God his help e'er *promiseth* 175

PROMPT

Holy Spirit, *prompt* us when 757
Prompt me now to do thy will 1761
Prompt to obey 1128

PROOF
Proof you are seeking 2337

PROOFS
Proofs of thine infinite kindness 713

PROPHECIES
For manhood's fuller *prophecies* 1779

PROPHECY
Prophecy will pass away 1192
The *prophecy* sublime 2074
There speaks the steadfast *prophecy* 46

PROPHESIED
Prophesied in days of old 290

PROPHET
Great *prophet* of my God 1035
The *prophet* gave the sign 1632

PROPHET-HOST
And the *prophet-host* in chorus 1213

PROPHETS
By holy *prophets* seen 197
By *prophets* long foretold 138
For our *prophets* and apostles 1280
Long by the *prophets* of Israel 660
Of *prophets* true and heroes 2179
Prophets and kings desired it 768
Prophets burning with his word 1071
Prophets have proclaimed it 501
Prophets swell the glad refrain 746
Thy *prophets* who have shown 191, 1445

PROSPECT
And the *prospect* dark appears 1775
The *prospect* doth my strength renew 861

PROSPECTS
Sweet *prospects,* sweet birds 795

PROSPER
And *prosper* in his reign 1454
Thou shalt see Jerusalem *prosper* 238

PROSTRATE
Behold, I *prostrate* fall 1230
Let angels *prostrate* fall 47

PROTECT
And *protect* us all 451
Both now, and ever, Lord, *protect* 1441
He will *protect,* defend 1331
Protect our homes, renew our 1884
Protect them by thy guarding hand 81
Protect them whereso'er they go 81, 418
Protect us by thy might 1225
Thou wilt *protect* us from danger 713

PROTECTED
And God the Lord *protected* still 2179
Protected by God's hand 431
Protected by his power 914

PROTECTION
Abide with thy *protection* 26
By his *protection* surrounded 1617
Our true *protection* find 45

PROVE
And *prove* the Savior friend 471
And *prove* thy good and perfect will 499
And who can *prove* a foe 1064
Believing where we cannot *prove* 1797
But we never can *prove* the delights 2266
Here may we *prove* the power 1032
I'll *prove* my faith in him 954
Then let us *prove* our heavenly birth 199
Thus may all our Sabbaths *prove* 1676
What best for each will *prove* 365
Would you *prove* him true in 2324

PROVED
How I've *proved* him o'er and o'er 2092

PROVIDE
All you may need he will *provide* 168
And *provide* a robe and crown 1711
Day by day *provide* us food 127
For all the meek thou will *provide* 72
For thee he will *provide* 885
God, our Maker, doth *provide* 359
I will abundantly *provide* 114

PROVIDED
Thus *provided,* pardoned 1058

PROVIDENCE
For thy *providence* that governs 1214
His *providence* hath brought us 1733
One *providence* alike they share 1446
That more and more a *providence* 39
Thy *providence* protected them 1448
Thy *providence* turns all to good 856
Whose *providence* is our defence 6

PROVIDES
Jesus *provides* a perfect salvation 504
Jesus *provides* a rest 2317

PROVOKE
Nor dare *provoke* his rod 337

PROVOKED
And *provoked* thee to thy face 554
Long *provoked* him to his face 395

PRUNING-HOOKS
To *pruning-hooks* their spears 198

PSALM
Sweet the *psalm* and sweet the carol 1182
Till *psalm* and song his name 1131

PSALMS

And sings the same sweet *psalms* 33
And the same sweet *psalms* we sing 1196

PUBLISH

And *publish* abroad his wonderful 2330
And *publish* thy praises abroad 2194
Publish glad tidings, tidings of 1551
Publish now salvation's story 542
We *publish* the Savior o'er mountain 1926

PUBLISHES

And *publishes* to every land 1932

PULSE

Pulse of waters, blithely beating 104
That every throbbing *pulse* of mine 23
Yea, while a breath, a *pulse* remains 30

PULSES

All the *pulses* of the world 62
Through all its *pulses* move 1778

PUNISH

Mine to *punish* or reward 738

PURE

O God, the *pure* alone 2273
Pure and free from sin's alloy 129
Pure and spotless let us be 1190
Pure I am not 1582

PURENESS

To manly *pureness,* manly 546

PURGE

And *purge* our hearts like sacrificial 1776
And *purge* the soul from sense and sin 194
Come, *purge* away the dross of sin 1401
Or *purge* with fire, if that must be 1582
Purge me from every sin 1774
Purge me from sin, O Lord 1219
Purge our pride and our vainglory 579
Purge out the shame 189
Purge thou each heart of secret sin 1385
Purge thou my sin away 1276
Purge us from lusts 1072
Purge us of low desire 1943
Purge your hearts of sin 1063
Them *purge* away shalt thou 1631

PURGED

When he had *purged* our stains 1653

PURIFIED

Purified by grace within 233
There forever *purified* 359

PURIFY

And *purify* the heart 2023

PURIFYING

The *purifying* will be all complete 1274

PURITY

For spotless *purity* 135
If 'tis for *purity* now that you sigh 905
Let *purity* awake 247
Where *purity* shall conquer sin 1412

PURPOSE

God's present *purpose* to fulfil 1593
Hath risen *with* purpose fell 19
His *purpose* must be done 1156
In the high *purpose* be strong 1098
That one redemptive *purpose* through 309
The *purpose* of his heart 2050
The unfailing *purpose* of our noblest 2198
Through whose deep *purpose* stranger 593
Thy holy, happy *purpose* 258
Thy *purpose* for thy world 1492
Thy *purpose* throbs in pulses 422
Thy *purpose* with a glad and holy 285
Thy servant's *purpose* ratify 2050
Thy wise, eternal *purpose* ran 67
To see thy mighty *purpose* 944
Whose *purpose* binds the starry 2028

PURSUE

And steadfastly *pursue* the way 2028
How long, unwise, will ye *pursue* 279
O Savior meek, *pursue* thy road 1660
Pursue it earnestly 1321
Pursue thine onward way 1911
We sweetly then *pursue* 1259

PURSUED

For me, who him to death *pursued* 94

PUSH

God, I can *push* the grass 1358

PUT

And those who *put* their trust 2023
And we *put* to flight 2180
He *put* within my heart 833
I shall *put* on glory then 810
Nor will he *put* my soul to shame 914
Put on the gospel armor 1786
Put your trust alone in Jesus 1076
These I *put* off and ponder 1291
Thou *hast* put all beneath 775
Thou hast *put* gladness in my heart 844

Q

QUARREL

Let the long *quarrel* cease 1768

QUEEN

And one was a *queen* 875

QUELL

And *quell* the sinner's pride 198
Quell the forces of temptation 470

QUELLS

And *quells* our rising fears 787

QUENCH

And *quench* the kindling fire 889
He'll never *quench* the smoking flax 2305

QUEST

Ne'er this searching *quest* allaying 51

QUESTION

And the *question* of his goodness 1957
But the *question* comes to me 805
I *question* not thy way, O Lord 1413
Nor any *question* ask 1382
Question not that God will use thee 296

QUESTIONS

Faith believes, nor *questions* how 77

QUICKEN

O do thou *quicken* us 2131
Quicken our spirits as we wait 422
Quicken the smouldering embers 1659

QUICKENS

And *quickens* all my slumbering 1233

QUIET

And a *quiet* in the air 1993
The *quiet* of a steadfast faith 1340

QUIETNESS

Blessed *quietness,* holy 1041
In *quietness* we come to ask 389

QUIT

"*Quit* these haunts of riot 939
Quit you like men, be strong 1081, 1997
Will ye *quit* the painful 1560

R

RACE

A heavenly *race* demands thy zeal 154
Even those that be of Israel's *race* 1898
God calls to every *race* 2100
Have I my *race* begun 154
My *race* is nearly run 1247
No alien *race,* no foreign shore 419
One *race* of ancient fame 2134
The *race* is not unto the swift 2226
Then shall the *race* of men confess 1061
To judge the human *race* 2037
Whate'er your *race* may be 919
When my *race* on earth is run 1710
When the *race* of life is run 2253
When, weary in the Christian *race* 1517
Who hath our *race* befriended 43
Ye children of the chosen *race* 72
Ye chosen seed of Israel's *race* 47

RACES

Here may all *races* mingle together 601
In Christ all *races* meet 284
O could my lifeblood as it *races* 23
Races and peoples, lo! we stand 438

RADIANCE

A *radiance* from the Cross afar 1962
But O, how fair the *radiance* bright 137
Into the *radiance* of the Savior's Cross 334
Let thy *radiance* on us shine 416
The *radiance* of those mansions bright 137
Through us thy *radiance* pour 191, 1445
Thy guiding *radiance* above us shall 110
To thy *radiance* we would flee 1084

RADIANCY

Come, the soul's true *radiancy* 341
What *radiancy* of glory 961

RADIATES

And *radiates* its deathless hope 309

RAGE

And calm amid its *rage* didst sleep 418
His *rage* we can endure 12

RAIMENT

And *raiment* fit provide 1364
But in *raiment* worn with travel 2254

RAIN

After the *rain* the sun 539
And *rain* and dew gave kindly drink 11
But the *rain* has only made 1270
For the *rain* and dew 409
Like a *rain* that falls from heaven 1041
Like *rain* on mown grass he shall 1454
The former and the latter *rain* 1146

RAINBOW

There's a *rainbow* 'round the throne 169

RAINS

And the *rains* of woe beat 1957

RAISE

Aloft your voices *raise* 50
And *raise* my head, and cheer 1519
And *raise* on high the victory song 2197
And *raise* that faithful servant's head 2331
And *raise* thy glorious throne 321
And *raise* to Christ our joyful strain 328
And *raise* up them that fall 244
And we to thee will ever *raise* 1037
But *raise* it to a flame 2305
Ever confessing thee, I will *raise* 1656
For thee this song of thanks I'd *raise* 23
He can *raise* the poor to stand 665
Here I *raise* my Ebenezer 340
High *raise* the note, that Jesus died 733
I *raise* the hymn to thee 1851
If thou our hearts wilt *raise* 33
Lord of all, to thee we *raise* 484
May *raise* the victor's strain 1854
Raise high your free, exulting song 1654
Raise, raise the song on high 2215
Raise the anthem manifold 1071
Raise the fallen, cheer the faint 994
Raise the glad strain 2333
Raise the song of harvest home 359
Raise the standard high 1769
Raise the stone, and
thou shalt find me 2006, 2017

Raise thy work and life anew 294
Raise your joys and triumph high 289
Raise your loudest, loftiest strains 669
Shall we not gladly *raise* the cry 2218
They best will *raise* their people 1453
To God, the Holy Ghost, we *raise* 2220
We *raise* it high, we send it 2164
We *raise* our songs of gratitude 1779
While we *raise* our hearts in love 105

RAISED

And hath *raise* up a mighty salvation 215
And *raised* the name of Jesus far 2334
Ere he *raised* the lofty mountains 356
He hath *raised* our human nature 1697
Raised from the dead and set on high 1670
That *raised* the dead to life and light 206
Thence *raised* from death we live 2090
Till soon it *raised* its head 11

RAISETH

The cast-down *raiseth* up 628

RALLY

Rally round the banner 1769
Up, it is Jehovah's *rally* 2157
We may *rally* to the fight 470

RANG

Rang out the angel chorus 551

RANGE

Still his words before us *range* 64

RANGED

Ranged in a quiet place we see 2182

RANK

High is the *rank* we now possess 194
Rank on rank the host of heaven 1060

RANKS

For our *ranks* are tried and true 2064
In crowding *ranks* on every side 1666
In our *ranks* you move united 62
In serried *ranks,* with fearless tread 1412
On and on the compact *ranks* 62
While her *ranks* are torn 1069

RANSOM

An everlasting *ransom* paid 1024
And *ransom* captive Israel 1336
He the *ransom* freely gave 894
Since only he could *ransom* us 206
That for our *ransom* bled 91
The *ransom* has been paid 965
The *ransom* pay that sets me free 1534
To him who for my *ransom* died 1241
To *ransom* me, the Son of God was willing 139
Your *ransom* and peace 73

RANSOMED

All his *ransomed* home to bring 1203
And sing with the *ransomed* the song 18
And the *ransomed* of every nation 699
But none of the *ransomed* ever knew 1983
But *ransomed* by Immanuel's blood 1137
Let none whom he hath *ransomed* 1551
Let the *ransomed* thus rejoice 1837
Ransomed, healed, restored 1618
That thou might'st *ransomed* be 827
The *ransomed* hosts surround 49
The *ransomed* own him 1703
When all the *ransomed* are gathered 167
When *ransomed* from the grave 1315
When with the *ransomed* in glory 881
Ye *ransomed* from the fall 47

RAPT

Rapt awhile from earth away 1085

RAPTURE

For the *rapture* which flows 1115
I sing in my *rapture,* Oh, glory to God 24
O the soul-thrilling *rapture* 2246
This my *rapture,* this my glory 1688
What *rapture* will it be 1234
What will our *rapture* be 1464
When with *rapture* I behold him 424

RAVISHED

Ravished from our wistful eyes 655

RAY

A *ray* of light divine is shed 654
And oft his mercy's *ray,* our dark 2104
And the broad sun's retiring *ray* 793
And with a pure and heavenly *ray* 1348
Like the sun's reviving *ray* 966, 1012
May its departing *ray* 861
Of wisdom's widening *ray* 191, 1445
When every *ray* of light had fled 2316

RAYS

A thousand *rays* of light 2085
As *rays* of light from yonder sun 1571
His golden *rays* are banished 1297
Slowly the *rays* of daylight 1927
When the sun's last *rays* are 429
With healing *rays* it gleams 309
With the early morning *rays* 1012

REACH

And *reach* my heavenly home 1421
And *reach* the goal 930
And we only *reach* that shore by 1991
Before we *reach* the heavenly fields 351
Can *reach* the heights 150
Ere we *reach* the shining river 1711
I shall *reach* the land of day 1682
I'll *reach* my port at last 2234
If it would *reach* a monarch's throne 1202
If you would *reach* the highest 2338
Lord, till I *reach* yon blissful shore 1237
May I but safely *reach* my home 2231
May I *reach* heaven's joys 177
Nothing then can *reach* me 431

O may I *reach* the happy place 1308
Soon we'll *reach* the shining river 1711
That when I *reach* the margin 737
The nearer I *reach* the banks 1913
The nearer I *reach* the end of time 1913
The nearer I *reach* the Fount of Love 1913
The nearer I *reach* the morning land 1913
They cannot *reach* the mystery 1458
They *reach* thy throne, encompass 2193
Thou didst *reach* forth thy hand 879
Through Jesus I shall safely *reach* 834
Till I *reach* the golden strand 986
Till I *reach* the vale of Jordan 863
Till I shall *reach* the realm 2234
Till we *reach* our home above 450, 756
Until it *reach* the shining sun 23
Until we *reach* that better land 1429
We *reach* the rest remaining 1341
We shall *reach* that lovely aiden 1991
When I *reach* my home 1500
When I *reach* that blissful shore 2043
When shall I *reach* that happy 1563
When they *reach* the land of strangers 1775
When we *reach* the glory land 2212
Yet they *reach* the home of 2004

REACHED

It *reached* this heart of mine 841
That when I've *reached* the great 1152

REACHES

That high it *reaches,* as deep 1840

READ

And *read* thee everywhere 1960
But thou canst *read* it there 2223
Gladly, I *read,* "whosoever may come 807
Have you *read* how in anguish he cried 696
Have you *read* how the dying thief 696
Have you *read* how they placed the crown 696
I can *read* his righteous sentence 1215
I *read* my duty in thy word 1226
I *read* my duty in thy word 1224
I *read* the wondrous story 1475
That I may *read,* with childlike eyes 797
The Bible they have never *read* 2245
We *read* our duty, day by day 300
We *read* thee best in him 1461
We *read* thee in the earth below 1461
We *read* thee in the flowers 1461
We *read* thee in the sky above 1461
We *read* thy name in fairer lines 1871
We *read* thy power to bless 1461
We'll *read* the meaning of our tears 1282

READING

They're *reading* it thro' and thro' 2281

READY

Be thou *ready* to receive it 175
Sick and helpless and *ready* to die 1983

REAFFIRM

We now *reaffirm* our undying 1372

REALM

Down in the *realm* of darkness 283
His *realm* is of the spirit 510
His *realm* shall spread like fire 377
Were the whole *realm* of nature mine 2236

REALMS

But press to *realms* on high 4
From celestial *realms* descending 217
Realms of heaven he forsook 290
The *realms* beheld his glory 1889
Thy *realms* shall last, thine own 1666
Where thou wilt in *realms* supernal 1516

REAP

And he shall *reap* the harvest 817
Reap life through the ages 1770
That we may *reap* contentment 712
Then *reap,* with toil and pain 1285
To *reap* thy harvest here below 686
We *reap* it on mountain 1298
You'll *reap* whatsoever you sow 1770

REAPED

Are *reaped* by the brave 1298
Since they *reaped* the golden ear 2299

REAPERS

But *reapers* are few, and the work 1540
But the *reapers* still are few 1783
Joyous, as when the *reapers* bear 1917
"More *reapers* for white harvest 1496
Reapers are few and the night 705
Where are the *reapers* 1540

REAPS

And *reaps,* from years of strife 1285
And *reaps* the fruit of all 1704

REARED

Reared at thine own command 1529

REASCENDS

Reascends his native heaven 655

REASON

And this is the *reason,* I walk 931
And this is the *reason* I'm pardoned 122
Let *reason* reign and right 2100

REASONS

Not for us to find the *reasons* 36

REBEL

For such as did *rebel* 2031
Rebel, ye waves, and o'er the land 1900

REBELS

Rebels he receives as friends 991
To bring us *rebels* back to God 1460

REBORN

Tells us that we, in thee, have been *reborn* 29

REBUILD

Rebuild her walls again 1497

RECALL

Could I but *recall* them now 1222
Let all *recall* hymns of gladness 770
We *recall* our Father's promise 2256

RECEIVE

All *receive* the grace atoning 339
"Almost persuaded," Christ to *receive* 85
Come and *receive* the blessing 2280
Faithful, approved, shall *receive* 1758
"For I will *receive* them 2245
Jesus will now *receive* you 2280
Just as I am thou wilt *receive* 1046
Just to bow and *receive* a new 1989
Lord, *receive* me, dying 937
May we in faith, *receive* thy word 393
O let me now *receive* that gift 444
O *receive* my soul at last 994
O *receive* whom God appointed 684
O when I *receive* it all shining 830
Receive and eat the living food" 2132
Receive in thine encampments 26
Receive it back unbought 241
Receive my latest sighing 98
Receive my thanks, O Lord 2035
Receive the homage of our souls 1090
That all whose souls the truth *receive* 83
There, dear Lord, we shall *receive* thee 42
There was none to *receive* him, none 1199
Thou shalt *receive* a blessing 1584
Thou shalt *receive* thy reward 1269
Thou sovereign God, *receive* 1899
Thou who didst *receive* the children 974
Thou wilt *receive* my soul 932
Will you *receive*, or his mercy reject 2
Ye all may *receive* 73

RECEIVED

Received on Calvary 113
Received our risen Lord 96
Thou hast *received* gifts for men 2031
Though the cloud from sight *received* him 77

RECEIVES

Into himself he all *receives* 146
Receives them, O so dearly 1535
When Jesus *receives* his own 953

RECEIVETH

"Christ *receiveth* sinful men 1735
On earth *receiveth* praise 28

RECKED

Recked they not of their own gain 485

RECLAIMED

Reclaimed from error's ways 278

RECLOTHE

Reclothe us in our rightful 386

RECONCILED

I through him am *reconciled* 2121
My God is *reconciled* 113
"O," be ye *reconciled* to God 799

RECORD

And while that wondrous *record* 1522
May I have a *record* whiter 1710
Our solemn vows *record* 15

RECREATION

God's *recreation* of the new day 1221

RECTITUDES

For truth's eternal *rectitudes* 1779

RED

Though they be *red* like crimson 2058

REDEEM

He will *redeem* and make whole 1331
Redeem me from distress 2244
Redeem the evil time 1576
Redeem the time, its hours too swiftly 322
Who doth *redeem* thy life, that thou 1513

REDEEMED

Christ hath *redeemed* us once for all 504
Hath *redeemed* us by his blood 77
He has *redeemed* me and I am 2136
He that *redeemed* my soul 1315
I am *redeemed*, but not with silver 1278
I am *redeemed*, set free, forgiven 2316
Redeemed and purchased with his 150
Redeemed and sanctified 150
Redeemed, and so happy in Jesus 1649
Redeemed at countless cost 278
Redeemed by grace divine 1027
Redeemed by him who bore 150
Redeemed by love, and though 13
Redeemed by the blood of 17
Redeemed by the blood of the Lamb 1649
Redeemed from earth and pain 1705
Redeemed through his infinite mercy 1649
Redeemed through thy mercy, made 1648
The Lord who *redeemed* us is coming 1926
Thou hast *redeemed* us by thy blood 1108
Thou hast *redeemed* us with thy blood 671
Till all whom he *redeemed* 33
To know he *redeemed* me 623
We, in thee *redeemed*, complete 1271
When *redeemed* by his side I shall 2246
Which none but thy *redeemed* 186
While those *redeemed* in ages 49

REDEEMER

Christ the world's *Redeemer* 1833

Earth's *Redeemer,* plead for me 77
For Christ is our *Redeemer* 763
Redeemer of the world 48
For such a *Redeemer* as mine 24
I am thy *Redeemer,* I will care 1808
Jesus, *Redeemer,* we look to thee 2004
My gracious *Redeemer,* my Savior 1246
My *Redeemer* is the light 913
O blessed *Redeemer,* all honor to thee 1855
Redeemer come, I open wide 1082
Redeemer of the world art thou 965
The great *Redeemer* lay 237
Thou *Redeemer* art to me 997
Thus my dear *Redeemer* meet 1222
To our *Redeemer* God 1105
To thee, *Redeemer,* now we cry 1859

REDEEMING

And with thy truth *redeeming* 26
But thou art the *redeeming* God 1440

REDEEMS

Redeems when oppressed 1894
Who *redeems* thee from destruction 1472

REDEMPTION

And *redemption* for all who believe 1115
But in *redemption,* O what grace 155
By thy grand *redemption* 2287
Now *redemption,* long expected 1106
O perfect *redemption,* the purchase 2102
Our full *redemption* won 283
Redemption also plenteous 1129
Redemption by his death I find 575
Redemption through his blood 241
That wonderful *redemption* 1830
There is plentiful *redemption* 1767
Thou for our *redemption* 1680

RE-ECHO

Re-echo through your starry 1725

RE-ECHOES

Re-echoes the praise of the Lord 1512

REED

The bruised *reed* he never breaks 2305
The bruised *reed* he will not break 848
The bruised *reed* thou didst not break 785
The bruised *reed* thou wilt not break 240

REFINE

The dross consume, the gold *refine* 686

REFINES

Refines our dross, and love divine 2090

REFLECT

Here *reflect* the bright and 399

REFRAIN

A glad and a joyous *refrain* 1958
Then list to the note of this solemn *refrain* 18

REFRESH

Now *refresh* the drooping heart 756
O *refresh* us, O refresh us 1125
Refresh and bless thy chosen 1716
Refresh thy people on their toilsome 585

REFRESHED

And hast *refreshed* me whilst I slept 545, 152
And when thou hast *refreshed* 2069

REFRESHMENT

And sweet *refreshment* find 777
Sweet *refreshment* here below 342

REFUGE

A *refuge* still, for all oppressed 1595
A *refuge* strong for all oppressed 1435
A *refuge* will he be for them 1887, 1888
And all the *refuge* of his grace 564
Be our *Refuge* and our Light 1603
Be thou her *Refuge,* and her Trust 1185
Doth *refuge* take in thee 166
Far from *refuge,* shelter, home 1837
For *refuge* from my cruel foe 2244
For *refuge* I will stay 166
For thou hast for my *refuge* been 1357
God also will a *refuge* be 1887, 1888
God is our *refuge* high 1258
"He is my *refuge* and my stay 1908
Jesus, my heart's dear *refuge* 1675
May such a blissful *refuge* be 132
My only *refuge* let me make 195
My *refuge* is the living God 932
My *refuge* sure, whate'er betide 1376
My sure and certain *refuge* 872
Other *refuge* have I none 994
Our *refuge* be 586
Precious Savior, still our *refuge* 2210
Refuge from danger 1656
Refuge thou and faithful Friend 2224
The sinner's *refuge* here below 2192
Thou the *refuge* of my soul 1682
To you who for *refuge* to Jesus 776

REFUSE

For, should I *refuse* to sing 1814
If you *refuse* him, O what will 569
Let those *refuse* to sing 351
Nor *refuse* thee blessing on thy 296
Shall we again *refuse* thee 1124
Will he *refuse* us a home 2000
Will ye still *refuse* to live 1736

REFUSED

Calmly he *refused* to win 268
Thy Lord *refused* not e'en to die 1823

REFUSES

Our blessed Lord *refuses* none 1343

REGALE

Now doth he *regale* in this 2041

REGARD

He shall *regard* and lend 2045
If, in my heart, I sin *regard* 50
Regard my prayer and hear 1395
When I *regard* the wondrous heavens 1450

REGARDED

That Christ has *regarded* my helpless 2249

REGARDEST

Can it be that thou *regardest* 101

REGARDS

He *regards* you from above 1099

REGIONS

Earth's remotest *regions* shall his 286
The *regions* in darkness its beauty 1855
Through earth's remotest *regions* 360
Till, past the cloudy *regions* here 685

REGRET

What *regret* must then be mine 1710

REGRETTING

Look not back, the past *regretting* 36

REIGN

Alleluia, the Crucified shall *reign* 160
And deathless it shall *reign* 1202
And let him *reign* within this place 114
And *reign* together in the sky 1432
And we shall *reign* with thee 671
And with Jesus *reign* forever 1044
Behind the *reign* of law, the love 2104
Blest *reign* of love and liberty 1443
Come and *reign*, and reign forever 227
Come now and *reign* within 1609
Come, O Christ, and *reign* among us 1760
Death, sin and hell no longer *reign* 49
"Doth the Lord now *reign* in me? 51
Everlasting is thy *reign* 746
For e'en now the *reign* of heaven 36
God omnipotent shall *reign* 676
He forever more shall *reign* 282
He shall *reign* from pole to pole 676
He shall *reign* when, like a scroll 676
He will *reign* through endless day 2342
His *reign* no end shall know 1917
His *reign* shall know no end 376
I shall *reign* with him on high 2002
May we ever *reign* with thee 1125
Now they *reign* in heavenly glory 677
O may thy gentle *reign* increase 87
Reign of love and light 501
Reign over me, Lord Jesus 920
Reign, reign without rival 719
Reign supreme, and reign alone 745
Reign thou my soul within 1645
Reign within my heart, O Father 461
Sure I must fight if I would *reign* 87
That we with him may *reign* 5
The Lord shall *reign* forevermore 1394
The Lord shall *reign* victoriously 1078
The *reign* of Christ bring in 1401
The *reign* of night is ended 770
They *reign* with him above 1869
Thy long *reign* is o'er 1599
Where is thy *reign* of peace 2073

REIGNEST

High in the heavenly Zion, thou *reignest* 1378
Reignest evermore in might 951

REIGNETH

Jesus, Savior, *reigneth* forever 1616
That the Lord who *reigneth* 2208

REIGNING

But now he is *reigning* forever 1229
Reigning where he was before 356

REIGNS

And now he *reigns* upon his throne 498
And *reigns* in glory there 1061
And *reigns* in heaven above 2179
And *reigns* in his eternal youth 377
God who *reigns* on heaven's high steep 610
He *reigns* and triumphs from the Tree 1921
He *reigns* and triumphs here 768
He *reigns* our King 1366
He *reigns* supreme 1882
He *reigns* with absolute control 1872
He *reigns!* ye saints exalt 1893
Jesus *reigns*, adored by angels 1697
Jesus *reigns* and heav'n rejoices 673
Jesus *reigns*, the God of love 673
Jesus, the Savior, *reigns* 1653
The Lord Jehovah *reigns* 148
Thy boundless power in all things *reigns* 43
Where Jesus *reigns* alone 1350
Where Jesus *reigns* in glory 1988
Who *reigns* and shall forever 328
Who *reigns* in light above 2151
Wide as he *reigns* his name be 1307

REINFORCEMENTS

Reinforcements now appearing 736

REINSPIRE

Reinspire me now 1000

REJECT

Can you *reject* such matchless 957
Do not *reject* the mercy 1584
I could not such a Friend *reject* 482
Just now, *reject* him no more 905
Nor *reject* the gracious call 1866
O do not *reject* him tonight 1542

REJECTED

By thine own *rejected* 35
Rejected and despised of men 426
Rejected, scorned, yet victor 510
Though *rejected* and denied 1109

REJECTEST

And thou *rejectest* none 240, 1428

REJOICE

And all *rejoice* with Christian heart 2197
And in my God *rejoice* 1700
Again we *rejoice* in the world 423
And do *rejoice* the heart 618
And in thee I will ever *rejoice* 1512
Believing, we *rejoice* to see 1279
Bidding *rejoice*, all in Jesus 1737
But we *rejoice* and sing to thee 2149
Can I enough *rejoice* 303
Come ye before him and *rejoice* 57
I cannot but *rejoice* 1759
I *rejoice* to know it's mine 25
In him *rejoice* in heart and voice 6
Let us all *rejoice* in thee 1181
Rejoice, all ye angels in chorus 1617
"*Rejoice*, for the Lord brings back 1983
Rejoice, give thanks and sing 1654
"*Rejoice*, I have found my sheep!" 1983
Rejoice, in glorious hope 1653
Rejoice in God's glad messengers 1652
Rejoice, O people, in the days (years) to be 1652
Rejoice, O people, in this living 1652
Rejoice, rejoice, his church on earth 1652
Rejoice, rejoice, O Christian 874
Rejoice that seeks the Lord 533
Rejoice that while the sin of man 1652
Rejoice this Easter day 1083
Rejoice to die with thee 391
So *rejoice*, though Satan be 1838
So we *rejoice* shall all our days 541
Thou rising morn in praise *rejoice* 41
Through them *rejoice* the heavenly host 1859
Thus may I *rejoice* to show 1687
To praise him, *rejoice*, and adore 701
We *rejoice* in the light and we echo 1995
With heart and voice we all *rejoice* 21

REJOICES

And *rejoices* the hymns of his own 765
Everything *rejoices* in the mellow rays 1800
My soul *rejoices* to pursue 7
The church on earth *rejoices* 33

REJOICEST

Yea, we know that thou *rejoicest* 101

REJOICING

And great our *rejoicing* through 2102

REKINDLES

Rekindles in our hearts 2090

RELEASE

Jesus can from all *release* thee 1577
May struggling hearts that seek *release* 32
Release the fettered heart 1497
To the suffering *release* 2227
Waiting still for sweet *release* 755

RELEASED

Released from earthly toil and strife 590
Until, *released* from carnal ties 1480

RELEASES

He from them all *releases* 854

RELENT

Shall make him once *relent* 2290

RELIEF

A sure and safe *relief* 348

RELIGION

Religion bears our spirits up 1739
Thy true *religion* in our hearts increase 585

RELY

And on thyself *rely* 4
Thou on the Lord *rely* 365
Who in Jesus *rely* 73

REMAIN

Secure, unmoved, I shall *remain* 2238
There we shall with thee *remain* 655
We cannot at the shrine *remain* 32

REMAINETH

The city of God *remaineth* 19

REMAINS

That firm *remains* on high 685

REMEDY

God's *remedy* for sin 1830

REMEMBER

And *remember* them no more 2058
Dear Lord, *remember* me 1509
I must *remember* thee 30
I will *remember* thee 30
Just *remember* that dark lonely 1956
Lord, we would *remember* thee 1173
Remember all his wondrous works 533
Remember, child, your mother's prayer 870
Remember Christ our Savior was born 599
Remember I'm the sinner 1830
Remember, Lord, thy works of old 1369
Remember me Lord, with that love 532
Remember me, O Mighty One 2251
Remember not our sin's dark stain 1369
Remember not past years 1053
Remember thee in all thy pains 30
Remember them each one 533
Remember thou his love of old 1651
Remember whence the glory came 1608
Still I *remember* mother's prayer 870
Still *remember* they are thine 488
When I *remember* that Jesus 806
Yet will I *remember* thee 672

REMEMBERED

I shall be *remembered* in my home 1808

REMEMBERS
For he *remembers* we are dust 1798

REMISSION
And through none other is *remission* 506
For the *remission* of their sins 215

REMOLD
Remold them, make us like thee 110

REMOVE
From thee shall not *remove* 1475
Remove from us the love to kill 1508
This holy seed *remove* 83

REMOVES
Removes his blest abode 1111

REND
O *rend* the heavens, come quickly 1032
Rend each man's temple-veil 522
Rend thou our little temple veils 1916

RENDER
But shall we only *render* 2230
O my Lord, what shall I *render* 415
We *render* back the love 762
What can we *render,* Lord, to thee 503
What shall we *render* to our God 1525

RENDS
Rends thy heart, to him unknown 71

RENEW
And thus *renew* our vow 1324
He doth still my trust *renew* 53
Oh God, *renew* with heavenly dew 2289
Renew in us each day our lofty 1388
Renew it boldly every day 1256
Renew my will from day to day 1231
Renew your solemn vow 348

RENEWER
Divine *Renewer,* graciously renew 1863
Divine *Renewer,* thee I bless 1863

RENOUNCE
Renounce at once thy stubborn 1343
Renounce thy works and ways 1514

RENT
And *rent* by endless strife 1328

REPAY
But drops of grief can ne'er *repay* 38

REPEAT
And oft *repeat* before the throne 494
And softly they *repeat* his name 2309
Often *repeat* the story 1773
Repeat anew the story o'er again 148
Repeat his mercy in your song 535
Repeat the blessed story 853
Repeat the sounding joy 1039
Repeat the wondrous story 6
'Tis pleasant to *repeat* 862

REPEATS
Repeats thy feast again 204

REPENT
O Lord, I do *repent* 183
They who *repent* and believe 353

REPENTANCE
In true *repentance* bow 348

REPOSE
A calm and undisturbed *repose* 132
O may my soul on thee *repose* 59
Who, with thy sweet *repose* 1383

REPROACH
With us *reproach* to dare 278

REPROACHES
No pained *reproaches* gave he 497

REPROVE
Oh, why dost thou thus *reprove* 1763

REQUEST
Let my *request* accepted rise 1434

REQUIEM
Above the *requiem,* "Dust to dust" 1446

REQUIRE
This, only this, dost thou *require* 1367

RESCUE
And to the *rescue* came 1630
He to my *rescue* came 2060
He to *rescue* me from danger 340
You may *rescue,* you may save 255

RESCUED
Rescued from its galling chains 1073

RESCUES
Rescues them from all their fear 1837
Rescues us from all our foes 1618

RESERVE
With no *reserve* and no delay 1045

RESIDING
God with man is now *residing* 103

RESIDUE
Myself, my *residue* of days 1144
Our *residue* of days or hours 1733

RESIGN
Freely I *resign* all my will 222
Here, then, to thee I all *resign* 1018

RESIGNED
Obedient and *resigned* 797

RESOLVED
I am *resolved*, and who will go 804
I am *resolved* to enter the kingdom 804
I am *resolved* to follow the Savior 804
I am *resolved* to go to the Savior 804
Thee, only thee, *resolved* to know 499

RESORTS
For thither Christ himself *resorts* 1809

RESOUND
The vales and hills *resound* with gladness 148

RESOUNDEST
Alleluia! Thou *resoundest* 78

RESOUNDS
Hallelujah *resounds* in the church 765

RESOURCES
Thy *resources* none can measure 2224

RESPECT
And have *respect* to all thy ways 270

REST
A *rest* from every turmoil 1988
A *rest* upon the way 203
Ah, with what a *rest* of bliss 1195
An endless *rest* of joy belongs 374
And calmly, gladly *rest* each future hope 2213
And I am thine, I *rest* in thee 1881
And I will give you *rest* 75
And in thee only *rest* 782
And let us *rest* beneath thy feet 1537
And my *rest* a stone 1044
And one their heavenly *rest* 667
And *rest* comes nearer 1578
And *rest* delay to come 902
And *rest* in the light of his beautiful 1909
And *rest* is for the weary 2120
And *rest* on Calvary 30
And *rest* on the blissful shore 1208
And then, O then, thine everlasting *rest* 98
And we shall be with those that *rest* 5
At *rest* till it finds rest in thee 2033
Bidding us *rest*, for night 1852
Come, Savior, ere we go to *rest* 2048
Come to him and *rest* 1114
Do you *rest* each moment 693
Far from *rest*, and home and thee 280
For *rest* and food and loving care 468
For *rest* of night 935
For *rest* the night 605
For there, in the *rest* that remaineth 1098
Forever would I *rest* 1476
God *rest* you safe from harm 1309
Here find the *rest* of God's own peace 32
Here is *rest* and plenty 939
"I am thy *rest*." 680
I can *rest* when he is at my side 2057
I often am longing for *rest* 1922
I *rest* in thy protecting arm 1297
I *rest* me in the thought 2012
I *rest* my soul on Jesus 854
I *rest* my weary soul in thee 1465
I *rest* on his unchanging grace 1244
I *rest* upon thy word 1003
I shall *rest* by her side 1986
If we from self could *rest* 1431
Jesus is calling the weary to *rest* 985
Let us *rest* in quietness 451
Longing for *rest* everlasting 263
May I *rest* me by his side 1218
May we *rest* this day in thee 1676
May we *rest* till morning light 632
Must *rest* in faith alone 1020
My *rest* a stone 1265
My *rest* in toil, my ease 2034
No *rest* is to be found 1259
Now *rest* my long-divided heart 1392
O happy they in God who *rest* 1446
O *rest* at Jesus' feet 1578
O *rest* beside the weary road 948
O Sabbath *rest* by Galilee 386
O shame on us who *rest* content 1397
O ye who would enter that glorious *rest* 18
Perfect *rest* to me is promised 66
Rest and reign with him in heaven 992
Rest beneath the Almighty's shade 271
Rest comes at length 670
Rest comes sure and soon 2320
Rest for the soul, and strength 1130
Rest in sleep and silence 1672
Rest in those mansions above 2317
Rest not day nor night 101
Rest on us from above 1373
Rest upon the Father's promise 1270
Rest upon this congregation 743
Rest upon us from above 1209
Rest where none weep 1737
Rest which the weary know 311
Rest with thee in heaven 2062
Rest your cause upon his holy 1769
Safely *rest*, all is well 381
Safely they *rest*, who on thy 464
Securely I *rest* 931
That *rest* not day or night 33
The blessed *rest* from inbred sin 575
The *rest* and the homeland of souls 2271
The *rest*, O God, is in thy hand 211
There alone is *rest* 1264
There is *rest* for friend 943
There is *rest* for you today 2252
There is *rest* from care and labor 943
There is *rest*, sweet rest 943
There is tranquil *rest* when day is done 810
There's a *rest* for little children 1988
There's for you a wondrous *rest* 562
There's *rest* in the home of thy Father 1494
They *rest* within thy sheltering care 1446
Thine is the Buddhists' *rest* 522

"This is my *rest,* here still 2205
Thy *rest,* thy joy, thy glory share 1170
To die is endless *rest* 979
To *rest* awhile with thee 199
We will *rest* where the steps of Jesus 1815
When I shall *rest* at the close 2235
Where'er I *rest,* where'er I go 1438
Where *rest* but on thy faithful word 1369
While I *rest* upon thy word 717
Yes, I *rest* in thee, Beloved 978

RESTING

Resting in Jesus I'm safe 2136

RESTING-PLACE

What a quiet *resting-place* 1041
Whose forgotten *resting-place* 485

RESTLESS

Why *restless,* why cast down 125

RESTORE

I *restore* to thee thy own 1144
Dost light and life *restore* 86
Let God *restore* the wasted years 1821
Long withheld, we now *restore* them 753
Restore and defend me, for thou art 1512
Restore and quicken, soothe 2008
Restore it thou again 724
Restore us with thy mystic might 389
Tenderly did he *restore* 611
Till thou *restore* us, with the blest 374
When to the Lord we *restore* our 2241

RESTORED

I am *restored* into his favor 2096
Lost, until by thee *restored* 346
O thou, who hast our peace *restored* 43
Restored my soul, and set me 1194
Restored to life, and power 1273
The name of him whose death the fallen race *restored* 13

RESTORES

Restores me when wandering 1894
Restores my soul by waters clear 1907
Restores the lost, and binds 1319

RESTRAIN

Restrain me from wandering on 1583

RESTS

And my Savior *rests* beside me 942
And *rests* not now by day 1856
Who *rests* within his firmament 1593

RESURRECTION

And *resurrection* power 86
Christ, himself the *Resurrection* 664
With *resurrection* light 1083

RESURRECTION-LIGHT

Still more in *resurrection-light* 1461

RETAINETH

And, since the Lord *retaineth* 2230

RETREAT

A safe *retreat,* where weary souls 1435
There is a calm, a sure *retreat* 511

RETURN

And let him *return* unto the Lord 2155
Brothers, this Lord Jesus shall *return* again 143
But let them not *return* to foolishness 909
O *return* while the Spirit in mercy 565
O *return* ye unto God 2058
Return, do not delay 158
Return now unto thine 2131
Return, O holy Dove, return 1347
Return, O Lord, in pity 1497
Return, thou weary wanderer 158
Return, ye ransomed sinners, home 241
Soon the Savior will *return* 1667
Suddenly *return,* and never 1190
They shall *return,* Christ, when thou 1737

RETURNS

For he *returns* to reign 160
Lo, he *returns,* our glorious head 1883

REUNION

Beyond the sunset, O glad *reunion* 207

REVEAL

And *reveal* thyself still clearer 563
But O, thyself *reveal* 1031
Now *reveal* his great salvation 339
Reveal the righteousness of God 1401
Reveal the things of God 1777
Reveal thy radiance through us 1359
Reveal thy secret way of visiting 2273
Reveal to us the Savior 149
Thyself in us *reveal* 515
To us *reveal* our emptiness 1776
Unto me *reveal* thy face 222

REVEALED

Revealed and ruled by thee 199
Shining *revealed* through every task 2200
Thou hast not yet *revealed* thy 387
Thou hast *revealed* thy will to mortal 1368

REVEALING

Divine and human, in his deep *revealing* 2200
Thy wondrous love *revealing* 29

REVEALS

Everything *reveals* God's goodness 1957

REVELATION

Thyself the *revelation* 1481

REVELS

The soldiers' *revels* in the midst of 37

REVERBERATIONS

In long *reverberations* reach 37

REVERE

Revere his great and holy name 958
That I no more *revere* his name 967

REVERENCE

And *reverence* his commands 1485
But more of *reverence* in us 1797
Here in loving *reverence* bow 1126
In deeper *reverence,* praise 386
In *reverence* he himself would 2050
With *reverence* and with fear 1171
With *reverence* crown the earnest 1526

REVIVE

And us again *revive* 587
Revive my soul and bless 2244
Revive our drooping faith 315
Revive our longing eyes 2073
Revive us again, fill each heart 2187

REVIVED

Revived my soul with grace 2223

REVIVES

Revives my heart, and checks 2117
Who *revives* my fainting heart 131

REWARD

A great *reward* provided is 618
A heavenly *reward* 26
And lo! we see the vast *reward* 97
Between our sins and their *reward* 99
Boundless is the pledged *reward* 1748
Give virtue's rich *reward* 311
God himself is thy *reward* 1748
Rich *reward* he offers free 679
This shall then be your *reward* 942
To a rich *reward* by his wondrous 941
What the high *reward* I win 131

RIBBED

Ribbed with the steel that time 2198

RICH

Both *rich* and poor, the bond 1898
Passing by the *rich* and great 665
The *rich* and poor, the great 1962
The *rich* may bring their wealth 1947

RICHES

And through the *riches* of his grace 150
Feasting on the *riches* of his grace 2002
For the *riches* of his grace 1837
For the *riches* we inherit 597
Its *riches* are unsearchable 1458
No *riches* of earth could have saved 1278
Not the *riches* safe and palling 62
Riches I heed not, nor man's 177
Riches in glory all his own 1216
Through the *riches* of Christ 111

RICHNESS

And the *richness* of thy grace 2019
Nor in thy *richness* stay 1911

RIDE

Ride forth, O conquering King 1945
Ride on in triumph 405
Ride on, ride on in triumph 48
Ride on till tyranny and greed 1507
Ride triumphant all around the 1073

RIDGES

Its *ridges* down dost press 410

RIGHT

And for the everlasting *right* 2075
And he will *right* the wrong 1998
And *right* the day must win 617, 2321
And *right* thy sceptre shall 2312
Battling for the *right* 1769
For his by *right* you are 348
For *right* is right, since God is God 617, 2321
For the *right* unflinching 1205
How long, how long, O God of *right* 1440
Of the *right* against the wrong 507
Right be her might 601
The *right* and wrong engage 1860
The *right* is marching on 507
Thine too by *right,* and ours 1146
With *right* he shall thy people 1454

RIGHTEOUS

But the *righteous* ever flourish 1066
For *righteous* is the Lord 1261
The Lord the *righteous* proves 1261
What can the *righteous* do 1261
Ye *righteous,* in the Lord rejoice 1889

RIGHTEOUSNESS

And all his *righteousness* fulfil 2161
And his untainted *righteousness* 1638
And in thy *righteousness* shall they 1390
And *righteousness* in fountains 661
And *righteousness* looks down 909
And *righteousness* thy constant shield 958
Be *righteousness* thy sceptre 1312
Before him *righteousness* shall go 1901
High *righteousness* and truth 1889
His only *righteousness* I show 1017
In *righteousness* alone can perfect 2098
In *righteousness* to judge the world 1887, 1888
No *righteousness* nor merit 872
O God of *righteousness* and grace 419
Righteousness and peace kiss 909
Righteousness and peace unite 1073
This is all my *righteousness* 2214
Thy perfect *righteousness,* O God 1387
Thy *righteousness* impart 2046
Thy *righteousness,* thy pardon 820
With no *righteousness* to call my own 977

RING

And *ring* from all the trees 1225
Ring across the golden fields 1665
Ring, happy bells, across the snow 1662
Ring in the Christ that is to be 1662
Ring in the nobler forms of life 1662
Ring in the thousand years of peace 1662
Ring out a slowly dying cause 1662
Ring out, O trumpets, sweet and clear 239
Ring out old shapes of foul 1662, 1663
Ring out, ring out, O bells of joy 148
Ring out the darkness of the land 1662
Ring out the false, ring in 1662, 1663
Ring out the narrowing lust 1662, 1663
Ring out the old, ring in the new 1663
Ring out the thousand wars 1662, 1663
Ring out the watchword true 516
Ring out, wild bells, and let 1663
Ring throughout the harvest days 1665
The vibrant chords of heaven *ring* 49
When they *ring* the golden bells 1991

RINGING

Flower bells are *ringing* 61

RINGS

It *rings,* and clings, and sweetly 2309
There *rings* a melody 833

RIPE

Ripe for the wine-press strife 170

RIPEN

They *ripen* on mountains of duty 1298

RIPENED

Ripened by his glorious sunshine 76

RIPENS

Ripens what we sow 1620

RISE

Alike we *rise* and fall 56
And as we *rise* again 391
And as we *rise* with thee to live 316
And ever let there *rise* to thee 418
And methinks when I *rise* to that 430
And *rise* to life and bliss 404
Against me many *rise* 1430
Before him *rise* in awful mirth 1889
But higher we shall *rise* 194
God calling yet! Shall I not *rise?* 558
How *rise* thy towers, serene 301
I *rise* from sin's dark sepulcher 1140
I shall *rise* again at morning 810
Let me *rise* to enjoy the blessing 2032
Let me *rise* with the wise 415
May we *rise* above our petty 944
May we *rise* renewed in thee 331
Rise, and join the Lord's command 36
Rise and shine 542
Rise ere the dawn be risen 2183
Rise from transitory things 1667
Rise, glorious at the awful day 59
Rise, God, judge thou the earth 1901
Rise, hope of the ages, arise, like 1768
Rise in the new creation 1089
Rise, my soul, and haste away 1667
Rise o'er sin and fear and care 980
Rise, shine, give God glory 2156
Rise to adore the mystery of love 298
Rise to all eternity 994
Rise up, and follow thee 386
Rise up, and make her great 1669
Rise up, and wonder, and draw near 1548
Shall *rise* our psalm of grateful 1446
Shall *rise* the glorious thought 1793
That we may *rise* from selfish 465
Then *rise* with lightened cheer 1431
They *rise* and needs will have 1255
They *rise* but never set 1933
They *rise* to heaven above 685
Thus evermore shall *rise* to thee 81, 418
Till *rise* at last, to span 2074
To hail thy *rise,* thou better Sun 1917
We *rise,* and all the distant 1183
We *rise,* how full of power 1183
We *rise* on thy free Spirit's wings 1380
We, too, may *rise* above the last of 260
Who *rise* to build the common weal 422
With him shall *rise* the ransomed 1895

RISEN

Christ is *risen,* Christ the first fruits 76
Christ is *risen,* he meets our eyes 552
"Christ is *risen,* praise the Lord!" 141
"Christ is *risen,*" today we cry 288
Christ our Lord is *risen* in might 412
"Christ, our Savior, now is *risen*" 354
For Christ the Lord hath *risen* 1854
For *risen* is our Savior 1418
Hath *risen* with purpose fell 19
He is *risen,* he is risen 664
Now is *risen* from the dead 76
Our Lord Christ hath *risen* 1599
Our *risen* King and Savior 49
Risen to a holier state 700
Risen with healing in his wings 675
Risen with him! allured by Love 264
That we have *risen* with Christ to 391
The Son of Man is *risen* 1879

RISES

He *rises* glorious from the dead 79, 1937
It is the Lord who *rises* 1759

RISETH

As he *riseth,* rise we too 412

RISING

His *rising,* his ascension 1883
Rising to the Father, in a chorus strong 61
The *rising* of the people 2176
Thy *rising* hath no setting 1089

RISK

Do not *risk* another day 2283
Risk not my soul on a moment's delay 353

RITE

And oft the sacred *rite* renew 2133

RIVER

A *river* flows whose streams 571
And our parting at the *river* 2246
And with Jesus they are walking where the *river* 1499
As from a pleasant *river* 92
Beyond the chilly *river* 2172
Blest *river* of salvation 1911
From many an ancient *river* 512
I plunged in that *river*, and Christ set 17
It from the *river* shall reach forth 1454
O *River* ever streaming 1317
River and mountain spring 733
Rolling *river*, praise him ever 104
The *river* running by 68
There life's crystal *river* 938
To the *river* draw thou near 1766

RIVERS

From *rivers* of thy pleasures 2080
From *rivers* of unfailing joy 2079
Our *rivers*, lakes, and fountains 515
Rivers to the ocean run 1667
The *rivers* of sorrow shall not 776
Where *rivers* of delight 834
Where *rivers* of pleasure I see 24

ROAD

A *road* to bring us daily nearer 1273
And although the *road* be rough 1983
And be the *road* uphill or down 1507
Journeying o'er the *road* 1680
Let the *road* be rough and dreary 367
Showing all around the *road* 742
The *road* that leads from banishment 1001
Thy *road* is ready and thy paths 405
True, 'tis a strait and thorny *road* 157
'Twas a toilsome *road* for the Lamb 864
Upwards by the starry *road* 346

ROAM

And wherever I *roam*, it is guiding 2066
Hither, hither, while they *roam* 1837
No longer I *roam* 931
O, why will you longer *roam* 1494
Why do they *roam* 326

ROAR

From Niagara's deep-toned *roar* 518

ROARED

Loudly *roared* the angry sea 521

ROARS

Wild *roars* the blast 1217

ROB

Thee to *rob* of God's tomorrow 175

ROBE

All holy is their spotless *robe* 1977
And a *robe*, and a crown shall be 2113
And *robe* of sorrow round thee 1124
I have a *robe*, 'tis resplendent 830
Of the beautiful *robe* and the crown 1751
Take we the *robe*, and the harp 228
The *robe* and palm of victory 2050
Thou, whose *robe* is gladsome 2308
Whose *robe* is the light 1546

ROBED

Are *robed* in their garments of white 1503
He hath *robed* him and he reigneth 610
Robed in dreadful majesty 1106
Robed in flesh, our great High Priest 77
Robed in his own glorious light 610
Robed in snowy white 900
Robed in the blooming garb 427
When *robed* in majesty and power 2037

ROBES

Bright *robes* of gold the fields 2120
In glorious *robes* arrayed 965
In *robes* of light arrayed 1931
Not in *robes* of purple splendor 2254
Our *robes* are white and clean 1597
Spotless *robes* and crowns of glory 2284
Whose *robes* are white and clean 1597

ROBEST

Thou *robest* in thy splendor 1089

ROCK

A *rock* that cannot move 2071
And my strong *Rock* is he 1258
And on a *rock* me raise 1903
Be thou our *Rock*, our life, our thought 502
Christ, o'er thy *rock*, nor death 1162
Dear name, the *Rock* on which I build 794
Gushing from the *Rock* before me 66
Firm as a *rock* his truth shall stand 184
Firm on the *Rock* and strong in thee 1170
Firm on the *Rock* of Ages 1675
From *rock* and tempest, fire and 418
From the smitten *rock* is shed 356
God my *Rock*, my Strength 951
He our *Rock*, our hope of eternal 1616
Hiding *rock* and treacherous shoal 1007
In God the *Rock* is all my strength 1258
O Jesus is a *Rock* in a weary land 1905
O near to the *Rock* let me keep 1489
O *Rock* divine! O Refuge dear 1905
O then to the *Rock* let me fly 1489
On Christ, the solid *Rock*, I stand 1244
On the *Rock* of Ages founded 541
Rock and high land 104
Stricken *Rock* with streaming side 1126
The *Rock* of Ages stands 685
Their *Rock* is our salvation 2164
Thou art my *Rock* and trust 1455

Thou blest *Rock* of Ages, I'm hiding 1477
To the *Rock* that is higher than I 1489
Upon the *Rock* of Ages they raise 489
Upon the solid *rock* we set the dream 2198
When the sheltering *Rock* is so nearby 1970

ROCKS

Let *rocks* their silence break 1225
Like the *rocks* of towering grandeur 606
'Mid rending *rocks* and darkening 1562
Rocks fall to dust, and mountains 1666
The *rocks* and rills, the vales and hills 148

ROD

For thou art with me, and thy *rod* 1904
Then the end; beneath his *rod* 676
Thy *rod* and staff my comfort 1876
Thy *rod* and staff shall keep us 2289
Thy *rod* shall defend me 1894

RODE

But, as he *rode* along 2230

ROLL

And the *roll* is called up yonder 2259
As you *roll* across the trestle 1076
Nor *roll* of stirring drums 1057
Onward *roll* from tongue to tongue 280
Roll back the veil of error 1497
When the *roll* is called up yonder 2259
You will *roll* up grades 1076

ROLLED

And *rolled* the stone away 260
My sins *rolled* away in the flood 17

ROLLETH

Rolleth the great new song 181

ROLLS

Around us *rolls* the ceaseless tide 199
Rolls a melody sweeter than psalm 430
Rolls on the glorious anthem 638

ROOF-TREE

And bless the *roof-tree* overhead 210

ROOM

And there's *room* for us all 1987
In every quiet upper *room* 204
No *room* in my heart for pleasures 1411
No *room* inside the hostel 918
Room and time now give to Jesus 692
Room at the cross 145
Room for Jesus, King of Glory 692
Room for pleasure, room for business 692
Room to deny ourselves, a road 1273
Saying, "Yet there is *room* 2026
That we, so lost, have *room* 1122
There is *room* at my side 2026
There is *room* in my heart for thee 2026

ROOT

But give it *root* in every heart 83
Root out all hypocrisy 1583
Thou *Root* of Jesse! David's Son 1470

ROOTED

Man's *rooted* enmity subdue 1026

ROSE

And as he *rose* at Easter 626
As when on blue Gennesaret *rose* high 1429
At once he *rose* to full belief's 785
For Jesus *rose* on Easter day 952
He *rose*, a victor crowned 283
He *rose* again; he rose again 33
I *rose*, went forth, and followed thee 94
In crystal and in *rose* 40
The hand that shaped the *rose* hath 40
The heavenly Savior *rose* 426
The *rose* I have in mind 1197
There *rose* a cry to the gate 1983
There *rose* the choral hymn of praise 2239

ROUND

Each annual *round* with bounties 21
Every *round* goes higher 2156
In our daily *round* of care 480
The trivial *round*, the common task 1273

ROUSE

If you cannot *rouse* the wicked 679
Rouse then, soldiers, rally round 1769

ROUTE

We the *route* for travel clearing 62

ROVE

Far did I *rove* and found no certain 1112
Mine to chide me when I *rove* 738
Nor *rove*, nor seek the crooked way 1035
Nor thoughts that idly *rove* 1301

ROYAL

Thou, David's *royal* Son 44

RUBIES

Of *rubies* and diamonds 1229

RUIN

Our *ruin* God has not intended 1290
You from sin's *ruin* to save 531

RUINS

The *ruins* of my soul repair 2202

RULE

And *rule* in equity 661
And thy just *rule* shall fill 520
His rod's stern *rule* has oft 2104
His *rule* is over rich and poor 1621
Now *rule* in every heart 338
O Father, that thy *rule* is just 43
Our *rule*, thy word 274
Rule and might o'er all possessing 1470
Rule in all our hearts alone 343
Rule in our hearts that we may ever be 421

Rule over everything 920
Simple *rule* and safest guiding 367
The *rule* of day is over 1297
The *rule* of his sceptered sway 1950
Thou, Lord, dost *rule* the raging 712
Thy *rule,* O Christ, begin 2073

RULED

One Spirit *ruled* them all 197
Our hearts be *ruled* 84

RULER

Be thou our *Ruler,* Guardian 585
He is a *Ruler* wise 534
Ruler of all mankind 592
Ruler of all nature 427
Ruler of sky, and land, and sea 1621
Ruler of the storm was he 521
'Tis well thou art our *Ruler* 43

RULERS

Our earthly *rulers* falter 1365

RULES

And *rules* the honest mind 377
He *rules* o'er earth and heaven 1653
He *rules* the nations by his might 1858
He *rules* the world with truth and 1039
Jesus *rules* the world alone 673

RULEST

Thou *rulest* in might 916

RULETH

God *ruleth* on high, almighty 2330
He *ruleth* o'er the nations 360

RUN

And may we *run* with faithfulness 1372
And *run* my course with even joy 499
And *run* not before him 1820
Awake, and *run* the heavenly race 157
Run its race and reach 930
Run the straight race through 477

RUNNETH

While *runneth* o'er each dear 1142

RUSH

What *rush* of hallelujahs 1836
When they *rush* into the fight 2264

RUSHES

The *rushes* by the water 68

S

SABAOTH

Lord *Sabaoth,* his name 12

SACRAMENT

In the solemn *sacrament* 42
In this our *sacrament* of bread 335

SACREDNESS

The *sacredness* of common things 1492

SACRIFICE

A joyful *sacrifice* 332
A pleasing *sacrifice* 31
A *sacrifice* of love divine 1534
A *sacrifice* of nobler name 1279
By thy one great *sacrifice* 269
God's own *sacrifice* complete 552
Himself the *sacrifice* 1564
I *sacrifice* them to his blood 2236
In *sacrifice* to die 86
In the *sacrifice* Jesus paid 1501
O Lamb of God, my *sacrifice* 30
O may this *sacrifice* to thee 2070
Our living *sacrifice* to thee 1491
Our *Sacrifice* is one 1579
That through thy *sacrifice* 855
The bleeding *Sacrifice,* in my behalf appears 113
The one true, pure, immortal *sacrifice* 99
The *sacrifice* that brings thy balm 596
Then as the evening *sacrifice* 1434
To pay thy morning *sacrifice* 152

SAD

For the *sad* and sinful 1787
If short, yet why should I be *sad* 1148
O how *sad* and sore distressed 140
Sad, sad, that bitter wail 85
When I am *sad,* he makes me glad 981
When I am *sad,* to him 981
Where the *sad,* the poor, despairing 716

SADNESS

And may there be no *sadness* of 1802
Does *sadness* fill my mind 2243
In our *sadness* bringing news of sins 1680
No longer in *sadness* I wander alone 1855
No *sadness* can enter the mansions 2271
Someone in *sadness,* yearning 1600

SAFE

All praise to thee, who *safe* hast kept 152
And *safe* in Jesus dwell 241
And *safe* in such confiding 921
And so we shall be *safe* 2131
How *safe,* how calm, how satisfied 1400
I am *safe* forever in Beulah 431
I am *safe* when I abide 963
I am *safe* when thou art nigh 1682
In Jesus I'm *safe* evermore 1257
In Jesus' keeping we are *safe* 1610
Not the riches *safe* and palling 62
Safe from dangers, free from 1647
Safe in the cross of Jesus 872
Safe shalt thou be 2139
We are *safe* if thou art nigh 1681

SAFETY

And hast my *safety* been 1484
Safety for my trembling soul 223
Their own *safety* scorned to seek 485
There alone is *safety* 1264
'Tis only there in *safety* and peace 1419
To him for *safety* I will flee 1908
To us doth *safety* bring 1390
Will all in *safety* keep 291
Will in *safety* keep 1565

SAGES

And lo! the eastern *sages* stand 2220
Sages, leave your contemplation 103

SAID

And *said,* "My peace be on all 1493
For God has *said,* "My spirit 1337
For the Savior *said,* "Whosoever 802
Have you ever *said,* "I thank thee 696
Jesus has *said,* "I'll never forsake 2152
Jesus *said* he would a place 2125
Then *said* the God of God 476
These are they of whom he *said* 1789
When the Lord *said,* "Whosoever 807

SAIL

I'll *sail* the wide seas no more 1257
Sail on in hope, thy flag 2190
So we'll *sail,* sail 2190
We *sail* along in the morning bright 2190
We *sail* along, there are shoals 2190
Ye clouds that *sail* in heaven along 41

SAILED

And *sailed* through bloody seas 87

SAILOR

When the *sailor* on the wave 2260

SAILORS

Sailors on the dangerous seas 488

SAINT

Did ever *saint* find this Friend 2000
For the *saint* and prophet born 1051
Let every *saint* thy beauty see 89
Till *saint* and martyr 1652

SAINTS

All his *saints,* by men rejected 1106
All the *saints* adore thee 749
All the *saints* with one accord 1726
And glorious with his *saints* in light 1864
And in thee thy *saints* shall rise 142
And let all those that are thy *saints* 2205
And *saints* on earth, with saints above 328
And to his *saints* makes known 575
And with thy *saints* adore 2178
Around his *saints* as watch and ward 1890
By saints below, and *saints* above 1351
For he his *saints* hath raised 1898
For thee the *saints* uplift 1651
Her *saints* shall shout forth 2205
Her *saints* shall shout with joy 114
How happy are the *saints* above 1223
I with the *saints* ascended 1552
In him his *saints* are blest 1430
"Jesus," let all *saints* proclaim 1912
Let all the *saints* below the skies 2105
Let all the *saints* terrestrial 324
Let all his *saints* with glad hearts 1670
Let the *saints* of every nation 227
O Jesus, Joy of *saints* on high 75
O ye *saints,* arise, be earnest 1222
Of *saints* and heroes wrought 385
On all thy *saints* 2099
Saints and angels crowd around him 1117
Saints before the altar bending 103
Saints below, with heart 1762
Saints will sing his praises 1114
Saints within his courts below 1623
So shall thy *saints* and martyrs 473
So the *saints,* from slumber blest 2299
Speaking to *saints,* to prophets 1368
Ten thousand *saints* adore 1959
That like thy *saints* we may 2115
That *saints* and holy martyrs trod 1108
The *saints* arrayed in white 33
The *saints* in countless myriads 1108
The *saints* in thy communion blest 364
The *saints* on earth unite 133
The *saints* will be with him 1926
Then shall *saints* and seraphim 748
Then with all the *saints* in glory 633
They were all of them *saints* of God 875
Thousand, thousand *saints* attending 1106
Thy *saints,* O Lord, thy name shall bless 628
Thy *saints,* to greet thy day of 2138
'Tis right and pleasant for his *saints* 1636
To him the *saints* in glory 853
To sing with *saints* his praises 854
Twelve valiant *saints,* their hope 1931
When martyred *saints,* baptized 1537
When the *saints* and the sinners 1990
When the *saints* of God are gathered 2127
Where *saints* and angels dwell 1369
Where *saints* are clothed in 1918
Where the *saints,* all immortal 1503
While *saints* address thy face 2203
While *saints* in heaven thy glory sing 2326
While *saints* their crowns within 642
With all thy *saints* on earth 335
With glorified *saints* 953
With *saints* above we hymn thy 642
With *saints* enthroned on high 1705
With *saints* redeemed in glory 1556
Ye fearful *saints,* fresh courage 577
Ye *saints* to come, take up the strain 2164

SAITH

And yet he *saith,* "I thirst 734
Where *saith* the Light of light 476

SAKE

And gladly, for thine own dear *sake* 235
Even (e'en) for his own name's *sake* 1904
For Jesus' *sake,* comes as thy right 553
For the *sake* of Jesus 290
For thy name's *sake* 629
Not for the *sake* of winning heaven 1235
Now for thine own name's *sake* 1255
O who am I that for my *sake* 2116
Worn and lonely for our *sake* 2255

SALE

From *sale* and profanation 1365

SALVATION

And by thy death was God's *salvation* 58
And his *salvation* ours 1785
And my *salvation* wrought 2309
And still to God *salvation* cry 1705
And thy *salvation* see 1590
And with *salvation* beautify 1634
Ascribing *salvation* to Jesus 2330
Blessed *salvation* once for all 504
Finding *salvation* from sin through 2337
For our *salvation* he hath yearned 1290
For the world's *salvation* bled 76
Great God of our *salvation* 1320
He of *salvation* is the God 2031

He only my *salvation* is 1258
His perfect *salvation,* his wonderful love 24
I shall full *salvation* find 800
Jesus my Savior *salvation* affords 1678
Let thy *salvation* set my soul 2078
O bring thy great *salvation* 82
O whence for me shall my *salvation* 2139
On thee, for our *salvation* 1341
Our great and sure *salvation* 2289
Our *salvation* have procured 971
Ours is such a full *salvation* 2065
Salvation and immortal praise 237
Salvation and peace have been 2084
Salvation full and free 827, 2077
Salvation full, at highest cost 575
Salvation, glory, joy remain 671
Salvation is at hand 587
Salvation is its bulwark sure 778
Salvation shall adorn her priests 114
Salvation through Jesus to sinners 1648
Salvation to bestow 498
Salvation to God, who sits on 2330
Salvation to his people, God 2078
Salvation to the Lamb 1705
Salvation to the Lord belongs 1430
Salvation whose fullness to all 1648
Thou didst free *salvation* bring 659
Thy free *salvation* is my shield 858
Till the *salvation* come 231
'Tis *salvation* full and free 912
To me *salvation* send 1719, 2116
Trusting thee for full *salvation* 811
Until in Christ's *salvation* 823
What a wonderful *salvation* 1041
When his *salvation* reigns within 1739
With all thy great *salvation* bless 1714
With thy *salvation,* O my God 532

SANCTIFIED

Sanctified my doings 415

SANCTIFY

And *sanctify* the whole 1021
And *sanctify* to thee 776
Come, *sanctify* wholly this temple 719
Let thy teaching *sanctify* 741
May *sanctify* each common task 235
Sanctify forever 1732

SANCTITY

Fount of love and *sanctity* 76

SANCTUARY

As, waiting in thy *sanctuary* 944

SAND

From sinking *sand* he lifted 926

SANDS

In vain the drifting *sands* 301

SAT

He *sat* on the flood 537

SATISFIED

I am *satisfied* to know 1848
"I am *satisfied* with thee." 805
I shall be *satisfied,* when 1764
Is he *satisfied* with me? 805
Jesus has *satisfied* 425
Satisfied the way he taketh 1643
That thou may'st be *satisfied* 1764
We shall be *satisfied,* and saved 721
We surely shall be *satisfied* 1631
Why art thou not *satisfied?* 1764

SATISFIES

It *satisfies* my longings 862
Satisfies its deepest longings 978

SATISFY

And *satisfy* her poor with bread 114
How *satisfy* the needs 817
Now none but Christ can *satisfy* 1322

SAVE

A never-dying soul to *save* 4
And only Christ can *save* 923
And *save* my soul from wrong 176
And *save* the world from war's decree 371
And wilt hereafter *save* 200
Didst *save* our lost and guilty 372
For who is God, and strong to *save* 858
God alone can *save* through the Son 2258
God *save* the people 2267
God *save* the state 557
He alone can *save* 2057
He will *save* you, he will save you 308
He will *save* you, save you now 1425
He will surely *save* them 286
Help, and *save* us, gracious Lord 288
If you would *save* your sinful soul 2338
Jesus is merciful, Jesus will *save* 1655
Jesus would *save,* but there's no one 705
Lord, thou canst *save* when sin 1162
My God that doth me *save* 1483
O *save* me from the snares of hell 176
O *save* the lost, the sinners turn 475
Of Jesus, who'll *save* whosoever 1257
Save all who dare the eagle's flight 81
Save, bless, and feed thy heritage 1455
Save her from pride and from luxury 601
Save him on the billows 1791
Save it from evil, guard it still 469
Save, *Lord,* by love or fear 2228
"*Save,* Lord, we perish," was their cry 475
Save me by thy blood 1000
Save me by thy grace 1607
Save me from every foe 265
Save me, Jesus, save me now 800
Save me, Lord, and keep me faithful 225
Save now, I pray thee, Lord 1484
Save our souls in mercy 922
Save thou the souls that slight thee 2497
Save thy servant that hath 2111
Save us, a present Savior thou 146
Save us from death, the death of sin 590

Save us from weak resignation 580
Save us, Lord, from seeking 925
Save us now, and save us ever 446
Save us, thy people, from consuming 762
Then *save* us now, by Jesus' power 1168
Thou canst *save*, and thou alone 488
Thou canst *save*, and thou canst heal 1681
Thou must *save*, and thou alone 1671
Who can *save* us, Lord, but thou 538
Would you have him *save* you so that 2324

SAVED

And *saved* me from my lost estate 153
And *saved* them out of all 1890
Be *saved* today 891
Dying, he *saved* me 1575
He *saved* my soul, and left 2016
I am so wondrously *saved* from sin 402
Is *saved* from endless woes 128
It has *saved* our fathers 2095
Now *saved* from gloom 2086
Saved by grace alone 631
Saved only through the Lamb 872
Saved, saved, by power divine 1678
Someone may be *saved* from ruin's brink 400
That *saved* a wretch like me 88
That, *saved*, we may thy goodness 2071
That we should be *saved* from our enemies 215
When the *saved* of earth shall gather 2259
Where the dear Lord, who *saved* us all 206
Wilt thou be *saved*? 1343
Who *saved* us from eternal loss 1425

SAVES

And *saves* me from the grave 1201
Come, and he *saves* us once for all 504
For my Savior *saves* me now 1222
God *saves* the meek 857
Hail him who *saves* you by his grace 47
He *saves* me every day and hour 482
He *saves* the oppressed 911
He *saves* to the utmost and keeps 1648
Jesus completely *saves* 891
There Jesus *saves* me and keeps 402
Those he *saves* are his delight 2232
Which *saves* us to the uttermost 93

SAVEST

Because thou *savest* them; let all 527, 1176
Thou *savest* me from ill 772
Thou *savest* those that on thee call 1023

SAVETH

He *saveth* by his might 573

SAVING

Saving, redeeming at measureless 326

SAVIOR

A dear loving *Savior* 830
A *Savior* who is Christ the Lord 2282
A wonderful *Savior* is Jesus 24
And O that my *Savior* were 830
And thou, blest *Savior*, thou art 1002
Be her *Savior*, Lord, and Guide 1033
But the *Savior* still is with me 895
Hail, thou agonizing *Savior* 659
He your *Savior* wants to be 891
How kind was our *Savior* 2245
I'm glad my blessed *Savior* 860
May we, gracious *Savior* 1034
My dying *Savior*, and my God 493
O, what a wonderful *Savior* 829
Pitying, loving *Savior* 964
Savior, we are thine 2287
That my loving *Savior* is your 830
Therefore thou alone, my *Savior* 1583
'Tis our God, our glorious *Savior* 2288
We would be more like the *Savior* 1694

SAVOR

So may the *savor* of thy grace 15

SAW

But Jesus *saw* them ere they fled 2245
He *saw*, and hailed his Lord divine 785
He *saw* me ruined in the fall 153
He *saw* the feet, the hands 1493
He *saw* thee risen 785
I *saw* his hands, all bruised 888
I *saw* his kind eyes glisten 892
I *saw* them each bearing 1941
Saw him then from judgment taken 140
Saw the glory 945
Saw the Lord's anointed taken 1263
Saw ye not the cloud arise 1695
They *saw*, and knew that it was good 2147
They *saw* the grace of thy dear face 2024
Until they *saw* the heavenly host 1928
"We *saw* no glory crown his head 2326
We *saw* the glory of thy new light 1984
What you *saw* and heard 1718
When she *saw* the Crucifixion 140
Who *saw* his Master in the sky 1931

SAY

And *say*, "Behold the way 1001
And *say*, was ever grief like his 1460
And *say*, when the death-dew 1246
And thou wilt *say*, 'twas better so 1821
How can I *say* ye (thee) nay 803
How many *say*, "In vain for help" 1430
How *say* ye then to me 1261
I of the Lord my God will *say* 1908
I *say*, more than they that do watch 1129
If I do *say* that darkness 1452
I'll say what you want me to *say* 955
My blessed Lord will *say*, "Well done" 1749
"No," *say* thy mountains 2267
O, can we *say* we are ready 2241
"O *say*, may I come in?" 841
Or who can *say* how great the jubilation 817
Say, "It is I, be not afraid" 650
Say, lest we sink to rise no more 475
Say, "Live forever, wondrous King 697

"*Say*, poor sinner, lovest thou me? 672
Say that for all Jesus suffered 908
Say to my trembling heart 417
Say to the billow, "Be at rest" 650
Say to the weakest, follow me 364
Say what God has done for thee 1703
Then *say* I, "What is man 775
Therefore will not *say* thee nay 330
They *say* I shall meet sorrow 1949
We cheerfully can *say* 1759
We must not *say* that these are dead 590
We'll never *say* "Good-bye" in heaven 2301
We'll *say* "Good-night" here, but 2225
What hast thou to *say* to me 1207
What more can we *say*, than to you 776
What shall I *say* thy grace 1018
Whereof I now will *say* and sing 513
You can *say* he died for all 679

SAYING

Making each faithful *saying* mine 1216

SAYS

And the Master *says*, "Well done" 480
For my Lord *says*, "Come 864
Jesus *says* to those who seek 2017
Tis God who *says*, "No longer mourn" 1657
What he *says* we will do 2266

SCAFFOLD

Yet that *scaffold* sways the future 1574

SCALES

O may his love the *scales* displace 89

SCAN

And *scan* his work in vain 577

SCATTER

Scatter all my unbelief 282
Scatter from the sad heart all its doubt 163
Scatter my sins as morning dew 545
Scatter sin and unbelief 1747
Scatter thy life through every part 1021
Yet when we *scatter* o'er life's fields 2174

SCATTERED

And *scattered* our might 2187
There is *scattered* myrrh most fragrant 299

SCATTERS

And *scatters* night away 1563
It *scatters* all their guilty fear 1017
Scatters fear and gloom 2010

SCENE

Before the mournful *scene* began 2132
Each changing future *scene* 1245
Through many a *scene* of strife 2072

SCENES

Above these *scenes* of storm and strife 1349
And when, in *scenes* of glory 862
In *scenes*, exalted or depressed 643
Scenes by the wayside 1831
Welcome, sweet *scenes* of rest 425

SCENT

And sweet the *scent* 946

SCHISMS

By *schisms* rent asunder 1845

SCHOLARS

As devout and patient *scholars* 2318

SCHOOL

In *school* and church, where all 1384

SCHOOL-DAYS

The *school-days* over, and the prizes 1274

SCHOOLED

And spirits *schooled* 84

SCIENCE

And *science* walks with humbler feet 1899

SCOPE

Broader than the *scope* of my transgressions 2315

SCORN

And wordly *scorn* assail us 2289
But those who *scorn* the right 1261
But with mocking *scorn* 2026
By loyal *scorn* of second best 1492
Didst not *scorn* a virgin's womb 1161
Nor *scorn* their humble name 1696
Or who should *scorn* or slight 201
Or will you *scorn* from his foes 984
Our wild hope who shall *scorn* 90
Scorn not, scorn not my soul 1239

SCORNED

Nor *scorned* that little children 763
Scorned and forsaken, derided 1015
Scorned by all they chance to meet 488
Yourself you *scorned* to save 1532

SCORNERS

Scorners shall seek, and saints 1914

SCORNS

Nor *scorns* the meanest name 2305

SCOURGED

Scourged, and crowned with thorns 140

SCREEN

No *screen* from thy all-searching eyes 2039

SCROLLS

Many diverse *scrolls* completing 242

SCULPTOR

Great *Sculptor*, hew and polish 649

SEA

A never-ebbing *sea* 917
A vast, unfathomable *sea* 2071
Across this troubled *sea* of life 1429
And so beside the silent *sea* 848, 2310
By *sea* or shore abiding 1906
Deeper than the deepest *sea* 1498
Deeper than the mighty rolling *sea* 2315
Down by the widest *sea* 1945
For azure, rolling *sea* 2303
From the eastern *sea* 1070
Nearer the crystal *sea* 1580
Of life's wide and restless *sea* 1096
On any *sea* or shore 956
On the stormy *sea* 1041
Or o'er the stormy *sea* 1822
Over *sea*, and land, and air 1305
Over the jasper *sea* 1675
Sweep across the crystal *sea* 77
The stormy *sea* sings praise to God 55
The wildest *sea* is calm 1462
Thou art a *sea* without a shore 788
Though deep the *sea* and wide 2134
Till, beyond the crystal *sea* 1055
Till, like a *sea* of glory 512
To him the spacious *sea* belongs 1334, 1335
Valiantly o'er *sea* and land 485

SEA-BILLOWS

Than great *sea-billows* are 1886

SEAL

And *seal* me for thine own 1230
And *seal* them in the sky 391
And *seal* them thine forever 642
Seal it for thy courts above 340
Seal me for thy courts above 222
Seal of immortality 346
Seal salvation on my heart 637
Seal thine image on my heart 1690
Seal us for service today 1694
Seal us just now, we pray 1694
Seal us with witnessing power 1694
Vainly they *seal* the dead 1200

SEALED

Sealed in the stone-cold tomb 2196
Sealed my pardon with his blood 1203
The blessed cross has *sealed* my peace 60
The flowing waters *sealed* 40
Thy broken heart my pardon *sealed* 60

SEAMAN

Some poor fainting, struggling *seaman* 255
Some poor *seaman*, tempest-tossed 255

SEAMEN

As shipwrecked *seamen* long for 29
Weary, helpless, hopeless *seamen* 474

SEARCH

In vain we *search* the lowest deeps 2181
In vain we *search* the lowest depths 917
Let the *search* for thy salvation 580
Search for us the depths of God 346
Search me, and try me, Master 691
Search me, Lord, and know my heart 222
Search me, O God, and know my heart 1438
Search my heart and my behavior 1583
Search out our hearts and make us true 189
Search, prove my heart 1519
Search, try, O God, my thoughts 2039
Then *search* in the highway, and pass 1540
Whilst we daily *search* thy word 127

SEAS

And sailed through bloody *seas* 87
Calm *seas* have their dangers 1114
Dark *seas* of trouble roll 1487
Great *seas* of new life giving 2135
In *seas* that swell, and streams 1461
Lord of *seas* uncharted 2274
Seas are calm and blue again 1305
The former *seas* have passed away 1111
The *seas* shall waste, the skies 1666
Through stormy *seas* to guide me 898

SEASON

And for a *season* slumber 2015
Let me in *season*, Lord, be grave 1128
No changes of *season* or place 795
Soon will the *season* of rescue 2068
Which in its *season* yields 1841
Yet a *season*, and we know 1667

SEASONS

A few more *seasons* wane 5
And in the *seasons* of the night 570
As *seasons* come and go 40
By him the rolling *seasons* 1734
His the *seasons* that inherit 1796
In *seasons* of distress and grief 1806
Or to know the times and *seasons* 36
The ever-changing *seasons* 1952
There shall be *seasons* refreshing 1981
Who, changing *seasons* brings 614

SEAT

And from thy celestial *seat* 341
In the *seat* of power enthrone him 1117
Thou in thy everlasting *seat* 1901

SEATED

And *seated* on thy throne 869
Now *seated* on his Father's throne 1968
Seated at our Father's board 486

SEAWARD

Skyward and *seaward*, let it 479

SECRET

I have the *secret*, I know where 506
In *secret* of his tent me hide 1903
In thy tabernacle's *secret* 730
That, in the *secret* of his presence 876
The *secret* of the Lord is theirs 229

This is the *secret* of proving 2337
Without the *secret* of thy love 844

SECRETS

Secrets that with thee are hidden 394
The *secrets* of thy Father's breast 1805
Thy blessed *secrets* tell 312

SECTS

Thy warring *sects* obscuring 1328

SECURE

Secure am I, if thou art mine 2034

SECURES

His word my hope *secures* 88

SEE

Again I *see* the life he lived 816
All that *see* and share his love 1623
And always *see* his face 1021
And bid us *see* him face to face 89
And Christ you *see* in his eternal 1063
And I shall *see* him face to face 1749
And I shall *see* his face 1339
And *see* each other's face 93
And *see* like thee, our noblest work 1468
And *see* no glimmering, guiding ray 1517
And *see* our Father's face 2090
And *see* the Canaan that we love 1966
And *see* the saints above, how great 530
And *see* thy glory there 965
And *see* thy wounded hands 2174
And *see* we him whose arm upholds 559
And though I cannot *see* him 860
And though I may not *see* his face 822
And we *see* where thy foot-prints 1815
Brethren, *see* poor sinners 'round 251
But when I *see* thee as thou art 794
By and by I shall *see* him and 1922
Come *see*, if there ever was sorrow 73
Come *see* the place where once he lay 264
Come, then, O Lord, that we may *see* 712
Come to Bethlehem and *see* 105
E'en now I can *see* through a mist 1868
For they shall *see* the Lord 1520
He shall his Lord with rapture *see* 2331
He was glad to *see* them there 1789
Here may we *see* those who are dead in sin 723
Here *see* the Bread of Life 355
I can *see* their gleaming banner 507
I cannot *see* another's lack 182
I *see* from far thy beauteous light 2033
I *see* her by the old armchair 870
I *see* his hand of mercy 874
I *see* how the thick shadows 509
I *see* my people falling 1943
I *see* the glory of a thousand years 1914
I *see* the scourgers rend the flesh 873
I *see* the sights that dazzle 1408
I *see* the stars, I hear 1437
I *see* the way he planned 431
I *see* thee death's strong fetters burst 1416
I *see* thee in thy weakness first 1416
I *see* thee not, I hear 1020
I *see* thy Cross; there teach 1778
I *see* thy light, I feel thy wind 1444
I *see* thy strength and vigor 1476
I shall *see* him and serve 884
I shall *see* him by and by 424
I shall *see* my Savior 900
I shall *see* them, I shall know 1499
In all that I can *see* 1259
Is to *see* that we grow 539
Let them *see* thee in thy glory 1686
Let us *see* thy great salvation 1190
Let us *see* thy power 563
Lo, *see* the earth with joy awake 1293
Look and *see* how charming 257
May we *see* our human family 974
My Lord, my Savior, when I *see* thee 1251
O could I *see* you now, my boy 2272
Once I was blind, but now I can *see* 1946
Only faintly now I *see* him 424
Savior, may we *see* thee bleeding 2279
See a long race thy spacious 1666
See all your sins on Jesus 1351
See barbarous nations at thy gates 1666
See from all lands, from the isles 660
See from his head, his hands 2236
See future sons, and daughters yet 1666
See God's people, thither tending 2153
See he is sinking; oh, hasten 2068
See, he lifts his hands above 655
See, he shows the prints of love 655
See heathen nations bending 1911
See heaven its sparkling portals 1666
See him all his life's blood pour 356
See him by Mary attended 1617
See him dying there for me 1564
See his anguish, see his faith 2247
See his banners go 1586
See his faith 2247
See his footprints all the way 2002
See how he hath everywhere 715
See how his enemies do 1015
See how his love is in Jesus 1617
See how the giant sun 151
See it break from yonder sky 2126
See, it bursts o'er all the earth 2154
See myself as crucified 1764
See o'er the world wide-open doors 433
See our fathers and our mothers 251
See that suffering, friendless One 2247
See the cloud and fire appear 541
See the Christlike host 1760
See the crowds the throne surrounding 600
"*See* the door still open 939
See, the feast of love is spread 2089
See, the foe is nigh 1769
See the gleaming from afar 1109
See the glorious banner waving 736
See the glorious orb of day 715
See the goodly land on the other 2153
See the King in royal state 1697
See the Lord of all 1792
See the Man of Sorrows now 1117

See the mighty host advancing 736
See the mighty host of evil 2064
See the sky above us 61
See the solemn pomp appear 1106
See the streams of living waters 538
See the whitening harvest languish 1136
"*See* the well-spread table 939
See that Christ is your conductor 1076
See thee on thy judgment throne 1671
See their feet are on the sands 488
See thou, O see, in misery 1239
See thy bright altars thronged 1666
See thy compassion in the Savior's 1368
See thy thorn-encircled brow 1005
See waters flowing 355
See what God hath done 2265
See where it shines in Jesus' face 1308
Seems now I *see* him on Calvary's tree 2144
Shall the true Messiah *see* 1106
So now they *see* his blessed face 118
So that we *see*, gleaming on high 1236
That all might *see* the reason we 1968
That I in thee might *see* the blessed 123
That I may *see* thy glorious face 1230
That I might *see* him face to face 1534
That we may *see* aright 1854
That we may *see* thee face to face 1520
That we may *see* thy glorious face 307
Then I'll *see* thy blessed face 2043
Then *see* before your very eyes 2340
Then shall I *see* and hear and know 1811
There our Lord we soon shall *see* 277
Thou and I will *see* him dine 627
Thou shalt *see* his cheering form 276
"Thou shalt *see* my glory soon 672
Though we *see* thee wounded 1005
Though him thou canst not *see* 685
To *see* thee face to face 234
To wrestle till we *see* thy face 1714
Until thou *see* God's kingdom 1651
Until thou *see* thy bitter travails 1177
We each, as dying Stephen, shall *see* 708
We may not *see* her King 886
We then shall *see* forever 252
We *see* and share the pilgrim's dream 1217
We *see* he is more lovely 1597
We *see* the beckoning vision 370
We *see* the imprint of thy hand 2277
We *see* the marriage splendor 1597
We *see* them as of you 957
We shall *see* him in all his beauty 699
We shall *see* the Lord of Harvest 167
We would *see* Jesus, dying, risen 2199
We would *see* Jesus, in his work 2200
We would *see* Jesus, in the early 2200
We would *see* Jesus, Mary's Son 2200
We would *see* Jesus, on the mountain 2200
We would *see* Jesus, other lights 2199
We would *see* Jesus, our weak 2199
We would *see* Jesus, the great Rock-foundation 2199
We would *see* Jesus, this is all we're needing 2199
We'll *see* that all the way he led 1274
When I *see* Jesus my Savior 2235
When I *see* the blessed Savior 1710
When I *see* thee as thou art 2261
When I shall *see* his 1763
When shall I *see* my Father's face 1563
When we all *see* Jesus 1731
When we *see* him in glory enthroned 2163
When we *see* thee face to face 1145
When we shall *see* him, the King 2129
Where none *see* the shadow 179
While I *see*, divine compassion 1813
While you *see* your soul's deep need 2283
Working in all we *see* 1382
You'll *see* his mercy through your tears 2269

SEED

And *seed* laid deep in sacred soil 1353
His *seed*, the growing light 191
His *seed* the sower sows 2076
Like *seed* into the ground 83
Like the *seed* when no man knoweth 36
Oft as the precious *seed* is sown 83
"That I thy *seed* establish shall 619
This holy *seed* remove 83
Ye chosen *seed* of Israel's race 47

SEEDLINGS

From little *seedlings* born 10

SEEDS

And the *seeds* of truth be sown 1567
But slowly growing from *seeds* 1840
Little *seeds* of mercy 1101
So children are the *seeds* God plants 10
Sowing *seeds* of kindness 1771
Sowing the precious *seeds* by the way 1693
The *seeds* by thee provided 2081
To swell the *seeds* and ripen fruit 1164
What then, if thousands of *seeds* 1840

SEED-TIME

Seed-time, harvest, cold, and heat 1799

SEEK

A song to all who *seek* his face 25
All they that *seek* the Lord 72
Alone thy will to *seek* 84
And who do *seek* the living God 212
And humbly *seek* thy blessing 642
And I *seek* my home 864
And *seek* a Father's melting heart 1657
And *seek* a grave 316
And *seek* an injured Father's face 1657
And *seek* for joys on high 91
And *seek* for them the shelter 505
And *seek* his face 477
And *seek* our rest above 1121
And *seek* the Savior's blessing 1911
And *seek* through all my days 2213
And *seek* to throne thee far 2038
And *seek* where we before have 1294
And vainly *seek* to comprehend 479
And will *seek* to obtain 1903

As they *seek* thee 1175
But they that truly *seek* the Lord 616
"Come, let us *seek* our God today!" 786
Do we *seek* to do our best 2241
Doth *seek* to work us woe 12
Early let us *seek* thy favor 1683
E'en though we *seek* him 1290
Ever *seek* thy mercy seat 129
Guilty, *seek* thy mercy 442
Henceforth we *seek* the things 264
How good to those who *seek* 1019
How they who *seek* in God their 1723
Humbly now we *seek* thy care 632
Humbly we *seek* the help 1316
I *seek*, by the path which my 1894
I *seek* for a brighter country 1411
I *seek* my place in heaven 779
I *seek* the treasure of thy love 1242
I, too, would *seek* thy face 434
I will *seek* a place of refuge 2257
I would *seek* this mighty gift 754
If you *seek* pleasure, no trouble 907
If you truly *seek* him 940
I'll *seek* the seas at his behest 826
Let others *seek* a home below 1243
May all who *seek* this door 1175
No more we *seek* thee from afar 1386
None that *seek* him will he spurn 2126
Now I *seek* the cross where Jesus 977
Now I *seek* thy saving grace 977
Now thee alone I *seek* 1220
Now to *seek*, and love, and fear thee 220
O let me *seek* thee and 1778
O *seek* not the world 2271
Of all who *seek* the land 274
Prepare themselves to *seek* thee 33
Seek and ye shall find 111
Seek Christ, his will 547
Seek the great Desire of nations 103
Seek the lost until she find 1033
Seek the right, perform the true 294
Seek those of evil behavior 1098
Seek thou this soul of mine 306
Seek thy face, thy mercies 1159
Seek us when we go astray 1683
Seek ye continually 533
Shall we *seek* thee, Lord, in vain 1181
So let the godly *seek* thee 772
Some *seek* a Father in the heavens 522
Thee they *seek* as God of heaven 1686
'Tis thee we *seek* 723
'Tis then I *seek* this Guide 134
To *seek* the eternal light 121
To them that *seek* thee, thou art 1023
We *seek* a loyal friend 1942
We *seek* one common goal 138
We *seek* thee as thy saints 2164
We *seek* thy grace alone 267
When we humbly *seek* thy face 589
When we *seek* relief 989, 1011
Where'er they *seek* thee, thou art found 1032
Which, *seek* through the world 1212
Who but *seek* to harm thee 1668
Who *seek* thee only 1289
Yet once again I *seek* thy face 2202
Yet, while I *seek* but find thee not 2033

SEEKERS

The *seekers* of the light are one 2030

SEEKEST

Thou *seekest* us in love 1386
"Whom *seekest* thou this morn?" 626

SEEKETH

For he *seeketh* ever in our 2300

SEEKING

Seeking to be, seeking to be 326

SEEKS

He *seeks* her wandering sons 1636
He *seeks* the wayward with a broken heart 2
He *seeks* to serve, to love 1930

SEEM

Few there are who *seem* to care 1056
Though oft I *seem* to tread alone 1400

SEEMEST

Be what thou *seemest* 703
Thou *seemest* human and 1797

SEEMETH

Yet it *seemeth* but a day 2299

SEEMLY

For it is *seemly* so to do 57

SEEMS

And rough *seems* the path 1489
More homelike *seems* the vast 956
Seems the earth so poor 2089
Whate'er *seems* best to thee 1828
When all that now *seems* so mysterious 1922

SEEN

A bleeding Savior, *seen* by faith 1038
And that I might have *seen* his kind 884
And thou, O God, by whom are *seen* 848
God manifestly *seen* and heard 2022
Hast thou not *seen* how thy desires 1637
Here have we *seen* thy face 15
I have not *seen*, but visioned 1533
I have not *seen*, though since my youth 1935
I have *seen* him, I have known 835
Ne'er have *seen* the brightness 517
O God, in Christ we've *seen* thy face 1356
They will never be *seen* 17
Was *seen* a wondrous thing 1113
We've *seen* thy glory like a mantle 2193
Whom we, that have not *seen* 1797
Yet, though I have not *seen* 1020

SEERS

This is he whom *seers* in old time 1558

SEES

Always *sees* what children do 1118
And *sees* true peace above 1480
He *sees* the Gideon who shall rise 473
Sees all thy children's wants 365
Sees naught but sunshine glad 1723
The aged Simeon *sees* at last 1488
Then at last, when on high he *sees* us 1815
Well he *sees* and knows it 968

SEEST

O *seest* thou not his pleading eye 195
When thou *seest* me waver 937

SELECTED

Your Shepherd *selected* the path 472

SELF

And, rejoicing, *self* deny 1271
Daily from *self* more free 1407
Let not narrow *self* your way 399
Let *self* die out, Christ shall suffice 547
My sinful *self* my only shame 203
Not for *self* and flesh to mar it 1835
So too are we, from *self* and sin 1948
"Some of *self* and some of thee!" 1498
Thine own dear *self* impart 204

SELF-DENIAL

More *self-denial*, like his 1219

SELF-LOVE

Thy *self-love* purge away 2226
Thy weak *self-love* and guilty 1333

SELF-WILL

Let no *self-will* within us lurk 2147

SEMBLANCE

Or in darker *semblance* 937

SEND

And *send* it from above 1259
And *send* us, after worldly pain 2332
And the Christ whom he did *send* 813
Father, *send* the glorious hour 581
From Zion shall Jehovah *send* 2138
God *send* his people peace 540
God *send* us men alert 603
God *send* us men of steadfast will 603
God *send* us men with hearts ablaze 603
Gracious Lord, *send* while I pray 1703
He will *send* thee comfort 987
Here am I, *send* me 679, 686
Lord of harvest, *send* forth reapers 429
Lord, *send* a beam on me 788
O *send* the day of joy and light 1174
O *send* us forth, thy prophets 419
Or *send* one twinkling vision 899
Send a gleam across the wave 255
Send down thy love, thy life 1699
Send down thy peace, O God 1699
Send down thy Spirit free 1699
Send forth the gospel, break 433
Send forth thy beams divine 311
Send forth thy heralds, Lord 1116
Send forth thy quickening breath 2013
Send light and might 770
Send me, Lord, where thou wilt send 1690
Send men, whose eyes have seen 1702
Send messengers o'er land 1948
Send now prosperity 1484
Send out laborers, Father 409
Send out thy light and truth 466
Send such, thy lost ones home 1702
Send the Comforter to teach 1703
Send the light 1985
Send the pentecostal fire 222
Send the proclamation over vale 2292
Send them forth with morn's first 429
Send them in the noon-tide's glare 429
Send them out, Christ, to be 1166
Send them thy mighty word 1116
Send them upon us, O Lord 1981
Send them where thou wilt come 1702
Send thy grace and show thy power 717
Send thy light and brilliancy 341
Send to those the joyful tidings 369
Send us thy help, remember 712
Send us thy salvation 467
Send us upon thine errand 1943
So *send* I you 126
Surely the Lord will *send* it the rain 1693
That he should *send* his Son to me 1534
Then *send*, O send, the Master's 156
Though he may *send* some affliction 2257
We *send* our love to every land 1930
Whom shall I *send* to shatter (loosen, succor) 1943

SENDEST

All that thou *sendest* to me 1265
Where'er thou *sendest* we will go 1382

SENDS

And *sends* his messengers to save 1930
And *sends* the blest Spirit to guide 701
He *sends* his showers of blessing 2307
He *sends* his word and melts the snow 2307
He *sends* refreshing showers down 791
He *sends* relief 791
He *sends* the harvest's golden grain 981
He *sends* the laboring conscience 911
He *sends* the sunshine and the rain 981
Sends deliverance from on high 1837
Sends the witness of the Spirit 664
Where he *sends* we will go 2266

SENSE

A *sense* of pardoning love 1038
And what from Eli's *sense* 797
Let *sense* be dumb 386
Making the springs of time and *sense* 39
Not when the *sense* is dim 613
The *sense* of godly sorrow give 1506
The *sense* of life that knows 2030
With quickened *sense*, and heightened 491

SENSIBILITY

A *sensibility* of sin 889

SENT

And all-discerning love hath *sent* 904
And God *sent* us salvation 551
As he *sent,* to spread the light 126
But *sent* the world his truth 1315
God has *sent* him as foretold 290
Hath *sent* us his Son to save 2208
It was *sent* from heaven above 833
O Spirit whom the Father *sent* 81
Sent by my Lord, on you I call 336
Sent by the Father from on high 1461
Sent from God and from the Savior 597
Sent from the heart of God 1969
Sent from the Savior above 1981
Sent him to die, I scarce can take 1437
Sent his Son from heaven above 126
That the Father had *sent* him to do 1115
Thou hast *sent* the glorious light 976
Thou who hast *sent* me many griefs 1387
'Tis he, my soul, who *sent* his Son 209
'Tis *sent* to announce a new-born 2220
To thee, by Jesus Christ *sent* 2118
Were ever *sent* away 348
Whom God the Savior *sent* down 302

SEPARATE

Separate from sin, I would 635

SEPARATION

Lest there be a *separation* 2297

SERAPH

While *seraph* unto seraph calls 437

SERAPHIM

More glorious than the *seraphim* 2333

SERAPHS

Lord of the *seraphs* serving day and night 595

SERPENT

The brazen *serpent* high 128

SERVANT

Am I his *servant,* then how 705
And each true-hearted *servant* 252
And O thy *servant,* Lord, prepare 4
And to each *servant* does the Master say 322
And to my *servant,* whom I loved 619
For still the more the *servant* hath 1396
He shall my *servant* be 1557
Let thy happy *servant* be 1144
Moreover, they thy *servant* warn 618
O happy *servant* he 2331
Should not the *servant* tread it still 550
Thy devoted *servant* make me 1690
Thy ransomed *servant,* I 1144
Thy *servant,* Lord, am I 910, 2219
Thy *servant,* sure, thine 910
Who wast a *servant* that we might be 58

SERVANTS

All his *servants* join to sing 665
All thy *servants* tell thy praise 485
And holy must thy *servants* be 1882
And thy *servants* still before thee 1159
For all the *servants* of our King 324, 1067
Forever through thy *servants,* Lord 2115
Freely may thy *servants* give 1760
From death's dread sting thy *servants* free 79, 1937
Let us thy *servants* be 1943
That at last thy *servants* may 662
Thy *servants* proclaim the renown 423
Thy *servants* true to be 2303
To guard his *servants* here below 117
We are *servants* of God 2113
Whose *servants* are the brave 1491
Ye *servants* of the Triune God 1627

SERVE

And if I now earnestly *serve* him 884
And *serve* the cause of such 1241
And *serve* the God they love 774
And *serve* thee better than 2122
And some there are who cannot *serve* 2088
But *serve* him, O serve him 1706
Gladly *serve* thee, and obey 966, 1012
Him *serve* with mirth 57
How many *serve,* how many more 396
I will joyfully *serve* him 1982
I would *serve* thee with all 1045
Lord, I would *serve,* and be a son 396
Might *serve* him without fear 215
O *serve* the Lord with gladness 1485
Serve and love thee best of all 970
Serve him while you may 941
Serve him with awe 1105
Soldiers who will *serve* him 3
Thee would I *serve,* if I might 613
They *serve* thee still 491
Therefore, let us *serve* the Savior 1066
Thus we would *serve* thee 2278
To *serve* each human need 138
To *serve* my God when I awake 59
To *serve* right gloriously 151
To *serve* the present age 4
To *serve* thee is to reign 1646
We can *serve* him as disciples 695
We gladly *serve* him 1707
We must *serve* as well as praise 1606
We *serve* no God whose work is done 1593
We will *serve* with gladness 1707
Who will *serve* the King 2287

SERVED

All who *served* and fell on sleep 485
He *served* with willing hand 145
We have not *served* thee as we ought 2170

SERVES

Who *serves* my Father as a son 919

SERVICE

All *service* sweeter for thy love 300
And then thy *service* prove 1142
Another year of *service* 106
Each noble *service* that men 1840
Faithful, loving *service*, too 891
For noble *service* thou art here 546
Forever ready at thy *service* 2186
Gracious *service* to the living 1606
His *service* is the golden cord 919
If in thy *service* every hour 1442
In grateful *service* would we now 1427
In his meek and lowly *service* 344
In the *service* royal 2287
In thine own *service* make us glad 99
Its cheerfullest *service* to claim 1098
Service meet may render 357
Sharing his *service* every one 396
The *service* glad and free 2074
The *service* of all in a world's 709
The *service* of my love 886
There in sweetest *service* would I 141
Thou dost our *service* own 240, 1428
To thy *service* set apart 1690
We in glad *service* bring 21
What may thy *service* be 1428
Would you do *service* for Jesus 2323
Would you in his *service* labor 2324

SET

And now I *set* the solemn seal 1137
And *set* me faultless there 2201
And *set* our hearts on wisdom's ways 1174
And *set* the prisoners free 671
And *set* the world with truth aflame 1469
And *set* their horn on high 1898
And *set* thy city free 1604
And *set* thy judgments on the earth 1349
And *set* thy soul ablaze 151
And thus he *set* me free 1422
Before me still the Lord I *set* 570
But *set* thy heart on things 1193
For he has *set* me free 361
He *set* my feet upon a rock 887
He will *set* thy heart to singing 1766
Here *set* up thy throne 719
How Christ hath *set* you free 549
Jesus has *set* the example 531
Jesus *set* the world to singing 1975
O mighty God, *set* us aflame 1467
Set at God's right hand 1572
Set free from death's dark prison 1724
Set free from present sorrow 1759
Set, Lord, a watch upon my mouth 1433
Set our feet on lofty places 580
Set our hearts at liberty 1190
Set the burdened sinner free 637
Set the meanest high in power 665
Set thou a seal upon my lips 1128
Set thy seal on every heart 1685
Set up thy standard, Lord 1373
Set up thy throne within 2044
Set waymarks for our doubtful feet 1548
The Lord doth *set* him free 1321
Thee may I *set* at my right hand 499
They *set* the cruel Cross on high 206
Thou canst *set* the conscience free 538
Thou on God hath *set* thy love 271
Thou that canst never *set* 1286
Those who *set* at naught and sold 1106
To *set* his servants free 1842
To *set* the captive free 661
Where thou hast *set* thy feet 285

SETS

God *sets* the prisoner free 1394
He *sets* the course, sail on 2146
He *sets* the prisoner free 1351
Lo! he *sets* in blood no more 289
Sets her evening lamps alight 382
Sets the kingdoms on a blaze 1695

SETTETH

Then on each he *setteth* 983

SETTLED

I could not have *settled* the least 122

SEVERED

Severed only till he come 2089

SHACKLES

Then shall all *shackles* fall 1319

SHADE

A *shade* by day, defense by night 1905
And in its *shade* like brothers rest 321
As *shade* of clustered palm trees 1849
In the *shade* of thy palms 236
'Neath the far-off temples' *shade* 1570
Shade creeps o'er wild and wood 1843
Shade, 'mid the noontide glow 311
Some sheltering *shade* where sin 2248
While through the *shade* beam the stars 1611

SHADES

Amid the *shades* of evening 1923
And the *shades* of evening fall 1685
From *shades* of night he calls 6
From *shades* of night to plains 926
In darkest *shades*, if thou appear 1240
Nor *shades* of death, nor hell 2289
Soon as the evening *shades* prevail 1932
The *shades* are longer growing 178
Through midnight *shades* thou 2039
When the *shades* of life are falling 1642
Who from deepest *shades* of night 275

SHADOW

And in his *shadow* safely hide 1908
And 'neath his *shadow* here to rest 1289
Beneath the *shadow* of thy heavenly 460
Beneath the *shadow* of thy wing 1795
Beneath thy *shadow* we abide 274
Calm in the *shadow* of thy wing 1795
In *shadow* of thy wings I'll joy 1172

In the *shadow* of his wings 943
In the *shadow* of the rock 1207
Its *shadow* falls on the burning 1970
The solemn *shadow* of thy Cross 240, 1428

SHADOWS

Amid the mystic *shadows* 1793
And death's dark *shadows* put 1336
And earth's vain *shadows* flee 27
And I'm looking through the *shadows* 1499
And life's long *shadows* break 670
And life's *shadows* flee 1793
And *shadows* flee away 16
And so the *shadows* fall apart 39
And the *shadows* flee 1793
And where no *shadows* intervene 491
Are the *shadows* lengthening 1606
Are you walking alone through the *shadows* 1499
Beyond the fleeting *shadows* 16
But behind the dark *shadows* 1956
In the *shadows* of night 1984
It may be through the *shadows* 1822
Lent's long *shadows* have departed 700
Like *shadows* and the billows' 725
Shadows are gathering 1743
Shadows around me, shadows 2152
Shadows of the evening 1302
Sowing in the *shadows* 1771
That *shadows* a dry, thirsty land 24
That *shadows* fall on brightest hours 1236
The evening *shadows* fall 1592
The *shadows* flee away 252
The *shadows* of departing day 1918
The *shadows* of the night 121
The *shadows* round thee fall 133
Then the *shadows* will be lifted 2158
There are *shadows* of death (doubt, fear) 1956
They are only *shadows* 1956
Thick *shadows* lie across our 2171
Till *shadows* end in glory 2168

SHAFT

No deadly *shaft* by day 1908

SHAKE

Shake off dull sloth, and joyful rise 152
Shake off thy guilty fears 113
What can *shake* thy sure repose 541

SHAKES

A sudden trembling *shakes* the ground 697
Shakes the trembling gates of hell 1695
The blast of war's great organ *shakes* the skies 37

SHAME

Bearing *shame* and scoffing 1203
Because of sin and *shame* 22
In *shame* my glory and my crown 2034
Its *shame* and reproach gladly bear 1561
O Lord, with *shame* and sorrow 1414
O *shame* most glorious 1251
O *shame,* thrice shame upon us 1414
On them the *shame* shall fall 2116
Shame on us, Christian brothers 1414
Shame our wanton, selfish gladness 580
Shame to the men who serve 1889
Till through our pity and our *shame* 86
Then, glorious from thy *shame* 1416
To *shame* and guide this life 390
We with *shame* our sins 1179
What *shame* that so long he entreated 1741

SHAMED

All ungrateful, *shamed* before thee 2308
Shamed by its failure or its fears 856

SHAPE

Which can *shape* the world to fitness 36

SHAPEST

Who *shapest* men to God's own law 1468

SHARE

And *share* in the glory 1540
And *share* thy joy at last 1150
And you will *share* his promise 2269
Before we *share* her glory 1274
Enough to *share* with loveless folks 883
God be with them while they *share* 555
I have a *share* in that atonement 139
Let it *share* that upreaching desire 1834
O let me *share* thy holy birth 1416
Share but one common birth 56
Share with him thy bread of blessing 2263
That, as we *share* this hour 86
Then *share* in the joy of the "harvest 1540
To love and serve thee is my *share* 1148
To *share* the gift divine 96
We *share* our mutual woes 232
Would not *share* her sorrow deep 140
When we *share* her wretched crust 1574

SHARED

And he *shared* their happiness 1789
But to have *shared* the travail 1344
Forever *shared,* forever 917
To have *shared* the travail 1164

SHARES

Who *shares* his life's pure pleasures 1880
Who so *shares* another's woes 299

SHAREST

Who *sharest* all our sorrows 1491

SHARETH

And he *shareth* in our gladness 1572

SHARPNESS

All the *sharpness* of the Cross 2089

SHATTER

And *shatter* the spear and sword 2208

SHAVINGS

Sweeping the *shavings* from his workshop 2262

SHEATHED

Sheathed his sword 676

SHEAVES

Bringing in the *sheaves* 1771
Christ's golden *sheaves* for evermore 2120
No gathered *sheaves* of life's fair 1285
Send them now the *sheaves* to 429
The golden *sheaves* of harvest 1734
The *sheaves* of good from the fields 1540
Their *sheaves* of golden grain 1166
When the harvest *sheaves* ingathered 2263
Yellow *sheaves* of ripened grain 1628

SHED

And hath *shed* his own blood for 2249
And *shed* a joyful light 327
And *shed* abroad a Savior's love 318
And *shed* for you his blood 549
For Jesus *shed* his precious blood 308
For me he *shed* his precious blood 1915
For us the Savior's blood was *shed* 43
For you he *shed* his precious blood 697
God *shed* his grace on thee 1311
O *shed* thine influence from 1781
O that it now were *shed* abroad 1458
On him then who *shed* it 1974
Rich the blessings he will *shed* 63
Shed forth thy Spirit, day by day 642
Shed o'er all his robes 771
Shed o'er the world thy holy light 1023
Shed on us from above 311
Shed on us thy deathless learning 242
Shed peace and hope and joy 321
Shed sacred glories there 272
Shed thy gracious radiance here 744
Shed upon us heavenly grace 76
Shed within its wall alway 281
"They were *shed* for one who had gone 1983
Thou hast *shed* thy radiance 1680
'Twas I that *shed* the sacred blood 873
Where Jesus *shed* his blood for me 1562
Ye have *shed* the gospel light 275

SHEDS

Sheds on our path the glow 1155

SHEEP

All we, like *sheep*, had gone astray 426
And for his *sheep* he doth us take 57
And the lost *sheep* dost gather 43
And when like wandering *sheep* we strayed 184
As a *sheep* by the shearers 2063
Calling the *sheep* who've gone astray 681
Come like poor wandering *sheep* 348
For the *sheep* he bled 983
For the *sheep* the Lamb hath bled 288
He's searching now for his wandering *sheep* 1970
My *sheep* should never fear me 892
The *sheep* astray on the mountainside 1970
Wandering *sheep* the Shepherd seeks 2126
With his *sheep* securely fold you 556

SHELTER

A *shelter* by thy power 1357
A *shelter* from judgment (harm) 20
A *shelter* from tempest, from wind 20
A *shelter* in the time of storm 1905
And his *shelter* was a stable 1572
But more for *shelter* for my guest 883
My roof's safe *shelter* overhead 182
No *shelter* or help is nigh 1208
Our *shelter* from the stormy blast 1375
Shelter me safe in that "haven 1266
This *shelter* from the world's unrest 1528
Thy *Shelter* and thy Shade 885
To thee, my *shelter* from the strife 2103

SHELTERED

Because I have been *sheltered,* fed 182
I am safely *sheltered* here 431
Sheltered o'er, sheltered o'er, with his love 1674
Sheltered, protected, no evil can harm 2136
That, *sheltered* near thy side 109
Where they'll be *sheltered* from the cold 681

SHELTERS

And *shelters* them tenderly 698
Shelters thee under his wings 1637

SHEPHERD

A *Shepherd* both mighty to save 20
A *Shepherd* who gives his life 20
But the *Shepherd* made answer 1983
Dear *Shepherd,* I hear and will follow 1512
Dear *Shepherd* of thy chosen few 1032
Good *Shepherd,* may I sing thy 1876
Good *Shepherd,* think of me 1476
How David, once a *shepherd* 2179
I am the *Shepherd* true 892
I have a *Shepherd* who leads 831
If I were a *shepherd* 933
I'll be a *Shepherd* to these lambs 2245
Jesus my *Shepherd,* Brother, Friend 794
Kind *Shepherd,* turn their weary steps 670
Like a *shepherd,* Jesus will guard 1616
Loving *Shepherd,* ever near 1197
My *Shepherd* is beside me 921
O risen Lord, O *Shepherd* of our dead 1532
Or why, as *Shepherd* he should seek 817
See how the *shepherd*-band 559
Shepherd and Savior and 1971
Shepherd of the wandering star 258
Still the faithful *Shepherd* feeds 990
Tender *Shepherd,* never leave them 633
The *Shepherd* climbs o'er mountain 1970
The *Shepherd* seeks his wandering sheep 158
Was there ever kindest *shepherd* 1767
When the *shepherd* on the moor 2260

Where dost thou, dear *Shepherd,* resort 1512
Where the *Shepherd* leads the flock 1207

SHEPHERDESS

And one was a *shepherdess* 875

SHEPHERDS

And *shepherds* every thought 1891
And unto certain *shepherds* brought tidings 599
As *shepherds* watched their sleeping flocks 1113
Come in, ye *shepherds,* straight 320
Happy were those *shepherds* listening 369
Those *shepherds,* through the lonely 1928
To Bethlehem *shepherds* of earlier days 1926
Of *shepherds* watching there 1487
Shepherds, haste to Bethlehem 542
Shepherds heard the angels 940
Shepherds in the fields abiding 103
Shepherds keeping vigil 945
Shepherds quake at the sight 1720
Shepherds saw the wondrous sight 524
Shepherds seek their wandering 1735
Shepherds trudging through the night 609
Shepherds, why this jubilee 105
Shepherds with wonder receive it 2317
That *shepherds* heard of old 138
The *shepherds* feared and trembled 551
Then to the watchful *shepherds* it was 298
While *shepherds* kept their watching 551
While *shepherds* watch are keeping 2215

SHEW

And *shew* unto their children dear 1541

SHIELD

A trusty *shield* and weapon 19
And *shield* me from all harm 1297
And *shield* my soul from sin 1408
And *shield* this child 1406
And will *shield* thee from each foe 63
Be thou my *Shield* and Hiding-Place 109
For he will *shield* us 1289
God *shield* his word 1156
He will my *shield* and portion be 88
He will *shield* thee from above 271
In God, our *Shield,* we will rejoice 1448
Let the *shield* of faith avail 1147
My *Shield* and Hiding-Place 794
My *Shield* and Tower 1864
My *Shield* divine 858
O my Savior, *Shield* and Sun 1814
O *shield* us through that last dread 644
Our brethren *shield* in danger's hour 81
Our *Shield* and Defender 1546
Our *shield* from foes, our balm 2289
Shield and banner bright 1769
Shield it, we pray from sin 2011
Shield me with thy mighty hand 448
Shield our land, and save 1159
Shield them from temptation's breath 760
Shield thou the mariner from harm 650
Shield us through our earthly 2009
Shield with thy might 455
Surely he would *shield* thee 987

SHIELDS

And *shields* me from the tempter's 812
Some are prone upon their *shields* 2182
Their golden *shields* defend ye 1309

SHINE

And always *shine* for him 1030
And *shine* upon us from on high 393, 651
Around and in us brightly *shine* 1402
Forever singing, as they *shine* 1932
Holy Spirit, *shine* thou on the book 757
How it did *shine* in this poor heart 1578
Let it *shine* forevermore 1985
O *shine* each mist away 1087
O *shine* upon them from above 2245
Shall *shine* as doth the day 252
Shine forth, and let the darkling 191, 1445
Shine forth, and touch the future 191, 1445
Shine forth, O Light, that we may see 191, 1445
Shine forth, O stars and reddening 507
Shine forth upon our clouded 85
Shine in our darkness 1163
Shine on my soul, and all is bright 247
Shine on our souls when day 1692
Shine on us through the light 825
Shine on us with thy face 1123
Shine out, O Light divine 240
Shine, shine on me 1084
Shine, sweet Spirit 1566
Shine thou, before the shadows fall 1424
Shine through nature's light 925
Shine upon us, Savior, shine 582
Shine within this heart of mine 745
So let us *shine* 968
So we must *shine* 968
They shall *shine* in their beauty 2229
Until, as *shine* upon the sea 1385

SHINES

As *shines* a star when weary day 334
He *shines* in all that's fair 2012
It *shines* in the light 1546
Jesus *shines* (brighter, purer) 427
Lord in thee *shines* man's perfection 1075
Now he *shines,* the long-expected 1558
One sun *shines* o'er us all 56
Shines in might victorious 1800
Shines on from age to age 1544
Shines on their march 1081
Shines to save, for Christ is here 742
Shines with a more enduring glory 170
So *shines* thy love on me 1462
That *shines* to endless day 1423
There *shines* upon our trusting souls 1385
Which *shines* upon men as they are 1098
Yonder *shines* the infant Light 103

SHINEST

Yet more wonderful thou *shinest* 798

SHINETH

It *shineth* for me 1855
It *shineth* like a beacon 1544
Shineth thy golden day 181

SHINING

Shining still before them 517

SHIP

Full-sailed, thy *ship* drives onward 1533

SHIPS

All the *ships* have reached the land 972
And the *ships* sail out to sea 1929
In many *ships* we seek one 522
Like *ships* by tempests blown 646

SHOCK

In vain the surge's angry *shock* 301

SHOCKS

Though earthquake *shocks* are 1539

SHONE

Brightly *shone* the moon that night 627
Shone as light amidst the gloom 1728
There *shone* a holy light 551

SHORE

And I am safe on that beautiful *shore* 2222
From *shore* to shore, from earth 1449
From *shore* to shore the anthems 1595
From *shore* to shore the peoples call 592
Now upon the farther *shore* 1303
On many a distant island *shore* 2291
On this wild rocky *shore* 5
On wave-lapped *shore* 604
Once along that rugged *shore* 521
Thou hast no *shore,* fair ocean 489
Thy tranquil *shore* we, too, shall see 1965

SHORES

Beyond the *shores* of time 135
By the *shores* of thy sea 236
From tropic *shores* and islands 149
Shores of the utmost west 733

SHORTCOMINGS

And o'er its own *shortcomings* weeps 306

SHOULDER

And on his *shoulder* gently laid 1876

SHOULDERS

For *shoulders* broad and strong 1346

SHOUT

And a *shout* of joy resounding 2297
And bid the *shout* of warriors cease 247
And now they *shout* and sing to thee 410
And *shout* anew the glorious refrain 148
And *shout* hallelujah 1648
And *shout* for Daniel's band 1788
And *shout* him welcome to the skies 697
And we *shout* with the ransomed 2113
Ay! we *shout* to the lovely 1995
Ere we *shout* the glad song 953
I will *shout* and sing 912
I'll *shout* with the millions on high 24
O, let them *shout* and sing 2099
Shout aloud hosanna 1769
Shout Hallelujah, for the Lord is King 433
Shout it forth with glad acclaim 2126
Shout salvation full and free 2169
Shout to the saints 683
Shout, while ye journey home 733
Shout with their shout of praise 151
Sons of God, that *shout* for gladness 104
That is why I *shout* and sing 2002
The *shout* of them that feast 961
The *shout* that every prayer for mercy 37
Then the glad *shout* of triumph 1987

SHOUTING

With *shouting,* and singing 509

SHOUTS

Let *shouts* of holy joy outburst 79, 1937
Shouts of salvation are rending 660
Their *shouts* of, "Crucify," appall 873

SHOW

And Jesus will *show* you 1338
And *show* a brother's love 792
And *show* his praise below 230
And *show* me the heavenly way 2084
And *show* the death of our dear Lord 266
And *show* thyself a God of love 2245
And *show* us that God is love 2208
And *show* us we are not alone 2122
Could only *show* its full overflow 22
How can I *show* my love for him 2213
How shall we *show* our love to thee 1439
More of thyself, O *show* me 1284
O *show* thy Cross to me 1475
O *show* us the true light 149
"O who will *show* us any good?" 526
Or *show* forth all his praise 532
Shall *show* that love by word 182
Show forth thy pity on high 608, 612
Show in the heaven thy promised 1836
Show me that scene in the garden 1831
Show me the living way 1323
Show me the tomb where thou 1050
Show me thy light, that I 1239
Show me thy ways, O Lord 2116
Show me what I ought to do 448
Show the brightness of thy face 582
Show the world just where 398
Show them that Jesus is All 1600
Show to me now the empty tomb 1050
Show thy reconciled face 1676
Show us anew in Calvary 1467
Show us every devious way 756
Show us that bright shore 989
Show us the way amid the darkness 466
Show us thy risen spirit 1275
Show us thy will, we ask 1468

They *show* thy power abroad 2195
Thou wilt me *show* the path of life 570
We *show* thy death, we sing 2132

SHOWED

He *showed* them why Christ came 975
Here awhile he *showed* his love 357
Showed to men the perfect 1728

SHOWER

As a gracious *shower* descend 743
In sunshine or in *shower* 6
Lord, *shower* upon us from above 1432
O for a blessed *shower*, filling 723
Shower, O shower them, Lord 1612

SHOWERS

And thou with gentle *showers* 2081
As *showers* on earth that fall 1454
As *showers* that usher in the spring 327
Beyond the gracious *showers* 1169
But for the *showers* we plead 1981
Showers of blessing over all 966, 1012
Showers of blessing we need 1981
Showers the thirsty land 1138
When summer's balmy *showers* 2250

SHOWEST

What thou *showest* to be true 1120

SHOWETH

God *showeth* his good will to men 43

SHOWING

Showing how pleasant and happy 1030

SHOWN

God has *shown* the world 542
Shown thyself in saint and seer 579
Who hath *shown* us our Savior 2187

SHOWS

And *shows* to life a richer prize 1523
From all illusive *shows* of sense 2038
Here Jesus *shows* the way to heaven 2117
If Jesus *shows* his mercy mine 1240
Jesus *shows* his smiling face 2001
O matchless kindness! and he *shows* 192
Shows his wounds, and spreads 395
Shows me the glories of my God 1201
To pardon he *shows* you the way 1925
When Jesus *shows* his smiling face 1980

SHRINE

And when within this *shrine* we kneel 642
To worship at his *shrine* 198
We cannot at the *shrine* remain 32
While to that sacred *shrine* I move 1392
Within thy Father's *shrine* 267

SHRINES

The *shrines* our fathers founded 1353

SHRINK

Nor *shrink* from roads that thou 893
Shrink not, Christians! will ye yield 1560
Shrink not from the loss 1794
We *shrink* before thy vast abyss 1495
Ye shepherds, *shrink* not 248

SHRINKS

It *shrinks* not, but with calm 420

SHUN

Shall I *shun* its brink 2032
Shun evil companions 2336
Shun not suffering, shame 552
Shun not the struggle, face it 174

SHUNS

And *shuns* not pain, nor shame 620

SHUT

And *shut* his glories in 38
Shut not that gate against me 1456

SICK

And I was *sick* with sorrow 892
For some are *sick*, and some are sad 136
May the *sick* be in thy care 416
Sick and faint—thy strength afford 346
Sick and sorrowful, and blind 1735
Sick at heart and weary 939
Sick, we come to thee for cure 442
The *sick*, O Lord, around thee lay 136
The *sick*, the poor the tried 121
The *sick* to cure, the lost to seek 1525
The *sick*, with fevered frame 2008
Till the *sick* and sad, in gladness 2047

SICKLES

With *sickles* of truth must the work 1540

SICKNESS

In *sickness*, sorrow, want 1371
In thee no *sickness* may be seen 960
Never a *sickness* that he cannot 407
No *sickness*, no sadness 953
Out of my *sickness* into thy health 1602
Sickness and sorrow, pain and 1563
So may *sickness*, sin, and sadness 2047
When worn with *sickness*, oft hast 2223

SIDE

Always on the Lord's *side* 2287
And he is at the Father's *side* 1893
Are you walking daily by the Savior's *side* 693
As *side* by side we onward go 1410
But on my *side* is power divine 2295
By the *side* of those most near 810
Ever I'm walking close to his *side* 2152
Ever near the Christian's *side* 755
Flowing from his pierced *side* 142
For the good or evil *side* 1574
Forever by thy *side* 2046

From thy riven *side* which flowed 1671
I am safe when by thy *side* 1682
Jesus at my *side* 62, 1574
"My pierced *side*, O Thomas, see 493
Nearer my Savior's wounded *side* 1267
O, may we never from his *side* 1374
O, why from his *side* flowed 1974
On every *side* I find thy hand 2039
On every *side* the walls are down 1467
Safe by thy *side* 2020
Still closer to thy *side* I press 1436
There, close by the *side* of that loved one 1986
Thou, Lord, wast at our *side* 2166
To dwell forever at his *side* 2
We are on the Lord's *side* 2287
When he was walking at their *side* 975
Who's on the Lord's *side* 1987

SIGH

Above the night-wind's *sigh* 2234
Every *sigh* was hushed forever 1499
For which our spirits *sigh* 16
I *sigh* for thee while waiting 1404
I *sigh*, when the evening shadows 1913
Inly I *sigh* for thy repose 2033
Not a *sigh* for the blessings of rest 1992
One *sigh* unheard, one prayer 1531
There is no secret *sigh* we breathe 1978
To every plaintive *sigh* 1

SIGHED

He *sighed*, "I bear this Cross for thee" 825
I *sighed* for rest and happiness 1322

SIGHING

There shall be no more *sighing* 137

SIGHS

A hymn of *sighs* shall rise to thee 23
And *sighs* from contrite hearts 1579
It *sighs*, "Where shall I find 724
Let *sighs* and sorrows cease 559

SIGHT

As in thy *sight* to live 4
Beyond the Father's *sight* 39
Dear to God's *sight* is his saints' death 910
Full in his *sight* his children stand 6
His *sight* is never dim 921
I am precious in his *sight* 2232
I shall ne'er get *sight* of the gates 864
If drunk with *sight* of power 583
Once the *sight* of Judah's seer 253
Sight to the inly blind 2051
Sight was gone, and fears 895
Still walking in your Captain's *sight* 1746
That glorious *sight* to see 2332
Then to my fainting *sight* appear 1517
Thou art precious in his *sight* 2341
Though *sight* and touch have failed 2168
Until that wondrous *sight* 1480
When forever from our *sight* 382
Well-pleasing in thy *sight* 1332

SIGHTS

From all ill *sights* would turn 1300

SIGN

And this shall be the *sign* 2282
At the *sign* of triumph 1586
"In this *sign* we conquer 507
There the saving *sign* display 1747
Though no *sign* was in the sky 2254
We bring them, Lord, and with the *sign* 9
Who by this *sign* didst conquer 762
Yet not the *sign* we trust 505

SIGNS

Signs of his coming multiply 982
We see the *signs* but see not him 89
What its *signs* of promise are 2154

SILENCE

All within keep *silence* 600
And *silence* holds the air 1552
In *silence* hast thou come 2168
In the consecrate *silence* know 2110
My lips no more can *silence* keep 34
What though, in solemn *silence*, all 1932

SILENT

Be not *silent* in your need 2268
O be not *silent*, lest I die 1455
Yea, when my tongue must *silent* be 23

SIN

A Savior who knows . . . from *sin* 20
All for *sin* could not atone 1671
All the *sin* of the world on the Savior 1268
Alone, thou Christ, with *sin* and death 123
And all our *sin* consuming 2086
And canst thou then, with *sin* beset 1514
And, lo, from *sin* and grief 2034
And of my *sin* thou freely didst 1314
And other's *sin* forgive 1930
And *sin* is backward hurled 148
And *sin* is slain, and death brings 1803
And *sin*, we shall be free 232
Away with *sin* and sorrow 2015
Be of *sin* the double cure 1671
Because of *sin* and shame 22
Beyond the present *sin* and shame 370
By *sin* unclouded 542
Come, and thy *sin* confessing 1584
Even me with all my *sin* 1735
False and full of *sin* I am 994
Far in *sin* to stray 1101
Fighting *sin* with all our might 1066
For man, the creature's *sin* 38
For *sin* can never enter there 135
Have I long in *sin* been sleeping 1138
Here 'mid earth's *sin* and sorrow 1829
I, who with *sin* was so defiled 2302
In thee to conquer *sin* 1187
Infinite, infinite, *sin* upon sin 1276
Is it *sin* that pains or grieves 1577

Just from *sin* and self to cease 2092
Let every *sin* be crucified 1230
Long has *sin*, without control 745
Look down on all earth's *sin* 82
Lord, I am *sin*, but thou art love 1018
My *sin* and guilt he canceled 870
My *sin* and misery declare 333
My *sin* hid not from thee 772
My *sin* I ever see 31
My *sin*, not in part, but the whole 2249
My *sin*, O the bliss of this glorious 2249
No matter how, if only *sin* 1582
None who in *sin* takes pleasure 1597
Nothing but *sin* have I to give 1001
O *sin* that hath no equal 1414
O *sin*, thou art vanquished 1599
O thou, who didst for *sin* atone 404
Sin, and want, and sorrow 968
Sin and want we come confessing 1681
Sin be banished from thy sight 951
Sin calls for ceaseless care 682
Sin cannot harm me there 1675
Sin had alarmed me 1262
Sin had left a crimson stain 837
Sin hath gone over me 1276
Sin of not loving thee 1276
Sin of not trusting thee 1276
Sin rebuke, and folly chide 1764
Sin shall then be overthrown 2126
Sin to rebuke, to break the 1511
Sin which laid the Cross 1271
Sin, with its follies, I gladly 1266
Some *sin*, that strives for mastery 1345
That *sin* might be forgiven 426
Then, from *sin* and sorrow 1745
There is no *sin* in heaven 1977
There shall be no more *sin* 2003
Thine own to be, from *sin* set free 21
Those who long in *sin* had strayed 1051
Thou didst for *sin* atone 2046
Though by *sin* oppressed 2094
Though *sin* and sorrow wound 1555
Though *sin* should fill me with distress 2295
Till we can *sin* no more 93
To falter would be *sin* 617, 2321
To guide and to save me from *sin* 2084
'Twas there from *sin* he set me free 1568
When from *sin* our hearts are pure 347
When *sin* abounds, and error 460
Where *sin* can never enter 872
Where *sin* no more shall sever 2207
Who are struggling hard with *sin* 251
Who from *sin* now saves us 290
Whose *sin* is wholly covered 772

SINCERITY

With *sincerity* and love 142

SINEWS

All our *sinews* feel new-strung 1305

SINFUL

And, suffering for the *sinful* 283
So *sinful*, so weary thine, thine 1477

SING

And I no more, as now, shall *sing* 1749
And *sing*, and love, and pray 600
And *sing* his bleeding love 1279
And *sing* his name to harps of gold 1308
And *sing*, in life or death 1245
And *sing* in sweetest notes the song 147
And *sing* my "Glory, glory" 1928
And *sing* the praises of thy name 1435
And *sing* the song of Moses 708
And *sing* the triumphs of his grace 1108
And *sing* the wonders of his grace 1864
And *sing* through endless days 1959
And *sing* with the ransomed 18
And *sing* with you this song 1081
And we'll all *sing* hallelujah 1499
But now we *sing* deeper 1298
Do *sing* everlastingly, "Holy! Holy!" 1213
For those who *sing* with saints 654
God be with them while they *sing* 555
Hallelujah we *sing* in the church 765
Hallelujah, we *sing*, like the children 765
Humbly *sing* until the day 1838
I shall *sing* his praises through 141
I shall *sing* thanks to God 1627
I *sing* aloud thy praises 1729
I *sing*, for I cannot be silent 1649
I *sing* for joy of that which lies 1723
I *sing* his praises, knowing 2109
I *sing* it again and again 1958
I sing it o'er and o'er 2309
I *sing* the beauty of the gospel 876
I *sing* the goodness of the Lord 877
I *sing* the wisdom that ordained 877
I, too, must *sing* with joyful tongue 528
I will *sing* of thy triumph 1648
I would *sing* only of thy power 893
I'd *sing* his glorious righteousness 1339
I'd *sing* the character he bears 1339
If you *sing*, and sing, and sing 1730
I'll *sing* upon a happier shore 1231
I'll *sing* with the glittering crown 1246
Incessant we shall *sing* 298
Let all *sing* hallelujah 952
Let us *sing* psalms to him 1334, 1335
Now to the Lord *sing* praises 599
O Gloria in excelsis *sing* 2306
O gratefully *sing* his power 1546
O Lord, I'd *sing* of thee 1557
O may we *sing* that song before 186
O *sing* in exultation, to Christ 1083
O *sing* of fragrant flowers' 1487
O *sing* of his grace 1546
O, *sing* the glad story old 2309
O *sing* ye praises to the Lord 1887, 1888
O *sing* ye the songs that 1768
Shall *sing* when songs on earth 604
Sing a cheery song 903
Sing above the battle's 2169
Sing all the earth to God 1486
Sing, all ye citizens of heaven 1330
Sing, and smile and pray 1730
Sing, choirs of angels 1330

Sing, creatures, sing; the dust 1727
Sing forth the honor of his name 50
Sing glory to God, and goodwill 1768
Sing his mercy and his grace 1731
Sing his praise with a ready 1706
Sing "Holy, holy, holy!" 1341
Sing how he intercedes above 147
Sing how he spoiled the hosts 697
Sing hymns that were sung by 1768
Sing in exultation 1330
Sing in holy convocation 1213
Sing in triumph o'er the tomb 2169
Sing it softly in the gloom 2169
Sing it with the saints in glory 895
Sing joyful hallelujah 952
Sing notes of love, that some 1548
Sing, O earth, his wonderful love 1616
Sing, O sing, of my Redeemer 894
Sing, O ye people, gladly adore 747
Sing of his dying love (rising power) 147
Sing of redemption he has wrought 2140
Sing of the boundless energy 2262
Sing of the great salvation 2140
Sing our harvest song 1620
Sing praise to him, and give him 1636
Sing praises to his name 2166
Sing praises to the Lord most high 1435
Sing, pray, and swerve not 904
Sing, sing, ye heavenly choir 788
Sing songs of love and praise 1734
Sing songs of the angels when Jesus 1768
Sing the ending of the fray 1728
Sing the Lord who came to die 1214
Sing the praises of the Lord 104
Sing the sweet promise of his 190
Sing the sweet songs of praise as you 130
Sing thy glory cheerily 208
Sing thy just and endless praise 227
Sing to God a hymn of gladness 76, 663
Sing to God a hymn of praise 663
Sing to him who found the ransom 356
Sing to the Lord of harvest 1734
Sing to the Lord with cheerful voice 57
Sing to the Savior who came 1617
Sing us sweet fragments 670
Sing we hallelujah 2118
Sing we here with glad accord 748
Sing when your trials are 1269
Sing, ye heavens, thou (ye) earth reply 289
Sing, ye islands of the sea 2169
Sing ye to him, sing psalms 533
Sing your Savior's worthy praise 277
So we *sing* the story 1205
That we all may *sing* for aye 287
Thee would I *sing* 1511
Then I will *sing* and praise thy 2078
Then shall I *sing*, with sweet 153
Then shall we *sing* to God our King 28
Then will we *sing* more sweet 2025
There to *sing* a nobler song 1118
They love to *sing* to God their King 28
They *sing* because thou art their Sun 788
They *sing* the name of Jesus 2172
Thou soon shalt *sing* the victor's song 1639
Thus they *sing* eternally 78
To God *sing* hallelujah 1164
To God, the *Savior*, sing 1449
To thee alone we *sing* 1481
To you we *sing* this glad Noel 918
We cheerfully *sing*, "Press onward" 1909
We shall *sing* on that beautiful shore 1992
We shall *sing* praise to the Lamb 167
We *sing* together hymns of praise 1591
We, too, *sing* for joy, and say 287
We, too, will *sing* to God our King 28
We would *sing* thee fairest 1034
We'll *sing* and shout the victory 1731
We'll *sing* in glad reunion 2061
We'll *sing* our Jesus, lovely name 2025
We'll *sing* the victor's song 1860
Who should louder *sing* than I? 1814
With those who *sing*, with those 1329
Yes, I would *sing* loudest hosannas 1831

SINGING

Birds are brightly *singing* 61
I'm *singing* them o'er and o'er 2066
There to thee, forever *singing* 78
Through the *singing* and the sobbing 1096

SINGS

And *sings* the same sweet psalms 33
Each little bird that *sings* 68
Joyful Zion *sings* 286
The stormy sea *sings* praise to God 55
Then *sings* my soul, my Savior God 1437

SINK

For how can I *sink* while 1868
I *sink* in contemplation 431
I *sink* in life's alarms 1202
Now I *sink* before thee lowly 394
Sink heart and voice oppressed 961
We *sink* beneath the water's face 316

SINKS

So peacefully he *sinks* to rest 793
When *sinks* my heart in waves 1519
While *sinks* life's lingering sand 1923

SINLESS

Where the songs of all the *sinless* 77

SINNED

Although thou hast *sinned* against 1494
Have you *sinned* as none else 1338
I have *sinned* against thy grace 554
Thou hast *sinned*, I'll pardon thee 836
Though we have *sinned*, he has 1743

SINNER

A *sinner* by choice, and an alien 1229
A *sinner*, condemned, unclean 881
A wretched *sinner*, lost to God 1137
But now I'm a *sinner*, saved 1262
Calling, O *sinner*, "Come home!" 1743
Come, *sinner*, come 680
For me, a *sinner*, is thy life-blood 1251

God and the *sinner* united 1617
I now am a *sinner* saved 1262
I'm only a *sinner* saved by grace 1262
"Nor let that ransomed *sinner* die!" 113
O the Savior is calling the *sinner* 2212
Once for all, O *sinner*, receive it 504
Or *sinner* find that he would not 2000
Over a *sinner* returning 353
Poor *sinner*, harden not your heart 1343
Sinner, do you love my Jesus 2156
Sinner, list to the loving call 1732
Sinner, O won't you believe it 2317
Sinner, will you let him in 692
That for me, a *sinner*, he suffered 880
The *sinner* am I, who on Jesus rely 73
The *sinner* is free 73
There is never a guilty *sinner* 1976
When the *sinner*, seeking life 2260
When the *sinner* shall hear his doom 1990
Who did for every *sinner* die 1777

SINNERS

And *sinners*, plunged beneath 1961
Can do helpless *sinners* good 358
Christ, who once for *sinners* bled 288
Come, *sinners*, see your Savior die 1460
Facing for *sinners* death 2144
For *sinners* interceding 1325
For *sinners* such as I 38
God and *sinners* reconciled 675
Guilty *sinners* to reclaim 227
He will the vilest of *sinners* forgive 829
Intercessor, Friend of *sinners* 77
Let *sinners* feel thy quickening word 2203
O thou for *sinners* slain 195
Once for favored *sinners* slain 1106
Praying for *sinners* 2144
Returning *sinners* to a Father's 435
Sinners, call ye on his name 1559
Sinners in derision crowned him 1117
Sinners Jesus came to call 358
Sinners to redeem and save 971
Sinners you can help to win 2339
That guilty *sinners*, such as I 109
The way, he'll *sinners* show 2116
There for *sinners* thou art pleading 659
Thou dost with *sinners* bear 2071
Thou Hope of *sinners* here 75
To praise the Lamb for *sinners* slain 316
To thee let *sinners* fly 1924
To wretched *sinners* condescends 1290
While *sinners*, now confessing 1911
Who didst for *sinners* die 404
Why, ye long-sought *sinners*, why 1736
Why, ye ransomed *sinners*, why 1736
"Worthy the Lamb, for *sinners* slain 1108
Ye *sinners*, come, 'tis mercy's voice 1924

SINS

Ah, Lord, our *sins* arraigned 1415
All thy *sins* shall be forgiven 1577
And my *sins*, which were many 2211
And take my *sins* away 5
And, when in *sins* and sorrows 2223
Bearing our *sins*, my Redeemer 1575
Come, with thy *sins*; at his feet 985
Crimson do my *sins* seems to me 214
For all my *sins* his blood 977
For all our *sins* we grieve 455
For his people's *sins*, chastised 140, 1263
For lo! between our *sins* 99
For our *sins* he suffered and bled 1616
For *sins* forgiven 1439
For *sins* not his own 73
For *sins* of heedless word and deed 189
For those whose *sins* he bore 147
From my *sins* O hide thy face 552
From our *sins* and fears release us 658
From *sins* which make the heart now cold 189
Have you *sins* that to men's eyes 112
He my *sins* did bear 900
Heavy though our *sins*, thy mercy 711
Here all your *sins* and sorrows 2155
I with all my *sins* draw nigh 1735
Let my *sins* be all forgiven 1013
Let our *sins* be all forgiven 1118
Lo, our *sins* on thee we cast 492
Made to cleanse my *sins* 214
My *sins* and faults of youth 1719, 2116
My *sins* are all under the blood 17
My *sins* are forgiven 122
My *sins* forgive, and let me live 1910
My *sins* he forgave 623
No more let *sins* and sorrows 1039
On the Lord thy *sins* were laid 2126
Our father's *sins* were manifold 648
Our oft-repeated *sins* 2036
Our secret *sins* are, in the light 1428
Our *sins* and follies, close in thine 385
Our *sins* confess, thy heart 325
Our *sins*, not thine, thou bearest 86
Our *sins* on Jesus laid 1846
Our *sins* were great and sore 368
The *sins* were mine, his body 825
Then are my *sins* by thee 1237
There our *sins* and sorrows hide 1028
This day's *sins* O pardon 446
Though your *sins* be red as crimson 1866
"Thy *sins* are sharper thorns 825
To shame our *sins*, he blushed 1555
'Twas my *sins* that crucified him 1709
Was it for *sins* that I have done 38
What though thy *sins* are like crimson 353
When I knew my *sins* forgiven 25
When my *sins* I must confide 2233
When Satan, by my *sins* made bold 1517
Your many *sins* are all forgiven 1867

SISTER

Moses' *sister* aided him 251

SISTERS

Sisters, will you join and help 251

SIT

And *sit* down upon his throne 1712
I *sit* in willing bonds 1035

Sit at the feast, dear Lord 721
There we *sit* in heavenly places 1697
To *sit* upon the throne 195

SITS

He *sits* at God's right hand 1653
He *sits* for grace and judgment 786
He *sits* on yonder throne 673
He *sits* upon the throne 283
Of him that *sits* upon the throne 323
To him who *sits* upon the throne 671

SITTETH

Nor *sitteth* in the scorner's chair 1841
Sitteth he in royal state 611

SKIES

And *skies* are chill, and frosts 2097
As those which are filling the *skies* 1095
Bright *skies* overhead 621
Bright *skies* will soon be 921
Brightening all the morning *skies* 127
Easter *skies* pour radiant light 412
Flushing the eastern *skies* 1089
For ample *skies* with glories 1779
For *skies* of golden splendor 2303
For the eastern *skies* are glowing 1993
It echoes through the *skies* 48
Its *skies* are not like earthly skies 1965
Just above are clouded *skies* that you 399
Must I be carried to the *skies* 87
Skies will be brighter some 1750
Skies will grow blue and sunny 903
Skies with crimson clouds aflame 1211
Still through the cloven *skies* they come 948
Sweetly sounding through the *skies* 684
The twilight *skies* adorning 137
Till the revolving *skies* had brought 237
When *skies* are dark, or when 383
When the *skies* are fair 1114

SKILL

Nor *skill*, nor might, nor merit 479
O *skill*, for human reach 2039
Our *skill* of hand and strength 1382
Skill of mind and hand and eye 1158
That by the *skill* of thy dear hands 388
The *skill* that teaches him to plan 414
This *skill* is thine, O Lord 414
What *skill* and science slowly gain 1168

SKY

Above the bright blue *sky* 1988
And fit it for the *sky* 4
But the *sky* is bright and cheery 1573
Far beyond the starry *sky* 424
Far, far above the starry *sky* 1243
In the evening *sky* 1102
In twilight *sky* it gleams 770
Now above the *sky* he's King 971
See the *sky* above us 61
Sky and sea, thine own creation 2308
Sky and sunlight, dream 1796
Than glows in any earthly *sky* 2001
That brightens up the *sky* 68
That the *sky* is blue 539
The glorious *sky*, embracing all 1960
The *sky* is dark, the foe is strong 1440
The *sky* is o'ershadowed 1208
When ever blue the *sky* shall gleam 520
When the *sky* is dark above 562
Your *sky* by the night be o'ercast 164

SKYLARKS

Skylarks, the earth forsaking 1724

SLAIN

And one was *slain* by a fierce 875
"For he was *slain* for us." 323, 671
Had Christ, that once was *slain* 2015
There was he *slain* in noble youth 1921

SLANDER

Who doth not *slander* with his tongue 2311

SLAVE

Once was a *slave* to doubts 624

SLAVES

Poor *slaves* of lies and sin 1373
Then *slaves* shall all be freedmen 781
Ye *slaves* of sin and hell 241

SLAY

A word shall quickly *slay* him 19
And *slay* the falsehood there 1373

SLEEP

A *sleep*, a dream, a story 1377
Above thy deep and dreamless *sleep* 1426
And quiet *sleep* will take 526
And sweet the *sleep* which follows 1810
And to send me quiet *sleep* 1304
And with sweet *sleep* mine eyelids close 59
Anywhere with Jesus, I can go to *sleep* 108
Be every mourners' *sleep* tonight 1801
But thine is still a blessed *sleep* 132
For those who *sleep*, and those 2207
From *sleep* and from damnation 1365
From thy *sleep* awaken 1668
I, ere I *sleep*, at peace may be 59
Nor shall my sword *sleep* in my hand 95
Scarce from *sleep* my thoughts 2308
Sleep in heavenly peace 1720
Sleep is for sons of night 682
Sleep not, when mercies loudly 1288
The *sleep* of ages break 733
Through *sleep* and darkness 1273
Until death's holy *sleep* 855
When in *sleep* mine eyelids close 2227

SLEEPETH

Behold, he *sleepeth* not, he 2139
While the Christian *sleepeth* 1668

SLEEPLESS

When in the night I *sleepless* lie 59

SLEEPS

She *sleeps,* sweetly sleeps 'neath 1986

SLIDE

Slide therefore shall not I 1043

SLIGHT

Do not *slight* the invitation 1866

SLIGHTED

And often I have *slighted* 497
Slighted thy word 607
So *slighted* by a rebel race 426

SLIGHTING

Though they are *slighting* him 1655

SLOPES

Where o'er the *slopes* of Persia 149

SLOTH

Cast all *sloth* away 2153
No faithless *sloth* be there 2147

SLUMBER

No careless *slumber* shall his eyelids 2139
O thou who canst not *slumber* 1377
Sleeping his first earthly *slumber* 369
Slumber sweet thy mercy send us 605
To be for such a *slumber* meet 132

SLUMBERED

But with the poor he *slumbered* 1199

SLUMBERETH

He *slumbereth* ne'er 2139

SLUMBER-GIFTS

Thy *slumber-gifts* our strength 1131

SLUMBERS

For "he *slumbers* not nor sleeps 2126
He *slumbers* not, nor sleeps 1093
He who *slumbers* not, nor sleeps 2275

SMART

Healing all its hidden *smart* 131

SMILE

And his *smile* drives their sorrows 1502
And his *smile* will be the first 2246
And *smile* at the tears I have shed 1512
By him victorious! *Smile* or frown 264
Each *smile* a hymn, each kindly 1319
His own most gracious *smile* 1959
His *smile* is upon me 1741
If a *smile* we can renew 1955
If you *smile,* and smile 1730
My *smile* beneath the tyrant's 2034
O let thy *smile* descend 723
Resting 'neath thy *smile* 978
Smile a bit as you journey 903
Smile on me, beautiful morning star 180
Then I can *smile* at Satan's rage 2231
Thou mayst *smile* at all thy foes 541
Though you have only a *smile* 907
Thy gladdening *smile* to meet 1805
Thy gladdening *smile* to see 234
Thy present *smile* a heaven imparts 89
We *smile* at pain while thou art 1459
What a Father's *smile* is thine 980
Yet just a *smile* from my Savior 2222

SMILED

And *smiled* on them 765
And *smiled* to hear their song 2230
And sweetly *smiled,* and kindly 2245

SMILES

And *smiles* have no alloy 489
The *smiles* and tones that make 1891
Welcome *smiles* on faces sad 2007
With *smiles* through the gates 1098
With thy *smiles* and sonnets 163

SMITE

And as they *smite* I feel afresh 873
But would *smite* the living 441
If not I'll *smite* your first-born 2240
Smite death's threatening wave 556
Smite us, and save us all 1365
Still *smite,* still burn, till naught 1373
The Lord shall *smite* each heathen 2138
Who shall *smite* in holy vengeance 2288

SMOOTH

Smooth let it be or rough 2083
Smooth the rough breaker's rising crest 650

SMOTE

That he who *smote* in Man for man 1630

SNARES

The daily *snares* of sin to spurn 161

SNATCH

Snatch them in pity from sin 1655

SNOW

After the winter *snow* a wind 1727
And I shall be whiter than *snow* 214
In winter's *snow,* in summer's sun 2277
On wings of silence, soft as *snow* 46
Snow had fallen, snow on snow 933
The crystal of the *snow* 40
When the *snow* lay round about 627
White as the *snow* they shall be 353
Whiter than *snow,* Lord, wash me 691
Whiter than *snow* you may be 1206
Would you be whiter, much whiter than *snow* 2323

SNOWFIELDS

Across the northern *snowfields* 33

SNOWFLAKE

Shekinah of the *snowflake* 1891

SOAR

I *soar* to reach immortal joys 2203
To thee should *soar* my song 1142
When I *soar* through tracts 1671

SOARED

His soul in vision *soared* 91

SOBBED

And *sobbed* with heart forlorn 626

SOD

And ever green the *sod* 520
And from the *sod* the flower 6
Beneath the earth's brown *sod* 11
Broken *sod* to living gold 1665
E'en when resting beneath the *sod* 729

SOFTENED

They *softened* every frown 956

SOFTNESS

Not in silken *softness* shod 2254

SOIL

O sweet and pleasant *soil* 960

SOLACE

A *solace* here I find 2243
Solace all its wide dominion 1042
Solace of my hours of night 972
Solace in the midst of woe 342
Yet he is himself my *solace* 1643

SOLD

How Joseph, *sold* by his brothers 2179
Ye who have *sold* for naught 241

SOLDIER

A *soldier* true 3
And one was a *soldier* 875
Soldier in the fight 1114
Soldier of the cross 2156
Strong-hearted like a *soldier* 1784
That a *soldier*, one day, thrust a spear 17
Then each faithful, loyal *soldier* 2064
When the *soldier* on the field 2260

SOLDIERS

Christian *soldiers*, onward go 1560
Faithful *soldiers*, we shall triumph 2159
Jesus calls for *soldiers* 3
Loyal *soldiers*, do and dare 262
On then, Christian *soldiers* 1586
Soldiers for the conflict 3
Soldiers of Christ, arise and enter 433
Soldiers of Christ, disciples 466
Soldiers who will serve him 3
While *soldiers* scoff and Jews 1333

SOLITUDE

All is *solitude* and gloom 552

SOMEBODY

Somebody bent so tenderly 1752
Somebody came, O, who could it be 1752
Somebody cares when you're tempted 1754
Somebody did a golden deed 1755
Somebody filled the days with light 1753
Somebody fought a valiant fight 1753
Somebody holds my hand each day 1752
Somebody made a loving gift 1753
Somebody thought 'tis sweet to live 1753, 1755
Somebody waits for your coming 1754
Somebody wants you to know him 1754
Somebody whispered, sweet and low 1752
Was that *somebody* you 1753

SOMEONE

Someone in darkness and sin 1757
Someone in silence is making the choice 1757
Someone is halting, and counting 1757
Someone is living in selfish delight 1757
Someone is spurning his love 1757
Someone is turning his face from 1757
Someone is walking a perilous way 1757
Someone the glorious King will see 1758
Someone will fail of the saint's 1758
Someone will gladly his cross 1758
Someone will greet on the golden 1758
Someone will knock when the door 1758
Someone will sing the triumphant 1758
Someone will travel the streets 1758
Someone will yield to the Lord 1757

SOMETHING

Something for thee 1689

SOMETIME

Sometime, sometime we'll understand 1282
Sometime with tearless eyes 1282

SOMETIMES

And *sometimes* how weary my feet 1489
O *sometimes* how long seems the day 1489
Sometimes 'mid scenes of deepest gloom 702
Sometimes where Eden's bowers bloom 702

SOMEWHERE

And *somewhere* always new 1852
There's surely *somewhere* a lowly 955

SON

Ah! ah! beautiful is her *Son* 257
And what the *Son* of Man that thou 1450
Christ, the everlasting *Son* 277
Dost to every *son* and daughter 2319
For this his *Son* to earth descended 1290
His only *Son* declared 2334
His *Son* thy righteousness 1454
How his only *Son* he gave 1783
In thee hath David's promised *Son* 1569
Jesu, *Son* of human mother 634

Jesus Christ, your Father's *Son,* bids 2276
Jesus, the Virgin's *Son* 1632
Lo, the *Son* of God is come 2154
My father's own *Son,* the Savior 1229
Now may Mary's *Son,* who came 2141
O *Son* of God, who lovest me 920
Or what the *Son* of Man that 775
The everlasting *Son* incarnate 1842
The Father's coeternal *Son* 775
The Lord to Hannah's *son* 797
The slain, the risen *Son* 1479
The *Son,* and him who reigns 1299
The *Son* of God commands 958
The *Son* of man, whom for thyself 2131
There David's greater *Son* hath fixed 786
There God the *Son* forever reigns 1563
Thy *Son* in love abiding 2021
To thee presenting, through thy *Son* 1733
To thee, who art with God the *Son* 2118
To us a *Son* is given 1917

SONG

A new and joyful *song* of praise 887
A new *song* to him sing 2329
A *song* of deliverance 1976
A *song* of glory to our God 887
A *song* of those who answer 956
A *song* of trust my soul can sing 867
A *song* with gratitude 23
A sweeter *song* shall then be heard 496
And a new *song* is in my mouth 1242
And Christ shall be our *song* 2025
And everlasting *song* 2105
And holy is their *song* 1977
And my *song* shall ever be 881
And our *song* will sound unceasing 450
And that *song* from afar has 1995
And the angels' *song* still rings 1095
And the *song* of our redemption 2256
For thee this *song* of thanks 23
Glad to join the holy *song* 1510
He put a *song,* a wonderful song 25
His *song* in them, in us 2164
In every *song* of every bird 1384
In joyous *song* our voices 1293
In the glad *song* of ages 2246
Jesus, Jesus, this is my *song* 65
Jesus, of thee shall be my *song* 65
Let the *song* of triumph 262
Lord, to thee our *song* we pour 1799
May my *song* ever be of the love 1268
May our evening *song* be telling 446
My *song* to him I raise 1455
My *song,* while climbing, shall 915
My thankful *song* thy mercy 2078
Now be the *song* of praise 1937
Oh, if there's only one *song* I can sing 806
One *song* ascendeth to the skies 1579
Our cheerful *song* would oftener be 2221
Our *song* shall be, "Hosanna 48
Our *song* shall rise to greet 33
Ours the *song* of praise 1205
Rang out the *song* 1366
Sing to the Lord a glorious *song* 1366
Some *song* to raise, or prayer 1689
Song of our spirits, rejoicing 2128
Still all my *song* would be 1265

SONGS

Amid thy people *songs* of praise 72
And here our *songs* ascend 2165
And his *songs* our tongues employ 1817
And in glad *songs* of praise 1704
And nobler *songs* above 2106
And *songs* ascend instead of sighs 2267
And *songs* at break of day 350
And *songs* of angels and of men 1592
And *songs* of gladness bring 1123
And *songs* of thy salvation 772
And the beautiful *songs* of the angels 1922
And the old, old *songs* that we used 2066
And victor *songs* ring clear 1604
But *songs* of peace and joy 2301
Glad *songs* that never cease 1959
Glad *songs* to thee we sing 332
Happy, how happy, the *songs* 2129
Hark, hark, my soul, angelic *songs* 670
Hark! the *songs* of peaceful 77
Holy *songs* of praise 1102
In loftiest *songs* of sweetest praise 1339
In *songs* of glad accord 1083
In *songs,* they shall sing cheerfully 50
Let merry *songs* be sung 160
Let *songs* of love and brotherhood 371
Let us in our most joyful *songs* 1334
Like morning *songs* his voice 327
My sweetest *songs* I'll raise 860
No earthly *songs* are half so sweet 1095
No *songs* of shallow welcome 1604
Of the *songs* that they breathe 1503
Our *songs* of praise 1342
Singing *songs* of expectation 2067
Songs are breaking o'er the earth 1100
Songs be in every mouth 733
Songs of his salvation never more 1833
Songs of praise arose when he 1762
Songs of praise awoke the morn 1762
Songs of praise shall conquer 1762
Songs of praise shall crown 1762
Songs of praise shall hail 1762
Songs of praise their powers 1762
Songs of praises, songs of 652
Songs of sinful man 101
Sweet are the *songs* when they together 666
The *songs* I cannot sing 2001
The *songs* of birds upon the wing 1461
Their joyful *songs* proclaim 559
Their *songs* of praise in heaven 374
Then let our *songs* abound 351
Thou with *songs* of deliverance 1314
To sing on high their festal *songs* 374
To thee sweet *songs* I raise 1387
Wafting the *songs* of the angels 181
We then our cheerful *songs* 28
What rapturous *songs* are mine 737
When our *songs* are glad with 1979
Where "*Songs* of the Lamb" through 1870

Where the *songs* of all the sinless 77
Why these *songs* of happy cheer 105
With *songs* and anthems I'll come 1621
With *songs* and honors sounding 2307
With *songs* on our lips 896
With the *songs* that angels sing 45

SONS

And all the *sons* of want are blest 1008
And his *sons* all good shall know 629
And *sons* of earth hold heaven in fee 1803
As *sons* who know the Father's will 370
Bursting from the *sons* of light 356
Fairer than the *sons* of men 1073
How many of the *sons* of men 1116
Hymned by the first born *sons* 1366
Let all her *sons* unite 2304
May our *sons* and daughters be 634
No longer, Lord, thy *sons* shall sow 1275
She calls her *sons* to pray 33
Patiently powerful for the *sons* 2262
Our *sons* and daughters guide 2291
So may the *sons* of men know 1474
Sons of earth from slumber waking 1109
Sons of men, awake to praise 1622
Sons of one Father, brothers 1254
Sons of men and angels say 289
Sons of men in battle long the enemy 431
Soon shall your *sons* be free 733
That so men's *sons* his deeds 628
The first-born *sons* of light 1458
The *sons* of earth are waking 1911
The *sons* of ignorance and night 420
The *sons* of men in their distress 731
That the *sons* of the day may 2180
Till all the *sons* of men become 309
Till, at last, her *sons* are gathered 42
Till *sons* of men shall learn thy love 2270
We *sons* of later days 1361
When *sons* of God around me pray 1569
When the *sons* of God shall prove 1647
With all the *sons* of God we shout 160
With us and with our *sons* abide 1174
"Ye *sons* of men, why will ye die? 2155

SOOTHE

And *soothe,* and hush, and calm it 820
Soothe thou each weary breast 455
Soothe thou my voyaging 476
When we *soothe* earth's weary 299

SOOTHED

Soothed by the pity of thine 1098

SOOTHES

It *soothes* his sorrows 794

SORROW

And *sorrow* crown each lingering 1459
And *sorrow* never come 2332
And through *sorrow* to arise 2255
And with that *sorrow* mingling 1849
Are we left in *sorrow* now 77
Brief *sorrow,* short-lived care 252
Come, see if there ever was *sorrow* like 73
Come to him, ye who, in *sorrow* 344
Ever from *sorrow* of earth be free 1758
Farewell to every *sorrow* 16
For all my *sorrow* giving a song 1047
For this thy dying *sorrow* 1475
Free from *sorrow* 947
Free from their *sorrow,* grief 1605
Grief nor pain, nor any *sorrow* 71
In *sorrow* he died, but in glory 623
In *sorrow* he's my comfort 834
In thee no *sorrow* may be found 960
Is this thy *sorrow* naught to us 86
Let not *sorrow* dim your eye 1560
Make us thy *sorrow* feel 86
Many a *sorrow,* many a labor 119
Never a *sorrow* that he doth not share 407
Never to *sorrow* more 2145
No longer *sorrow* as without hope 368
No more from want and *sorrow* 1
Not a *sorrow* we share 2266
Not from *sorrow,* pain, or care 449
O'ercast with *sorrow,* pain, and fear 1517
Our hearts' most bitter *sorrow* 1849
Sharing their *sorrow* and shame 326
So free from all *sorrow* 896
Some are down-hearted, in *sorrow* 1600
Sorrow and love flow mingled 2236
Sorrow and sadness take their 137
Sorrow and sighing shall be 982
Sorrow can never be 476
Sorrow vanquished, labor ended 119
Sorrow will change to unending 1763
The deepest *sorrow,* like a passing 16
The *sorrow* thou dost treasure 534
Then away from my *sorrow* and care 1503
There shall be no more *sorrow* 1404
There is no *sorrow,* nor any sighing 913
Through *sorrow* or through joy 1245
Thy mortal *sorrow,* and thy life's 35
To comfort us in *sorrow* 2165
Whatever *sorrow* vex the mind 75
When in *sorrow,* when in danger 741
When *sorrow* flows from eye to eye 792
When to follow thee brings *sorrow* 2276
Who in each *sorrow* bears a part 1967

SORROWED

I *sorrowed,* O, I sorrowed 825

SORROWFUL

All the *sorrowful* drew near 2255

SORROWING

Thou, *sorrowing* at the helpless cry 372

SORROWS

All our *sorrows* left below 1667
And all my *sorrows* borne 834
And earthly *sorrows* light 1480
And 'mid earth's *sorrows* 1722
And *sorrows* like the rain 1952
And *sorrows,* sometimes how they sweep 1489

And *sorrows* still increase 1059
Did not its *sorrows* prove the path 666
For thy *sorrows* we adore thee 1813
Fruitful let thy *sorrows* be 1686
Grievous were the *sorrows* he bore 214
Have you *sorrows* that no one 111
He all my *sorrows* shares 854
He who all our *sorrows* bore 521
In all my *sorrows,* conflicts 1509
In *sorrows* taught to shine 2273
On thee, when *sorrows* rise 392
Our *sorrows* still remain 960
Out of earth's *sorrows,* into thy 1602
The *sorrows* of thy servants 1927
The *sorrows* ye endure 1391
Then our *sorrows,* in a moment 2158
Thy *sorrows* make my own to cease 60
When shall my *sorrows* have an end? 960
When *sorrows* like sea-billows 2249
When *sorrows,* round me press 178

SOUGHT

All I've *sought,* or hoped 980
And *sought,* but never found 768
As thou hast *sought,* so let me seek 1170
At last I *sought* them in his sheltering 1112
Father, who hast *sought* and found 470
He *sought* me ere I knew the way 1907
I *sought* at once my Savior's side 1421
I *sought* his love in lore of books 878
I *sought* his will to know 1822
I *sought* the cross of Jesus 872
I *sought* the Lord, he answered me 1890
I *sought* the Lord, he heard 616, 1902
Jesus *sought* me when a stranger 340
Jesus, too late I thee have *sought* 1002
Sincerely I have *sought* thee, Lord 189
Sought out they are of every one 1638
Sought peace and rest 1220
Sought thee wandering 672
There they *sought* unto thee only 1553
Thou hast *sought* us and found 578
Thy mercy *sought* me 60
We've *sought* and found thee in the secret 2193

SOUL

A never-dying *soul* to save 4
Ah! *soul,* are you here without 430
All, all thine own, *soul* 1778
All my *soul* to thee upbringing 1085
All that my *soul* has tried 425
And all my *soul* be love 493
And for each humble *soul* and sweet 2115
And may each *soul* salvation 1232
And my *soul* athirst may be 66
And, my *soul,* be swift to bring 1993
And o'er my *soul* shall sweep 1585
And *soul* by soul, and silently 886
And still my *soul* in slumber 558
And still my *soul* would cleave to thee 392
And the high *soul* climbs the high way 2101
And the low *soul* gropes the low 2101
And with my *soul* I know 926
As thus my inmost *soul* 1237
Be calm in thy *soul* 1820
Because my *soul* in confidence 166
Because my *soul* in death's abode 570
Both *soul* and body bear your part 1729
But above all the *soul* distressed 263
But, O my *soul,* forget him not 1514
But on the *soul* thick midnight 1131
But only that my *soul* may feed 822
But the *soul* that is trusting 1976
But thou, my *soul,* ere slumber 1309
Can my thankless *soul* forget 1709
Christ to every *soul,* and mine 339
Close beside my Savior would my *soul* 403
"Come hither, *soul,* I am the way." 1001
Each glad *soul,* its free course winging 104
Enter, poor *soul,* and be saved 2
Eternal *Soul,* our souls keep 2115
Every *soul* now laud him 1838
Feasting my *soul* on manna sweet 1267
Fill my *soul* with love divine 1690
Flooding my *soul* with glory 2152
For a precious *soul* is born again 1664
For her *soul* of joy bereaved 140
For my *soul* is filled with his goodness 1847
For there my *soul* the Lord may see 1569
He doth my *soul* redeem 854
He thy *soul* will strengthen 987
He to the lowly *soul* doth still 229
He your *soul* will sure defend 1996
He'll not let my *soul* be lost 2232
Here let my *soul* retreat 352
His *soul* in vision soared 91
His *soul* shall dwell at ease 2116
His *soul* was once an offering 1351
"Ho! every thirsting, sin-sick *soul* 1970
How pure the *soul* must be 420
If no *soul* to me can say 1710
If thy *soul,* with power uplifted 2263
In my *soul* the heavenly joys 1573
In thee my *soul* hath shelter 1134, 1376
In thee my *soul* is satisfied 1436
Is your *soul* burdened down 694
It is well, it is well with my *soul* 2249
Jesus, for my *soul* is caring 2257
Keep on praying for the *soul* 1048
Let every *soul* be Jesus' guest 336
Let my *soul* look up with steadfast 808
Let my *soul,* revolving round thee 1055
Let our whole *soul* an offering be 1776
Let the earth-bound *soul* arise 668
May each *soul* be rekindled with fire 2187
May every *soul* thy praises sing 1921
My captive *soul* from prison bring 2103
My guilty *soul,* revived, made whole 134
My inmost *soul* with longing cries 135
My ransomed *soul* shall be 1689
My *soul,* bless thou the Lord 1547
My *soul* bowed down is longing 1395
My *soul* do not leave destitute 1433
My *soul* doth thirst for thee 1172
My *soul* faces home 931
My *soul* for that great day 5

My *soul* found no relief 772
My *soul* from lasting doom 13
My *soul* has often found relief 1806
My *soul* he doth restore 1904
My *soul* in mercy to reclaim 926
My *soul* in its conflicts and sorrows 1477
My *soul* is dark and guilty 868
My *soul* is satisfied to know 822
My *soul* is so glad 1926
My *soul* is well content, Lord 1818
My *soul,* O Lord, is thine to keep 1844
My *soul* rejoices to pursue 7, 1933
My *soul* shall boast of God 616
My *soul* shall ever love thee well 786
My *soul* shall in Jehovah boast 1902
My *soul* thee follows hard 1172
My *soul* to him may take its flight 1749
My *soul* waits for the Lord 1129
My *soul,* with courage wait 567
My *soul* with fairest day 134
My *soul* with heavenly thoughts 59
My *soul* without it dies 444
My steadfast *soul,* from falling 1021
My thirsty *soul* doth pine 125
My thirsty *soul* longs vehemently 783
My troubled *soul* found sweet relief 1194
No higher than the *soul* is high 1358
No *soul* to save 967
Not one *soul* with which to greet 1222
Now may man's *soul* arise 1727
Now my raptured *soul* can only sing 2335
Now my *soul,* with joy awaking 1703
O, be swift, my *soul,* to answer 1215
O for a *soul* washed white 1920
O, how my *soul* delights to hear 1867
O, let all the *soul* within you 2157
O let my *soul* with ardor burn 156
O may my *soul* on thee repose 59
O my *soul,* praise him, for he is 1637
O, my *soul* within me yearneth 1772
O, shall your *soul,* through doubting 1740
O *soul* bowed down with harrowing care 196
O *soul* in grief and sorrow 1331
O *soul* in sin, and bondage 1331
O *soul* near despair in the 931
O thou my *soul,* do thou return 857
O why, my *soul,* art thou cast down 1700
O wondrous Lord, my *soul* would be 769
Raising my *soul* from out the dead 2316
Seeking *soul,* to Jesus turn 2126
Seems now some *soul* to say 85
Since the Lord my *soul* unbound 1559
Sinful *soul,* thy debt is paid 2126
So be thy *soul* as if it shared 1784
So my *soul* derived from God 1667
So now herself my *soul* 1940
Some precious *soul* may help decide 400
Some *soul* for thee 1152
Soul and body, soul and body shall his 1510
Soul and body thine to be 800
Soul, be thou glad, for hell's 1765
Soul, be thou healed in the waters 353
Soul by woe oppressed 1114
Soul do not permit thy sorrow 175
Soul, now rejoice, though all hell 1765
Soul of mine, continue pleading 1764
Soul of mine, must I surrender 1764
Soul of mine, my heart is clinging 1764
Sweetly my *soul* shall rest 1675
That his pardoned *soul* is worthy 110
That my *soul* may serve him better 411
That *soul* is body, mind and heart 1844
That *soul,* though all hell 776
The bleeding *soul* to cure 674
The captive *soul* to free 594
The *soul* can split the sky 1358
The *soul* her sacred page 1576
The *soul,* O Lord, is ours to keep 1844
The *soul* of Christ lives on 1879
The *soul* that on Jesus hath leaned 776
The *soul* thou hast redeemed 1387
Their *soul* is Christ's abode 229
Then my *soul* shall fear no ill 863
Then shall my *soul* her conflict 1349
Then shall my *soul* new life 2203
There my burdened *soul* found liberty 2335
This *soul* in safety keep 291
Though your *soul* is sorrow-bowed 169
Through her *soul,* in anguish 1263
Thus every *soul* illuming 2086
Thy fainting *soul* Jesus can 1737
Thy *soul* they will enslave 158
Till every *soul* of thee hast heard 1169
Till my guilty *soul* imploring 2335
Till my raptured *soul* shall find 986
Till my *soul* is lost in love 1684
Till then, my *soul,* pray on 1639
'Tis thine each *soul* to calm 1592
To my *soul* best comfort give 758
To sanctify the *soul* 315
To win that *soul* for thee alone 1152
What he did for my *soul* 50
When all around my *soul* gives way 1244
When my poor tested *soul* 2096
When my *soul* is faint and thirsty 942
When the *soul* waketh 1793
When your *soul* is burdened 2252
Where my *soul* in joyful duty 1588
Who would not his whole *soul* 1367
Will your *soul* be ready for the mansion 693
With which the *soul* will long 306
Yes, a *soul* is rescued from his sinful 1664
Yet to each waiting *soul* speak 2273

SOUL-REDEEMING

Name of *soul-redeeming* fame 13

SOULS

All Christly *souls* are one in him 919
All *souls* are his, and here 2163
All *souls* are thine 590
All *souls* are thine, and here or there 1446
All *souls* that sin and pray 1880
And faithful *souls* have yearned 2075
And humble *souls* rejoice 786
And laden *souls,* by thousands 670

And reverent *souls* adore 419
And *souls* to be freed 1987
And *souls* shine like stars 1770
And young *souls,* meekly striving 1947
Believing *souls,* rejoicing go 575
Bidding sinful *souls* draw nigh 442
Bringing to hungry *souls* the bread 762
But for all faithful *souls* 1442
But *souls* new-born arise 90
By thee the *souls* of men are fed 2120
Can we, whose *souls* are lighted 512
Christ of our *souls,* who savest 162
Cleansing *souls* from every stain 1126
Come, all ye *souls* (every soul) by sin oppressed 336
Come, and be all *souls* fed 2183
Come, Holy Ghost, our *souls* possess 314
Come thou within our *souls* 1819
"Come, weary *souls,* for Jesus bids you 670
Do thou our troubled *souls* uplift 43
Ever may our *souls* be fed 245
Fain would our *souls* feel all 447
For our own *souls,* for all 1316
For *souls* redeemed, for sins 1439
For the *souls* that go astray 488
For the *souls* that overcome 1748
For the *souls,* who voyage, Lord 2274
For 'twas to bless such *souls* 1696
From famished *souls,* from sorrow's 2270
God, who did your *souls* retrieve 1736
Happier *souls,* that find a rest 1612
Happy *souls!* their praises flow 1612
Have in our inmost *souls* 1819
In *souls* most sullen thou art 385
It is not thus that *souls* are won 550
Jesus our weary *souls* invites 1122
Longing *souls* he satisfies 1622
Lord, for these our *souls* shall 1628
Lord, on thee our *souls* depend 1181
Loving *souls,* on thee reposing 446
May lift our *souls* on high 55
May our *souls* be filled with thee 331
May our *souls* find rest in thee 331
May our *souls* find strength in thee 331
May our *souls,* on thee relying 993
May our *souls,* refreshment 519
May our *souls* thy peace possess 589
Millions of *souls,* in glory now 1875
Never from our *souls* remove 439
Now our *souls* with manna feed 759
"O foolish *souls,* come near me 892
O happy *souls,* that pray 1167
O let our *souls* on thee be cast 1714
On our *souls* thy graces 743
On *souls* that follow Christ shall break 2016
Other *souls* to Jesus win 1573
Our cautioned *souls* prepare 2037
Our sinful *souls* to spare 965
Our *souls* are his immortal breath 328
Our *souls* are lost in thee 1464
Our *souls* from folly would secure 1300
Our *souls* from Satan's grasp 206
Our *souls* he hath released 1313
Our *souls* in worship bend 2107
Our *souls* shall drink a fresh supply 157
Our *souls* the joys celestial seek 1716
Our *souls* to thee in worship 1149
Our *souls,* we know, when he appears 194
Our *souls* with all thy fullness fill 1163
Prayerful *souls* may find him 2300
Shepherd of *souls,* who bringest 436
Showing to wandering *souls* 762
Souls all pure and white 1706
Souls in danger, look above 891
Souls, newborn, O Lord, in thee 142
Souls rise above the sod 170
Souls that passed and left no name 1280
Souls that perish, heed the message 474
Souls will be whiter 1750
Telling *souls* in darkness 108
That all whose *souls* the truth receive 83
The new-born *souls* whose days 278
The *souls* for whom Christ prays 1545
The *souls* he died to save 1734
The *souls* that hunger, feed thou 1317
Their *souls* with saving grace endow 9, 706
There are *souls* to rescue 1985
There are weary *souls* who perish 1955
Thither faithful *souls* do soar 217
Thou shalt have *souls,* precious 705
Through our surrendered *souls* 1819
Through *souls* of saints and prophets 2115
Till *souls* of all, the Crucified 1275
Till then, to thee our *souls* aspire 300
'Tis beckoning now to the *souls* 1868
Weary *souls* fore'er rejoice 755
Where better *souls* have trod 107
Where fainting *souls* are fed 204
Where meek *souls* will receive him 1426
Wherein at last our *souls* 2029
While our waiting *souls* adore 993
While the *souls* of men are dying 697
With thankful *souls,* behold we 2070
Ye doubting *souls,* dismiss your fear 1924
Ye mournful *souls,* be glad 241

SOUND

A *sound* of God comes to my ears 788
And a glad *sound* comes 322
And *sound* a nobler call 1609
And *sound* his power abroad 190
Its *sound* is sweet 850
Let the amen *sound* from his 1637
May thy gospel's joyful *sound* 1676
No *sound* of jarring strife 654
O could I *sound* the glories 1339
O let the gospel *sound* 1156
Or *sound* the depths 150
Shall lift the joyful *sound* 28
Sound his praises, Jesus who bore 1616
Sound his praise, tell 1070
Sound now the final chord 682
Sound the charge against the foe 262
Sound the loud triumphant lay 1728
Sound through the world the joyful 239
The joyful *sound* proclaim 512
The sacred gospel's joyful *sound* 786

The *sound* compelling startles 1533
The *sound* of the harp and the angels' 2271
Their *sound* through all the earth 1862
Too full for *sound* or foam 1802
Where *sound* the cries of race 2270

SOUNDED

He has *sounded* forth the trumpet 1215
Sounded through the wide creation 1214

SOUNDETH

Hark! what *soundeth* 2157
Soundeth the heaven 228

SOUNDS

And clearer *sounds* the angel hymn 40
And ever o'er its Babel *sounds* 948
Earthly *sounds* are none 1672
It *sounds* like music in mine ear 1967
Loud *sounds* the world's appeal 1951
Now all the myriad *sounds* of earth 1385
The echoing *sounds* grow fainter 37
The tempting *sounds* I hear 1408

SOURCE

And trembling to its *source* return 1521
Bounteous *source* of every joy 1628
Come, thou *source* of sweetest 743
He the *source*, the ending 1558
Source and giver of all good 485
Source of all life, unnumbered 712
Source of all strength thou art 332
Source of hope forever present 2318
Source of life, and truth, and peace 1760
Source of purest pleasure 1004
Source whence all our blessings 1628
The *source* of human woe 1381
The *source* of wisdom and of love 155
To thee, the *source* of all our joy 645

SOVEREIGN

My *Sovereign* bids me tell 799
O *Sovereign* meek and lowly 1470

SOVEREIGNTY

Thy *sovereignty* has held our hearts 2193

SOW

And knowing, we may *sow* the seed 596
Sow blessings, and blessings will 1770
Sow hatred, and hatred will grow 1770
Sow hope, and receive its fruition 1770
Sow in our hearts the seeds 712
Sow love, and its sweetness 1770
Sow love, and taste its fruitage 703
Sow mercy, and reap sweet 1770
Sow peace, and reap its harvest 703
Sow sunbeams on the rock and moor 703
Sow weeds, and of weeds reap 1770
We *sow* our seeds, lo! tares 1285

SOWER

Chiming to the heavenly *Sower* 1665

SOWN

How, *sown* of martyr's blood, the faith 91
Oft as the precious seed is *sown* 339

SPACE

Although in *space* and time apart 197
High in the trackless *space* that paves 595
Lord of interstellar *space* 96

SPAKE

As he *spake* by the mouth of his 215
As once he *spake* in Zion 1943
Spake through the trumpet voices 2115
The Savior *spake* in anguish 497
Thus *spake* the seraph, and 2282
When he *spake*, and it was 1762

SPAKEST

Thou *spakest* not to them alone 838

SPAN

The *span* of time is brief ere we 2096

SPARE

Spare not the stroke 649
Thou didst not *spare* thine only Son 1439
We can *spare* them, loving Savior 2275

SPARROW

Behold, the *sparrow* findeth out 783

SPEAK

Aloud they do not *speak* 1862
And round us, when we *speak* thy 100
And *speak* in every heart 1777
And *speak* some boundless thing 190
And *speak* within the soul 1526
And while we *speak* he's near 2331
Be thankful unto him, and *speak* good 1310
Blessed Master, *speak* thou still 219
He will *speak* your sins forgiven 1996
If you cannot *speak* like angels 679
Lord, I was dumb, I could not *speak* 1140
Lord, *speak*, and make me whole 803
O *speak*, and I shall live 444
O *speak*, and make me listen 1408
O, *speak* the word, thy servants 465
O *speak* to reassure me 1408
Shall *speak* thy praises, Lord most 186
Speak, and behold, we answer 1943
Speak, and make me blest 1207
Speak but the word 803
Speak his sorrows ended 2204
Speak just a word 1773
Speak, O eternal Lord 332
Speak, O God, and I will hear thee 1588
Speak oft with thy Lord 1820
Speak or thou never hence 333
Speak that I may follow faster 1207
Speak that my soul may hear 1774
Speak that word of love again 1735
Speak the old words again 2069
Speak the word of power 1138

Speak through human kindness 925
Speak thy pardoning grace 637
Speak to each heart the mighty 364
Speak to me by name, O Master 1207
Speak to my heart, in blessing 333
Speak to my warring passions 417
Speak to our fearful hearts 762
Speak to our hearts, and let us 1824
Speak to the heart of love, alive 2262
Speak to the shadows of the night 650
Speak to us, thy erring children 2049
Speak with the voice that wakes 1659
Speak ye peace, thus saith our God 363
Speak ye to Jerusalem 363
That I may *speak* with soothing power 1170
Whate'er I *speak* or frame 1228
When they *speak* the solemn words 2264

SPEAKS

And *speaks* of heaven 1589
God *speaks* to us in far (darkest, every) 604
He *speaks,* and eternity, filled 1512
He *speaks,* and in his heavenly height 1900
He *speaks,* and listening to his voice 1351
He *speaks,* and the sound of his voice 819
He *speaks* the drooping heart 1867
He *speaks*—'tis done 676
He *speaks* to me everywhere 2012
Here *speaks* the Comforter 355
Jesus *speaks,* and speaks to thee 672
Jesus sweetly *speaks* to me 800
So now he *speaks* again 1943
Speaks all the promises 190
Speaks of many a wrong to thee 538
There *speaks* the steadfast prophecy 46
While your Savior from above *speaks* 259

SPEAR

Bring me my *spear,* O clouds, unfold 95
Not by warrior's *spear* and sword 275

SPED

The three sad days are quickly *sped* 79, 1937

SPEECH

All *speech* flow to music 1768
But clearer far the friendly *speech* 592
Day unto day doth utter *speech* 40
How purely hath thy *speech* come down 301
In *speech* that flows to melody 419

SPEECHES

From all the easy *speeches* 1365

SPEED

And *speed,* O speed the blessed day 592
And *speed* the hour when wars 490
Both *speed* them to their source 1667
God *speed* his word 1156
God *speed* the day, when those 433
O *speed* thy work, victorious 1442
Speed forth thy flight 2051
Speed on thy word 1156
Speed on with eager feet 2074
Speed, speed thy work 550
Speed the foot and touch 1686
Speed to Bethlehem's walls 1110

SPEND

I *spend* the hours of parting day 861
Spend much time in secret 1820
Why do ye *spend* your strength 2155

SPENDEST

And all thou *spendest* Jesus will 1551

SPENT

And *spent* too soon her golden 1918
Because I *spent* the strength thou gavest me 183
Have I *spent* one for thee 2077
To die, to suffer, and be *spent* 1412
When half *spent* was the night 1107

SPHERE

O, how shall I, whose native *sphere* 420

SPHERES

The brave procession of the *spheres* 46
Ye higher *spheres,* and cloudy 1898

SPILT

Not *spilt* like water in the ground 590

SPIRIT

A broken *spirit* is to God 31
A right *spirit* me within 31
Ah, then my *spirit* faints 494
And a Christ-like *spirit* everywhere 1985
And every Christ-like *spirit* 1879
And if the tired *spirit* should falter 1098
And in whose *spirit* is no guile 1314
And let thy *Spirit* brighten 1377
And on my naked *spirit* bear 420
And *Spirit* evermore 91
And with thyself my *spirit* fill 152, 545
As among us doth thy *Spirit* 1092
Baptize them with thy *Spirit* now 9
Blessed *Spirit,* brooding o'er us 1681
Breathing o'er my troubled *spirit* 1772
Brightly doth his *Spirit* shine 1721
By thine own eternal *Spirit* 658
By thine own *Spirit* fostered 1849
By thine unerring *Spirit* led 274
Creator *Spirit,* work in me 1863
Ever God's *Spirit* is saying 807
For every generous *spirit* 1529
For the *Spirit* born to bless 483
For the *Spirit* who protects us 242
For thou the *Spirit* art of life 1401
For thy *Spirit* new-creating 1686
For with you the *Spirit* will not always 1542
He the broken *spirit* cheers 665
His *Spirit* dwelleth in me 1571
His *Spirit* is guiding my pilgrimage 871
His *spirit* of heroic love 309
His *Spirit* only can bestow 2151
His *Spirit,* through the Savior 2090

Holy *Spirit,* dwell with me 635
If he his *Spirit* and love 908
In my *spirit* I hear 236
In *spirit* and in truth thy will 944
Let nothing your *spirit* dismay 164
Let the good *Spirit* show all men 1014
Let thy *Spirit* dwell in me 554
Life-giving *Spirit,* o'er us move 1398
Long my imprisoned *spirit* lay 94
Lord Jesus, both *spirit* and life 1583
Lord, on us thy *Spirit* pour 1145
Lord, the *Spirit* she doth bless 1213
May then through me thy *Spirit* 1410
May thy *Spirit* here give rest 1567
More of his *Spirit,* the wanderer 1219
My fallen *spirit* to restore 2202
My *spirit* loudly sings 1247
My *spirit* pants for thee 249
My *spirit* seems in heaven 1237
My *spirit* trusts exultingly 1416
My weary *spirit* waits 1404
O may thy *Spirit* gently draw 2011
O may thy *Spirit* guide my feet 1143
O may thy *Spirit* seal 459
O my *spirit* longs and faints 1612
On the parched *spirit* rain 744
Our *spirit* upward springs 1480
Poor in *spirit* would I be 1218
Rather must *spirit* vanquish 170
Setting my *spirit* free 2315
So does God's *Spirit* bring 120
Spirit and life are all his words 263
Spirit, breathing from above 1195
Spirit consoling, let us find 1780
Spirit creative, give us light 1780
Spirit of Christ, do thou our first 1291
Spirit of God, my teacher be 1216
Spirit of light, explore 1132
Spirit of love and truth, breathing 613
Spirit of love at evening time 1780
Spirit of our God, descending 1058
Spirit of purity and grace 1589
Spirit of truth and love 2051
Spirit redeeming, give us grace 1780
Spirit to spirit thou dost speak 1318
Spirit, who our hearts dost raise 1748
Still let thy *Spirit* unto us 762
Strong *Spirit,* burning with mankind 1355
The restless *Spirit* still 2273
The *Spirit* is tenderly pleading 1925
The *Spirit* meek, the guileless 1453
The *Spirit* sent from heaven 1341
The *Spirit* to the brethren 781
The *Spirit* who in them did sing 2164
The wounded *spirit* heal 393
Thee in man's *spirit* we behold 591
Then, Jesus, be thy *spirit* ours 205
Thou the anointing *Spirit* art 313
Thy present *Spirit* waits to fill 1360
Thy *Spirit* calls to all 1919
Thy *Spirit* can their flames control 546
Thy *Spirit* ever lead and guide 770
Thy *Spirit* is more strong than they 546
Thy *Spirit,* Lord, bestow 1027
Thy *Spirit,* O send down 1699
Thy *Spirit* send with grace 1149
Thy *spirit* to thy father 98
Thy *Spirit* trains our souls 1523
Thy tender *Spirit* stoops to bless 1363
Till his *spirit* he resigned 140
Till thou my patient *spirit* guide 1003
To believe that *spirit* triumphs 110
To him your *spirit* give 547
Truthful *Spirit,* dwell in me 635
Unto each the *Spirit* came 1036
When my *spirit,* clothed, immortal 66
When the *spirit* rests from sin 1744
When thy *Spirit* is repeating 219
Where from thy *Spirit* shall I go! 1452
Who hath a guileless *spirit* 772
Whose *Spirit* breathes the active 146
Whose *spirit* trusts alone in thee 1167
With a *spirit* large and free 639
With thy *Spirit,* Lord, endue me 798
With thy *Spirit* recreate me 606, 615

SPIRITS

And all thy kindred *spirits* dwell 1569
And heroic *spirits* answer 110
And mortal *spirits* tire and faint 157
And our broken *spirits* heal 756
And our *spirits* shall sorrow 1992
As *spirits* go, from strength to strength 1294
By prostrate *spirits* day and night 1234
For thee our waiting *spirits* yearn 502
Of those whose anxious *spirits* 1806
Our broken *spirits* pitying see 1184
Our inmost *spirits* purify 189
Our restless *spirits* yearn for thee 1023
Our *spirits* are thine 110
Our *spirits* schooled 84
Our *spirits* yearn to feel thy 447
Our stubborn *spirits* bend 311
Spirits yearning for the word 296
The *spirits* that surround thy throne 420
Unto thy children's *spirits* teach 1360
With all the good for which our *spirits* sigh 16
With *spirits* as fresh as the dew 1909
Ye *spirits* blest, God's own victorious 1725

SPLENDOR

A *splendor* greater yet while serving 2193
And *splendor* clothes the sun 414
And glorious is the *splendor* 1874
In the *splendor* of the dawn 309
Lo, how its *splendor* challenges 1397
Now all the heavenly *splendor* breaks 1843
So full of *splendor* and of joy 1236
Splendor he makes on earth 732
Splendor, light, and life attend him 53
What lasting *splendor* crowns 1658

SPLENDORS

The solemn *splendors* of the night 40
There heavenly *splendors* shine 96

SPOILED

Majestic from the *spoiled* tomb 1078

SPOKE

Dying, he *spoke* my name 2143
How he *spoke* to the disciples 996

SPOKEN

Be *spoken* from thy word 1094
Spoken through the silence 1787

SPOT

How many a *spot* defiles the robe 1920
No *spot* is so dear to my childhood 1986
That in the darkest *spot* of earth 1236
There's a hallowed *spot* 'neath the 2066
Till not a *spot* remains 854

SPOTLESS

Spotless to the last 143

SPRANG

Sprang at once to sight 143

SPRAY

And thy *spray* on the dust 236
Though heavy oft with drenching *spray* 826
Washing up its silver *spray* 1711

SPREAD

And *spread* abroad his fame 1485
And *spread* his kingdom wide 377
And *spread* it everywhere 1
And *spread* o'er all the earth 2135
And *spread* the truth from pole 1932
And *spread* thy table in our heart(s) 165
Far *spread* the conquests of thy grace 1449
Let me *spread* abroad the story 1573
Now *spread* from shore to shore 1089
O *spread* thy covering wings 1364
O *spread* thy pure wing o'er 1944
O *spread* thy truth's bright precepts 640
One night will *spread* its pall 56
Should *spread* from clime to clime 91
Spread abroad the Victor's fame 1117
Spread all the world around 28
Spread aright the gospel light 126
Spread our wants before thy feet 589
Spread the blessed tidings all 2292
Spread the brightness of his glory 684
Spread the feast today 1664
Spread the gladness all around 2169
Spread the kingdom of the Lord 1783
Spread thou the mantle of thy love 422
Spread thy golden pinions 718
Spread thy love's broad banner 144
That *spread* the flowing seas 877
Then *spread* the banners, and unfold 1921
To *spread* abroad the firmament 81
We have *spread* forth to thee 99
Who will *spread* the message 1997

SPREADS

And *spreads* his hands 395
He daily *spreads* a glorious feast 2294
It *spreads* from pole to pole 512
More and more it *spreads* and grows 1695
Now it *spreads* along the skies 1695
Now *spreads* the fame of his dear 1487
So bright, that all which *spreads* 1965
Spreads so warm and blue 61
Spreads throughout the world like leaven 36
There *spreads* a heaven of light 700

SPREAD'ST

Thou *spread'st* a table in my sight 1876
Thou *spread'st* the curtain of the night 1233

SPRING

And life's yet finer *spring* 21
And *spring* adorns the earth 1354
And still, now *spring* has on 1146
From thee the overflowing *Spring* 157
Insatiate to this *Spring* I fly 1555
It has no *spring* of action sure 1202
Life's everlasting *spring* hath robbed 1727
Spring thou up within my heart 994
Spring up, and never cease 1463
The *Spring* of our new life 1318
There everlasting *spring* abides 1966
They *spring* up every day 2195
Thou the *spring* of all my comfort 1607
Thy health's eternal *Spring* 125
Who, creation's Lord and *Spring* 1566

SPRINGETH

Beauty *springeth* out of naught 53
It *springeth* up alway 191

SPRINGS

Are *springs* of joy that never fail 1038
It *springs* from the fountain of blood 17
Like thy *springs* and running waters 606, 615
Making the *springs* of time and sense 39
The hidden *springs* of truth whence 1951
The *springs* of comfort seem to fail 392

SPRINGTIDE

Thee, Lord, we praise for *springtide* days 21

SPRINGTIME

And another *springtime* 922
Springtime in triumph marches 1724
There's *springtime* in my soul 2001

SPRINGTIME'S

In *springtime's* bright array 1083

SPRINKLE

Sprinkle me ever with thy blood 493
Sprinkle our works with Jesus' 397

SPRINKLED

Of *sprinkled* water, name them thine 9
Oft as it is *sprinkled* 544

SPRINKLES

And *sprinkles* now the throne of grace 113

SPURN

Thou wilt not *spurn* contrition's broken 1395
To *spurn* the fleeting things of earth 91

SPURNING

Not *spurning* what is small 1291

SQUADRONS

The winged *squadrons* of the sky 1660

STABLE

Behold, in *stable* rude and bare 320
But ah! Within that *stable* 918
Happy they within the *stable* 369
Rudely in a *stable* sheltered 2288
Softly to the little *stable* 257
Not in that poor lowly *stable* 1572

STABLE-PLACE

A *stable-place* sufficed 933

'STABLISH

'Stablish our work in thee begun 456

'STABLISHED

And *'stablished* it upon the flood 1080
Hath *'stablished* it fast by a changeless 1546

STACKED

Since they *stacked* the balmy hay 2299

STAFF

Fainting, be my *staff* and rod 1516
Going each with *staff* in hand 2284
Lord, send us forth, nor *staff,* nor scrip 1169
Thy *staff* be my stay 1894

STAGE

Thy daily *stage* of duty run 152

STAIN

Dark is the *stain* that we cannot 1206
Flowing o'er till every *stain* 977
From their *stain* I am clean 17

STAINED

Very deeply *stained* within 891

STAINS

Sin *stains* are lost in its life-giving 2323
To wash my crimson *stains* 854

STAMP

Man, the *stamp* of thy Creator 104
Stamp deeply thy likeness 719

STAMPED

Stamped with his image today 1694

STANCH

And *stanch* the spring of guilty 1582

STAND

Active and watchful, *stand* we 467
Always for thee to *stand* 1027
And *stand* at last with joy 594
And *stand* before the Lamb 118
And *stand* complete at last 1746
And when all alone I *stand* 448
Bold shall I *stand* in thy great 1024
Come, *stand* in awe before him 360
Doth ever *stand* at my right hand 570
Father, we *stand* prepared to do 466
I cannot *stand* alone 820
I *stand* on the mount of promise 1847
I *stand* on the mountain of blessing 1741
"I'll *stand* by until the morning 474
Jesus no longer will *stand* at the door 2
Let him *stand* between you and 1210
Lord, who shall *stand,* if thou 1129
My Jesus, he will firmly *stand* 1915
O may we *stand* around thy throne 965
O may we *stand* before the Lamb 1111
Or *stand* within his holy place 1080
Stand at the last accepted 2120
Stand faithful to the last 1784
Stand fast for Christ thy Savior 1784
Stand fast, whate'er betide 1784
Stand firm, everyone 1769
Stand in awe, and sin not 1565
Stand in his strength alone 1786
Stand, then, in his great might 1746
Stand in our midst, dear Lord 2048
Stand up, and bless his glorious 1785
Stand up, speak out, and bravely 174
Stand ye in awe before his face 72
Still I *stand* the tempest's shock 2056
Still may we *stand* before thy face 1105
That they may *stand* secure 244
Then shall we *stand* as Mary stood 1275
They *stand,* those halls of Zion 961
Till we safely *stand* in our 989
Trembling they *stand* before his throne 644
Until we *stand* at thy right hand 2289
We *stand* beneath thy banner 48
We *stand* to bless thee ere our 1679
When I *stand* before the throne 2261
When we *stand* with Christ in glory 2261
Who steadfast *stand* at God's right hand 325
Would you *stand* among the victors 2064

STANDARD

Let the *standard* be displayed 1994
Round his *standard* ranging 2287
To the *standard* of our Captain 2064
Under the *standard,* exalted 2128

STANDARDS

Standards of worth o'er all 2110

STANDEST

There, there thou *standest* pleading 1325

STANDETH

And *standeth* still, and still shall 1784
And *standeth* sure while earth 2197
Standeth God within the shadows 1574

STANDING

Here in our midst he's *standing* 347

STANDS

And falling, *stands* again 1526
He *stands* in the midst of nations 1998
He *stands* like friends who never 377
Here *stands* the house, O God, we built 1287
Immovable she *stands* 1539
It only *stands* unbent 1202
Jesus ready *stands* to save 358
Jesus *stands* ready to aid 1765
Mount Zion *stands* most beautiful 646
Nor *stands* in sinners' way 1841
Stands the gem-built throne 356
Still for me the Savior *stands* 395
Still *stands* thine ancient sacrifice 583
There *stands* he with unhurrying 96
Who is he that *stands* and weeps 2286
Yet One *stands* ready to help 506

STAR

A *star* their journey guiding 1878
And the *star* rains its fire 1995
And to follow the *star* wherever 1861
As surely as a *star* 96
Behold the bright and Morning *Star* 1381
But through them all hope's *star* 882
By that guiding *star* 517
Christians, lo, the *star* appeareth 299
Did the guiding *star* behold 129
Following yonder *star* 2196
"From Jacob shall a *star* proceed 2220
Hail the *Star*, that from far 52
Heaven's *star* shone brightly forth 524
Her *Star* is risen, her Light 2149
Higher yet that *star* ascends 2154
In every *star* thy wisdom shines 1871
Let not my *star* of hope grow dim 1245
Like the morning *star* he rose 1051
Likewise a bright *star* in the sky 1650
O bright and Morning *Star*, draw near 247
O God, thou *star* of dawning day 408
O Jesus, while the *star* of grace 2220
O star of wonder, *star* of night 2196
Star and angels gave the sign 1189
Star of faith, when winds are 1791
Star of hope, gleam on the billow 1791
Star of hope, in danger cheer 1603
Star of our hope thy softened 1155
Star of our night, and hope 1162
Star of the coming day 1086
Star of the East, the horizon adorning 254
Star of wonder, star of night 2196
Star upon our path abiding 367
Star with royal beauty bright 2196
The pole *star* in the north 149
The *star* is dimmed that lately 2091
There is a voice in every *star* 55
There the bright and Morning *Star* 986
There's a *star* in the sky 1995
There's a *star* to guide the humble 367
This *star* drew nigh to the northwest 1861
'Tis he o'er whom the blazing *star* 320
'Tis the *star* that will shine through 130
Ye have seen his natal *star* 103

STARLIGHT

In the fading of the *starlight* 1993
In the *starlight*, in the shadows 936

STARS

Although by *stars* thou dost not lead 1520
Amid the *stars* a stranger 1878
And all the *stars* obey 877
Beyond the *stars*, beyond all space 91
Countless *stars* by night that shine 1211
In *stars* and mountain summits 1698
Like the *stars* of the morning 2229
May the *stars* proclaim thee 2274
O morning *stars*, together 1426
Of *stars* by night revealed 107
Slowly the bright *stars*, one by one 1927
Stars and angels sing around 1040
Stars are hid and compass 488
Stars begin to peep 1302
Stars shining bright 935
Stars upon their way 143
That bright *stars* may be mine 809
The ancient *stars*, the ancient faith 1217
The *stars* above are shining bright 2306
The *stars* and rainbows are thy 385
The *stars* are brightly shining 1399
The *stars* are sparkling bright 1095
The *stars* he numbers, and their names 155
The *stars* in the bright sky 159
The *stars* keep watch above our way 507
The *stars* nor pause nor cease 46
The *stars* now tell the story 1552
The *stars* of heaven still shine 1095
The twinkling *stars* come one by one 1939
Thou who the *stars* in their courses 578
When, like *stars*, his children 1572
Where glad *stars* sing together 1928
While all the *stars* that round her 1932
While the *stars* in heaven glisten 1100
Will there be any *stars* in my crown 809
With all the morning *stars* we sing 160

START

From journey's *start*, to 490

STARTED

And *started* the life-giving flow 17
I *started* in shame and in sorrow 1941

STARVING

And the *starving* fed 2007

STATE

Come, Lord, again in kingly *state* 2024
In whatever worldly *state* 449
Ne'er yet was regal *state* 368
Till man's first heavenly *state* 298

STATION

In her everlasting *station* 610
Truly blessed is this *station* 1813

STATUTES

His *statutes* are inclined 212
O that thy *statutes* to observe 212
The *statutes* of the Lord are right 618
Thy *statutes* teach thou me 270
Upon thy *statutes* my delight 270

STAY

And *stay* by my side until morning 159
Art thou not our *stay* 837
As their *stay* thy promise taking 1775
Come to me, I'll be thy *stay* 837
Ever will he be thy *stay* 276
For Jesus close to me doth *stay* 867
God calling yet, I cannot *stay* 558
Here might I *stay* and sing 1255
Here would I ever *stay* 425
I'd *stay* in the garden with him 819
My guide and *stay* can be 27
O Jesus, ever with us *stay* 1023
O *stay* thou close beside us 1850
Or *stay* to serve thee in homes 713
Stay, let me weep 1832
Stay our wayward feet, O Lord 127
Stay thou, guide now our souls 1402
Stay thou near by 868
Stay not till all the holy (lowly) 1911
Will be our *stay* tomorrow 6

STAYED

And on his God is *stayed* 1394
Stayed upon Jehovah 1091

STAYS

And if he *stays* with me 954
And *stays* our sin 817

STEAD

Jesus is bearing it all in my *stead* 1015

STEADFASTNESS

Naught thy *steadfastness* can bend 2224

STEALING

And pardon o'er our sinful spirits *stealing* 29

STEEP

And up from the rocky *steep* 1983
Awhile upon the barren *steep* 161
Would *steep* my heart in sin 178

STEEPLES

Even when *steeples* are falling 263

STEERS

Unerringly he *steers* thee home 2146

STEM

From tender *stem* hath sprung 1107
Must I not *stem* the flood 87

STEP

Each *step* of my journey can see 701
For *step* by step he will lead me 867
From *step* to step it wins its way 325
One *step* enough for me 1053
Only a *step*, only a step 1584
Still step by *step* he will lead me 867
The freer *step*, the fuller breath 2030
When we *step* from the earth 2225

STEPS

And all my *steps* to thee-ward 2033
As with joyful *steps* they sped 129
Guiding thy *steps* as may best 2322
Here thou our fathers' *steps* didst 640
His sacred *steps* pursue 2334
How beautiful to walk in the *steps* 2129
In his master's *steps* he trod 627
In his *steps* we go, facing 2159
Let the great Master's *steps* 703
No more my *steps* to roam 1421
On our *steps* from heaven above 144
Our devious *steps* attend 311
Savior, where'er thy *steps* I see 1519
The *steps* of him I love 7
Though my weary *steps* may falter 66
Trying to walk in the *steps* 2129
Walking in thy *steps* below 1197
When in his *steps* we tread 1515
When my *steps* wander 1656
When the last feeble *steps* 1922
Where their *steps* have led the way 1499
While on in Jesus' *steps* I go 1733

STERN

To face the *stern*, to wrestle 1352

STEWARDS

Faithful *stewards* of the word 485
We but *stewards* of thy bounty 1760

STILL

And *still* the ocean's roar 2081
And *still* this throbbing heart 1020
Come, Holy Spirit, *still* my heart 1349
Still my doubting, calm my fear 1772
Still our mind with truth's 440
Still their strife and my confusion 730

STILLED

Stilled our rude hearts 578
Who *stilled* the waves, and stayed 371

STILLNESS

A holy *stillness*, breathing calm 654

STILLS

And *stills* the stormy wave 327
And *stills* the tempest of my throbbing 1284

STING

From death's dread *sting* thy servants free 79, 1937
Where is death's *sting* 27

STIR

And still *stir* up thy gift 1521
And *stir* us up to pray 2037
Lord, I was dead, I could not *stir* 1140
Stir in me the same emotion 140
Therefore, I *stir* my inmost heart 1444

STIRRED

Be *stirred* up his holy name 1513
Stirred by deep devotion 517
Stirred the slumb'ring chords 2002

STIRS

Stirs on the earth 683

STONE

Each *stone* has now a million 2174
In vain with *stone,* the cave 1078
That *stone* is made head 1484
Till not a *stone* was left on stone 1124

STONES

Here be living *stones* prepared 1567
Polished well those *stones* elect 217
Stones thy pillow 500
Sure the very *stones* would speak 1814
The *stones,* our silence shaming 2230
Who, of living *stones* art builded 217

STOOD

As mute I *stood,* fear overwhelmed 878
At last it *stood,* with thousands more 11
He once *stood* fast for thee 1784
He *stood* at my heart's door 1741
His truth at all times firmly *stood* 57
It was alone the Savior *stood* 957
So to the Jews old Canaan *stood* 1966
Stood the mother, worn with weeping 1263
Stood the mournful mother weeping 140
The Lord Christ *stood* on Easter Day 626
When Moses *stood* with arms 2221

STOOP

Cans't thou *stoop* again, yet lower 369
Stoop down, and drink, and live 842
Stoop to my weakness, mighty as 1778

STOOPED

Even as I *stooped* to drink 1322
For thou hast *stooped* to ask 1234
I *stooped* to kiss away the marks 888

STOOPS

And O, when *stoops* on Judah's path 2239
But *stoops* a servant low 2334

STOP

And there it did both *stop* 1861

STOPPED

At last I *stopped* to listen 892

STORE

A boundless *store* from his 771
To bless the toiler's *store* 21

STORES

Autumn's rich o'erflowing *stores* 1628

STORIES

Stories and tunes and kindly 1629
Stories of Jesus, tell them 1831

STORM

Above the *storm* are shining still 1217
As o'er the *storm* ariseth 1874
Be then no more by a *storm* 1840
Come not in flashing *storm* 2273
Far below the *storm* of doubt 431
In *storm* and in calm, his strong arms 623
In *storm* or battle, with thine arm 650
Storm and flood and ocean's roar 1211
The *storm* cannot hide his 1848
The *storm* is changed into a calm 773
The *storm* may roar without me 921
The *storm* that I feared may 1848
Thou, when the *storm* of death 476
Through life's *storm* and tempest 2188
Through the *storm* I safely ride 2056
When loud the *storm* and furious 712
When the *storm* of life is past 1682
Where no *storm* ariseth more 2275

STORM CLOUDS

Often have the *storm clouds* gathered 1270
When the *storm clouds* lower 256

STORMS

A few more *storms* shall beat 5
Above the *storms* of passion 1408
After the *storms* your skies will all 1270
And if a few more *storms* shall 2146
And *storms* of sorrow fall 2231
And when the *storms* are its branches 1840
No *storms* will threaten 207
Out of life's (earth's) *storms* and into thy 1602
So when the fiercer *storms* arise 1429
Storms cannot shake nor stain 2183
Storms obscure the light of day 2056
The raging *storms* may round us 1905
Though *storms* of hate may rage 309
Though the *storms* may gather 1004
Through the *storms* he doth send 2096
When the howling *storms* of doubt 1790
When the *storms* are near us 1180
When the *storms* are raging sore 755
When the *storms* of fierce temptation 1603
Where no *storms* ever beat 896

Where the *storms* are sweeping 403
Ye *storms* and winter snow 1936

STORM-TOSSED

Storm-tossed and beaten more 2146

STORM-WINDS

And *storm-winds* drift us 475

STORY

A *story* of peace and light 2208
A *story* of truth and sweetness 2208
Ancient Israel, the *story* of his 611
And to tell the old, old *story* 1044
Beautiful the *story* 6
But best of all is the *story* 2179
Keep telling the *story*, be faithful 2281
Let the sweet the joyful *story* 581
No *story* so divine 1255
Repeat the wondrous *story* 6
Shall be the endless *story* 1419
Story of man's wondrous journey 2318
Telling o'er and o'er the *story* 411
Telling still the ancient *story* 1295
The *story* of pardon to tell 529
The wide world's wondrous *story* 92
Then a wonderful *story* told 1199
This is my *story*, this is my song 213
'Tis the Lord, O wondrous *story* 2286
To tell the *story* 1578
'Twill be the old, old *story* 862
While degradation's *story* 923
Who will go, salvation's *story* 433
With the *story* of his worth 1070
Ye who sang creation's *story* 103

STRAIGHT

And *straight* are in the way 212
It grew so *straight*, and tall 11

STRAIGHTNESS

Like the *straightness* of the pine trees 606

STRAIN

And echo back the mighty *strain* 49
And the angel *strain* was this 1718
Beneath the angel *strain* have rolled 948
Come heaven's melodious *strain* 272
One the *strain* that lips 2067
That one *strain* of the song which 430
This is the *strain*, the eternal strain 1936

STRAINS

And *strains* of sweetest music 2172
And then in *strains* of glory 872
But, oh, the *strains*, how full 1592
For which in joyful *strains* 1543
In celestial-like *strains* 430
In what are sund'ring *strains* 138
Let *strains* of heav'nly music rise 851
The *strains* of all its holy throng 2120
With *strains* of love and power 55

STRAND

From India's coral *strand* 512

STRANGER

A *stranger* and a pilgrim 869
And there a *stranger* journeyed too 888
But no more a *stranger* 524
Dear little *Stranger*, born in a manger 1199
Hail, little *Stranger*, laid in a manger 1504
I once was an outcast *stranger* 1229
The *Stranger* was their Friend 975
To *stranger*, as to kin 210
When the *stranger* asks a home 2260

STRAY

And when I so often would *stray* 701
Else I must surely *stray* 2083
From thee that I no more may *stray* 889
How shall we *stray* 578
How wide and far we *stray* 240
Let me never from thee *stray* 637
Lest from thee we *stray* abroad 127
Nor let me ever *stray* 1227
So shall we never *stray* 1401
That I from thee no more may *stray* 1230
Trusting thee, I cannot *stray* 1684
Where'er I *stray*, still from above 815
Wherein no blinded child can *stray* 39

STRAYED

Perverse and foolish oft I *strayed* 1876

STREAM

Free to all, a healing *stream* 986
Gently down the *stream* of time 1682
Not Jordan's *stream*, nor death's 1966
Streams from the fount of heavenly 1052
That life-giving *stream* will continue 17
The narrow *stream* of death 1067

STREAMING

And from it love's pure light is richly *streaming* 29

STREAMS

And for all *streams* and rills 1224
And Niger's deadly *streams* 149
It *streams* from the hills 1546
Its *streams* the whole creation 2071
Its *streams* will soon run dry 1193
Let the healing *streams* abound 994
See, the *streams* of living waters 541
Streams ever copious are gliding 660
Streams of mercy, never ceasing 340
The liquid *streams* forbear to flow 2307
The *streams* of his dread agony 266
The *streams* of heavenly radiance 2147
The *streams* on earth I've tasted 1923
What *streams* I have to cross 387
Where *streams* of living water flow 1876
Whose *streams*, aglow with fountains 1951

STREET

And, day far spent, the very *street* 2174
In crowded *street,* by restless 2008
No city *street* is dumb 1943
Singing in the quiet *street* 1100

STREETS

All the *streets* with gold 938
All thy *streets,* and all thy bulwarks 217

STRENGTH

All in his *strength* and beauty 626
And in his *strength* unto the end 1860
And in my quiet *strength* again 362
And in the *strength* thy grace 2107
And perfect *strength* in weakness 820
And *strength* to strength oppose 1786
And *strength* yet stronger grow 2134
As then our *strength* in time of need 588
Be our *strength* in days 1084
Be our *Strength* in hours of 441
Be thou my *strength* and stay 178
Be thou still my *Strength* and Shield 652
Be with us, thy *strength* supplying 470
But for *strength* that we may ever 441
Christ is thy *Strength,* and Christ 477
Daily *strength* for daily needs 380
Did we in our own *strength* confide 12
For all its *strength* and beauty 1529
For *strength* and peace which gladden 1329
For *strength* to do, and will 1346
From *strength* to strength go on 1746
Gathering *strength* from every nation 669
Give of the *strength* of your youth 531
God is his people's *strength* 1455
God is our *strength* and song 1785
Great your *strength,* if great your 1560
Happy, whose *strength* in thee doth 782
He is my *strength* from day to day 981
He who is the Savior our *strength* 2336
He'll be our *strength,* our refuge 791
His *strength* shall bear thy spirit up 1823
His *strength* the more is 707, 2290
I have no *strength* or goodness 820
In *strength* of which we travel 1716
In *strength* or weakness may we see 1424
In the *strength* of the Lord let me labor 809
In the *strength* that cometh by 293
In thee my *strength* renew 406
Israel's *strength* and consolation 343, 658
Jehovah all *strength* to his people 537
Jehovah is my *strength* and shield 1455
Jehovah still thy *strength* supplies 958
Jesus will your *strength* renew 2252
More *strength* to carry crosses 1219
My life's *strength* is the Lord 1903
My *strength* and my salvation do 1258
My *strength* is in thy might 727
My *strength* proportion to my day 1519
My *strength* was spent with grief 772
My waning *strength* increase 1387
Nor *strength* and gladness lead astray 1495
O God of *strength,* be thou to us 1361
O let my *strength* be as the day 1509
Our *strength* is dust and ashes 1943
Our *strength* renew 342
Our *strength,* thy grace 274
Our *strength* thy Spirit 1873
Put on thy *strength,* the nations 116
Strength aiding still the strong 2267
Strength and health are mine 2224
Strength and honor give to his holy name 1616
Strength and life sufficiently 51
Strength for the conflict, victorious 2314
Strength for thy labor the Lord will 1655
Strength for today and bright hope 647
Strength in the Lord Jehovah dwells 778
Strength is within his holy place 1486
Strength, joy, and willingness 2199
Strength of all that lives 1158
Strength of mine is only weakness 225
Strength to serve thee, hour by 42
Strength to the end 1656
Strength unto our souls afford 127
Strong in the *strength* which God 1746
Strong in thy *strength,* we will battle 2128
Strong in your Captain's *strength* 1081
That in thy *strength* we evermore 828
That we may go in *strength* upon 422
The Lord almighty and his *strength* 533
The *strength* and portion of my heart 932
The *strength* of joy, the zest 2040
The *strength* of youth we lay at Jesus' 516
The *strength* those weaklings 2164
Their only *strength* thy grace 1432
Then is my *strength* by thee 1237
Thine ample *strength* release 1359
Thine is the Roman's *strength* 522
Thou dost my *strength* assure 839
Though thy *strength* be small 1114
Thy *strength* shall never fail us 2289
To be my *strength* and stay 869
To thee our earliest *strength* we vow 1424
What *strength* for warfare 1237
Whene'er my *strength* shall fail me 1818
Who in the *strength* of Jesus trusts 1746
With all his *strength* endued 1746
With all his *strength,* to thee 1367
You in his *strength* 906

STRENGTHEN

But *strengthen* and sustain 240
I'll *strengthen* thee, help thee 776
O *strengthen* me, that while I stand 1170
O *strengthen* our infirmity 456
Strengthen hand and heart 997, 998
Strengthen me in fullest measure 225
Strengthen my feet with steady pace 1953
Strengthen my trust in thee 463
To *strengthen,* save, and make us whole 317

STRENGTHENED

Seeking to be *strengthened* 1102
Strengthened with bread, the food 466
Strengthened with might 264
Strengthened with the bread 1560
Thus, *strengthened* with all might 1171, 1506

STRESS

Be near us in the *stress* of life 1401
Whose stern, impassioned *stress* 1311

STRETCH

And *stretch* his hand 1
Far *stretch* the shining paths 1951
I may *stretch* out a loving hand 1170
Stretch o'er her lands and isles 321
Stretch thy love, a tent 730

STRETCHED

Stretched the hand and strained 1686

STRETCHES

Where wild Judea *stretches* far 272

STREW

In the place of briers, *strew* 163
Sometimes they *strew* his way 1255
Strew ye palms along the way 1726

STREWN

Strewn with wrecks and stained 1760

STRIDING

To the gates of heaven *striding* 51

STRIFE

Amid the world's increasing *strife* 1508
And *strife* shall cease upon the highway 720
From the *strife* of class and faction 1280
God calls from deadly *strife* 2100
Here in overwhelming final *strife* 1803
If, after the *strife* is ended 1411
In all the *strife* of mortal life 2289
In keenest *strife*, Lord, may we stand 1204
In the *strife* of truth with error 507
In the *strife* of truth with falsehood 1574
No *strife* shall rage 198
O may no angry *strife* destroy 1432
Once more, from earth's tumultuous *strife* 1385
Our *strife* of speech and sword 2076
Preparing for the bitter *strife* 1417
Strife will vanish where thou 1402
The last and fiercest *strife* 1660
The *strife* at last is ended 43
The *strife* is not man against man 170
The *strife* to rescue souls 2189
The *strife* will cease 1
The *strife* will not be long 1786
When o'er the *strife* of nations 1652
When the *strife* of sin is 2253
When the world's sharp *strife* 2264
Whilst in strange and awful *strife* 288
Yet *strife* and tumult rage 2098

STRIKE

And *strike* each cheerful chord 1895
Strike! Let every nerve and sinew 2157

STRIKES

Comes the Lord when *strikes* the hour 36
He *strikes* the fetters from the slave 1930
Strikes for a kingdom, and his 2262

STRINGS

No longer let your *strings* 1362
Strings and voices, hands and hearts 1623

STRIPE

For every martyr's *stripe* 507

STRIPES

By his *stripes* I am healed 122
His *stripes* hath healed us 426
Lord, by the *stripes* that wounded thee 79, 1937
Only by his *stripes* we are healed 214

STRIVE

And *strive* to serve him well 325
Blindly they *strive*, for sin darkens 506
In vain we *strive* to rise 318
Should *strive* afresh against 1630
Should *strive* and should prevail 1630
Strive for souls while still 1222
Strive for the right, for the Lord 378
Vainly will *strive* when the door 1758
Who *strive* and bleed, with courage 1593

STRIVING

Striving to please him in all that I do 1104

STRIVINGS

From vain *strivings* cease 344
Holy *strivings* nerve and strengthen 71
Till all our *strivings* cease 386

STROKE

No fatal *stroke* shall thee 1908
Without one *stroke* of battle 1874

STRONG

Shall the *strong* retain the spoil 1136
Through him we are *strong* 1620
'Tis also *strong* to save 327
To wrestle with the *strong* 1352

STRONGHOLDS

For captured *strongholds* of the foe 2185
His *strongholds* are spoiled 1599
Sin's *strongholds* it now o'erthrows 1695

STROVE

The more I *strove* against its power 1001

STRUGGLE

In *struggle* which thou never did ordain 183
Long as ye *struggle* here 682
Vainly you *struggle* from him 984

STRUGGLES

A few more *struggles* here 5

It is enough earth's *struggles* 1610
Then all the *struggles* of the day 2048

STRUGGLING

To those who are *struggling* near 529

STUDY

And *study* war no more 198
Study, science, all the treasure 1158

STUMBLE

Blindly we *stumble* when we walk 1059
Lest thou shouldst *stumble* in the way 201

SUBDUE

There let him *subdue* 143

SUBDUES

Subdues the powers of hell 1897

SUBJECTION

That never in *subjection* 26

SUBMITS

Submits to death, nay, bears 2334

SUBSTANCE

And all our *substance* and our strength 828

SUCCESS

Till all *success* be nobleness 1311
When *success* attends their mission 1775

SUCCOR

And for my *succor* flying 1475
And the weakest and poorest some *succor* 1987
Do thou thy mighty *succor* give 1406
He will *succor* and defend 480
My *succor* and salvation 1003
Who unto him for *succor* turned 72

SUE

To *sue* for mercy 435

SUFFER

He will not *suffer* that thy foot 2139
I will *suffer* naught to hide 1004
I would be strong, for there is much to *suffer* 897
If best that I must *suffer* loss 135
It must not *suffer* loss 1786
It shall never *suffer* loss 1846
Nor for fear or favor *suffer* me 937
Nor *suffer* him to die in vain 336
Nor *suffer* me again to stray 1953
Nor *suffer* thee to live in vain 1821
Since God's own son must *suffer* thus 206
Suffer a sinner whose heart 1262
"*Suffer* little children to come 2245
Suffer me to come to thee 523
Suffer me to leave thee never 1690
Suffer not our steps to stray 1197
"*Suffer* them to come to me 1789
"*Suffer* these little ones to come 949
Suffer to redeem our loss 971
They *suffer* with their Lord 1869
Thou didst *suffer* to release us 659

SUFFERED

And *suffered* and died alone 881
And *suffered* there for me 957
But he *suffered* thus not in vain 214
Gladly, Lord, with thee they *suffered* 677
He has *suffered* to redeem me 805
He *suffered* all for thee 348
He *suffered,* bled, and died alone 957
I am not worth all he *suffered* 1971
I *suffered* much for thee 827
Jesus *suffered* in the sinner's 2125
Suffered uncomplaining 357
There *suffered* to maintain the truth 1921
To the cross where he *suffered* and bled 1114
'Twas for thee he *suffered* 1114
'Twas there on the cross Jesus *suffered* 17
What thou, my Lord, hast *suffered* 1475
Who *suffered* there for thee 203
Who *suffered* with nail-pierced hands 2212

SUFFEREDST

Thou *sufferedst* all for me 2077

SUFFERER

Mighty *Sufferer,* draw us 950

SUFFERING

All his *suffering* ended 622
Through *suffering,* thou, O Christ 1948

SUFFERINGS

All his *sufferings* for mankind 339
Lo, these are they from *sufferings* 774
Till, our *sufferings* ended, we 752

SUFFERS

Nor *suffers* one true word 1360

SUFFICE

He shall *suffice* me 683
Suffice it if—my good and ill— 2248

SUIT

O do not our *suit* disdain 1181

SUM

And in their *sum* how passing 1452
This is the total *sum* 1456

SUMMER

And the *summer* of life was gone 1941
For long *summer* days 61
Like *summer* in the soul 120
My *summer* would last all the year 795
Summer and winter, and springtime 647
The pleasant *summer* sun 68
The *summer* will be ended 1337
Where the *summer* smiles 1070

SUMMON

'Tis not to *summon* you from human mirth 279

SUMMONED

Summoned forth its fruit 579

SUMMONS

Ready as he *summons* me to go or stay 108
'Tis a *summons* to the conflict 2064
Waiting the *summons* from on high 132

SUN

A *sun* with healing in its wings 1810
A *sun* without a sphere 788
After the *sun*, the rain 539
And thee no *sun* by day shall 2139
And thou my rising *sun* 1240
And where the *sun* that shineth 1397
Bright as the *sun* ever it glows 1559
But Christ, my *sun*, ascendeth 1552
But Christ, the *Sun* of gladness 1297
Christ, her *Sun*, all sloth dispelling 668
Clearer than the *sun* at noon 742
Earth's *sun* in the calm lake 1208
E'en though the *sun* withholds 1803
Fair as the *sun* when night 29
For the *sun* and showers 409
Gently as life's setting *sun* 1744
God is our *Sun* and Shield 1167
God is their *Sun*, whose cheering beams 774
Great *Sun* of Righteousness, arise 1871
Hail, the *Sun* of Righteousness 675
Heaven's better, brighter *Sun* 2332
Here the *sun* is always shining 431
High above the kingly *sun* 1305
If thou art my *sun* and my song 795
In them he for the *sun* 1862
Keep on praying till the *sun* 1048
Last like the *Sun* it shall 1454
Majestic like the *sun* 7
Man's clouded *sun* shall brightly 2267
'Neath India's glowing *sun* 149
'Neath *sun* or moon, by day or night 885
O for the *Sun* of Righteousness 1920
O *Sun* of Righteousness, appear 247
One *sun* shines over all 56
Our heavenly *Sun*, our glorious 1286
Rising o'er me like the *sun* 717
Sun and moon and stars decay 1667
Sun and moon, bow down before him 1618
Sun and moon, rejoice before him 1626
Sun and moon-bright 104
Sun and shield alike thou art 1612
Sun and stars are singing 258
Sun, moon and stars convey 1871
Sun, moon and stars forgot 1265
Sun, moon and stars in their courses 647
Sun of grace, the shadows flee 1085
Sun of our life, thy quickening 1155
Sun of Righteousness, arise 292
Sun of the soul, thou Light 1402
The Lord whom *sun* and moon 1865
The midsummer *sun* shines but dim 795
The radiant *sun* hath vanished 1297
The rolling *sun*, the changing light 1871
The setting as the rising *sun* 1795
The smiling *sun* placed on 11
The summer *sun* and air 1146
The *sun* gone down 1265
The *sun* himself hath vanished 1552
The *sun* is falling fast 279
The *sun* may stand in zenith 1131
The *sun* shines out in glory 1949
The *sun* shone out with fairer ray 1037
The *sun* that bids us rest 1856
The *sun* that from his amber bower 2250
The *sun* that lights its shining 479
The *Sun* that lights mine eyes 1723
The unwearied *sun*, from day to day 1932
Thou burning *sun* with golden 41
Tomorrow's *sun* may never rise 1343
To see thee in the *sun* by day 1384
Warm as the glowing *sun* 1462
Well might the *sun* in darkness hide 38
When *sun* and moon shall shine no more 535
When the constant *sun* returning 605
When the *sun* of bliss is 934
Where brighter than the *sun* he glows 1543
Ye *sun*, and moon, and stars 2328

SUNBEAM

A *sunbeam* kissed the hidden spot 11
Be a golden *sunbeam*, bright and pure 163
Bright as a *sunbeam*, pure as 1605
I'll be a *sunbeam* for Jesus 1030

SUNBEAMS

Sunbeams scorching all the day 500
There the *sunbeams* are ever shining 913
Till the *sunbeams* bring us 935

SUNDERED

Though *sundered* far, by faith they meet 511

SUNG

Sung by flaming tongues above 340
'Tis *sung* in words, and *sung* in deeds 1113

SUNK

When has *sunk* yon glaring sun 2261

SUNLIGHT

And the *sunlight* falls in gladness 2256
Come into the *sunlight* 931
Fairer than the *sunlight* 1034
For the Lord will be *sunlight* 1870
Heavenly *sunlight*, heavenly 2152
In the bright *sunlight*, ever 2152
Like the *sunlight* from the sky 1041
Mine is the *sunlight* 1221
No need of the *sunlight* in heaven 1946
Not of the *sunlight*, not of 1550
O tranquil, radiant *Sunlight* 1359
Sunlight and shadow moving on 385

The *sunlight* is glowing o'er armies 509
True *sunlight* of the soul 1463
Walking in *sunlight* 2152
When *sunlight* through darkness 953
With thy golden *sunlight,* dry the dewy tear 163

SUNRISE

From *sunrise* to its setting 284
O that will be *sunrise* for me 2235
Sunrise in glory is waiting 2235
Sunrise tomorrow, sunrise 2235
Sunrise will chase all the darkness 1763
Sunrise with Jesus for eternity 2235

SUNS

A few more *suns* shall set 5
Do flaming *suns* his footsteps trace 96
Long as *suns* continue, it shall stand 286
Nor *suns* with scorching ray 774

SUNSET

At *sunset* with us be 1094
Beyond the *sunset* a hand 207
The *sunset* and the morning 68
The *sunset* glows dividing 1878

SUNSHINE

Fair is the *sunshine* 427
For the *sunshine* warm and bright 273
In *sunshine* or in shower 6
In the *sunshine,* in the air 936
It may be in the *sunshine* 954
Let his radiant *sunshine* flood 1210
Like *sunshine* at noon day 1946
O there's *sunshine,* blessed *sunshine* 1980
Ripened by his glorious *sunshine* 76
Rising in his *sunshine* joyous 663
Sowing in the *sunshine* 1771
Sunshine and gloom are alike unto 1611
Sunshine and rain, harvest of grain 981
Sunshine, darkness, cloud 1071
Sunshine of my Father's face 978
The golden *sunshine,* vernal air 1439
There is *sunshine* in my soul 1980
There's a little of God's *sunshine* 1957
Through cloud and *sunshine,* Lord abide 27
Through the *sunshine* and the shadow 801
Thy *sunshine* hath no shade 1089
Why from the *sunshine* of love 985
With thy joyous *sunshine* blest 1085

SUP

There *sup* with us in love divine 165, 1716

SUPPER

Thy *supper,* Lord, is spread 204

SUPPLIANTS

Suppliants at thy mercy-seat 2047

SUPPLIES

And new *supplies* each hour I meet 631
The hand that gave it still *supplies* 7

SUPPLIETH

And *supplieth* every need 2252

SUPPLY

I will *supply* her daily need 114
My soul with heavenly thoughts *supply* 59
Well *supply* thy sons and daughters 541

SUPPORT

And will *support* me until the end 1756
Its sure *support,* its noblest end 1241
Still *support* and comfort me 994
Still *support,* control, protect 989

SUPPORTED

Supported by thy word 87

SUPPORTS

The Lord *supports* the fainting 911
Supports the fainting heart 685

SURETY

And *surety* that we shall be 383
Thou art my *surety,* now and 1829
Your *surety* he is 73

SURGE

Not a *surge* of worry 1091

SURGES

And *surges* swell no more 5
But should the *surges* rise 902
Now like angry *surges* meeting 678

SURPRISE

And it will *surprise* you what the Lord 2265

SURRENDER

Here I *surrender* all my grief 2096
I *surrender* all 70, 1688
Surrender your all today 1822
To whom shall I myself *surrender* 2140
When you *surrender* your life 2337
Will you *surrender* to this Savior 1425

SURRENDERED

Freely *surrendered* and wholly 2128

SURROUND

And thus *surround* the throne 381
Like them, let man the throne *surround* 55
Surround me as I go 1463

SURROUNDED

Now scornfully *surrounded* 1475
Surrounded by Jehovah's might 1569
Surrounded by thy power 2039

SURVEY

If I *survey* the ground I tread 877

SUSTAIN

Do thou in love *sustain* us 43
Sustain their faith, whate'er befall 1379

Sustain, we pray, each lifted head 495
Thou wilt *sustain* us till its work 447

SUSTAINETH

Who everything *sustaineth* 853

SWALLOW

The *swallow* also for herself 783

SWARE

Jehovah *sware* and made decree 2138

SWATHED

Swathed and cradled in a stable 1718

SWAY

Nor times' destroying *sway* 1064
The mighty *sway* of evil 1328
Thy silent *sway* fashions the nations 593
To scorn the senses' *sway* 1825
To thy *sway* all creatures bow 715

SWAYS

He *sways* my soul with divine 1847

SWEAT

But *sweat* drops of blood for mine 881
When on the *sweat* of labor 2262

SWEEP

Sweep across the crystal sea 77
Sweep over my spirit forever 430
Sweep through the earth, keen 1609

SWEEPING

Sweeping on o'er hill and plain 1109

SWEEPS

There *sweeps* no desolating wind 1965

SWEETEN

It would *sweeten* my bliss 809
Then *sweeten* thy labor with song 1098

SWEETENS

And *sweetens* every bitter cup 2192

SWEETER

O there he'll be still *sweeter* 2108

SWEETNESS

And let them all thy *sweetness* know 1232
Thou *sweetness* most ineffable 1405, 1409

SWELL

Alleluia, *swell* the strain 282
And surges *swell* no more 5
Swell high the note on every tongue 371
Swell one hymn round the throne 748
Swell the mighty flood 544
Swell the triumph of his train 1106

SWELLS

Like heav'nly music *swells* 22
There *swells* the sobbing human 1397

SWEPT

Jesus *swept* across the broken 2002

SWERVED

That, wheresoe'er my feet have *swerved* 39

SWING

Swing, bells, in every steeple 1724
Swing it straighter and higher 1834
Swing the heart's door widely open 692

SWORD

A single *sword* to thee 1365
And point Orion's *sword* 96
From the *sword* at noonday 271
Nor shall my *sword* sleep in my hand 95
Our *sword* is the Spirit of God 2180
Our *sword* the Word of God 413
Overcoming daily with the Spirit's *sword* 1790
Sword and crown betray his trust 53
The *sword* of thine own deathless 1702
'Tis a *sword* for spirit-wielding 2319

SWORDS

Our *swords* to plow-shares 1930
The *swords* of scorn divide 1365

SWORN

And thou hast *sworn* to hear 1146
He by himself hath *sworn* 1864
Sworn to be Christ's soldiers 2157
Sworn to yield, to waver, never 2157

SYMBOL

A holy *symbol* to declare 1093
In *symbol* here we see 234
Symbol of the peace within 1744
Symbol of the world's redemption 1728
That *symbol* of his flesh he 2133
'Tis the *symbol* of our faith 507

SYMBOLS

O Master, through these *symbols* shared 204

SYSTEMS

Our little *systems* have their day 1797

T

TABERNACLE

Within thy *tabernacle* I 1357

TABERNACLES

The pleasant *tabernacles* are 782
The *tabernacles* of thy grace 782

TABLE

And at his *table* dine 2294
Around thy *table,* Lord 15
At his *table* we'll sit down 251
Lo, the *table* is spread and the feast 565
My *table* thou hast furnished 1904
O let thy *table* honored be 1232
Shall about the *table* meet 238
This is the heavenly *table* 727
This *table* now, we spread 1324
Thou art coming, at thy *table* 2018
Thou at the *table,* blessing, yet 335
When at his *table* sits the Lord 89

TAKE

And gladly *take* my station 1806
And going *take* thee to their home 1032
And shall *take* his harvest 359
And *take* his wanderers home 147
And *take* me home, what joy 1437
And *take* my sins away 5
And *take* salvation's waters 2155
And *take* the bliss thy love 1924
And *take,* to arm you for the fight 1746
And though they *take* our life 19
But *take* as from thy hands our tasks 1291
But *take* away our pride 1365
But *take* the dimness of my soul 1778
Come and *take* thy royal throne 227
Freely let me *take* of thee 994
God will *take* care of you 168
He'll *take* thee, at thy parting breath 1256
He will *take* you home to heaven 1996
Holy Spirit, *take* possession 1688
I *take* my cross and follow him 1822
I *take,* O Cross, thy shadow 203
I with her would *take* my place 1263
I'll *take* it, joy or sorrow 1949
It will *take* us all to heaven 2095
Lord Christ, we *take* the torch from thee 1608
Lord, I'll *take* it 2032
Lord Jesus, *take* this spirit 291
Nor *take* reward will he 2311
O *take* it to God in prayer 111
O, *take* my burdened heart 2046
O, will you not *take* him today 1925
Old and young *take* up the story 1272
Or *take* me to thee up on high 795
Or *take* us from our Shepherd's side 2174
Savior, *take* the power and glory 1106
Shouldst thou *take* my life 1690
So *take* our work into thy loving 1287
Take all hindrances away 1147
Take all my guilt away 1227
Take all the failures, each 388
Take away our sin and shame 1676
Take away the love of sinning 1190
Take Christ as your Savior, then all 1542
Take for thyself the flower of youth 2291
Take from our souls the bitterness 944
Take from our souls the strain 386
Take his easy yoke and follow 1577
Take home the wandering sheep 291
Take in thy keeping those, who 595
Take it, O Lord, and make it clean 1383
Take it, then, where'er you go 1817
Take it to the Lord in prayer 2210
Take its guidance, and be wise 742
Take me now, Lord Jesus, take me 1690
Take me to thy heavenly home 976
Take me, when I die 1013
Take my feet, and let them be 1816
Take my guilt and grief away 717
Take my hand and ever keep 973
Take my hands, and let them move 1816
Take my heart, it is thine own 1816
Take my intellect, and use 1816
Take my love, my Lord, I pour 1816
Take, my soul, thy full salvation 980
Take my spirit to thee 613
Take my voice, and let me sing 1816
Take my will, and make it thine 1816
Take my will forever 2123
Take myself, and I will be 1816
Take not thy thunder from 1365
Take our sins and guilt away 287
Take part with me against 2038
Take the crown that love immortal 1710

Take the King of Glory in 655
Take the manna of today 380
Take the name of Jesus ever 1817
Take the praise that brims 1158
Take the task he gives you gladly 697
Take the thanks of a boy (man) 613
Take thou my heart, I would be 1219
Take thou my heart to be thy 724
Take thou our courage, for thy 1157
Take thou our fears that weaken 1157
Take thou our hearts, O Christ 1819
Take thou our lives and use them 762
Take thou our love, for thou 1157
Take thou our selves, O Lord 1819
Take thou our strength, for thou 1157
Take thou our truth 1157
Take thou our wills 1819
Take thou the hands we lift 1604
"*Take* thy cross and follow 814, 2032
Take thy great power and reign 2128
Take thy sweet flowers of peace 334
Take thy throne our hearts 1049
Take to God your plans 561
Take to Jesus all your want 2252
Take up the battle-cry 958
"*Take* up thy cross and follow 888
Take up thy cross; let not its 1823
Take up thy cross; nor heed the shame 1823
Take up thy cross, then, in his strength 1823
Take up thy cross, with willing 1823
Take us, and make us holy 1943
Take us in thy arms 929
Take us in thy care 928
Take us, Lord, to dwell with thee 1745
Take your appointed post 1081
Take what I am and what I have 2213
Thankful I *take* the cup 417
That I must *take* to dwell 319
That no one can *take* away 139
That we must *take* to dwell 310
Thee for my Savior let me *take* 195
Then *take,* O God, thy power 1660
Then *take* thy power, and reign 1836
Then *take* up the glad refrain 1975
Then *take* with rejoicing from Jesus 1974
They may *take* heart, if you show 907
Unless thou *take* the veil away 1777
Which thou didst *take* to save 1177

TAKEN

And thou hast *taken* count of all 1812, 1478
Who hath *taken* him away 552

TAKES

It *takes* its terror from the grave 2192
Jesus *takes* the highest station 1117
Which *takes* the humbler part 306

TAKING

Just from Jesus simply *taking* 2092

TALE

The wondrous *tale* is written 2072

TALENT

Ev'ry *talent* I will bring 801
Here for all your *talent* you may 399

TALENTS

Offering *talents,* time and treasure 579
So many *talents* wasted 1849

TALES

Tales of the sea 1831
Wondrous *tales* of it are told 656

TALK

And *talk* of all thy truth at night 1811
Let us *talk* of all his wondrous love 2259

TALKETH

Comfortable words he *talketh* 71

TALKS

And he *talks* with me 819

TARES

But, ah, what *tares* the evil one 666

TARRIED

We've *tarried* for the Bridegroom 1597

TARRY

E'en though he *tarry* late 682
Gladly will I *tarry* in Beulah Land 431
I can *tarry* but a night 913
If you *tarry* till you're better 358
O why do you *tarry* so long 2293
Tarry no more without 1463
Tarry not in all the plain 1866
Why do you *tarry,* why linger 2068
Why should we *tarry* when Jesus 1743

TASK

A *task* beyond our powers 100
And when my *task* on earth is done 702
And with the *task* sufficient 1468
Every *task,* however simple 1022, 2006
For the daily *task* and challenge 331
In its sweet *task* to bear thy part 600
Our *task* is no greater than that 1372
Take the *task* he gives you gladly 697
The *task* thy wisdom hath assigned 499
Thou my daily *task* shalt give 380
Till every common *task* seems great 1393
We take up the *task* eternal 62

TASKS

And the sweet *tasks* of love 205
From daily *tasks* set free 199
The *tasks* he gives are those 2160

TASTE

And *taste,* before him lying still 1431
But now they *taste* unmingled 1223
Here shall ye *taste* unmingled joys 778
Here *taste* afresh the calm 727
I *taste* even now the hallowed bliss 1348

O *taste* and see that God is good 616, 1902
Taste of the glories that there 1758
That God is good, O *taste* and see 1890
Though bitter to the *taste* it be 417
We more than *taste* the heavenly 779
We *taste* thee, O thou living Bread 1023
When we *taste* the mystic wine 1028

TAUGHT

He *taught* our hearts to rise 231
He *taught* us how to rule the wild 2104
Taught by the Bible 804
Taught by thee, we covet most 636
Taught me to pray 2316
Taught to lisp the holy praises 633
Thou hast *taught* me it is so 1195
Thy grace has *taught* me to believe 60
'Twas grace that *taught* my heart to fear 88

TAUNTS

With *taunts* and scoffs they mock 1251

TEACH

And *teach* me in all things 1583
And *teach* me where to cast the net 838
And *teach* our hearts, in highest 316
And *teach* our hearts 'tis goodness 1184
And *teach* their hearts to love thy law 1495
And *teach* them in that word 785
And *teach* us, as we sound thy praise 1384
And *teach* us in our youth 78
And *teach* us now to walk 793
And *teach* us to know that humble 1594
And thou didst *teach* their feeble 1361
He will *teach* me how to live 1218
Him shall he *teach* the way 2116
I shall you *teach* to understand 1321
Lord, *teach* us how to pray 1506, 1641
O blessed Lord, *teach* me thy law 789
O *teach* me from my heart to say 1231
O *teach* me, Lord, just what to say 1056
O *teach* me, Lord, that I may teach 1170
O *teach* thou us to count our days 1174
O *teach* thy wandering pilgrims 1544
Savior, *teach* us so to rise 552
Should *teach* his brethren, and 1630
Teach it salvation's song 406
Teach me as seemeth best 1828
Teach me by love 1828
Teach me by pain 1828
Teach me by that bitter cry 2059
Teach me highly to regard 1583
Teach me how to do God's will 758
Teach me how to grow in goodness 973
Teach me, Lord, on earth to show 2261
Teach me now thy patience 2043
Teach me the patience of unanswered 1778
Teach me the struggles of the soul 1778
Teach me the way that I should go 2244
Teach me the wayward feet 1466
Teach me thus thy steps to trace 1687
Teach me thy patience 1466
Teach me thy truth, O Christ 1323
Teach me thy way 1828
Teach me thy way, and in thy truth 54
Teach me thy will 868
Teach me thy will to heed 2244
Teach me thy wondrous grace 1828
Teach me to be pure and true 448
Teach me to die, that so I may 59
Teach me to do thy will most 1645
Teach me to fear 765
Teach me to feel that thou art always 1778
Teach me to know, each hour 1828
Teach me to know thy word 1828
Teach me to live, that I may dread 59
Teach me to live, to die 1828
Teach me to love thee as thine 1778
Teach me to love thy sacred 457
Teach me what to do and say 976
Teach mortal tongues 641
Teach our hearts to love thee 579, 451
Teach our tongues to praise 451
Teach the little children 2245
Teach the mysteries of God 275
Teach their souls to thee to bend 2264
Teach them, O thou heavenly King 1570
Teach them to learn in thy great 371
Teach thou, and we shall know 596
Teach thou my lips to sing 1828
Teach thou my soul to cry 1828
Teach thy wisdom to my heart 554
Teach us all thy voice to hear 1197
Teach us aright to number 1377
Teach us, as ever in thy sight 1371
Teach us beyond our striving 1359
Teach us delight in simple 445
Teach us, great Teacher 596
Teach us how to love each other 1040
Teach us how we ought to pray 1147
Teach us in Christ to find 1313
Teach us, in every state 902
Teach us in thy love to learn 2253
Teach us in watchfulness 1026
Teach us, Lord, at length 1581
Teach us, Lord, thy wisdom 925
Teach us purity 2049
Teach us that lowliest duty done 596
Teach us the lesson thou hast taught 1371
Teach us the strength that cannot 445
Teach us thy majesty, thy calm 596
Teach us thy will and way 1943
Teach us to ban all ugliness 419
Teach us to bear the yoke in youth 445
Teach us to build; upon the solid 2198
Teach us to feel the sins 1184
Teach us to follow the Master of all 584
Teach us to know our faults 189
Teach us to know our God 317
Teach us to know the Father 313
Teach us to know the love which 1545
Teach us to know the truth 1819
Teach us to know the way of Jesus 1374
Teach us to know our sin which needs 1545
Teach us to look in all our ends 445
Teach us to love the true 1291
Teach us to redeem the time 219

Teach us to rule ourselves 445
Teach us to seek our heavenly home 437
Teach us to share thy ageless 1417
Teach us to speak thy word of hope 1130
Teach us where'er we live 1291
Teach us, with repentant grief 756
Teach us with thee to mourn our sins 1187
Then *teach* us, whatsoe'er betide 1371
There *teach* my heart to cling 1778
Thou didst *teach* us when we pray 1196

TEACHER

A silent *teacher*, Lord 559
Therein my *teacher* be 2116, 1719

TEACHERS

Nor e'er to other *teachers* range 317

TEACHING

And this was all their *teaching* 2072
And to its heavenly *teaching* turn 1052

TEACHINGS

By thy *teachings* sweet and holy 220

TEAR

Ah! *Tear* it thence, and reign 2033
And even the penitential *tear* 1237
And every *tear* be dry 351
No *tear* to wipe 967
Soon shall every *tear* be dry 1560
Wiping every *tear* 983

TEAR-DROP

Never a *tear-drop* and never a moan 407

TEAR-DROPS

And the *tear-drops* fall 1643
And when the *tear-drops* start 1896

TEARS

A few more *tears* 5
All their *tears* are wiped away 2275
And *tears* are of those former things 1977
And *tears* be wiped away 781
And *tears* no bitterness 27
And *tears* thy face have marred 1414
And where the *tears* are wiped 1397
But all their *tears* and sighs 644
By thy *tears* of bitter woe 1145
Do the *tears* flow down your cheeks 112
For her my *tears* shall fall 859
For thee, my Savior, scarce my *tears* 1251
For us his *tears* and blood 1168
He had no *tears* for his own grief 881
Here we no *tears* to shed 1333
Human *tears* for thee are flowing 1686
It is not thy *tears* of repentance 1974
Let us all, with *tears* of sorrow 668
Nor *tears* of sorrow flow 1959
Only a few more *tears* 1675
Our bitter *tears* he's staying 1535
Tears and smiles like us he 1572
Tears and sorrows never enter 2125
Tears unavailing, no merit 1262
There are no *tears* within their eyes 491
There the *tears* of earth are dried 1303
Though my *tears* flow all the night 401
Where all *tears* are wiped away 1682
Where *tears* are ever banished 489
With my *tears* his feet 1813

TELL

And *tell* him I love him still 2272
And *tell* him thou hast died 109
And *tell* its raptures all abroad 1392
And *tell* me, if thy name be Love 333
And *tell* my trouble and my woe 2103
And *tell* of all thy mighty works 1043
And *tell* of the King's highway 2125
And *tell* the golden harvest's yield 1327
And *tell* the story, saved by grace 1749
And *tell* what he has done for you 2269
And they *tell* me that no tears 1502
And, thrilling, we *tell* out our joyous 1725
Come, *tell* me all that ye 362
Does he *tell* you in communion 695
Go *tell* him how the Lord can bless 156
Here *tell* your anguish 355
I can never *tell* his love 1573
I can never *tell* how much 1573
I cannot *tell* how all the lands 817
I cannot *tell* how he will win 817
I cannot *tell* how silently he suffered 817
I cannot *tell* how soon 'twill be 1749
I cannot *tell* the depth of love 824
I *tell* him all my doubts and griefs 942
I'll *tell* of grace that keeps 912
I'll *tell* of mercy's boundless 912
I will *tell* the wondrous story 894
I would *tell* these little children 996
None call *tell* what pangs 2059
O Savior, *tell* my mother I'll be there 2237
O *tell* of his might 1546
O they *tell* me of a land far away 1502
O they *tell* me of an unclouded day 1502
O they *tell* me that he smiles 1502
Someone must *tell* them the news 1972
Tell all your troubles unto him 1640
Tell forth the wondrous story 2303
Tell her that her sins I cover 363
Tell him all thy grief 987
Tell him that Jesus loves him too 2272
Tell how Christ, the world's 1728
Tell how he died for you 1773
Tell how he helps you live 1773
Tell how he liveth again 1832
Tell how he stooped to save 1551
Tell how the angels in chorus 1832
Tell how the sparrow that twitters 1831
Tell how, when at length the 1728
Tell it out, let others share it 1703
Tell it out, through all the land 398
Tell it to Jesus 112
Tell it to me again 2317
Tell it to the captives waiting 1833
Tell it with a joyful voice 700
"*Tell* me all thy sorrows 680

Tell me, in accents of wonder 1831
Tell me the same old story 1830
Tell me the story always 1830
Tell me the story most precious 1832
Tell me the story often 1830
Tell me the story simply (slowly, softly) 1830
Tell me thou art mine 1772
Tell me thy name 333
Tell me thy secret, help me 1466
Tell me when thou wilt be free 158
Tell mother I'll be there 2237
Tell of Christ, the joyful message 2125
Tell of his excellent greatness 1616
Tell of our Redeemer's love 1783
Tell of the Cross where they 1832
Tell of the days that are past 1832
Tell of the grave where they laid 1832
Tell of the sorrow he bore 1832
Tell of the strength and comfort 1773
Tell of the years of his labor 1832
Tell old Pharaoh, to let my people go 2240
Tell the honor of your name 275
Tell the hungry nations 1833
Tell the joyful news wherever 2292
Tell the joyous tidings 1664
Tell the poor wanderer a Savior 1655
Tell the story far and wide
Tell the sweet story of Christ 1601
Tell them all about the Savior 251
Tell them how the Father's will 1783
Tell them of Jesus the mighty 1655
Tell them of the Lord of glory 542
Tell them of the Spirit giv'n 1783
Tell them that he will be found 251
Tell them to me 1831
Tell this word of grace to all 1735
Tell to all the blessed story 542
Tell to sinners far and wide 2169
Tell us, pilgrims, what you hope 2284
Tell us where the seraph 1718
Tell us, ye blest ones, that in it 1538
Tell ye forth his might 1211
That ye may *tell* posterity 646
Then will I *tell* to sinners 1001
They *tell* thy love, O God 2195
They *tell* thy love to all humanity 1919
To know that naught in man can *tell* 100
To *tell* the old, old story 862
To *tell* the world the peace 624
To thee I *tell* each rising grief 392
We cannot *tell* what pains 1963
We will *tell* the story 2127
With none to *tell* them of the 1551
Yes, *tell* my darling mother I'll be 2237
Yet how or why, I cannot *tell* 926
You can *tell* the love of Jesus 679
Zion, *tell* the world his fame 611

TELLING

What is this that they are *telling* 1100

TELLS

All that *tells* the world is loss 2089
And he *tells* me I am his own 819
And *tells* me I am born of God 113
He *tells* me every care on him 834
It *tells* me of a Savior's love 1967
It *tells* me of his precious blood 1967
It *tells* me what I am 872
It *tells* me what my Father hath 1967
It *tells* of benediction 350
It *tells* of One whose loving 1967
Till you have done what he *tells* 2337
When he *tells* us we may cast 2093

TEMPER

Temper my spirit, O Lord 1834

TEMPERANCE

Temperance in every pleasure 470

TEMPERED

God has *tempered* it with mercy 1957

TEMPEST

A little while of *tempest* 2172
A Shelter from *tempest* 20
And the *tempest* rises high 2056
From rock and *tempest*, fire and foe 81
If there's a *tempest*, your voice 905
Listening 'mid the *tempest* 1264
'Midst the *tempest* I have been 223
Nor a *tempest* can cast away the soul 1533
The *tempest* brings no fear 1462
The *tempest* may sweep o'er the wild 1257
The *tempest* that surges I will not 1868
There will be no *tempest* sweeping 1738
Thine, too, the *tempest* or the zephyrs 595
Though the *tempest* rave 2298
Through the *tempest* and the sunshine 863
What time the *tempest* rages 1377
While the *tempest* still is high 994

TEMPESTS

And *tempests* blow by order 877
And we shall be where *tempests* cease 5
E'en now, when *tempests* round 1026
In the *tempests* of life, on its wide 1477
Tempests will change to ineffable 1763
When the wild *tempests* rave 557

TEMPLE

A *temple* meet for thee 222
And now within thy *temple* 1529
Come to God's own *temple*, come 359
Each one in his *temple*, his glory 537
Early in the *temple* met 752
For the *temple* near thy throne 1567
God is in his *temple* 563, 600
In his *temple* shall appear 103
Is my *temple* and my tower 53
Let it be thy *temple* 1588
May each a living *temple* be 307
May this new *temple* prove 1175
Or *temple* altar's lambent flame 1088
No *temple* can with thee compare 1569
Shall one great *temple* rise to thee 496

Temple builded for my God 1835
The *temple* courts were dark 797
This *temple*, reared to thee 332
Thy *temple* deign to make us 1402
Thy *temple*, Lord, ere now it should 724
To this *temple*, where we call thee 281
Tow'r and *temple* fall to dust 53
When we in thy *temple* meet 589
Whose *temple* ever stands 2165

TEMPLE BELLS

Like echoes to sweet *temple bells* 29

TEMPLES

All earthly *temples* excelling 263
And we, as living *temples*, thine 502
For *temples* of worship all time 959
Starry *temples*, azure-floored 104
Still we our earthly *temples* rear 263
Surely in *temples* made with hands 263
Temples still undone o'er crumbling 2198
Thy true *temples*, Holy Spirit 718

TEMPT

And Satan *tempt* me sore 834

TEMPTATION

Awhile from thy *temptation* learn 161
In my *temptation*, provideth 573
In *temptation* he's my strong 834
Temptation with its flaming brand 1440
When *temptation* sorely presses 993

TEMPTATIONS

Are *temptations* so alluring 1709
Be with me when *temptations* 178
By *temptations* pressed 462
If *temptations* round you gather 1817
Safe from the world's *temptations* 1675
Temptations cannot last for long 1639
Temptations, hidden snares often 2127
Temptations lose their power 868
The manifold *temptations* that death 1391
Though *temptations* gather round my pathway 108
When *temptations* almost win thee 1642
When *temptations* come alluring 989
When *temptations* throng around you 398

TEMPTED

And if I *tempted* am to sin 176
And *tempted* like as we 1412
For the *tempted*, Lord, we pray 488
He himself was *tempted* that he might help me 108
O thou, once *tempted* like as we 161
Someone is *tempted* to turn from 1600
Tempted and tried I need a great 865
When I shall *tempted* be 463
Whenever I am *tempted* 2296

TEMPTER

That if the *tempter* cross my way 176
The *tempter* is foiled 1599
When the *tempter* would prevail 2232

TEMPTERS

Tempters seek to lure astray 2056
Though *tempters* strong beset thy way 546

TEMPTS

And Satan *tempts*, and human 460
When Satan *tempts*, and doubts 906

TEND

May all within us upward *tend* 1883
Tend them in sickness 458
To whom we ever *tend* 421

TENDED

Sweetly, fondly, safely *tended* 633

TENDERNESS

And now he is watching in *tenderness* 830
Let thy *tenderness* so loving 1691

TENDS

Father-like he *tends* and spares us 1618
Forward *tends* to his abode 1667

TENT

A *tent* or a cottage, why should I 1229
Be my *tent*, and in thy covert 730

TENTS

He *tents* within the lonely heart 1891
Let *tents* of ease be left behind 413

TERROR

Before thee *terror* is withdrawn 1088
From all that *terror* teaches 1365
My *terror* kill, be gracious 1239
What *terror* can confound me 567

TERRORS

No nightly *terrors* shall alarm 1908

TEST

No matter what may be the *test* 168
We *test* our lives by thine 917, 1428, 2181

TESTAMENTAL

Thy *testamental* cup I take 30

TESTED

Is *tested* by his way 185

TESTIFY

And *testify* to all mankind 1777

TESTIMONIES

And his *testimonies* heed 629
Thy *testimonies* all in faithfulness 598
Thy *testimonies*, every one 1886
Thy *testimonies*, Lord, in faithfulness 1882
Thy *testimonies* make me glad 789

TESTIMONY

God's *testimony* is most sure 618

THANK

And I *thank* thee for thy care 1013
And *thank* thee for thy saving grace 316
Father, dear, we *thank* thee 61
I *thank* thee, Lord, for health (hope, strength) 882
I *thank* thee, Lord, that here our souls 1236
I *thank* thee, Lord, that thou hast kept 1236
I *thank* thee more for bread 883
I *thank* thee more that all our joy 1236
I *thank* thee much for bread (place) 883
I *thank* thee now in word and deed 2302
I *thank* thee, too, that thou hast made 1236
I *thank* thee, uncreated Sun 1953
I *thank* thee, who hast overthrown 1953
I *thank* thee, whose enlivening 1953
I'll *thank* my Pilot true 2234
O *thank* him for his goodness 43
So Lord, we *thank* thee for that 2278
Thank him for life, for joy 1293
Thank him, thank him all ye little 1191
Thank him who gives to each one 1633
Thank him who gives us welcome 1633
Thank you for the birds that sing 1839
Thank you for the food we eat 1839
Thank you, God, for everything 1839
We *thank* thee, Father, for each word 1388
We *thank* thee for each mighty one 2115
We *thank* thee for him, thy 2194
We *thank* thee for life 423, 2194
We *thank* thee for love, that most 2194
We *thank* thee for the flowers 2195
We *thank* thee for the grace of home 1346
We *thank* thee for the hopes that rise 1186
We *thank* thee for the love divine 2115
We *thank* thee for the sunshine 2195
We *thank* thee for the ties that bind 1186
We *thank* thee for the word of might 2115
We *thank* thee for these years 2040
We *thank* thee for thy boyhood 1468
We *thank* thee, Lord, for sunshine 712
We *thank* thee, Lord, for they have won 491
We *thank* thee, Lord, that ours has been 1287
We *thank* thee, O God, for all things 2194
We *thank* thee that thou madest 2195
We *thank* thee that upon us fall 1346
We *thank* thee that thy church 1856

THANKED

And God anew he *thanked* 2133

THANKFULNESS

Dissolve my heart in *thankfulness* 38

THANK-OFFERINGS

Let them all *thank-offerings* bring 1622
Thank-offerings I to thee will give 910

THANKS

All *thanks*, O Lord, to thee 1851
And after *thanks* and glory 2133
And grateful *thanks* we bring 1464
And give thee *thanks* forever 43
And oft' my *thanks* renew 2234
And *thanks* for the harvest of beauty 1298
And *thanks* never ceasing, and infinite 2330
Eternal *thanks* to thee I'll give 123
Give *thanks* to thee for life divine 23
Let everlasting *thanks* be thine 7, 1933
No *thanks* to them abideth 12
O *thanks* with all my heart 2302
O'er *thanks* exalted far 100
Such *thanks* the blessed Mary 1186
Thanks be to God that such 956
Thanks we give and adoration 1125
Thanks we give to thee, our God 518
Thus shall my *thanks* be thanks 182
To him shall *thanks* and praise 1700
Yet *thanks* to thee for souls aflame 1916

THANKSGIVING

And with glad *thanksgiving* 1066
Lord, we would with deep *thanksgiving* 1280
Thanksgiving and honor and praise 1298
To him the loud *thanksgiving* raise 1108
To thee, in our *thanksgiving* 2165
With high *thanksgiving*, thee 1873

THANKSGIVINGS

Thanksgivings we bring in our songs 959

THEME

Be this *theme* my song and story 1688
Its never-changing *theme* is sweeter 2309
No *theme* is like redeeming love 1122
Our Jesus shall be still our *theme* 2025
The angels' *theme* in heaven 2192
The eternal *theme* of praise 2022
The same sweet *theme* 2164
Their everlasting *theme* 1869
This is the *theme* of the hymns 228
This shall be our *theme*, as we walk 1707
Thou art every creature's *theme* 1214
'Tis the grandest *theme* 2094
'Twill be my endless *theme* 833
'Twill be my *theme* in glory 862

THIEF

The dying *thief* rejoiced to see 1961
When a *thief* lifts up his eyes 110

THIEVES

How long shall *thieves* and robbers 405

THING

And every good *thing* is supplied 553
But there no evil *thing* may find 2201
But this one *thing* I know 954
Is there a *thing* beneath the sun 2033
No good *thing* will he deny 111
O what a fearful *thing* is sin 206
One *thing* I of the Lord desired 1903
Seeking for some great *thing* to do 443

So shall no wicked *thing* draw near 117
That so the *thing* that might have been 1383
This is that great *thing* 131
This one *thing* is needful, all 1583
'Tis the very *thing* to plead 2268

THINGS

Adrift from dear and anchored *things* 1294
Ah, no; when all *things* else expire 1514
All the vain *things* that charm 2236
All *things* are possible 472
All *things* are ready, come away 1875
All *things* both new and old 1378
All *things* in Christ are ready 336
All *things* in earth and heaven 1423
All *things* in Jesus I find 506
All *things* living he doth feed 1074
All *things* living show his hand 715
All *things* that live and move, by sea 2186
All *things* to him I owe 1016
All *things* living, thanks are giving 770
All *things* obey thy sacred word 1406
And all *things* else recede 1407
And all *things* in thy hand 856
And all *things* large and small 602
And all *things* new become 1332
And for the *things* to be 1505
And he with me doth all *things* 2294
And in all *things* trust him to supply 1565
And, of all *things* on earth 617
And outward *things* are strong 176
And still to *things* eternal look 499
And the dark *things* shall be plain 424
And *things* celestial thee shall own 373
And *things* terrestrial, Lord 373
And pondering all *things* in her heart 1488
And, when earthly *things* are past 129
Bright *things* they see, sweet harps 117
But in earth's common *things* he 1698
Evil *things* are there before thee 369
For all *things* serve thy sovereign will 417
For *things* that are we thank thee 1505
Freedom's good *things* we bring 2183
Great *things* he hath done 2102
Great *things* he hath taught us 2102
Here earth's bitter *things* grow 1271
Here earth's precious *things* seem 1271
Humbler *things* we ask thee 1036
In all *things* may I see 1825
In all *things* near and far 1891
Let all *things* praise the Lord 1625
Mighty *things* it can effect 1147
Of the *things* that are and have 1558
Of thee three *things* I pray 379
Rich in *things* and poor in soul 580
Seeking the *things* which are above 1670
Sending us *things* which bless our eyes 1633
Showing the *things* of Christ to me 1216
So many glorious *things* are here 1236
That, having all *things* done 1746
The higher *things* which every day 383
The *things* of earth have filled 2170
The *things* through mists 197
There its hidden *things* are clear 1303
Things deemed impossible I dare 1238
Things I would ask him to tell me 1831
Things that are higher 804
Things that are nobler 804
Things that once were wild alarms 1195
To flee from all *things* wrong 244
To follow all *things* holy 244
To touch unseen, eternal *things* 1294
When old *things* shall be done away 1332
Who wondrous *things* have done 1299
Whom all *things* serve from day 1865
Wonderful *things* in the Bible I see 806
Wondrous *things* the Lord may do 400
Ye creeping *things*, birds on 2328

THINK

And all we *think*, and all 459
And when I *think* of the Cross 1249
And when I *think* that God, his Son 1437
But let me only *think* of thee 856
Do you *think* I'd made a soldier 2156
Do you *think* he ne'er reproves 942
I should *think* 'twould make 996
I *think* of him all the day long 1649
I *think* of his hands pierced 880
I *think* of my blessed Redeemer 1649
Let me *think* how thy dear Son 449
Let us *think* how heaven and home 2089
Nearer now than I *think* 1580
Ne'er *think* the victory won 1256
Nor *think* till death to lay it 1823
O *think* of the friends over there 1503
On all I *think*, or say, or do 654
Think God's thoughts after thee 1490
Think how all-seeing God 152
Think no more of friendships 1577
Think that Christ has promised you 2265
Think what Spirit dwells within 980
Think, when you see those whom sin 908
When I *think* of the prize 1751
Whene'er I *think* of her so dear 870
Whenever I *think* of him 1847
Yet *think* thou on in me 1383

THINKETH

And as he *thinketh* in his heart 2311

THINKS

He *thinks* he was not made to die 1797

THIRST

And *thirst* our souls from thee 1023
I *thirst* for springs of heavenly 1242
I *thirst*, I faint, I die to prove 1458
My *thirst* was quenched, my soul 842
That *thirst* were all for me 734
They nor *thirst*, nor suffer hunger 2275

THIRSTY

That shadows a dry, *thirsty* land 24
To the *thirsty* desert 983

THORNS

And *thorns* put forth a rose 1727
And *thorns* thy brow encircle 1414
But of *thorns* 119
By *thorns* with which they crowned thee 1124
For me the cruel *thorns* he wore 825
New *thorns* to pierce thy steady brow 1124
Nor *thorns* infest the ground 1039
Or *thorns* compose so rich a crown 2236
That *thorns* remain 1236
The *thorns* in my path are not 1848
Thine the sharp *thorns,* so mine 2201
With *thorns,* thine only crown 1475

THORN-TREE

The *thorn-tree* had a mind 947

THOROUGH-FARE

A *thorough-fare* for freedom beat 1311

THOUGHT

And cold my warmest *thought* 794
And every *thought* of holiness 1589
And every *thought* to him aspire 1640
And every *thought* within us sings 1380
And I *thought* I heard him say 892
And not a *thought* our bosoms 1184
And on the wondrous *thought* 1571
And sweeter is the *thought* of thee 844
And when my *thought* is all 1383
Be my last *thought,* how sweet 1801
Each *thought* and each motive 1820
Each *thought* is fraught with love 2309
Each wayward *thought* reclaim 1592
Every *thought* is praise 409
For, far above the *thought* 536
Forever in my *thought* the Lord 2238
God's *thought* to earth thou bringest 1490
Hast thou no *thought* for heaven 196
He *thought* not of his agony 2242
He *thought* of you and me 2242
I *thought,* how, as the day had come 840
In kindling *thought* and glowing word 1170
In noble *thought* and deed 520
In silent *thought,* or friendly 1884
In sinful *thought* and word 2155
Let every trembling *thought* be gone 157
Let every *thought,* and deed 1398
Let every *thought,* and work 1230
Let my every *thought* be thine 1566
Lord of *thought* and Lord of will 1049
Nerving simplest *thought* 1077
No *thought* can reach, no tongue 1025
Nor *thought* I how soon they 1941
Now thine errant *thought* collect 1766
O *Thought* in flesh enshrined 1490
O wondrous peace, in *thought* to dwell 100
O wondrous *thought,* for me he careth 852
O'er every *thought* and step preside 310, 319
Our highest *thought* thy will 1386
Scarce a *thought* to wisdom lent 1179
She *thought* she heard the gardener ask 626
So shall each murmuring *thought* 417
That every *thought,* and word, and deed 1844
The secret *thought,* the hidden 1386
The *thought* of thee is mightier 856
Then in *thought* I go to thee 2247
This *thought* is so precious, although 2055
Thou my best *thought,* by day or by night 177
Thought of that now clouds 1222
Thy will was in the builders' *thought* 67
Which all our better *thought* inspires 481
With loving and adoring *thought* 2313

THOUGHTFUL

Be *thoughtful* and earnest 2336

THOUGHTS

All evil *thoughts* expelling 1853
All my sinful *thoughts* forgive 1218
All our *thoughts* his love exceeds 990
And all thy secret *thoughts* surveys 152
And so our *thoughts* are ever 1535
And why with vexing *thoughts* 1483
And winging *thoughts,* and happy 1938
Be *thoughts* of thee a cloudy screen 2239
Calling our *thoughts* away 721
Evil *thoughts,* perverse behavior 446
For all gentle *thoughts* and mild 484
From the *thoughts* that oft beguile 1055
Guarding our *thoughts* and our passions 578
Hallowed *thoughts* we turn to thee 521
Hence, all *thoughts* of sadness 1004
How good thy *thoughts* toward us 1130
How precious also are thy *thoughts* 1452
Let evil *thoughts* and spirits flee 1289
Let holy *thoughts* be ours where 1289
Let not self thy *thoughts* control 1668
May our *thoughts* be undefiled 962
My secret *thoughts* are known to thee 2039
My *thoughts* rejoice at Jesus' name 1308
New *thoughts* of God, new hopes 1273
Nor with idle *thoughts* and vain 233
Of our *thoughts* and actions too 1118
Our earliest *thoughts* be thine 1289
Our evil *thoughts* assuaging 1162
Our *thoughts* lie open in thy sight 240
Our *thoughts* lie open to thy sight 1428
Sinful *thoughts* and words unloving 1179
So many gentle *thoughts* and deeds 1236
The *thoughts* that move the heart 414
Then with my waking *thoughts* 1265
These are thy *thoughts,* Almighty Mind 414
Thine are their *thoughts,* their works 590
Thoughts of wisest meaning 657
Through all our *thoughts* thy voice 784
Thy *thoughts* of love to me surmount 2039
To make our *thoughts* and actions 1549
To my *thoughts* attentive be 710
To thee may all our *thoughts* arise 1105

Until with braver *thoughts* shall rise 826
Where all our *thoughts* are drowned 2071
While our *thoughts* his greatness 1178
Yea, all my *thoughts* afar to thee 1452

THOUSAND

He's the fairest of ten *thousand* 834
Ten *thousand thousand* are their 323

THOUSANDS

And *thousands* press within 1440
At last it stood, with *thousands* more 11
Behold how many *thousands* still 1551
But there are many *thousands* who 2245
Thousands of children stand 118
Thousands of *thousands* stand 788
Thousands only live to bless thee 101

THREATEN

Should *threaten* to undo us 12

THREE

But the greatest of the *three* 1192

THRESHOLDS

On shadowed *thresholds,* dark with 2270

THREW

Threw his loving arms around me 895

THRILL

A *thrill* of hope, the weary world 1399
And in my heart I feel the *thrill* 2
With joy does *thrill* me now 13

THRILLS

How it *thrills* our souls 1817

THROES

Who is he, in Calvary's *throes* 2286

THRONE

A *throne* without thy blessing 1457
And, humbly bending at thy *throne* 1134, 1376
And thou art on the Father's *throne* 965
And upon the *throne* be wrong 1579
And when, before the *throne,* I stand 837
Around its glorious *throne* 1959
Around the Savior's *throne* 1931
Around the *throne* on high 1592
Ascending to the *throne* 1080
At the *throne* doth intercede 480
Before his *throne* rejoice 304
Before our Father's *throne* 232
Before the *throne* my Surety stands 113
Before thy *throne,* O Lord of heaven 1927
Before thy *throne* we sinners bend 452
But thy coming, and thy *throne* 2018
By the *throne* of God now flowing 1766
By thy high majestic *throne* 269
Ere to his *throne* he passed 1579
Faultless to stand before the *throne* 1244
Forth from the *throne* of God 355
From his shining *throne* on high 995
From his *throne* in heaven, God is 1270
From the highest *throne* of glory 1214
From the *throne* of heaven's glory 227
From thy *throne,* as April shower 1516
Gathering round the great white *throne* 2191
He on his *throne* shall rest 661
Here from the *throne* sweet waters 279
High on the eternal *throne* 1106
His *throne* he hath established 778
His *throne* is built on high 1897
His *throne* is fixed, he reigns 1882
It shall be thy royal *throne* 1816
Jesu, from thy heavenly *throne* 962
Let me at a *throne* of mercy 1607
Let Satan from his *throne* be hurled 1026
Low before thy *throne* we fall 1179
More about Jesus on his *throne* 1216
My glory-circled *throne* 827
My great Redeemer's *throne* 1350
Nearer the great white *throne* today 1580
Now before thy *throne* of grace 222
Pointing to his *throne* of light 518
Presenting at the Father's *throne* 1143
Round his *throne* of triumph 1833
Round thy *throne* of light 101
So be it, Lord, thy *throne* shall 1856
Soon, descending from his *throne* 2126
The *throne* of grace, I dare 2295
There is the *throne* of David 961
They, round thy *throne* a shining throng 642
Though returning to his *throne* 655
Throne in her heart the unseen 601
Thy *throne* is fixed of old 598, 1886
Till around thy *throne* we stand 1028
Till before our Father's *throne* 1197
To him who sits upon the *throne* 1366
To thy *throne* their tributes 208
To thy *throne* united raise 1213
Trembling at thy *throne* of grace 538
Until at the glorified *throne* 880
Who is he that on yon *throne* 2286

THRONED

High *throned* on heaven's eternal 1367
Not *throned* above the skies 1515
The Lord is *throned* on high 1261
Throned above celestial things 1161
Throned in endless might and power 288
Throned in thy vast infinity 1163
When Christ is *throned* as Lord 284
When *throned* where glory dwelleth 1923

THRONES

Not *thrones* alone, but men 2267
Not *thrones* and crowns, but men 2267
Thrones and dominations 143

THRONG

And all the martyr *throng* 961
And *throng* with joy 1366
O that with yonder sacred *throng* 47

Shall *throng* the sacred floor 540
Then when with yonder *throng* 2309
There, with the blood-washed *throng* 181
There, with the ransomed *throng* 434
They *throng* the silence of the breast 956
To thee with all the white-robed *throng* 23
Which long ago the heavenly *throng* 1916
Yea, the martyred *throng* of yore 1213

THRONGS

Among these restless *throngs* abide 2270
While happy *throngs*, with 2024

THROW

And *throw* off your burden of sin 2293
But *throw* out the life-line 2068
Just now, *throw* open the door 905
Throw down your branches at his feet 1604
Throw thy radiance o'er them 517
Throw wide the door, each willing mind 192
Throw your heart open wide 694
Throw your soul's fresh, glowing ardor 531
We never will *throw* off his fear 329

THRUST

And *thrust* my willful hand across 183
And *thrust* of driving trade 2160
That a soldier, one day, *thrust* a spear 17
Thrust in our sickles at thy word 1496
Who, *thrust* in prison or cast 1204

THUNDER

By the deep *thunder* of its want 1277
In *thunder* the God of the glory 537
It is the *thunder* of the Lord's appearing 683
The *thunder* and the shower 55
Thunder like a mighty flood 77

THUNDERS

Loud as mighty *thunders* roar 2150
The *thunders* of his hand 1897
Ye *thunders*, echoing loud 1936

TIDE

Boundless as ocean's *tide* 2051
But such a *tide* as, moving 1802
From every swelling *tide* of woes 511
Hark, that glorious *tide* of song 669
Its *tides* bind strand 2134
Nearer the fountain's crimson *tide* 1267
On the rising *tide* it can never 2298
The *tide* of time shall never 661
Then I'll be with him, where the *tide* 1044
This holy *tide* of Christmas 599
There is flowing a crimson *tide* 1206
When its *tide* of glory 1034
With its crystal *tide* forever 1711

TIDES

High above the restless *tides* 485
Mighty *tides* about me sweep 2056
When the strong *tides* lift 2298

TIDINGS

Are longing that the *tidings* 149
Glad *tidings* from the throne 1169
"Glad *tidings* of great joy I bring 513, 2282
"Glad *tidings* of great joy to all 1866
Glad *tidings* of our God to bring 2220
How sweet the *tidings* are 768
Immortal *tidings* in your mortal hands 720
Let the *tidings* roll 2094
O *tidings* of comfort and joy 599
Tidings bringing 945
Tidings of a gospel true 945
Tidings of Jesus, redemption and 1551
Tidings old, ever new 1261
Tidings sent to every creature 1136
Unto you the *tidings* 940
What glad *tidings* did you hear 105
When Thomas first the *tidings* 1493
With them the joyful *tidings* first begun 298

TIE

Ev'ry human *tie* may perish 2341
Tie in a living tether 1365

TIES

By all sweet *ties* of home 1254
Thine am I by all *ties* 855

TILLAGE

Tillage has been turned again 1665

TILLS

He *tills* the holy land 1880

TIMBRELS

Timbrels soft and cymbals loud 1625

TIME

A gracious *time* for planting 1598
And in the *time* of plague 2104
And just the *time* I need him 874
And so, midst boundless *time* 1495
And the *time* is drawing near 574
And there, some *time*, we'll understand 1282
And *time* shall be no more 2259
Can *time* undo what once 2044
Each *time* my feet in some sin 1249
Every *time* that you read it you'll learn 130
For the solemn *time* is coming 78
For *time* nor space can us divide 2174
Fresh'ning *time* with truth 1077
From all *time* where thought can soar 610
From henceforth, the *time* redeeming 1179
From oldest *time*, on farthest shore 1576
Have you any *time* for Jesus 692
In such a *time* he shall thee seek 1314
In the *time* of wealth and ease 993
In *time* of trouble thy face from us 1873
In your *time* of sore distress 2268
It may be a *time* of sorrow 2297
It may be the last *time* you'll ever hear 1337
Let not the *time* be lost 1292
Let this *time* of worship be 1010

Let Zion's *time* of favor come 116
New rising in this gospel *time* 1810
New *time,* new favor 1288
No *time* for rest, till glows the western 322
Now is the *time* to know him 2280
Now is the *time* to own him 2280
O how soon the *time* will flee 1598
O what a *time* of rejoicing will come 167
O'er these dark hills of *time* 5
Precious *time* and talents 1703
Some *time,* some time we'll understand 1282
Some *time* with tearless eyes 1282
Soon will your *time* of probation 2
That all the best of endless *time* 2027
That in our *time,* thy grace may 445
The sowing *time* is ours 1169
The *time* that shall surely be 574
There's no *time* for idle scorning 1955
This is now our *time* of need 759
This is the *time,* no more delay 336
This is the *time,* O then be wise 1343
Thou hast no *time,* bright day 489
Thy precious *time,* misspent redeem 152
Thy *time* is now and evermore 788
Till the appointed *time* is nigh 2059
Till *time* and tide shall cease 2309
Till *time* shall be no more 21
Time appointed may be long 2018
Time for the world with its glittering 705
Time, like an ever-rolling stream 1375
Time long foretold by seers 1443
Time makes ancient good uncouth 1574
Time now is fleeting 1743
Time shall soon this earth remove 1667
What *time* my heart is overwhelmed 1357
What *time* soever I awake 1452

TIMES

All *times* this shall be on record 2045
At *times,* to faith's foreseeing eye 494
At *times,* with sudden glory 1874
In ancient *times* didst give the law 1336
In old *times* when dangers darkened 611
In our *times* of deep distresses 993
In quiet *times* of trustful peace 1363
In the *times* of grief and pain 993
In *times* when temptation 1477
Seven *times* he spake, seven words 1333
Ten thousand *times* ten thousand sound 788
There are *times* of sore affliction 1957
There are *times,* when tired 1954
With prosperous *times* our cities 1185
With ten thousand *times* ten thousand 2019
Worthiest art thou at all *times* 653

TINSEL

All its *tinsel* perisheth 175

TINTS

While their bright *tints* are glowing 2320

TIRE

Nor *tire* along the heavenly road 157

TITLE

My *title* there I read 872

TOCSINS

The bloody *tocsins* ring 592

TODAY

And still is ours *today* 1299
But *today* accept his grace 2283
God, only God, *today* as yesterday 1914
Heaven is won *today* 2204
"Hell *today* is vanquished 2204
Just for *today* 1128
O, *today* is "time accepted" 692
O, that *today* they might fall 1981
Perhaps *today* there are loving words 955
There are many who are perishing *today* 2125
Today he rose and left 2014
Today let healing waters be 1379
Today my sail I lift 826
Today on weary nations 1341
Today, our week, but new begun 2036
Today shines as the past 1087
Today the dream is visible 1287
Today the saints his triumph 2014
Today to these thy children 1344
What if it were *today* 982
What thou shalt *today* provide 1647

TOIL

And earth's vain *toil* and wandering 1424
And often *toil* seems dreary 2120
And *toil,* till all are thine 1386
Are you weary and worn from its *toil* 694
But our *toil* he doth richly 2266
But that *toil* shall make thee 293
By the *toil* of lowly workers 1160
Full of *toil* and care 903
Gladly I will *toil* and suffer 2042
Hallowed is *toil,* if this 1825
Henceforth I must *toil* for 1941
I'll bear the *toil,* endure the pain 87
Like them of old, in vain in *toil* 712
'Mid the *toil* and heat 1114
'Mid *toil* and tribulation 1845
Nor in *toil* nor sorrow 925
Oft we *toil* amid the shadows 2256
Our daily *toil* may tend 1301
Praying through every *toil* 1238
The *toil* that prospered harvests 1852
The *toil* of my work groweth 1848
There *toil* seems pleasure 1578
Till *toil,* and grief, and pain 1519
Toil and sing 'neath the banner 1994
Toil by the truth, life 1511
Toil on, faint not, keep watch 550
Toil on, nor deem, though sore 1531
Toil on till the Lord of the harvest 1540
Who *toil* along the climbing way 948

TOILED

For thee they *toiled* and prayed 1312

Thank we those who *toiled* 242
They who bravely *toiled* amongst 2275
While others *toiled* hard 1941
Who *toiled* and fought and lived 875

TOILER

Here may the busy *toiler* 1529
"Welcome, *toiler,* I've prepared for thee 1710

TOILERS

Toilers at the furnace blaze 485
Toilers in the mine and mill 485

TOILING

By the *toiling* servant's side 71
Toiling on, *toiling* on 2113

TOILS

A few more *toils,* a few more tears 5
And all the *toils* that foes do 2103
And, strong amid the *toils* 1416
From earthly *toils* lift up thine eye 196
Nothing seen but *toils* and dangers 1775
O what are the *toils* and labors 1411
That we, when all earth's *toils* 2301
The *toils* of day are over 1851
Then the *toils* of the road will 1922
Toils evermore, with power 1593

TOILWORN

Toilworn, and sad with 491

TOKEN

In *token* let him feel 2050

TOKENS

Are *tokens* of blessing in thy 959

TOLD

And it *told* thy love to me 808
For 'twas you who *told* me of 1710
O God, he *told* us of thy grace 1356
One half hath not been *told* me 1419
The half has never yet been *told* 844
Till they came, who *told* the story 242
Told how his will was sacrificed 1755

TOMB

As at Bethany's *tomb* 236
Majestic from the spoiled *tomb* 1078
No *tomb* shall my spirit confine 871
The rending *tomb* proclaims 2023
While this liquid *tomb* surveying 2032

TOMORROW

And for *tomorrow* whate'er it be 1756
Even let the unknown *tomorrow* 1759
Never for *tomorrow* be thou anxious 1838
Tomorrow comes the song 174
Tomorrow has no promise that 1337
Tomorrow his grace may be ending 1925
Tomorrow is eternity 1337
Tomorrow may bring you the darkness 1542
Tomorrow you may call in vain 692
What *tomorrow* may betide 1647

TOMORROWS

My *tomorrows* are all known 969

TONE

Every tribe's familiar *tone* 1036

TONES

All the enticing *tones* of ill 1772
Its *tones* so sweetly are calling 1986
Soft are the *tones* which raise 349
With all *tones* of waters blending 610

TONGUE

And canst thou, my *tongue,* be still 1814
And every *tongue* confess his name 1968
And every *tongue* shall sing 33
By every *tongue* be God's eternal 1781
Every *tongue* confess him 143
For in my *tongue,* before I speak 1452
How shall my *tongue* describe 2315
I, too, must sing with joyful *tongue* 34
In every *tongue* and nation 33
Let every tongue *confess* with one accord 58
Let no *tongue* on earth be silent 1558
More than thy *tongue* can tell 827
My *tongue* did him extol 50
My *tongue* repeats her vows 786
My *tongue* shall praise him 2144
My *tongue* would bless thy name 1035
No mortal *tongue* their joys can tell 192
No *tongue* can tell the numbers 325
Nor *tongue* nor pen can show 1019
O thou, who by an infant's *tongue* 9
Of every *tongue* redeemed of God 1108
One *tongue,* one faith, we claim 2134
Sinless be *tongue* and hand 1934
The *tongue* of secret slander 1557
There shall each raptured *tongue* 147
Till every *tongue* and nation 1089
Till every *tongue* confess him 1945
To him let every *tongue* be praise 2106
What *tongue* can speak thy worth 1464
When this poor lisping, stammering *tongue* 1961
Yea, when my *tongue* must silent be 23

TONGUES

And myriad *tongues,* in one great anthem 1368
But God from infant *tongues* 28
From men's *tongues* thy servant 730
In the *tongues* of all the peoples 2318
Let mortal *tongues* awake 1225
Like to quivering *tongues* of flame 1036
Little *tongues* are saying 1102
Many *tongues* of many nations 1182
No *tongues* of flame desire 1090
Our *tongues* inspire his praise 1398
Pleading in the thousand *tongues* 258

Shooting out *tongues* of flame 2262
Sweet the countless *tongues* united 253
Ten thousand thousand are their *tongues* 671
The wrangling *tongues* that mar thy praise 496
Thee may our *tongues* for ever bless 1409
Tongues of earth or heaven above 636
Tongues that each might hear 1036
Who in a hundred *tongues* repeat 592

TOOK

And *took* our sins away 1487
But when I *took* him at his word 926
He *took* his seat above 1653
He *took* me from destruction's pit 887
He *took* me from its clutch 1249
He *took* my sins and my sorrows 881
He *took* them in his arms 949
O'er Bethlehem it *took* its rest 1861
Then *took* the cup, and blessed 2132
Took from thee the name of day 233
'Twas not so much that I on thee *took* hold 879
Who *took* our place at judgment bar 1080

TORCH

The *torch* to their devotion lent 1353

TORE

He *tore* the bars away 1200

TORMENT

Which from endless *torment* 544

TORN

And *torn* with many a rift 826
Torn with nails, and crowned 2288

TORRENT

Troubled *torrent,* madly rushing 104

TORRENTS

Torrents of sin and of anguish 1208

TORTURE

Yet, in the midst of the *torture* 1015

TOSSED

Just as I am, though *tossed* 1046
When *tossed* by storm and flood 2310

TOUCH

And lo! Thy *touch* brought life 2008
And *touch* of hand 604
And with his *touch* of love 845
At his *touch* our burdens fall 1295
Blest are all that *touch* thy scepter 1073
By the *touch* of his hand on mine 1954
Here would I *touch* and handle 727
How oft at the *touch* of that nail 1868
In the *touch* of his hand 1954
O *touch* my lips with fire divine 686
O, *touch* the hem of his garment 1713
One *touch* of its finger will make 1868
Only a *touch* of thy hand 1585
Shine forth, and *touch* the future 191
Still his *touch* upon the soul 521
The wondrous *touch* of God 11
Thy *touch* has still its ancient power 136
Thou whose *touch* could heal 2049
Touch me and heal me 691
Touch our hearts and turn 2049
Touch thou our dust with 1780
Touch thou the sad, discordant keys 388
Touch with thy pierced hand 721
We *touch* him in life's throng 917, 2181
We *touch* thee (him) in life's throng 240

TOUCHED

But now, as *touched* with living 1140
Touched by a loving hand 1655
Touched by the lodestone 1029
Touched with a sympathy within 2305
Who *touched* my broken heart 134

TOWER

My never-failing *tower* 872
The *tower* to which I flee 1376

TOWERS

Building proud *towers* which shall not 438
Her lofty *towers* tell 646
Its glittering *towers* the sun 1243
Lifting the *towers* of her lightning-lit 601
The *towers* of Zion tell 2312

TOWN

"To you, in David's *town,* this day 2282

TOWNS

The wail of famine in beleaguered *towns* 37

TRACE

And as we *trace* our weary way 1285
Do flaming suns his footsteps *trace* 96
I *trace* the rainbow through the rain 1465
Through him thou canst not see, nor *trace* 685
Trace we the Babe who has 298
We *trace* the working of thy hand 1353

TRACED (TRAC'D)

Trac'd upon our dial 1091

TRACK

Have marked my erring *track* 39
His *track* I see, and I'll pursue 1001

TRACTS

Dim *tracts* of time divide 2044
Ye *tracts* of earth and continents 1936

TRADE

For crafty *trade* and subtle snare 189

TRADES

Who *trades* with heaping measures 1880

TRADITION

From war's grim *tradition* 709
Let old *tradition* die 2076

TRAFFIC

O'er which our *traffic* runs amain 81

TRAIL

Where once the crooked *trail* in darkness 720

TRAIN

But *train* me for thy will 396
In reverent *train* to meet him 2180
Lo! the apostolic *train* 746
Train us in thy garden 928
With all thy Father's dazzling *train* 2037
With his angel *train* 143
With his seraph *train* before him 253, 1178, 1673

TRAINED

Trained in wisdom, led by love 756

TRAINS

She *trains* the eye to look 1186

TRANQUIL

Tranquil you lie, your knightly 1532

TRANSCEND

O could my voice *transcend* the spaces 23

TRANSCRIBE

I would *transcribe* and make 1226

TRANSFIGURATION

In heaven's bright *transfiguration* 23

TRANSFORM

Transform me by thy grace 1027

TRANSFORMED

Transformed by his wonderful grace 17

TRANSGRESSION

Mine, mine was the *transgression* 75
To take away *transgression* 661

TRANSGRESSIONS

Alleluia our *transgressions* 78
And the *transgressions* of whose life 1314
But as for our *transgressions* all 1631
For my *transgressions* I confess 31
My *transgressions* I confess 554
On him were our *transgressions* 426

TRANSLATED

He, our Enoch, is *translated* 1697

TRANSPORT

And O what *transport* of delight 1876
O this *transport* all divine 1195

TRANSPORTED

Transported with the view, I'm lost 2223
When clothed in his brightness, *transported* 24

TRAPPED

All *trapped* and frightened 1103

TRAVAIL

And the *travail* of our spirit 1993
To thee the *travail* deep was known 373

TRAVAILED

Has *travailed* long in pain 284

TRAVEL

Nevermore will he *travel* that 2063
We the route for *travel* clearing 62

TRAVELER

Now, like a weary *traveler* 1923
Traveler, ages are its own 2154
Traveler, blessedness and light 2154
Traveler, darkness takes its flight 2154
Traveler, lo! the Prince of Peace 2154
Traveler, o'er yon mountain's height 2154
Traveler, yes, it brings the day 2154

TREAD

All the path which thou shalt *tread* 63
And though I *tread* a darksome path 1967
For the matchless Lord of Life doth *tread* 309
If onward ye will *tread* 1391
O may we *tread* the sacred road 1108
O *tread* the city's streets again 2270
Oft we *tread* the path before us 2256
They who *tread* the path of labor 1022
Thou didst *tread* this earth 1058
Tread in his steps, assisted by 298
Tread softly, tread softly, the Master 172
Tread the path of darkness 2204
Tread the path that Jesus trod 716
Tread them to dust beneath 1157
Tread where his feet have trod 1669
We shall *tread* the streets of gold 1731
We *tread* the road the saints above 413
When I *tread* the verge of Jordan 652
When we *tread* death's valley 983

TREASON

Alas, my *treason,* Jesus hath undone 35

TREASURE

Bringing down the richest *treasure* 743
God, thou art unfailing *treasure* 2224
He your *treasure* and your 1838
Lord, this *treasure* I am shielding 2319
My dearest *treasure,* the light of 1104

My Savior has my *treasure* 921
O *treasure* each word 172
Precious *treasure,* thou art mine 738
The priceless *treasure,* freely spent 1921
Treasure of the Spirit's love 1005
What a *treasure* I have in this 430
What a *treasure* is mine 139
Where eternal *treasure* lies 233
Who life's *treasure* gather 657

TREASURE-HOUSE

It is a *treasure-house* of gold 2087

TREASURES

All our costliest *treasures* bring 129
And better are these *treasures* 1947
And the *treasures* they ever unfold 553
And these shall be the *treasures* 1947
And with the *treasures* of his grace 674
For *treasures* that may rust 2189
He *treasures* up his bright designs 577
New *treasures* still, of countless 1273
Or its sordid *treasures* 937
Richer than all earth's *treasures* 638
Should *treasures* vanish from our life 383
The *treasures* of the earth and sea 1441
Whose *treasures* are far beyond telling 179

TREASURY

My never-failing *treasury* filled 794

TREAT

And will ye *treat* me so 1414
You *treat* no other friend so ill 192

TREATED

I would be *treated* as a child 443

TREE

And though the *tree* by its might 1840
By the *tree* of life so fair 2191
He groaned (suffered) upon the *Tree* 38
He prayed on the *Tree* 73
He shall be like a *tree* that grows 1841
Like the sheltering *tree* that groweth 36
'Neath the *tree* where the wild flowers 1986
O *Tree* of grace! the conquering sign 1921
Thereby itself like a *tree* 1840
Though the *Tree* was so heavy 2063
'Twas on a *Tree* they slew him 947
Where the *tree* of life in eternal 1502

TREES

Dead and bare the tall *trees* stand 2299
From under the *trees* they drew 947
Fruitful *trees* and ever verdant 951
The tall *trees* in the greenwood 68
Ye forest *trees,* in God rejoice 2328

TREMBLE

And though I *tremble* when I think 822
And *tremble* as they gaze 1476
I *tremble* to know that for me 880
Or *tremble* at the tempter's power 2295
That will not *tremble* on the brink 1348
We *tremble* not for him 12

TREMBLED

Then I *trembled* at the law 2335
Trembled the mariners 476

TREMBLES

And Satan *trembles* when he sees 2221
And *trembles* in the air 683

TRIAL

Deeming each *trial* a part of my cross 1104
Gives me grace for every *trial* 66
In *trial* sore and dark temptation 1896
Never a *trial* that he is not there 407
Shall we, in this her *trial* 923
Shall not we thy *trial* share 500
When shall we, out of *trial* 2170

TRIALS

Have we *trials* and temptations 2210
He is with me in my *trials* 805
How little then the *trials* of life will seem 16
How often when *trials* like sea billows 1477
In fiery *trials* will pour from heavenly 573
Long as our fiery *trials* last 1714
May *trials* well endure 194
My strongest *trials* now are past 1247
Neither *trials* lay me low 942
No *trials* yonder, all the testing 1274
Only a few more *trials* 1675
The *trials* that beset you 1391
Then *trials* cannot vex me 1949
Though *trials* come through passing days 824
Trials fall across the way 2002
When after all our *trials* 2096
When *trials* sore obstruct my way 1509
Where *trials* never come 1959

TRIBE

Let every kindred, every *tribe* 47
Of battling *tribe* and clan 46
When every *tribe* and nation 781

TRIBES

All *tribes* and tongues, shall flow 198
Hark! all the *tribes!* "Hosanna," cry 1660
Him shall the *tribes* of earth obey 1917
In thee our *tribes* appear 786
Soon may all *tribes* be blest 321
The restless *tribes* and races feel 1467
The *tribes* of God go thither 843
Thither the *tribes* repair 540
Till *tribes* and tongues the world 2107
To God the *tribes* of ocean 55
Who to thy *tribes* on Sinai's height 1336

TRIBULATION

Through *tribulation* great they came 1108

TRIBULATIONS

All my *tribulations,* all my 1808

TRIBUTE

Again our grateful *tribute* bring 15
Give our *tribute* due 1110
Its thankful *tribute* to present 1362
Still with *tribute,* treasure laden 299
Their tuneful *tribute* bring 55
Your morning *tribute* bring 2332

TRIED

Cheerfully *tried* a load to lift 1755
I *tried* the broken cisterns 1322
If I *tried,* I could not utter 942
Tried, they were, and firm they stood 677
Tried to make him sin through pride 268

TRIFLES

And *trifles* of the passing hour 2170

TRIM

And *trim* the golden flame 2331
Trim your feeble lamp 255

TRINITY

O *Trinity* of love and power 81
One sacred *Trinity* 1940

TRIUMPH

Alleluia, his the *triumph* 77
And I will *triumph* in the works 2112
And in *triumph* victorious 2031
And *triumph* evermore 1653
And *triumph* in the dying hour 575
By thy *triumph* o'er the grave 269, 1761
Easter *triumph,* Easter joy 142
He, in *triumph* from the grave 260
His seeming *triumph* o'er God's 473
How we *triumph* in thy reign 1073
I *triumph* still, if thou 27
In *triumph* meet to praise thee 1505
Its *triumph* let us tell 1846
My *triumph* is begun 1247
Not ours but thine the *triumph* 1359
Now is the Victor's *triumph* 1937
The Easter *triumph* sing 626
The *triumph* of the Christ shall 1860
There the glorious *triumph* waits 655
Their *triumph* to his death 530
They may with us in *triumph* 460
Triumph o'er the shades of night 292
Triumph with cheerful voice 532
When, through his mighty *triumph* 1418
With a mighty *triumph* o'er his foes 1200
Zion in *triumph* begins her mild 660

TRIUMPHED

Him who *triumphed* o'er the grave 131
It *triumphed* o'er disease and 2008
The Lord hath *triumphed* gloriously 1078, 1883

TRIUMPHS

May she holy *triumphs* win 1033
O Christ, thy *triumphs* now begin 1660
The scanty *triumphs* grace 1812, 1478
The *triumphs* of his grace 1351
The *triumphs* of his justice 360
Triumphs in their breasts 1110
Triumphs of mercy, wrought for thee 116

TROD

And he patiently *trod* all 2063
And *trod* the path of youth 1526
And when they *trod* the wintry 1354
For thee I *trod* the bitter way 836
He *trod* in old Judea 1556
Thou, who hast *trod* the thorny road 1978
Trod the path of duty 1205
With the Savior I have *trod* 835

TROOPS

These *troops* with heaven for home 90

TROPHIES

Earnestly beseeching *trophies* for the King 297
Our *trophies,* fetters broken 1320
Rich the *trophies* Jesus brings 1117
Till my *trophies* at last I lay down 1561

TROPHY

A *trophy* of thy grace 2107

TROUBLE

The doubts that *trouble* pass away 2
In *trouble* and distress 75
In *trouble* he's my stay 834
In *trouble,* too, in every changing 1896
Is there *trouble* anywhere 2210
Thou shalt from *trouble* keep me 1314
Trouble nevermore to borrow 1738
We, where no *trouble* distraction 1538
When I by *trouble* am distressed 1376
When *trouble* is at hand 571

TROUBLED

Are you *troubled* at the thought of dying 112
O'er *troubled* sea 702
Thou hast been *troubled,* tempted, tried 136
When the *troubled,* seeking peace 2260
When we are *troubled* sore 956

TROUBLES

Farewell to all the *troubles* of today 16
Let *troubles* rise, and terrors 1064
The *troubles* that afflict the just 1321
Thy *troubles* to bless 776
Troubles almost 'whelm the soul 2056
What *troubles* have we seen 93
When *troubles* great o'erwhelm 1134

TRUE

All that is not *true* 143
Have we been *true* to the trust 2241
Let us then be *true* and faithful 1731
So *true,* and kind I always find 134
The Lord will keep thee *true* and strong 1639
The *true* thy chartered freemen are 301

To the *true* and faithful there is rich 1997
We must be *true,* we will be free 1608
We will be *true* to thee till death 428

TRUMP

And *trump* and timbrel answered 2239
The gospel *trump* is sounding 1320
The *trump* of God shall sound 1653
The *trump* of jubilee 1320
The *trump* shall resound and the Lord 2249
The *trump* that angels quake to hear 2228
'Till *trump,* from east to west 2015

TRUMPET

God's *trumpet* wakes the slumbering 620
The gospel *trumpet* hear 241
The *trumpet* sounds, the graves 644

TRUMPET CALL

The *trumpet call* obey 1786

TRUST

A little more *trust* in the will 10
A *trust,* O Lord, from thee 2167
All my *trust* on thee is stayed 994
And for them who will *trust* and obey 2266
And let me ne'er my *trust* betray 4
And now henceforth I'll *trust* in thee 1248
And put our *trust* in him alone 317
And through the *trust* I have in thee 1413
And *trust* his constant care 777
And *trust* his power to save 2234
And *trust* in his redeeming blood 1963
And *trust* in things divine 1927
And *trust* me with thy future 836
And *trust* thee though thou slay 1171
And we who *trust* his word 1906
And we will ever *trust* each 447
And with all who *trust* 2266
And yet we *trust* it comes 1797
Because on him my *trust* is stayed 2238
Because thy *trust* is God alone 1908
But still we *trust* thy word 1520
But to *trust* and obey 2266
But *trust* thee for grace each day 529
But *trust* till the danger is past 164
He doth still my *trust* renew 53
I dare not *trust* the sweetest frame 1244
I *trust* his love, he knoweth best 847
I will *trust* thee 223
I *trust* him now, I'll trust him 981
I *trust* in thee, whose powerful word 453
I *trust* the Cross of Jesus 872
If we *trust* in his grace 1956
I'll always *trust* in thee 1260
In God I'll *trust,* that all 2054
In simple *trust,* like theirs 386
In thee do we *trust* 1546
In thee my *trust* abideth 2119
In them that *trust* his love 1636
In *trust* that triumphs over wrong 1466
Jesus, Jesus, how I *trust* him 2092
Let all that *trust* in thee be glad 527, 1176
Let no other *trust* intrude 358
My God, in him my *trust* shall be 1908
My *trust* is set on thee 1433
O how sweet to *trust* in Jesus 2092
O Lord, I *trust* in thee 2116
O to *trust* him then more fully 1643
O, will you not *trust* him today 1925
Once was afraid to *trust* a loving God 624
Only *trust* him now 308
Our *trust* and hope secure 283
Our *trust* and hope thy grace 1873
So *trust* in God, however dark 16
Somehow I *trust* him for today 1756
Still I can *trust* him, I know 2136
Still *trust* in God; for him 1483
Still *trust* in his word 1820
Still will we *trust* in God 1794
Surely I can *trust* my blessed 2057
Sweet it is to *trust* in thee 2062
Then *trust* in God, through all 1282
They who are willing to *trust* 353
They who *trust* him wholly 1091
Thou art my only *trust* 392
To all who *trust* in him, our Lord 1621
To free all those who *trust* in him 599
To him I wholly *trust* 291
To one fixed *trust* my spirit 2310
Trust and obey, for there's no other 2266
Trust, and thy trusting soul shall prove 477
Trust for our trembling, and hope 2322
Trust God, and he'll employ 125
Trust God if thou desirest 534
Trust him evermore 1114
Trust him, then, and forward go 63
Trust him, then, ye fainting 356
Trust him to carry you through 908
Trust his rich promises 904
Trust in God and do the right 367
Trust in him from day to day 2283
Trust in his promises 1804
Trust in the Lord and take heart 1269
Trust in the Lord, for ever trust 778
Trust not in princes, they are 1621
Trust only Christ, thy Captain 548
Trust the heart of Jesus 987
Trust, thou, in his word 922
Trust ye in Christ, our God 1621
We cannot *trust* him as we 1431
We may *trust* him fully 1091
We *trust* in thee 586
We *trust* thee for the grace to win 1412
We *trust* thee on some height 2027
We *trust* thy love and merit 291
We *trust* thy sacrifice 404
We *trust* thy wisdom, love, and 1518
With childlike *trust* that fears 1473
While such as *trust* their 157
While we *trust* thy love and power 42
Whom shall we *trust* but thee 1369
Will you not *trust* him, so faithful 569
Yes, 'tis sweet to *trust* in Jesus 2092

TRUSTED

And *trusted* in his grace 778

I *trusted* also in the Lord 1043
Or if he *trusted* it to me 564
The God they *trusted* guards 1354
We *trusted,* Lord, with thee 1146

TRUSTING

By *trusting* in his word 308
I am *trusting,* Lord, in thee 800
Trusting Jesus, that is all 1721

TRUSTS

Who *trusts* in God's unchanging 904
Who *trusts* in him is blessed 616, 1902
Who *trusts* in him shall blessed be 1890

TRUTH

All *truth* to love 603
Almighty God of *truth* and love 889
And all *truth* and knowledge see 667
And all thy *truth* and righteousness 1451
And for thy *truth* the world endure 1286
And his *truth* endureth from 1310
And let thy *truth* within us 397, 1149
And the *truth* make her free 601
And through the *truth* that comes 428
And while the *truth* of God remains 2071
And with thy *truth* redeeming 26
Blessed *truth* enduring always 1707
But simple *truth* be on our tongue 1301
Do thou thy *truth* impart 332
Each thought-revealing *truth* 1388
Eternal *truth,* attends thy word 508
Ever faithful to the *truth* 1125
For his *truth* unchanging 2287
For such thou dost no *truth* conceal 1094
For *truth,* and righteousness 1045
God's *truth* abideth still 12
His saving *truth* reveal 1398
His *truth* at all times 57
His *truth* be thine affiance 567
His *truth* confirms and seals 1897
His *truth* doth hallow the temple 263
His *truth* forever stands 911
His *truth* is marching on 1215
His *truth* to triumph through us 12
How sweet the *truth* those blessed strains 670
In *truth* and patience wrought 199
Infinite *truth* and mercy shine 1514
Let simple *truth* be on our lips 1934
Let the gospel *truth* speak plainly 219
Let *truth* thy buckler be 958
May thy whole *truth* be spoken 2142
May *truth* reveal its power 1529
O blessed Lord, thy *truth* 28
O do thou *truth* and grace 1134
O for thy *truth* and mercy's sake 2202
O God of *truth,* whom science seeks 419
O God, thy *truth* and grace 1376
O Jesu, full of *truth* and grace 2202
O *Truth,* before whose shrine 1424
O *Truth,* unchanged, unchanging 1544
Of a *truth* I know Jesus loves me 1501
Of *truth* that spread from shore 191, 1445
On thy *truth* relying 937
One for his *truth* we stand 1156
So when thy *truth* began its race 1871
Such was thy *truth,* and such 1226
Sure as thy *truth* shall last 859
Teach me thy way, and in thy *truth* 54
That *truth,* may guide where'er we go 1389
That *truth* to keep 2023
That we, through *truth* and mercy 2165
The God of *truth* and love 1653
The *truth* and its brave fight 120
The *truth* divine that maketh free 596
The *Truth* himself is here 1488
The *truth* how may I know 1097
The *truth* is her prophetic gift 1576
The *truth* is marching on 507
The *truth* of his word 423
The *truth* of thine indwelling 784
The *truth* that censures and the grace 522
The *truth* that makes me free 1323
The warfare of the *truth* 84
Then, God of *truth,* for whom 1373
Then to side with *truth* is noble 1574
Then *truth* begins to shine 1405
Thou art full of *truth* and grace 994
Thou art the *truth;* thy word 2023
Through me thy *truth* be shown 406
Thy perfect *truth* shall dwell 1373
Thy *truth* beyond the clouds 1362
Thy *truth* display 265
Thy *truth* doth reach the clouds 2080
Thy *truth* I will pursue 265
Thy *truth* is still the light 1511
Thy *truth* my light 780
Thy *truth,* O Lord, send down 1699
Thy *truth* shall break through every 731
Thy *truth* unchanged hath ever stood 1023
To his sure *truth* and tender care 365
To sow thy *truth* poured out 1873
To thee, whose faithful *truth* 2118
Truth in its beauty, and love 2322
Truth in the inward parts 1171, 1506
Truth meets with mercy 909
Truth reveals the promised day 275
Truth springs from earth 909
When *truth* in conquering grandeur 1443
Which heavenly *truth* imports 1960
Who its *truth* believeth 1180
Who *truth* doth ever keep 1394
With flaming *truth* and love 120
With *truth* all girt about 413
Yea, Lord, this *truth* we know 2098
Yes, Jesus, is the *Truth,* the Way 308
Yet 'tis *truth* alone is strong 1574

TRUTHS

Here what delightful *truths* are giv'n 2117
His *truths* upon the nations 7, 1933
How well thy blessed *truths* agree 1065

TRY

And, if I *try* to follow 860
And *try* his works to do 1963
Try heart and reins 1043
Try me, my thoughts to know 1438

Try to help others, ever be kind 378
We'll *try* our best to please him 1947
While we *try* to preach the word 251

TUMULT

And *tumult* of her war 1845
If now perchance in *tumult* 2076
Life's *tumult* we must meet again 32
That in the *tumult* and the strife 1323
The *tumult* and the shouting dies 583
The *tumult* of each sacked and burning 37
There no *tumult* shall alarm thee 271
There's a *tumult* of joy o'er 1995

TUNE

In vain we *tune* our formal songs 318
Tune my heart to sing thy grace 340
Tune our lips to sing thy praise 1181
Tune we heart and voice anew 412

TUNES

Tunes every mouth to sing 774

TURMOIL

Above earth's *turmoil* peace 915
Turmoil will change into infinite peace 167

TURN

Almost persuaded, *turn* not away 85
And scarcely can we *turn* aside 199
And though we *turn* us from 2029
And *turn* my face to thee 1444
And *turn* our seeking minds to thee 1389
And *turn* the darkness into day 845
And *turn* their darkness into light 650
And *turn* to gain our loss 1325
And *turn* unto the Lord in fear 1858
And will not *turn* our prayer away 791
He cannot *turn* away the presence 113
He will not *turn* thee away 985
Let us early *turn* to thee 1683
May I never *turn* aside 780
Nor *turn* from thee at all 2131
Nor *turn* you from your purpose 1469
O *turn* again and comfort me 1387
O *turn* not thou away 158
O *turn* thy face on me 476
O *turn* us not away 648
To thee we *turn* 2100
Turn back the foes that would assail 334
Turn from all created things 1583
Turn from all of earth's ambition 1764
Turn, Lord, to us in our distress 1174
Turn me not away unblest 717
Turn my darkness into day 745
Turn my dreams to noble action 587
Turn not away from us thy face 114
Turn not from his grief away 552
Turn our sadness into praise 1028
Turn thou *away* my sight 1826
Turn thou for us its darkness 1679
Turn thou mine eyes in dying 98
Turn thou our darkness into light 1424
Turn us again, Lord God 2131
Turn us and us restore 587
We *turn* from the world, with 1909
We *turn* to thee ourselves to find 784
We *turn* unfilled to thee again 1023
When to the Cross I *turn* my eyes 30
Wilt thou not *turn* and hear our voice 587

TURNED

But *turned* my soul perversely 183
He *turned* with, "Daughter, be of good" 1713
I *turned* away from One 841
I *turned* from the sin that deceives 1941
I *turned* that day to Christ 841
If I have *turned* aside from want 901
That ever *turned* at sorrow's prayer 206
Turned thy darkness into light 672
We've *turned* us each to his own 2155
Who has not *turned* my prayer from 361
Who *turned* not my prayer from him 50
Yet he *turned* aside to make all 2255

TURNEST

And *turnest* my mourning 856

TURNS

And love still *turns* where the Godhead 1095
He *turns* our spears to pruning hooks 1930
It *turns* their hell to heaven 1017
Turns to joy the mourner's tears 665
Who *turns* the wrong down 1880

TWILIGHT

It may be at *twilight* 953
Then, when *twilight* falls 1044
Toiling in *twilight* flickering 2262
Twilight and evening bell 1802

TYPE

The *type* of heaven's eternal rest 1704
Type of the stainless worship 1849

TYPES

Old *types* now disappear 1488

U

UNBELIEF

Blind *unbelief* is sure to err 577
Unbelief or trials seize thee 1577

UNBIND

That *unbind* all feeling 1034

UNBOSOM

Unbosom all our cares 393

UNBROKEN

Unbroken by the last of foes 132

UNCHANGED

Unchanged by changing place 1576

UNCOMPREHENDED

Uncomprehended and unbought 1461

UNCORRUPTED

'Tis, *uncorrupted,* undefiled 231

UNCREATED

With *uncreated* light aflame 1088

UNCTION

Come, and thy sacred *unction* 375
Come with *unction* and with power 743
Thy blessed *unction* from above 313
Thy gracious *unction* from above 642
Thy *unction* grace bestoweth 1876

UNDEFILED

He is still the *Undefiled* 524

UNDERSTAND

And *understand* the utterance 1914
And we cannot *understand* 2127
But we'll *understand* it better 2127
Though oft I cannot *understand* 1413
To *understand* they are so slow 2
Too high to *understand* 1452
We cannot *understand* the woe 1525
We will *understand* it better by and by 2128
Which all men *understand* 14

UNDERSTANDS

Jesus *understands* your need 2252

UNDERSTOOD

A providence of love is *understood* 39
With One who *understood* 549

UNDIMMED

Undimmed by human tears 1311
Undimmed by time, the word 1368

UNDISTURBED

May I *undisturbed* draw near thee 1588

UNDIVIDED

Undivided God we claim thee 746

UNDONE

Alas, my treason, Jesus hath *undone* thee 35

UNDYING

And we will love thee with a love *undying* 29

UNFAITH

From old *unfaith* our souls 1124

UNFATHOMED

O thou from whose *unfathomed* law 40

UNFOLD

And will *unfold* his wisdom 534
Each day it would *unfold* 11
The radiant morns *unfold* 40
Wide *unfold* the radiant scene 655

UNFOLDEST

Unfoldest blessings on our way 41

UNFOLDING

Things of Christ *unfolding* still 346

UNFULFILLED

No longer *unfulfilled* remain 1579

UNGODLY

The *ungodly,* filled with guilty fears 644

UNHARMED

Unharmed by Satan's malice 244

UNHEARD

Unheard by mortals are the strains 2091

UNHELPED

Unhelped by thee, in error's maze 1059

UNHINDERED

Unhindered and unresting 534

UNINJURED

Uninjured in the day of earth's 460

UNION

For a *union,* heart to heart 2158
That from that *union* evermore 1523
When *union,* sweet and dear 792

UNISON

In *unison* with all our hearts 1086

UNITE

Thus *unite* we to adore him 253, 1178, 1673
Unite my heart, that I thy name 54
Unite our hearts in love to thee 667
Unite the hymns of praise 45
Unite us all who own thee 284
Unite us in the sacred love 1185
Unite with one accord 533
We now *unite* with all who seek 1329

UNITED

Through thee, *united* worshipping 454

UNITY

All hail, eternal *unity* 45
And these are but a *unity* 1844

UNIVERSE

All the *universe* must be doomed 2319
That *universe,* how much unknown 2177
Throughout the *universe* it reigns 2071
Throughout the *universe* of bliss 2022
Thy *universe* unfolds thee 2303

UNKNOWING

Far and wide, though all *unknowing* 1686

UNKNOWN

And, behind the dim *unknown* 1574
For nothing falls *unknown* to him 6
Only good and only true, God *unknown* 53

UNLOCK

He only could *unlock* the gate 1963

UNLOCKED

I'd rather he *unlocked* the day 564

UNLOOSE

Lord, *unloose* my stammering tongue 1814

UNMEASURED

Unmeasured is my peace and light 1569

UNMOVED

Thou art *unmoved* and steadfast 1251
Unmoved by threatening 1003
Unmoved my soul remains 1430

UNOBSERVED

Unobserved and very near 36

UNREST

Out of *unrest* and arrogant pride 1602

UNRIGHTEOUSNESS

I am all *unrighteousness* 994

UNSEAL

Unseal our lips to sing 1149

UNSEALS

And God *unseals* his eyes 1727
Unseals our eyes 605

UNSEEN

Though *unseen* by mortal eye 2339
Though *unseen,* now be thou near us 2279

UNSEVERED

Unsevered and unblighted 1457

UNSHEATHED

Still *unsheathed* the Spirit's sword 1747

UNSPOTTED

Unspotted is the fear of God 618

UNSWERVING

And thy love *unswerving* 35

UNTHANKFULNESS

Forgotten in *unthankfulness* 1315

UNWASTED

Unwasted by the lapse of years 1576

UNWORTHY

Though I *unworthy* be 1259

UPHELD

Still I shall be *upheld* by thee 1438
Upheld by my righteous 776

UPHOLD

Uphold and keep me to the end 845
Uphold me in the doubtful race 1953
Uphold thou me, and I shall stand 494
Uphold us by thy word 1873
Yea, I will *uphold* thee 1787

UPHOLDETH

The Lord *upholdeth* all that fall 628
When I faint, his grace *upholdeth* me 65

UPHOLDS

The Lord *upholds* the poor and meek 1636

UPLIFTED

Not in vain for us *uplifted* 950
"*Uplifted* are the gates of brass 1081

UPLIFTS

The Lord *uplifts* his aweful hand 1900
Uplifts my soul, O God, to thee 654

UPPER ROOM

The *Upper Room* has not 2174

UPRAISED

Let it be to God *upraised* 1766

UPRIGHT

All ye that are *upright* in heart 164
The *upright* shall behold his face 1261

UPRISING

Uprising from all lands today 82

URGE

And onward *urge* thy way 154
I *urge* no other plea 2046

USE

And *use* the lives thy love 1168
But thou canst *use* our weakness 1943
From earthly *use* for heaven's employ 1082
I'd *use* for thee, O God of glory 23
O *use* me, Lord, *use* even me 1170
Seemly *use* of earthly treasure 470
Such boasting as the Gentiles *use* 583
Use it in the world for thee 634
Use us to fulfil thy purpose 1160
Use us to make the earth 1819

USHER

And *usher* in the morning 248
Then *usher* in that glorious day 156

USURPER

Where the rebel *usurper* holds 1987

UTMOST

O do thine *utmost* for their souls' 99

UTTER

And *utter* forth a glorious voice 1932
Day unto day doth *utter* speech 40
They *utter* forth no word 1862

UTTERED

And all thine *uttered* words 1140
If I have *uttered* idle words 901
So solemnly *uttered* by Jesus the Lord 18

V

VAIL
The opening *vail* reveals the way 1562

VAIN
All is *vain,* unless the Spirit 251
Nor is my boasting *vain* 967
Vain the stone, the watch, the seal 289

VALE
In death's dark *vale* I fear no ill 1876
In peopled *vale,* in lonely glen 1116
Or walking the shadowy *vale* 1489
This dark *vale* will be behind us 1738

VALES
The *vales* with corn are clad 410
To the sweet *vales* of Eden they 2246

VALLEY
By mountain pass, or *valley* low 81
Down in the *valley,* or upon 403
In the grey *valley* let us hear 1780
In the *valley* of the shadow 224
Say, why in the *valley* of death 1512
The *valley* holds no dread for you 2269
Through the *valley* and shadow of death 1894
Valley and lowland, sing 733

VALLEYS
In *valleys* fair and smiling 149
Let the *valleys* rise to meet him 363
The *valleys* laugh and sing 1734
The *valleys* shall be exalted 1998
The *valleys* stand so thick with corn 2120
There let the *valleys* sing 1936

VALUES
Keeping eternity's *values* in view 705

VANGUARD
Thy *vanguard* in the distant land 495

VANISH
These things shall *vanish* all 19
Vanish at thy bidding 258

VANISHES
And ere it *vanishes* over 1550

VANITIES
Then earthly *vanities* depart 1405, 1409

VANQUISHED
And o'er the *vanquished* powers of sin 82
And *vanquished* all our foes 1704
He has *vanquished* sin 1697
Jesus has *vanquished* death, and all 1610
Thy foes are *vanquished* 49

VANQUISHER
Thou, his *vanquisher* before 500
Vanquisher of darkness, bring 2204

VARIES
It *varies* with the wind 1202

VAULT
While the *vault* of heaven rings 1117

VEIL
No sudden rending of the *veil* 1778
O lift the *veil,* if veil there be 89
The rending *veil* shall thee reveal 1020
The *veil* of night is no disguise 2039
The *veil* of sense hangs dark 1020
Then, the *veil* uplifting 1800
Thou within the *veil* hast entered 77
Veil their faces to the presence 1060
When within the *veil* I meet 2121
With the shadowy *veil* of death 810

VEILED
But *veiled* within the shroud of 2273
Veiled in flesh the Godhead see 675
Veiled in the softened splendor 1457

VEILS
God kindly *veils* the distant skies 847
Which *veils* the glory now 559

VEIN
From the mountain's deep *vein* poured 104
Life mounts in every throbbing *vein* 40

VEINS
Rejoicing through my *veins,* so run 23

VENGEANCE

Fiercely then his *vengeance* flowed 611

VENTURE

Venture on him, venture wholly 358
With this I *venture* nigh 109

VESPER

And *vesper* hymn and *vesper* prayer 32

VESSEL

A lowly *vessel* at thy feet 686
Now the frail *vessel* thou hast made 1242

VESSELS

A Pilot who bringeth all *vessels* to land 20
Vessels, instruments of grace 752

VESTURES

But, in heavenly *vestures* shining 280
In all thy *vestures* of the earth 385

VEX

Though still thou dost *vex* us 1599
Vex not thyself in vain 1283
Whatever sorrow *vex* the mind 75

VIBRATIONS

With solemn, sweet *vibrations* 37

VICE

From *vice,* oppression, and despair 2267

VICTIM

Christ the *Victim,* Christ the Priest 142
Christ the *Victim,* undefiled 288
He who on the Cross a *victim* 76
Mighty *Victim* from the sky 142
O *Victim* of thy love 1251
The spotless *Victim* all divine 372
Thou on earth both Priest and *Victim* 77
Was not for them the *Victim* slain 1232

VICTOR

Anywhere with Jesus I may *victor* be 108
He is the *Victor,* Savior, King 1418
More than a *victor* I may ever be 285
O *Victor,* aid us in the fight 1078
The *victor,* palm branch waving 763
Victor after hard-won fight 356
Victor in wars our weakness 1157
Yet I would the *victor* be 224

VICTORIES

By the *victories* of meekness 1160
Come, *victories* of peace 2134
Victories and failures, tell 1210

VICTORS

Victors in the midst of strife 1040
Victors o'er the tomb 983

VICTORY

And a royal *victory* win 268
And didst the *victory* win 1187
And every *victory* won 1589
And ours the *victory* 1482
And the *victory* won 3
And thine the *victory* 1482
And *victory* remains with love 1333
Each *victory* will help you some 2336
Endless is the *victory* 2010
From God the *victory* I receive 858
From *victory* to victory 1786
High King of heaven, my *victory* won 177
His the *victory* alone 77
How the *victory* he giveth 894
O, glorious *victory* that overcomes 413
Of *victory* now o'er Satan's power 575
On to *victory,* waving high 2159
Our *victory* cannot fail 473
The Lord is leading on to certain *victory* 1860
The *victory* may depend on you 2064
The *victory* of faith to loyal 958
The *victory* of life is won 79
Then the *victory,* my brother 2064
"To Christ does *victory* belong 239
To them the *victory* yield 514
Victory is nigh 736
Victory soon shall tune your song 1560
Where, grave, thy *victory* 27
Who has gained the *victory* 76
With shining *victory* meet 1345

VIEW

And *view* my Savior there 787
And *view* the landscape o'er 1966
And bids us *view* his pierced hands 89
And to our wondering *view* reveal 315
The wide horizons grander *view* 2030
Though hidden to the *view* 14
Till glory breaks upon my *view* 7
View the Lord of Life arraigned 552
We shall *view* our home supernal 1738
We *view* his wisdom, pow'r 1658
Where is the soul-refreshing *view* 1347

VIGOROUS

Sleep that shall me more *vigorous* wake 59

VILENESS

Thou dost my *vileness* fully cleanse 839

VILLAGE

Every peaceful *village* in our land 2300
In lowly *village* stall 368
The tumult of each sacked and burning *village* 37

VINDICATED

Vindicated and enthroned 2018

VINE

I am the *Vine* of Life 170
Thou art the *Vine,* to thee we 2082
Though *vine* nor fig-tree 1759
Vine of heaven, thy blood supplies 245

VINES

To tend the *vines* 396

VINEYARD

The *vineyard* of the Lord 97
This *vineyard* of the Lord 682
This *vineyard* which thine own right 2131
Working in his *vineyard* 2124

VINEYARDS

Ye *vineyards* shout hosannas 510

VINTAGE

He is trampling out the *vintage* 1215

VIRGIN

A *Virgin,* born of David's line 1632
Of a *Virgin* lowly 290
The lowly *Virgin* brings 1488
The *Virgin* sings her lullaby 2215

VIRGIN-BORN

O Lord, the *Virgin-born,* to thee 1865

VIRGINS

"Come forth, ye *virgins,* night is 2149

VIRTUE

A healing *virtue* flows 128
And by *virtue* of his merits 217
And every *virtue* we possess 1589
And *virtue* bless where'er we live 1389
By active *virtue* crowned 2090
May *virtue,* piety, and truth 2011
Your knightly *virtue* proved 1532

VIRTUES

In whom man's *virtues* shine 1490

VISAGE

How does that *visage* languish 1475

VISION

A heavenly *vision* appeared in 1650
Again with *vision* kindled 1361
And faiths' fair *vision* changes 586
But the *vision* must be sure 2018
If clearer *vision* thou impart 1582
Let the larger *vision* 925
No more the far-off *vision* 2172
O thou who dost the *vision* send 1468
Only for keener *vision* that may greet 385
Still be my *vision;* O Ruler of all 177
The poet's rapt *vision* 709
Thy *vision* fades in ancient 2044
Thyself the *vision* passing by 40
Till with the *vision* glorious 1845
With *vision* clear and mind equipped 603
With *vision* ever clear 434
"*Vision* of peace," that brings joy 1538
Vision dear, of peace and love 217
Vision true to keep them noble 974
What glorious *vision* did ye see 2326

VISIONS

Beautiful *visions* of glory 1678
Beautiful *visions* will there behold 1758
Brighter *visions* beam afar 103
In my *visions* and dreams 896
That, even in *visions* of the brain 1383
To *visions* of a larger good 82, 1079
Visions of rapture now burst on my sight 213

VISIT

And *visit* it with thine own ardor 306
And *visit* this thy vine 2131
Come, *visit* every humble mind 375
Visit me with thy salvation 415
Visit, then, this soul of mine 292
Visit us with thy salvation 1190

VISITED

And *visited* and cheered 503
For he hath *visited* and redeemed 215

VISITEST

When once thou *visitest* the heart 1409

VOICE

A *voice,* a chime, a chant 840
A *voice* comes floating in the air 870
A *voice* from heaven was heard 2228
A *voice* of heavenly joy steals 796
A *voice* that invites 2
All with one sweet *voice* explain 29
And a *voice* through the waiting 2110
And every *voice* a song 674
And every *voice* adore 49
And grateful *voice* we'll raise 149
And his the gentle *voice* 1589
And the *voice* I hear falling on my ear 819
And the *voice* of thy love 236
And the *voice* that subdued 1922
And when my *voice* is lost 911
And yet I hear a *voice* that bids 2201
Beyond thy *voice,* thine arm 590
But if by a still, small *voice* 955
But surely God hath heard my *voice* 50
Can I his loving *voice* despise 558
Deep from thy *voice* we drink 751
Each glad *voice* its free song 104
Every *voice* in concert ring 1558
Hark! A *voice* from yonder manger 52
Hark! the *voice* of one that crieth 363
Hark! 'tis the *voice* of angels 1675
Hearing his *voice* in every line 1216
Hearing now his blessed *voice* 431
Here may his loving *voice* 723
Here the Redeemer's welcome *voice* 457
His mighty *voice* commandeth 1874
His pardoning *voice* I hear 113
His *voice* commands the tempest 327
His *voice* could not deceive me 892
His *voice* is calling all the day 836
His *voice* so gentle bids me 2
His *voice* sublime is heard afar 1900
His *voice* to each loving heart reacheth 1098

His *voice* to me is calling 819
How welcome is their *voice* 768
I hear once more the *voice* of Christ 37
I hear the *voice* of joy and health 1242
It is the *voice* of Jesus that 2201
Let the *voice* of hope be heard 1747
Let thy *voice* be one with theirs 151
Let thy *voice* call me home 2026
Lift up your *voice* and with us sing 41
Listening, ever listening, for the still, small *voice* 1707
Longing for thy *voice* that cheereth 1208
May her *voice* be ever clear 1033
My *voice,* Lord, do thou hear 1129
My *voice* shall echo the message 955
No human *voice* can utter 252
No other *voice* but thine 868
No *voice,* but those that sweetly sing 654
No *voice* of terror heard 128
Nor *voice* can sing, nor heart can 1019
O blessed (cheering, loving, welcome) *voice* 350
O Christ, whose *voice* the waters heard 418
O could my *voice* transcend the spaces 23
O for a *voice* to praise our King 1920
O still, small *voice* of calm 386
O *voice* divine, speak thou to me 604
O *voice,* I know thee who thou art 1533
O *voice,* which through the ages 1545
Sing to the Lord with cheerful *voice* 57
Soon shall thy *voice* comfort 1737
That I, with *voice* of thanksgiving 1043
The loving God your *voice* will hear 1640
The Master's *voice* still calling 1880
The *voice* of God hath reached 558
The *voice* of Jehovah comes down 537
The *voice* of Jehovah in majesty 537
The *voice* of Jehovah is mighty 537
The *voice* of Jehovah the cedars 537
The *voice* of Jesus sounds o'er land 670
The *voice* of prayer is never silent 1856
The *voice* of salvation awakes every 509
The *voice* that rolls the stars 190
The *voice* to lisp a prayer 1186
The worldwide *voice* of God 1914
Their *voice* is never heard 1862
Then, when thy *voice* shall bid 1679
There is a *voice* in every star 55
There's a *voice* in the wilderness 1998
These hear his *voice* 1366
Though the accusing *voice* within 538
Through the *voice* of woe 819
Thy dear *voice* alone obey 998
Thy pardoning *voice* I hear 2046
Thy secret *voice* invites me 2033
Thy *voice* comes strange o'er 2044
Thy *voice* of love, in gentlest tone 1400
Thy *voice* their idols shall confound 116
'Tis God's all-animating *voice* 154
'Tis mercy's *voice* invites thee 1657
To God my *voice* imploring 2103
To hear thy *voice,* like spoken word 1384
To hear thy *voice* we need but love 1386
To hear thy *voice,* where time's is 1795
To thee whose faithful *voice* 2118
Unto my supplications *voice* 1129
Voice of joy that cannot die 78
Voice, that oft of love hast 1672
We hear thy *voice,* O Son of Man 2270
What though no real *voice* 1932
When his tender *voice* is pleading 969
When suddenly a *voice* divine 797
When the Master's tender *voice* 810
With low, sad *voice* he calleth 196
With that *voice* so gentle 680
With the still, small *voice* of love 2279
With *voice* and lyre, in happy choir 437
Ye lights of evening, find a *voice* 41
Yet still my *voice* it seems to be 873

VOICES

Again to thee our feeble *voices* 435
All earth's thousand *voices* 1800
All the world's distracting *voices* 1772
Aloft your *voices* raise 50
And angel *voices* greet us 2172
And infant *voices* shall proclaim 1008
And myriad, myriad human *voices* 817
And to our *voices* tones 1410
Angelic *voices* swell 559
Come to him, all sweetest *voices* 344
Earth's bitter *voices* drown 1699
For prophet *voices* gladly heard 1388
Hark, angelic *voices* cry 287
Let all their *voices* raise 1898
Let us our *voices* raise 1556
Mid tempters' *voices* calling 2251
Once again sweet *voices* ringing 678
Our *voices* and our skill 55
Our *voices* join to sing 1329
Ringing *voices* and eyes alight 1706
Sweet as harp's melodious *voice* 2261
Sweetest angel *voices* 52
Ten thousand *voices* say 1242
The bells, like angel *voices* 33
The *voices* echo nearer 1604
The *voices* of our playmates 1629
The *voices* of the harpers 2172
The *voices* that have mingled 2030
Thee, Jesus, may our *voices* bless 1405
Thee their tiny *voices* praise 976
Their grateful *voices* raise 1165
To him our *voices* raise 1334, 1335
To thee our *voices* raise 2175
When a thousand *voices* cry 488
While their *voices* high are swelling 1100
Whom the *voices* of the prophets 1558
With *voices* united our praises 2188
Your *voices* in his praise employ 328
Your *voices* raise to the Lord 1211

VOID

If there's a *void* this world 905

VOLUME

But the blest *volume* thou hast 1871

VOLUNTEER

A *volunteer* for Jesus 3
Will you be enlisted as a *volunteer* 3

VOUCHSAFE

And upon us *vouchsafe* to make 2131
Here then, my God, *vouchsafe* to stay 1824
Here *vouchsafe* to all thy servants 281
Vouchsafe thy presence now 1427
Vouchsafe thy sevenfold Spirit 1325
Vouchsafe to bring us by thy grace 1543
Vouchsafe today thy presence 1344

VOUCHSAFED

Vouchsafed to earth by heaven 923

VOUCHSAFES

And yet *vouchsafes,* in Christian 1441
Jesus *vouchsafes* to be my tower 2295

VOW

Christian *vow* and fight 1179
That *vow* renewed shall daily hear 1392
The broken *vow,* the frequent 1478, 1812
The *vow* is past beyond repeal 1137
When the sacred *vow* is made 760

VOWS

And there our *vows* and homage 786
Breathing first to heaven above holy *vows* 555
For thou, O God, my *vows* hast heard 1376
For thou, O Lord, My *vows* 1134
For thou the *vows* that I did make 1357
Lord, I my *vows* to thee renew 152, 545
My *vows* to pay 1045
My *vows* will daily pay 1134, 1376
O'er *vows* and promises unkept 1285
Our solemn *vows* record 15
Our solemn *vows* we pay 728
Our *vows,* our prayers we now 1364
Our *vows* to thee alone 200
To thee *vows* paid shall be 1631
We all with *vows* and anthems 1733
When the *vows* that they have made 2264
When to thee my *vows* are taken 2308
Where broken *vows* in fragments lie 388

VYING

I with them will still be *vying* 1510

W

WAFT

And *waft* it to the skies 1184
Waft it on the rolling tide 2169
Waft them on to India's plains 1070

WAFTS

Wafts its praise on high 544

WAGE

And *wage* thy holy war 471
Wage to the end the glorious strife 1108

WAGES

Content to ask no *wages* 1166

WAIL

Sad, sad, that bitter *wail* 85
The *wail* of famine in beleaguered towns 37
Wail of the tempest wind 476

WAIT

All in white shall *wait* around 1572
And so I *wait* on shore 2234
And *wait* beneath thy feet 392
And *wait* for thee, sweet hour 1806
And *wait* the promise of our Lord 1132
And *wait* with patience for the morn 16
Be silent, and *wait* on 172
But they who *wait* upon the Lord 685
Do not *wait* to shed your light 399
For I shall *wait* his lead 1283
Here let we *wait* with patience 1675
I *wait*, but he does not forsake 558
I *wait* for God, my soul doth 1129
I *wait* the muffled oar 848, 2310
Left behind, we *wait* in trust 1303
Many are helpless and *wait* for your 1600
On him we *wait* 557
Only be still, and *wait* 904
Silently now, I *wait* for thee 1587
Some *wait* around him, ready still 117
Then, lowly kneeling, *wait* thy word 1679
Thou dost not *wait* till human speech 1386
To pray, and *wait* the hour 2037
Wait and worship while the night 382
Wait but a little while 1959
Wait for the others, coming 1605

Wait for thy unguarded 295
Wait, meekly *wait*, and murmur 1531
Wait not for what the years 1706
Wait on the Lord, and keep his way 1935
Wait, thou, His time 536
Wait till I see the morning 1675
Wait till the darkness is over 1742
Wait till the night is o'er 1675
Wait till the tempest is done 1742
We humbly *wait* thy blessing 1853
We *wait* for thy command 1951
We *wait* on thy decree 1146
We *wait* thy certain word 2076
We *wait* thy revelation 1124
We *wait* thy will; on thee 1163
We *wait* to feel thy power 1872
We *wait* until thy help appears 1174
While we *wait* at Jesus' feet 759
Who *wait* the last, clear trumpet 1532
Yea, none that *wait* on thee 2116

WAITED

And patiently *waited* an entrance 1741
Has *waited* long, is waiting still 192
Ye that have *waited* long 733

WAITEST

Thou *waitest* to be gracious 2071

WAITETH

He *waiteth* to bestow 348

WAITING

Christ is *waiting* to receive us 2284
For he is *waiting* even now 2
Jesus is *waiting* for thee 353
Jesus is *waiting* to save thee 353
Lovingly now he's *waiting* 1584
Patiently Jesus is *waiting* 1743
Waiting on Jesus when I am strong 2148
Your Savior is *waiting* to give you 2293

WAITS

And *waits* the hour when 1080
Come, he *waits* for thee 1584
He patiently *waits* to receive you 1925
He patiently *waits* to save 1257
He *waits* to give strength in the way 1925

She *waits* the consummation 1845
Waits his mercy to fulfil 611
Which *waits* us in the skies 97

WAKE

And *wake* dead souls to love 2013
But *wake,* my soul, before him 1552
That fruits of earth shall *wake* 21
Then *wake* your golden lyres 1895
Wake, and lift up thyself, my heart 152
Wake, and resound Jehovah's 1807
Wake and sing, good Christians 1792
Wake, and the song of joy 1807
Wake every heart and every tongue 147
Wake, for night is dead 2183
Wake, my soul, awake and sing 715
Wake, my spirit, clear my sight 761
Wake on earth a song of glory 581
Wake the immortal strain 2317
Wake up the slumbering conscience 244
We shall *wake,* where none 1738
When I *wake* with the blest 809

WAKED

I *waked* because the Lord sustains 1430

WAKEN

Knowing I shall *waken,* never more to 108

WAKENED

Wakened by kindness 1655
Wakened by the solemn warning 668
Wakened up from wrath to flee 2261

WAKES

From which none ever *wakes* to weep 132
She *wakes,* she rises from 2149
Wakes above, beneath, around 676
Whatever *wakes* my heart 1444

WALK

And *closely* walk with thee to heaven 499
And I will *walk* with him 921
And they *walk* in peace and light 1066
And we will *walk* the weeded field 1327
Anxious and despairing, many *walk* 1565
Come now and *walk* the fields 2277
"Come, *walk* with me today 1880
Do *walk,* and do not stray 212
I *walk* and I talk with 931
I *walk* secure and blessed 1378
I *walk* with the King 931
If you *walk* in the light before him 111
If we *walk* in his love they will 1956
I'll *walk* with thee today 838
Let me ever *walk* with thee 2043
Nevermore to *walk* alone 2256
Nor if I'll *walk* the vale with him 849
Now they *walk* in golden light 677
O Lord, then *walk* will I 54
O may we ever *walk* in him 230
Only let me *walk* with thee 2042
Or *walk* the golden streets 351
Or we'll *walk* by his side in the way 2266
Round Zion *walk,* about her 646
Safe I *walk* 780
Saviour, let me *walk* with thee 2042
So shall I *walk* aright 2083
So shall my *walk* be close 1347
That those who *walk* the ways 383
That we, with thee, may *walk* 445
The Lord be with us as we *walk* 1884
There I *walk* amid the shades 2247
Though thou *walk* through hostile region 271
Thus shall I *walk* with thee 1276
Tis better far that I should *walk* 822
Walk as Jesus walked below 752
Walk humbly, gently, leaning 465
Walk in his way, his word 1651
Walk in thy light, and in thy temple 1666
Walk the straight and narrow 2339
Walk thou beside us lest 762
Walk thou not as one benighted 296
We are young who *walk* 1796
We *walk* by faith as strangers here 231
We *walk* in the light when we follow 1946
We will *walk* and worship 1711
We who *walk* forth in thy greatness 578
We'll *walk* the heavenly way 804
While we *walk* the pilgrim pathway 1731
Who *walk* with us no more 956, 2163
Would you *walk* with him within 2324
Yea, though I *walk* in death's 1904

WALKED

He who *walked* with God, and 1697
I *walked* and sank not 879
If I have *walked* in my own 901
Of him who *walked* upon the sea 1487
One who of old *walked* in Eden 946
When he *walked* the fields, he drew 2255
When Jesus *walked* in Galilee 949

WALKEDST

Who *walkedst* on the foaming deep 418

WALKETH

Who *walketh* not astray 1841

WALKS

And he *walks* with me 819
And *walks* the honest road 1880
Beside us *walks* our brother Christ 2160
He *walks* with me and talks 874
He who *walks* in godly fear 629
Yes, Jesus *walks* beside us 1535

WALL

A *wall* of fire about me 834
Till within the jasper *wall* 1721

WALLED

Nor *walled* with shining walls 1515

WALLS

And is not trusting in *walls* 1840
And *walls* of strength embrace 786
For thou, within no *walls* 1032

Her *walls* before thee stand 859
High *walls* of ignorance around 1168
Its bright, jasper *walls* I can see 896
Its *walls,* defended by his grace 778
Long may its *walls* in beauty 2107
O Father, deign these *walls* to bless 67
The *walls* of gold entomb us 1365
These *walls* for thine own sake 1427
Unmoved her *walls* shall stand 571
Where the *walls* are all of jasper 1712
While round these hallowed *walls* 1530, 2052
With salvation's *walls* surrounded 541
Within these *walls* let holy peace 393, 651
Within these *walls* may peace 540, 1809
Within whose foursquare *walls* 1397
Yet these are not the only *walls* 199

WANDER

And *wander* away 806
And *wander* wide and long 2029
Nor *wander* from the pathway 1408
O why should I *wander,* an alien 1512
Prone to *wander,* Lord, I feel it 340
Should we *wander* from thy fold 589
Why will ye *wander* 279

WANDERED

And we've *wandered* in the darkness 2127
Far off you may have *wandered* 2280
Father, I have *wandered* from thee 214
He *wandered* far and wide 145
I long have *wandered* 913
Lord, we have *wandered* forth through 447
O thou who, homeless, *wandered* 1527
Once *wandered* o'er earth 1229
Sinful, wretched, I have *wandered* 1703
Thou hast *wandered* far away 939
Though I have *wandered*
God knows where 870
Though I've *wandered* far from his fold 214
Though you've *wandered* so far from 565
Those who've *wandered* far 517
Ye who have *wandered* far 348
You have *wandered* far away 2283

WANDERER

For the *wanderer* now is reconciled 1664
O *wanderer,* come 85
Some *wanderer* sought and won 1689
The *wanderer* reaches a shelter 179
The *wanderer* there a home 1965
Though, like a *wanderer* 1265

WANDERERS

Jesus is seeking the *wanderers* yet 326
Waving *wanderers* onward to their home 256
Ye restless *wanderers* often rest 336

WANDERINGS

For *wanderings* sad and lone 827
In our *wanderings* be our Guide 441
O when shall all my *wanderings* 2033
Till all our *wanderings* cease 1364

WANDERS

Forsaken Israel *wanders* lone 2239

WANE

A few more seasons *wane* 5

WANT

All that I *want* is in Jesus 506
And we *want* our loving Father 929
Do you *want* to be made a blessing 111
For *want* and weakness 1242
For *want* my plentiful supply 2034
From all *want* and danger free 633
From *want* of faith in work 1518
I *want* a true regard 1003
I *want* my life to tell men 890
I *want* my life to testify 890
I *want* no better Friend 981
I *want* the world to know 890
I *want* to be a light 890
I *want* to help to make his crimson 890
I *want* to live as Jesus lived 890
I *want* to love as Jesus loved 890
I *want* to please and honor him 890
I *want* to serve and honor him 890
I *want* to tell the blessed story 890
Lord, I *want* to be more 1139
No more from *want* and sorrow 1
No *want* shall turn me back 921
No *want* thy fullness knows 1367
Out of my *want* and into thy 1602
That they may *want* him too 549
The *want,* the waste, the hate 46
Thou, O Christ, art all I *want* 994
To go where *want* and sorrow are 2147

WANTS

All our *wants* by thee supplied 2009
And to all their *wants* attends 1581
Each other's *wants* may we 1432
He your Savior *wants* to be 891
It *wants* the breeze to nerve 1202
It *wants* the needed fire 1202
Jesus *wants* me to be loving 1030
My *wants* are treasure 1578
Now, our *wants* and burdens leaving 1295
Or how my *wants* shall be supplied 2295
Our deepest *wants,* our highest aims 300
Simple *wants* provide 621
Till all their *wants* are satisfied 1317
Your *wants* shall be his care 2060

WAR

All they who *war* against them 1505
And *war* no more its death-blast 1930
And *war* with all its woe 1401
And when the *war* is over 3
By *war* without and fears within 109
For *war* has blighted every land 2100
From *war* and woe he brings 1930
God calls that *war* must cease 2100
In *war* my peace, in loss 2034
Of man at *war* with man 46

Of nations freed from *war* 46
Onward to the *war* divine 262
That *war* may haunt the earth 1340
That *war* throughout the world may 371
The holy *war* shall cease 1204
Though *war* against me rise 1903
When *war* shall be no more 720

WAR CRY

Their *war cry,* "We will seek 1702

WARD

Ward off, while yet we dwell below 372

WARFARE

And her *warfare* now is over 363
Faith's *warfare* ended, won 1204
That, in the *warfare* I must wage 285
The *warfare* of the truth 84
Thine was the *warfare* with 1482
When the *warfare* is finished 1987

WARM

And *warm* and bright and good 2142
And *warm* my heart with 770
Come, *warm* my heart 1462
Warm and cheer us forth to go 966, 1012

WARMED

And *warmed* its earthly bed 11

WARMEST

Thou *warmest* my heart 1462

WARMS

And *warms* our lives with heavenly 481

WARMTH

And the *warmth,* the living 1942
And the *warmth,* the loving 1942
And the *warmth,* the pulsing 1942
Thou giveth man both *warmth* and light 41
Warmth to give, and pleasant 976

WARRIORS

As *warriors* brave and true 1948
As *warriors* through the darkness 1654
Warriors all and free men 1205
Warriors fighting for the Lord 1071
Warriors wielding freedom's 485

WARS

By *wars* and tumults, Love is mocked 438
In *wars* and tumults loud 2104
Our *wars* of class and nation 2076

WASH

He will *wash* away my sin 995
Jesus Savior, *wash* away all that 1304
O *wash* me in thy precious blood 5
Or *wash* away the stain 1279
So, *wash* thou me without 1582
Wash all our guilty stains 206
Wash me and keep me thine forever 1219
Wash me, and make me thus thine 493
Wash me, and mine thou art 493
Wash me, but not my feet 493
Wash me, cleanse me 839
Wash me in his precious blood 637
Wash me in the blood of the Lamb 214
Wash me in the blood that he shed 214
Wash me, make me pure within 554
Wash me, Savior, or I die 1671
Wash me whiter than the snow 554
Wash out its stains, refine 1519
Wash the stains of guilt away 342
Wash, thou, my soul this day 1276
Wash, thou, our wounds in 75

WASHED

And have *washed* their robes in blood 677
And *washed* our souls from sin 2090
And *washed* us in his blood 2106
Are you *washed* in the blood 693
For he *washed* my sins away 833
He *washed* it white as snow 837
Him who *washed* us with his blood 669
Washed all my sins away 1961
Washed us from each spot and stain 543
Who hath *washed* us in the tide 142

WASHES

That *washes* white as snow 308

WASTE

The want, the *waste,* the hate and rage 46
Waste no part of these precious years 1706

WASTED

If I've *wasted* all the talents 1710

WASTES

Then all these *wastes,* a dreary 1116
Through weary *wastes* bewildering 92
Wastes rise in verdure 660

WATCH

Always *watch* and prayer?" 293
And no *watch* are keeping 1668
And the night *watch* seemed 1993
And *watch* the glad appearing 1906
Asking thee to *watch* and keep 1304
But, *watch* and wrestle as I may 1582
His *watch* the temple child 797
I *watch* to shun the miry way 1582
In vain the *watch* kept ward 1078
Keeping *watch* above his own 1574
Let me *watch* as a winner of souls 809
Let us *watch* thee in the garden 2276
Lo! Her *watch* thy church is keeping 1136
O *watch* and fight and pray 1256
One in the faithful *watch* they keep 1453
Short as the *watch* that ends 1375
Their *watch* around us while 117
Their *watch* let angels round him 1406
Those who *watch,* thy presence 416
Thou thy *watch* wilt keep 1672
Vainly they *watch* his bed 1200

Watch against the devil's snares 1668
Watch against thyself, my soul 1668
Watch and fight and pray 2153
Watch and pray, my soul 2153
Watch and see, lest there be 1668
Watch and ward o'er thee 271
Watch did thine anxious servants 475
Watch each sleeping child 1685
Watch for the boatmen, wait 1605
Watch for the breaking of day 1742
Watch for the time is drawing nigh 982
Watch lest with her pomp 1668
Watch, let not the wicked world 1668
Watch my sleep till morning 1013
Watch o'er them day by day 514
Watch o'er thy church, O Lord 469
Watch the curves, the fills 1076
Watch, the tempter's snares 2153
Watch thou my wayward feet 1645
Watch: 'tis our Lord's command 2331
Watch with him one bitter hour 552
We *watch,* and wait, and pray 1
When lone my *watch* I'm keeping 2251

WATCH-CARE

Needing his *watch-care* so true 1754
Under thy *watch-care* safe I shall be 226

WATCHED

As he *watched* the childrens' games 1789
Jesus *watched* the children play 1789

WATCHERS

And thy trusted *watchers* fly 1642
The *watchers* of the north 1878
We are *watchers* of a beacon 487

WATCHES

But the slow *watches* of the night 2075
Christ *watches* me, his little lamb 1928
For Jesus *watches* and cares for me 1756
He *watches* o'er me day 981
He *watches* o'er you 378
Jesus *watches* children still 1789
Or *watches* at thy gates 797
Through the day *watches,* Father 462
Through the silent *watches* guard us 2062
Through the silent *watches,* think 1565

WATCHEST

Watchest where thy people be 1681
Who *watchest* sun give place 1361

WATCHETH

He *watcheth,* through the night 573

WATCH FIRES

I have seen him in the *watch fires* 1215

WATCHING

Above thee *watching* 2139
Watching for you and for me 1743
We are *watching* not in vain 2158

WATCHMAN

Watchman, does its beauteous 2154
Watchman, let thy wanderings 2154
Watchman of Zion, herald 747
Watchman, will its beams alone 2154

WATCHWORD

O let the *watchword* ring 1906
One only *watchword*—love 1579
Our *watchword,* the Incarnation 2180
This shall our *watchword* be 1945

WATER

Be it by *water* or by fire 1582
Let the *water* and the blood 1671
No *water* can swallow the ship 1208
Of sprinkled *water,* name them 9
The living *water,* thirsty one 842
The *water* of life 2
Thou flowing *water,* pure and clear 41
Thou living *water,* come 1463
Water cannot wash them away 214
Water like a stone 933
With *water* from the rock 1716

WATERED

Watered by his hand 928

WATERFALLS

Waterfalls that never sleep 1211

WATER FLOODS

Lord, the *water floods* have lifted 610

WATERS

And living *waters* flowing 1341
And on, ye *waters,* roll 512
And the sunlit *waters* in the 2274
And the sweet *waters* flow 403
And the *waters* sink to sleep 972
And *waters* veil the sky 2307
As the *waters* cover the sea 574
As the *waters* fill the shallows 331
But, ah, the *waters* failed 1322
But by Babylon's sad *waters* 78
By *waters* calm, o'er troubled sea 702
For jewelled *waters,* wind-caressed 1779
For the *waters* of the earth have failed 1242
From the *waters* lifted me 891
Is by living *waters* cheered 2319
Its *waters* call with entreating 1970
Like the *waters* of the sea 912
Not forever by still *waters* 441
O'er the *waters* it soundeth 1987
On these baptismal *waters* 316
The closing *waters* hide 391
The flowing *waters* sealed 40
The *waters* of Marah he'll 472
The *waters* of the springtime 2081
Though foaming *waters* roar 571
Thy *waters,* Gennesaret 236
Waters dancing, sunbeams 208
Waters in the desert rise 1612

We are nearer its *waters* each 2004
"When through the deep *waters* 776
While the nearer *waters* roll 994

WAVE

And every *wave* like crystal 737
And not a *wave* of trouble roll 2231
E'en death's cold *wave* I will not 702
Not an angry *wave* shall our bark 2298
O *wave* your green palm branches 510
Sinking 'neath the *wave* 474
Through the *wave* that drowns the foe 142
Wave advancing, wave retreating 104
Wave the answer back to heaven 736
We *wave* our palms before thee 48
When upon the tossing *wave* 521
Who *wave* their palms in triumph 283
Will their heads before him *wave* 76

WAVED

And *waved* green palms for love 2024

WAVE-NOTES

And while the *wave-notes* fall 1587

WAVER

Yea, nevermore did *waver* 2035

WAVES

And though the *waves* roll high 820
And when towering *waves* 2096
And when the towering *waves* 2096
Beyond the *waves* of woe 2172
Boisterous *waves* obey thy will 1007
Breathing thy *waves* of balm 181
Do hungry *waves* thy craft 2146
For amber *waves* of grain 1311
For though, like *waves* on Galilee 1487
Gold *waves* the corn 1164
Hark! again like *waves* retreating 678
In spite of *waves* and angry 2146
Like thy dancing *waves* in sunlight 606, 615
Lo, over the *waves* of the wide-flowing 537
Now like moonlight *waves* retreating 678
On thee, when *waves* of trouble 392
So that the *waves* which raged 773
The *waves* of strife be still 2013
The *waves* of the river are dark 2004
Though dark *waves* roll o'er the silent 1737
Through *waves* and clouds 536
To others the *waves* run fiercely 2004
Unknown *waves* before me roll 1007
When *waves* would whelm 1052
Where the *waves* of sin and sorrow 1603
While all around him *waves* 322
While the dark *waves* roll he will 1954

WAX

As *wax* before the Lord they flow 1889

WAY

A *way* thy steps may go 534
Afar from thine and wisdom's *way* 1517
All the *way* from earth to glory 411
Along the sacred *way* where thou 1177
Although my *way* is often steep 1907
And although the *way* be cheerless 989, 1011
And in the right and perfect *way* 2244
And in thy good and holy *way* 1826
And my *way* I cannot see 224
And pointing the *way* to the heavenly 1868
And the *way* grows weary 401
And will be all the *way* 134
And yet by him the wicked's *way* 1394
Are you weary, does the *way* 906
Back to the narrow *way* patiently 1655
Be thyself the *way* 964
But toiling in life's dusty *way* 1489
By the *way* of redeeming love 1500
Confronting me in the *way* 529
For all my *way* hath miry been 1582
For, groping in my misty *way* 564
For the *way* is growing brighter 812
For why the *way* of godly men 1841
Have thou thy *way* at any cost 135
Have thou thy *way* in all my life 1413
Have thou thy *way* in me 135
He is the living *way* 804
His blessed *way* to live 547
His *way* can never grieve me 2216
His *way* will lead me unto rest 847
How oft the *way* to thee I trod 1569
How sweet the *way* divine to take 2016
I am the *Way*, the Truth, the Life 1097
If rough and thorny be the *way* 1519
If the *way* be drear 989, 1011
If the *way* of the Cross I miss 864
If your *way* be dark and drear 2268
In every *way* try to please him 1030
It is the *way* the Master went 550
Jesus is the true, the only Living *Way* 2292
Leading still the ancient *way* 299
Looking this *way*, yes, looking 1605
Most perfect is his holy *way* 858
My *way* in life which thou shalt choose 1413
Never forsaking the *way* 1047
No broader is the *way* 432
Now a living *way* I see 864
O, how sweet to walk in this pilgrim *way* 2209
O *Way*, through whom our souls 1424
On the *way* from earth to 1642
Or climbing the mountain *way* steep 1489
Or if my *way* lie where storms 2020
Pressing my *way* to mansions 2152
Shining so brightly all the *way* 1984
Singing if my *way* is clear 1721
So shall my *way* be safe 1463
Sometimes the *way* is rough 847
That so thy wondrous *way* 2099
The *way* I journey soon will end 888
The *way* I know—I know my Guide 1318
The *way* into heaven could not 1278
The *way* is dark and drear 178
The *way* is dark before me 737
The *way* is open now 1597
The *way* of the Cross leads home 864
The *way* that leads to glory 2005
The *way* the holy prophets went 1001

Them safely in thy *way* to guard 9
There is a *way* for man to rise 420
There let the *way* appear 1265
There's no other *way* but his way 2293
There's no other *way* but this 864
This is the *way* I long have sought 1001
This is the *way* of life 539
Thou all my *way* dost know 815
Thou art the *Way* the holiest 1511
Thou art the *Way*, the Truth 714, 2023
Though dark the *way*, still sing 1282
Though long the weary *way* we tread 1459
Through him alone who hath our *way* 1794
Through their childhood's onward *way* 760
Thus, all my toilsome *way* along 1729
Thy *way* is in the sea and air 1467
Thy *way* to God commit 1708
To aid you on your *way* 1063
To cheer them in their onward *way* 1410
To Christ, the *Way*, the Truth 1097
To show the *way* that thou 1474
To teach the *way* of life 2167
Too long the darkened *way* 1699
Treading not the straight and narrow *way* 2125
Trusting through a stormy *way* 1721
'Twas best for him to have his *way* 2324
Walking sadly life's dark *way* 2288
Walking steadfast in his *way* 519
Walking with him, how blessed the *way* 1782
Walking with Jesus in the narrow *way* 2125
We upon our *way* would go 144
We'll be happy all the *way* 1066
When rough and dark my lonely *way* 815
When the *way* is dim, and I cannot see 1954
When the *way* is gloomy 163
Whene'er thy *way* seems strange 434
Whereas the *way* of wicked men 1841

WAYS

All other *ways* have proved 2135
All thy *ways* are worthy of thyself 641
All *ways* are thine, and thine the glorious 1852
And all thy *ways* of wondrous grace 234, 1805
And her *ways* are ways of gentleness 886
By quiet *ways* through mornings 604
For the grassy *ways* 61
For the *ways* of sin grew dreary 892
Holy and true are all his *ways* 1893
In thee love's *ways* we find 1490
In *ways* of love and truth 1186
Just and true are all his *ways* 951
Meek and lowly were his *ways* 2255
Most sure in all his *ways* 1630
Mourning o'er our sinful *ways* 1028
My *ways* are known to thee 1438
Nor in unsimple *ways* ensnared 1478
Of weary *ways* or golden days 849
So we go the unknown *ways* 62
Such in his *ways* do walk 212
Thou wouldst my *ways* direct 212
Through all our *ways* thou takest 534
Through desert *ways*, dark fen 720
Walking ever in his *ways* 238
When the crooked *ways* are 424
Where in life's common *ways* 1515
Whose *ways* are brotherhood 1397

WAYSIDE(S)

By *waysides*, if wounded ones 1098

WAYWARD

He seeks the *wayward* with a broken heart 2
The *wayward* and the lost 278
Though I was often *wayward* 2237

WEAK

Are we *weak* and heavy-laden 2210
For I am *weak* and weary 1830
For we are *weak*, and need 447
Here may the *weak* a welcome find 1595
I am both *weak* and sinful 860
Strong in battling for the *weak* 485
Strong the *weak* to save 1205
The *weak* and wavering strengthen 244
They are *weak*, but he is strong 995
Yea, the *weak* and helpless shall his 285
Yet *weak* and blinded though we be 240

WEAKLINGS

To *weaklings* as we are 100

WEAKNESS

All our *weakness* thou dost know 1058
All your *weakness* he will strengthen 344
And in our *weakness* thou dost make 464
Dying in *weakness*, but rising 228
I am *weakness*, full of weakness 766
In our *weakness* and distress 492
In *weakness* and in want we call 67
In *weakness* my almighty power 2034
Leaning on thee, in *weakness* I am 1284
My *weakness* changed to glorious 1194
Never a *weakness* that he doth not feel 407
Now in my *weakness*, seeking thy favor 226
Our *weakness* pitying see 1589
Though our mortal *weakness* raise 753
To him in my *weakness* for strength 1741
Weakness needs the Strong One near 682
Weakness will change to magnificent 1763

WEAL

And for our country's *weal* 515
O do thine utmost for their soul's true *weal* 99

WEALTH

A *wealth* I know that was not meant 182
And *wealth* increase with lowly 1595
For the *wealth* of all heaven is mine 871
For they are *wealth* beyond compare 789
Our *wealth*, our wisdom perish 2076

The *wealth* in every mine 2294
The *wealth* of land and sea 199
Though their *wealth* increase 1565
Thine the *wealth* of land and sea 1760
We have no *wealth* or learning 1947
Wealth and rank possessing 627
Wealth upon the needy shower 665
With all its *wealth* untold 1857

WEAN

Wean our hearts from all below 2279
Wean us and train us with thy rod 189
Wean us from earth, through all 1778

WEANED

More *weaned* from earth 1432

WEAPON

A trusty Shield and *Weapon* 19
From every *weapon* death can 1037

WEAPONS

No *weapons* in his hand are seen 128

WEAR

And *wear* a crown with Jesus 1867
And *wear* in endless glory 548
But then shall *wear* the crown 252
May we *wear* the crown 262
We shall *wear* a crown 262
Wear it ever, night and day 295

WEARETH

He *weareth* in this hour 19
He *weareth* it for you 1391

WEARIED

For I was *wearied* sore 303

WEARINESS

But when through *weariness* 2221
May *weariness* and sadness be 1853
No toiling yonder, and no *weariness* 1274

WEARY

Are you *weary,* distressed and lonely 111
I was *weary* too 293
Still the *weary,* sick, and dying 2047
'Tis *weary* and worn and sad 1950
The *weary* find eternal rest 1008
Thou art he who, never *weary* 1681
Thou art very *weary* 293
Thy world is *weary* of its pain 82
To the *weary* and the worn 11

WEAVE

Thy God can *weave* the strands 1821
To *weave* a crown for May 21

WEB

And through the ceaseless *web* 1495

WEEP

And we shall *weep* no more 5
If I must *weep* with thee 1245
Stay, let me *weep* while you 1832
We *weep* for sin and wrong 247
Weep o'er the erring one 1655

WEEPS

He *weeps* when his own Son you 2338
Jesus *weeps,* and loves me still 395

WEIGHT

O the *weight* of her affliction 1263
Our heavy *weight* of mortal toil 121
There is never a *weight* of woe 1976
When *weight* of sin oppresses 2251

WELCOME

And a *welcome* that all may receive 1115
And *welcome* peace, away with strife 160
And *welcome* spring, and everywhere 160
And *welcome* youth, for he is young 160
Come and *welcome,* come and 2284
His *welcome* will make thy heart 1494
I can peacefully *welcome* the night 1751
In Christ a hearty *welcome* find 336
O how *welcome* thy voice 1742
Soon he's coming back to *welcome* me 2002
Then thy Lord's sweet *welcome* 297
Then *welcome* beauty, he is fair 160
Then *welcome* honest labor 1252
There is *welcome* for the sinner 1999
Thy *welcome* shall proclaim 674
Welcome him to enter in 1726
Welcome now the blessed day 1272
Welcome to our pilgrim band 1272

WELCOMED(S)

And Anna *welcomes* Israel's Hope 1488
And *welcomed* at any cost 529

WELL

The deep, sweet *well* of love 1923
There is a *Well* in a desert plain 1970
When the living *Well* is so near 1970

WELLS

Its *wells* are broken cisterns 1193

WELLSPRING

Wellspring of heavenly peace 1463
Wellspring of my heart's delight 972
Wellspring of the joy of living 1040

WENT

As they *went* where'er he sent 695
For my Lord *went* first 864
To thee they *went*—the blind 2008
Went down to dust beside thee 1124
Went the Savior alone on his knees 1268
With palms before thee *went* 44

WEPT

But never *wept* for thee 1322
I *wept* to see a crown of thorn 825

WHEAT

The *wheat* may be there, though 1540
Wheat and tares together sown 359

WHEELS

His chariot *wheels* are heard 958

WHILE

A little *while,* and then shall come 1592
A little *while,* faith's flickering 1352
A little *while* for patient 1352
A little *while,* the earthern pitcher 1352
A little *while,* to keep the oil 1352
A little *while,* to sow the seed 1352
Just a little *while* before me 1499
Let the little *while* between 2089

WHISPER

And *whisper,* "It is I" 820
But *whisper,* "Thou art mine" 190
He can *whisper* words of comfort 863
How its gentlest *whisper* 983
I'll *whisper* as I take the cross 135
What matter who should *whisper* blame 201
When lo! a *whisper* from the tree 825
Whisper, "I am near" 1672
Whisper, O Truth of Truth 476
Whisper softly, "Wanderer, come" 755

WHISPERS

And *whispers* I am his 1240
He *whispers* in my breast 1723
He *whispers,* there is wealth 120
The last low *whispers* of our dead 2181
To attend the *whispers* of thy grace 1824
Unto me, he *whispers* words 812
While he gently *whispers* 755
While he *whispers* in my ear 1195

WHIT

I am every *whit* made whole 800

WHITENS

That *whitens* o'er the plain 1166

WHOLE

That *whole* and sick, and weak 2008

WICKED

Let the *wicked* forsake his way 2155
The *wicked* are not so 1841
The *wicked* oppressing now cease 2166

WICKEDNESS

That doth in *wickedness* delight 527, 1176

WIDENESS

There's a *wideness* in God's mercy 1767

WIDOW

The *widow* and the fatherless 911
When the *widow* weeps to thee 2260

WIDOWS

Nor *widows* desolate 1836

WIELD

And *wield* the sword of truth 285

WIELDS

He *wields* a mighty scepter 2005

WIFE

Goods, honor, children, *wife* 19
In thy *wife* thou shalt have gladness 238

WILD

If in this darksome *wild* I stray 1519

WILDERNESS

In the pathless *wilderness* 492
In the *wilderness* astray 1837
In this dark *wilderness* 178
Or alone in this *wilderness* rove 1512
Suffering in this *wilderness* 738
The *wilderness* is fruitful 2081
Till *wilderness* and town 1699

WILDS

They that *wilds* inhabit 286
Though in desert *wilds* thou sleep 271

WILL

According to thy *will* and word 1332
All thy holy *will* to trace 127
Alone thy *will* to seek 84
And in that *will* I now abide 1822
And knowing now thy perfect *will* 491
And my oft-rebellious *will* 972
And my *will* be lost in thine 808
And the *will* of God 1069
And thy holy *will* obey 582
And *will* to generations all 619
But Lord, the *will,* there lies 2173
By whom thy *will* was done 419
Each to work with ready *will* 555
Gladly all thy *will* obey 1197
God's *will* to earth thou bringest 1490
He who, with calm, undaunted *will* 620
His sweet *will* so precious will be 1707
His *will* e'er right remaineth 2216
His *will* I have joy in fulfilling 1848
His *will* obey, him serve 1651
His *will* to learn 603
In them the *will* of God the Son 1859
In thy great *will,* O Master Mind 1951
In *will* and deed, by heart 314
Into thy blessed *will* to abide 1602
Is it thy *will,* O Father 2267
Learning all his *will* to feel 294
Let his *will* enfold you 143
Let me be slow to do my *will* 1128
Let thy *will* be done indeed 1588
Loyal to thy holy *will* 1120
May thy *will* and mine be one 1644
May thy *will,* not mine be done 1644

More of his holy *will* discern 1216
My consecrated *will* surrender 724
My Lord, thy *will* be done 1245
My weakened *will,* Lord, thou canst 1829
"My *will* is best." 564
My *will* is not my own 1202
No other *will* I own 2046
Now thy *will* and mine are one 972
May thy *will* be mine 1245
Our *will* to dare great things 185
Ready for all thy perfect *will* 1521
Ready, my God, thy *will* to see 1587
Save that his *will* be done 1940
The *will* to win it makes us free 370
Then shall thy perfect *will* be done 1579
Thy righteous *will* be done 1281
Thy *will* alone let all enthrone 1165
Thy *will* alone we ask 1951
"Thy *will* be done." 1231
Thy *will* is just 590
Thy *will!* It strengthens weakness 1281
Thy *will* move strong and swift 1844
Thy *will,* not mine, be done 1324
Thy *will* was in the builder's thought 67
To catch the wandering of my *will* 889
To do his *will* my highest 832
To do my Master's *will* 4
To do the *will* of Jesus, this is 1610
To do thy *will* we come 1496
To his *will* I'd gladly bow 1222
To know thy *will* and keep from sin 789
To thy blest *will* our wills 1482
To thy most holy *will,* O Lord 388
Who have done his *will* 1102
"Whosoever *will,*" forever must endure 2292
"Whosoever *will* may come." 2292
"Whosoever *will,*" the promise is 2292
"Whosoever *will,*" 'tis life forever 2292
Will of his glorious Son 1052
Yet, Lord, to thy dear *will* 1592
Yet, while thy *will* we would 1131
Yielding his *will* to the will 2143

WILLED

We will not fear, for God hath *willed* 12
Who therewith hath *willed* forever 217

WILLEST

And what thou *willest* be 1228
That as thou *willest* I might live 1228

WILLING

If he had not been *willing* 2063
May I be *willing,* Lord, to bear 1050
O, how much he was *willing* to bear 1982
Thou hast made us *willing* 2287

WILLINGNESS

By thy *willingness* to die 1145

WILLS

And our *wills* uplift to thine 416
Free *wills* to us thou givest 1490
In *wills* empowered to witness 2165
Just as he *wills* my path 847
May we our *wills* resign 1184
Our *wills* are ours, we know not 1797
Over our *wills* and affections 2128
Stilling the rude *wills* of men's wild 92
Strong be our *wills,* through praise 2027
Thus shalt our *wills* from hour to hour 414
To brace our *wills,* to prove 120

WIN

And he must *win* the battle 12
And *win,* like them, a crown of life 1108
And *win* the well-fought day 1746
Thou shalt *win* at last 293
To prize it, *win* or lose 120
Win a crown of life 941
Win and conquer, never cease 1554
Win or lose, to keep the same 930
Win the crown, my soul 2153
Win through thy blood, our pardon 235

WIND

All-powerful as the *wind* he came 1589
And the *wind* blows stronger 627
And the *wind* that sweeps from 1929
Be wild the *wind* and fierce 2146
Come as the *wind,* with rushing 1776
Come *wind,* come weather 2290
For over it the *wind* doth pass 1798
In *wind* and wave I hear 815
It is the *wind* of God, that dries 826
Like mighty rushing *wind* 1132
No rushing mighty *wind* we ask 1090
O *Wind* of heaven, by thy might 81
Stormy *wind,* fulfilling only his 1624
The changing *wind,* the flying cloud 2307
The cold *wind* in the winter 68
The murmuring *wind,* the quivering 1459
Thou rushing *wind* that art so strong 41
True *Wind* of heaven, from south 1398
While *wind* and wave unite 1385

WINDOWS

And all the *windows* of my heart 39

WINDS

And in the *winds,* from unsunned 2248
And so the west *winds* play 39
And stormy *winds* around me 1907
And though abroad the sharp *winds* 2097
Great *winds* thy clarions 612
In *winds* that drift the clouds along 604
'Mid rising *winds* we hear 1429
No chilling *winds* nor poisonous breath 1563
O, let the *winds* your message bear 239
Soft fragrant *winds,* blue skies 1293
The wild *winds* hushed 475
"The *winds* and the waves" shall obey 1208
The *winds* obey his will 1900
The *winds* of hell have blown 1846
The *winds* that sweep the mountain 2250
Thou art Lord of *winds* and waves 1775

When stormy *winds* fulfil thy will 1370
Whom *winds* and seas obey 365
Wild *winds,* that do his word 1898
Winds of temptation, and billows 2068
Ye *winds* of night, your force 1900
Ye *winds* on pinions light 1936

WINE

And here for you the *wine* of love 362
For the *wine,* which thou hast poured 486
The *wine* how rich, the bread how sweet 89
The *wine* shall tell the mystery 266
Wine of the soul, in mercy shed 246

WINEPRESS

Where the *winepress* alone 1115

WING

And *wing* my words that they may reach 1170
And *wing* to heaven our thought 1785
I shall *wing* my flight to worlds 2002
On joyful *wing* our songs 2107
Or if on joyful *wing* 1265
Resting 'neath his sheltering *wing* 2002
Wing your flight o'er all the earth 103

WINGS

And 'neath thy *wings* we rest 1939
And on the eagle *wings* of love 324
Beneath his *wings* of love abide 168
Beneath his *wings* shalt thou 1908
Beneath thy own almighty *wings* 59
But oftener on *wings* of peace 1363
But, on *wings* of prayer 1553
He made their tiny *wings* 68
I shall, on eagle's *wings* upborne 1864
If I the *wings* of morning take 1438
My Savior, 'neath thy sheltering *wings* 1436
'Neath his *wings* securely hide you 556
On cloudy *wings* let glad words fly 239
On eagles' *wings* they mount 685
On *wings* of love our souls shall fly 157
On *wings* of silence, soft as snow 46
Rising then on *wings* of praise 555
The *wings* of peaceful love 1776
Their *wings* are faith and love 685
Thy *wings* shall my petition 1806
Upward for aye on *wings* 1602
When, on the *wings* of prayer 1237
Wings an angel, guides a sparrow 1214
Wings its flight to realms of day 66
With the *wings* of his protection 271

WINS

Long endurance *wins* the crown 71
Now it *wins* its widening way 1695
There he *wins* our full salvation 356

WINTER

Amid the cold of *winter* 1107
As *winter* flies away 21
When *winter* binds in frosty chains 2250
Who have *winter,* but no Christmas 369
Winter long is over and the spring 1270
Winter shapes the leaves of spring 1075

WINTERS

And why are my *winters* so long 795

WIPE

And *wipe* my weeping eyes 2231
God shall *wipe* away all tears 938
He'll *wipe* every tear, roll away 2225
He'll *wipe* my tears away 1949
Where God himself shall *wipe* away 888
Wipe away thy tears 987
Wipe from your brow the sweat 362
Wipe sorrows tears away 1227

WISDOM

And he whose *wisdom* guides the world 6
And with *wisdom* kind and clear 635
Be thou my *wisdom* and thou 177
Deep his *wisdom,* passing through 53
Eternal *wisdom* is their guide 767
God is *Wisdom* 566
Here the *wisdom* from above 742
Here, *wisdom* shines forever bright 155
His *wisdom* and his power 1899
His *wisdom* ever waketh 921
His *wisdom* is unsearchable 1636
In *wisdom* and uprightness 1557
In *wisdom* guide, with faith 1165
Is it *wisdom* that you lack 2268
Let there be *wisdom* on the earth 1072
Let *wisdom* broaden with the day 1526
No *wisdom* of my own 820
O loving *wisdom* of our God 1630
O *Wisdom* from on high 1544
Supreme in *wisdom* as in power 685
Thine endless *wisdom,* boundless 1234
Those whose *wisdom* still directs us 242
Thy *wisdom* is unerring 1794
Thy *wisdom,* Lord, thy guidance 1595
Thy *wisdom* shall the way prepare 1238
To speak his *wisdom* all divine 155
True *wisdom* is with reverence 1899
Until true *wisdom* from above 419
Wisdom and strength for each day 578
Wisdom comes to those who know thee 242
Wisdom and riches and strength evermore 228
Wisdom in strength's decay 613
Wisdom true impart, O Lord 127
With *wisdom,* light and knowledge 307

WISE

All things *wise* and wonderful 68
How *wise,* how good to choose 120
Wise to conquer every foe 780

WISH

I *wish* that his hands had been placed 884
My God, I *wish* them there 1260

O let my *wish* be crowned 1259
Therefore I *wish* that peace 843
'Tis all I *wish* to seek 1824
When one their *wish*, and one their prayer 667
Whose *wisdom*, love, and power 1344
Wish and fulfillment can severed 1538
Without a *wish* or thought 1940

WISHES

And *wishes* thine increase 786
Fervent *wishes*, earnest thought 753
Our *wishes* all above 792

WITHDRAW

If thou *withdraw* thyself 444

WITHER

And *wither* and perish 916
Nay, they *wither*, root and stem 483

WITHHOLD

He will not *withhold* one blessing 561
How can I, Lord, *withhold* 855
To give or to *withhold* 39

WITHHOLDEST

Nor *withholdest* aught that may 449

WITHSTOOD

I have long *withstood* his grace 395

WITNESS

And he the *witness* gives 839
And *witness* with the blood 1777
Constant *witness* to God's mercy 2318
God's *witness* of celestial things 1810
Of *witness* for thy love 106
Ours to bear the faithful *witness* 36
Thy sacred *witness* bear 338
Thy *witness* in the souls of men 1467
True *witness* of thy love 1175

WITNESSER

Witnesser of Jesus' merit 1138

WIVES

Our *wives* and children we commend 712

WOE

And in deepest *woe* pray on 449
And *woe* he lightens 566
Deep the *woe* of her affliction 140
Doth seek to work us *woe* 12
"Flee from *woe* and danger 52
For through many a *woe*, to our home 989
In *woe* they rise, but all their tears 644
Let *woe* and waste of warfare 1072
Seeking this Savior from all earthly *woe* 302
To banish mortal *woe* 1924

WOES

All his *woes* are over now 700
Bearing all my *woes* 1000
But with the *woes* of sin 948
O Savior Christ, our *woes* dispel 136
Ours were the *woes* he bore 426
So by my *woes* to be 1265
The *woes* of life he knew 1252
When free from the *woes* that on earth 2225
When the *woes* of life o'ertake 934
With *woes* that none can number 1505
Would God my *woes* were at an end 960

WOKE

But *woke* to life and hope 11
I *woke* to find my dream was true 825

WOLVES

And *wolves* devour thy fold 2073
Though the *wolves* may ravin 983

WOMAN

That all of *woman* born may see 1776

WOMB

In Mary's *womb* vouchsafed to dwell 1865

WOMEN

From *women* struggling sore 1397

WON

And Christ has *won* the victory 1418
Christ has *won* the victory 700
For Christ has *won*, and man 1078
For he hath *won* the victory 1083
For Jesus *won* the world 2321
He has *won* me by his grace 835
Hers, who *won* God's benediction 1263
The victory of life is *won* 79, 1937
Thou hast *won* my heart to serve 1470
Which thou hast *won* for us 1177
Won by thy deathless love 406
Won safe from sinner's madness 1889

WONDER

And then no more thou'lt *wonder* 1698
And we *wonder* why the test 2127
And *wonder* how he could love me 881
"O, what a *wonder* that Jesus loves me!" 806
O *wonder* of wonders, can it be 2063
Though with a scornful *wonder* 1845
To see the *wonder* God has wrought 298
Wonder of wonders, Jesus is mine 2148
Wonder of wonders that he should love 829
Wonder that he cares so fatherly 1838

WONDERFUL

The *Wonderful*, the Counsellor 1917

WONDERS

And all his *wonders* tell 2014
And *wonders* of his love 1039
But O these *wonders* of thy grace 1863
For great thou art, and *wonders* great 1901
For the *wonders* of creation 1214
For the *wonders* of his word 1837
His *wonders* to the nations show 1061

Lord, great *wonders* workest thou 715
Lord, how thy *wonders* are displayed 877
Its *wonders,* O what thought can trace 155
Such the *wonders* of his ways 665
The *wonders* of his love proclaim 958
The *wonders* of redeeming love 203
The *wonders* of thy grace 1122
The *wonders* of thy love 1419
The *wonders* of thy name 40
The *wonders* that our fathers told 1369
The *wonders* thou in me 2039
Thy noblest *wonders* here 1871
Thy *wonders* in their days performed 1448
Two *wonders* I confess 203
Why should the *wonders* he hath wrought 209
Wise are the *wonders* of thy hands 731
Wonders of grace to God belong 535
Wonder of *wonders,* O how can it be 1015

WONDER-WORKING

O *wonder-working* name, of 13

WONDER-WORKINGS

In *wonder-workings,* or some bush 1698

WONDROUS

For they are all so *wondrous* 2195
Wondrous is thy sacred story 243

WONT

Where all are *wont* to meet 540

WOOD

Be it through *wood* or valley 1818
Wood and island 104

WOODLANDS

And in the *woodlands* cool 2195
Fairer still the *woodlands* 427

WOODS

All the *woods* are new in leaf 1305
Out of the *woods* my Master 947
Thy *woods* and templed hills 1225
When through the *woods* and forest 1437
Woods are soft and tender 1305

WOOS

He *woos* me again to his side 701

WORD

A *word* from the heart 2
A *word* in season, as from thee 1170
A *word* shall quickly slay him 19
And in thy *word* believe 455
And to take him at his *word* 2092
As true as God's own *word* is true 473
Be loyal to God's holy *word* 547
Be thy gracious *word* fulfilled 2253
But by the *word* of grace 1716
But in God's *word* the light 1571
But in thy blessed *word* I trace 2117
But the *word* of our God endureth 1998
By God's *word* at last my sin 2335
By his *word* and Spirit led 480
By the living *word* of God I shall 1790
By thy perennial *word,* lead us 1715
Come thou incarnate *Word* 338
Each his *word* from God repeating 242
Each spoken *word,* each silent 1438
Enduring *Word,* thy strength abides 1658
Every *word* he whispers 169
Flowing in the prophet's *word* 1077
For his *word* shall never 1786
For idle *word* and trifling thought 1518
For right is God's *word* 2329
For the *Word* incarnate cries 282
Forever, O Lord, is thy *word* established 2084
God's *word,* for all their craft 19
Grand in the poet's winged *word* 1366
Hallelujah! let the *word* 676
He, the *Word,* was born of woman 1728
He whose *word* cannot be broken 541
He whose *word* rebuked the storm 169
Here in his *word* he hath shown 347
His blessed *word* of love 205
His brethren's *word* he would not take 785
His tender *word* I hear 2296
His very *word* of grace 190
His *word* ere long shall run 1156
His *word* he will surely fulfil 553
His *word* is tried 858
His *word* my hope secures 88
His *word* of truth I am believing 1896
If he according to thy *word* 270
If his *word* they still obey 629
In friendly *word* where neighbors 2277
In your every *word* and action 398
Inspiring *word,* thy truth imparts 1658
Just a little *word* of Jesus' love 400
Kind is the *word* 1804
Let me no wrong or idle *word* 1128
More about Jesus in his *word* 1216
More of believing his marvelous *word* 10
No sinful *word,* nor deed of wrong 1301
No *word* from thee shall fruitless 136
No *word* of man can ever tell 1912
Nor how believing in his *word* 849
Not any *word* can be 1452
Now the *word* doth swiftly run 1695
O let thy *word* for e'er be heard 2086
O may thy holy *word* 28
O Savior, whose almighty *word* 418
O *word* of comfort, through the 1545
O *word* of hope, to raise us nearer 1545
One gracious *word* can set the sinner 803
One little *word* shall fell him 12
One *word* of thine could save 1429
Only a *word* from thee 1585
Only a *word* of love 1585
Resting on thy *word* of power 2018
Revealing Jesus through the *word* 849
Shall the *word* with terror 2032
Sowing the *word* with prayer 1693
Supported by thy *word* 87
That his *word* is never broken 363
That *word* above all earthly 12
That *word* and life thy truths 191, 1445

The *word* he speaks, it cannot die 852
The *word* of blessing give 1537
The *Word* of life and truth impart 317
The *word* that tells of peace 2178
Then thy *word* doth cheer us 1180
Then, when the *word* is given 1067
Thou in thy *word* hast said 712
Thou whose *word* could still 2049
Through him whom thy *word* hath 2084
Through his *word* he says 259
Thy beloved *word* obeying 221
Thy holy *word* forget 270
Thy quickening *word* shall raise 453
Thy sovereign *word* restores 1233
Thy whispered *word* from housetops 594
Thy *word* above the storm rose 475
Thy *word* alone true wisdom 2023
Thy *word* can bring a sweet relief 392
Thy *word* have I hid in my heart 2084
Thy *word* I cherish in my heart 789
Thy *word* I in my heart have hid 270
Thy *word* into our minds instil 1478, 1812
Thy *word* is like a deep, deep mine 2085
Thy *word* is like a morning star 2086
Thy *word* is like a starry host 2085
Thy *word* is true 590, 1446
Thy *word,* O Lord, will safely lead 789
Thy *word* of truth believing 1317
Thy *word* our law 555, 1610
Thy *word* shall be my chief delight 789
'Tis the Bible, *word* of life 2319
To God, the *Word,* on high 2243
To thee, O *Word,* our merry hearts 1725
Trusting his *word* in thankfulness 1670
Until thy mighty *word* prevails 1916
Waiting for thy gracious *word* 1207
When his *word* commanded 1624
When the *word* of life is given 662
Where prophets' *word,* and martyrs' 1496
Word of consolation 1180
Word of God, and inward light 761
Word of life, who thee receiveth 2319
Word of the ever-living God 1052
Word of the Father, now in flesh 1330
Yet no ungentle, murmuring *word* 2217

WORDS

All the *words* he ever spoke 990
All thy *words* we would fulfil 752
And from ill *words* thy tongue 1321
And gentle *words* of kindness say 1536
And wild and sweet the *words* 840
And with *words* of love draw near 668
And with *words* that help and heal 635
And *words* of peace reveal 768
Attracted by those loving *words* 75
Beautiful *words,* wonderful *words* 1732
Breathing *words* of absolution 1049
By whom the *words* of life were spoken 246
Calmly now the *words* we say 1303
Comfortable *words* he talketh 71
Fairer than our *words* can say 662
For the *words* which thou hast spoken 486
His *words* of welcome 207
In all his *words* most wonderful 1630
In everchanging *words* of light 40
In gladsome *words* I would rejoice 1444
Little *words* of love 1101
Lord, the *words* thy lips are telling 610
May our *words* be true and mild 962
No parting *words* shall e'er be spoken 2301
No *words* can sound the music 325
No *words* can tell what sweet 1237
Not vain, unthinking *words* 1942
O Christ, whose *words* make dear 1417
O how passing sweet thy *words* 1772
O how shall *words,* with equal 2223
O, that my *words* might magnify 890
O *words* of gentle worth 1093
O *words* with heavenly comfort 702
Seven *words* of love 1333
Still his *words* before us range 64
Still with healing *words* replying 2047
Sweeter are thy *words* to me 780
That his *words* "well done" may greet me 411
That thy *words* may prove 297
Their *words* to earth's remotest 1862
These are the *words* of the Savior 353
Those gentle *words* should raise 190
Thy *words* with pleasure we recall 1026
Well may we their *words* resound 1100
What sweet *words* do they repeat? 1100
What wondrous *words* of love 2132
Wonderful *words* of life 1732
Words and deeds of Christ our Master 2318
Words flow apace when we complain 2221
Words full of kindness 1831
Words, idle *words,* for earnest deeds 1285
Words of comfort meet us 1787
Words of counsel, wise and pure 742
Words of kindness always say 2339
Words of life and beauty 1732
Words of life so urgently 219
Words of life we have from thee 219
Words of promise, bright and sure 742
Words to bring us greater gladness 1100
Words to chase away our sadness 1100
Words which thou thyself 811

WORE

He *wore* a crown on Calvary 2242

WORK

A *work* of such a curious frame 2039
Alike at *work* and prayer 2243
And a *work* of lowly love to do 443
And man's rude *work* deface 520
And the *work* that we have builded 656
And *work* and joy with others share 1591
And *work* crown all our prayer 2147
At *work* for God, in loved 1810
Blest by the *work* the Spirit 1865
Earthly *work* is done 1672
For holier *work* above 106
For if thy *work* on earth be sweet 1148
For the joyful *work* and true 273
For *work,* and all the lessons 2162

For *work* and rest, for home 1518
For *work* itself is love 1977
"Go *work* today." 322
Great the *work* they have 1783
He will your *work* reward 682
His *work* most honorable is 1638
His *work* my hoary age shall 1241
His *work* to do 603
How they *work* within 293
I *work* or wait, still following 1284
I would *work* ever for the right 1045
If firm thy *work* shall be 534
In all our *work*, in all our play 456
In Jesus' *work* below 322
In our *work* and in our play 962
In thy *work* to share 928
In us the *work* of faith fulfil 146
In *work* and worship so divine 209
In *work* that gives effect to prayer 1492
Let his *work* your pleasure be 679
Love's redeeming *work* is done 289
May our *work* be keen and willing 1158
My Father's *work* to do 1468
No *work* of sin I'll suffer 1557
None for the Master's *work* 705
Now Lord, the gracious *work* 1801
O blessed *work* for Jesus 1578
O'er each *work* of thine 101
O let thy *work* and power appear 1541
On homeliest *work* thy blessing 199
One little *word* for Jesus, O speak 1292
Our Father's *work* to do 1468
Our Master all the *work* hath done 396
Our *work* is glad, in thee begun 1380
Savior, thy *work* revive 723
So shall thy *work* be done 365
Some *work* of love begun 1689
Somebody's *work* bore joy and peace 1755
Strong Son of God, whose *work* was his 1130
That love may dare thy *work* 84
That *work* awaits our hands 370
That *work* of thine shall finish 534
The meanest *work* divine 1825
The *work* accomplished by our hand 1174
The *work* with little fervor 2170
Then *work*, brothers, work 1098
Then, *work* done, ran happily 930
There the *work* of life is tried 1303
There's a *work* to be done 1987
They who *work* without 1022, 2006
Thine is the *work*, and only thine 1018
Thou must *work* all good 220
Though our *work* is hard 1620
Thy arduous *work* will not be done 1256
Thy finished *work* retrace 434
Thy *work* of grace we sing 965
To do his *work* again 547
To do his *work* and will 145
To *work*, and think, and speak 1521
Until at last when earth's day's *work* 1393
Up and *work* while yet 'tis day 1222
We have hard *work* to do 174
We *work* with thee, and go 1130
We'll *work* 'til Jesus comes 1421
When fully he the *work* hath wrought 536
When he first the *work* begun 1695
When Jehovah's *work* begun 1762
When man's *work* is o'er 2320
When my *work* on earth is ended 805
When the *work* of grace is done 672
Whispering words of peace to cheer 2279
With us the *work* to share 278
Work, brethren, work 682
Work, for daylight flies 2320
Work for the good that is nearest 1098
Work 'mid springing flowers 2320
Work never can bring weariness 1977
Work shall be prayer 199
Work, though the world may defeat you 1098
Work through the morning hours 2320
Work through the sunny noon 2320
Work 'til the last beam 2320
Work while strength endureth 297
Work while the day grows brighter 2320
Work while the dew is sparkling 2320
Work while the night is darkening 2320
Work with heart (lips, prayer) 297

WORKER

But the lonely *worker* also finds 2017
Each *worker* pleases when the rest 396
For where there is a *worker* 1252
Must be a *worker* too 1252

WORKERS

Hail the hero *workers* of the mighty past 657
Hail then, noble *workers*, builders 657
Hail ye hero *workers* who today do hear 657
Hail ye hero *workers*, ye who yet shall come 657
Hail ye, then, all *workers* of all lands 657

WORKETH

And *worketh* righteousness 2311

WORKING

In *working* or in waiting 106

WORKMAN

O *workman* true, may we fulfil 1492
Thou Master *Workman*, grant us 1492
Where the tired *workman* sleepeth 2006
Workman of God, O lose not heart 617

WORKS

Again thy *works* of wonder 312
All his *works* are done in verity 2329
All thy *works* before thee stood 748
All thy *works* shall praise thy name 749
All thy *works* with joy surround 1040
All *works* are good, and each 396
And for his *works* of wonder 773
And wondrous *works* my mind 1451
And *works* by thee are done 54
And *works* his sovereign will 577
For thou, Lord, by thy mighty *works* 2112

Glorious in his *works* and ways 277
God's mighty *works* who can 532
Gracious in his *works* and ways 1622
Great thy *works* and deep thy 951
His wondrous *works* and ways 1315
His wondrous *works* through ages 1899
His *works* do show him clothed 1886
His *works* most wondrous he hath 1638
In all his *works* he doth excel 2216
In all my *works* thy presence 499
In all thy *works* art thou 50
In his *works* his mercy read 1622
In *works* that keep faith sweet 1466
Let not our *works* with self 1478
Let *works* of darkness disappear 1646
Man's feeble *works* grow old 1658
Matchless thy *works* abide 265
My father *works* in and through 170
Nor *works* my faith to prove 2310
O'er all his *works* his mercy is 628
On thy mighty *works* I ponder 394
So let our *works* and virtues shine 1739
So the wondrous *works* of God 1036
The mighty *works*, or mightier name 190
The *works* of God, above, below 1960
The *works* of men decay 1998
The *works* that only love hath 371
Their *works* of pure unselfishness 471
These nobler *works* of thine 1863
Through all his mighty *works* 1897
Through the *works* thy hands 951
Thy mighty *works*, and wondrous grace 775, 1450
Thy *works* all praise to thee afford 628
Thy *works* of grace, how bright 1811
To practice wicked *works* with men 1433
Viewing here the *works* of God, I sink 431
Who *works* for justice, works for thee 1360
Who *works* in love, thy child 1360
With no *works* that my Redeemer 1710
Works of love on man bestowed 752
Works with skill and kindness 1214

WORLD

A little further from the *world* 1345
A ransomed *world* at last 300
A stricken *world*, despairing 1328
A *world* that knew not when he came 194
Above the *world* is stretched the sky 1358
All men the whole *world* through 14
All the *world* is God's own field 359
Although all the *world* should forsake 1583
And a *world* of trouble and care 1929
And all the *world* his glory 1123
And all the *world* in awe 2099
And all the *world* is singing a glad 510
And all the *world*, with the birds 1750
And let the *world*, adoring, see 116
And o'er a dark and ruined *world* 1449
And so the Savior, Savior of the *world* 817
And the whole *world* give back the song 948
And the *world* had ceased to woo me 892
And the *world* grew mirthful-hearted 2254
And the *world* is wrapped in fear 668
And the *world* looks cleaner 1305
And through this *world*, with devils 12
And were this *world* all devils o'er 19
And wide o'er all the peopled *world* 1449
But in this *world* of sin 1426
But O, in a *world* where our Father 1929
By this dark *world* unknown 194
Christ is coming, o'er the *world* 1616
Come ye aside from all the *world* holds 362
Counting all the *world* but loss 1196
Did the *world* from darkness bring 1566
Doth the *world* redeem 544
Ere through the *world* our way 1801
For God so loved the *world* 22
For O, in this *world* of our Father 1929
For the *world* has never known 912
For the *world* I pined 802
For the *world* to Christ must now be 400
From that *world* by thee redeemed 748
From the *world*, the flesh, deliver 446
From world to *world* one song 1893
Glorious ere the *world* began 798
Guarding, in a *world* of strife 1196
Has the *world* my heart been 1138
He's in the *world* today 874
In all the *world* around me 874
In him the *world* shall onward move 377
In that blest *world* above 1977
In the *world* where thou dost send us 486
In the *world* you've failed to find 2283
In this *world* of darkness 968
In whom his *world* rejoices 1299
Is this vile *world* a friend to grace 87
Jesus is all this poor *world* needs 506
Leading the *world* in the triumph 601
Let all the *world* 2099
Let all the *world* fall down 1555
Let not the wicked *world* 1668
Let the round *world* keep 1854
Let the *world* in thee find rest 581
Let the *world* take up the story 1272
Let the *world* true praises sing 1559
Lightly by the *world* esteemed 748
Not of this *world* his kingdom 510
Now let the *world* to peace 1930
O how the *world* to evil allures me 865
O that the *world* might know 1777
O that the *world* might taste 1017
O, the *world* is full of sighs 1955
O'er a faithless fallen *world* 1747
O'er all the *world* thy glories shine 1447
Of the whole wide *world* the throne 268
Or the *world*, a tempting snare 963
Over the *world* afar 180
Over the *world* must this message 1972
Round the *world* his praise be sung 665
Savior of the *world* to be 521
Shall all the *world* command 198
Should the *world* and sin oppose 480
So shall the *world* become 1401

Spread all the *world* around 28
That the *world* cannot enslave thee 175
That through the *world* thy truth 1442
That with the *world,* myself, and thee 59
The Savior of the *world* is here 1082
The Savior of the *world* took bread 2133
The weary *world* rejoices 1399
The whole round *world* complete 284
The whole wide *world* around 1169
The whole wide *world* rejoices 1078
The *world* and all its pomp to flee 2189
The *world* could not help me 931
The *world,* doth it offer a refuge 2271
The *world* established is 598
The *world* established stands 1882
The *world* for Jesus now 1945
The *world* has waited long 284
The *world* in slumber lies 1297
The *world* in solemn stillness lay 948
The *world* is also stablished 1886
The *world* is bright with the joyous 875
The *world* is ever near 1408
"The *world* is full of sorrow 1949
The *world* is glad to hear your chime 1661
The *world,* it is thy word 1444
The *world* its hate hath shown 1846
The *world* like a dream will vanish 1411
The *world* my soul would gladly cheat 2302
The *world* now is waiting the harvest 1540
The *world* redeemed, the will 1177
The *world* revolved from night to day 840
The *world* rushes on 1820
The *world* shall be reborn 90
The *world* stands out on either side 1358
The *world* takes up the chant 1661
The *world,* the flesh, and Satan dwell 176
The *world* to Christ we bring 278
The *world* to glory bring 1945
The *world,* with sin and Satan 708
The *world* with song is vibrant 48
The *world* without may rage 1432
Therefore in all the *world* thy glories 653
There's a *world* of toil, and a world 1929
Thine is the Greek's glad *world* 522
Though all the *world* deceive 2119
Though all the *world* forsake me 834
Though all the *world* his love neglect 482
Though the *world* may be deriding 175
Though the *world* may change its fashion 450
Through each bright *world* 155
Through the *world* far and wide 2051
Through this changing *world* below 1684
Throughout the *world* proclaim 241
Thy *world* is open everywhere 1467
Thy *world* is weary of its pain 82, 1079
Till the whole *world* knows 912
Till the *world* for Christ 1069
'Tis he who this round *world* hath 1080
To a *world* of sinners revealed 214
To all the *world* the message 1368
To receive from the *world* 953
To redeem the *world* 1198
To save a *world* Christ sends you 1469
To save a *world* undone 283
To that bright *world* of endless day 153
To tell the *world* the peace 624
To tell to all the *world* that God is 1551
To the *world* a stranger 524
To thee the *world* beholden 1457
Triumphant o'er the *world* and sin 1864
Vain *world,* farewell! from thee 558
Watching the *world* till the breaking 1611
We are making God's new *world* 309
We to the *world* belong 26
What though the *world* deceitful prove 1400
When all the *world* looks up because 2262
When the old *world* drew on toward 373
When the *world* around is smiling 993
When the *world* to thee seems drear 63
When the *world,* with tempting 2153
Wherever in the *world* I am 443
Whereon the Savior of the *world* 298
Which can shape the *world* to fitness 36
Which have been since the *world* began 215
While Christ is all the *world* to me 1021
Wide as the *world* is his command 184
Winning the *world* to that last 1374
Yet doth the *world* disdain thee 1415

WORLDING

When the *worlding,* sick at heart 2260

WORLDS

All the *worlds* to him belong 1211
In brighter *worlds* above 7
In *worlds* by the undying trod 321
Let all the *worlds* give answer 283
Midst flaming *worlds,* in these arrayed 1024
New born *worlds* rise and adore 53
Of shining *worlds* in splendor 585
The watery *worlds* are all his own 337
The *worlds* awake to cry 151
The *worlds* of science and of art 199
Through thee the *worlds,* with all they bear 414
Worlds and men and angels 1034
Worlds are charging, heaven beholding 2157
Worlds his mighty voice obeyed 1626

WORMWOOD

O the *wormwood* and the gall 552

WORN

When *worn* with sickness, oft hast 2223

WORRIES

Foolish *worries,* fretting troubles 2224

WORRY

A little less *worry* of what may come 10

WORSHIP

All on earth shall *worship* thee 50
And every knee shall *worship* 33

And I will *worship* in thy fear 527, 1176
And thy *worship* God's employ 294
And *worship* face to face 252
And *worship* him as God alone 1858
And *worship* him in humbleness 41
And *worship* near thy throne 1230
And *worship* only thee 1347
And *worship* reverently 54
And *worship* thee with trembling hope 1234
Both high and low shall *worship* 360
But simply *worship* thee 100
But *worship* and adore 1632
Come and *worship* 103
Come, *worship* at his throne 337
He would *worship* God alone 268
Him *worship*, all ye angels 1889
How they *worship* thee in heaven 1085
I *worship* thee, and pay my vow 72
Our *worship* doth thy name deride 1916
Such the *worship* that upraises 1606
The holier *worship* which he deigns 1319
'Tis the Lord himself we *worship* 299
To *worship* rightly is to love 1319
We *worship* only thee 522
We *worship* thee, God of our fathers 2188
We *worship* thee in joyful song 1356
We *worship* thee, we bless thee 1481
We *worship*, we adore thee 1089
With thy *worship* shall be blest 1173
Worship and thanks to him belong 328
Worship at his holy hill 611
Worship Christ the new-born King 103
Worship, honor, power and blessing 659
Worship there the infant Savior 542
Worship we our Jesus 1189
Worship we the Godhead 1189

WORSHIPPED

The angels *worshipped* as he lay 9
Worshipped the Beloved 933

WORTH

All are too mean to speak his *worth* 1035
Learning all the *worth* of pain 2247
Life's *worth* in fellowship 456

WOULD

All that I *would*, but fail to be 390
And fain I *would*, but though 2033
Fain I *would* be as thou art 523
I *would* be like Jesus 411
I *would* not if I might 2083

WOUNDED

Lord, by the stripes that *wounded* thee 79, 1937
Once *wounded* for me, by his stripes 122
Or, if *wounded* some should fall 2264
Powerful the *wounded* soul to 417
The *wounded* looked, and straight were 128
Though thou hast *wounded* me 1015

WOUNDS

Five bleeding *wounds* he bears 113
Hide in the *wounds* 2
Lord, thy *wounds* our healing give 245
Rich *wounds*, yet visible above 376
The very *wounds* that shame would hide 136
Thy cruel *wounds* my own have healed 60
Thy *wounds*, O Savior, bring salvation 724
To heal earth's *wounds* and end 762
To the *wounds* of Calvary 813
Wash thou our *wounds* in that dear blood 75
Will all my *wounds* and sorrows 1585
Wounds or sickness may divide us 366

WOVEN

Woven the thorns for thy tortured 1015
Woven through thy history 521

WRAP

Wrap now thy peace, like a mantle 578

WRAPPED

All meanly *wrapped* in swathing 2282
But thou wast *wrapped* in 475
Not *wrapped* in dreamless sleep 590
Not *wrapped* in morning cloud 2273

WRAPS

It *wraps* me 'round with 1462

WRAPT

Wrapt in the silence of the tomb 237

WRATH

And oft a people's *wrath* may flash 1281
Be thou, long-suffering, slow to *wrath* 2239
By thy *wrath* and judgment just 554
Can my God his *wrath* forbear 395
He, swiftly marching in his *wrath* 2138
His *wrath* and justice stand 1897
In *wrath* and fear, by jealousies 438
Let not thy *wrath* in its terrors 607
The *wrath* of sinful man restrain 1369
Though Satan's *wrath* beset our path 2289
Whether the *wrath* of the storm-tossed 1208

WREATHS

For all *wreaths* of empire 143
My choicest *wreaths* are always wet 362

WRESTED

He *wrested* from the hand of sin and death 148

WRESTLE

And *wrestle* till the break of day 333
Wrestle, and fight, and pray 1746

WRESTLED

I've *wrestled* on toward heaven 1923
They *wrestled* hard, as we do now 530

WRESTLERS

To *wrestlers* with the troubled sea 1170

WRETCH

That saved a *wretch* like me 88

WRIT

And *writ* the blessing in thy word 1065

WRITE

And will he *write* his name 1897
And *write* all these thy laws 1133
And *write* their names upon 9
Write me as one of thine 1027
Write on my heart every word 1832
Write thou deeply in my heart 715
Write thy new name upon 1350

Y

YEAR

A glad new *year* to all the earth 34, 528
Another *year* is dawning 106
Another *year* of God 107
Another *year* of happy work 107
Another *year* of leaning 106
Another *year* of life's delight 107
Another *year* of progress 106
Another *year* of summer's glow 107
Another *year* of training 106
Another *year* of trusting 106
Another *year* with thee 106
Each *year* that passes o'er us 1952
For the *year* before us 1787
In the new *year* of God 796
Still each *year*, through midnight 1100
The fresh and fading *year* 1146
The opening *year* thy mercy shows 643
The *year* in beauty flows 40
The *year* is going, let him go 1662
The *year* of jubilee is come 241
The *year* with good thou crownest 2081

YEARN

As shipwrecked seamen *yearn* for morning 29
Yearn for the sign, O Christ 683

YEARNED

I *yearned* for them, not thee 1322

YEARNING

And so for thee, O Christ, men's hearts are *yearning* 29
Love him who with love is *yearning* 52

YEARS

Afflicted through the weary *years* 1174
All the weary *years* of strife 63
And as the *years* shall come and go 2107
And that future *years* shall see 1558
And *years* wherein we ill 1096
Down weary *years* to learn thy name 1088
For, as *years* pass, a fuller sense 882
For *years* are fleeting fast 820
For *years* in the fetters of sin 931
God of the coming *years* 586
Great Lord of *years* and days 151
How dread are thine eternal *years* 1234
In the glad eternal *years* 1096
Just a few more *years* with their toil 1044
Long *years* were spent for me 2077
Many *years* my heart has strayed 977
My *years* for thee be spent 2077
O the *years* in sinning wasted 1222
Of *years* so radiant with 2027
Our fourscore *years* of joy 725
Our *years* are like the shadows 1377
Shall life's sweet passing *years* 558
So shall added *years* fulfil 380
So the *years* go, speeding fast 2299
Sweeter as the *years* go by 1556
The rolling *years* his furrows are 191
The *years* that he gave I had wasted 1941
Though our *years* are far and ranging 1796
Through endless *years* declare 234
Through endless *years* to live 1108
Through *years* unnumbered 2144
Thus, with thirty *years* accomplished 1728
To endless *years* the same 1375
When rolling *years* shall cease 184
When with the ever-circling *years* 948
While the *years* of eternity roll 430, 896
Whose *years*, with changeless virtue 267
With thee a thousand *years* 725

YESTERDAY

But *yesterday* it was a viewless 1287

YIELD

Abundant the *yield* of ripe 959
All we *yield* to thee 1680
At his second coming *yield* 76
But let it *yield* a hundredfold 83
Didst *yield* the glory that of right 58
For the grain field's plenteous *yield* 518
For the valley's golden *yield* 1799
He surely will *yield* to love 2272
I only *yield* thee what was thine 1231
I would *yield* that heart to thee 1690
I *yield* my flickering torch to thee 1465
I *yield* my powers to thy command 1233
I *yield* myself, O Lord, to thee 825
Its *yield* of riches has no end 2087
Jesus, to thee I *yield* my all 2016

O, will you not *yield* while you may 1925
Shall we not *yield* him, in costly 254
We must never *yield* or falter 62
We *yield* ourselves to thee 1819
We *yield* them up to thee 1696
Yield allegiance to the Master 2159
Yield now to the Savior who 1925
Yield to him now, O yield 1925
Yield to his pleading 569
Yield to me now, for I am weak 333

YIELDED

I have *yielded* him my life 259
I *yielded* myself to his tender 1257
While I am waiting, *yielded* 691
Who *yielded* his life an atonement 2102

YIELDEST

Freely thy life thou *yieldest* 98

YIELDING

Yielding allegiance, glad-hearted 1104

YOKE

And 'neath his *yoke* their rest 666
Come to him, his *yoke* is easy 344
May thy *yoke* be meekly worn 1120

YOKES

He *yokes* the whirlwina 1900

YOUNG

Both *young* and old exalt 1898
Calling the *young* and old to rest 263
The thoughtless *young*, the hardened 1116
The *young*, the old be strengthened 1529
The *young*, the old inspire 1132

YOUTH

And teach us in our *youth* 28
And *youth* renewed and frenzy 2008
Bright *youth* and snow-crowned age 1654
From *youth* to age, by night and day 1654
God of our *youth*, be with us yet 588
If *youth* in all its bloom 1442
That *youth* may love and age adore 1424
Valiant *youth* goes striding forth 1796
We offer thee our *youth* 84
Youth soon disappears 1706

Z

ZEAL

Could my *zeal* no respite know 1671
His *zeal* inspired their breast 530
Holier *zeal* impart 925
I would not with swift-winged *zeal* 1142
Let their *zeal* revive again 1775
March on with relentless *zeal* 1069
More *zeal* to labor, more courage 1219
Nor did their *zeal* offend him 2230
To their *zeal* thy wisdom lend 2264
With flaming *zeal* your hearts 2325

ZEPHYRS

Like evening *zephyrs* blowing 2109

ZESTS

Youthful *zests* are keener 1305

HOW TO USE THE JUDSON CONCORDANCE TO HYMNS

1 Starting with a known line—

"And all the twinkling starry host"

2 Locate the KEY WORD.
The Key Word is usually the first verb or common noun in the line. In this case it is—

HOST

(For exceptions see "How to Use This Concordance" in the introductory pages of the book.)

3 The Key Word will lead you to the complete line in the LINE INDEX and a REFERENCE NUMBER.

Sweet *hosannas,* sweet hosannas	1099
With glad *hosannas* ring	237
With your glad *hosannas* make	1833

HOST

A mighty *host,* by thee redeemed	1507
Against me though an *host* encamp	1903
And all the twinkling, starry *host*	427
And ever with the heavenly *host*	307
Christ hath our *host* surrounded	283
Heaven's *host* their noblest praises	1105
His sacramental *host*	1081
Lo! the angelic *host* rejoices	684
Part of his *host* have crossed	324, 1067
Satan and his *host* defy	1788
The angel *host* on high	28
The whole triumphant *host*	1864
Thy ransomed *host* in glory	1880
Till Satan's *host* is vanquished	548
Till, with all the angel *host*	357
Who for God had been a *host*	1788

HOSTEL

The *hostel* rang with song	918